WITHDRAWN

Nietzsche's Teaching

Nietzsche's Teaching

An Interpretation of *Thus Spoke Zarathustra*

LAURENCE LAMPERT

Yale University Press

New Haven and London

Designed by James J. Johnson
and set in Zapf Book types.
Printed in the United States of America by
Thomson-Shore, Inc., Dexter, Michigan.

Library of Congress Cataloging-in-Publication Data

Lampert, Laurence, 1941–
    Nietzsche's teaching.

    Bibliography: p.
    Includes index.
    1. Nietzsche, Friedrich Wilhelm, 1844–1900. Also
sprach Zarathustra.   2. Philosophy.   I. Title.
B3313.A43L36   1986   193   86–9209
ISBN 0–300–03560–8

*The paper in this book meets the guidelines for permanence
and durability of the Committee on Production Guidelines
for Book Longevity of the Council on Library Resources.*

10   9   8   7   6   5   4   3   2   1

Für U. K.

Acknowledgment

For more than five years this book has benefited from the careful attention lavished on it by David Frisby. Beginning as typist, but immediately taking upon himself the tasks of informant, critic, and editor, he became indispensable to me in working through both Nietzsche's text and my own. His analytic persistence and unflagging generosity have made my book more nearly worthy of its subject than I could have made it by myself.

Thus man grows out of everything that once embraced him;
he has no need to break the shackles—they fall away
unforeseen when a god bids them; and where is the ring that
in the end still encircles him? Is it the world? Is it God?—

—NIETZSCHE, *"Mein Leben,"* written 18 September 1863, at
the age of nineteen

Contents

Abbreviations

Nietzsche's works are cited in the text by section number. For the sake of convenience all references to *Zarathustra* utilize chapter numbers, though Nietzsche left all the chapters unnumbered. References to the notes printed in the *Kritische Gesamtausgabe* are by volume, notebook, and section number—e.g., volume VIII, notebook 15, section 30, is VIII 15 [30].

A	*The Antichrist*
AO	*Assorted Opinions and Maxims* (*HH*, vol. II)
BGE	*Beyond Good and Evil*
BT	*The Birth of Tragedy*
CW	*The Case of Wagner*
D	*Daybreak*
DD	*Dionysos Dithyrambs*
DS	*David Strauss*
EH	*Ecce Homo*
GM	*On the Genealogy of Morals*
GS	*The Gay Science*
HC	*Homer's Contest*
HH	*Human, All Too Human*
KGW	*Kritische Gesamtausgabe*
NCW	*Nietzsche Contra Wagner*
PTG	*Philosophy in the Tragic Age of the Greeks*
SE	*Schopenhauer as Educator*
TI	*Twilight of the Idols*
UD	*On the Uses and Disadvantages of History for Life*
WB	*Richard Wagner in Bayreuth*
WP	*The Will to Power*
WS	*The Wanderer and his Shadow* (*HH*, vol. II)
Z	*Thus Spoke Zarathustra*

Introduction

> Some day . . . it might even happen that a few chairs will be
> established for the interpretation of *Zarathustra*.
>
> —NIETZSCHE, *EH*, "Books," 1

No chairs have been established yet for the interpretation of *Thus Spoke Zarathustra*. At the time Nietzsche made this suggestion, his book had baffled even the most intelligent of the few readers it had attracted—and this was perfectly in order, Nietzsche said (*EH*, "Books," 1). *Zarathustra* was not the only book of Nietzsche's that readers found incomprehensible; when he published a second edition of his previous book, *The Gay Science*, he offered aid to the reader in the form of a preface that explained the perspective from which "Mr Nietzsche" had written his book. But there he admits that such a book may require many prefaces, and that prefaces alone may never prepare anyone for contents that demand similar experiences in order to be understood. *Thus Spoke Zarathustra* has no preface—and who has had similar experiences? Had chairs for the interpretation of *Zarathustra* been established, Nietzsche's extravagant claims for it might, by now, have been acknowledged as warranted, and the book might have assumed the pivotal place in the study of his thought that he knew it merited. But this has not happened, and a full century later Nietzsche's book remains, as he said privately after completing it, dark and hidden and ridiculous to everyone (letter to Köselitz, 2 September 1884). Still, Nietzsche judged that in *Thus Spoke Zarathustra* he had accomplished exactly what he had wanted to do—but what had he wanted to do?

When Friedrich Ritschl said in recommendation of his student Nietzsche that he would be able to do simply anything he wanted to do, he could have had no inkling of what Nietzsche would eventually want to do, for Nietzsche himself discovered only slowly what it was possible for a human being to want to do, and only slowly did he set his mind to want that for himself. Even with the advantage unavailable to Ritschl of being able to judge what Nietzsche wanted to do long after he did it, serious impediments stand in the way of our recognizing it. The way has been

1

blocked accidentally by a handful of fortuities that have cast a shadow over Nietzsche that he could not control, beginning with the accident of his madness. But it has also been blocked deliberately, by a shadow that he could control, the shadow cast by his practice of the cheerful vice courtesy, one of whose forms is irony, the art of appearing more stupid than you are (*BGE* 284, 288). Courtesy belongs to "the three hundred foregrounds" that Nietzsche chose to place between ourselves and his task as he came to understand it. It would have been a discourtesy both to himself and his reader to portray that task directly, without benefit of masks, for such a portrayal would have been an invitation to the reader to assign it to the realm of fantasy or megalomania. Nietzsche's ambition so far transcends ordinary ambition that it is scarcely recognizable or credible, and when intimations of its scope first dawn on us, we are compelled to regard it as preposterous—or "Impossible," to quote the sign that Nietzsche hung over the way taken by his Zarathustra.

Simply put—one of many simple statements in this introduction that will be justified in the interpretation that follows—what Nietzsche set out to do was to become a "philosopher," but a philosopher in a sense quite different from the senses now prevalent or from the senses prevalent in 1871 when his Basel colleagues refused him the chair of philosophy for which he had applied.[1] Part of what Nietzsche meant by the word is apparent in those books about Nietzsche that he entitled *Schopenhauer as Educator* and *Richard Wagner in Bayreuth*, and especially in his book about "philosophers of the future" entitled *Beyond Good and Evil*. But in none of these three books does he portray the task of the philosopher as his own; consequently, they paint a more modest picture of Nietzsche's ambition than is finally warranted. For all his courtesy Nietzsche is above all not modest. His immodesty, the immodesty of a philosopher, is best shown in *Zarathustra*, a fable that chronicles the evolution of a philosopher who grows into the task that has befallen him as a result of what he has learned about mankind and its history.

WHY ZARATHUSTRA?

What does Nietzsche suggest about what he wanted to do by choosing Zarathustra as his mouthpiece? Zarathustra, the ancient Persian prophet, is better known by the inaccurate name the Greeks gave him—Zoroaster. Zarathustra/Zoroaster is not just any ancient prophet, and in order to understand what is at stake in Nietzsche's *Zarathustra*, it is helpful to know what his namesake had accomplished. Therefore, because no one had asked, as they should have asked, what the name "Zarathustra" meant to him, Nietzsche felt constrained to ask this question of himself in *Ecce Homo*, a book that could be counted among the prefaces to *Zarathustra*. Nietzsche says that Zarathustra/Zoroaster's uniqueness lies in his being the first thinker to see morality, the battle of good and evil, as the very wheel in the machinery of things (*EH*, "Destiny," 3). He is the first prophet to proclaim that a happy immortality is to be gained by moral behavior, by enlisting on the side of the good cosmic forces, which are pitted against the evil cosmic forces in the great drama that is the meaning of history. He is the author of the grave view of personal responsibility, according to which one will be held accountable for all one's deeds on a coming Day of Judgment, when those deeds will be weighed, and eternal bliss or eternal woe meted out to their doer. He is likewise the author of the grave view of the passage of time, according to which time is history and moves morally toward its consummation, when time will be arrested and the whole drama of a thousand acts brought to a welcome end. Zarathustra/Zoroaster is the founder of the linear view of time, the first to formulate the mighty vision that time is the progressive escalation of the struggle of good and evil, culminating in utopia for the worthy.

Prophetic religions, both sacred and profane, that appeal to an authority higher than the ancestral or the civil and that speak for the great march of history are customarily thought to have originated with the prophets of the Old Testament. But, as Nietzsche holds, they originated with Zarathustra/Zoroaster; they are "his work," work that was taken over as their own by the Hebrew prophets, servants of a jealous God, during their Babylonian captivity, just as it was taken over by Greek philosophers.[2] His work was also appropriated by later, modern apocalyptic preachers, who aimed to turn the world upside down to set it right. The revolutionary tradition of the West reformulates again and again the moral vision and religious mission of which Zarathustra is the founder.

In *Thus Spoke Zarathustra* that most portentous of founders returns— but not to become his own follower. Because he has remained a practitioner of his highest virtue, the honesty, or will to truth, that is also his work, he has finally come to recognize his calamitous error, the error around which the world has turned (*EH*, "Destiny," 3). The scope of the new Zarathustra's ambition—or of what Nietzsche wanted to do—is to be measured by the ancient Zarathustra's achievement. The founder of the view that time is progress in the moral overcoming of earthly life returns to bring a different teaching, one that is true to earthly life—a new teaching around which the world will turn. No prophet, fanatic, or preacher demanding belief, Nietzsche's Zarathustra appears as a seducer, a tempter, an "immoralist" to those moral in the old way (*EH*, Preface, 4).

Of course it is no part of Nietzsche's book to argue for the historic primacy of the ancient Zarathustra or to give him his due as the founder of the teaching that has come to prevail in the West. Like other books of Nietzsche's, *Zarathustra* focuses on the Platonic Socrates and on Christianity as the sources of the teaching through which the moral interpretation of temporal phenomena gained sway in the West and on modern teachers who inherited that tradition as part of their blood (*KGW* VIII 15 [30] = *WP* 765). The identity of these ancient and modern teachers is not spelled out, because the rhetorical requirements of *Zarathustra* forbid their being named; but just who they are becomes clear in the descriptions of their teachings.[3] *Thus Spoke Zarathustra* overthrows their teachings by telling the truth about them and begins to replace them with an alternative understanding of temporal or mortal things, rooted in the enigmatic teaching of eternal return.

DRAMA AND STRUCTURE

Thus Spoke Zarathustra exists as a vehicle for the thought of eternal return, "the highest formula of affirmation that is at all attainable" and "the fundamental conception" of *Thus Spoke Zarathustra* (*EH*, "Books: *Zarathustra*," 1). Eternal return first came to Nietzsche in August 1881 during a walk through the woods along Lake Silvaplana, in the high Alpine valley where he spent his summers. But it was only during the following winter, on long walks around the Bay of Rapallo, not far from Genoa, not far from Columbus's city, that Zarathustra first came to him as the fitting voice for his new thought.

Zarathustra is the only book that Nietzsche ever wrote with a dramatic narrative.[4] The title identifies it as a book of speeches, but the dramatic devices—characters, events, setting, and plot—are not extraneous, and to ignore them is to pretend inappropriately that the book is a treatise.[5] To divorce the speeches from their context is to make them too general, as if they were suitable for all occasions and all audiences; such a practice refuses the lessons quietly taught by a book that enacts its subtitle and gradually shrinks Zarathustra's audience from "All" to "None." Pretending that the book is a treatise obliterates the main feature of the drama, the transformation of Zarathustra into the new philosopher. Viewed from the end, the point of the drama is to show how Zarathustra grows into the task required of the philosopher in that destitute time that Nietzsche diagnosed as the terminal nihilism of Western culture, how he is educated to the task of a new founding.

By composing a fable that gives this task to one "younger and stronger" than himself, Nietzsche was able to avoid the praise of oneself that offends good taste (*BGE* 283; *GM* II. 25), while still chronicling the steps by which he arrived at his most important and most novel teaching. One of the metaphors used privately by Nietzsche to describe his book was that of an "entrance hall" (letters to Overbeck, 8 March 1884 and 7 April 1884, and to von Meysenbug, end of March 1884 and beginning of May 1884). This architectural metaphor suggests the process whereby Zarathustra enters the completed structure of Nietzsche's thought. By retracing the route taken by Zarathustra, the reader too can enter Nietzsche's philosophy, if not in the precise way of the one who opens that route, nevertheless as its friend or follower.

But the metaphor of the entrance hall can be misleading, because it suggests that the completed structure of Nietzsche's thought can be found elsewhere. Some have thought that the seven books completed after *Zarathustra* represent the completed edifice, or at least a systematic advance over *Zarathustra*. But Nietzsche unequivocally assigns these books the preliminary role of dismantling the old; each advances in its limited sphere until it arrives at a point where it says that the next and harder steps are the ones already taken in *Zarathustra;* each is in its own way a preface to *Zarathustra.* Others have thought that Nietzsche's notebooks contain the guide to the completed structure. But the notebooks, for all their fascination as glimpses into the planned *Hauptwerk,* seem to me not to add anything essential to what *Zarathustra* had already shown, and it is precisely structure that they lack, the artistic form that Nietzsche knew to be essential to the presentation of his thought.[6] Still others suppose that Nietzsche, who mistrusted systematizers as liars (*TI*, "Maxims and Arrows," 26), had no such structure in mind, because it is in the nature of his thought to destroy structure. But a philosopher has "no right to isolated acts of any kind" (*GM*, Preface, 2), and in Nietzsche's writings "a long logic of quite determinate philosophical sensibility" is at work, "not a confusion of a hundred indiscriminate paradoxes and heterodoxes" directed against whatever order happens to stand (letter to Brandes, 8 January 1888).

In the teaching of eternal return, Nietzsche points to a new and comprehensive center of gravity. Because *Zarathustra* exists to present that thought, Nietzsche could say that "among my writings my *Zarathustra* stands alone" (*EH*, Preface, 4). Now that Nietzsche's illness has deprived us of the Hauptwerk he was planning, *Zarathustra* is the only book that affords entry into Nietzsche's essential thought. It is the explosive core of the work of the philosopher who could say, "I am dynamite" (*EH*, "Destiny," 1);[7] and it is that core because it does more than destroy, it begins to construct what Nietzsche could call the new temple (*GM* II. 24).

THE EDUCATION OF ZARATHUSTRA

Because *Thus Spoke Zarathustra* describes a transformation, the answer to the question "Who is Nietzsche's Zarathustra?" must be given serially. As I will try to show, the main point of the action of *Zarathustra* is to demonstrate first the need for a new teacher, then the nature of his teaching in the discoveries of will to power and eternal return, and finally the founding of that teaching by Zarathustra himself.

In part I Zarathustra descends from his solitude and describes for all the need for a new teaching, grounding that need in the desolation of the old teaching—"God is dead"—and in the base motive concealed in that old teaching. A new teaching loyal to the earth is to be brought by some future teacher, there called the superman. After learning the lesson of the prologue, that he cannot move the people, Zarathustra turns to the making of followers, gradually succeeding in that intention, until, at the end of part I, he is able to address a band of disciples. While the high point of part I, chapter 15, "On the Thousand Goals and One," presents a comprehensive account of Zarathustra's teaching on human goals, that teaching is still incomplete for the two reasons given in the chapter itself: the ground of all goals, the will to power, has been named but not yet fully exhibited, and the thousand-and-first-goal, itself a voice of the will to power, has not yet been glimpsed. In part I Zarathustra is merely the herald of the superman, a maker of disciples who are to prepare the way for his coming. Zarathustra is, for now, the "teacher from the ground up," who "takes all things seriously only in relation to his pupils—even himself" (*BGE* 63).

In part II Zarathustra descends a second time, this time to further the education of his disciples. Their instruction complete, he sings three songs (chapters 9–11) which prepare him for the insight related in the decisive chapter, "On Self-Overcoming" (12). There he elaborates his fundamental discovery of will to power into a comprehensive teaching about beings as a whole. This new teaching discloses that the highest human beings are philosophers who exercise the most spiritual will to power over all beings. Consequently, this chapter is addressed only to philosophers, "you who are wisest," for the new teaching threatens to terminate the dominion that their most spiritual will to power has enabled them to exert over mankind. Later, in chapter 20, the most astonishing of all the chapters in the book, Zarathustra, under the influence of uncontrollable dismay, reveals that the teachings that have prevailed until now embody a spirit of revenge against mortal life. This revelation points for the first time to the content of the new teaching: redemption from the spirit of revenge requires that the most spiritual will to power will the eternal return of beings as they are. Human will to power thus creates the new ideal of the most high-spirited, alive, and world-affirming human being, who exercises his love of life and loyalty to the earth by saying to the whole of the past, present, and future: "But thus I willed it!" Zarathustra's caution in presenting the decisive discoveries of part II shows that he has learned that "when a philosopher these days lets it be known that he is not a skeptic ... everyone is annoyed" (*BGE* 208).

In part III Zarathustra prepares for the new affirmation of the whole of things. The preparations include a sea voyage, during which he reveals for the first time his new insight into eternal return (chapter 2). The select audience for that revelation is excluded from the deepest and most revealing speech, which is addressed to the silent sky (chapter 4). Zarathustra's preparations also take him on long travels among men to discern the contours of modern nihilism. The insights gained during these travels lead to the creation in solitude of half-written law tablets, which are to be delivered on the third and final descent to mankind that he is now planning. His preparations complete, Zarathustra wills eternal return in solitude, and part III ends with four chapters that interpret that event and demonstrate how eternal return will bring the world under a new and joyous rule. Zarathustra has thus become a philosopher in Nietzsche's sense, "the man of the most comprehensive responsibility who has the overall development of mankind on his conscience" (*BGE* 61). This is the end of the book. Part IV, added later as an afterthought, is an "interlude."[8]

Zarathustra's education in what needs to be learned includes lessons in what can be taught. Like every great teacher introducing a novel teaching, he is opposed by a world not yet aware that it could desire such a teaching or that it might be in need of it. Moreover, he rediscovers the old truth that the people have the laws on their side, as well as sacred tradition and the values that confer worth on their actions; they necessarily oppose a new teacher as a deadly enemy. By having Zarathustra begin by addressing the people, pass of necessity to the making of disciples, and end by addressing only himself, the book appears to present his failure as a teacher. But, contrary to first appearances, he does not fail as a teacher for his disciples await his return. By having Zarathustra end in solitude, the book focuses on what is preliminary for a teacher: success as a learner. It shows Zarathustra preparing himself to become the new teacher by making the new teaching his own, and his success as a learner fits him for the "Great Noon" anticipated throughout the book. On that day Zarathustra will become the teacher of eternal return, the one who pronounces a day of judgment on all teachings of the Day of Judgment. By moving from all to none, Nietzsche's book shows that there exists as yet no audience for the teaching that Zarathustra gradually learns, but it is the aim of the book to create the audience that it shows Zarathustra failing to find.

NIETZSCHE'S ART OF WRITING

Through the dramatic aspects of his book, Nietzsche is able to temper the excess that seems to flare out of Zarathustra's speeches, for the drama introduces a quality that seems inconsistent with excess, a delicate and lovely subtlety that transforms the deeds and speeches of fable into lessons for his friends. By means of this careful blend of excess and reserve, Nietzsche presents matters that he knew would offend his intended readers if he stated them directly. It is no offense to such readers to have Zarathustra say, "I am Zarathustra the godless," but it would be an offense to them were Nietzsche to say that he is no longer a skeptic, that he has himself discovered the true teachings necessary for the dark times in which we live. Attuned to that offense, honoring its legitimacy while knowing that it could cost him the free spirits who are his potential friends, Nietzsche came to practice an art of writing aimed at tempering offense and winning over free spirits.

That art leads into temptation. It practices the enticements of the tempter god, bewitchingly described at the end of *Beyond Good and Evil*. It would be wrong to claim that Nietzsche engaged in the art of politic speech in the manner of Plato, or in "enigmatical, folded writing" in the manner of Bacon or Descartes. But Nietzsche the philologist rediscovered and put to use the difference between the esoteric and the exoteric known to all philosophers before the modern age of equality (*BGE* 30). He shows his Zarathustra learning the necessity of artful speech for the introduction of his novel teaching, but an artful speech that is different from Plato's because it does not need to pretend that it is ancient, and different from Bacon's and Descartes' because it does not need to pretend that its novelties can be accommodated to what is already revered. Instead, it presents itself as utterly novel, a wicked allurement, a thing of the devil—though in its way it is a vindication of the gods. When Nietzsche makes that quiet suggestion in *Beyond Good and Evil,* it appears as the contrary of what his friends most fear: having just heard his teaching on will to power presented in as direct a way as his method of temptation would permit, his friends react in honest horror, fearing that in Nietzsche's teaching God is refuted but the devil not (*BGE* 36, 37). But in his emphatic response, "On the contrary! On the contrary, my friends!," Nietzsche suggests that in his teaching the devil is refuted but God is not. His friends are thus invited to wonder if the "devil" could be that supernatural God whose jealous claim to supremacy caused all the other gods to die laughing (III. 8), and who cursed the earth with single vision. They are invited, further, to wonder if "God" could be what that heavenly monotheism deemed the devil, an earthly power who rules a world deemed fallen.

Through this inversion Nietzsche can accommodate his teaching temporarily to the vulgar speech still spoken by worried friends who fear his teaching because they are, while free spirits, only partially free of the clumsy dogmatism that two thousand years of Platonism and Platonism for the people have made second nature. In the end, however, Nietzsche supplants these rigid categories of religious monotheism with a manner of religious speech that is far more refined, not only because it deals with mystery, but also because it addresses those who no longer like to believe in God and gods and so must avoid giving offense whenever it steps beyond skepticism (*BGE* 295). Twice captive, once to a supernatural or anti-earthly monotheism, then to the pandemonium of welcome censure that abolishes it, the now impoverished, almost ruined words for the sacred are reintroduced with great restraint in Nietzsche's artful speech.

The spiritual warfare in whose service the new art of writing is placed continues to make war on God, but it promises a return of earthly gods who need not be flattered with omniscience or supreme goodness, since for them supreme power suffices (*KGW* VIII 10 [9] = *WP* 1037). The mystery is not profaned in the telling, but Nietzsche anticipates the return of Dionysos and Ariadne, earthly gods of earthly celebration. Willing to risk offense because he had grave doubts as to whether there could be a world whose center is not God (*BGE* 150), Nietzsche dares to have Zarathustra crown the newest aristocracy of thought with "saints of knowledge" (I. 10), establish a new ladder of values whose highest rung is the holy (I. 15), peer into a future of playful, dancing, philosophizing gods (III. 12, §2), and prophesy that the singing of his songs will bring from across the sea on a golden boat the one at whose arrival all living things dance and leap on feet made light and marvelous by his coming (III. 14). *Thus Spoke Zarathustra* is the masterwork of the writer who rediscovered the art of seeming, the art of the tempter god, Dionysos, who makes his reappearance with Ariadne, mysterious and nameless, at the very climax of the book.

"I tell every one of my friends to his face that he has never considered it worth his while to *study* any of my writings" (*EH*, "Books: *Wagner*," 4). This is the reproach to be expected from the philologist who rediscovered the lost arts of writing and reading and wants his friends to understand that his books require special attention (*BGE* 30). The preface to *Daybreak*— added in 1886, "late but not too late," for Nietzsche's issues take time and have time—identified Nietzsche as "a friend of *lento*," "a teacher of slow reading," whose venerable art of philology trains one to read well, "slowly, deeply, looking cautiously fore and aft, with reservations, with doors left open, with delicate eyes and fingers." All Nietzsche's books indulge "the art of nuance which constitutes the best gain of life" (*BGE* 31). This best gain is most present where least evident, in the vehemence of *Zarathustra*, in which all nuance seems to be submerged by the unconditional. The product of more than three years of concentrated labor by a most gifted writer schooled in a long apprenticeship of careful writing, now at the height of his powers and with no other duties to deflect him, *Thus Spoke Zarathustra* is an astonishing blend of fervor and restraint, which demands the most careful attention and yields the greatest reward.

INTERPRETING NIETZSCHE

A way of thinking as novel, comprehensive, and tempting as Nietzsche's quite naturally gives birth to a varied family of interpreters, friends and enemies of the one who fathered them, and friends and enemies of one another. Within the varied family of Nietzsche interpreters, the two who have been most important for my work are Martin Heidegger and Leo Strauss, readers who share the currently unfashionable view that Nietzsche's writings present a specifiable teaching about beings and human being. They maintain that the old philologist who warned constantly of the dangers of too little philology, and who knew well the problem of taking an interpretation for the text itself, nevertheless wrote interpretable books in full awareness of the pleasures and problems bequeathed to his readers. Both Heidegger and Strauss judge Nietzsche to be the teacher of our age, the philosopher who gives voice to what now is.[9] Heidegger, often taken to be Nietzsche's greatest follower, in the end judges Nietzsche to be a teacher of revenge, whose teachings we must "lose" if we are to lose the wretched age of which they are a part. Strauss, customarily regarded as an enemy of Nietzsche because of his loyal opposition to the modern in favor of the ancients, in the end, as I read him, judges Nietzsche to be the "complementary" man, the philosopher who in an amazing way replaces Plato.[10] Indebted to both Heidegger and Strauss, and learning from each of them how to side with Nietzsche, my interpretation of Nietzsche's teaching attempts something that has not been done before. In setting out to follow the new route opened by Nietzsche, I retrace Zarathustra's path serially through all the events and speeches of *Thus Spoke Zarathustra*. His path discloses itself as the upward way of spirited discovery, leading to the new teaching, but because, as Heraclitus held, the way up is also the way down, Zarathustra's course is also a descent to the things of the earth that gives them weight and importance again. Retracing the route opened by Zarathustra leads to an affirmation of Nietzsche's teaching as the comprehensive wisdom that can guide the most spiritual beings, human beings, in their pursuit of the most spirited ends, the ends of knowledge, within a framework that lets things be what they are by willing their eternal return. Nietzsche's teaching, so far from being the "nihilism" with which it is customarily accosted, shows modern man how he can be spared the oblivion of eternity and the ignorance of the highest good.

My book is, of course, not the work of a philosopher in Nietzsche's sense, but of a "philosophical laborer" (*BGE* 211). I do not demean myself by this term, for the "noble models" of philosophical laborers are Kant and Hegel, and the work of such laborers is "an enormous and wonderful task in whose service every subtle pride, every tough will can certainly find satisfaction." Still, such work is different from that of the philosopher in Nietzsche's sense, and, in "pressing into formulas" a positing of values like Nietzsche's, in "abbreviating" it, and attempting "to make it manageable," such work as mine runs the constant risk of losing "the art of nuance," and hence of threatening this least dogmatic of philosophers with a dogmatic interpretation. I have tried to remember that "everything unconditional belongs in pathology" (*BGE* 154), while remembering too that even Nietzsche had to say that pathologically.

Whereas the philosophical laborer is always dependent and works within a horizon, the philosopher Nietzsche aimed at absolute independence. He knew what it meant to stick fast and to break away, and he privately exulted in being the most independent man in Europe (*BGE* 41; letter to von Meysenbug, end of July 1888). But in the end even he yields to something other. He is the commander who learns from life itself that the highest commanding is a kind of obeying (II. 12). What he obeys is his nature, that which is given in himself, an instinct, a passion, a "great stupidity," but one that expresses itself in "the ideal of the most high-spirited, alive and world-affirming human being," who wants "to have what was and is repeated into all eternity, insatiably shouting *de capo* . . . to the whole play and spectacle" (*BGE* 56, 231). In him the natural instinct in love with natural things finds voice, a voice whose song at last drowns out the ancient siren song of those metaphysical bird-catchers who have piped at us all too long that we are more, we are higher, we are of a different origin (*BGE* 230). Having discovered the passionate origin of that old song and recognized the great stupidity to which it gives voice, the singer of the new song teaches us to delight in its discrediting and in our actual, earthly origins which it would have us repudiate.

"Thus man grows out of everything that once embraced him; he has no need to break the shackles—they fall away unforeseen when a god bids them" ("Mein Leben," 18 September 1863).[11] When Nietzsche recounted that experience at age nineteen, he went on to ask himself, "Where is the ring that in the end still encircles him? Is it the world? Is it God?—" It is neither, for Nietzsche shows Zarathustra outgrowing everything that has encompassed him and, in his address to the empty heavens (III. 4), acknowledging that nothing but depth and silence encompass man. And yet it is both, for in the teaching that Zarathustra enters a new and human center of gravity is provided by the will that cries insatiably, "Once More!", to the whole marvelous spectacle, and mankind finds itself encircled by the open sky and earthly gods.

Part I

Whoever is a teacher from the ground up takes all things
seriously only in relation to his pupils—even himself.

—NIETZSCHE, *BGE* 63

THE ACTION OF PART I

Part I is the provisional presentation of an unfinished teaching. It consists
of two sections, "Zarathustra's Prologue" and "Zarathustra's Speeches,"
the first serving as an introduction to the second. Though both sections
present the same teaching, that the superman is the meaning of the earth
and Zarathustra his herald, they do so in different ways. Zarathustra's education in what mankind needs had begun during ten years of solitude
prior to the opening of the prologue. His education in how to teach mankind what he alone knows it needs begins in the prologue itself, for there,
at the very beginning of his teaching, he suffers the shock of seeing his
ideal of the superman scorned by the people it was meant to move. This
first step in determining the proper audience for his teaching requires that
he turn to the making of a few disciples to carry it forward and eventually
bring about the advent of the superman. This resolve governs "Zarathustra's
Speeches"; they are acts of persuasion aimed at attracting disciples to the
cause on which the meaning of the earth depends. His strategy works,
and in the final chapter of part I we see him leaving the city, followed by
his newly won disciples.

But later events counsel caution in the interpretation of part I, with
its dominant image of Zarathustra as herald of the superman. The role of
herald recurs, to be sure, in Nietzsche's next book, *Beyond Good and Evil*,
in which he appears to be smoothing the way for unknown philosophers
of the future. And to be John the Baptist to such redeemers would seem
to be ambition enough for any man. But, as will be argued, the action of
Zarathustra shows that such ambition falls far short of the actual ambition
that spurs the one who came to understand the whole course of human
history as Nietzsche did, the one who stands at the gate of the future,

13

having witnessed the tremendous struggles and transitions of the past (*BT* 15). Such a one, charmed by his vision of the struggle, must take part and fight. *Zarathustra* chronicles the way in which Nietzsche came to understand the magnitude of the role that fell to him. What Zarathustra merely heralds in part I, he comes to recognize as his own task in part II and sets out to accomplish in part III. The role of herald must be seen as provisional, for the teachings of part I are not merely amplified in the later parts but are surpassed and grounded in an unanticipated way. Nietzsche well knew that Zarathustra's task was more than that of herald of the superman. Zarathustra had come to him as the means of showing the way into his thought of eternal return, and that thought has not yet dawned on Zarathustra in part I.

ZARATHUSTRA'S PROLOGUE: A HERMIT'S FOLLY

(Prologue 1) Jesus not only died too soon; he taught too soon, his forty days in the wilderness at age thirty insufficient to overcome his hatred of the world, despite his noble character (I. 21). Zarathustra's frequent comparisons of himself with Jesus always show him to be superior, and here, at age thirty, he leaves his home and the lake of his home (not Galilee but Urmi, the lake in Persia associated with Zarathustra) to spend not forty days, but ten years in the wilderness. Unlike Jesus, who is driven into the wilderness, Zarathustra enters of his own accord; he is attended not by angels but by the wild beasts; he neither suffers in his solitude nor is tempted, but instead enjoys his spirit and his solitude.

Part I, like parts II and III, begins with an initial ascent into solitude, but only his descent is depicted, the clearest glimpse of his solitude being the speech that ends it. This first speech is addressed to the rising sun, still large and golden on the horizon from Zarathustra's vantage point high in the mountains. Unlike the ancient Zarathustra, who prayed to the sun as a god, Nietzsche's Zarathustra is a modern man who addresses the sun as "you great star," a heavenly body similar to other stars except for its proximity. From this opening speech it is evident that Zarathustra considers there to be nothing in the heavens superior to him. He does not, like Aristotle, found his own worth on the greatness and regularity of the heavens; nor is he, like Kant, reduced to insignificance, to a mere speck, by the starry heavens above.[1] Zarathustra expresses gratitude for the sun, but he interprets the sun's happiness as dependent on his gratitude; the sun's apparent autonomy masks a dependence, for it would grow tired of its course were it not for those who await its light every morning. Zarathustra is like the sun in this dependence, for he too needs those who can receive his light. But he is like the sun in a second way, for, reminding the rising sun of its coming descent into the sea, he says that he too must, as men say, "go under." Like the sun that descends into the sea, bringing light to the underworld, he must descend to bring wisdom to mankind, to "pour gold into the sea out of inexhaustible riches, so that even the poorest fisherman will row with golden oars" (III. 12, §3).[2] Zarathustra descends to bring a comprehensive teaching that will alter the experience of all mankind.

Zarathustra's closing request for the sun's blessing compliments the sun for being able to look on a great happiness like his own and feel no envy. In this, it is unlike human beings, who always envy the happiness of others. In Zarathustra's speeches, envy and the related passions of hatred and revenge come to light as basic to human achievement. While teaching that envy can be a deadly poison, Zarathustra does not teach that it can or should be eradicated; rather, it must be purified and put to use in the contest of overcoming that alone makes the earth meaningful. The capacity of the sun to gaze without envy on the happiness of others is thus seen to be a lack, a lack that is not enviable, for the sun is not superhuman but subhuman, not a god but a stone. Nevertheless, Zarathustra is shown to be envious of the sun insofar as it is a light-bringer. This envy does not poison him, but rather spurs him to do what he will counsel followers to do: act in such a way as to emulate the envied, with a view to surmounting it, or eclipsing it.

Zarathustra's final words, that he wants to become man again by rejoining the company of men, imply that solitude is an unnatural state for human beings, and even though his later speeches include praise of solitude, this opening implication is confirmed not only in other speeches, but also in his repeated abandonment of solitude. "To live alone one must be a beast or a god—says Aristotle. Leaving out the third case: one must be both—a philosopher" (*TI*, "Maxims and Arrows," 3). However necessary solitude may be for the philosopher Zarathustra, it is a provisional condition, a prelude to becoming man again.

The single italicized word in the first speech of a speaker who speaks frequently in italics is *untergehen*, "going under." Although its use implies a comparison between Zarathustra's descent and the setting of the sun, *untergehen* is also the word for the sinking of a ship and for death and destruction generally. This emphatic, ominous word is qualified as the word that men would use to describe Zarathustra's act. But it is used again at the end of Zarathustra's very first speech: "Thus began Zarathustra's going under," and the same words are used at the end of the prologue (10); even Zarathustra uses *untergehen* from time to time to describe his course. Near the end of part III his animals say as a benediction: "Thus ends Zarathustra's going under" (III. 13). Going under, the first act of the prologue, is featured at the openings of each of the other parts as well, and part IV will end with the promise of yet another descent, the meaning of which depends on the meaning of all the previous descents. Zarathustra's first going under is literally a descent from his mountain to mankind in the valleys below; he descends as the bringer of light and is then ready, part I suggests, to set as the sun sets, or die (I. 21). His going under is also a return to the earth and to the body that celebrates the things to which he descends. Going under thus opposes the tradition of ascent to higher, non-earthly, nonbodily things. Men schooled in this tradition would name Zarathustra's descent *untergehen*, but he descends to demonstrate that transcendent things are products of earth and body, thereby calling for a revaluation of both the things descended to and the traditional ideal of ascent, with its hatred of the earthly and the bodily.

But *untergehen* is not the only word used by Zarathustra to describe his course; he too speaks of ascent, though without implying transcendence of the earthly. Images of ascent, of climbing, dancing, and flying, are even more prominent than images of descent. The movement that men call "going under" includes, both in Zarathustra's address to the rising sun and at prominent points later, a rising or dawning, an ascent into the sky. Zarathustra depicts himself as a bird-spirit flying free, defying gravity. The force that draws the bird-spirit downward is named "the spirit of gravity," Zarathustra's "archenemy," who draws downward, to himself as center, everything that falls within his sphere of influence; it is said of this spirit that he is "the master of the world" (II. 10). Zarathustra's battle with the spirit of gravity persists throughout the book and provides the basis for his own account of his culminating action; whereas the animals speak at the end of his going under, he himself speaks of flying (III. 16, §7). The contrasting images are not contradictory, but rather, different and complementary ways of characterizing Zarathustra's course.[3]

The first section of the prologue is an exact repetition of the last section of *The Gay Science* (342) but for the small omission of the name of Zarathustra's lake and the larger omission of the title: *Incipit tragoedia*. Is Zarathustra's going under a tragedy? While Nietzsche omits the revealing title here, it is unlikely that he has changed his mind about the meaning of Zarathustra's descent, for at the end of his going under the god of tragedy, Dionysos, makes a mysterious appearance (III. 14). This appearance accords with another feature of the unfolding narrative that is consistent with tragedy; the dominant imagery of part I, the sun imagery associated with Apollo, is superseded, but not replaced, by other imagery of the sky, the depth and silence that lie beyond the brightness of the heavenly bodies.

(Prologue 2) In his first encounter with a human being upon descending from his mountain cave, Zarathustra is given a wise and true warning, which he ignores. He meets an old saint who lives a solitary life and who recognizes Zarathustra despite the ten years that have intervened since he first saw him "carrying his ashes to the mountain." The old saint's first address to the one who now returns as fire to the valley warns him not to go down to men. Zarathustra's reply is quite possibly his first statement to a human being in ten years: "I love mankind." But he seems to retract this revealing answer when the old saint says that mankind is not worthy of his love. Denying that he spoke of love, Zarathustra says instead that he brings mankind a gift. Despite his persistence, the old saint is unable

to take away Zarathustra's belief in mankind, but his warnings show that he is better acquainted with the ways of the world than Zarathustra, even though he is no lover of mankind. At a loss, finally, in the face of the old saint's insistence that he, a fellow solitary, not go to mankind, Zarathustra asks, in effect, "Why should one stay in solitude?" When the old saint responds that he maintains his solitude in order to praise God, the compassionate and gift-giving Zarathustra continues on his way, turning even his separation from the old saint into a gift to man, for he departs so as not to take away from the old saint the belief that makes his solitude possible. In parting they laugh at one another, each knowing the folly of the other's belief, Zarathustra's in mankind, the old saint's in God.

Having left the old saint, Zarathustra expresses his amazement that the old man has not heard that God is dead. His astonishment is instructive, for it shows that Zarathustra's purpose in descending is not to teach the death of God. Such a teaching would be superfluous in the world to which he thinks he is returning, for, as he understands that world, everyone in it but the solitary saint must know by now that God is dead. What Zarathustra intends to teach are the consequences of the death of God. The God who once lived and provided a sun for this earth is now dead, and the earth grows colder; a new epoch has been born, in which God no longer supplies a horizon to man's world (GS 125). Zarathustra descends believing that he comes at the decisive hour with the decisive choice; he returns to offer a mankind that has lost its belief in God the supreme gift of a new meaning for the earth, the superman. His return with this "fire" suggests that his "carrying his ashes to the mountain" ten years earlier was a retreat, burned out, from a world grown meaningless through the death of God, that he entered solitude so as to discover how to love the world and mankind now that God is dead. Or, in terms of the parable of Nietzsche's previous book, he entered solitude as "the Madman" who knew the death of God to be imminent, and that it would be a catastrophe for mankind. It is the answer to that catastrophe, an answer that has rekindled him in his solitude, that he now brings.

The encounter between the solitary lover of mankind and the solitary lover of God demonstrates how the two solitudes differ. The old saint's solitude is relief from mankind's perpetual unworthiness; it can be permanent and even end in solitary death (IV. 6), because it is shared not just by animals but by God; he need have no hope for mankind. But Zarathustra's solitude is shared only by his animals. Unlike the old saint, he must return to mankind to share the hope he has won in solitude, because for him there is nothing that could bring comfort to complete solitude. He entered solitude not to redeem his own soul, but to ponder the redemption of mankind. Thinking himself to have solved the problem of the meaning of the earth, the problem that became acute with the death of God, he must now return to mankind, for if mankind can have no God, it can still have a future.

When Zarathustra returns, he is like some new Prometheus bringing a gift from the gods against the gods' own will. But the gift he brings cannot be welcomed, because he is mistaken about the world to which he brings it; the old saint is not the only one who still believes in God. Zarathustra has not yet learned that the death of God must be followed by a long twilight of piety and nihilism (II. 19; III. 8), in which men will show the gruesome shadows of the god for centuries in caves (GS 108). Zarathustra's gift of the superman is given to a mankind not aware of the problem to which the superman is the solution. Eugen Fink says that "the central theme of part I of *Thus Spoke Zarathustra* is the death of God,"[4] but it should be added that this theme is seldom made explicit because it is simply assumed. In this assumption, we see where *Zarathustra* stands in relation to Nietzsche's later books; in teaching the death of God, the latter describe the events preceding Zarathustra's descent to mankind. In this respect, though written after *Zarathustra*, they resemble *The Gay Science;* for where they end, Zarathustra begins.[5]

(Prologue 3–5) When Zarathustra arrives in the nearest town, the people are already gathered in the marketplace awaiting the performance of a tightrope walker. But first they hear Zarathustra's three speeches "On The Superman And The Last Man" (the title of the prologue in the first edition of *Zarathustra*, which contained only part I). Though the speeches are intended to instruct the assembled citizens they draw instead reactions that instruct Zarathustra. The hermit Zarathustra speaks as if the people have all experienced the need he himself knew ten years earlier, as if they are all waiting for the redemption he has found for that need. Their mocking response to his first speech causes him to vary his manner of speaking in his second speech, but the basic concern remains the same, the description of the future goal, pursuit of which overcomes the lassitude resulting from the death of God. The people allow this second speech to run its course, and at the end they merely laugh. But their laughter is enough to show that Zarathustra has failed yet again; he therefore devises a different strategy for his third speech, a strategy aimed at shaming the people into action. But this fails too, and the rest of the prologue is taken up with the lessons of these failures and with devising yet another strategy, which will be enacted in "Zarathustra's Speeches." This last shift in strategy is much more radical than the shifts in the prologue itself, for, rather than trying to move the people as a whole, Zarathustra will now attempt to win a few special followers away from them.

The three speeches in the marketplace are probably the best known of all of Zarathustra's speeches. Arresting and memorable, they threaten to eclipse everything that follows, as if what follows were mere amplification of this emphatic beginning. But, instead of allowing the beginning to determine the interpretation of what follows, the reverse seems to me to be necessary, with the beginning measured by the end. Zarathustra himself guides such interpretation by his frequent retrospective assessments of his own actions, assessments that are unanimous in their verdict: this beginning was folly. Of course, his verdict does not entail the conclusion that all the ideas in these opening speeches are abandoned, but it does entail that caution be exercised in judging these incautious words.

Zarathustra begins abruptly and emphatically, as if it is his message that the people are waiting for, rather than the act of the tightrope walker. "*I teach you the superman.*" These opening words are repeated three times in the first speech, each time following a different image of the superman— as the goal of a willed evolution, the cleansing sea into which a polluted mankind streams, the lightning that kindles the greatest experience for mankind.[6] The theme common to these three images is that of mankind as defective or contemptible, able to justify itself only in the achievement of something higher than itself.

The first image of the superman makes him the goal of the whole evolutionary history of life. Zarathustra pictures evolution in a linear way, as the creation by each species of a species higher than itself. Man stands at the summit of this evolutionary achievement not as its glorious termination, but as a step to something higher, from whose perspective—the perspective that already enables Zarathustra to measure man—man is shameful. "The superman is the meaning of the earth" because he is the goal toward which the evolutionary process tends, the goal that must now be willed by the species mankind. The earth has no meaning apart from the future superman; at present it is only potentially meaningful. The meanings that have been given to the earth in the past have been sins against the earth. Under the injunction "Be loyal to the earth!" Zarathustra describes the ways in which mankind has been disloyal by dreaming otherworldly dreams. He takes it for granted that for the people God has already died. Moreover, the death of God spells death for the immortal soul, and these two deaths have left earth and body in ruins. God and the immortal soul, the very foundations of virtue, the postulates of moral experience for philosophers as different as Plato, Descartes, and Kant have been rendered incredible by modern life, and Zarathustra comes to announce a new foundation. Because it is the future that will provide the new ground for meaningful action, the greatest experience now available is contempt for the past and the present; the speech thus becomes a litany inviting contempt for the five most honored things: mankind's happiness, reason, virtue, justice, and pity.

At this point, Zarathustra is interrupted by a voice from the crowd. The speaker jokingly takes this speech to be the introduction to the tightrope walker, and the latter begins his performance, taking the joke as his cue.[7] Although Zarathustra is amazed by what has happened, he is not daunted and begins a second speech on the superman, shifting the focus away from contempt to what he loves about mankind. The point remains the same, however, for only that which squanders itself on behalf of the future is lovable.

Fittingly, the theme of the speech is going under, with its implications of plummeting and perishing. While the tightrope walker crosses the square high above the people's heads, Zarathustra states that mankind too is a crossing over, a rope and a bridge suspended between animal and super-man above an abyss. Pictured in its high exemplar, the tightrope walker engaged in his dangerous crossing, mankind is seen as moved by two complementary passions, contempt for what is behind and longing for what is ahead. This speech runs its course with no interruption and ends with Zarathustra's identification of himself as the herald of the lightning to come, who dies once his message has been given.

Zarathustra's sensational teaching on the superman, both here and in later speeches, makes it clear that he does not herald the coming of super*men:* nowhere does he picture such a plurality. On only one occasion does he use the word in the plural (II. 17), and then only as a test for a pious disciple, in which he links his own teaching with the "gods and supermen" dreamed up by the fancy of poets. Furthermore, despite the gravity of his message and the fervor with which he proclaims it, he never once urges any of his hearers to aim at becoming the superman; rather, he urges them to prepare the way for the superman, to be his worthy forerunners. In part I the superman is still a long way off, in a future to be created by the effort now being initiated. By the consistent use of the singular and by setting the goal a long way off, Nietzsche forces us to raise the question of the relationship of the audience to the superman. Many readers have wanted to see the superman teaching as a general, edifying call to human greatness and have pluralized or democratized it, bringing it into their immediate present by thinking that it was addressed to their becoming super*men,* or to the creation of a new class of authentic men, or even a new species of man.[8]

Although Nietzsche had long regarded mankind as justified only in its superior specimens, it is only in *Zarathustra* that he elaborates the idea of the superman,[9] and there the idea undergoes important changes. In part I Zarathustra does not aim at the creation of a band of supermen, or even of a single superman from among his audience; his goal is rather to initiate a historic project the culmination of which will be the superman. The most important feature of the future superman is revealed in the teaching on peoples: he will be the founder of a new and global people (I. 15). After part I, speech about the superman is sharply and surprisingly curtailed. As I will show, this comparative silence is linked to a still more important change quietly taught by the book's dramatic development, for Zarathustra takes upon himself the tasks he had once thought would be the responsibility of his followers and his followers' followers. In the pro-logue and part I, Zarathustra presents the superman as an evolutionary phenomenon, but this image is subsequently abandoned, and we are pre-sented instead with the evolution of the man Zarathustra. The path taken by Zarathustra in the later parts can thus never be a model for admirers to duplicate or improve on, because it terminates in the singular and su-preme act anticipated in part I: the act performed by the founder of the new people, the superman.

Caution with respect to the teaching on the superman can be seen to be in order if one measures the beginning of Zarathustra's course by its end, for he begins as the teacher of the superman but ends as the teacher of eternal return. The first teaching requires a linear concept of time, with the meaning of time's passage dependent on the future achieve-ment of those who have contempt for the past. But the final teaching seems to contradict the notion that time is linear, that the past is worthy only of contempt, and that the future alone can be the ground of meaning. Inter-pretation of the superman teaching requires that it be reconciled with the teaching of eternal return.[10]

Zarathustra's first commandment is: "Be loyal to the earth!" Thus "to sin against the earth is now the most dreadful thing." This command to be true to the earth is given in a book that emphasizes its natural setting of mountains, seas, sun, and storms. The injunction and the setting pre-dispose the reader to find in Zarathustra's teaching a stance toward the natural world that honors nature as it is and learns to love the limitations nature sets. But Zarathustra's view of nature is much more nuanced than appears from these first impressions. Judged by its context, the command "Be loyal to the earth!" means that the earth is not to be disparaged by otherworldly dreams, but is rather to be won back from the hatred ex-pressed in the judgment that it is inferior to heaven, in the judgment that "the wisest men of all ages" have made about life, that "it is no good" (*TI*, "Socrates," 1). The earth to which Zarathustra commands loyalty is the earth that was regarded as merely the "apparent world" by those who believed in a "true world" beyond it; "Zarathustra begins" at the point at which this "true world" invented by Plato is abolished (*TI*, "True World"). But when the true world is abolished, the apparent world is also abolished, and man is left with the task of discovering how to live with the world that remains. "Zarathustra begins" with a new conception of the meaning of the world.

In Zarathustra's opening speeches to the people, his new conception is described as man's taking possession of the earth; the people are to sacrifice themselves so "that the earth may one day belong to the super-man." His coming confers meaning on the earth; apart from his possession, it has no meaning. In taking possession of the earth, the superman does not merely yield to a meaning that the earth already has. Whereas the first mention of the earth in *Zarathustra* states that "the superman is the mean-ing of the earth," the last mention makes it the table on which the gods play dice, the object of their creative new words (III. 16, §3). Is the earth simply at the superman's disposal then? Does Nietzsche's thought, ap-pearing at "the moment when man is about to assume dominion of the earth as a whole," facilitate and certify that dominion as Martin Heidegger

PART I

so powerfully and influentially argues?[11] Does it fulfill Descartes' project of making man the master and possessor of nature? Although *Zarathustra* abstracts from the infinity of devices created by the modern mastery of the earth and presents Zarathustra in a fully natural setting, the spider, the snake, the leech, the cows, the lion, and all the other living things referred to in his speeches are used to draw lessons, and it is not immediately apparent that any of the lessons drawn is the lesson of Montaigne, who, having spoken at length about animals, concludes: "I have said all this to demonstrate the resemblance that there is between things animal and human, and to bring us down to join the ranks of all living creatures."[12] When William Earle says that "nothing could be more foreign to Nietzsche's heart than deference,"[13] he names the trait whose utter absence seems to determine Zarathustra's own disposition toward the earth. Beginning with his celebratory account of evolution and the willful tasks it assigns to mankind, Zarathustra's way does not open by taking its bearings from the harmonies and rhythms of nature. The word *nature* is used only once in the book and, like the single use of the plural of *superman*, occurs in the chapter on poets, where it is said that nature is a poet's fancy, and that poets imagine nature to be in love with them and to whisper privileged truths in their ears (II. 17). Zarathustra seems, at first, to find nothing numinous in nature, and as he grows into the task that falls to him, he seems to come close to the biblical view of man's proper relation to the animals and the earth as declared in God's command to Adam to exercise dominion over them.[14] Thus *Zarathustra* could be thought to confirm Heidegger's judgment that true "loyalty to the earth" depends on "losing" Nietzsche.[15] Nevertheless, for all its initial persuasiveness, Heidegger's judgment against Nietzsche seems to me to be wrong. It takes its bearings from *Zarathustra*'s beginning, not its ending; from the opening invocation of the superman, not the closing amen songs which express a desire for the eternal return of beings as they are. At its mysterious climax Zarathustra's teaching allows the return of a god who shows forth in himself the cycles of nature. The meaning of Zarathustra's loyalty to the earth is to be found in that mysterious deed and in the songs it gives rise to, songs of natural beings celebrating the cyclical coming and going of things (III. 13). The status of nature is one of the questions that *Zarathustra* addresses and answers; it may even be said to be *the* question that *Zarathustra* addresses, though the complexities of the answer are not at all clear at the opening, in the command to be loyal to the earth. I hope to show that Zarathustra's course refutes Heidegger's judgment; that the task is not to lose Nietzsche, but to find him, for it is through Nietzsche's teaching that loyalty to the earth can be won.

The immobility of the people in the face of the challenge of the superman elicits astonishment from Zarathustra and a change in strategy. In the reflective moment after his speech he recognizes that their refusal of his teaching comes from their having been raised to admire and treasure their own things, and he sees now that it could not be otherwise. He later calls his rash and ill-advised speech "the folly of a hermit," the folly of supposing that what he had learned only with the greatest difficulty in a long solitude could be shared so easily with everyone (IV. 13. §1).

His silence after the speeches on the superman is a thoughtful silence preparatory to a new speech embodying a new strategy. But even this new strategy involves contempt for what the people most value, despite his recognition that his contempt is the cause of their rejection of his teaching. Such contempt is necessary, however, if Zarathustra is to sever the people from what they now respect and move them to something completely novel. The problem he faces is the problem of giving the people a gift that he alone knows they need; he must therefore create in them a sense of their need for his gift by depriving them of their present contentment; he must create a sense of poverty precisely where there is thought to be plenty. The new strategy is an appeal to their pride, an attempt to demonstrate that what they treasure is "the most contemptible." This speech on "the last man" will be a direct lesson in what he previously called "the greatest experience," the experience of having contempt for what one has most prized. His appeal to their pride is intended to shame them, to turn their pride in their "culture" to contempt, and to initiate a move away from what is present and treasured to what is absent. But the people show that they cannot be shamed by Zarathustra, that they are closed to his greatest experience, for they terminate his speech on the last man with the outcry: "Give us the last man and you can have the superman!"

It could be said that in the reflective instant between his two speeches Zarathustra learns a fundamental lesson taught by Francis Bacon. In recounting the story of Prometheus, whose gift of fire made possible the culture that its recipients have come to love, Bacon says: "The opinion of having enough is to be accounted one of the greatest causes of having too little."[16] Men do well to complain of Prometheus that he has not given them enough, Bacon says, for only thus will they come to desire more, or to desire what it is possible to have. It is therefore as necessary for Zarathustra as it was for Bacon to characterize what is on hand as overrated or meagre, unbefitting a race that could have more. The strategy adopted by Zarathustra in the speech on the last man also follows the lesson of John Locke, who taught that "the chief, if not only spur to human industry and action is *uneasiness*."[17] Zarathustra, teacher of the greatest action that first gives meaning to the earth, learns from the people's response to his teaching that "whatsoever good is proposed," "if a man be easy and content without it," he will have no desire for it nor be moved to achieve it. Thus Zarathustra turns away from the teaching of a future good and attempts to inculcate uneasiness through shame.[18]

A special urgency is given to Zarathustra's strategic speech on the last man because of the historic moment in which it is made. The people addressed are like all other peoples in preferring what is on hand to what a teacher of novelty promises; but they differ from all other peoples insofar as they are well along in the process of acquiring the qualities of the last man. For Zarathustra's speech articulates the inchoate modern ideal to which they are drawn; they are already under way, not to the superman, but to the last man. In proclaiming its preference for the last man, his audience proclaims its loyalty to the modern age. The approaching universal domination by the last man poses the greatest threat to the project of the superman; the victory of the last man would preclude the coming of the superman and thereby prevent the earth from having any meaning. Zarathustra therefore attempts to teach modern men that they take pride in a shameful diminution of man, a debasement of the human species that thwarts the appearance of anything higher. Enlightened by Hobbes and Locke to the fear of death as the fundamental fear, Zarathustra's audience is in the process of surrendering all aspiration except for comfortable self-preservation. "Wretched contentment" is Zarathustra's name for this Lockean ideal. Basing their lives on a calculated self-interest that uses others for their own spiritual and physical advantage, as they are themselves used by others, last men content themselves with a universal and uniform society in which all differences are abolished, in which all are "recognized" or acknowledged as having the same worth.

Zarathustra's teaching on the last man is the essential counterpart to his teaching on the superman; it is not a general description of human mediocrity or everydayness, any more than the teaching on the superman is a general description of human authenticity. Last man and superman represent the two extremes made possible by the malleability of man, "the as yet undetermined animal" (BGE 62). Both belong to the period of Western history subsequent to the death of the Christian God. They represent two quite different atheisms. The atheism of the last man is still informed by the ideals of modern teachers who took their view of man's condition from Christianity and taught the formation of a civil society based on a calculated self-interest that aimed to overcome man's alleged "state of nature," a contemptible state of war and penury. The speech on the last man is the first of many speeches on the fate of modern man as heir to a kind of Christian morality while free of the Christian God. As Zarathustra presents the historical crisis in the prologue, the death of God means that mankind can either decay into the spiritual nihilism of the last man or revive himself by reaching for the superman. The passion of his speeches is rooted not so much in ten years spent in solitude by a lover of mankind, as in what Nietzsche later describes as dread for "the whole future of mankind," a future "in which no hand, and not even a finger of God [takes] part as a player" (BGE 62, 203). Like a prophet proclaiming the end time as a time of doom, Zarathustra proclaims that the ascendancy of the last man will terminate the possibility of human magnificence. Universal sway by the last man is the condition toward which the present tends, and it is this movement that Zarathustra seeks to arrest with his appeal to shame. But the people's reaction shows him how completely the ideal of the last man has already infected them.

The speech begins positively by stating that "the highest hope" can still be planted in human soil, and that "the dancing star" can be created from the chaos still within man. But both fruitful soil and fruitful chaos are in danger of growing barren because the last man sees himself as the culmination, and hence perfection, of evolution. Because history is progress, the last man knows himself to be superior to everything that has gone before; he surveys the past from the vantage point of its fulfillment and gathers what is interesting or useful while proclaiming it primitive or prep- aratory to himself. He is that "Posterity" of which past generations dreamed and for the establishment of which they sacrificed themselves. He lives the humanism that survives the death of God; but he does so modestly, tending to his health and avoiding strenuous extremes. Through the avoidance of extremes, equality prevails among last men, for there are neither rich nor poor, ruler nor ruled; uniformity prevails, and the one who feels differently goes of his own accord into the madhouse, the appearance of a deviant need being self-evidently the outbreak of a treatable madness. The last man still loves his neighbor or feigns such a love, for he needs the warmth his neighbor brings. The happiness "invented" by the last man is a fragile happiness, for it requires reassurance and recognition by others like himself; in return for approval, the last man approves. The last man is modern "psychological man" or "therapeutic man": "The last man, the lowest and most decayed man, the herd man without any ideals and aspirations, but well fed, well clothed, well housed, well medicated by ordinary physicians and by psychiatrists is Marx's man of the future seen from an anti-Marx point of view."[19]

What modern man sees as his proudest achievement, Zarathustra identifies as shameful. The last men are the men of technological mastery, not ruled but managed by one another, living comfortably with their neighbors, serviced by the line and race of inventions springing from their science of nature. They are products of the charitable efforts of modern technology in relief of the human estate or in the "humanitarian emen- dation" of nature (BGE 22). Representing the technological overcoming of inequality and scarcity, and of fear in the face of unmanageable forces of grace or chance, last men experience overwhelming confirmation in the global spread of their teachings and products. Collectively the technological masters of nature, they acknowledge no masters and no gods; they are humanists or atheists of a refined sort, who *want that some day there should be nothing more to be afraid of!"* (BGE 201). But it is precisely this that Zarathustra is most afraid of, and in his fear he repeats a theme that had long been present in Nietzsche's work, one that is expressed most directly in *On the Uses and Disadvantages of History for Life*. Speaking of noble purposes pursued in the name of the great and the impossible, Nietzsche addresses the overwhelming danger menacing his age in the true teachings of "the sovereignty of becoming," "the fluidity of all concepts, types and kinds," and "the absence of any cardinal difference between man and animal." These three teachings are "true but deadly," and their truth will crush and destroy, if they "are flung at the people for one more lifetime" (*UD* 9).[20] Only the coming of the superman can save mankind from these true but deadly teachings.

After the prologue, Zarathustra abandons the term *last man*, but not the concept, for in a much later reminder of the "last man" (its only other use in the book), he links the last man with "the good and the just" (III. 12, §27).[21] Although not used in his speeches to the people, the phrase "the good and the just," which Zarathustra learns from the jester (Prologue 8), occurs frequently in subsequent speeches. The danger of the last man is subsequently expressed as the danger of "the good and the just," a pressing danger in that "the damage [done by] the good is the most damaging damage" (III. 12, §§26–27) because it destroys hope for the future of mankind. "The good and the just" is a more comprehensive designation than "last man," for Zarathustra holds that the good and the just are present in every society; they are those who teach contentment through the given norms, and who treat any new teacher as a "destroyer." In his contempt for them Zarathustra later presents himself as making common cause with "one who once saw into the hearts of the good and the just and said: 'They are Pharisees' " (III. 12, §26).[22] Zarathustra thus claims to share a war with Jesus against the inertial weight of the good and the just, the shepherds of the herd, but whereas hatred of the good and the just defeated Jesus and turned him to a hatred of life (I. 21), Zarathustra's ten years of solitude have made him immune to such hatred. The modern good and just whom he opposes teach that eventually there will be only last men, for the state will wither away, religion will be abolished, and philosophy will be transformed into science.

The project of the superman implies a praise of progress. But the critique of the last man separates that praise from much of what has counted as progress in the modern world and raises the question of where Zarathustra stands with respect to the characteristic modern teaching of progress. An adequate answer to this question cannot be puzzled out of the oracular utterances of the prologue, nor does it need to be, for Zarathustra will later unfold a comprehensive view of human history that makes clear the ways in which he embraces progress—the progress of inquiry, for instance—while refusing as madness unrestrained progress in the alteration of nature.

Zarathustra's remarkable speech on modern man is answered by the rude, but appropriate, interruption: "Give us the last man and you can have the superman!" Jubilation and clamor follow this collective outburst, but Zarathustra's rueful soliloquy puts the crowd's reaction in the proper perspective. Despite the long solitude that has caused this hermit to misjudge the people, he is able to see through their laughter to the hatred that they have come to feel for him; but he is spared the consequences of that hatred by his care for the tightrope walker.

(Prologue 6–10) At the end of the speech on the last man Nietzsche states: "Here ended Zarathustra's first speech, which is also called 'the Prologue.'" What follows is the lesson to be drawn from the prologue, a lesson already suggested by the old saint, but one that Zarathustra must learn for himself. The lesson is not learned easily, because it requires the surrender of hope for the people, the very hope that brought him down from the mountain.

After the scheduled entertainment comes to an abrupt end, when the jester causes the fall of the tightrope walker, Zarathustra is after all able to give the gift of his teaching—not to all but to one. Knowing himself to be dying, the tightrope walker resigns himself to the fate to which his life of danger condemned him; nor does he expect anything from Zarathustra's compassion. But it belongs to Zarathustra's very honor that the devil and hell, so feared by the dying man, should not exist; it dishonors life to fear such an afterlife. But his attempt to comfort arouses discomfort, for if it is true that the soul dies before the body, is not life itself worthless? Is not the life of the tightrope walker, one of cruel punishments and meagre rewards, reduced to nothingness if he has nothing more to fear nor to hope for after this life than have flies or ants? No, his life is worthy in itself. By making danger his vocation, he has lifted himself high above the crowd and made himself the model for an ideal contrary to the crowd's ideal of risk-free contentment. In living heroically, he has distinguished himself by a manliness worthy of Zarathustra's respect. The two part as friends, Zarathustra promising to bury the tightrope walker, the tightrope walker acknowledging his gratitude for a teaching that redeems his already spent life.

Although able to console the dying tightrope walker, Zarathustra is unconsoled. For now the ten years passed in solitude appear to be pointless, so too the termination of that solitude in order to bring mankind the gift won there. He recognizes that his speeches must have sounded to the people like the ridicule of the jester to the tightrope walker. At the end of the first day, a day on which he was to have been triumphant, this new fisher of men[23] reflects that he has caught only a corpse. But while carrying the corpse out of the town at night, he is favored with a private communication from the jester. In his whispered words on the secret motives of the people, the jester comes to light as the serviceable cynic described as a "jester" in Beyond Good and Evil. There Nietzsche says that a philosopher should congratulate himself when such a cynic speaks out in his presence, for the cynic provides the "shortcut" in the philosopher's indispensable study of the average man (BGE 26). The jester's words confirm Zarathustra's suspicion that to the people he is in the middle between a fool and a corpse: he has been a fool; they will make him a corpse. Moreover, the jester's words are a mockery of heroic effort by one who believes that mankind belongs in the tower, in stasis. In the superiority of his cynicism he knows that his alone is the art of the high wire; only cynicism, bitter knowledge of man's ignoble origins and vain ends, transcends everyday life; he will leap over Zarathustra too, another foolish tightrope walker. Zarathustra says nothing to the jester; he neither thanks him for his warning nor challenges the superiority that he has implied.[24]

On his way out of the town Zarathustra meets the grave-diggers, who call him a grave-digger. But Zarathustra will not dig a grave for his companion; he will leave him in the hollow tree in which he had temporarily placed him to protect him from the wolves. The grave-diggers accuse Zarathustra of being a thief (confirming the old saint's prediction), although they think he has stolen only a "dog." After he has learned his lesson, Zarathustra confirms their view of him by attempting to steal not their dogs but their most prized offspring, those who, like the tightrope walker, rise above the crowd in pursuit of danger. Attributing to him a wickedness worthy of the evil one, the grave-diggers curse him with their devil, it being no part of *their* honor that the devil not exist. But his silence demonstrates to the grave-diggers that he is content to let the dead bury the dead.[25]

Zarathustra's final encounter is with another outsider, an old hermit troubled by uneasy sleep. The old hermit is moved by charity, but an indiscriminate charity that refuses to distinguish between living and dead in its offer of bread and wine, the Eucharist or thanksgiving meal. The bitter hermit with his forced philanthropy finds no joy in giving; his surly response shows that Zarathustra's innocent "wisdom"—that the one who feeds the hungry finds his own soul refreshed—is not true of him. Later, after he learns his lesson, Zarathustra states that he intends to sing to the hermits. His song will enable these outsiders to be of good cheer and to distinguish living from dead in the giving of gifts; it will be a grateful gift in return for the gift of discriminate giving taught unintentionally by the bitter hermit.

When Zarathustra awakens at noon the next day, he does so with a new insight into his task, derived from his encounters with the crowd and the outsiders. He knows now how to continue as a teacher in the face of the people's resistance, for now he intends to win from them a few "companions" for his teaching, "disciples," though that word is pointedly withheld until he has successfully carried out the intention he here declares. This new intention provides the essential introduction to the speeches of part I: they aim at winning a few select friends for the new teaching. Zarathustra's new aim shows that he has learned an old lesson about the introduction of new teachings: "Nothing is more difficult to deal with nor more dubious of success nor more dangerous to manage than making oneself the head in the introduction of new orders."[26] Any such introduction necessarily takes place in a setting already shaped by tradition, and the people thus shaped, "the adversaries," "have the laws on their side." Not only are the people unable to welcome the novelty of a wholly new teaching because they think they already know the things worth doing, but they treat the advocate of such novelty as "the paragon of all wicked-ness."[27] The gravity of the people's reaction, the intensity of their hatred of him and his teaching, becomes apparent to him when he likens the people to a herd. For, while they are like a herd to him, he must be like a wolf to them, and he learns from this imagery that the herd's desire to protect its lambs turns the killing of wolves into a virtue. He protected the corpse of the tightrope walker from howling wolves; but he has himself become a wolf in the eyes of the herd. Welcoming the people's judgment that he is a beast of prey, Zarathustra sees that he will have to win their prized offspring in the face of the people's censure. The guardians of that censure, the shepherds of the herd, he now describes by the two epithets learned from the cynical jester: "the good and the just" and "the faithful of the true faith." These attentive guardians of the people's faith inevitably see him as a "destroyer," though he knows himself to be a "creator"; as a "criminal," though he knows himself to be the bringer of a new law; as a teacher of evil, though he knows himself to be the bringer of the essential gift. The antagonism and rivalry between Zarathustra and the people whom he had only yesterday come to win has today become complete, or to the death. To Zarathustra it is a battle for the future of mankind itself; to the people, a battle for the survival of what in their view are the highest things. Zarathustra's insight into the people deepens the seriousness of the speeches he is about to deliver, by putting them in a setting of conflict, a conflict that pits him against the modern crowd in a world-historical battle for the good of mankind.[28]

At the end of the prologue (10), as a benediction on his new insight, Zarathustra welcomes the return of his animals, the eagle and the snake. The eagle, an omen to the Greeks, flies in wide circles above him, while the snake, the eagle's traditional foe, winds itself in wide loops around the eagle's neck. These animals with whom Zarathustra shared his ten-year solitude were once the animals of Zeus (the eagle) and Apollo (the snake) and symbolize the virtues of pride and cleverness, vices from a Christian standpoint.[29] They symbolize too the new epoch as the overcoming of the epoch of Zarathustra/Zoroaster: the eagle was once the animal of Ormuzd and a symbol of light, the snake the animal of Ahriman and a symbol of darkness. Their intertwining symbolizes the overcoming of the old dualisms of light and darkness, heaven and earth, good and evil; their intertwining is beyond good and evil, a harmony of earth and sky.[30] Reflecting Zara-thustra's own twofold spirit, the proud eagle soars high above the earth while the clever snake dwells nearest the earth; but the pride of soaring is not condemned, nor are nearness to the earth and its concomitant clev-erness seen as a curse.[31] At the end of the prologue Zarathustra desires to learn from his animals, because he is still inferior to them in pride and cleverness. Later, however, his superiority in both respects requires that he hide his pride from them with cleverly told fine lies (IV. 1). Whereas

Zarathustra's growth in pride is simply a consequence of his achievements, his growth in cleverness or prudence arises from his discovery that he will have to abandon one kind of prudence whose presence holds him back (II. 21) and to cultivate another kind whose absence would endanger him (III. 5, 6). For Zarathustra, learning the place of prudence means learning the immoderation of thought and the moderation of speech.

The prologue as a whole ends exactly as its first section ended: "Thus began Zarathustra's going under." The repetition points to the prologue as a false start in Zarathustra's teaching; he must begin again in a new way and he does so in the speeches of part I. He has not been as wise as a serpent in going among men, as Jesus counseled his disciples to be when he first sent them out into "the midst of wolves."[32] In his last speech in the prologue Zarathustra thinks ruefully of the old saint and prays the fitting prayer that he may become as clever as his snake. But then, because that seems impossible, he asks instead that his cleverness be always accompanied, not by the harmlessness of a dove, but by the pride of an eagle; when his cleverness abandons him, so may his pride abandon him also. This is not a prayer for humility, but for a cleverness worthy of his pride. Although Zarathustra is chastened by his failure, the gift to mankind won in solitude is still intact, and in his speeches he will attempt to create worthy recipients of that gift.[33]

Ascent and descent in the prologue can be seen as repeating, but correcting from a contrary perspective, the ascent and descent described in connection with the most prominent symbol of Western philosophy, the cave in Plato's *Republic*. Having ascended burned out, Zarathustra rekindles himself through solitude, and at the end of his restoration addresses the sun as a mere star. The sun is not the symbol of the Good, beyond being in dignity and power;[34] it is rather the symbol of giving and going under. Zarathustra's sun, like the sun of our heavens, is not always at the zenith holding in being and intelligibility the things that have being and intelligibility; rather, it rises and sets, and is thus a symbol of coming into being and passing out of being. Moreover, this rising and setting is symbolic of its worth, not its worthlessness. The old Platonic "sun of a fundamental moral judgment and standard of highest value" (GS 7) is itself setting, and a new sun is rising, one that takes its bearings from the judgment that the old Platonic sun is dead. By addressing the sun as a rising and setting star, Zarathustra has "unchained this earth from its sun"; he has wiped away "the entire horizon" formed by construing the sun as symbolic of the permanent Good (GS 125).[35] But this act creates a new horizon, for Zarathustra's descent to the cave is intended to bring the light of a new sun to enlighten the cave. His first attempt fails, and the light-bringer finds himself in danger of being killed by the watchful guardians of the cave.[36] Avoiding death by a lucky act of compassion, he escapes and learns Plato's lesson for himself, that the cave-dwellers must love their own things and view as a corrupter of morals one who brings a novel teaching. Recognizing thereby his capacity to harm, as well as the danger of his being harmed, Zarathustra will enter the city with his new strategy to speak to the few. He will adopt a rhetoric that will be an indispensable instrument for his teaching; its purpose will be to lead potential followers to his teaching by liberating them from the charms of the opinions that now hold them.[37] Despite his new caution he will have to speak as a "flatterer" to those who now falsely believe themselves to be the natural sons of great "families," sons of the time and place in which they were born and whose things they have come to identify as their own. He will weaken and break the family ties by telling the sons the truth about their origins, and in so doing evoke the hatred of the faithful and bring upon himself the opprobrium due an outlaw. Knowing the danger to which he exposes himself, he will speak gently in his approach to young men, though even that may not spare him private plots and public trials that the shepherds of the herd will set for him.[38] He adopts this strategy not because he is solicitous of the cave-dwellers who may be harmed by his teaching; his speech appears not to be animated by a spirit of social responsibility or a justice that seeks to avoid doing harm; he adopts his strategy in order to avoid being harmed and to further the project that will give meaning to the earth. For Zarathustra does not go under at the beginning of his work merely to observe and pray, nor does he, like Socrates, have to be kept in the place he descends to by a threat of force;[39] he has descended from his solitude with a mission to transform mankind through the teaching of the superman. His speech is, after all, animated by a spirit of social responsibility of a certain sort, by a justice that gives to each what is his due when the meaning of the whole or the good itself is the future superman. Although he will invite his special audience to ascend to solitude, that ascent will be portrayed not as an ascent to the true light, but as an ascent of discovery preparatory to a subsequent descent to rule, not because duty dictates that the one who has ascended return, contrary to his natural inclination, to rule the city which made it possible to ascend, but because the best desire to rule (III. 12, §21).[40] The people will not desire that the best rule, nor can they be persuaded that this is desirable;[41] the rule of the best will have to be achieved through means other than those employed in the hermit's folly of the prologue.

ZARATHUSTRA'S SPEECHES: THE TEACHING THAT MAKES DISCIPLES

"Zarathustra's Speeches" implement the new strategy or apply the political education of the prologue. They aim to make disciples through the attractive presentation of the novel teaching. Heeding the lesson learned in the prologue, Zarathustra begins in a politic way by describing the appealing features of spirit necessary in those who would follow him (I. 1). His next six speeches merely demean the old teachings while intimating a new, more attractive teaching (I. 2–7). They succeed in attracting special hearers (I. 8). Only then, in another series of six speeches, does he begin to reveal to

them that the new teaching is in fact a call to war, a fight to the death
with the preachers of death, which requires a complete separation from
what have been taken to be one's own things (I. 9–14). At the peak of his
teaching in part I, Zarathustra shows that human creativity has grounded
all peoples in the past, and that the present calls for a new act of human
creativity that will ground a future people, mankind (I. 15). The next six
speeches prepare for the new creativity by establishing new conventions
(I. 16–21). Finally, Zarathustra speaks privately, outside the city, to those
persuaded by his speeches, for the first time calling them disciples (I. 22).
The speeches of part I are thus framed by the appropriate opening and
closing challenges and fall into three distinct groups separated or hinged
by two turning points.[42]

"Zarathustra's Speeches" teach both the possibility and the desirability
of the superman. Since the superman is the meaning of the earth, the task
of preparing his way is the measure of all previous teachings and all present
actions. Like every revolutionary teacher, Zarathustra distinguishes between
what has long been authoritative and what "I say unto you."[43] His new
teaching holds that all values are human creations; that they control human
affairs; that hitherto values have paraded as objective and life-serving, although they have actually been subjective and life-denying; and that the
superman will self-consciously create values that are life-serving. All values
are rooted in the body, even when they conspire to transcend the body
or diminish its worth, but Zarathustra does not advocate a bodily hedonism
or surrender to its passions; he counsels discipline instead, a spiritualization of the passions, his own sort of transcendence of the body through
mastery of its inclinations for the good of mankind. All passions and actions
submit to a single measure of worth in the austere teachings of part I: only
what serves the coming of the superman is of worth. The extent to which
private passions must be transformed into service for mankind comes to
light only slowly because of the need to make his teachings attractive.
Nevertheless, Zarathustra concludes part I with teachings on birth and
death that make being born and dying worthy only insofar as they promote
the coming of the superman. Like Nietzsche, Zarathustra will show himself
to have "a stricter morality than anybody" (draft of a letter to Rée, last week
of December 1882).

Gifts of Spirit (Chapter 1)

The first of "Zarathustra's Speeches" has a special prominence. Coming
on the heels of his new insight that he can fulfill his mission to mankind
only by finding fit companions and singling them out from the "herd" to
which they now belong, it defines what is required in such companions.
But the definition not only sets out the requirements; it also flatters and
entices, for Zarathustra does not simply await the appearance of spirits
like those he describes; he seeks, through his teaching, to create them.

Aside from the prologue, there is no introduction to inform the reader about the circumstances of this first speech; nevertheless, the prologue shows that the speech is addressed to a general audience with the intention of drawing away from it the few suited to be Zarathustra's companions. Moreover, at the end of the speech (and three other times, at I. 8, I. 22, and III. 8), it is said that the speeches of part I were given in the city called "The Colorful Cow," a name that suggests the rich but indeterminate diversity of the modern democratic city, as well as the domesticated character of its inhabitants.[44] Plato's Socrates, who inhabited the most open and democratic city in ancient Greece and loved to speak with young men, held that democracy is the most "colorful" of regimes, because it displays all types of men, and that it is therefore the suitable setting for the philosopher, who studies all men and attracts some. To attract the special few suited for his teaching, Zarathustra takes advantage not only of the colorful diversity of the democratic city but also of the other feature illuminated by Socrates' account, its permissive openness which allows even philosophy, a useless or dangerous pursuit from the standpoint of a less permissive, less bovine, city.[45]

Zarathustra's first speech describes the three states of the spirit necessary for his companions (camel, lion, child), but it describes only two transformations (from camel to lion and from lion to child). On the first transformation, from the spirit's prior state to camel, Zarathustra is silent, apart from declaring it to be necessary. This silence, which is surprising, given the promise of the title, "On the Three Transformations," in fact follows necessarily from the political lesson of the prologue: the transformation to camel cannot be taught. The camel spirit comes to light as the heroic spirit, that of the tightrope walker, the spirit that asks of heroes what the heroic labors are, in order that it may perform those labors itself and thereby prove to itself that it possesses heroic qualities. While Zarathustra's teaching aims to produce the qualities it deems worthy, it depends initially on a quality that is simply given, a gift of the spirit that Zarathustra cannot give. But those gifted in this way, the spiritually adventurous already disposed to undertake the heroic, Zarathustra can instruct if they learn to ask of him what the heroic is. By beginning this way, Zarathustra limits his appeal to spirited natures of a special and rare sort, those whose qualities of spirit already single them out from the people as a whole.

It is sometimes supposed that the camel spirit is one that Zarathustra only criticizes because it demands a "strong reverent spirit that would bear much," the supposition being that Zarathustra shuns reverence and calls his followers only to the lion and child transformations, to destruction and creation.[46] Although the camel is a homely and domestic beast, possession of its qualities renders the spirit noble and heroic. Zarathustra already exhibits a camel spirit, one that takes upon itself what is hardest. In this speech aimed at making followers, it is altogether appropriate that Zarathustra should insist first of all on the willingness to bear much, for in the speeches that follow he asks of them that much be borne; without the camel's qualities no beginning can be made on the way he prescribes.

Zarathustra is willing to bear much because he has a great reverence for the superman. But this opening speech does not name the superman, nor does it imply the existence of any goal in the name of which the spirit burden itself. Prior to the articulation of any such goal, the spirited nature must feel impelled to difficult acts simply for the sake of their difficulty; it must be driven to follow "whatever whim's most difficult / Among whims not impossible."[47] The spirit that would bear much asks of heroes what it is that they have found most difficult and seeks to duplicate it, not merely to be acclaimed heroic, but to be so. The sole motive for heroic behavior as described here is the delight of the spirit in its own strength. Such spiritedness is not honor-loving but victory-loving; it is not in love with being loved, but only with winning the victory, even if the victory is known only to itself.[48] Zarathustra describes the spiritedness he requires as a kind of cruelty toward the self with respect to both knowledge and one's relationship with others. Of the six hardest measures with which the spirit undertakes to burden itself, the first, third, and fifth all concern wisdom or knowledge, the second, fourth, and sixth independence of others. The camel spirit refuses itself both the comforts of any traditional wisdom and the comforts of any community; it burdens itself by subtraction. In taking upon itself what is hard (schwer), it anticipates Zarathustra's primary conflict with the spirit of gravity (Schwere). Such a heroic spirit seems perfectly free in its pursuit of wisdom, since it does not take its measure of itself from the acclaim of others. It is a free spirit where "bound spirits are the rule" (HH I. 225). But later, Zarathustra is forced to acknowledge in private to a young man with heroic yearnings that this seemingly perfect freedom faces a deadly enemy (I. 8).[49]

Why is the reverent spirit that would bear much not enough? Why must it flee into the desert and be transformed into its seeming opposite, a destructive lion? Zarathustra's answer to his own question is that the camel must become a lion precisely because the spirit that would bear much must bear the heaviest burden of destroying what it has come to revere. This act of destruction is the last and most difficult rung on the ladder of spiritual cruelty climbed by the heroic spirit. No motive is given for the lion's cruel act other than the hard conscience that belongs to the camel as camel. The lion does not act out of its own rage; its rage to destroy whatever gives it repose is the willful creation of the camel spirit. Zarathustra had used the word brothers for the first time when he asked why the reverent spirit was not enough. To become Zarathustra's brother, it is necessary for the most reverent spirits to perform the destructive act of intellectual conscience that removes at a stroke values that have withstood the millennia, ancestral values that come out of the past bearing the imperative gravity of the sacred and honored things. It is a stroke that plunges the spirit into a homeless nihilism.[50]

But once the lion has been formed and his single deed done, what necessity transforms it into the child? The lion cannot suffice because its destructive act leaves the spirit homeless; it is not enough to worship the stone. The lion spirit is transformed by the need of the spirit for a home, not the ancestral home, but one it builds for itself, against which it need not rage. The rage of the best or most spirited of men is abated when revolt is total, or when there is nothing more to bring down. Then, according to Zarathustra's promise, the spirit is born again, free of rage because free of the need for revolt, fully at home in a world in which no dragon exists. The spirit that has lost the world by destroying all previously created worlds is thus transformed into the child spirit. The spirit born of destruction is free of the camel's need to burden itself. Zarathustra describes the child spirit's free, creative play, its yes-saying after the consistent no-saying of the camel and the lion, but he does not describe what it creates. The goal as described in this first speech is a renewed spirit, self-generating and therefore free of rage against the past, self-fulfilling and therefore not in need of a future to redeem it. Still, it befits a child that it mature, that its promise and potential take a still to be determined form. While the child of promise is here the goal, this is only the beginning; Zarathustra's teaching as a whole aims at manliness or supermanliness, the maturity to which the creative child is father.

It is fitting that this first speech aimed at making companions defines not the task but the disposition necessary for the task; those who lack this disposition, as Nietzsche said at a similar juncture in his next book, "listen in without permission" (BGE 30).

Few of Zarathustra's speeches have been as abused as this one by the customary act of divorcing the speeches from their setting in a developing narrative. It has the limitations appropriate to the first speech in a series, but these limitations have usually been ignored, and the imagery has been taken as Zarathustra's final word on the transformation of the spirit instead of his first, inviting words.[51] That it is no such final word is clear from Zarathustra's own subsequent transformations. According to the old saint (Prologue 2) Zarathustra has already been transformed into a child. But there are further transformations, including the fundamental one depicted in part III (III. 2), which cannot be subsumed under the imagery of this first speech to potential companions. The images employed in describing that later transformation are completely different. On the other hand, the three transformations described here can well be read as a preview of the rest of the speeches in part I, the first group of which burden their listeners with an account of the worthlessness of the teachings in which they have been raised (I. 2–7); the middle group of which create lion spirits for the battle against the old teachings (I. 8–14); and the final group of which suggest what will be required of those who take up Zarathustra's project (I. 15–22).

School for Insurgents (Chapters 2–7)

The group of speeches that follows the opening, flattering speech can be treated as a unit because they all develop the contrast between the old teachings which the young men inherit in the old ways and Zarathustra's new teaching. The first and mildest speech allows the old teachings to speak for themselves (I. 2). The next three speeches each dissect some aspect of the old teachings, showing how the modes of human experience held to be transcendent to mere body—gods and afterworlds (I. 3), reason and spirit (I. 4), the virtues (I. 5)—are in fact products of the body. The primacy of the body is then exhibited by a criminal case in which transcendence of the body failed (I. 6). The final speech (I. 7) points to the new possibility in an especially attractive way. Fittingly, the chapter that follows this series relates a private conversation outside the city between Zarathustra and a singular young man attracted by these speeches.

"On the Chairs[52] of Virtue" (I. 2) is uncharacteristic in that the speaker for most of the chapter is not Zarathustra. Instead, one of the famous teachers of virtue is allowed to speak, while Zarathustra joins the young men sitting at his feet, as if to share their subjection to his demands.[53] According to his account of the rival teaching, an account kept from the young men, it holds the highest virtue to be sleep and knows the forty disciplines necessary to achieve it.[54] It warns against the terrors of the night, and, though it has no clear teaching on life after death, practices ritual defenses against the night. The old wisdom teaches submission to power, for it is beyond the power of the sage to remedy the crooked paths of the powerful. It loves the poor in spirit precisely because of their poverty, for it prefers what it can pity to what might arouse its envy. In all its precepts this ancient wisdom holds that wakefulness exists for the sake of sleep, or, by extension, that life is to be lived for the sake of a good death or a good life after death. Its highest dream is a dreamless sleep, a blessedness bereft of thought, completely mute. It is precise and didactic and can present itself as a full science of behavior. Although Socrates, Plato, Aristotle, Epicurus, and other ancient philosophers can all be heard in the old teaching as Zarathustra recounts it, it seems that no particular teacher is characterized here, but rather the whole tradition of wisdom in which young men are schooled, a tradition which teaches that life is to be lived for the benefits of the transcendence of life, a tradition that consistently judges that life is no good (*TI*, "Socrates," 1).[55] The rigorous disciplines taught by the old sage anesthetize the body to facilitate its transcendence. Through submission to this teaching, ardent and unanesthetized youths learn obedience and self-renunciation, thereby learning to grow old while still young. Zarathustra, on the other hand, desires that the young become as children. This chapter also displays the old way of discipleship as youthful surrender to the old and authoritative wise, a way that requires constant repetition in order to create the controls of habit that tame a youthful nature, which, left to itself, would favor innovation or indulgence of the passions now beginning to be experienced.

After hearing the old teaching, Zarathustra states to himself that the old teacher is a fool, but that the young men are not entirely foolish to submit to his teaching. He acknowledges that if life had no meaning, he would himself choose this form of meaninglessness, the old wisdom of death over a meaningless life. He does not condemn the young men for submitting to this teaching, for they have had no opportunity to discover that life has meaning apart from any transcendence of life. Zarathustra understands the old teaching better than its honored teachers do, for his temperate commentary on it draws attention to its hidden surrender to the meaninglessness of life. His opposition is founded on his conviction that life has a meaning, a future meaning that he will describe for the young men in speeches to come. The time is up for the old teachings, even though their time has been all of human history till now, and Zarathustra ends this most moderate of his speeches with the frequently repeated joke that these old teachers of sleep should now take their teaching seriously—and nod off. While these teachers nod, less moderate assessments of their teaching will be made as enticements to their pupils.[56]

The next three speeches unmask three specific aspects of the teaching that the young men are accustomed to hearing. But what Zarathustra reveals, they are not accustomed to hearing, for he discloses the motives behind the teachings on the afterworld, reason, and virtue. He discredits the teachings by discrediting the teachers; he makes himself attractive to his young listeners by showing that the onerous teachings inflicted on them stem from their teachers' afflictions.

Having spoken of the old philosophy, Zarathustra now speaks of the old religion ("On the Afterworldly,"[57] I. 3). Its teachers also renounce the body, but, unlike the old philosophers, they believe in an immortal soul tended by a moral God. Zarathustra meets his listeners on their own grounds, acknowledging that he too once believed in God or gods, if not exactly in their way. At one time the world seemed to him too to be the creation of a god; but because it seemed imperfect, he imagined its creator god to be himself imperfect, a sufferer who created the world to heal himself. This experience made the source of his own god and all other gods apparent to him. "Believe me my brothers," he says with twice-repeated urgency, the creative source of all afterworlds is that special sort of body that despairs of the body. This despairing body alleges that it "heard the belly of being speak to it"; but it is only the body that speaks when gods and afterworlds seem to speak, and it speaks only of its own despair of itself and its need to be delivered. As in the previous speech, the traditional teaching is countered by uncovering its secret despair at the meaninglessness of life on earth, a despair it translates into dreams of a new earth and a new body.

Zarathustra then declares a principle that prevails throughout part I as the ground of his affirmations: "The belly of being does not speak to man at all, unless as man." This derogatory phrase for the object of philosophical inquiry is highlighted in its two uses by contrasting it with the head—not the head that inquires into the nature of being, or the highest being, in a rational and disciplined way, but the head as battering ram that crashes through the ramparts of the world to reach "that other world." But neither the head as battering ram nor the belly of being provides a way to a world beyond.[58]

The inventive, despairing body of the first part of the speech gives way in the second part to the healthy, but still inventive body. While "being" is always difficult to prove and to bring to speech, the "I," or ego, is the best proved of all beings and the one that speaks most honestly in its contradictions and confusions. The creating, willing, valuing I is "the measure and value of things," while all gods and afterworlds have been its creation. The history of honest speech prior to Zarathustra is the history of the modern discovery of the subject as the ground of meaning. Although Zarathustra is in the mainstream of this historic movement, he identifies himself as the one in whom the discovery has ceased to be blind, in whom it has become self-conscious. His "new pride," grounded in the self-conscious subject, learns to create an earthly meaning for the earth, while his "new will" affirms the primacy of the subject that frightened even those predecessors who discovered it.

At this point he returns to his Feuerbachian debunking of the gods, grounding belief in the gods in sicknesses of the body. He thus turns physician, mild to the sick, encouraging them to convalescence, to that health of the body that will cure them of otherworldly needs. The speech ends in a reenactment of the historic modern contest, in which the voice of the healthy body speaks for the youngest virtue, honesty, against the old virtues of faith. Zarathustra's elevation of the virtue of honesty, or intellectual probity, and his adherence to it throughout his course, despite its costs to himself and his audience, show how little he shares the "absolute lack of intellectual integrity" of those for whom "it does not matter whether a thing is true, but only what effect it produces." (KGW VIII 10[184] = WP 172). Zarathustra is in the vanguard of the newly appearing honesty that is grounded in the subject and that demythologizes everything transcendent to the subject. In the next chapters he continues the project of demythologizing by disclosing the bodily sources of rationality and virtue. Thus, it "is perhaps the first insight reached by" Zarathustra's capable listeners, that he is "a psychologist ... who has no equal" (EH, "Books," 5).[59]

"On Those with Contempt for the Body" (I. 4) begins and ends by addressing those with contempt for the body, but it does not aim to reform them. It aims rather to reform the young men, addressed in the central part of his speech, by inviting their contempt for the old teaching of a radical distinction between soul and body. In this speech—part of his contribution to the project begun by Descartes to "assassinate the old soul concept" (BGE 54)—Zarathustra goes beyond the previous speech to show that the creative I is itself not fundamental but is founded on what he calls the *self*, the body in all its aspects. He recommends a return to the wisdom of the child who has awakened from the sleep of the old wisdoms that honor soul, reason, and spirit as if they were transcendent to mere body, though they are only its instruments. Using political terms and metaphors, he describes man as a regime with the self as the ruler who utilizes his instruments of senses and spirit for hearing and seeking. Through these ministers, the ruling self "compares, subdues, conquers, destroys"—a crescendo of activities which serve the self in its end of absolute rule. It exercises dominion through its subsidiary or ministerial functions, while uniting in itself power and wisdom, the prerequisites for perfect rule. As absolute ruler, the self or the body determines all experience of pain and pleasure, imperially dictating to the I when and where it should feel pain or pleasure. The reasoning of the I is grounded in those pains and pleasures, for it must calculate how best to avoid them or procure them.

After thus claiming that thought serves the purposes of the body, Zarathustra addresses those whose thought makes the body contemptible. Such an address is necessary, because their contempt poses a riddle for his account of the primacy of the body: if it is the single source of thought and action, how can it produce thought and action aimed at its own demise? Zarathustra's answer is that the body turns suicidal when it knows itself to be thwarted in its creative essence. It belongs to the body to create beyond itself, but because it has become "too late" for this, it wills its own annihilation; there is no surcease from willing for "man would rather will nothingness than not will" (GM III. 1, 28). The suicidal body has created fables of a nonbodily soul, rationality, or spirit that have served as the rationale for its debasement.[60] But why has the self or body judged that it is "too late" to create beyond itself? At the end of his speech Zarathustra names the ground of that judgment: "unconscious envy." Zarathustra does not intimate the object of envy, only that an unrecognized envy has given rise to contempt for the body and to teachings which carry that contempt into action. Envy, the malignant passion which comes as the uninvited response to the success or superiority of others, focuses on what one wills for oneself but knows to be lacking. As envy, it is malevolence directed in the first instance at those who do create beyond themselves, but who, in so doing, make it "too late" for others. But envy then takes the form of malevolence directed at the self for its incapability. Zarathustra's analysis remains dark, because envy is not clarified; it is named in an accusation, with no attempt to demonstrate the truth of the accusation. Still, these are the opening speeches meant to attract young listeners to a new teaching not yet enunciated in those speeches and the mere accusation that the vice of envy is the basis of the virtuous teachings on the renunciation of body is enough for Zarathustra's purpose. Envy will be the theme of many later speeches, but what appears here as envy will then be explained in a deeper, more telling way as revenge. Revenge will itself be elaborated in stages, as revenge against those with the capacity one lacks (II. 7) and revenge against time itself, the primary revenge that is responsible for all previous teachings (II. 20). Thus Zarathustra's analysis goes beyond the uncovering of the old vice of envy to a deeper vice seen in a novel way.

The last sentences of the speech intimate for the first time how the healthy body creates beyond itself, and what that creation is for which it is not too late. Zarathustra says that those with contempt for the body are not the "bridge to the superman." It is the first time in these speeches to the young men of the Colorful Cow that he names what he had named in his very first sentence in his rash and useless speech to the crowd. Having stated at the end of his previous speech that the healthy body speaks the meaning of the earth, now, at the end of a speech describing the body as the creative source of all meaning, he names the superman. Now that his strategic lesson has been learned, he unveils the goal of human creating more enticingly, while at the same time breaking the charm of the old teaching.

Zarathustra celebrates the primacy of the self as body, for that self erects everything sublime; but reducing the essence of man to body does not make him mere machinery. Zarathustra denies that Cartesian dream of man's full accessibility to rational inquiry. His effort to "bring Reason itself to reason" (HH I, "Epilogue") recognizes that the heart of man is elusive. Still, there are no moral curbs on inquiry into that elusive core, nor is there any defense for a salutary skepticism which limits knowledge in order to make room for faith. The elusive self will be partially captured later by being named "will to power."

Although the title of the next chapter, "On Enjoying and Suffering the Passions" (I. 5), names joys and passions, its subject is virtue. Still, the title is fitting, for Zarathustra speaks first of the joy of virtue and then of the suffering caused by the separation of virtues from their ground in the passions. In this chapter the psychologist unriddles the virtues just as he has previously unriddled the gods and rationality, by showing the bodily sources of the anti-body teaching on virtue. The speech breaks down the distinction between virtue and passion, first by ignoring it and pointing to the cherishing of passion, then by showing how the old virtues have arisen from passions, and finally by showing that they are themselves still kinds of passions.

Zarathustra begins by speaking in the singular to "my brother" on how to be virtuous. He shows that he is not a teacher of virtue who multiplies by four the ten commandments in the interests of deadening the body and inducing sleep; he is a teacher of virtue who allows the young man his private virtue or passion. A virtue is a dearly held private possession that one can hardly resist playing with and naming. But to name it makes it common and forces it to be public and shared; it is far better that it retain its nameless private character. Virtue is a passion that moves a young man's soul to both agony and sweet delight; it is the hunger of his very entrails, too exalted to be named. Zarathustra is himself moved in his very entrails by a virtue or a passion, as he will reveal in the final speech made to the young men attracted by these teachings (I. 22, §1), but here he follows his own counsel and does not name his virtue. He keeps it completely private until he wants what naming it will do for it: cause it to be shared by others and move them as it has moved him.

If his brother simply must speak of his beloved passion or virtue, Zarathustra gives him a model speech, said to be stammering and unsure of itself. In fact, the speech is a most attractive gift, given as an example of how Zarathustra thinks young men are to live with their passionate natures, for it allows him to keep what is his, rather than embark on that program of habitual extirpation learned at the feet of the traditional teachers. Zarathustra teaches the young man to say of his virtue that it is his, his own good, and that he wants it simply to be his; for it is not God's law, nor does it mark the way to something higher or other than itself. It is not what the great teachers of virtue, Aristotle and Kant, have said virtues are, for it is not prudent, and least of all does it derive its validity from universalizability. It is a bird that flew here from somewhere and built its nest here: it should be welcomed and harbored and allowed to hatch its golden eggs. What is remarkable about this model speech on virtue is not only its attractiveness but its permissiveness, for it allows the young man to nurture his waxing passion, whatever it may be. In his later speeches Zarathustra will be much less permissive; he will attempt to channel or sublimate the passions into what he sees as the single hope for mankind. Still, breaking the authority of the ancestral by learning to treasure one's own private virtue remains an important part of the complete break with ancestral authority described later (III. 11).[61]

The passions that Zarathustra has quietly assumed to be virtues were formerly regarded as evil and were gradually transformed into what were formerly regarded as virtues by an act of domestication. Uninvited passions such as anger, lust, fanaticism, and vengeance have all been made manageable or turned into virtues that can be regarded as chosen. This transformation of passions into virtues has left man tame; no longer impassioned, he is at peace, and nothing evil grows out of him anymore.

Or so it seems. But there is an exception to man's domestication: the evil in man caused by the battle of virtues. The virtues have not become house pets subject to their master man, for they master him by making him the battlefield of virtues. In some lucky cases like his own, a single virtue reigns preeminent, and such a one, with no division in himself, goes "easily over the bridge." While it is a distinction to have many virtues it is also a hard lot and in depicting this hard lot, Zarathustra describes the virtuous man. He does not follow the advice of the old teacher (I. 2) to possess all the virtues and to tame each with a little indulgence, even though he accepts the old teacher's ground for that indulgence, namely, that the virtues quarrel like women over the child that each wants to possess for herself. Many have gone into the desert, not to kill the dragon of "Thou Shalt" or of virtues a thousand years old, but to kill themselves because they can no longer bear to be the battlefield of virtues. But is war evil? Zarathustra does not answer this question here, but later he will teach the merits of war to those singled out by his teaching (I. 10). But even if war is evil, it is a necessary evil because of the way in which envy, mistrust, and calumny have come to characterize relations among the virtues. Each passionately desires to be highest, to rule over the whole spirit; each is jealous of the others and jealousy among the virtues is a terrible thing, because a virtue will kill its possessor rather than exist as less than first. Zarathustra does not see jealousy as a virtue and envy as a vice in the way that Aristotle did.[62] Instead, he sees jealousy as self-destructive and envy simply as a passion that must be made conscious because of its dangers. When conscious, envy among the virtues can be transformed into an order that ranks them. This account of envy, while limited in that it omits the harm to the envious described in the previous speech, is consistent with what Zarathustra will later teach about the uses of envy (I. 8, 10); the battle among envious virtues could serve as a model for the battle for preeminence to which Zarathustra will invite his followers.[63]

As a result of the long history of attempts to domesticate the passions, mankind has been transformed into a battleground for conflicting virtues. Only sleep, the unmastered master of the passions, can put an end to this warfare, according to the old sage. But Zarathustra draws a different conclusion, one that refuses surrender: mankind must be overcome. Zarathustra teaches his followers to enjoy their virtues as if they were one's own. But virtues are passions which come uninvited and exercise imperial rule; one suffers them and even perishes of them, because they master and are not mastered. Mankind is not yet good enough, because it is subject to its virtues; to be man is still to be mastered by what is not man. Zarathustra acknowledges man's enslavement to uninvited forces, but, unlike the old sages, he does not see this as man's perpetual state and so does not agree that sleep or death is a preferable state. Enslavement now takes a form dictated by the ancient virtues themselves, by their passion for preeminence and their jealousy of rivals. Zarathustra's teaching is itself a virtuous rival, and therefore it must engage in warfare with other virtues willing to go to war for preeminence. Zarathustra's solution to the problem of enslavement is that mankind must be overcome in the direction of mastery. Uninvited virtues should not be extirpated but loved. It is not simply the enjoyment of the passion that lies behind Zarathustra's counsel to love it but the greater goal of overcoming mankind and mastering the mastering passions. Only slowly, in view of the sensibilities of his audience, does Zarathustra disclose how little his teaching is preoccupied with the self; neither the means nor the goal is self-absorption, the therapeutic healing of an injured self, or the authenticity of an alienated one. The inwardness sought is an overcoming of self in the service of a historic possibility.

The reevaluation of gods, reason, and virtue just completed (I. 3–5) will be taken up again later in a more vehement assault, but neither the frequency nor the vehemence of the attacks should obscure their limits, for each of the matters attacked as a product of the unhealthy body is subsequently rehabilitated on the basis of the healthy body. Most enigmatically, the gods, here assailed unequivocally, later reappear in an unexpected way, at the culmination of Zarathustra's course.[64] The assault on reason (I. 4) is qualified immediately by its rehabilitation as the rationality of the healthy body whose tools and toys are sense and spirit. Whatever sacrifices Zarathustra may call his followers to make, they do not include "the sacrifice of the intellect" (*BGE* 23) or of intellectual honesty. The assault on virtue, which roots virtues in the passions (I. 5), is made by a teacher of virtue who will promulgate the novel virtue of the gift-giver, of sacrificing oneself for the future of mankind (I. 22). This virtue too is a transformed passion whose nature will be made explicit only much later (III. 10).

These three speeches also come to light as explications of items first enumerated in Zarathustra's opening speech in the prologue (3), where the greatest experience is said to be the hour in which one experiences contempt for one's happiness, one's reason, and one's virtues. Since the gods have been contrived for one's happiness (I. 3), contempt for that happiness contributes to the greatest experience, as does contempt for what has been seen as reason (I. 4) and as virtue (I. 5). Zarathustra's list also includes contempt for justice and pity, and the next two chapters focus on these virtues.

"On the Pale Criminal" (I. 6) deals with justice, with a single case of crime and punishment that shows why the prevailing justice must be treated with contempt, whether it be the justice one man administers to himself or institutional justice. Zarathustra continues to demonstrate himself to be a psychologist who understands the soul because he understands the body. Here his knowledge of the body displays itself as capable of unriddling the secrets of even the most unhealthy exception. Having first thought and then performed his deed, the pale criminal proves unequal to the remembrance of it, and he condemns himself for his single exceptional deed. But this "madness after the fact" was preceded by a "madness *before* the fact." The pale criminal is not a robber who committed murder arbitrarily and inexplicably, as his humanitarian judges suppose. He is a murderer who explicably robbed. His soul wanted blood, but his poor reason persuaded him that blood was not a legitimate ground for action and demanded its own reason, robbery. Now that the soul has had its blood, that same poor reason makes him pale with guilt at the image of himself as a murderer. What is this man? He is a heap of diseases whose sick body produces its means of destruction through guilt, even when it invents no afterworlds or higher reason or virtue. Found guilty by the hanging judge of his own reason, the pale criminal suffers from an incurable disease. But in drawing his hard lesson from this case, Zarathustra condemns not only the pale criminal, for, while the pale criminal is a casualty of the faulty reason created by the suffering body, the learned and censorious judges

are also casualties of the same process. Himself a criminal in the eyes of
the good and their watchful guardians (Prologue 9), Zarathustra prefers
the madness of the pale criminal to the sanity of the "good" represented
by the judges.

This repellent speech, in which Zarathustra says that he prefers a
man who is "a heap of diseases" and "a ball of wild snakes" to those in
authority who consider themselves the good, ends on the appropriate note
with Zarathustra describing himself as a railing beside a passing stream
and saying: "Grasp me, those who can grasp me! But your crutch I am
not." Those who would grasp this teaching must separate themselves not
only from the old constraints, but from the great majority who know themselves to be the good and to whom the new teaching is a crime. The next
chapter develops the theme of grasping Zarathustra but in a more pleasing
way, for he there makes himself attractive for his listeners by turning away
from the diseased body to the healthy body at play.

"On Reading and Writing" (I. 7) is the culmination of the series of
speeches just delivered, the last speech before Zarathustra's private meeting
with a young man both drawn to his teachings and repelled by them (I.
8). Having listened to the teaching to which the young men now attend
(I. 2) and discredited it (I. 3–6), Zarathustra now flaunts the attractions of
his own new teaching and shows how it can charm those made attentive
to his words through his assault on the old. But "On Reading and Writing"
also raises directly the question of companions, which links it with the
succeeding chapter. The links are not emphasized, for Zarathustra practices
the art of speaking he recommends, an art that does not do everything for
the reader. In the first of the two chapters (I. 7) he speaks in general terms
about followers, with a view to attracting a special few; in the second (I.
8) he exhorts a young man who has felt himself singled out by Zarathustra's
speeches. The qualities described in the first chapter as worthy of emulation
are discussed in the second; but what is held up as exemplary in the first
chapter is shown to thwart the young man in the second. Both chapters
speak of climbing mountains and culminate in the image of flying. Together
they demonstrate the power of Zarathustra to both attract and repel; but
they also show him going out of his way to befriend a young man both
attracted and repelled.

The theme of "On Reading and Writing" is speaking and being spoken
to. The first part distinguishes among those spoken to, while the second
part shows in a poetic and playful way the one speaking. The self-de-
scription at the end is presented as exemplary for those singled out by
the first part. Those addressed are taught the last of the five contempts
that constitute the greatest experience, contempt for their pity. They are
taught to harden their hearts against what lies beneath them and to be
pitiless.[65] According to Aristotle, whatever men fear for themselves will
arouse their pity when it befalls others.[66] In refusing to look down, in looking
only upward to what is higher, Zarathustra's followers are to become fear-

less and to feel themselves exempt from what befalls others. But in the next chapter he shows that they are not exempt from the dangers presented by what is higher. For, in hardening their hearts against pity, they become vulnerable to envy of the pitiless one above them.

The speech opens with a series of aphorisms that ends in an aphorism explaining aphorisms and their purpose. Aphorisms are a form of writing able to avoid or evade the evils of writing, which are described aphoristically as writing's availability to all and the coarsening and leveling consequences of conceding to that availability and attempting to speak to all. Although aphorisms can be read by all, they speak differently to different people and do not speak at all to most. Because of the effort required to understand them, they engage only the "tall and lofty" in the elevating task of unriddling them or ascending to their meaning. They create their proper readers by drawing them up a privileged route into experiences and insights that, left to themselves, they might never have gained. This art of writing distinguishes the worthy by making them prove their worth, and flatters those who succeed by allowing them to judge that they belong among the worthy few. Through invitation and flattery from what is above them, they achieve "hardness of heart" as judged from below them. In the effort of understanding, intimacy is established; the understanding reader becomes an accomplice in the things understood by sharing in their discovery. The aphorism is an instrument of seduction aimed at those fascinated by riddles; those with a taste for the bold, the quick, the impetuous; those fit by nature for the spiritual warfare to which Zarathustra attracts the young men.[67] The shared act of ascent makes "alien blood" after all understandable and lifts the bold and impetuous young man who understands above the crowd of readers for whom the writer of aphorisms intends to do nothing. The aphorisms themselves state why the writer of aphorisms shuns a literary form that takes pity on its readers; they state why *Thus Spoke Zarathustra* takes the form that it does instead of the form of the treatise or essay.[68]

Irony, "appropriate only as a pedagogical tool," is practiced by Zarathustra in a way that does not feign ignorance; instead, it takes the way of display without flaunting everything known. It conceals the full measure of its thought in the little abysses of its aphorisms and, thus spared becoming base or falling into arrogance, becomes a pedagogical tool of selection (*HH* I. 372). In the irony or aphorisms of this chapter the writer Nietzsche has his pure speaker Zarathustra speak of writing and its limitations just as Plato had his pure speaker Socrates do in the *Phaedrus*. Although Zarathustra does not directly state the superiority of speaking, as Socrates does, he shows how writing can be made to be most like speaking and thus overcome its characteristic limitation of opening what is said to everyone, rather than modifying the words to suit the audience addressed. Nietzsche's art of writing, the literary form of aphorism, avoids what is shameful in writing and what corrupts spirit by turning it into something common, just as Socrates' speech avoids the "shameful" speech that does not speak beautifully or take into account the character of its hearers. The words selected by Nietzsche to record, apparently for all, what Zarathustra intended only for some, select their audience, just as Platonic writing modeled on Socratic speaking plants its seeds not artificially in Adonis's garden but only in carefully prepared ground.[69]

The opening aphorisms which distinguish the listener sought by Zarathustra[70] end on the laugh of his courage, which drives away ghosts while creating for itself friendly spirits of earth and hearth that inhabit his heights, even as spirits were said to inhabit Heraclitus's height in the famous story recounted by Aristotle.[71] With this playful description of himself Zarathustra begins the longest part of his speech in which he distinguishes himself from others. He shifts from the singular to the plural "you," and marks himself off from others with words that place him on a mountain peak, laughing at the clouds below that frighten those beneath them—the motto for part III.

As Zarathustra's occupation of the height becomes the paradigm for the ascent of others, he turns to exhortation and shifts to "we." This speech, which contains many of the images that appear later at moments of crisis, tells how Wisdom, a woman, wants her warriors, and how these warriors are to stand towards Life. Zarathustra, here the playful lover of both women, Wisdom and Life, will later, in two dancing songs, be less courageous and more troubled; he will himself be mocked for a conflict of loves, for Wisdom and Life are not as easily loved as Zarathustra here avows (II. 10; III. 15). As his speech turns to the theme of the dance, he identifies the only god whom he could ever believe in, without saying whether such a god exists. But the devil he can believe in does exist; he is "the spirit of gravity," "of whom they say that he is 'the master of the world' " (II. 10). Zarathustra asserts that levity is the answer to his devil's gravity, but when the spirit of gravity reappears later, laughter is insufficient to banish him. Zarathustra's battle against the spirit of gravity subsequently becomes the most important image of his essential task (II. 10; III. 2, 11). But for now, claiming that he has learned to walk, run, and fly, he ends this celebration of his exemplary self flying above himself with a god dancing through him. This account of flying will be seen to be premature when Zarathustra later rebukes himself with the statement that one cannot fly into flying (III. 11, §2); still, his course ends on an act of flying (III. 16, §7).

However the images of this speech are later modified, they are now the means by which Zarathustra parades his exalted state as a challenge to others. But it is precisely this ascendant Zarathustra that thwarts the young man of the next chapter, driving him away instead of attracting him. That chapter marks a major turning point in "Zarathustra's Speeches." Having begun with a description of the spiritedness required of those who would become his companions (I. 1), and having delivered six speeches (I. 2–7) contrasting the old teaching with the new, first emphasizing the unattractive qualities of the old, then gradually revealing the enticing, intoxicating qualities of the new, Zarathustra must now counteract one of the effects of his teaching. For while it has succeeded in attracting the talented young man, it has also evoked in him a disturbing revulsion that must be remedied before he can become Zarathustra's "companion."

Envy's Evil Eye (Chapter 8)

No narrative comment (aside from the repeated "Thus spoke Zarathustra") occurs between chapters 2 and 8. In chapter 2, Zarathustra was pictured in the Colorful Cow sitting with the young men at the feet of the traditional sage. But now that his own speeches have begun to break the hold of the old teaching, chapter 8 shows him outside the city speaking in private to one young man, for Zarathustra's teaching has evoked a response in him that he is only beginning to identify and that forces him to avoid Zarathustra. His avoidance and Zarathustra's refusal to accept it lead to one of the few private conversations in part I.[72] As in the other chapter that contains a private conversation at the opening (I. 18; see also II. 17), Zarathustra controls the situation, forcing the dialogue to open in a certain way and follow the course he desires. The title ("The Tree on the Mountainside"), the setting outside and above "The Colorful Cow," and Zarathustra's praise all indicate that the young man who avoids him is no ordinary adolescent, but is superior and has already transcended all his contemporaries in the city. "Zarathustra's eyes" and what they can see form a recurring theme in the chapter, for they have seen not only the young man's avoidance, but the reasons behind it; they have seen the envy in his eyes, his "evil eye."

One evening, on a walk in the mountains above the city, Zarathustra "found" the young man seated by a tree. This apparently fortuitous circumstance may well have been arranged by Zarathustra, for when he speaks, his words are well planned for just this occasion. Without announcing himself, speaking from behind the tree so that the young man cannot see him, he tells a flattering parable calculated to draw out the young man's reasons for avoiding him. The young man recognizes the voice and confesses that he has just then been thinking of Zarathustra. Zarathustra has seen that he was responsible for the young man's avoidance; he can also see the invisible forces in the young man symbolized in the parable by the invisible wind that bends and torments the tree.

His words have startled and confused the young man, and in this unguarded state he continues his confession. When Zarathustra speaks of the tree stretching upward into the light by rooting itself deeper into the darkness of the earth, into evil, the young man fervently answers, for the first of three times, confirming Zarathustra's interpretation of his state. He wonders how Zarathustra could have discovered the secrets of his soul, and when Zarathustra's answer suggests that they are the secrets of his own soul, he deepens his confession with a long speech describing his experience of ascent. But his effort has forced failures and uncertainties on him for the first time, and in his shame he mocks the lack of aptitude which his need for effort seems to reveal. He uses Zarathustra's words "contempt and longing" to describe his condition but laments that they grow simultaneously, thereby applying to himself Zarathustra's image of the tree growing upward by descending downward. But what he now secretly feels threatens his ascent. Shamed by his newly experienced incapacity, he comes to hate the one who can already fly and confesses revulsion for the whole project of ascent. No wonder he has avoided Zarathustra while thinking constantly of him.

But Zarathustra is not yet done with his parable, for it still has not made the young man fully aware of what Zarathustra has seen as the ground of his avoidance. Zarathustra now presents the final image of his parable, one that flatters the young man by comparing him to a tree that has already outstripped all its neighbors and now reaches up and waits— but for what? Could it be awaiting "the first lightning," the bolt from the clouds that will strike it down or consume it in flames? The young man is even more vehement in confirming this interpretation of his secret feelings. His hatred of what is above him and his surrender in the face of it are an invitation to the lightning to consume and destroy him. Moreover, he identifies what draws the lightning: envy of Zarathustra. He has come to hate his own height because there exists one higher whom he cannot help but envy.[73] Thinking himself already destroyed by his envy of one who can already do what he can only dream of doing, the young man at the depths of his confession, or of his insight into how envy has poisoned him, cries bitterly in the presence of the one envied. Zarathustra puts his arm around him, and they walk off together. By Zarathustra's contrivance the young man's avoidance has resulted in this conversation, confession, and embrace; but his act of befriending the young man is not over.

In his final speech he seeks to terminate the young man's avoidance by helping him understand his envy. But he abstains from using the word that exploded from the young man in his agitated state; his speech teaches, but it also tempers and calms. He refrains from naming what poisons the young man's ambition, and from introducing his new teaching on envy. Zarathustra knows full well that envy can poison, for it has poisoned the young man into a hatred of what is higher, and it poisons those who, unconscious of their envy, come to have contempt for the body (I. 4). Such poisonous envy can be eradicated, and that promise comforts the young man enflamed with envy. But Zarathustra refrains from stating what will later be the main theme of his teaching on envy, namely, that envy is a useful passion, a goad to action necessary for the project of the superman with its continual surpassing of what is envied. For envy is not by itself shameful, however much his newly attracted listeners, trained by their previous teachers to a condemnation of envy, feel shame at their envy of him (I. 10). Nor is it one of the "deadly sins," "the evil eye," as they had been taught. Zarathustra's later lessons on envy—given to an audience that presumably includes this young man, now saved from his poisonous envy by his pride—will be lessons on a kind of friendship or discipleship as yet unknown to the young man. They teach a lesson that Nietzsche learned early about the "gulf of ethical judgment" separating the Greeks from ourselves; and they take the side of "the older Greeks" in honoring envy as a spur to emulation, a way of esteeming the superior by desiring to surmount it. The young man on the mountainside who has not had the benefit of learning from Hesiod or Aristotle will learn from Zarathustra that "the greater and more sublime a [man] is, the brighter the flame of ambition that flares out of him" (HC). What Zarathustra presents as novel, he in fact takes over from the Greeks. On the single occasion on which he names the Greeks he quotes as typifying them the words of Peleus to his son Achilles: "You shall always be first and excel all others" (I. 15).[74] In Aristotle's terms, what the young man now experiences as the vice of envy will have to be transformed into the virtue of jealousy[75] in order that Zarathustra's superiority not daunt him, but goad him to surpass it. The surpassing of Zarathustra by his young listeners is essential to his mission as herald; the eventual appearance of the superman depends on followers who will surpass their teacher, and for that surpassing, envy is a necessary passion.[76]

Walking with his arm around him, Zarathustra acts as if the young man had not said that the danger came from above, from Zarathustra himself. Whereas the first part of Zarathustra's final speech refers obliquely to the danger posed to the young man by envy, the second and longer part refers to the danger posed by being envied, a danger to which both the young man and Zarathustra are exposed. Zarathustra thus reduces the apparent difference between them by speaking of what they share. In the first part Zarathustra utilizes his ability to see the invisible, and he identifies as base the envy that the young man feels. Zarathustra's superiority, the cause of that envy, is never in doubt, but it is not paraded by any reference to the legitimacy of the young man's envy or the ends to which it can be put. Instead, Zarathustra speaks of a potential freedom from envious instincts that turn the one imprisoned by them to deceit and meanness. Those "bad instincts" contend with the longing that the young man also feels. The plea to the young man to rekindle his love and hope is based on Zarathustra's exhibition of love and hope and appeals to the young man's spirit, the spiritedness that loves victory and could lead the young man to surpass him.

The second part of the speech is silent on the young man's envy; instead it flatters him as noble, as both enviable and envied. It teaches him mastery of the poisonous envy that comes from others. Learning how to acquit himself with the envious involves learning a distinction between the noble and the good on the question of innovation: the good are loyalists who desire that things remain the same, whereas the noble are revolutionary and create novelty. The good discern the nobility of the noble, but they hate it and want to poison it with their evil eye. While showing how the noble are endangered by the good, Zarathustra does not mention all aspects of the danger—the enticements of esteem and wealth that the good are later said to offer to the potentially noble (I. 11, 12), or the ruin that the good worked on the noble Jesus by turning him to a hatred of the earth (I. 21). He discusses only the danger that the spirit be broken by the false and base teaching that spirit is reducible to sensual pleasure and can be fully gratified by it. Noble men known to Zarathustra have submitted to this false teaching and been broken by it. Zarathustra's emphasis on this danger seems to indicate that it is the one that faces this young man, that his spiritedness is tied to a manly *eros* that could easily be turned to the merely sensual. His erotic nature thus requires instruction in the noble and the base,[77] as it will require instruction on chastity (I. 13) and on woman (I. 18).[78]

Zarathustra's private and befriending speech ends with a second plea to the young man: not to throw away the hero in his soul and to keep holy his highest hope. These injunctions begin to specify the heroic qualities of spirit first presented in the images of Zarathustra's opening speech (I. 1); they will be repeated in later speeches in which the theme of the heroic is developed (I. 10; II. 7, 13). The silence observed in this speech on the most heroic matter, dedication to the superman, is necessary because of Zarathustra's recognition that envy of the high threatens to ruin this young man's aspiration. Instead of trying to move him to aspiration through description of the goal, this speech must focus on what is to be avoided because it is beneath him. The aspect of envy that had to be skirted in this private speech will be elaborated to a broader audience (I. 10) after Zarathustra has spoken in a general way on previous teachings (I. 9). "The Tree on the Mountainside" signals a turning point in "Zarathustra's Speeches" by showing that those speeches are having the desired effect on their listeners.[79]

School for the Lion-Hearted (Chapters 9–14)

In the next six chapters Zarathustra returns to the traditional teachings already described and speaks more frankly to those attracted by his earlier speeches. He speaks openly for the first time about the insight that came to him at the end of the prologue as the ground of his resolve to create companions, namely, that the people are a herd who must preserve their own things by engaging in a struggle to the death against wolves with a teaching different from the herd's. In these speeches Zarathustra begins to disclose the demands of discipleship to those attracted by the liberating promises of his opening speeches. Beginning with preachers and passing to warriors, statesmen, and intellectuals, he makes a case for solitude as the prerequisite for gaining a perspective on pressing contemporary issues.[80] These speeches can therefore be thought of as presenting Zarathustra's political philosophy, the theme that becomes explicit especially in "On the New Idol" and "On the Flies of the Marketplace" (I. 11, 12). All six speeches can be construed as descriptions of the lion spirit, the willful spirit that conquers all the thousand-year-old values that proclaim "Thou shalt." The speech that follows, "On the Thousand Goals and One" (I. 15), marks another turning point, for it addresses the question of peoples and their values in the most comprehensive way. It is succeeded by another series of six speeches (I. 16–21) which, as revaluations of specific values, can be seen as descriptions of the child spirit.

"On the Preachers of Death" (I. 9) is not addressed directly to followers; it is in its way a preaching of death addressed to the preachers of death. Although its opening words suggest that preachings of death exist because they are needed by the many who are comforted by such teachings, they can also be interpreted as meaning that the preachers of death need to have death preached to them. In fact Zarathustra repeats frequently that preachers of death should be consistent and follow their teaching into death. The speech is a list which extends the identification of preachers of death to the whole field of religious teachers already canvassed, as well as some new ones. Included in the list of condemned is the Buddha, whose encounters with the invalid, the aged, and the corpse after his protected life in the castle led him to conclude that "life is refuted." The final category of preachers of death are modern servants of the work ethic, products of the Christian ideal of service, who submerge life in frantic labor, fleeing from themselves in the fast, the new, and the strange, and concentrating only on the moment. This speech on those who malign life on religious grounds separates two speeches addressed to prospective followers on the theme of envy of Zarathustra (I. 8, 10). It too concerns followers in that it teaches that the old teachings are not merely about waking and sleeping (I. 2), but about life and death; as such they engage the new teacher in a life and death struggle or a war as the next speech makes clear.

"On War and Warriors" (I. 10), addressed to "my brothers in war," states what is required of Zarathustra's followers. It goes beyond what was said privately to the young man on the mountainside and shows that all potential followers must learn novel lessons about envy and how to put it to use.

Zarathustra begins by begging permission to speak the truth, presumably because the truth could harm them. But he vows that he speaks this potentially damaging truth out of love for them. Furthermore, in identifying himself in order to win their permission, he claims to be their best enemy and says that warriors must honor their enemies and not wish to be spared by them. The hard truth that requires this careful preparation is precisely the truth that caused the young man on the mountainside to avoid Zarathustra. "I know the hatred and envy of your hearts," he says, after he has steeled them and vowed his love for them. Aspirants to greatness, they are not yet so great as to be spared the presence of those still greater, whose greatness they must hate and envy. In the order of rank named in this chapter, the highest rank accorded is "saints of knowledge." Such sainthood would presumably be beyond hatred and envy. Desiring, but still lacking, such sainthood, Zarathustra's listeners are invited to employ their hatred and envy as warriors of knowledge, testing their manliness and strength on the very hatred and envy they feel. Instead of thinking it shameful to be subject to hatred and envy, they must learn to treasure those feelings as a goad to battle. Instead of the mortification and ill will occasioned in the young man on the mountainside, recognition of Zarathustra's superiority is to occasion their attempts to outstrip him.[81] Although Zarathustra does not distinguish between the hated and the envied, both being cause for a contest of overcoming, it is clear that the hated are the larger class, and that whereas the envied may elicit a kind of hate, the hated for the most part are not enviable. While himself an object of envy, he must teach what is to be hated, or what is at issue in the great war yet to be fought.

In this Machiavellian chapter, Zarathustra, while avowing his love for his followers, seems to be indicating that where the goal is the superman, it is better to be envied than loved. He counsels his warriors to think only of war, even during times of peace; still, because his audience consists not of princes but of prospective followers who are prospective superiors, he must teach them the virtue of obedience, of submission to a cause greater than their own success. Whereas earlier speeches had emphasized liberation from constraints onerous to young men, Zarathustra here emphasizes constraint through obedience to a commander. This obedience is also preparation for the possibility that the warrior will himself become a commander one day. He ends his speech to warriors as he ended his speech to the young man on the mountainside, with a plea to live for their "highest hope." But the mode of address is no longer mere entreaty; rather, he speaks as a commander addressing warriors who want to hear "Thou shalt" rather than their own "I will." They need to be told the things worth fighting for, and Zarathustra obliges with a series of commands based on their love of life, ending with the command that their love of life be a love of their "highest hope," and that their highest hope be their "highest thought of life," namely, that "man is something to be overcome." If they are obedient to the command to live only for the superman, their hatred and envy can be turned to Zarathustra's purpose.

Zarathustra desires to make himself admirable in order that he be envied. By arousing the salutary envy of the young men, he appeals to their ambition and love of victory and facilitates his own overcoming in the direction of the superman.[82] His existence, like his teaching, argues against being at peace, for peace is wretched contentment. By exhibiting envy of Zarathustra's superiority, the young men to whom he appeals give evidence of their spiritedness. Unlike the crowd in the prologue, they are responsive to an appeal to their pride. Roused to shame by the very presence of a height they do not occupy, they will be delivered from peace into war, into the intemperate love of victory. By drawing the envy of the spirited young men to himself, Zarathustra begins to show them what is most enviable or what the task is that is worthy of their spirit of victory. The spiritedness of these ambitious few must aim at something higher than the status or rule to which they now aspire, for such aspirations are governed by love of honor, where the honorable is defined by the good and the just. Lessons about honor will form the core of the political instruction in the next chapters (I. 10, 11).

War imagery comes easily to Zarathustra, for he sees himself engaged in a campaign for the very future of mankind, and he argues the virtues of war in some of the best-known sayings of the book, their fame resting on their startling and unsettling character as celebrations of war. But Zarathustra's "warrior of knowledge" is no soldier; his warfare is spiritual warfare, his wars the ones already declared and opened in Nietzsche's books. To say, as Zarathustra does, that "it is the good war that hallows any cause" is not to say that all causes can be made holy by war. Only the good war sanctifies, and Zarathustra is in the process of defining the good war as opposition to what has been successfully fought for until now. In this warfare even the contemplative natures must take part and fight. But this is no novelty, for the wisest and most saintly have always been warriors in Zarathustra's sense and have always known themselves to be engaged in spiritual warfare, which does not necessarily require taking up arms. "War (but without gunpowder!) between different thoughts! and their armies!"— this is the warfare to which Zarathustra calls his listeners (*KGW* VII 16 [50], Fall 1883). Nietzsche need not be remade into a mild pacifist to be spared the travesties foisted on him by his sister and her Archive, who managed to transform the war for mankind's future into a war for Imperial Germany and ruin Nietzsche's reputation for decades.[83]

In the next two chapters, "On the New Idol" (I. 11) and "On the Flies of the Marketplace" (I. 12), Zarathustra addresses followers in a new way. Now that he has warriors at his command, he speaks openly about the insight that came to him at the end of the prologue and first sent him in search of companions, an insight attesting to the presence of strong rival claims on the spirited youths he seeks. To secure their loyalty to him, he must sever their loyalty to their own things, acquired automatically in their rearing. "Convictions are more dangerous enemies of truth than lies" (*HH* I. 483), and these two speeches break their convictions about the superior virtue of modern democracy by telling the truth about its origins and aims. As examples of "philosophizing with a hammer," these chapters are true to Nietzsche's explanation of that enterprise in *Twilight of the Idols*, for, however much the primary and arresting sense of that phrase stands, it is to be supplemented by another sense, according to which idols or values are tapped with a hammer, as with a tuning fork, in order that they ring with the sound that betrays their true nature. The hammering is performed for the sake of prospective companions, to afflict them with shame at what they have honored till now, to persuade them to scorn the honor offered by political or public life in a modern state.

The two chapters analyzing the politics of the modern European state begin with a contrast that honors an ancient politics not of states but of "peoples." Later, in the chapter devoted to the fundamental political theme, "On the Thousand Goals and One" (I. 15), Zarathustra will show that his critique of the modern state issues in a kind of restoration of the ancient way of "peoples" through the establishment of a completely novel people, "mankind." The unveiling of that goal adds a dimension to Zarathustra's political philosophy absent in the present chapters, in which the critique of the modern state culminates simply in refusal and severance. These two chapters begin the reenactment of the old rivalry between politics and philosophy by having as their aim the liberation of potential followers from the charms of the political realm. For now, Zarathustra limits his rival claims to a call to separation from the political realm in the name of something higher; but in calling followers to the new loyalty to the coming superman, he calls them to politics of a new sort. Begun here with a fitting limitation, Zarathustra's political philosophy expands in later chapters to the most extreme or total political ambition. Inasmuch as Nietzsche said that, to understand a philosopher's assertions, one does well to attend to their moral or political meaning, Zarathustra's political aims would seem to be of special heuristic value in understanding his teaching as a whole (*BGE* 6, 211).[84]

"On the New Idol" is a political speech addressed to "my brothers." Its language is inflated and hortatory, and although this is not uncharacteristic of Zarathustra, the rhetoric here is especially heightened and pressing, as if he had to adopt in augmented degree the rhetoric with which his rival, the modern state, addresses his prospective followers. His opening words show him to be the inhabitant of a modern European state, Leviathan, the "cold, lying monster" whose primary lie consists in declaring that it is the people, thereby imputing to itself the honors to be accorded peoples. But Zarathustra differentiates peoples from states on the grounds that peoples are founded by great creators who give their creation "a faith and a love," whereas states are founded by "destroyers," because the new "idol" destroys the older, more honorable forms of worship. Genuine peoples still exist, but they rightly hate modern states as the evil eye that will destroy them by means of a spiritual imperialism that erodes what they worship. Although the faith and love of a people is always narrow and excludes the neighbor as an outsider, it gives identity and resolution to those who know themselves to be citizens, for it teaches them what is sacred and fitting. Peoples serve life, Zarathustra says, in what amounts to the highest praise of peoples, whereas the modern state serves death, because it appeals only to the "sword and a hundred appetites." Zarathustra implicitly criticizes Locke and other teachers of the modern commercial state by condemning the emancipation of acquisitiveness, or of the desire for more than one needs, that such teachers counseled as the basis of a new political order. The modern state also appeals to might, and while Zarathustra has just roused the martial spirits of his listeners, he judges ignoble the appeal to might in the modern state, because it is in the service of either mere appetites or justice as equality.[85]

He presents himself as a reader of signs and says that the sign of a people is that its good and evil is clear and consistent and its own, whereas that of a modern state is a confused plurality of good and evil. In this confusion the state serves as an instrument of the many. Still, the many must make use of the superior few in their midst, and to achieve this end, they offer the temptation of honor to the ambitious young. Himself flattering the ambitious young by calling them "you great souls," Zarathustra relates their temptation in the words of the devil's third temptation of Jesus:[86] they will be given everything if only they bow down and worship the state. They will be given positions of administration and management and will become the shepherds of the herd, if they are willing to serve the interests of the state. Zarathustra's "brothers" must see through the modern state to the many whom it serves through its universal education, its public media, and its pursuit of wealth. Ambition has moved those to whom he speaks, but now that he has unmasked the context of that ambition by using "his unsurpassable and inexhaustible power of passionate and fascinating speech for making his [listeners] loath, not only socialism and communism, but conservatism, nationalism and democracy as well," now that he has "taken upon himself this great political responsibility,"[87] he must teach them a more worthy political goal. He concludes his speech with a plea to escape to solitude. They are to look beyond the state, not simply for the sake of solitude, but in order to see that where the state ends stand "the rainbow and bridges of the superman." In this way Zarathustra invites his audience to repeat the young Nietzsche's experience of severance from his own things at their moment of acclaimed triumph and thus to become solitary and untimely wanderers, not sons of their times but stepsons concerned with the excellence of mankind in general (SE 3).[88]

In using the superman as the new political vision that sets his listeners against their own things, Zarathustra calls them to a political courage that lacks completely the element of loyalty to one's own things that Plato defined as political courage.[89] Zarathustra, the revolutionary teacher opposed to the modern state, does not find it necessary or desirable to cover himself with a mask of loyalty to the things of his city as Plato does. Because the rule of the philosopher envisaged by Plato depends on grace or chance, that rule is extremely unlikely; consequently, the city will remain what it is, and the philosopher who lives in it must appear to be a loyal citizen.

But Zarathustra's project of bringing the whole world under the rule of the superman replaces the apparent Platonic surrender to grace or chance as the only means for the coincidence of wisdom and power; in this way the rule of the philosopher is to become both possible and desirable.[90]

"On the Flies of the Marketplace" (I. 12) continues the theme of flight from the honors offered by modern democracies but does so in a somewhat calmer tone. It is addressed in the singular to "my friend" or "my brother," and the one thus addressed may be presumed to have heard the public speech of the preceding chapter. What he now learns in private is a further lesson contrasting the love of one's own things with the love of the good, but what he hears undermines the most estimable of contemporary things.[91] This speech marks Zarathustra's return to the marketplace, the scene of the prologue, but he now offers no public speeches, only a private speech about the marketplace. The marketplace has become, as it was in the prologue, the place for the exchange of ideas. But in place of the one jester, there are now many jesters, for what counts in the new marketplace of ideas is showmanship. That marketplace is ruled by the "great men" who shape opinion, and these are served by "the flies of the marketplace," popularizers and publicists, intellectuals who trade in these opinions. Zarathustra intimates that the great men are themselves secretly ruled, both by their ambition for fame or recognition and by far greater creative thinkers who were moved by a passion unknown to the marketplace and whose values govern the "great men" whose opinions seem to make the world turn. Wiser about the marketplace now, all Zarathustra adds to its clamor of voices is the temptation to abandon it, to spurn the best that it offers, fame, the "last infirmity of noble mind." Zarathustra holds out this temptation to those already bedazzled by the impressive feats of the "great men" but he neither criticizes their feats nor promises something higher; rather, he focuses on something lower, the little stings already inflicted by the flies of the marketplace. The bulk of his speech is a stinging antidote to the poison already spread by the mass of intellectual communicators, the "unconditional and pressing men," "sudden men," who demand that everyone take sides immediately on the issues that matter to them.[92] The young man, moved by the ladder of achievement so evident in this exciting marketplace, naturally wonders, in the manner of the ageing Yeats, how "I could have proved my worth / In something that all others understand or share."[93] But what all others understand or share belongs to the flies of communication, and everything rare and magnificent escapes them. Vulnerability to the common is not what Zarathustra warns against most vehemently, however, but vulnerability to revenge. The impulsive need of the flies to have others recognize their ideas, either by sharing them or combatting them, engenders a need to revenge themselves on what is different. Revenge is a communicable disease, carried by a poison that infects the one stung. Only solitude, withdrawal from contemporary debates in the marketplace of ideas, makes it possible to gain a perspective that allows ideas to come to light as what they are, as what Zarathustra sees them to be.

The invitation to special men to flee into solitude continues in the next chapter with an invitation to a particular form of solitude, chastity (I. 13). This chapter and the next ("On the Friend") continue the theme of the other, but the private, special other, not the other of the marketplace (I. 12) or the state (I. 11) or the other who is the enemy (I. 10) or the old teachers (I. 9). The speech on chastity has no addressee, as if there were none among his audience who could welcome it. It begins in a way that connects it with the account of the marketplace, by contrasting city and forest, the city being the place of feverish and debilitating sensuality. Chastity may seem a peculiar topic for a teacher who began by announcing a new understanding of the healthy body and its pleasures. But the speech shows how little Zarathustra's celebration of the body implies mere surrender to its drives. He too is a teacher of sublimation, of the transformation of bodily drives into spirit, as was apparent in his warning to the young man on the mountainside (I. 8) regarding the dangers of eros. This speech introduces Zarathustra's teaching on channeling or curbing the passions for the sake of a transcendent goal. It is also the beginning of his account of the virtues, where virtue is understood as action that facilitates the good that is the superman. Virtue so understood provides the essential perspective on the earlier, inviting speech on passions and virtues (I. 5), which had implied a tender indulgence of the passions for their own sake.

Zarathustra's speech on chastity is in part a witty response to Wagner's celebration of chastity in *Parsifal*, a celebration radically different from Zarathustra's in that Wagner exalts the redemptive efficacy of chastity and the pursuit of pity.[94] But in calling followers to a solitary existence, Zarathustra is not calling all of them to chastity, for he teaches that only a few are worthy or capable of it; others it embitters and destroys because they are not inwardly chaste. Like the apostle Paul, Zarathustra teaches that it is better to marry than burn with passion;[95] and for those of his followers who lack the gift of chastity, he subsequently prescribes a certain kind of marriage (I. 20). Himself chaste, he is not a teacher of chastity but uses the occasion of a praise of chastity for a condemnation of mere sensuality. He offers no direct counsel on sexuality (see III. 10) beyond what is implied in the description of the bitch sensuality leering out of the enviously chaste, or stalking the city in search of the unwary. The speech ends in gratitude for the gift of chastity, the chaste state being very like the state Nietzsche describes later in an account of the philosopher as ascetic out of an inner, praiseworthy necessity (*GM* III. 8, also 10).[96]

"On the Friend" (I. 14), which follows a series of speeches on the unworthy other, teaches the uses of the worthy other. In reviving the theme of friendship as contest, Zarathustra echoes Bacon's judgment that there is little friendship in the world, and that what there is is appropriately between superior and inferior.[97] Zarathustra holds that there are no completely worthy friends, a lack that transforms friendship into utility, the most worthy friend eliciting longing for the friend who does not exist, the superman. Friends of Zarathustra must clothe themselves in allurements for each other's sake, portraying themselves as better than they are; for in that excellence, even if it is feigned, friends kindle in one another the desire to outdo the excellent. Correspondingly, a friend respects the way his friend clothes himself: not even in his dreams should he desire to peer into what his friend dreams. Still, in unguarded moments, in sleep, the feigning friend inadvertently shows himself to be all too human, displaying in himself that mankind is defective, "a heap of diseases," something that must be overcome. But the lack of excellence in the friend kindles a desire for the excellent; thus Zarathustra's friends are spurred both by the friend's excellence and by his flaws to achieve a greater excellence. The mutual striving of friends to outdo one another is not a friendship in which there is repose; it is not the contemplative friendship of the like-minded defined by Epicurean philosophers. It is an agonistic friendship in which each loves to triumph even over his friend, friendship of the sort Nietzsche saw in Greek greatness prior to the rise of philosophy, that "decadent" counter movement to ancient noble taste (*TI*, "Ancients," 3).

Zarathustra shows his friends that, while collectively they may be a community of warriors vying with one another, their highest goal cannot be to win respect even from the respected. Taught to shun the honor offered by the public, they must learn to shun the honor offered by the community of friends or the recognition of any single friend. The friend is the occasion not for mutually reflected honor but for victory: the friend's flaws send one to solitude to make of oneself what not even the friend is yet. The solitary thus wins a victory not for the sake of honor, not even for the sake of victory itself. According to Zarathustra, what is now to move the spirited is the desire for victory for the sake of that most victorious solitary yet to come, the superman. The spirited thus put themselves at the disposal of the future of mankind.

Through this series of speeches, the young men have become acquainted with the lion spirit, which, in the solitude to which Zarathustra invites them, encounters the great dragon with thousand-year-old values glittering on its scales. Those with the willingness to bear much must transform themselves into lions in order to break the hold of ancient values.

The Way of Peoples (Chapter 15)

Zarathustra's teaching in part I reaches its highest point in "On the Thousand Goals and One" (I. 15). The prospective disciples now learn that the grounds for the destruction of the old go far beyond the lion's rage, for there exists an impetus for destruction grounded in the vision of a new people, mankind. This pivotal chapter can be seen as preparing the transformation from the lion's rage to the child's creative play. Zarathustra here returns to the contest between the way of peoples and the way of the modern state. The future alternative to the modern state is elaborated in a setting of adventure, not the adventures of "A Thousand and One Arabian Nights" told to a passionate king by a mistress in fear for her life, but the comprehensive adventure of mankind as a whole, the thousand peoples hitherto. The unusual but precise wording of the title, *Von tausend und Einem Ziele*[98] points to the argument of the chapter itself, the replacement of the indiscriminate variety implied in "a thousand" by the particular thousand and first yet to come, the novel and greatest adventure with which the chapter will close.

Zarathustra begins with a display of credentials: like Odysseus, he has seen many lands and many peoples and has known their minds. But unlike Odysseus he does not now seek his homecoming, his return to the quiet life of hearth and home. On his travels he has discovered not only the good and evil of many peoples, but also that there is no greater power on earth than good and evil. Necessary to every people is its own good and evil, its own way of esteeming, which marks it off from its neighbors by proclaiming itself good and its neighbors outsiders or strangers to that good, and hence deluded or wicked. Every people has needed its noble lie in order to ground its actions, or make them weighty and meaningful by enclosing them within a sacred necessity exclusive to itself. This is not merely the rediscovery of the cultural relativism of ancient sophism or modern liberalism, however, for Zarathustra claims to have discovered the sole basis of all created good and evil. That discovery requires the establishment of the thousand-and-first goal that will encompass and master all others.

The tablet of the good that hangs over every people is said to be a tablet of its overcomings. A people seems to depend on the camel spirit, for it sets before those born within its sacred precincts a hierarchy of hard achievements pointing toward the greatest achievements, those remembered most vividly and held highest as most worthy of emulation. The hierarchy of achievement, or the upward way in every people's tablet of the good, has three levels: what is hard is held to be praiseworthy; what is both hard and indispensable is held to be good; and what is hardest, rarest, and liberates from the highest need is held to be holy. The praiseworthy, the good, and the holy provide the means whereby a people "rules and conquers and glitters, to the dread and envy of its neighbor." What marks it off in this way, what accords it recognition and acknowledgment through the fearful gaze of its neighbor, a people holds to be "the highest, the first, the standard of measure, the meaning of all things." This plurality of achievements has a single name, "the law of a people's overcoming."

What Zarathustra has here described is what Nietzsche earlier called "the preconditions of culture" (*HH* I. 25) and later explained in detail in *The Antichrist*. There, in his account of the origins of the law of Manu, he described the origins of "every great code of laws" or "holy lie" as a codification that sums up "the experience, prudence and experimental morality of many centuries," and that decrees the end of experimentation and the beginning of loyal repetition and emulation of the truth arrived at through that long experimentation. The legislator comes late; he belongs to "the most insightful stratum" of a people, those who see furthest both backward and forward and, on the basis of what they see, codify the people's ways. To give authority to the codification and weight to the people's actions, they show that "God *gave*" the law and "the forefathers *lived* it," or that the law has sacred origins and has been in effect since the earliest or greatest times, the ancestral times, which saw the founding of the important things, the retention of which is now the people's task. A people lives by its loyalty to the ancestral and achieves its greatness within the horizon of the worthy codified by its most insightful members (A 57).[99]

The long view backward afforded the most insightful Zarathustra is not confined to the experience of a single people at whose origins stand the forefathers or the gods. It encompasses the experience of all thousand peoples and brings to light the whole experiment of mankind. It is the longest view, which confers the greatest responsibility, the one that has always fallen to the most insightful. But the new codification, because it views the whole history of mankind, cannot be particular to this or that people and its ancestral ways. Furthermore, the ancestral way as such is no longer available, because the look backward now provides no "feeling of the grandeur of man by pointing to his divine origins." As Nietzsche said in *Daybreak*, the way backward "has now become a forbidden way, for at its portal stands the ape, together with other gruesome beasts, grinning knowingly as if to say: no further in this direction!" (D 49). But the task of the creator of the people mankind has been made even more problematic by the invention of the individual and by the achievements of the modern state. These novel conditions require a novel act of founding, whose character cannot yet be discerned beyond the recognition of its necessity and its historic and global magnitude. It remains the undefined task for the future superman. The present, definable task is to create the conditions out of which he might arise. Thus, although Zarathustra has seen furthest backward, he sees forward only dimly, to one who must come to weld mankind into a noble unity that overcomes the base disunity of modern states.

But Zarathustra has also seen furthest downward. After he announced that the tablet of good was the tablet of a people's overcoming, he went on to say that "it is the voice of its will to power." The phrase *will to power* appears only once in part I; it appears in two later chapters (II. 12, 20), but there too will to power is spoken of guardedly. The one appearance in part I is not offhand. It occurs at the rhetorical peak of the chapter in which the greatest power on earth, good and evil, is identified. All peoples have grounded themselves by tying their thoughts and deeds to the divine or to nature. Only once does the chapter provide a glimpse at what grounds those grounds, or at what the real foundations are of the teachings about god and nature that all peoples have given themselves. After twice ordering his audience to "Behold," Zarathustra makes visible the ground of the greatest power on earth by naming it "will to power." That which is even more fundamental than the greatest power on earth is not further eluci- dated in this speech, for he passes immediately to a more detailed account of what is enacted by that power in the peoples' tables of values. Never- theless, at the end of his speech, when he turns away from examples of tables of values and from a description of creators of values to demand that a new table of values be created, it is clear that the will to power is once again to enact legislation to create a people, this time, the people mankind.

Good and evil and the teachings about god and nature that justify them are all conventions, or in Nietzsche's language, art. But convention itself seems to be grounded in nature, for peoples share a common nature, a will to power that grounds their apparently most fundamental teachings. Because conventions exist in great variety, and because they do not re- semble the shared ground in whose service they exist, it seems implausible at first that they could all stem from such a ground. But Zarathustra makes no effort whatever to persuade his audience that he has discovered the fundamental truth about nature and convention, the truth which philos- ophy had sought in vain since its beginnings. Apparently only philosophers need to be persuaded of fundamental matters, for the next time will to power arises, Zarathustra speaks exclusively to them and makes a special effort to persuade them (II. 12).

The one and only naming of will to power in part I shows how cautious Zarathustra is in speaking about the deepest things, his apparent loqua- ciousness notwithstanding. Attention is called to this careful manner of speech by the very occasion on which it is most absent (II. 20). When Zar- athustra speaks of will to power again, he does not address a general au- dience nor repeat the claim made here; instead, on the basis of further discoveries about will to power, he addresses only those who exercise its most spiritual form and claims that all life must be understood as will to power. Many interpreters have judged that with this claim Zarathustra enters what Karl Jaspers called a "blind alley" and makes a "mistake";[100] they hold that will to power is plausible, if at all, only with respect to human values and actions, and that the teaching should be taken no further than the statement given in "On the Thousand Goals and One." But, for Zarathustra, this is only the beginning. It seems fitting that what has hap- pened among Nietzsche's interpreters parallels what happened to the dis- ciples drawn by Zarathustra's speeches in part I; for although the latter are persuaded by the speeches on the body and its created values, they do not follow Zarathustra on the new route he opens regarding the fun- damental ground, will to power.

After returning to the surface or to the consequences of will to power,

Zarathustra speaks of peoples in general and gives four specific examples. Both the general description and the examples point to triumphant peoples, those who are "the dread and envy of their neighbors," whose good and evil has enabled them to fulfill their will to power. For each of the examples, Zarathustra quotes "the law of its overcoming," the ladder whereby each ascended to its hope. Only the Greeks are named, and they are placed first on the list, ahead of Zarathustra's own people who are listed second. What defined the Greeks and moved them to their greatness was the passion contained in Peleus's advice to his son Achilles: "You should always be first and excel all others; your jealous soul should love no one, except the friend."[101] Zarathustra does not say he belongs to the people described next, only that they gave him his name, a name that points to his responsibility as founder. This people, the Zoroastrians, or Persians, took up his teaching "to speak the truth and to know well how to handle bow and arrow," the teaching that by Herodotus's time defined the education that Persians gave their boys.[102] Described third are the Hebrews, the people who were to "honor father and mother and do their will even from the roots of the soul," and who were promised that their days would then be long upon the land.[103] Zarathustra adds that their days were in fact made eternal, and the people made mighty by this incorporation of the parental into their own souls. The fourth people are defined by their loyalty: "Practice loyalty and for the sake of loyalty risk honor and blood even in evil and dangerous causes." Some have thought that Zarathustra was referring to the Germans or the Prussians, and that in alluding to them, he was pointing to the task of the new founder.[104] But it seems more likely that all four peoples are pre-Christian, and that the fourth people are the Romans, whose founder was Aeneas the pious, who was loyal to the ancestors and the sacred hearth, and from whose devout and heroic fidelity there would spring, so Jupiter promises Juno, a race who would "outdo both men and gods in its devotion."[105] The loyalty of the Romans led to their conquest of self and made them pregnant with their · "great hopes" or gave birth to an empire.

Zarathustra does not identify himself with any of the historic examples of value creation that he has drawn from Homer, Herodotus, the Bible, and Virgil. Instead, he uses these greatest examples, which parallel Machiavelli's greatest examples,[106] as the basis for describing the project with which he does identify himself. But first he draws the general conclusions from his examples for "you creators." Values are conferred by human creators, and those creators were at first peoples and only later individuals. Zarathustra's distinction between peoples and individuals is not a call to individuality, but an elaboration of the insight of the prologue (9) regarding the relationship between the herd and its founding teachers (see also I. 11). Addressing creative men regarding the creative greatness that has become possible at this point in the history of mankind, Zarathustra maintains that the individual is the latest creation. When peoples created, they were moved by a love that found its joy in the herd, not in the "I"; during the long reign of the herd, only the bad conscience said "I." But the latest creation, the individual, springs from an "I" rooted in bad conscience, one that is described as clever and calculating, for it seeks its private advantage in the advantage of the greatest number. This utilitarian "I" is not, as Utilitarians have argued, the origin of the herd that was supposed to have arisen through some original contract of mutual advantage drawn up by calculating individuals. It is, rather, the death of the herd or the death of the ancestral way of peoples; in this way Zarathustra certifies his claim that the modern state is the death of peoples (I. 11). It is not a people over whom hangs an ancestral "faith and love," but a leviathan moved by individual, utilitarian calculation of advantage. The rise of the modern state cannot be accounted for on the ancestral principle of the thousand peoples but stems from the rise of the individual through bad conscience. Zarathustra later describes this rise as the destruction of peoples through the impact of Christianity and its modern heirs (II. 3–8), but here he is content to acknowledge the historic achievement of the individual by pointing to its dubious roots. Still, the way of the individual is not to be overcome by a return to the way of the herd, for the achievement of dignity through the view backward, the ancestral way, is now forever thwarted by the rise of the individual, just as it is thwarted by the leering ape now seen in the more truthful view backward to stand at the head of the tribe. The ancestral view that mankind, or this portion of mankind, has divine or heroic origins is destroyed forever by the deadly truth that there is no cardinal difference between man and the animals. Creation of the people mankind, whose realization is now assigned explicitly to the labors of the superman, will not involve a return to ancestral ways but will incorporate the historic achievement of the individual that was the death of peoples. It will thereby ennoble yet another matter with base origins and carry further the evolution described in the speeches of the prologue.

To conclude his speech, Zarathustra, reasserting his Odysseus-like credentials as a knower, summarizes his teaching on the power of good and evil in order to draw its final imperative for creators and lovers of mankind. The work of lovers of mankind, their gift of good and evil, is defined as "the power of praise and blame" and also as "a monster" with a "thousand necks" that has never been yoked and brought under control. Yoking the powerful monster is the task of the lovers of mankind, the voice of their will to power. The thousand-and-first goal that yokes the thousand goals hitherto will for the first time draw mankind together into a single people. This is the culmination of Zarathustra's political teaching in part I, and it shows the extent of his ambition for man. The thousand peoples who have existed hitherto have been local and particular, and no universal system of harmony or historic necessity has governed their chance appearance or yoked them together into something meaningful. The coming of the superman will weld the thousand peoples into one global people.

The effect of this supreme act will be to overcome both the uncontrolled particularity of the thousand peoples hitherto and the ignobility of the modern state, whose march toward global dominance appeals only to the sword and the appetites and brings about only the universality of last men. The preconditions of the superman include the whole history of the human race so far, a history now seen as the long preparation for his coming. That most powerful man who will weld mankind into a whole must possess "an unprecedented knowledge of the preconditions of culture." Whereas Nietzsche had thought that the "great spirits of the next centuries" would have to busy themselves with this "monstrous task," here that task falls to the superman (*HH* I. 25)[107]

It is from the perspective of this commanding speech on the highest ambition that the earlier speeches, especially the opening speeches (I. 2–7), come to light as limited, as strategic enchantment aimed at attracting disciples to the one task that matters. The good of mankind is the superman, a good that does not yet exist. The new good determines the new virtues: virtue is what contributes to the appearance of the good which is the superman. The chapters defining the virtues required for the realization of the greatest good (I. 16–21) culminate in the private disclosure of "the highest virtue" (I. 22).

School for the Virtuous (Chapters 16–21)

The next six speeches reevaluate specific conventions in the light of the good that is the coming of the superman. The new account of what is worthy of praise and blame treats love of neighbor (I. 16), solitude (I. 17), man and woman (I. 18), justice (I. 19), marriage and child-rearing (I. 20), and death (I. 21). These six speeches correct in detail the impression left by the six earlier speeches implementing the strategic plan devised at the end of the prologue (I. 2–7), the impression that, as against the onerous disciplines and constraints of the old teaching, the new teaching gives license to free-spirits. Here Zarathustra shows the discipline required of one who loves the superman and introduces potential followers to the creative possibilities of the child spirit, which wins a new world for itself after the lion spirit has rendered itself homeless through the destruction of thousand-year-old values (I. 9–14). He shows how all passions are to be transformed into a single virtue identified only at the end, the gift-giving virtue that derives its worth from the superman.

"On Love of the Neighbor" (I. 16) attacks the teaching of love for the nearest, replacing it with exhortations to love the farthest, the superman. Appropriately, as a variant of Zarathustra's enduring theme of a schooled contempt for one's own and an acquired longing for the distant, it follows the contrast between the loves that occur within the horizon of a people's good and evil and the greater love that founds new peoples through the creation of a new good and evil. The love of the far, or innovation that serves mankind, evokes the enmity of those who love the near. Love of the near must therefore be discredited for love of the far to flourish, and it is unmasked as a dishonest, uncertain love of the self, in contrast to the healthy love of the self in the service of the far. But a fitting love of the near survives this attack, the love of the creative friend that can serve as a goad to will the superman. That creative friend has a gift to give, a complete world, whose dispersal and reassembly is made to resemble some general course of things. Zarathustra thus recommends himself as the creative friend who is near, the giver of a complete world, whose gift of friendship points forward to the farthest, the final cause for the sake of which the nearest deeds are performed.

Zarathustra then speaks in private to a young man setting off into the far, into solitude. "On the Way of the Creator" (I. 17) is reminiscent of Zarathustra's earlier private speech to the young man on the mountainside (I. 8). But with this young man it is not poisonous envy that dictates separation from Zarathustra, but the desire to imitate and surpass him. Zarathustra's speeches have slowly created the audience that he has sought from the beginning, an audience of "creators" who will create beyond themselves to the superman. Zarathustra is now an examiner, who demands of the young man entering solitude in obedience to his teaching that he prove his right to it. He has previously flattered his special audience by distinguishing it from the people, but here he asserts that the young man carries with him into solitude the internalized voice of the people. That voice, the voice of conscience, will sound like his own voice, condemning him for betraying his own people. But these pangs of conscience are merely the unexorcized remnant of the herd's imprint on him, and by detaching himself from this last refuge of ancestral constraint, he will become self-legislating, not simply free, but responsible only to what he sets for himself, the actions that prepare the way for the superman. In solitude he will discover in himself that man is "the as yet undetermined animal" (*BGE* 62). Still, the morality to which Zarathustra invites him is "stricter" than anyone else's (draft of a letter to Rée, December 1882) and requires that he be lawgiver, judge, and avenger of his own law. If the sole ground of his courage is merely the desire to be a free spirit, his courage will break in solitude, and he will cry out: "I am alone!" Utterly alone, with no measure outside himself for the high and the low, he will lose sight of the exalted and see only the low in himself; he will then cry out a second time: "Everything is false!" If he does not succeed in murdering the passion that produces this final cry of conscience, the passion that it ought not to be so, it ought to be otherwise, it ought to be higher, better, firmer—if he cannot murder the passion of nihilistic conscience, it will murder him.

The many from whom the young man separates himself will not forgive his separation. Out of envy they will hate him, but he must learn to welcome their envy, even though it is unjust. Zarathustra gives him words to say to them that calmly grant the justice of their injustice, words that would seem calculated to heap coals of fire on their heads.[108] Still, the greatest danger for the solitary comes from himself, for, although "the way of the creator" is the way of a lover, when the beloved is the self, it is the lover's way to despise the beloved for not being good enough. The young man will encounter in solitude not simply the self honored until now by his contemporaries and even by Zarathustra, but a self that requires the highest victory over itself. Zarathustra prophesies that under the young man's own demands, lover's demands, the self will come to seem like a heretic, a witch, a soothsayer, a fool, a doubter, an unholy one, a villain. The lover in his cruelty must burn these seven devils in his own flame and rise, a god, out of his own ashes. Drawn by Zarathustra and his teaching and inspired now by the project that awaits him, the young man must leave Zarathustra to pursue his own victory in solitude, where he will not be able to measure himself by Zarathustra or by Zarathustra's regard, but only by what he sets for himself. Zarathustra knows well the cruelty of such a spirit and he certifies him fit for solitude by the tears he sheds for him.[109] The spiritedness he sees in the young man is what he sees as best in mankind, and its presence in a young man who follows his way is the sign of the success of his speeches.

Zarathustra's next speech, "On Little Old and Young Women" (I. 18), is also delivered in private to a single follower, but this time he speaks under cover of a growing darkness about something he is hiding. He speaks because a "brother" asks him to speak, but the brother has been seduced into asking by Zarathustra's ostentatious furtiveness. What he hides under his cloak is "a little truth" he has just been given. Following his brother's bold suggestions, he calls what he is hiding both a treasure that he has been given and a child that has been born to him. He does not speak of the third suggestion that he, the friend of evil, is off on a thief's errand. He hides what he has because it would "cry too loudly" if uncovered by his hand and cloak.

He then tells his brother the occasion of the birth of this loud child with whom he has to be so careful. Earlier that evening, while walking alone, he had been stopped by a little old woman who had sought him out to question him. She had heard his teaching and found it to be addressed to women as well as men, but now, in private she wants him to rectify his failure to speak about women.[110] He refuses, alleging that it is meet to speak about women only to men, but she gets him to relent by maintaining that she is a special woman, one who is completely forgetful owing to her age. Much of the speech that follows consists of injunctions relevant only to young women. Zarathustra has, therefore, presumed that the old woman is lying about her forgetfulness, and that she will relay his teaching to the women whom it concerns. The young women will thus learn his teaching in the appropriate way, from an old woman. But the injunctions intended for young women he now tells in private to a young man; in this way he speaks appropriately of women only to men, telling the young man how women want him to behave.

The old woman had sought Zarathustra out and elicited his teaching with a lie; she welcomed it as she heard it, and finally made her own contribution to it. The young man, on the other hand, was provoked into asking about it by Zarathustra's curious behavior; Zarathustra thereby forces him to hear what may well be a teaching unwelcome to him.[111] His teaching on woman is a teaching on man and woman that distinguishes them as complementary, man providing woman with a child, woman providing man with danger and play. Man is the means to woman's end, whereas woman provides recreation for man, whose end is achieved among other men. A man should be raised for the manly or for battle, a woman for the recreation of such a warrior. While the child is woman's end, it can serve Zarathustra's end, the superman. The teaching that the old woman is to convey to young women contains the new hope that they will bear the superman, that the child they love as their own may also be lovable in himself, because he could become the greatest man. Woman's way is not the way of honor but of love. Thus the lying old woman is to transmit the appropriate variant of Peleus's counsel to his son Achilles, a woman's spirit of victory: always love more than you are loved and never be second. Man is to fear woman's love and woman's hate as that which is nearest to a woman but to him a mystery, but the fear is not to debilitate him or temper his actions, for woman loves, man wills. Fear of what woman loves and hates is to make man more willful, for what woman hates in a man is weakness of will. To be worthy of a woman's love, a man must will; whereas a woman's worthiness consists in yielding to the commanding will of a man.

The old woman's response to this speech acknowledges that its proper audience is young women, not herself. She finds it strange that the solitary, chaste Zarathustra should know so well the truth about woman. But the explanation she suggests attributes to women the grounds of his truths, for if "nothing is impossible with woman," everything said about her could be true of her or made true of her. Having received the gift of Zarathustra's teaching on woman, a teaching that is not fit for a man to address to a woman, the old woman repays him with a gift of her own, a teaching that is not fit for a woman to address to a man, at least to a man not likely to forget it. In saying that she is old enough to give this gift, she implies that no man would use it on her. It is she who tells him to be careful with her gift, to wrap it up and cover its mouth lest its cry be heard where it shouldn't be heard. She also calls her gift "a little truth," and although she does not call it a child, she treats it like a child. It is the child Zarathustra has apparently fathered on her by his teaching on woman; it is what the old woman makes of that teaching when she addresses its apparent father. Would she make something else of it if she were addressing young women?

She gives Zarathustra the gift she has borne but only after he has commanded her. Thus spoke the old woman: "You are going to women? Do
not forget the whip!"[112]

This child born of Zarathustra's teaching on woman cries too loudly
if not covered, yet he uncovers it for his brother after forcing him to ask
about what he hides. The child could be understood to be Zarathustra's
actual offspring, especially in view of the whip's later appearance as a sign
of his own increasing manliness, a sign of what happens between the man
Zarathustra and the woman Life. The manly Zarathustra will be portrayed
as lover of the woman Life (II. 10, 12), but their love will not be consummated
until late in part III, after he remembers the whip in going to the woman
Life (III. 15). She may object—she could hardly do otherwise—but she loves
him to be willful and impetuous and submits to his will when she hears
it. The fruitful marriage that follows provides the mysterious climax of the
whole book (III. 16). Because it proves to be a prelude to this climax, what
Zarathustra gives and gets from the old woman cannot be cast aside as
some private misogyny on Nietzsche's part, better ignored for a true appreciation of Nietzsche's teaching as a whole. The teaching on man and
woman points to an essential matter in *Zarathustra, the* essential matter
even, mankind's relation to nature. But, as elaborated so far, that teaching
contains an equivocation not yet open to resolution. The old woman's
formulation of Zarathustra's teaching incorporates famous imagery of man's
forceful mastery of woman and of nature. Machiavelli taught that fortune
is a woman who loves her men impetuous; although she will yield to a
calculating prudence that plans its controls well in advance, she is "a friend
of the young because they are less cautious, are fiercer, and with more
audacity do they command her." "She lets herself be overcome," but "if
one wants to keep her down, it is necessary to beat her and knock her
down." She is a woman who has already yielded to the most willful men
by taking "whatever form they pleased."[113] Francis Bacon speaks of a marriage bed prepared for the nature of things and for her partner, the imperial
mind of man; from that marriage bed of willful man and pliant nature
spring the line and race of inventions that will improve the human estate.[114]
Yet it is the old woman's words, her child, that suggest continuity with
this view of malleable, female nature at the disposal of willful male. Has
this child been fathered on her by Zarathustra? Her own words and their
source suggest another possibility, for the power she attributes to woman—
"with woman nothing is impossible"—usurps the power that the angel
attributes to God when announcing to Mary the miracle of her virgin birth.[115]
Is it possible that the old woman has after all given birth without the aid
of a male? What she infers from his teaching may well be a virgin birth,
despite its long life as Nietzsche's teaching on women. Zarathustra's own
words on man and woman seem to attest to the presence of something
contrary to the willful mastery of a merely pliant nature, for man and

woman are treated as simply given in what they are, and man and woman seem to bespeak a natural givenness more comprehensive than the sexes. This teaching on male and female seems to attest to the presence of limits already assigned by nature and assented to by human beings. Male and female as a desirable complementarity granted by nature elicit from Zarathustra a response that will be increasingly evident as fundamental to his teaching: gratitude. Against a modern teaching on woman that aims to overcome what has traditionally been held to be given in male and female or that treats that difference as primarily conventional, Zarathustra seems to insist on the difference as natural and to honor the natural difference by yielding to it.[116] Although the word *nature* is used only once in *Zarathustra*, and although that usage makes emphatic both the association between nature and woman and the apparent pliancy of nature through its surrender to a poet's words (II. 17), what comes to light in Zarathustra's counsel on male and female seems to be a refusal of mere pliancy in the name of nature. Rather than viewing nature as infinitely malleable, Zarathustra seems prepared to see her as she is and to alter his reaction to her unalterable ways. But what is the place of the whip when Zarathustra finally goes to Life? Only in the mysterious relationship between Zarathustra and Life as it develops in parts II and III does an answer to that question emerge. In that relationship Nietzsche presents the resolution of what he had earlier defined as philosophy's twofold task of discernment and action: "To me . . . the most vital of questions for philosophy appears to be to what extent the character of the world is unalterable: so as, once this question has been answered, to set about *improving that part of it recognized as alterable* with the most ruthless courage" (WB 3).

With no other teaching that he presents to the young men does Zarathustra take such precautions as with his teaching on man and woman. Still, he does present it, whereas he has kept silent about his teaching on will to power except for a single naming. Of all Zarathustra's teachings on conventions, only this one cries too loudly, however loudly the others may cry. What he covers, however, is not his teaching on woman but a conclusion someone else draws from his teaching, the only such conclusion directly stated in part I. He intimates in this way that his teaching can be put into dangerous and blunt words that are not easily forgotten and that seem to annul, at least for the forgetful, the delicate and subtle words he himself chooses for such subjects. This is not the only speech from which a listener might draw a conclusion that is more severe or more brutal than the one drawn by Zarathustra.[117]

Zarathustra's teaching on conventions continues with his teaching on justice or what is due other human beings ("The Adder's Bite," I. 19). It is presented in the form of a parable that baffles his disciples (so named here for the first time) and requires an unparabolic explanation.[118] It confines itself to half the traditional or political definition of justice and teaches how to harm enemies, how to benefit friends having already been discussed many times, especially in the speeches on warriors and on friends (I. 10, 14). The parable concerns a poisoning, a harming that fails because the means are inadequate, a hurt administered in such a mode that there remains a fear of vengeance, though Zarathustra proves to be above such action. This explication ends with a harming that succeeds because the means are adequate albeit extreme: kill the hermit you have insulted. The Machiavellian teaching[119] that ends this chapter, unlike the Machiavellian teaching that ended the previous one, is a conclusion drawn by Zarathustra, and it does not seem to require concealment. Perhaps it does not cry too loudly because it confines itself to hermits, and the people are suspicious of hermits anyway (Prologue 2).

Zarathustra's teaching on what is due one's enemies explicitly opposes the New Testament's justice of requiting evil with good, of disarming the enemy and ending enmity; instead, it arms the enemy and aims at enmity. Near the end of his speech he refuses what he calls being fundamentally just, just from the ground up. Such justice requires lying for the good of others so as to give to each what is his own or what is due him. Such justice might well be understood as the philosophic justice that Socrates practiced without explicitly defining, the justice of doing good to friends who are good and not harming anyone, the justice of prudent and ironic speech practiced by the philosopher.[120] Shunning such reserve or speech that lies for the good of others, Zarathustra promises to give to each only what is Zarathustra's own; his teaching on justice thus takes its bearings not from the good of others but from the good that is the superman. By giving to everyone what is his own, he gives to most a contempt that turns them into enemies. This reckless course of intentionally making enemies out of those who might justly be lied to seems directed especially at the good and the just named near the beginning of the chapter as those who charge him with being the annihilator of morals. But the parable with which this teaching began portrays him as a dragon invulnerable to the poison of a mere snake or to the attacks of the enemies he desires to make through his reckless speech. In making enemies, he measures them and does what is necessary to defend himself against them; were he to insult a hermit rather than the people, he would kill him too. He can insult the people without taking such extreme measures because they have short memories and are therefore not perpetually enemies.

The last two speeches before Zarathustra's departure from the city speak of the fundamental matters of birth and death and the conventions surrounding them. They emphasize the virtuous austerity of his teaching by making specific his demand that fundamental passions be controlled in the name of the good. The conventions that he recommends for birth and death are to be governed by the single good which is the coming of the superman. Marriage is certified or utilized by Zarathustra, but only under certain circumstances ("On Child and Marriage," I. 20). How rare those circumstances are is shown by the privacy of the speech, made to "you alone," a young man contemplating marriage, and by the disgust that Zarathustra expresses over marriage as customarily practiced. He sees no defense for the customary practice, but though it demeans those who engage in it, he has no interest in reforming marriage in general. He requires only that his young follower not marry for any of the customary reasons—animal passion, loneliness, discontent with oneself—but that he marry for the only reason that any of his followers perform any decisive act; he is to marry to raise children and raise children to prepare for the superman. Followers who lack the gift of chastity are to turn their private pleasures into service for mankind and the superman. No less than Plato's city built in speech—though without Plato's repeated questioning of the possibility and desirability of the extirpation of the private, whether the loves of a man and a woman in a family or the love of a philosopher for wisdom—Zarathustra's "city built in speech," his dream of progress toward the superman, requires the transformation of private passion into public service. Either the family serves history by nurturing forerunners of the superman, or it decays into contemptible privacy, which can have no historic justification. Just how austere Zarathustra's commands are to transform private passions into public good can be measured by his own apparent fall into the private in the next chapter.

Zarathustra's reevaluation of conventions concludes in a telling way with the teaching on "free death" (I. 21), a teaching of special interest because he refuses it. Death is free, or is not the final compulsion to which men are subject, when death is willed. Zarathustra's teaching on death is a novel teaching on suicide addressed only to the special few whom he first names "disciples" in the next chapter; the opening explicitly excludes the many and lets them die under compulsion. This final speech in the Colorful Cow replaces the teaching on death that Zarathustra had heard from the traditional sage at the beginning of his stay there (I. 2). It singles out for special scorn the old teaching that life be lived in the service of death, for death is to be mastered by life. But in serving life, it must serve the meaning of life and hence the superman. But how can death be made to serve the superman?

Unlike the Epicurean teaching on suicide, according to which life may be terminated when it is no longer pleasant, and unlike the Stoic teaching, which counsels suicide in the face of personal distress that cannot be mastered, Zarathustra's teaching requires that a free death be undertaken solely for its effect on an audience. Death becomes glorious as done for them; it can serve their purposes by being the occasion for swearing earnest vows to also live sacrificial lives. Like Lykurgos's death, it can show the living what their lives are to serve—no longer Sparta or an order that already exists, but solely the coming of the superman. To those few like himself who measure all their actions in the pure light of the good, the act of death can be a gift to the living. Such men must seize death at the right moment, the singular moment in which their historic contribution to the historic good reaches completion, in which their gift has been given and heirs created. This is a fitting teaching for one who understands mankind to be a bridge or a rope reaching toward a future that alone justifies it. Death as the culminating deed of life restates for the heirs what is worthy and causes them to harden their resolve that the meaning of life be exhausted in the cause of the superman. To live after the gift has been given is to live spent, a burden on the earth, no longer serving the historic task that alone gives life meaning. At the very end of his speech, Zarathustra says that he wills such a death for himself in order that his friends may love the earth more, for his sake, adding that in this way he returns to the earth and finds rest in the earth that bore him. This funeral oration for himself utilizes the edifying language of surrender to an earth seen as a mothering and superior force to willful man, but the one who delivers it is the one who does not surrender, even to inexorable death, but rather wills the moment of his death just as he wills the meaning of the earth. Speaking in the past tense, he says that he had a goal, and he commands his friends to be the heirs to his goal, to be those very ones the having of whom makes now the right time for him to die.

But Zarathustra betrays his own teaching when, instead of giving his disciples a riveting example of death in the interest of the superman, he lingers as a spectator of what he anticipates will be the historic drama of their march toward the superman. He wants the pleasure of observing the Posterity that alone makes his life worthwhile, even if it betrays his own teaching of a dramatic death for the sake of that Posterity. He asks to be forgiven for a desire that is merely personal and private, one that therefore has no meaning from the perspective of his sole standard of meaning. He needs forgiveness from his disciples because he is depriving them of an occasion for resolve, perhaps even *the* occasion. More than that, it would seem that his own example cannot help but weaken their resolve to serve only the superman, because he, the teacher of the superman, here serves only his private pleasure. In serving himself and not his disciples he fails his disciples; for he himself holds that free death, or martyrdom for the cause now at its very beginnings, is what disciples need. His disciples would have done well to have thought hard about forgiving him, for they have become disciples of a master less dedicated to the cause that he himself invented than were those masters, those "covert suicides" (AO 94), whose teachings on life and death he aims to supplant—Socrates, whose death gave Plato the transforming example of how life is to be lived when life is thought, and Jesus, whose death gave St. Paul the transforming example of how life is to be lived when life is the service of sinful man to sovereign God.

But if Zarathustra had died then, he would have joined the few who died too soon, for he would not have achieved the pinnacle of what was possible, one that at age forty seemed unattainable both for himself and his hearers, since it could be attained only at the end of a long chain of gift-givers like himself. By refusing his own teaching on death, he preserves a possibility that he has until now denied himself. For although he leaves his disciples with the impression that his own work is completed, that he has thrown the golden ball of his teaching as far as he can and that the task of throwing it further is now theirs, this impression is false according to the assertion with which part II opens, that Zarathustra had closed his hand while it still contained gifts to be given. Measured by this assertion Zarathustra has shown himself to be less than he is. Not only has he held back much that he might have given to his disciples, but he has shown himself flawed, in need of forgiveness, capable of being surpassed. He ends his speeches in the city on an act of grace that consists of diminishing himself so that they may make themselves great or greater than he, an act that befits a teacher who has made envy the dangerous spur to greatness. His serious followers can think themselves more serious than their teacher in dedication to the one achievement which gives meaning to the earth.

With his teaching on death, Zarathustra ends his presentation of what might be called his "provisional maxims,"[121] those principles of behavior that hold until the superman comes, and that aid in bringing the superman with his definitive teaching for mankind. Those prepared to live by these maxims now follow Zarathustra out of the Colorful Cow.

The Farewell Gift (Chapter 22)

The last speeches of part I, given in the final chapter entitled "On the Gift-Giving Virtue" (I. 22), differ from the other speeches in their location, audience, and intent. They are delivered outside the city, at the crossroads, to those who now call themselves disciples and whom Zarathustra for the first time calls "my disciples." Their frequent echoes of Jesus' farewell speeches to his disciples outside the city flaunt Zarathustra's hostility to the otherworldly self-denial that Jesus demanded of his followers.[122] These speeches attest to the success of his previous speeches in that he now has disciples to address, those whose task it is to carry his teaching further. His teaching, the meaning of the earth, now becomes their responsibility. The chapter is divided into three parts, each containing a single speech, and the speeches are separated by silences marking changes in both Zarathustra's mood and his strategy. Together, these speeches are the culmination of all Zarathustra's speaking in part I. They resemble the initial speeches delivered to the people in the prologue; but now Zarathustra has created their appropriate audience.

He leaves the city to which his heart has become attached, taking his disciples with him. Knowing that he is to leave them, his disciples bring a parting gift as an expression of their gratitude: a staff with a golden handle

showing a serpent coiled around the sun. The staff resembles that of Asklepius, god of healing, who received it from his father, Apollo, as the symbol
of the healing art. Apollo gave the staff to Hermes after Zeus had Asklepius
killed, and through Hermes, herald of the gods and guide of souls, it became
the sign of the messenger or herald. Zarathustra, both healer and herald,
gives the disciples, as his parting gift, the name of his virtue and what it
implies. Leaning on the staff for the first speech, he takes the staff as his
text. His speech is the most complete and revealing account of who the
Zarathustra of part I is; in describing for the first time his single virtue, the
gift-giving virtue,[123] it describes Zarathustra himself. Here the teacher who
had once counseled his listener not to name his virtue lest it become public
or shared (I. 5) names his own virtue in order that it be shared. In so doing,
he names the hunger of his entrails, what gives both agony and sweetness
to his soul (I. 5). True to his earlier teaching, he describes his own virtue
as transformed passion, for the passions of contempt for mankind and
longing for the superman are the source of the gift-giving virtue. He flatters
his disciples by assuming that they have become like him; he thinks, or
alleges, that he sees in them what he knows in himself to be the most
severe liberality, the squandering of one's self as a gift to mankind's future.

Having just left the city, Zarathustra delivers a speech contrasting his
perspective with the city's. Its theme is gold, which has come to have the
highest value and is pursued for itself by the city based on commerce. But
for Zarathustra, gold is merely an image of what is valuable for itself; a
fitting image, nevertheless, for, like the highest virtue, it is uncommon, and
its worth is not grounded solely in utility. Those he has drawn out of the
city are those with gold in their veins. Moved by the gift-giving virtue, they
are unlike those they have left behind in the city; they are not common,
in that they do not merely calculate their private utility; their giving is not
based on calculations of taking. In fact, the reverse is true; their taking—
says the one who has taken them from the city—though insatiable, in that
it desires to draw everything to itself, is a taking based on the passion to
give. His own taking will make him seem like a "wolf" or a "robber" to the
city (Prologue 9), but he explains to those he has taken how he differs from
a wolf,[124] how his robbing is for the sake of giving. The contrast between
his way and that of the city initiated by the reflection on gold comes to
focus on the word *selfishness,* used here for the first time in an attempt
to win selfishness back from the meanness of modern utilitarianism and
the hedonistic egoism of last men. Although Zarathustra and his kind
openly take for themselves, their selfishness is preparatory to an act of
giving for the sake of mankind. Although the men of the modern city openly
describe their actions as altruism, these actions are calculated selfishness,
a "sick selfishness" that says, "All for me," and that is grounded in the
correct perception of a self in need. The two kinds of selfishness bespeak
two kinds of selves; one that is decadent—and decadence is the very worst
condition because it keeps everything low by holding it to be low—and

one that is noble and aspires to move upward from base beginnings. Zarathustra's new selfishness does not turn private, nor does it manipulate an inattentive public for its private good; in projecting itself outward onto the world, it becomes its measure-giver, for love of the self leads to love of the world.[125] Whereas part I began with Zarathustra's going under, this speech at the end of part I commends the upward way, the way of advance and elevation moved by a selfishness grounded in the passion of gift-giving, a selfishness of independent, solitary selves that differs from the needy selfishness of the city.[126] Zarathustra may have named his virtue, but names given to virtues are only signs hinting at the presence of passions, which alone are noble or base. The one who desires to understand "the passage of the body through history" or its present stand in history must be a reader of signs who can detect the noble and base passions that underlie the greatest power on earth, good and evil. In describing the two kinds of selfishness, Zarathustra shows that he is such a reader, and he calls his disciples to watchfulness for the five signs of the spirit that mark the onset of their own new virtue.[127] The new gift-giving virtue is a mastering thought enclosed in a prudent soul, like the golden sun enclosed in a coiled golden serpent.

The second private speech is more apprehensive than the first. The plea of the prologue, "Be loyal to the earth!", is now addressed to its proper audience. The mastering thought and prudent souls of Zarathustra's friends are to be put in the service of the meaning of the earth, not otherworldly hopes. Mankind's disloyalty to the earth consists in its judgment that the earth is not good enough; but it is Zarathustra's judgment that only mankind is not good enough, and the task that he sets for himself and his disciples is that of making it good enough. Success in this historic task is made problematic by mankind's past of otherworldly concerns, which continues to take its toll. For, as heirs to millennia of attempts to deny the earth and body, mankind today inherits a marred and limited capacity to be loyal to the earth. It is dangerous to be heir to the long experiment that mankind is, because the accidental, experimental past is not inherited as accident, but as its opposite, necessity.[128] Products of that now necessary past, Zarathustra and his friends must be physicians who heal themselves and thereby help mankind to heal itself. The abused body's healing balm is knowledge, not just of the past, but of an open, experimental future that stretches from the present in a thousand untrodden paths. This speech does not prophesy the end of the world but the opening of a new future; disciples are not to "watch and pray" but to "watch and listen"; they are not to avoid falling into temptation but to try the tempting paths not yet taken.[129] The historic responsibility to bring to an end "that gruesome rule of nonsense and chance that has been called 'History' till now" (*BGE* 203) differs from the responsibility assigned to man by Hegel or Marx, because it is not the case that the world has been unfolding as it should, or that the best order is being actualized by History. Superintended by neither a spiritual nor a material dialectic, a process in which not even this finger of God has taken part as a player, human history is subject to mere accident, and the accidents that have governed the appearance of the present imperil the future. Though they are to watch and listen, Zarathustra and his disciples are not permitted the luxury of mere observation; because they have on their conscience the whole future of mankind, they must intervene (*BGE* 61, 62). Zarathustra ends his second speech with a restatement of his vision of the future from the prologue, with mankind as the bridge to the superman. But now that redeeming future depends not on mankind as a whole, but on this small band of followers whom he addresses with all the urgency of his great longing. Evoking now the image of Moses speaking in the desert to the chosen people whom he has led out of Egypt toward the promised land, Zarathustra, grasping the rod symbolic of his power,[130] speaks to the followers he has led out of the city into solitude and toward the promised land of the superman. They represent the hope of mankind, and he prophesies that out of them will spring a "chosen people"[131] from whom will spring the superman, the messiah who will give the earth its meaning and redeem mankind from its past.

In falling silent for a second time, a long time, Zarathustra makes it clear that he has not finished speaking; his silence prepares his disciples for his final words by increasing their anticipation. Balancing the staff they have given him in his hand, he appears doubtful about what he is to say. What he finally says, what he long knew he would finally say to them, must startle them, coming from the one they have learned to love, he whom they have sold everything to follow. His words are reminiscent of Jesus' words to his disciples, but oppose them in content, for he tells them to find themselves by losing him, and promises that only after they have denied him will he return to them.[132] Where the goal is the coming of the superman, the disciples made by the herald must break with him by surpassing him toward the goal. His last speech commands their overcoming of mere discipleship, their refusal to let a statue slay them.[133] Zarathustra's promise to return to seek them with other eyes and to love them with another love serves as the motto for part II, in which he returns to disciples who have denied him and exhibits a different love.

Zarathustra promises not only a second coming, but also a third, in which they will celebrate "the Great Noon," the point in human history midway between animality and the superman.[134] This third coming seems to coincide with his own evening, for he links the noonday sun with the setting sun, as if mankind's noon were his setting. But he refers as well to the rising sun that marks the dawn of the new day. The promise of a third coming is not fulfilled in *Zarathustra* but it is elaborated in later speeches and points to the return prepared at the end of part IV, the meaning of which depends on the intervening events of Zarathustra's career. Zarathustra's last words to his disciples echo his first words to the people and complete his teaching in part I; the "last will" of the disciples, the will appropriate to the Great Noon, is that the superman live now that all gods are dead.[135]

THE PROVISIONAL TEACHING OF PART I

Part I ends with Zarathustra defining discipleship to disciples. Urgency and pathos mark his definition, for these disciples are the tiny handful on whose future achievements the future of mankind depends. Nevertheless, echoing a judgment that many have made on the basis of the final speech of part I, Werner Dannhauser says categorically, "Zarathustra wants no disciples."[136] But in part I, Zarathustra wants disciples above all else, because he thinks that the meaning of the earth depends on disciples loyal to the cause of the superman. At the very end of part I, where he seems to repudiate discipleship in the name of an independence of masters that many have thought the most edifying part of his whole teaching, he in fact repudiates only the Christian understanding of discipleship, as he must, since in his view there has not yet been a redeemer-superman worthy of imitation. Because something that has not existed before must be created, discipleship cannot be mere imitation, it must involve a passionate exertion to outdo even the master who brings the teaching. But it is not inconsistent with this surpassing that disciples stay loyal to Zarathustra's teaching. They are to be disciples "who will follow themselves—wherever I want" (Prologue 9). The loyalty proper to his disciples is disloyalty to him only insofar as they are to outdo him on the way to the superman; they are not to be disloyal to his goal of the superman. The disciples exist as means to the superman; overcoming mere discipleship to Zarathustra entails submitting themselves to his ideal.

Zarathustra, the unarmed prophet of a novel teaching, necessarily arms himself with disciples for the spiritual warfare that lies ahead. The model of discipleship he appropriates in part I derives from the Greeks, not the New Testament. As Nietzsche portrays the Greeks, all of life was a contest; poetry was a contest, philosophy was a contest; Euthymides wrote right on the magnificent amphora he had painted, "Euthymides son of Polias painted it," and on the other side, "as Euphronios never [could]."[137] The ideal of zealous emulation with the goal of surpassing its model was fundamental to Greek achievement, and Nietzsche at twenty-eight described it with awe and admiration in "Homer's Contest," as his own zealous emulation of the highest Greek achievements was beginning to be awakened. In describing such emulation, Aristotle says, "it is a good feeling felt by good persons," especially "by the young and by persons of lofty disposition."[138] But the emulation Zarathustra recommends adds a dimension foreign to the Greeks in that it transforms the goal of surpassing into service for mankind as preparation for the appearance of the superman. Such striving is not "narcissistic," but rather a kind of charity that gives the highest gift of oneself to mankind.

It might be thought that the Zarathustra who "wants no disciples" is the Zarathustra of part III who has left his disciples and returned to solitude. But the return to solitude cannot be interpreted as a rejection of disciples, as if the joys of solitude were enough, as if it were not necessary to return to the world of men with the achievements of solitude. Stanley Rosen says that Zarathustra's "isolation has been overcome by the possibility of a new historical epoch."[139] The new epoch overcomes Zarathustra's isolation, not because the thought of it comforts him nor because he can dream of the day when disciples will found it, but because he himself is moved to found it. This seems to me to be the appropriate conclusion to draw from the events of parts II and III. Although the specific conditions of discipleship will therefore change, discipleship of some sort will be required in order to secure the new epoch.

In part I Zarathustra holds that the superman is the meaning of the earth, and that life in the present is meaningful only insofar as it is a gift given for the future. The teacher of the gift-giving virtue says nothing about the antecedents of his virtue, preferring to treat it as a historic novelty, his own gift to mankind. Aristotle's account of liberality, magnificence, and magnanimity, culminating in praise of "the great-souled man," is in some respects an antecedent, most particularly in the competitive desire to be superior in giving.[140] But Aristotle's praise of gift-giving lacks the historical dimension present in Zarathustra's teaching. For Zarathustra the meaning of gift-giving lies in its contribution to the goal of the superman, whereas for Aristotle it consists in being recognized as magnanimous. Because the history of mankind depends on it, Zarathustra's emphasis on giving oneself away for the superman sounds a far more impassioned note than the deliberate, distant greatness of the man who has "the crown of the virtues," magnanimity, and who is honored because he merits honor.

This emphasis on self-sacrifice makes the Christian virtue of charity seem a more direct antecedent of Zarathustra's gift-giving virtue.[141] But Zarathustra parades his virtue as "selfishness," as if to distinguish it from Christian charity. Although his selfishness is not the degenerate selfishness that says, "All for me," it is nevertheless a celebration of self, not its denial for the sake of others. Giving oneself in Zarathustra's sense elevates the self. Zarathustra's apparent self-emptying at the beginning and end of part I is only a metaphor for the outpouring of his teaching, while the teaching itself aims to bring into being the most elevated of men. Whereas "God chose what is foolish in the world to shame the wise ... what is weak in the world to shame the strong ... what is low and despised in the world ... to bring to nothing things that are,"[142] Zarathustra cultivates and encourages what is wise or mighty while aiming always at the wisest and mightiest of all. Whereas charity sacrifices the self for the lowly, the gift-giving virtue squanders the self for the great. Whereas charity "pulls down the mighty from their thrones and exalts those of low degree,"[143] the gift-giving virtue seeks power, for it aims at becoming the new form of the greatest power on earth.

The most direct antecedent to Zarathustra's virtue seems to be the modern progressive virtue that measures worthy actions by their contribution to the future development of mankind. In its image of a bridge or rope constituted of members living for a future, the gift-giving virtue echoes the ethic of service to Posterity advocated by some of the thinkers of the modern Enlightenment. "Posterity is for the philosopher what the other world is for the religious," Diderot claimed, arguing that if there were no Posterity to serve, if it could be proved that at a future date a comet would collide with the earth, totally destroying it, there would be "no more ambition, no more monuments, poets, historians, perhaps no more warriors or war."[144] Service to Posterity is the virtue peculiarly suited to a teaching of progress, because the present generation surrenders its own benefit for benefits that accrue only to future generations. Zarathustra relies on a teaching of virtue to move spirited young men to take up his ideal of progress, since he could not rely on the means more characteristic of the modern doctrine of progress. In the fundamental teaching of Locke, it is not the forever delayed gratification of an ethic of service or any love of Posterity that provides the basis for progress; instead, the private pursuit of wealth, "the desire of having more than man needed," redounds to everyone's benefit and effects the long term improvement of nature by correcting her niggardliness.[145] Similar expectations of progress in the common good through pursuit of private ends ground Kant's "mechanism of nature" or "concord through discord."[146] And Hegel's Providence realizes its goal of freedom and self-consciousness through the private passions of ambitious men seeking neither freedom nor self-consciousness, but acknowledgment of their own greatness in concrete deeds. Hegel could speak ironically of "the cunning of Reason," which had been shrewd enough to spare itself while using and using up perishable men in compulsory and ignorant sacrifice to the achievement of freedom and wisdom.[147]

The progress Zarathustra seeks is yet to come and depends wholly on the actions of men guided by a new knowledge of what is desirable. He cannot look confidently backward on a long progress superintended by Providence, nor can he assume the miraculous transformation of private passion into public good. Because he cannot trust to miracle, he is forced to rely on virtue. That virtue is grounded in the passions of longing and contempt; his appeals to live and die for a future a long way off present themselves as a pure love of Posterity, of mankind in the form of the superman, aided by contempt for the present so clearly expressed by another progressive, Condorcet: "The human race still revolts the philosopher who contemplates its history."[148] The crisis of outcome is authentic for Zarathustra, because no "invisible hand," no "mechanism of nature," no "cunning of Reason," fuses private passions and public benefits, and the teaching based on such miracles threatens to bring into being the dominion of last men. Gift-giving Zarathustra gives the gift of "uneasiness" or contempt for what is already at hand. Because of Nietzsche's fame as the teacher of the death of God, it is easy to misread Zarathustra's counsel of contempt as directed primarily against the religious tradition grounded in the Bible. But though such contempt is present, it is mostly presupposed. Zarathustra has returned to a world in which God is already dead, and although he loves to push over what is already toppling (III. 12, §20), his most vehement contempt is reserved for what still stands and what is coming to stand as a consequence of what is toppling, namely the modern teaching on progress, the modern form of pride that interprets the history of mankind edifyingly, in the form of self-congratulation, as the long struggle for democratic politics and universal enlightenment now reaching its culmination. It is the alleged freedom and alleged enlightenment of progressive modern man that provokes Zarathustra into declaring war and calling on the best youths to share his revulsion for the things nearest them, the good as defined by democratic politics, the true as defined and certified by democratic science. Zarathustra's counsel of contempt for the things that modern man has been taught to honor most is counsel to disloyalty or treachery from the perspective of the watchful guardians of the modern herd, to whom Zarathustra is a wolf preying on their young, a teacher of evil, a nihilist opposed to civilization itself.

The subsequent parts do nothing to allay the suspicions and fears of such guardians, but they do show that the teaching of part I, the teaching of a herald, needs to be treated with the caution appropriate to a provisional teaching. Part I assumes that there will be continued progress through the disciples up to the superman, but part II shows Zarathustra learning the limitations of disciples and losing faith precisely where faith is necessary for a teacher of progress, in the ability of followers to improve on his work. But it also shows Zarathustra, moved by his discoveries about will to power and by his own spiritedness, coming to understand that the task he has assigned to his disciples is not theirs but his. At the beginning of part III he abandons his disciples in order to take the impossible path himself, the way of the superman. Eric Voegelin's judgment is apt: having just defined "Platonism in politics" as "the attempt, perhaps hopeless and futile, to regenerate a disintegrating society spiritually by creating the model of a true order of values, and by using as the material for the model realistically the elements which are present in the substance of the society," he goes on to say with regard to Nietzsche that "the man with the Platonic temper will try the impossible." "Impossibility" is the sign that hangs over the path Zarathustra takes in part III, and the labor of the superman that lies at the end of that path could well be seen as Voegelin's "Platonism in politics."[149]

The teaching of part I is incomplete, while pointing to what would complete it. That the herald of part I becomes the one heralded is indicated by dramatic changes in Zarathustra's role. In part I he is wholly teacher, the one who "takes all things seriously only in relation to his pupils—even himself" (*BGE* 63). Later he ceases to be pure teacher and becomes once again a learner and a solitary. What he learns in solitude he does not address to disciples (II. 12) except when uncontrollable dismay forces him to speak to them in the way he speaks to himself (II. 20). These changes in the teacher point to still more fundamental changes in what he has to teach or what he has come to learn. The changes are shown most simply by Zarathustra's deepening reflection on his single, defining virtue, the gift-giving virtue (III. 10, §2). Having unmasked the virtues of others, he unmasks his own. The gift-giving virtue hides a passion that has finally become clear to him because of what he has learned about will to power. The one who advocated the virtuous gift of one's self for the sake of mankind's future now gives a new name to the "nameless" passion he feels within himself; he calls it "the passion to rule," while acknowledging that even this improved name is inadequate. He is not shocked by his unmasked virtue, nor does he renounce it; instead, he prepares himself to cultivate it more knowingly, to remedy the deficiency of will for which he was taunted at the end of part II. He prepares himself for the highest act of gift-giving, the act of ruling or founding which brings the book to its climax.

Zarathustra learns other important lessons. Revenge, an incidental theme in part I (I. 6, 12, 19), becomes the pervasive sickness from which all mankind needs to be redeemed (II. 8, 20). Whereas in part I Zarathustra presents himself as having fully convalesced from the sicknesses of mankind (I. 3, 22, §2), his convalescence continues when he discovers new ways in which mankind and he himself are diseased by revenge (II. 20, III. 13). But the most important change is in the fundamental matter, his understanding of life or of beings as a whole. "The belly of being" that speaks to no man unless as man, according to the skeptical Zarathustra of part I (I. 3), speaks to Zarathustra—but as Life herself (II. 10, 12). Her speech forces him to abandon the skepticism that had made life simply unfathomable in favor of an unexpected possibility, the true if dark teaching that life is will to power. Discovery of the scope of will to power proves to be the fundamental discovery of *Thus Spoke Zarathustra*, for it leads to the teaching for the sake of which the book exists. The thought of eternal return—absent from part I, though said by Nietzsche to be "the fundamental thought" of *Zarathustra*, and though present at the end of Nietzsche's previous book as an introduction to *Zarathustra* (*EH*, "Books: *Zarathustra*," 1; *GS* 341, 342)— appears first in part II as the consequence of Life's secret and emerges in part III as Zarathustra's essential task. Eternal return is not only the teaching loyal to the earth, but also the novel teaching that founds the new age, the teaching brought by the superman.

If Zarathustra subsequently takes upon himself the labor of the superman, the teaching of part I must be understood as provisional. What the superman teaches is different from what his herald teaches, for, whereas his herald teaches the austere view that all actions must be measured by the good that is the superman's coming, the superman himself comes to teach a new good, eternal return, of which the herald has no inkling. Whereas the herald teaches that the meaning of the earth lies in a future achievement, the superman teaches eternal return, with its completely different perspective on the passage of time, one that renders obsolete the progressive view that the present is justified only by the future. *Zarathustra* as a whole does not teach that life is to be lived for the future superman; rather, that life is to be lived *sub specie aeternitatis*, where *aeternitas* is the eternal return of beings as they are. Just how Zarathustra progresses to that teaching is shown in detail in parts II and III and constitutes Zarathustra's entrance into Nietzsche's philosophy.

From the later perspective, the teaching in part I can be seen as Apollonian with Zarathustra exhibiting the calm mastery that was always Apollo's trait and gift. Images of light-bringing Apollo are present from Zarathustra's opening address to the morning sun to his closing invocation of the Great Noon. His teaching is itself like a sun, a "golden ball," bringing enlightenment to the world. Like Apollo, who is honored for developing boys into men, Zarathustra comes to win youthful disciples to a teaching that will make them worthy men and forerunners of the superman. Zarathustra follows the great archer Apollo by himself becoming an archer whose arrows are his teachings. As if to honor Apollo, god of prophecy, Zarathustra appears as prophet of a new teaching. Apollo's animal, the snake, is one of his animals. Apollo is the god of medicine, father of Asklepius, and Zarathustra appears among men as the healer of the ancient sickness that hates the body and the earth. Apollo is also the patron of light-bringing philosophy, forefather of Plato himself, and in part I it is as if the philosopher Zarathustra has come to replace the teachings of the philosopher Plato with a truer presentation of the things of Apollo. But the teaching of the new light-bringer Zarathustra is revealed as Apollonian especially after he discovers a "midnight wisdom." The characteristics of that wisdom are Dionysian, and at the mysterious climax of the book Zarathustra welcomes the return of Dionysos.

Part II

> When a philosopher these days lets it be known that he is not
> a skeptic . . . everyone is annoyed.
>
> —NIETZSCHE, *BGE* 208

THE ACTION OF PART II

Part II describes the decisive action of *Thus Spoke Zarathustra*, the discovery
of the teaching required to fulfill the historic mission left to some future
superman in part I. The speeches of part II are given on "the blessed isles,"
the place of future hope where Kronos once ruled over the heroes of old
amidst peace and plenty, or where the worthy few were rewarded for surviving their three incarnations in innocence.[1] In the first chapter Zarathustra
utters "a cry and a shout of joy" like an ancient hero and pictures himself
sailing "across broad seas" to "the blessed isles where my friends are waiting." Zarathustra's blessed isles are not a final resting place but the dwelling
place of his disciples, his hopes for a new future. But at the end of part
II Zarathustra leaves his disciples, and at the beginning of part III he sails
away from the blessed isles and from the hope for the future that he had
invested in his disciples. Whereas the early chapters of part II further the
education of the disciples as means to the superman, the later chapters
show them to be incapable of surpassing Zarathustra toward the superman.
By the time Zarathustra sails away, the making of disciples who will prepare
the way for the superman is no longer the goal of his life, though his life
continues to have the goal of realizing the superman. Part II, framed by a
hope and its destruction, contains the dawning of a new and necessary
ambition for Zarathustra. He is the one who now asks, "Who is Zarathustra?"

Whereas in part I Zarathustra's learning was confined to lessons on
politic speech, in part II he learns the truth about the fundamental phenomena: that life is will to power and wisdom its most spiritual form.
These discoveries lead to the additional discovery that all previous wisdoms,
including his own, share a property that he names "revenge." In his most
revealing speech in part II, a speech that in its inwardness and intensity

forgets its audience, Zarathustra shows that he himself is not yet "redeemed" from the spirit of revenge (II. 20), although he now knows what is necessary for redemption. The discoveries of part II do not eliminate the need for the superman; on the contrary, they give definition and content to the labor of the superman in a way that the speeches of the herald did not. These discoveries signal an expansion of ambition almost unthinkable to the herald, for it becomes obvious that it is given to him to undertake what he had pictured as the task of superior heirs. The act of sailing away from the blessed isles at the beginning of part III bespeaks Zarathustra's willingness to undertake those labors himself.

The pure teacher of part I exhibits a surprising reticence about his discoveries in part II, for he does not pass them on to his disciples. The fundamental discovery that life is will to power is suggested in three oblique and obscure songs (II. 9–11), and the speech in which the discovery itself is recorded is addressed not to the disciples but only to "you who are wisest" (II. 12), as if they were the only ones who need take an interest in it. Will to power is not mentioned again until the speech in the disciples' presence that Zarathustra regrets as too revealing (II. 20). It is too revealing not only because it shows the disciples that their teacher is not redeemed, but even more because it shows that redemption requires what might be thought impossible, willing eternal return. Not even Zarathustra is ready for this teaching. In his new reticence Zarathustra practices ways of speaking that are much less direct than the persuasive speeches of part I. Part II therefore contains many remarkable chapters whose meaning is hidden in a play of parable and song. The parables are no longer explained, and the aphorisms are no longer simply invitations to occupy the height already occupied by Zarathustra. In ceasing to be the pure teacher of part I, Zarathustra frees himself from the limitations of the teacher; he now takes all things seriously, not in relation to his pupils, but in relation to a task in which pupils play no part.

The overriding theme of part II is wisdom. In the first chapter Zarathustra receives in a dream the sign that permits him to return to his disciples bringing them the fruits of his new wild wisdom (II. 1). He delivers the new wisdom in six speeches and rekindles their ardor for the task of preparing for the superman. The new wisdom provides them with an alternative to the rival teachings that have attracted them in his absence (II. 2–7). There follows an interlude of inwardness in which Zarathustra addresses the wisest men, having discovered the secret of their wisdom (II. 8–12). He then turns to other forms of wisdom (II. 13–19), the final three of which draw his disciples into misapprehensions about him and the nature of his wisdom. In the climactic chapter Zarathustra reveals what it is that man still needs to be redeemed from and the seemingly impossible means to that redemption (II. 20); here wisdom is seen as both the curse of mankind and the means of redemption from that curse. Having thus revealed the inner connection between will to power and eternal return, part II closes quietly on the theme of practical wisdom, with Zarathustra resolving to terminate one aspect of his prudence (II. 21) and consequently taking leave of his disciples (II. 22).[2]

What gradually becomes clear in this account of wisdom is that it pictures the contemporary situation of philosophy and science, though the limitations of rhetorical form dictated by a fable set in no historical time or place conceal to some extent the European present actually depicted. In the metaphors of open sea and open sky, of sailors and fliers driven to explore them, *Zarathustra* depicts what for Nietzsche is the highest and defining aspect of mankind, open-ended investigation of the enigmatic world of which we are a part. Although modern philosophy and science have jointly brought low the ancient order that forced them to serve otherworldly ends, philosophy itself has fallen into servitude to its offspring science, and both have become servile to a base politics that threatens a permanent end to their independence. The future of mankind is at issue in this relationship of philosophy, science, and politics. In speaking of the whole great history that has fated the present age, Zarathustra speaks "with greatness—that means cynically and with innocence," cynically because he refuses to believe the grounds customarily given for that history, and with innocence because he refuses to lament that history as if it were guilty of some crime against what went before (*KGW VIII* 11 [411] = *WP*, Preface, 1).[3] In its own way *Zarathustra* thus continues the essential theme of *Human, All Too Human* by calling Europe back to the task that belongs to it, carrying forward Greek science (*HH* I. 475). According to Nietzsche's insurgent history of philosophy, this task of precise, joyful inquiry into earth and sky was interrupted by the advent of Christianity, what Yeats called the one "Asiatic vague immensity" that managed to cross "the many-headed" Aegean to Europe, its crossing smoothed by the Platonic teaching on the pure mind and the good in itself.[4] As the character and dimensions of the task for philosophy in the present age become clear, so too does Zarathustra's or Nietzsche's relationship to it; no longer herald of an undertaking obscure to him, he must take up the impossible task himself.[5]

WILD WISDOM (CHAPTER 1)

Part II begins in a way that invites comparison with the opening of the prologue, by describing an initial ascent, a long period of solitude, and the reasons for ending that solitude. But whereas the ten years of solitude reported in the prologue were years of enjoyment, the years of solitude between parts I and II are filled with impatience and longing, because Zarathustra now has disciples whom he loves. Because he assumes his absence to be necessary to them, he can permit himself to return only after they have taken advantage of his absence to deny him. But he waits impatiently, like a sower who has cast his seed, not only because he wants to see them grow, but also because he has more seed to sow. The free and open giving of part I had been a strategic withholding as well, albeit one occasioned by love. The love that denies itself by not giving all it possesses to the beloved is a gracious love that withholds only what cannot be received, or which measures the beloved and spares him what would harm him. But now that the recipients of his gift have met the condition of denying the giver, now that their prolonged reflection on his teaching has turned it into something he must oppose, he can give them what he had previously withheld. In its severity his new gift is fitting only for them; they have qualified for it by attempting to think through his previous gift, even if that attempt has ended in what looks like failure.

While the action of the prologue began at dawn with an address to the sun, the action of part II begins in the darkness before dawn with Zarathustra speaking to his own heart. (Part III begins and ends at midnight.) Zarathustra is awakened before daybreak by a dream telling him that his disciples have denied him. But the dream brings joy, for the denial was expected, and it grants him permission to return. The title of the chapter, "The Child with the Mirror,"[6] thus refers to a disciple whose three transformations (I. 1) are complete, but whose immature creativity reflects a Zarathustra who, to Zarathustra's eyes, has become a devil. By his innocent invitation to Zarathustra to behold himself in his mirror, the child shows himself not to be ashamed of the way he reflects his master; what to Zarathustra is denial seems to him praiseworthy service. The nature of a denial that can seem an affirmation becomes clear from the speeches that Zarathustra will deliver to his disciples. The only italicized word in his speech interpreting his dream shows that Zarathustra's *teaching* is in danger when his disciples fail to mirror it faithfully, for his teaching depends on disciples carrying it forward to the coming of the superman.

The dream that has awakened him causes a transformation, which he describes to his startled animals.[7] His speech is the ardent utterance of a lover long denied his love. Still, though unrestrained and impassioned, he knows that he must excuse himself for his lack of restraint, for having forgotten the need for silence. In excusing itself, this speech apologizes in advance for the unrestrained speeches soon to be made to his friends (II. 2–7). The speech abounds in images describing Zarathustra's fervent state on his return. He is a lake from which a river rages out of the mountains, pouring eventually into the sea; a warrior springing into a chariot of storm and whipping the storm to battle or leaping astride his wildest horse with the aid of his spear. Like the warriors of part I, he is grateful not only for friends, but also for enemies on whom he can vent the tension of the storm gathered in his own breast. As the bringer of lightning and hail, he is more than the heavy drop of rain that signals the coming storm in the prologue (4). To end the speech anticipating his return, Zarathustra speaks compassionately of his friends, warning that they too may shrink from the new storms he brings. While regretting that he cannot win them back with "shepherd's flutes" (were the winning speeches of part I "shepherd's flutes"?), he exults in his new wild wisdom, pictured as a woman who has just given birth and is searching for a bed for her young. Zarathustra again abandons his solitude out of love for mankind, this time to return to his disciples to impart the new offspring of his wild wisdom.

WILD WISDOM'S YOUNG (CHAPTERS 2–7)

Unlike the opening speeches of part I, the opening speeches of part II are not aimed at attracting disciples; they do not have to begin mildly in order to make a novel teaching appealing to unprepared listeners. And, unlike the later speeches of part I, they do not have to provide instruction on the new goals and conventions. Addressed only to those already schooled in his teaching, they make that teaching even more harsh and demanding by refusing any compromise with rival views. They seek to win back from those who inadequately reflect his preliminary teaching only those who can bear a complete break with teachings they still revere. In emphasizing Zarathustra's own experience, these speeches are much more personal than those of part I, revealing more of the experience that he presumes to be unique to himself but that he needs to share with others if his private vision of the superman is to be realized. The speech which follows these new requirements for discipleship marks the transition by being addressed only to the famous wise men and not to the disciples (II. 8).

The speeches that reveal wild wisdom's young to lapsed disciples address what are presumably the reasons for their lapse. They excoriate in uncompromising fashion a series of teachings on God, compassion, redemption, virtue, the people, and the ideal of equality, all of which must be portrayed as general teachings on God and man in order to maintain the literary fiction of a timeless time. Nevertheless, the specific historic forms of these teachings come to light as Christian forms—Christian belief (II. 2), Christian compassion (II. 3), Christian asceticism (II. 4), a Christian moral world order (II. 5), the modern consequences of Christian teachings on man and society (II. 6), and the modern teaching on equality rooted in Christianity (II. 7). These speeches thus remedy a lack in the teaching of part I to which Zarathustra himself had called attention: by giving an account of the rise of the individual whose appearance is the death of peoples (I. 11, 15), they show how modernity has developed out of Christianity. The speeches end by pointing back to the way of the Greeks (II. 7) as superior to the way taken by Christianity.

The speeches thus reveal what Zarathustra makes of the image that he saw in the mirror. His anxiety for his teaching arises not because it looks demonic to others—of course it looks demonic to others—but because, as reflected by his disciples, it looks demonic to him. Because Zarathustra's devil is the spirit of gravity, the disciples' denial of him must have been their inattentive harmonizing of his teachings with contemporary teachings, all of which stem from "the master of the world," the spirit of gravity. The disciples have after all remained loyal to their own things, to modernity and its pervasive appeal. Though they thought themselves loyal to Zarathustra, they denied him by flirting with his devil. They have not understood the basis of his teaching if they have supposed that there could be such a thing as a Nietzschean Christianity or a Nietzschean socialism. Consequently, Zarathustra now assaults contemporary teachings with a view to separating them entirely from his own and rendering untenable any irenic interpretation by syncretist disciples, trimmers who say "Peace, Peace, where there is no peace." In the face of his disciples' pliant both/and, Zarathustra sharpens his either/or in an attack that conforms to an image used in the final speech (II. 7): he rakes at the webs of attractive teachings in order to draw forth the ugly spider that spun them. In developing this contrast between hidden motives and alluring surfaces, Zarathustra implies throughout, but states only at the very end, a singular challenge to his disciples: they are to raise the question of his own motives. Does his soul too churn with the revenge he detects in his enemies? Is he too a teacher of revenge? The demands of discipleship become more stringent as the singular and exclusive content of the novel teaching becomes more emphatic and as the disciples' stance towards it comes to hinge on a matter they have to decide for themselves.

Zarathustra reappears to his disciples as suddenly as he had first appeared to the people. In his first speech to them, he makes no reference whatever to the reasons for his return, or to his disciples' denial of him and the consequent danger to his teaching.[8] Still, his disciples can be presumed to have remembered that he promised to return only after they had denied him, and that he would then seek them with different eyes and love them with a different love (I. 22, the motto to part II). The first speech bringing wild wisdom's young opens with an image of Zarathustra as a north wind causing ripe figs to fall and break open; his ripe teachings, like figs, fall before his disciples, who are invited to drink their juice and eat their flesh. Although it is an afternoon in the fall, full of the promise of harvest, and they stand amidst a natural abundance, they are to gaze into a distant future, to the still more abundant time of the superman. The opening image of an easy and bountiful harvest contrasts with the harsh image of a hammer on stone with which the first speech closes. The opening image of ripeness also contrasts with what Zarathustra says in the closing speech of part II; there, speaking for the last time to his disciples, he reports that a private voice has said to him, "Your fruit are ripe but you are not ripe for your fruit" (II. 22).

Zarathustra begins his first speech by reminding his already schooled listeners that the goal of his teaching is the superman, and that this goal is incompatible with any teaching of God or gods.[9] Judging by this first speech, God or gods are the special temptation to which his disciples had fallen prey. While gods thwart the creative will, the superman spurs it;

while gods cannot be thought by the will to truth, the superman is its logical outcome. But Zarathustra interrupts his argument for a revelation in the form of a hypothetical syllogism. After preparing his disciples with the noteworthy claim that he reveals his heart completely, he says: "*If* there were gods how could I bear not to be a god! *Therefore* there are no gods. Though I drew this conclusion, it now draws me." This complete revelation of Zarathustra's heart points to its ruling love of victory. It is not mere antitheological ire that moves him in his attack on the gods, but a rivalry that would be unbearable if such rivals existed. The death of God is no tragedy for Zarathustra. His envy wills gods dead. His disciples have been taught to distinguish among forms of envy, to purify themselves of its poison, and to exploit its potency. Is it a poisonous envy that moves Zarathustra to envy what has been attributed to uncreatable, unthinkable gods? Having once drawn the conclusion that no gods exist, a victory-loving man governed by the will to truth is drawn by the conclusion that man is the highest being and the creative thinker the highest man. For such a one, the highest thinkable victory must be seen as possible, the whole world must be seen as potentially at his disposal. Like Alcibiades, he prefers to die rather than live with great achievements while being denied the possibility of still greater achievements; having conquered all of Greece, such a one prefers to die rather than live on under the condition that he not be permitted the attempt to conquer Persia.[10]

The rest of Zarathustra's speech describes the effect of the idea of God or permanence on the human will.[11] At the culmination of a series of aphorisms on the permanent and the transitory, he makes a memorable change in the memorable conclusion of the most famous poetic work in the German language, Goethe's *Faust*. (A disciple who is present remembers the memorable change later [II. 17].) After correcting the most revered poet on the issue of the permanent and the transitory, Zarathustra adds: "And poets lie too much."[12] The lies of creative poets have given the people their gods, as Epicurus also taught. These lies have secured the people's transitory world within ramparts of permanence guarded by their gods. The primary fears of men have been allayed by ministering or lying poets, who allege that the walls of man's world will not crumble because the gods who created it hold it in being, and that the world loved by men is lovable in itself because it is loved by the gods.[13] Zarathustra teaches that the permanence guaranteed by the gods imperils, rather than preserves, the lovable because the lovable does not yet exist. The creativity of poets who attribute the world to the creativity of gods is to be replaced by the creativity of men who know themselves to be creating a human world. Whereas ministering poets have celebrated the gods and a deathless permanence as the antidote to the primary fear, the fear of death, Zarathustra calls for poetry to become a praise and justification of the passing or the mortal. Such poetry would celebrate and reflect the creative life that is itself a series of deaths or transformations. In part I, Zarathustra's teaching on

death had described only the useful death of those who live for the superman (I. 21). Now his teaching becomes more general in that it gives instruction not only on how to die, but also on how to celebrate that whose
nature it is to die. Zarathustra does not simply stand beyond the primary
terror like an Epicurean philosopher, observing its effects on an impassioned mankind always prey to it. An earlier Greek response to that terror
seems to guide him, the response described at length in Nietzsche's praise
of the Greek achievement of beauty in the face of a folk wisdom that peered
steadily into the abyss (*BT* 3, 4, 7, 9). Creation of beauty in the celebration
of mortal things seems to be the poet Zarathustra's response to the primary fear.

Having refuted gods for the sake of a human creator yet to come, Zarathustra goes on to describe what this creator must be like. According to
this first speech to those who are already disciples, the creator must grow
through transformations of many kinds, not just the three transformations
outlined in the first of the speeches that made them disciples (I. 1). Speaking
of his own transformations, he says that he has suffered a hundred births
and has often taken leave of beloved things. To those beloved ones from
whom he had many years earlier taken leave, Zarathustra gives assurance
that leave-takings are simply necessary, thereby granting them absolution
for having taken leave of him. He speaks of himself as fated to heart-breaking
leave-takings but then corrects himself in the interests of honesty. He is
not fated external to his will for his creative will creates his fate. He does
not suffer his transformations but generates them himself. With respect
to will and fate, he teaches that his will fates; with respect to will and
freedom, he teaches that "willing liberates." He does not add what he will
later be forced to add, that the liberating will is itself imprisoned; the discovery of that truth (II. 19, 20) leads him to his own most liberating act of
will. Having spoken of will and fate, he speaks of will and knowledge: in
knowledge he experiences his will's delight in begetting and becoming.
Knowledge is not the dispassionate apprehension of some permanent
knowable accomplished by curbing the desires. Nor does it even dream
of a complete explicitness of things but loves the whole as an enigma that
invites willful inquiry.

Zarathustra's speech ends with a vivid and illuminating image of what
he intends for mankind. Distant now from the opening image of a north
wind and soft fruit, he sees himself as a hammer and mankind as stone.
Within that "hardest and ugliest stone" he has caught a glimpse of a shadow
imprisoned and his hammer rings against the stone in an attempt to release
the shadow. Fragments shatter from the stone, but they mean nothing to
the one moved by the shadow, that stillest and lightest of things that once
came to him. Turned away from gods by his creating will, Zarathustra
turns to a still hard and ugly mankind as the sculptor who will make of
it a beautiful creation that will justify its existence. Here too he reveals his
heart to his disciples. Have they thought his teaching too hard? His storming

wild wisdom, leaving all reserve behind, insists on the greatest hardness as necessary for mankind's redemption. The images of the coming of the superman take on a fiercer hue. Rainbow, bridge, and rope are replaced by a hammer ringing on unyielding stone. What Zarathustra closed his hand on in part I was apparently this hard teaching on the creative will. His restraint had held back from new disciples the full implications of the gift he had given them.

"On the Pitying" (II. 3) exhibits the hardness of heart or the unpitying stance toward mankind that Zarathustra called for at the end of the previous speech. It speaks of the second most important limitation on the creative will; having broken the limits set by ideas of God and permanence, the will must break the limits set by an inappropriate love of mankind as it is. Without saying so explicitly, Zarathustra here addresses the Christian way of being with others as inimical to the will that wills beyond mankind to the superman. The words mimic the Sermon on the Mount just as the contents mock it. Zarathustra thus begins to specify the implications of "the greatest recent event"—that the old god is dead. The extent of those implications remained unknown as long as the old morality seemed capable of surviving the death of the old god, but the time is coming when "the whole of our European morality," which is propped up by that old faith and grown into it, will be known to be untenable without it. In the following speeches Zarathustra prepares his friends for the death of the moral principles founded on the now dead god, just as Nietzsche prepares his readers for those events in the books after *Zarathustra* (GS 343).[14]

Zarathustra has heard a criticism of himself, one to which his disciples may well have been attentive: he has been assailed for his pride, for thinking himself above mankind. He corrects the criticism by making it stronger, confirming that pride is necessary and speaking of "the knower" as rightfully proud. "Knowers" was the flattering appellation used in the previous speech for his disciples, but they cannot be knowers in the full sense, because he has to tell them what knowers know. In giving his account of the knower or the enlightened man, Zarathustra secures the perspective from which mankind is to be measured. Whereas the low must be understood from the perspective of the high, the high must understand itself as the result of a long transformation and sublimation of the low. From the perspective of the knower, both man and the history of man come to light in a new way, for the knower sees man as "the red-cheeked animal" and the history of man as "shame shame shame." But this does not make mankind simply shameful, for man's red cheeks bespeak his pride, his awareness of the shameful. Being ashamed at the shameful transfigures shame. Although it is true that "with regard to origins, everything human deserves ironic reflection" (*HH* I. 252), that reflection does not reduce man to the low, for man transcends his origins in transfiguring acts worthy of pride, the proudest now aiming at the transfiguration of man into superman. That the high is built on the shameful is not shameful. But more than knowledge is needed, and Zarathustra now moves from the knowing man to the noble man. The noble man is presumed to be a knower, though the knower is not presumed to be noble. The noble knower makes two resolves that bespeak his nobility. First, he resolves not to cause shame or call attention to the shameful. Still, the very existence of the noble man causes shame or causes the shameful to be aware of itself (I. 8). Second, he resolves to feel shame at suffering, not to feel pity, and to harden his heart in the manner described in the rest of the speech.

That this speech is necessary implies that Zarathustra's enemies have won his disciples to the way of compassion, having diminished him in their eyes as proud and disdainful. Disciples, seeing him now through the eyes of virtuous enemies, who teach that compassion is the highest virtue, will surely hear in this speech a "teacher of evil," for Zarathustra speaks well even of devils, encouraging the possessed to rear them up into something magnificent. Zarathustra himself was addressed by a devil once, perhaps the devil that he is possessed of; but has he reared it into something magnificent? His compassionate friends will be forced to wonder, because the devil's words condemn compassion. According to the devil's report, mankind too could die of pity for mankind if it does not harden its heart and create beyond mankind. What Zarathustra reared from the devil's revelation is a new second commandment, which becomes the first now that God has died, and which has nothing to do with compassion: "I sacrifice myself to my love, and my neighbor as myself."[15]

"On the Priests" (II. 4) is separated from the two previous speeches by the passage of time; it opens with the first use of the word *disciple* in part II, as if his disciples have become loyal again during the time that has elapsed. This is the only speech in the series that contains a dramatic event as its setting, and both the event and Zarathustra's statement about it are remarkable. The Zarathustra who loves enemies because they justify his warfare against them avoids a confrontation with the priests whom he names his enemies. Are they unworthy enemies, enemies for whom he has contempt (I. 10)? No, for his blood is related to theirs, and his speech behind their backs shows just how close that blood relationship is.[16] Perhaps he avoids a confrontation because his warfare with Christianity, being a matter of good manners, is very far from holding individuals responsible for the fateful calamity of millennia (*EH*, "Wise," 7). The priests are merely victims. Still, these victims have acquired a sting. Does he avoid a confrontation because he is a coward afraid of their sting? Later, at the end of this series of speeches, he will provoke the sting of other teachers (II. 7) and will make explicit what is implicit here: his friends will have to judge for themselves whether he differs from his kin in the ways that he claims.

Though his private speech resonates with sympathy for his priestly kin and the heroic self-sacrifice through which they became victims of their passions and their redeemer, Zarathustra never permits himself to express directly the "profound gratitude" so characteristic of Nietzsche's accounts of what the cruel priestly spirit has achieved in human history by transforming mankind out of animality and making it more subtle, more interesting, more profound. "This tyranny, this caprice, this rigorous and grandiose stupidity has *educated* the spirit" (*BGE* 188; see *HH* I, 40; *KGW* VIII 5 [58] = *WP* 54). "Let us not be ungrateful," Nietzsche says many times, because the qualities it has created, albeit "merely moral," prepare the way for what is higher, and eventually even for that "high spirituality" which makes mankind capable of aiming for the highest goal (*BGE* 209, Preface; see *GM* III. 12).

Zarathustra is related to the priests by blood; they are kin in the ascetic cruelty they practice on themselves. But they are unrelated in taste, a much better measure of truth. Zarathustra has been given his blood but has had to win his taste, and the cruelty through which he has won it has reversed the priestly cruelty toward the self. Blood, the worst witness to the truth, fully persuaded the priests, and their passionate hearts came to control their minds, turning their minds cold and calculating in the service of their hearts.[17] Zarathustra's cruelty toward himself has moved in a different direction: his free mind has tethered his passionate heart, his passions have been bound over in service to the goals set by his free mind. Whatever sacrifices his thought may call for, it is not the sacrifice of the intellect to some passion of the heart (*BGE* 87, 23). The cruel priests have been too easy on themselves in not letting their minds judge their hearts. Worse still, they have let their hearts be redeemed by a redeemer from another world; they have felt their hearts so reprobate and unforgivable that they had to invent a comfort that would deliver them from themselves and from the earth. Their asceticism has proved total: they long to be rid of everything they are. The newly won taste that longs to be loyal to the earth and the body is capable of hard judgment: "I name Christianity the *one* great curse, the *one* great innermost corruption, the *one* great instinct of revenge, for which no means is poisonous enough, stealthy, subterranean, or *small* enough—I name it the *one* immortal blemish on humanity" (*A* 62). But here, in the reeducation of those who are already his friends, and who are to judge for themselves, Zarathustra is less categorical in his condemnation, ending with a tribute to the priests' strength. Their faith or obstinacy made them successful in transforming their tribal and ancestral god into a universal and sovereign God; they have remained heroically loyal to him, despite the fact that he has "contradicted and harmed them," as he has contradicted and harmed human and earthly things in general. Their teaching of equality, the equality of all as slaves before a sovereign Master, has been the path by which the herd has passed into its modern and secular future, as the next speeches show.

Having spoken of his own pride, Zarathustra now speaks to his disciples' pride ("On the Virtuous," II. 5) by treating them in a demeaning manner as disappointed and fractious children in need of toys. In de-

scribing their flawed behavior, this speech appears to be a remonstrance
directed at wayward disciples by the returned master. It is a speech on
virtue addressed solely to "the virtuous" who are the disciples, for, although
he describes twelve ways in which virtues have come to be held by others,
he says that he has no interest in teaching those others the error of their
ways. Because the disciples have been disloyal, Zarathustra has to scold
them; while he can learn through a quiet inward address, they must be
shouted at. By flaunting the differences between himself and them, he
seems to desire to ignite their envy with their pride. In teaching the gift-
giving virtue, Zarathustra had taught that there is no reward for virtue,
and even that virtue is not its own reward; but his disciples had felt betrayed
by that teaching, because they had still expected to be rewarded. The old
fiction of the necessary conjunction of virtue and happiness has, in a novel
form, again been "lied into the very ground of things," or understood to
be a necessary postulate of the moral life, and the disciples seem to have
fallen for some such Kantian metaphysics of morals, though Zarathustra
baits them as being too refined for a teaching that makes revenge, punishment, reward, and retribution characteristics of things themselves. He
ends by treating them like naughty children, for linking his teaching with
this pale northern relic of the old "true world" fable (*TI*, "Fable"); but if he
is a wave that has swept away their toys, they are not to cry, for he will
bring them new and better ones. They are to persist in their virtue, not
because of a promise of happiness, but because of the sting of shame and
because of a distant future that they will never themselves enjoy.

Zarathustra's assault on the post-Christian temptations faced by his
disciples continues with speeches on the practice (II. 6) and theory (II. 7)
of equality. In "On the Rabble" (II. 6) he describes what can ruin the sweetness of life for him. In the presence of his compassionate friends, what he
had earlier called the "herd," and still earlier the "people," he now calls
the "rabble." He says he curbs his tongue among the people, but among
friends he can confess that for him too life has a feature that almost refutes
it: the apparent necessity of the rabble. That necessity was so abhorrent
to him that he almost condemned life itself because of it. But his confession
leads to a claim of redemption: he saved himself from his crippling thought
by his dream of a future where the rabble no longer existed. For life to be
uncompromisingly sweet, it will have to be sweetened by the elimination
of what threatens to refute it. Here in particular his friends could ask, as
his enemies have, whether he is moved by a poisonous passion, for his
confession shows that he shares that most destructive modern passion,
the dream of a perfect future to be built through the annihilation of what
the dreamer loathes. But when he discovers what genuine redemption
requires, it is precisely this abhorrence that he will have to swallow, for
no such future will redeem him and mankind, but only the ideal of eternal
return—and that requires of him that he will what almost refutes life for

him. Eternal return is a remedy for even his own passion to alter the unalterable.

Zarathustra then turns to the theory of justice advocated by the "rabble," the modern teaching of justice as equality ("On the Tarantulas," II. 7). According to this speech, Zarathustra's teaching on justice had, more than any other, caused confusion among his disciples, for they thought they heard in it the modern ideal of equality. This final speech in the reeducation of his disciples is one of the high points of part II; as the culmination of the storms of his wild wisdom aimed at identifying his enemies for his disciples, it makes most explicit the grounds of his spiritual warfare. The chapter begins and ends with parables involving a tarantula, a wolf spider of southern Europe that springs out of its cave to kill its victim with a poisonous bite. It opens with Zarathustra inviting such an attack and ends with him suffering it. The parable at the beginning depicts his method of exposé, a method that is more than simple unmasking. By raking at the webs of teachings spun by others, he invites a counterattack. He forces his enemies out of hiding and into the open so that they can be identified not by the attractive teachings they spin, but by the motives they have for spinning them. But his attack on them can be used on him: Is he exempt from what he detects in them?

Zarathustra and his enemies clash most directly over the primary good of modern societies, equality, the foundational good that in its self-evidence provides the center around which the virtues array themselves and from which they derive their reflected worth. The chapter depicts a battle between advocates of justice as equality and a single advocate of justice as inequality. The battle is waged first in a dialogue between enemies, conducted in front of the interested audience of disciples. After the dialogue, both voices of which are provided by one of the advocates, Zarathustra addresses his friends in order to expound its lessons, the justness of justice as inequality. Although it treats the theme of justice, the chapter speaks at greatest length about revenge, for in Zarathustra's view, revenge produces the ideal of justice as equality. Near the beginning of his speech he proclaims as his "highest hope," that *mankind be redeemed from revenge.*" His speech leaves the impression that overthrowing the teachers of equality would effect mankind's redemption from revenge, but when redemption is finally defined later, the revenge from which mankind needs to be redeemed appears as something far more comprehensive (II. 20).

Zarathustra shows how the arbiters of "current moral fashion" (D 174) speak to themselves, before allowing them to speak for themselves. What they say to themselves explains why they publicly advocate justice as equality. Their justice is a convention which becomes desirable for them after they have recognized the unfair portions meted out by nature. Having seen that nature is unfair, because it gives the gift of superiority to some and the punishment of a recognized inferiority to others, and, in particular, having seen nature's niggardliness to themselves, they seek to remedy nature's unequal gifts by inculcating a will to equality. Victims of a natural order of rank, these teachers of virtue plan the correction of nature. They secretly plot the overthrow of, first, "all whose equals we are not" and, second, "all who possess power," the overthrow of both the naturally and conventionally powerful. Zarathustra pounces on their secrets with the explanation that their preaching of equality is motivated by envy and the desire for power. Teaching the virtue of equality to the powerful enables the preachers of equality to vent their "repressed envy" and achieve their calculated ambition for power. Zarathustra thinks he sees in the "spiritualized malice" (*BGE* 219) of these modern teachers the envy and conceit of the fathers that breaks out as revenge in the sons; what was borne silently by the fathers becomes deed in the sons, who, for the sake of the fathers' honor, take reprisal for the wounds long inflicted on them.

At the end of the dialogue Zarathustra refers to "you preachers of equality" as "they," and addresses his audience of friends. His aim is not to reform the preachers of equality, but only to enlighten his friends about their now powerful teaching. The preachers of equality are said to have sublimated their deepest feelings into qualities that are praiseworthy; thus their revenge makes them seem inspired, their envy makes them refined and cold, and their jealousy has even led them into the path of the thinker. In this way they mimic the highest achievements of religion and philosophy, but they expose their mere mimicry by always going too far. In giving his friends these means of identifying the motives of others, Zarathustra again awakens suspicion about his own: what moves him in his teaching, he who is by turn inspired, refined, and cold, he who is a thinker and goes so far?

The way of revenge has come to hold that the highest state, the state of very blessedness, is to be judge. As judges, the teachers of equality are accorded final authority, their judgments taken as binding and carried out by functionaries. Guided by the highest court, the whole world will rage against privilege or superiority, punishing its every appearance. From this depiction of the teachers of equality turned judges, Zarathustra draws the conclusion that he wants his disciples to draw: mistrust all in whom the drive to punish is powerful, all who talk much of their own justice.

Now Zarathustra can turn to the problem that has necessitated his return, his having been confused with others and taken for what he is not. The specific confusion here is that his novel teaching has been taken to be akin to other modern, revolutionary teachings that also attack the established view.[18] Confusion has deepened because these modern teachers of equality speak well of life and in that respect too sound like Zarathustra. But the modern teachers of a revolutionary equality who speak well of life are said by Zarathustra to harbor a fundamental hatred of life and of their own lives. The justice of equality is a desire to do harm to enemies, and thereby to protest life for being good to some, but stingy to most. A fine historical irony exists in the tarantulas' vengeful act of harming the powerful, for the entrenched powers against whom they preach are themselves "preachers of death," representatives of Christianity grown powerful in a worldly way. In enviously attacking the entrenched powers with a view to themselves becoming judges who wield the greatest power, modern teachers of equality attack those who are kin to themselves, those who, through *their* teaching of revenge, have ascended to positions of power. The modern heirs of Christianity who teach a revolutionary kind of equality, not the equality of unequals before God but the radical equality of the last man, share the envy and revenge of their forebears but turn their envy and revenge against their own forebears grown powerful. If it were otherwise, Zarathustra says, the tarantulas themselves would say so, for they would have an excellent weapon; that they remain silent about the revenge that moves their powerful and entrenched Christian enemies, shows that they dare not accuse their enemies of what they recognize only too well in themselves. By refusing to remain silent on the secret motive of revenge in other revolutionary modern teachers who speak well of life, Zarathustra provides the dangerous criterion by which he himself is to be measured.

In order that his friends not confuse his teaching with others Zarathustra states his own standard of justice or what is due other human beings. When justice speaks to him, it says: "Men are not equal," and he adds on his own the emphatic determination that they not become equal. Equality is not a desirable goal. How could the teacher of the desirability of the superman be thought to have taught otherwise? The disciples' insistence on seeing these teachings as related shows how firmly the modern teaching holds them. Zarathustra speaks as clearly as possible about the differences. The motive of envy in the tarantulas makes them speak of a peaceable equality, the motive of love in himself makes him speak of war and inequality. The tarantulas allege that they are advocates of life, but Zarathustra accounts himself life's true advocate, for he sees life as just in assigning different portions. The natural order of rank is protested only by those who judge themselves to be harmed by it. Zarathustra addresses those who have been favored by nature and could be presumed to have no quarrel with her, or at least not the quarrel that moves the teachers of equality who desire the correction of nature or the "humanitarian emendation" of nature (BGE 22).[19] This account of life by an advocate of life expands the opening image of Zarathustra's first speech to the people, in which life continually strives to overcome itself. The wars he praises and welcomes are wars against a teaching of equality grown powerful, wars on behalf of self-overcoming life, whose next stage depends on willful man, in whom life's self-overcoming has become self-conscious. But the man on whom life now depends himself depends on life, on the natural and unasked-for gift that life has granted, the gift of strength and command, which his poisonous enemies envy and resent.

The teachers of equality make an additional claim that Zarathustra wants to refute, a rhetorical claim meant to establish their title to noble origins. He calls his listeners back to his opening parable by pointing again to the cave of the tarantula; there the ruins of an ancient temple rise. What is the true relation between the tarantula and the temple? Zarathustra has shown modern teachers of equality to be kin to the ancient Christian teachers they attack as alien; now he shows that they are alien to the ancient Greek teachers they claim as kin. Here at the very end of the speeches to his disciples that have shown the historic role of Christianity in the formation of the modern world, Zarathustra turns back to the Greeks, a turn made problematic by the claim of kinship with the Greeks already made by the modern teachers of equality. Refuting that claim recovers the Greeks from their modern interpreters. Calling on his disciples to look with enlightened eyes on ancient things only traces of which remain, Zarathustra causes them to see that the one who built the ancient temple was like the wisest in knowing "the secret of all life," for even the beautiful exhibits struggle and inequality and war for power. A godlike striving to be first is visible in the stones of the ancient temple. Its builder knows what the wisest know because he was taught by Homer, by that one of the wisest whose songs of excelling built the ancient culture of which the temple is a part.[20] The legitimate kin of that noble teaching exhibits his legitimacy by exhorting his friends to strive against one another and against him, to be like gods driven by the passion to be first, worthy of turning friends into enemies in that passion. But after this exhortation, an enemy of a different sort reappears. Zarathustra's attack on teachings of equality has succeeded, for the tarantula has sprung from its hole and bitten him on the finger. His enemy has responded to his attack with a counterattack. Behind its bite is the thought that there must be punishment and justice; elevating itself to the final court of judgment, the tarantula means to poison Zarathustra with its own poison; its justice is revenge.[21] The sought-for enmity of the tarantula is one that is useful to Zarathustra, for it can reveal to those who watch the combat, the difference between the combatants.

In the previous chapter on justice (I. 19) he also suffered a poisonous bite, but the bite of a mere adder could not do the monster Zarathustra its intended harm. There, in response to his disciples' confusion about the meaning of the bite, he had explained his teaching on the justice of harming enemies and had seemed to be above mere poison. In the present chapter on justice, however, the disciples are not given any assistance in interpreting the harming bite of an alleged justice. Has Zarathustra been harmed?—harmed into revenge? Zarathustra makes the problem of interpretation the responsibility of his disciples by putting the bite not only at the end of his speech, but at the end of the whole series of speeches intended to mark him off from the teachers of revenge with whom he has been confused. It would seem that a new teacher elicits the greatest confusion and the greatest enmity with his teaching on justice, for how can a novel teaching on justice appear just?

Has Zarathustra been poisoned by the bite of the tarantula? His speech
has interpreted justice by peering into the souls of two teachers of justice
in order to discern what really moves them in their teachings. In biting
Zarathustra, the tarantula wants his soul to whirl with revenge; it engages
in Zarathustra's own strategy in order to show that his motive for attack
is itself revenge. In contrasting the parable of the ancient temple with that
of the tarantula, has Zarathustra contrasted things that truly differ? Is there
a godlike striving that is not poisoned by revenge? And even if there is, is
it possible that the teacher of the virtue of envy possesses it, the teacher
who desires to make enemies of the powerful by openly arousing suspicions
of depravity against them? The challenge to Zarathustra's friends is made
clear by the Homeric note on which the chapter ends, a note that likens
him to one of the greatest of the Greeks, he whose successful odyssey was
made possible by that in which he was greatest, wisdom. In order that the
strategy of the tarantula not succeed and his soul not whirl with revenge,
Zarathustra asks his friends to bind him to the column of the ancient
temple. In his precautions against the onset of revenge, Zarathustra shows
himself to be akin to Odysseus, who asked his friends to tie him to the
mast so that he could hear the Sirens' song without yielding to its charms.
Zarathustra wishes to be tied to the ancient column, so that he can hear
the song of sweet revenge without being driven mad by it.[22] Having taken
these precautions, he ends his speech by asserting his innocence of revenge.
A wind at the end of the previous chapter, he declares himself at the end
of this one not to be a wind that whirls, a cyclone. Although he is a dancer,
he does not dance the tarantella, the southern Italian dance named after
the tarantula, which, while thought to be the antidote to its bite, exhibits
precisely the same symptoms of whirling alleged to be caused by the bite
itself. In binding him to the ancient column, his friends bind one who has
just told them emphatically to mistrust all whose desire to punish is powerful and who talk much of their justice. Having just talked much of his
justice and exhibited his powerful desire to punish by the precautions
taken against it, he shows that they must apply these warnings even to
him. They are to mistrust him, to strive against him in the suspicion that
he too is a teacher of revenge. Rather than aid his disciples in interpreting
his justice, he presents them with a challenge aimed to test their mettle
by forcing them to test him. He invites them to measure his teaching by
the standard of revenge. Having dared to accuse his enemies of a poisonous
motive visible only to him, he invites his friends to peer deeply into his
own assaulting soul, suspicious that it too harbors the revenge that he has
discerned in others.

Accepting, in effect, Zarathustra's challenge, Martin Heidegger agrees
that overcoming revenge is the essential task, but he judges Nietzsche not
to have succeeded.[23] The question of what moves Zarathustra, the question
of the place of revenge in his teachings, cannot be answered fully until
the end of his course; at this point it appears to be necessary that he be

bound to what is admirable in ancient Greece, so as not to be moved by revenge. Nevertheless, caution can already be raised about Heidegger's interpretation, which places Nietzsche among the teachers of revenge by placing him among the modern teachers as their fulfillment. Just this chapter has complained about the mistaken judgment that detects a continuity between Zarathustra's teaching and modern teachings in general; just this chapter has pointed to the difference between them, that whereas modern teachings have a powerful quarrel against nature and seek to alter her cruel inequality, Zarathustra's teaching sides with nature in praising what she grants. Heidegger argues that Nietzsche is a teacher of the conquest of nature, the philosopher of our technological time; but Nietzsche's Zarathustra presents a teaching on loyalty to the earth, on man and woman, on mortality and on an order of rank that seems opposed to such conquest. These teachings plus that final teaching still to come, eternal return, provide the grounds on which Zarathustra's friends can judge him on the question of revenge.

In likening Zarathustra to Odysseus, the man of many guiles, wisest of Homeric Greeks, the end of "On the Tarantulas" brings to an end the whole series of speeches addressed to his friends with the purpose of distinguishing his teaching from other modern teachings and it does so by anticipating a voyage, Zarathustra's own private odyssey in pursuit of wisdom, an odyssey that takes him back to the Greeks and to an understanding of their wisdom. The words *wisdom* and *wisest* have not been used in the discussion of Christianity and modernity (II. 2–7), except at the very end of "On the Tarantulas" where the Greeks are introduced. After that introduction, wisdom is made the theme of the coming chapters (II. 8–12). At the end of his odyssey, Zarathustra will address "you who are wisest" with the secret that he has discovered about all wisdom, one that will demonstrate that "Alas, my friends, we must overcome even the Greeks!"—even the ancient temple to which Zarathustra himself has appealed (GS 340).[24]

LIFE'S WISDOM (CHAPTERS 8–12)

"On the Famous Wise Men" (II. 8) begins a series of five chapters dealing with wisdom. They record a most remarkable transformation in both Zarathustra and his wisdom. Disciples, the essential audience for the instruction so far given in part II, are present only incidentally, in the middle chapter. The select audiences for the opening and closing speeches (II. 8, 12) are men of a different order, wise men whose wisdom he unriddles. Here, at last, begins what Thomas Pangle calls Zarathustra's "warfare against peers";[25] here he finds enemies he need not despise, worthy enemies in whom he can take pride (I. 10). Two separate acts of unriddling occur in these chapters, the first addressed to the famous wise, the second to the simply wisest. The secret motive of the wisest is different from that of the famous wise, and to understand that motive, Zarathustra has to be taught a fundamental, but unwelcome, lesson by Life herself. Between the two chapters that unriddle the wise are three songs, the first in the book. It is in these songs that he comes to recognize that he has something more to learn before he can unriddle the wisdom of those who are simply wisest. What he learns marks an epoch in his life; it is not just one of a hundred transformations.

In the first chapter on wisdom he addresses only "you famous wise men" and shows that he knows their wisdom better than they do because he possesses a wisdom closed to them. The speech opens with a contrast between the famous wise and the "free spirit" that is maintained and developed throughout the whole speech. The famous wise whom it addresses are not all those who are famous for their wisdom but only those currently honored as wise by the people whom they champion. This chapter thus advances the theme of the previous two chapters, on the people and their justice, by providing an exposé of the celebrated modern philosophers who have successfully taught the people how to achieve power in the modern age. It claims that the famous wise belong to the people and possess their spirit, for their "will to truth" is a will to prove the people right in what they revere.[26] These partisans of the people possess a spirit that has shrewdly calculated its own advantage and attached itself as loyal servant to the master who could best serve its ambitions. This master turned out to be the mass of servants, the people itself; the famous wise serve the servants. Through the calculating advocacy of their loyal wise, the many have risen to power. Responsibility for the successful modern revolution lies not with the multitude it benefits, but with the few teachers who set it in motion, the philosophers, the aristocrats of thought who "broke rank" to lead the plebs, thereby becoming the secret spiritual rulers of the modern age.[27] These famous wise teachers of modernity seem not to be moved by revenge (see II. 7) but by a love of glory; by appointing themselves advisors to the budding tyrant, the people, they have achieved their goal of immortal fame. But Zarathustra seeks to shame them by showing that Hobbes and Hegel are wrong, that there is a wisdom free of the need for glory or recognition. Although the "free spirits" well know, with Hesiod, that "men are exalted in the speech of others or remain unknown,"[28] they have freed themselves from a need for exaltation, while submitting themselves to a need for victory that may well banish them to the solitary desert.

The philosophers responsible for the revolutionary rise of the people have not been believers in the people's sense, and the people have known it. Still, the people have tolerated this form of unbelief because what these famous wise men did believe, or at least teach, served the people's interests by making them powerful. The honored wise differ from the hated wise, the "wolves" on whom the people set their dogs. The people hate the unbelief of such "free spirits" because it is not curbed by the desire to be honored by the people and therefore does not cater to them; such spirits are willing to go into the desert in search of the truth that they honor more than fame. Although the famous wise have wrapped themselves in the lion's skin, that skin covers the spirit of an ass harnessed to the people's wagon. Not they, but the free spirits, possess the lion's spirit. Because the famous wise have remained in the cities to serve the people, their spirit lacks refinement, being ignorant of what can only be learned by those who go into the desert to take upon themselves what is hardest. Zarathustra thus gives the famous wise a lesson in "spirit," for neither they nor the people know that form of spiritedness which is the love of victory. Though the famous wise teach the meaning of spirit, they themselves know no higher spiritedness than the love of honor, and they make the need for recognition the engine of history. The spiritedness that moves Zarathustra is different, for the solitary spirit that loves victory is free not to take its bearings from the other, but from itself. Its freedom is cruelty practiced on itself. "Spirit is the life that cuts into life." From the perspective of the famous wise or the people themselves, such a solitary pursuit unchecked by the other can result only in madness. Does it not begin in madness? For is it not mad to desire victory that no one else can recognize or certify?

In addressing the famous wise, Zarathustra does not seek to reform them; he treats the gifts of spirit as unteachable, as the gift or curse laid on certain natures to practice cruelty on themselves that may well blind them or cripple them but that they cannot gainsay. At the end of his speech, he contrasts the famous wise who simply stand there with the wise who are driven by the "strong wind or will" and anticipates that he himself will be driven onward. It is the third speech in a row that ends with an image of the wind.[29] In the three songs that follow, the wind of Zarathustra's will blows the sail of his wisdom over the sea of his spirit. In this metaphoric odyssey into himself, Zarathustra's will discovers the fundamental wisdom. Then he will be able to address the simply wisest as the one who has understood their wisdom.[30]

Abruptly and unannounced, Zarathustra sings for the first time in the book ("The Night Song," II. 9). The song is a lament on being the singular and solitary spirit described in the last part of the previous chapter, the freest of spirits bound by its own necessity to practice on itself the cruelty of the most driven knower.[31] Written in Rome, the city of fountains, the Night Song opens by likening Zarathustra's soul to a fountain which speaks more loudly at night, when everything else is still. Alone at night, he sings his lament at being the gift-giver, at being what he had from the beginning understood to be his single and novel merit. After hearing the many ways in which Zarathustra speaks to others, the reader is now privileged to hear how he speaks to himself,[32] and will, from this point on, be led ever more deeply into his solitude.

He sings of the dark night of the gift-giving soul, of its craving for what it thinks impossible for it, respite from giving through the experience of receiving. The "poverty" of such a soul is that it knows no repose from the extravagance of its own giving or creating. But it experiences more than poverty; the teacher who has taught others to distinguish between a poisonous envy that stings one into acts of revenge and a useful envy that spurs one to outdo the envied, here, for the only time in the book, confesses to an envy that leads him to contemplate revenge on the envied, on those who can be what he cannot be, receivers. While his friends follow his invitation to probe for revenge in his teaching, his own probing discloses a desire for revenge that is no mere residue of the tarantula's bite but is rooted in his very being as gift-giver. Desiring to vent itself on his friends, it seems to be an instance of that most powerful form of revenge, complete insight into which affords an understanding of all previous teachings (II. 20). Still, the envy that here moves him to desire revenge may yet be useful if transformed into emulation of those blessed to receive.

The imagery of the song reproduces the images of the sun and of shining, but from a perspective different from their earlier occurrences, where they were images of Zarathustra's joy at gift-giving. The imagery of the Night Song signals what will prove to be a great shift in Zarathustra's imagery of wisdom, culminating in the triumph of night over day, of sky over sun. The night wisdom will supersede the day wisdom celebrated until now, though without replacing it.

The longing to receive that moves him to desire even revenge is not simply the ever-present dark side of his virtue. Rather, the next songs show it to be the anticipation of a transformation from pure gift-giver to receiver of an unprecedented gift. The Night Song is remembered later by Zarathustra's mothering solitude as the central of three occasions on which he was forsaken, the only one that does not directly involve being forsaken by others (III. 9).[33] There has been no hint in the actions of this gift-giver of any reason for feeling forsaken. His sense of forsakenness does not concern disciples and their loyalty or disloyalty; it would exist even if all the world had accepted his teaching and he had become the most famous of all wise men. The next song shows that the crisis of the Night Song has nothing to do with the dispensing or sharing of his wisdom. As Nietzsche said in the commentary on this song of suffering in *Ecce Homo*, the song needs an answer. The answer which comes in the Dancing Song is essential but incomplete, for it is not, by itself, what Nietzsche said would be needed as an answer: "Ariadne." How Ariadne can be the answer is a mystery that will be solved only later in Zarathustra's course. But it is clear that the longed-for gift is not something that friends can give. As the lament of the passionate wanderer in search of the truth, the Night Song anticipates wisdom's repose—but repose in a way appropriate to Zarathustra—the discovery of truth through being shone upon with life's wisdom of will to power. And as the lament of one endangered by the desire for revenge, it anticipates the overcoming of revenge in the new teaching of eternal return. When it receives its answer, lament is transformed into thanksgiving. In language that is not Zarathustra's, the Night Song can thus be said to anticipate the end of nihilism through the teachings of will to power and eternal return.[34]

"The Dancing Song" (II. 10) is the central and decisive song. Before an audience of dancers and disciples, conflict breaks out where there was thought to be harmony, for Zarathustra's love of life defies his love of wisdom and leaves him despondent. At the beginning Zarathustra is walking with his disciples in a forest. It is evening, and while seeking a fountain, they come across a meadow in which young girls are dancing with one another. As soon as the girls recognize Zarathustra, they stop dancing, as if they see in him neither a dancer nor a fit audience for their dancing. He corrects their mistaken impression with a friendly gesture and reassuring words; he is "no spoil sport" with an evil eye; he is "no enemy of young girls." In the bright meadow he must appear to the girls as "a forest and a night of dark trees," but while they are surely frightened of the dark, he promises that those who look into his darkness will find there bowers of roses. They will even find Cupid there, asleep by the fountain; and he commends himself to the girls as an advocate of their favorite god. Awakened from his daytime drowsiness by the chastisement that Zarathustra risks even in front of the young girls who love him, Cupid yearns to dance with the girls. Zarathustra sings the song for their dance in advocacy of Cupid, or Eros, offspring of Hermes and Aphrodite.

He calls his song a dancing and mocking song on the spirit of gravity. In his own eyes, the spirit of gravity is his "most supreme and powerful devil," while others say of him that "he is 'the master of the world.' " Both characterizations accord him high honor, but neither is specific enough to secure his full identity. However, inasmuch as the song mocks Zarathustra's wild wisdom, it suggests that the spirit of gravity is a form of wisdom, one that has mastered the world and still bedevils Zarathustra, even though he desires to defeat it. But to mock the spirit of gravity is not yet to defeat it; that deed needs further preparation and will crown part III.

The imagery of the first part of the song, a dialogue between Zarathustra and Life, is imagery of the hunt which is fishing, a mysterious and dark hunt in which distance separates the hunter from his unseen quarry. But who is the quarry of whom? Zarathustra and Life both put themselves in the role of the hunter. Zarathustra opens his mocking song with a confession to Life, but she mocks him for the gravity of his wisdom which has called her "unfathomable,"[35] and which caused him to grow dizzy when it recently looked into her depths—possibly that despairing look into the depths which is the Night Song. But, having fished him out of his despair with her golden fishing rod, Life denies that she is unfathomable, even if he, like "all fish," has taken her to be so, concluding that what he has not fathomed is unfathomable. Addressing the virtuous and grave Zarathustra, Life confesses to be a woman in every way and not virtuous. Her words accuse him of sharing with other suitors the manly virtue of imposing on Life their own idea of virtue; whereas others have called her "deep," "loyal," "eternal," "mysterious," he has imposed on her the virtue of being "unfathomable." In response to this mockery of his search and his conclusion, Zarathustra ends the dialogue by calling her "the incredible one" and saying that he never believes her when she speaks ill of herself.

But he is wrong not to believe her. For Life to suggest that she can be fathomed is not to speak ill of herself—as will be shown in the first chapter after the songs. Zarathustra's refusal to believe that Life can be fathomed means that he continues to bestow on her the virtue of his wild wisdom that makes life unfathomable. But in saying that she can be fathomed, Life suggests—in the image of the Night Song—that she can give him an unprecedented gift, for she is more than the various features that virtuous men have bestowed on her. What she suggests is itself a wisdom, a rival to his "wild Wisdom." She cunningly begins her suit for the lover Zarathustra with the suggestion that his lover Wisdom, Wisdom herself, is mistaken. While changeable and untamed, Life is fathomable in herself, and when Zarathustra finally accepts her invitation to fathom her, he discovers that she is will to power, a discovery that necessitates abandoning his own wild Wisdom and all wisdom hitherto. The gift that Life gives Zarathustra will show life to be something not only fathomable in itself but good in itself. But for now she remains "the incredible one," and Zarathustra's dancing and mocking song turns to his other love.

He speaks in secret[36] with his wild Wisdom. She is angry with him out of jealousy at his love for Life, and she berates him for his reason for praising Life: "You will, you want, you love, that is the only reason you *praise* Life." He says that he almost answered wickedly and told the angry woman the truth, the woman who is his wisdom. In withholding the truth from her, he shows himself to be wiser than his wild Wisdom. He knows that his reasons for praising Life—will, want, and love—are the best of reasons, though they are not Wisdom's reasons.

In the first two episodes of this mocking song on the spirit of gravity, Life mocks Zarathustra, whereas Zarathustra could have mocked his grave Wisdom but forbears. In private, he reflects on the lovers' triangle in which he is caught; to himself he can say what he cannot bring himself to say to his wild Wisdom, that his love for her is a case of mistaken identity. His passionate pursuit of her was undertaken as if wisdom were life itself; he even thought that she possessed the golden fishing rod that can fish him out of the abyss into which he sinks when he looks into the meaning of life. Although his confusion of wisdom and life, or his identification of life with wisdom, may be beginning to seem mistaken he does not blame himself, but rather wisdom's charm.

The final episode of the song begins with Life asking him about her rival: What is wisdom after all? Zarathustra is rash with Life where he was reticent with Wisdom and answers fervently and foolishly, confessing his love for Wisdom to her rival. But Life, unlike his wild Wisdom, is not angered by the truth; she chooses instead to flatter herself by purposely misunderstanding. Life is more forgiving than his Wisdom, but then she can afford to be, for she suspects what he confesses in private, that he loves only Life from the heart. Zarathustra's rash answer returns to the images of the unsuccessful hunt used in his first conversation with Life, and his words about Wisdom are very like, but still unlike, the words used by Life about herself. Most remarkably, while he does not believe Life when she speaks ill of herself, he finds Wisdom most seductive precisely when she speaks badly of herself. For Wisdom to speak badly of herself would be for her to speak a skepticism or even ignorance; Wisdom's attacks on wisdom make her forever elusive and forever seductive to "the old carps" like Zarathustra who yearn to catch her. Having fallen prey to her seductive skepticism, it is no wonder that he is mistaken about Life; for such a wisdom it belongs to the very nature of Life that it be unfathomable.

In speaking badly of herself, Wisdom implies the impossibility of possessing her, and Zarathustra's enflamed speech about her confesses that he has not possessed her. But when Life—from Zarathustra's mistaken perspective—speaks ill of herself, she speaks precisely of the possibility of possessing her. Life, who is not virtuous, who is beyond good and evil, offers herself to be possessed if Zarathustra will cease being like the virtuous men who impose their own virtue on her, having judged her to be no good. Virtuous Wisdom who cannot be possessed demands fidelity from those who love her nevertheless; chaste, she sinks to indignation when she suspects that her suitors seek a lover they can possess. Whereas Zarathustra's love of his wild Wisdom has necessarily been futile or fruitless, his love of Life, until now futile because of his mistaken wild Wisdom, will eventually be consummated.

While Zarathustra delivers his bootless praise of her rival, Life modestly closes her eyes. But finally she laughs and says, "But of whom are you speaking? Of me, surely?" She too knows the wicked truth he has withheld from his Wisdom, that his reasons for loving Life are the best reasons, reasons that preclude his continued love of his wild Wisdom. But she is not angry, and she coyly invites him to begin now to speak of his Wisdom, now that the way matters stand among the three of them has become clear to two of them. But he can no longer speak of his Wisdom, for Life has opened her eyes again. The song ends with Zarathustra unable to praise his Wisdom and seeming again to sink into the unfathomable.

But his speech to the wisest following the songs shows that his confusion is only temporary, for Life has communicated her secret wisdom to him. Her final words seem to supply the clue: she invites him to wonder if his knowledge of wisdom is not itself knowledge of life. In coyly taking his praise of Wisdom to be praise of herself, she invites him to think that the secret of the wisest is at the same time the secret of life, that life as a whole is revealed in the experience of the most spirited form of life, in which alone it becomes conscious of itself. Ever elusive wisdom thus provides the clue to hitherto unfathomable life, for if life resembles wisdom in the essential respect, wisdom's quest is, in a way, fulfilled when unfathomable life is fathomed as will to power. But then jealous wild Wisdom must be abandoned. Zarathustra is no longer a skeptic, though he is very far from having become a dogmatist, for the true teaching of will to power does not fully banish the enigma of things; it does not make all being thinkable.

In the Dancing Song, Life seems to favor Zarathustra in a way that she has not favored any of the virtuous men who have fished for her, although they too have thought themselves to be so favored, and they too have named her. Whether Zarathustra has been truly favored with the fathomable secret of life, he leaves to his friends to decide, after making clear how great a problem it is to discern the truth from the lie in these matters (II. 17).

The dance ends, the girls leave, and Zarathustra grows sad. The sun has long since set, and a chill moves out of the woods asking why Zarathustra is still alive. It is no wonder that such questions come to him uninvited after the setting of the sun of his beloved wisdom. That setting is like death itself, for his life has been his wisdom; he has thought the two identical.[37] The girls who danced to his song would ask such questions too if their love failed them, if Cupid died. After voicing the despairing questions that arise of their own accord, Zarathustra becomes aware of his disciples' presence and attempts to hide his despair from them. But his courtesy is betrayed by his confusion. While begging their forgiveness, he alleges that what spoke was only the customary gloom of evening. But he asks them also to forgive him that evening has come. He cannot evade responsibility for his sadness by blaming evening if evening itself is his responsibility. But in fact he is responsible for neither; he can no more hold back the questions than he can hold back the evening. Nevertheless, he needs to be forgiven once again by his disciples. This time it is not merely a private passion forbidden all whose overriding passion is the coming of the superman that must be forgiven, but an even more serious breach in what he has represented to them until now, if evening has come to his wild Wisdom.

In the Dancing Song, Zarathustra does not dance. Much later Nietzsche says that Zarathustra is a dancer (EH, "Books: Zarathustra," 6); but first he must learn to dance. In part I he is never said to dance, though once, in a speech that anticipates the imagery of the Dancing Song, he says that a god dances through him in order to kill his devil, the spirit of gravity (I. 7). But it is only in "The Other Dancing Song" (III. 15) that Zarathustra himself dances, and then there are no onlookers and no other dancers, for he dances alone with Life. There he again begins by looking into Life's eyes but he ends in praise, not in a dizzy sinking into the unfathomable. That dance with Life is made possible only by transformations stemming from Life's offer to be fathomed.

Although Zarathustra has already given counsel on how women want their men and has even received from the little old woman the praise that, though inexperienced with women, he is right about them, his own ways with women are not displayed until the Dancing Song. He knows well how to please young girls with attractive words and song but he is less successful with the women Wisdom and Life. The woman Wisdom wants her warriors "brave, unconcerned, mocking, violent" (I. 7), but he is cautious with his shrewish, scolding wild Wisdom; he seems solicitous of her jealous fears, and refuses to mock her. But his strategy fails, for she rightly suspects that he is unfaithful. He is not drawn into a quarrel with her; he seeks neither to manage her nor to alter her, not even with the means suggested by the little old woman. Although he is now silent with his Wisdom, he praises and blames her openly to Life her rival. But what Life says of herself, he can only disbelieve, for he finds it demeaning to her, prejudiced as he is by her rival. When he speaks incautiously to Life, it is not with the manly "bravery" or "unconcern" of Wisdom's warrior, but rather, in the foolish confusion of a lover on whom it dawns that his beloved may be flawed or, worse, not even worthy of him. Life is no fool, and when he blurts out his self-justifying praise and blame of wild Wisdom, she knows that she can afford to be coy with him and toy with him. Zarathustra, the self-assured purveyor of manly counsel on woman, shows himself to be incapable of following his own advice with Life, not man enough for it.

But with women such as Wisdom and Life, Zarathustra is perhaps not to be blamed, especially now, just when he becomes unsure of the identity of his love and whether she is worthy of him. Although he reveals himself in this song to be confused as a lover, his way of behaving is, after all, not contrary to his teaching on man and woman. Even his confusion could be seen as manly in that it shows his lack of calculation or cunning. He betrays himself to Life with a noble forthrightness that shows that he is moved from within, or for himself and not by his need to move her: his happiness is "I will." He treats his beloved Wisdom, on the other hand, with a noble reserve that spares her what would pain her. And both women speak in the way appropriate to those whose happiness is "he will," those who are dependent on the external means of his will for the achievement of their end. That dependence on the external breeds guile in order to elicit from the other the essential act: the magnet must be strong or made stronger to draw the iron to it. The arts of dissimulation are the female arts, practiced and honed over aeons of manipulating the means to their happiness, and Life practices these arts on Zarathustra through her modesty, humility, and self-beautification. Zarathustra, dizzied by her appearance, is oblivious to his own. No master of the art of seeming, he shows instead how he is. Still, while Life's speeches are blandishments or acts of appearance for the purpose of winning him, she too will finally be forced to show how she is. Her blandishments include an offer appropriate to a man taken up or turned aside by interests other than herself, public interests, the interests of mankind: she offers herself. She thereby intimates that she differs from her rival. For all her beauty and for all the efforts of the greatest men, Wisdom remains, like Athena, virginal and unpossessed, whereas Life, like Aphrodite, can be possessed.

Life and Zarathustra are true to the natural strife between the sexes or the natural complementarity of male and female as represented in Zarathustra's teaching. In his self-forgetfulness the man Zarathustra is moved by the public realm, by the future of mankind; in her self-possession the woman Life is moved by the private, by the need to win over the means to her happiness, her progeny. Their complementary needs do not founder on a conflict of public and private, nor is one satisfied at the expense of the other; for the heroic is here mated with the private things of home, and the progeny will be a new people, who are at home on the earth. Life draws Zarathustra to his public task, not to the privately erotic. Life's love is not harmful to the hero Zarathustra, for it promises something even higher than the heroic. The marriage symbol par excellence for Nietzsche is the marriage that followed the abandonment of a woman by a heroic man with civic duties to perform, the marriage of Ariadne and Dionysos that followed the abandonment of Ariadne by Theseus. It is toward this mystery that the fable of *Zarathustra* moves, the mystery of male and female culminating in marriage, in the fruitful complementarity of Zarathustra and Life.[38]

In the Dancing Song Zarathustra is shown not to have succeeded in his love of Life. But his very failure seems to presage success, for when he next speaks (after the third song), he is able, by means of Life's wisdom, to unriddle the wisdom of the wisest. But Life's revelation of how she is to be fathomed is not the end, for when she and Zarathustra next appear together (III. 15), he is willful with her in a way that he cannot be now, and she yields gladly and submits to a fruitful marriage (III. 16). Zarathustra's way with women is not to be measured in that moment of wavering when his love is uncertain of its object. In the Other Dancing Song he dares to argue with Life, but his argument draws her admiration and her love, for his whispered conclusion proves to her that he loves her as she is and does not aim to alter her.

The title of the third and final song, "The Song at Grave-side" (II. 11), refers to the funeral song sung by the open grave, but the last word, "resurrection," names its theme or its resolve as the refusal of a final leave-taking. The song has no audience; it is sung on an unidentified island far from the blessed isles and is as inappropriate for disciples as the Night Song would have been. The song begins with Zarathustra's resolve to sail to an island. But part II itself began with such a resolve, to sail to "the blessed isles" where his disciples dwell. Here he sails to the island that harbors the tombs of his own past; this too is a voyage of hope that addresses a beloved audience and requires loyalty of it. This song of hope suggests what the narrative of the rest of part II and part III will confirm, that Zarathustra's redeemable hopes lie not on "the blessed isles" of his disciples, but on this island of his own buried past or buried nature.

The Song at Grave-side consists of a lament, a curse, and a resolve, each addressed to its appropriate, if absent, audience. The opening lament is addressed to the now silent and absent visions of his youth, whose memory still brings him comfort. Zarathustra and these youthful visions were made to be loyal to one another, and he has come to see their absence as an act of disloyalty. But now he discovers that they no more deserted him than he them; their departure was not an act of disloyalty, but a murder aimed at killing him.

In the next and longest part of the song, Zarathustra, standing before the sacred tomb of his visions, addresses his enemies with a solemn curse. He grants the success of their murderous deeds but at the very end expresses hope for the resurrection of his visions. His enemies, identified only by their murders, seem to be everything that opposes him by making his visions seem impossible. The visions spoke of sacred things: "Divine shall all beings be to me"; "all days shall be holy to me." That "joyful wisdom" looked to the happy augury of birds and "vowed to renounce all nausea." When these visions first presented their holy and noble paths, Zarathustra was blind; but he will recover them consciously through an act of will in his final wisdom. His account of the deeds of his enemies ends with a singular event and shifts from the plural to the singular. Once he wanted to dance away over all heavens, but the best singer was lured away from him, and his dance was terminated. It is that great singer, now turned pious enemy, whom Zarathustra now addresses; his betrayal has ruined the possibility of Zarathustra's dance and left his "highest hope" "unspoken and unredeemed." Having pleaded with others that they not abandon their highest hope (I. 8, 10), he now resolves not to abandon his. Redemption from the fall that has cost him his visions will be brought about through his own song, "The Other Dancing Song" (III. 15).[39]

In the resolve that ends the song, Zarathustra returns to his present, to marvel at still being alive despite the murderous deeds of his enemies. Unlike Achilles, who was vulnerable only in the heel, he has been vulnerable everywhere except in his will. In the image of *Daybreak* (455), the acquisition of a "second nature" has not dried up his "first nature"; his will, or first nature, has instead grown mature, and he will prove snake enough to throw off the skin of his second nature. Or, in the image of *Beyond Good and Evil* (229–31), the cruelty of Zarathustra's spirit enables him to recover what is deepest in him, "the unteachable, the granite of spiritual fate," the unchangeable "This is I." As Zarathustra describes his life in this song, no grace or chance has assisted at his rearing and protection as a philosopher;[40] abandoned in his youth, he will recover through his own will what his enemies have killed. And yet this song attests to the presence in him of things that are simply given, as if by grace; he has been favored with visions, and if they are now dead for him, he has been favored too with an indomitable will that refuses to accept their death. The song ends with Zarathustra addressing his invulnerable will, through which the visions once thought disloyal will rise from their graves on this island of his youth.

Zarathustra has never said before that he had a past like this. He has never said to those he teaches that he enjoyed visions in his youth, that teachings learned later had killed those visions by making them seem impossible, that he still suffers under those teachings, and that his visions are still dead except in willful promises to himself. A prophet of a new future, he has previously spoken of the whole past, including his own, as something to be redeemed through a new future. All that has been revealed of Zarathustra's own past up until now is that at thirty he had entered solitude (Prologue 2), that his years from thirty to forty had passed in a victorious solitude (Prologue 1), and that he had once believed the world to be the creation of a god (I. 3). When the past becomes the central problem in later chapters, it will be the past as a whole that he has to redeem, and the visions from his own past will play a part in that redemption.[41]

The interlude of the three songs thus comes to an end, but the fruit of the songs appears immediately in "On Self-Overcoming" (II. 12), for Zarathustra now shows himself able to unriddle the wisdom of the wisest, those virtuous men who have bestowed on life her virtuous names. Addressing now not merely the famous wise of the modern age (II. 8), but the simply wisest, Zarathustra engages in that conversation which is the privilege of genius described by Nietzsche ten years earlier, when he spoke of the "timeless simultaneity" of "the republic of geniuses," in which "one giant calls to the other across the bleak interval of the ages ... undisturbed by the unruly noisy dwarfs who creep about beneath them" (UD 9). This speech addresses only "you who are wisest," informing them of the real will hidden behind the virtuous "will to truth" with which they had purported to fathom life. Zarathustra calls to the wisest across the ages with the new truth that unriddles their hearts and destroys their ark of values, an ark that has been obediently carried forward by the stream of mankind. Unriddling the will to truth of the wisest breaks the hegemony of the wisest hitherto; this act of destruction presents itself as literally faithful to life in being the self-overcoming of the wisest by the one who has made himself wiser. The matter here revealed by the wise Zarathustra is explosive, a lightning bolt in Zarathustra's imagery, "dynamite" in the word Nietzsche used to describe himself (EH, "Destiny," 1). It intends not only to dynamite the wisdom of the wisest but to redirect the whole stream of mankind.

This is the decisive speech. It provides privileged access to a conversation among philosophers from which others are excluded. It is not only a conversation, however; it is a contest among mighty rivals for the highest human achievement, with the latest claimant to wisdom revealing the discovery that gives him the victory over his rivals. Speeches of a similar range or ambition occur later in the book, but none have occurred before. When they occur later, they will be speeches for which there are audiences only

inadvertently (II. 20) or by special invitation (III. 2), or for which there is
no audience whatever (III. 4, 14–16).

What lies behind the vaunted "will to truth" is the theme of Zarathustra's speeches both before and after the songs (II. 8, 12). The second
such speech shows that Zarathustra is able to unriddle the will to truth
of the wisest because he has learned the fundamental matter. His speech
to the philosophers begins abruptly, triumphantly, by announcing what
unriddles the secret of their hearts; only after he has stated his new insight
into their wisdom does he try to persuade them of its truth. But he does
try to persuade them; the speech is uncharacteristic in that it attempts to
justify its opening claims, grounding them in exceptional observations.
Zarathustra's attempt to persuade the wisest relies first on his own authority and second on a speech made to him by the highest authority, Life
herself. He tries to win the philosophers to a single insight and at the end
invites them to consider that insight together in a community of inquiry.
But while this chapter confines itself to insight and persuasion, the insight
leads to actions of destruction and construction. The destruction is made
clear in the speech to its victims, but the construction to follow is alluded
to only at the very end.

Zarathustra begins by naming the motive that the wisest have piously
attributed to themselves. But he names it slyly, in a leading question that
pictures their high and honored pursuit as a state of drivenness, fueled
by a burning lust. He sees their will to truth as a passion that he names
"the will to the thinkability of all beings." In his explanation of the ambiguous phrase "thinkability of all beings," he pointedly avoids the terms
that philosophy has developed for its inquiry, just as he avoids the word
philosophy. In particular, he avoids the term *being,* speaking instead of "all
beings,"[42] or "life";[43] and he avoids the term *nature,* speaking instead of
the "way," or "manner," of life. The wisest will to make all beings thinkable
but their will is grounded in their well-founded doubt as to whether beings
are thinkable in themselves. Moved by that doubt, the wisest will the bend-
ing and yielding of all beings. Not yet thinkable, or in themselves unthinkable, all beings yield to the will of the wisest and take the appearance of
the thinkable. Summing up in a single phrase his insight into their "whole
will," Zarathustra tells the wisest that it is "a will to power," adding immediately that it is present even when they speak the completely different
language of "good and evil," the greatest power on earth, the moral language
to which beings have hitherto yielded. The hidden reason for the moral
metaphysics of the wisest is their desire for a world before which they
could kneel, a world fit for reverence, worthy of their submission. The
world that has become thinkable under the force of the wisest is the world
of a permanent order of good and evil to which human beings are subject.
The moral demand for the thinkability of all beings is, for Nietzsche, a
demand first made by Socrates, but one felt by all Socratics, the first and
greatest of whom was Plato, "the most beautiful growth of antiquity." Plato

commanded "the greatest strength any philosopher has so far had at his disposal," and since Plato, "all theologians and philosophers are on the same track" (*BGE*, Preface, 191). This speech to "you who are wisest" thus translates Nietzsche's understanding of the Socratic-Platonic roots of Western civilization into *Zarathustra's* idiom of fable.

Zarathustra first follows the will of the wisest in the direction of its effect. Speaking of how the wisest are related to the unwise, he shows how the wisest have ruled, how philosophers have become kings, the secret spiritual rulers of the age. The unwise or the people are like a river directed forward by an ark of values invented by the wisest and given to them as a gift; they are the dutiful slaves of the mastering will. From time to time, out of the flowing river, waves of protest may arise against the honored ark, but they break ineffectively against the keel. The people and their protests are no threat to the mastering will that gave the river its direction; nor are the famous wise who represented the people and directed their protest in the modern age against ancient values, for their protest is itself a species of Platonism and does not alter the essential direction of mankind. But a danger does exist, a threat to the whole will to power of the wisest, in another will to power of similar magnitude. The one who sees the will to truth as the will to power is not simply a critic of the wisest who refutes their pious claims; for what he sees does not diminish the wisest but recognizes them to have been the best and most powerful of men. His insight is a celebration of them and their power, and precisely in that celebration he announces his rivalry. His own will to power aims to overcome theirs, to strike their ark of values not just as a wave that breaks into foam against the keel, but in a way that will destroy it and give the river of becoming that is mankind a new direction, with a new ark of values to carry forward. Zarathustra here presents in an image the account of Western history that Nietzsche gave in his first book. There it had already been granted to him, a contemplative man, to view the tremendous struggles and transitions set in motion by "the one turning-point and vortex of all so-called world history," Socrates, and the charm exercised by the insight into those struggles had already called the one who viewed them to take part and fight (*BT* 15).

To the wisest whom he has threatened Zarathustra now offers what he rarely offers, a detailed defense of his claim; he offers to teach the wisest as he has been taught. His speech on the will to power of the wisest therefore turns in the opposite direction, away from the effect of that will to power on all beings and on the history of mankind and toward its source or ground. He attempts to make his claim about the wisest plausible to them by grounding it in the fundamental phenomenon; in order that they understand and credit his teaching on good and evil, he offers them his teaching on life.[44] In doing so, he certifies himself to the wisest as the canniest observer of the most mysterious of observed things: when life is mute, he "hears" what is spoken in its eyes; when life speaks, he "sees"

what was reflected in its speech. By listening to the visible and seeing the
audible, he has discovered the way or the manner of life itself. He does
not claim to have discovered its "nature."[45] The philosophers' search for
the nature or nameable structure of things is doomed and is replaced, not
by a complete skepticism about "the belly of being," but by an insight into
the way or manner of things, into that changeability or becoming that,
though elusive, cannot completely resist capture.

In the Dancing Song, in which eyes are so important, Zarathustra's
look into Life's eyes twice caused him to sink into the unfathomable; now,
however, he claims to have heard life's speech in its eyes and goes on to
list the three things that he has heard there: first, that every living thing
is an obeying thing;[46] second, that what does not obey itself is commanded
by another; and third, a matter that needs more explanation, even for the
wisest, though it asserts to commanders the simple claim that commanding
is more difficult than obeying. The obvious reason for this greater difficulty,
which the wisest presumably know already, is that the commander assumes
the burden of the commanded and may well be crushed by it. The additional reason appeared only to Zarathustra: in all commanding, the one
who commands experiments and risks himself. His risk consists in having
no ground for his commanding external to himself; in legislating, he becomes the judge, the avenger, and the victim of his own laws (see I. 17
and II. 7). The commander is the ungrounded ground-giver. But what persuades the living to take such a terrible risk?, Zarathustra asks. Having
observed that mastery and slavery are the very way of life, he must ask
himself, Why would the master risk himself for mastery?

Before grounding the riddle of the master in the insight that came to
him alone, Zarathustra pauses to address a request to the wisest. What
he has heard in life's eyes, they can hear in the ordinary way, in his spoken
words; but they are to test his words seriously, for they say something
extraordinary. They are to ask themselves if he has discovered the very
heart of life, and thereby the heart of the wisest. Has he discovered the
ground of all things, whose persuasion cannot be refused even by the
highest commanders who risk everything in the highest obeying?

The conclusion drawn by Zarathustra from the puzzle presented by
the wisest is that the living are persuaded to risk everything to command
by what they are, will to power. Wherever he found the living, he found
the will to power—not only in those who risk everything to become master,
but even in those who yield. He gives examples of the yielding and the
mastering in order to persuade the wisest of the truth of his conclusion
regarding what persuades all the living. The weaker yields to the stronger
because it wills its own mastery over the still weaker. But even the strongest
yields to something for the sake of power; it yields to the persuasive ground
of all living things, the will to power. Master and slave have not engaged
in a fight to the death for the recognition that each is more than mere
aliveness, as Hegel would have it, celebrating man above all living things

in this manner. Master and slave and master and master engage in a fight to the death for the sake of power; in so doing, they demonstrate themselves to be continuous with all life; their act is not a negation but an assertion of life itself. This is the solution that Zarathustra has guessed to the riddle of mastery: mastery obeys the persuasive will to power that it is, and in that obedience gives expression to the highest, most spiritual form of life.

Zarathustra ends the part of the speech based on his own authority with a noteworthy claim: where sacrifice, service, and amorous glances are found, where yielding is found, there too is the will to be master. By stealth the weaker creeps into the fortress of the strong and steals power from the strong. These examples suggest something more than their initial impression that even in the apparently contrary phenomena of yielding and surrender a canny will to power is at work, for, after calling attention to the calculated yielding on the part of the weaker, Zarathustra turns immediately to the secret he has himself won from Life. By what means has he crept into the secret heart of Life herself and stolen power? What is noteworthy about his final claim regarding will to power is that it suggests that he has stolen power from Life by the devious means of creeping into her fortress, that he, the weaker, forced Life, the stronger, to yield her secret to him through canny means of sacrifice or service or amorous glances. He has fathomed Life, whereas all the other virtuous men have merely imposed their own virtue on her. His speech now turns to a report of how the highest authority betrayed the fathomable truth to him.

Ordering Zarathustra to "see" what she says, Life begins emphatically, with a description of herself, and ends repeating that she is will to power. In "On Self-Overcoming" it is Life who says of herself: "I am that which must always overcome itself." Zarathustra had observed the mastery and slavery of beings in relation to one another, but Life who speaks for the whole of beings speaks of "self-overcoming"; Life itself enslaves and slaves. She describes from inside the fortress what Zarathustra saw from the out- side. For her secret to be seen, she must make a long didactic speech. Although presenting herself as fathomable, she nevertheless treats herself as a mystery, a secret to be "guessed" at. She begins her speech in the familiar plural, as if she were addressing Zarathustra simply as one of the wisest, and continues with the plural as long as she is describing what the wisest have guessed her to be. But she switches to the familiar singular halfway through, when she reveals to him alone the secret that unriddles all the wisest, including himself. The wisest generally, those virtuous men who have bestowed their virtue on Life, have given her many names, seeing in her the procreative will, or the drive to the telos, to the higher, more distant, more manifold. But these virtuous names for Life who is not vir- tuous cover a single secret, a unity in the whole, and Life would rather go under, become not life, than give up this one thing. Where there is going under, life sacrifices itself for power. The one who guesses what her will is simultaneously guesses what "crooked" ways her will must take. Although she creates and loves, she must in time overcome the very thing she creates and become the opponent of her love, forcing it to go under. There is no repose in her love, nor does she make what she loves immortal. Having vowed her infidelity, Life speaks to her lover in the singular, to "you, knower," proclaiming her mastery over him, not only in his mortality, but in his very being, for he is only her plaything, whose very will to truth is but an expression of her will to power. She thus reduces him to a momentary modification of herself, even in his highest aspiration. Still, she has allowed him to be the first to discover her real name. Assertion of her mastery over him has cost her her secret; the weaker has by superior guile wrested the secret from the stronger.

Life tells Zarathustra that there is no "will to existence" and even gives an argument, albeit specious, to prove it: neither the dead nor the living can possess such a will, because the dead are not, and the living already exist. But beyond her narrow argument she describes what is willed by the living: where life is, there also is will, not will to life but will to power. This emphatic declaration is interrupted at mid-point by her statement, "So I teach you"—in the singular. Life confesses that mere aliveness is not the highest; the living value something higher than mere life—the will to power. Life ends the speaking that Zarathustra must see with the phrase "will to power"; this is the secret of life that is higher than mere aliveness and to which mere aliveness yields.

Although Life admits that the most powerful men have imposed their virtue on her, she does not thereby imply that she is infinitely malleable to their will. Rather, she denies it in her claim that the wisest are moved by the most spiritual form of what she is. For what she is cannot be altered, however plastic its forms. Whereas the virtuous Zarathustra, schooled by his wild Wisdom, had once believed that life was unfathomable, he has now learned to fathom unvirtuous life. He now knows that Life was not speaking ill of herself when she suggested that she could be fathomed; he now believes her when she says that she is will to power. Only the partial eclipse of his virtuous, if wild and skeptical, wisdom allows him to learn that life is will to power. Whereas he had held that "the belly of being does not speak to man, unless as man" (I. 3), Life herself has now spoken to him and forced him to abandon his virtuous skepticism.

Zarathustra says to the wisest, to whom he has betrayed the secret that Life gave him, "Thus Life once taught me," and with life's secret he unriddles their hearts, just as she had unriddled his heart in the middle of her speech. In the chapter on self-overcoming, Zarathustra uses that word only after he has learned its extent from Life. Now he can make explicit his threat to the "good and evil" legislated by the will to power of the wisest. Good and evil must overcome themselves, or the will to power of the new teacher must overcome the good and evil legislated by the wisest hitherto. Having crept into the heart of life, he can creep into the heart of the highest form of life, the wisest, and see the force and violence of the legislation of values by these "value assessors." Now that their secret is out, he promises that a still more violent force will grow out of their values and repeats for them his old lesson that a creator must be a destroyer. These creators, who themselves destroyed the old to create their once new ark of values, will in their turn be destroyed by the new creator, the superman to come. Zarathustra ends the threats of his speech with a term well known to the Socratics he addresses, "the highest Good." Belonging to the highest good, as Zarathustra understands it, is "the highest evil." The new highest good is "the creative," and this new definition signals the demise of the highest good as the permanent ground of permanent being and does so by revealing that it too was created; such destruction is the "highest evil" where evil is what breaks the good or the customary.

Here Zarathustra breaks off his speech. Now conciliatory toward his adversaries, having shown the means to eventual triumph over them, he invites them to speak with him about what he has said. The few philosophers are to speak in private about the most momentous discovery of one of them, a discovery that is "as theory, a novelty—as reality, the *primordial fact* of all history" (*BGE* 259). Acting as if he has won their allegiance with this invitation, Zarathustra speaks in the plural, ending with what purports to be the prayer of all the wisest. Now that the house of being has been destroyed, the house of creative becoming must be built.

The rest of Zarathustra's course is set by this fundamental speech. Having unriddled the ambitions of the wisest with the truth about life, victory-loving Zarathustra is set upon his own course. To become wise as the wisest are wise, to seek the highest victory, to take upon himself the heaviest burden, means now to enact a new will to power over "all beings." Prior to that act its appropriate character must be discerned, and that discernment occurs only with the subsequent discovery that all wisdom hitherto has perpetrated "revenge" on the unwillable past (II. 20). The new act of will to power must be free of revenge, and hence must learn to will the seemingly unwillable past through willing the eternal return of beings as they are. That most spiritual act of will to power, that tyrannical act of founding philosophy (*BGE* 9), takes place at the end of part III; but it must be followed by a less spiritual, more political act, the descent that will bring the new ark of values that the river mankind will carry forward.

This decisive chapter touches the fundamental matter in Nietzsche's philosophy, the discovery of what was once called nature or being. Fittingly it treats that discovery as a mystery and speaks of it in the appropriate terms of poetry and privileged conversation. What has transpired between the manly Zarathustra and the woman Life that she has yielded her secret to him? Their meeting, with its emphasis on secrets and guesses parallels the challenge recounted later, in which the more than heroic Zarathustra scorns the guiding thread the hero Theseus found necessary in the labyrinth and invites his readers to be more than heroic, to guess rather than deduce (III. 2). There is no guiding thread fashioned by some Daedalus for what Zarathustra has here discovered. Because he speaks of the fundamental matter, he speaks of something not simply demonstrable, something that cannot be proved by an appeal to phenomena more fundamental than itself or by an appeal to agreed-upon criteria for measuring what is true. What the wisest must judge for themselves in the challenge raised by Zarathustra's claim is made more explicit in Nietzsche's next invitation to reflect on his claim to have discovered the fundamental phenomenon: "This too is only interpretation" (BGE 22). Can there be a true interpretation of the fundamental phenomenon? Is will to power that interpretation?

Zarathustra presents the challenge in the fable of a heroic deed. To the one who has by stealth won his way into her fortress, Life tells the unchangeable secret of her changeable nature. As loving, if not virtuous, female, she yields the secret of her nature, and Zarathustra draws the fitting conclusion for a willful and virtuous male, for if life is changeable and a woman in every way, if she is will to power, then she yields to the orders imposed on her by the most powerful men through the most spiritual will to power. Life announces the defeat of the lovers of Wisdom through her own favored lover. Although they appeared to master her through their virtuous names, she won at the beginning because their naming merely expressed what she is, and she wins at the end because she is not loyal to their virtuous names but allows her lover to overcome them.

As an imposition of meaning on life, Zarathustra's wild wisdom had made it seem as if life itself were mute, as if life as changeable were necessarily unfathomable. And even now, after life has spoken her secret, wisdom is seen to be the imposition of meaning on life. How has it become possible, then, that Zarathustra can receive the truth about life and not command it, that he can by guile or any other means be passive or receptive to the ultimate wisdom that wisdom is not passive or receptive but is the imposition of will? The literal answer of *Thus Spoke Zarathustra* is: with mirrors. This literal answer intimates that whereas no miraculous harmony exists between the mind of man and the nature of things, nevertheless, the way in to the nature of things is not simply closed, nor is the nature of things simply opaque. The elusive secret of being lies in the elusive heart of the highest or most spiritual beings; the nature of nature comes to light in the highest natures. Their commanding is an obeying; in obedience to nature they enact nature's most spiritual deeds. The soul is "the ladder with a hundred rungs on which to climb to knowledge" (HH I. 292), and the fortress into which Zarathustra has crept is the fortress of his own life, or the secret of his own victory-loving spirit. The truth about life as such is revealed in the truth about his own life, a life of the most unrestrained self-overcoming. The final question that he had put to life after his scrutiny of life as mastery and slavery, or as mastery and yearning for mastery, was: How is it conceivable that there be striving for mastery even at the cost of life? Is life not highest? The answer given by Life confirms his suspicion that mere life is not highest, that the highest end is power, and the persuasive force a will to power. Still, this means that life *is* highest, life as will to power. The dialogue between Life and Zarathustra reveals that the highest commanding of nature is an act of obedience to nature, that philosophy, imperial philosophy, is surrender to life's passion. The fable that pictures Life in her fortress attempting to retain power over the one who has by stealthy scrutiny won entry there, pictures her attempting to retain her power precisely by yielding her secret. She succeeds, for when changeable life speaks her unchangeable truth, she reveals that her secret is itself an enigma, a perpetual invitation to the highest spirits to wonder. Because life is will to power, it is not simply intelligible or thinkable; if there were gods, they too would philosophize (*BGE* 294, 295).[47]

This most extensive speech on will to power in *Zarathustra* serves the purpose of the narrative or of Zarathustra's education; it does not serve the purpose of explaining will to power. Although Zarathustra's speech is unusually bent on persuasion, it is still fragmentary in its persuasiveness in that it is addressed only to the wisest, with the sole purpose of unriddling their wisdom. If they find his insight persuasive, they can accept his invitation to reason together on these dark matters. But, willingness aside, they may be forced to reason with him, for his teaching on "life" is the rival of previous teachings on the nature of "all beings," those Socratic-Platonic teachings that have sought to make all beings thinkable or calculable. Saying that "all beings" are will to power asserts that they are unthinkable, enigmatic in themselves, while at the same time accounting for their malleability or their susceptibility to the will of philosophers, who have made the changeable world seem a pale reflection of an unchanging and infinitely more worthy reality that is in principle closed to inspection, or who have made the changeable world into a calculable, manipulable world that yields to alteration by men bent on correcting an existence made to appear unsatisfactory. The one who invites the wisest to reason with him is one bent on destroying what they have created and replacing their rule with his own. His rivalry with the wisest vindicates the way of the master over the way of the slave, where master and slave are understood spiritually as the wisest and the unwise. The way of such masters is not a dead end just because it depends on the work of the slave. For history has not been made by the coarse work of slaves, but by the spiritual will to power of their masters; the slaves have only changed the world in accord with the will of the masters whose real point has been to interpret it, to create a human world. But these are very delicate matters, fit to be spoken of only among the wisest, among those whose high spirituality (*BGE* 219), beyond good and evil, enables them to see the spiritual sense of mastery and slavery and to see that they themselves are mastered by the most spiritual will to power. Reasoning together, Zarathustra and his like will aim to bring their thinking into accord with their being, through a mastering thought that is not a negation. In this way, the second chapter to mention will to power points to the third and final chapter to mention it, for the discovery of philosophy's secret, will to power, points to the new philosophy, eternal return. In the new wisdom of Zarathustra, the wise man, the spirited knower, is a lover who transforms the beloved into something still more beautiful than she is, and she is beautiful as she is. Zarathustra's act of artistic transformation begins with the judgment of a lover and bids the beloved to eternally return. In this way Zarathustra answers what Nietzsche had said was "the most vital of questions for philosophy," for he discerns the extent to which "the character of the world is unalterable" and embraces unalterable life as its lover. But with this act of discernment Zarathustra prepares for the second part of what Nietzsche said was philosophy's task: "to set about *improving* with the most ruthless courage *that part of [the world] recognized as alterable*," including "the very much alterable judgments of mankind" (*WB* 3).

The title of this chapter that unriddles philosophy as will to power might seem to encourage a limited interpretation of will to power as simply an injunction to human beings to overcome themselves, to practice an honorable self-mastery or independence. But "On Self-Overcoming" is not characterized by exhortation, nor is it addressed to everyone. Unlike so much of *Zarathustra* until now, it does not tell anyone to do anything; it simply puts before the wisest, and only the wisest, a thought regarding the riddle of their wisdom and its ground. Only at the very end does it suggest a task, a task of the greatest magnitude in that it involves redirecting the river mankind by reevaluating all beings and creating a new ark of values.

HOUSES OF WISDOM (CHAPTERS 13–19)

Having ended his speech to the wisest with the challenge that there is many a house for them yet to build, Zarathustra turns to the houses of wisdom that now stand in the modern world. Although the deconstruction of these houses is stressed in his speeches, he honors what has been undertaken in each and points to the construction of the new house of wisdom. The most profound of modern knowledge-seekers have been laid low by the deadly truths they have discovered in their praiseworthy search (II. 13). Modern education has looted the thousand peoples without having resources of its own to ground a people (II. 14). Modern philosophy and modern science practice a praiseworthy objectivity, but their pursuit of mere objectivity leaves them barren precisely where they need to be productive (II. 15). The art of scholarship that Zarathustra himself once practiced has prostituted itself in the service of unworthy masters (II. 16). Zarathustra is still a poet (II. 17), as well as a teacher of revolution (II. 18), but his is not modern poetry or modern revolution. As poet and revolutionary he is threatened by the modern teaching of nihilism, which comes to him as a prophecy that causes a nightmare (II. 19). But out of the nightmare of nihilism there comes at last, as a kind of revelation, clarity about what is necessary for mankind's redemption (II. 20). The four chapters on poetry, revolution, nihilism, and redemption mark the return of the disciples to the narrative. In a series of three tests they are found wanting, and Zarathustra is forced to shake his head three times, first at one of the disciples (II. 17), then at all of them (II. 18), and finally at the most beloved disciple (II. 19). But then he betrays to his disciples his own unredeemed state and finds it necessary to beg forgiveness for his unguarded speech (II. 20). From their failure and his own, he learns the proper meaning of prudence and imprudence (II. 21), and part II ends with Zarathustra practicing a form of his newfound prudence (II. 22).

"On the Sublime Ones" (II. 13) opens with an image of hidden serenity that recalls, by contrast, the images of stormy seas with which both part II as a whole and the chapters on wisdom began (II. 1, 8). Himself a combination of serenity and storm, Zarathustra differentiates himself from the "sublime ones," heroic modern seekers of knowledge. These seekers have discovered truths of great value and have freed themselves from the old superstitions, but they have been left skewed and lack the beauty of serenity that ought to be present in the most sublime. He never calls the sublime ones "wise" (see II. 8, 12), but neither does he say that they are moved by a desire for fame. His look into their souls confirms that they live lives of service to knowledge as adherents of the youngest virtue, honesty, or intellectual probity. "Man's life is thought," they think, and after "ravening, raging, and uprooting" "through century after century," they

come
Into the desolation of reality: \
Egypt and Greece good-bye, and good-bye, Rome![48]

They are the ones who have hunted down the deadly truths of sovereign becoming, the fluidity of all concepts, types, and species, and the lack of any cardinal difference between man and animal (*UD* 9). In the words of *Beyond Good and Evil*, they are the ones who sacrifice God to stupidity and worship the stone (55).[49] In describing one of the sublime ones whom he has just seen, Zarathustra presupposes, but cannot name, Kant's views on the sublime, that the sublime is a feeling of reverence and awe in the face of the unmeasurable or the terrible in nature, and at the same time a feeling of power and elevation that fears no limit because it knows itself to be the locus of limit and measure. While admiring those who achieve this sublimity in themselves, Zarathustra's "taste" finds the sublime one deficient, and taste is the standard under which all of life comes into disputation. In this witty fashion opposing Kant on taste, Zarathustra accuses even the greatest modern knowers of failing to duplicate the sublime achievement of the Greeks. Opposing Hegel as well, Zarathustra corrects him regarding the inability to leap over one's own shadow or escape one's own time, and in so doing, implies that the one who leaps is himself the sun that casts shadows. The description of the sublime ones culminates

in counsel that the hero addressed ascend beyond the heroic. Hegel, admirer of world-historical heroes whose deeds can be understood only in
retrospect by the wise man who can look only backward, could well be
counseled to celebrate himself, to become the white bull who walks for
once in front of the plowshare, to become beautiful and, holding the mirror
for once before himself, tremble like Narcissus at his own beauty. Then
the admirer of the heroic ascends in dreams to the superhero or himself.
The heroic labors of these highest men of science, Kant and Hegel—albeit
a Kant and Hegel who refuse themselves any residue of Christian superstition—have uncovered time as history, and shown that the world of concern to us is ungrounded in anything higher. But for all their greatness,
the labors of these "philosophical laborers" are insufficient and point to
the labor of the "genuine philosopher," the creation of values that beautify
the world of concern to us (*BGE* 211).[50] In this way Zarathustra shows why
science must pass into the care of philosophy.

With the Greeks, knowledge of the terrifying truth had led to the highest
achievements, the creation of the beautiful, as Nietzsche had argued in
his first book, in which the beauty of Greek tragedy was seen as the pinnacle
of their encounter with life as it is. Moderns like the sublime one here
addressed have begun to share the Greek knowledge of life as tragedy, but,
clothed in their ugly truths, they are "penitents of the spirit," whose penance consists in their absolute renunciation of any comfort. Zarathustra's
counsel for the heroic sublime one consists of instruction in the beautiful.
But "beauty is of all things the most difficult for the hero," because he is
possessed of a violent and powerful will that has not learned measure; his
great virtue—or, *"our"* great virtue, as Nietzsche puts it in *Beyond Good
and Evil* (224), in which he places himself provisionally among "the free
minds" like the sublime ones—is unrestrained, measureless, half barbarian.
But the beautiful is power that has learned measure; it is an act of grace,
"power that becomes grace and descends into the visible." Having looked
into the secret of the souls of the heroic seekers of knowledge, Zarathustra
ends by disclosing what he calls simply "the secret of the soul": the heroic,
Theseus with his guiding thread, is not enough (III. 2). When the soul
"trembles with godlike desires," the heroic abandons the soul, but when
the soul is left abandoned by the hero, there approaches in a dream that
which is still higher, "the superhero." This is the first time in *Zarathustra*
that the mystery of Theseus, Ariadne, and Dionysos appears in recognizable
form.[51] This mystery of the divine superseding the heroic becomes more
prominent, if persistently mysterious, as Zarathustra follows his course to
its end; in the way appropriate to fable, it separates the highest from the
high, philosophy from science.

By bringing together truth and art, this chapter provides another episode in the long history of Nietzsche's reflection on what he came to
regard as the "problem of science itself," a problem raised in his first book,
in which "science is viewed under the optics of the artist, and art under

that of life" (*BT*, "Self-Criticism," 2). These are the never abandoned optics of one who knows—because "he experienced it, he has perhaps experienced nothing else—that art is worth more than truth" (*KGW* VIII 17 [3 §4] = *WP* 853). This statement on Nietzsche's experience never found its way into the new preface to the *Birth of Tragedy* for which it was projected, perhaps precisely because it could mislead on the essential matter by eliciting the inappropriate conclusion that therefore truth is worth little. On the contrary, it matters very much to Nietzsche whether a thing is true or not; those who say, "It does not matter whether a thing is true, but only what effect it produces," exhibit "an absolute lack of intellectual integrity" unknown to Nietzsche (*KGW* VIII 10 [184] = *WP* 172). The art that is nevertheless worth more than truth, which is worth so much, the art that passes beyond the truth uncovered by the modern heroes of truth, is not indifferent to truth nor an opponent of it. Art must accord with the world known to modern science and in this accord ennoble and dignify that world. As his honoring of modern truth-seekers shows, Zarathustra does not aim to undo their work but to ground it and justify it and allow the great hunt to proceed.

The next three chapters speak of three reasons for pride in modern achievements: educational pluralism or liberalism (II. 14), objectivity in philosophical and scientific research (II. 15), and assiduous, disinterested scholarship (II. 16). But each of these aspects of modern education is found to hide something shameful. Still, Zarathustra does not seek to educate the educators, only to destroy confidence in them. His criticism is not of education, science, and scholarship but only of their contemporary misuse. Modern education casts a cold eye on the whole of human history, gathering from it the interesting or the quaint (II. 14); but it ends up with the bad conscience consequent on possessing nothing high of its own except the study of the other (II. 15, 16). Zarathustra once admired the historical and philological modern sciences as a practitioner of them, and his speeches show that their achievements are admirable and irreversible. Nevertheless, inasmuch as modern educational ideals reflect a democratic bias and a suspicion of anything noble or magnificent, they suffer from the general subjection of modern science to modern politics.

At the beginning of "On the Land of Education" (II. 14), Zarathustra returns from his own distant futures, where he has no contemporary, and addresses his most advanced contemporaries.[52] They think of themselves as progressives directed toward the future, having encompassed and incorporated the whole of the past. Decked out with a knowledge of all beliefs and permissive of all, these products of modern education have made themselves "unworthy of belief" in Zarathustra's eyes. In their lack of belief and lack of longing they resemble last men. In another echo of the prologue, Zarathustra, the traveler of worlds and underworlds, compares the "realists" of the present unfavorably with the long dead inhabitants of the underworld who were capable of vigorous belief and action. He modifies and intensifies

Achilles' judgment on the underworld, for he would prefer to be an in-
significant day laborer among the shades of the bygone in the underworld
than to be anything at all among educated moderns. Now a fugitive in
every city, Zarathustra the educator has hopes only for his "children" and
his "children's land," the land that will be created by the disciples whom
he creates.

Zarathustra turns to a noble aspect of modern education in "On Immaculate Perception" (II. 15), a deep inquisitiveness that can pride itself
on something uniquely its own, the ideal of complete objectivity developed
in modern philosophy and modern science. In one of a series of references
to his own past as a search among modern options for knowledge that
could satisfy his own passion for the truth, he says that he was once persuaded that the objectivity of modern scientific researchers was a genuine
attempt to grasp the knowable, by ridding the self of the distortions of
personal and local perspectives. He had admired as divine the aspiration
of the modern philosopher or scientific researcher to become the per-
spective-free viewer of the thing to be known, to achieve what they themselves want to call "contemplation."[53] But this tribute to the objective spirit
is unabashedly subjective; it is an excessive and impassioned speech full
of sexual imagery that would embarrass and appall those who seek the
extirpation of their own passions in order to achieve disinterested knowledge. But, while recognizing that objectivity can never be " 'contemplation
without interest' (which is a nonsensical absurdity)," Zarathustra is far
from abandoning objectivity. "Let us not be ungrateful" for the impossible
objectivity of the immaculate perceivers, for it prepares a "future
'objectivity,' " Zarathustra's objectivity, "the ability to *control* one's Pro and
Con and to dispose of them, so that one knows how to employ a variety
of perspectives and affective interpretations in the service of knowledge"
(*GM* III. 12). Here, a controlled Zarathustra employs a con in the form of
ridicule; his exposé of the disinterested accuses them of being moved by
shame at the impurity that they feel in their own passionate bodies. Desiring
separation from their own bodily grounds, their spirits reinterpret the earth
as a place congenial only to spirit.

The parable with which this speech begins and ends equates the ideal
of objective knowledge with the reflective and passive moon, the modern
moon that can no longer sustain the traditional imagery which attributed
to it a female fecundity. In Zarathustra's parable, the moon is barren, its
apparent pregnancy a lie; rather than female, it is a sterile, staring male,
the jealous eye of mere observation. The barrenness of the moon, of objective knowledge, leaves the earth itself barren; and the "pure perceivers"
are cursed with the necessary consequence of impotence, that they will
have no offspring. Contrary to all appearances, which seem to argue otherwise, Zarathustra claims that modern philosophical and scientific objectivity will have no progeny, but will be eclipsed by the offspring of a
new fertile sun. "Pure observers" are invited to observe how the rising sun

pales the setting moon. The rising sun of the new age is the rival that will
dim them, Zarathustra's sun, an active, virile force that will have progeny
by drawing the things of earth to its own spiritual height. Zarathustra's
claim of barrenness would seem to be a challenge to the ultimate fruit-
fulness of modern technological science, the science that would, according
to Bacon, one of its founders, produce from the marriage of mind and
nature a "line and race of inventions" to relieve the human estate. Bacon's
promise of mechanical progeny was surely warranted, but Zarathustra
nevertheless accuses the modern scientific enterprise of barrenness. Although necessarily almost silent on modern technology because of the
constraints of its literary form, *Zarathustra* raises the question of the modern mastery of nature, while asserting the necessity of human mastery of
a certain sort. Present here only in the metaphor of the barrenness of scientific objectivity, Zarathustra's assault on the effects of modern technological science, while remaining metaphoric, becomes more explicit later
when he resumes his travels among modern men and describes what he
sees as their diminution (III. 5).

"On Scholars" (II. 16) shows that Zarathustra was himself once a scholar
who knows their ways. He is still a scholar to the child and to those who
are not scholars in the old way, but the opening parable shows a sheep,
a scholar, nibbling at the ivy wreath on his head and drawing the conclusion
from this mere taste that Zarathustra is no longer a scholar. But if he is
no longer a scholar, he can no longer be authoritative for scholars, and
the sheep abandons Zarathustra, assured of his superiority.[54] Zarathustra
welcomes this abandonment, for the estrangement that has grown up between himself and scholars is necessary and desirable. He claims not to
have been driven out of the fellowship of modern scholars but to have
moved out of his own accord, having recognized the distance between
them.[55] But the intensity of his attack on scholars is grounded in something
other than their being merely parasitical and petty. Laboring under false
ceilings that they have erected in order to partition themselves off from
everything high and to make plausible their denial of its very existence,
they perform an essential service for their political masters: they demonstrate conclusively that there can exist only the common, that all men
are driven by the most common of desires that the most common of men
are able to control. Against the efforts of modern scholarship, Zarathustra
finds it essential to assert that men are not equal, that some men experience
desires unfelt by most, desires that are not explicable as immoderate out-
breaks of the low. Like Hegel who delighted in Odysseus's pummeling of
Thersites while himself pummeling "psychological valets,"[56] Zarathustra
attacks scholars for being in the service of modern democracy, and hence
commissioned to explain or explain away experiences and ambitions like
his own by reading into them the low grown to unlawful or freakish proportions. Since he moved out of the house of scholars, he has been heard
least by the most scholarly. Unlike the previous speeches, which were ad-

dressed to their subjects, this speech does not address the scholars but only describes them from a distance.

With the problem of the poet, Zarathustra's account of the ways of wisdom takes an important turn. Because poetry (II. 17), revolution (II. 18), and nihilism (II. 19) all belong so essentially to Zarathustra's way, his followers face the constant danger of wrongly identifying his versions with other, more familiar forms. The disciples' failures in these three chapters exhibit the gravity of such misinterpretations, as well as how easy it is for even the best of followers to make them. These are the only chapters in part II in which the disciples speak, and they do so only to show their failure to understand their master as poet, revolutionary, and nihilist. After each failure Zarathustra shakes his head. Through this disenchantment with his disciples, he begins his severance from them. That the disciples are not wholly to be blamed for their failures is clear, not only from these chapters, but more directly from the next chapter (II. 20), in which Zarathustra shows himself to be blameworthy. The subsequent chapter (II. 21) is a meditation on prudence, which enlightens him about his relation to his disciples, and the next and final chapter of part II effects his separation from them. The elaborate preparations for the break between Zarathustra and his disciples focus on their misunderstanding of his teaching. Recognizing that misunderstanding to be necessary, he abandons his hope that disciples will be able to carry his teaching further than he can.

"On the Poets" has three parts: an exchange on belief between Zarathustra and a believing disciple, a speech by Zarathustra to his disciple that properly makes him angry, and a speech by Zarathustra apparently to himself. Zarathustra initiates the dialogue by repeating to a single disciple a statement he had made earlier to all his disciples (II. 2). The disciple remembers not only what Zarathustra says that he said, but exactly what he said next. It is not surprising that the disciple remembers, for he shows himself to be a lover of poetry, and what Zarathustra has repeated is his transformation of the claim made by the most famous and authoritative poet at the end of his greatest work of poetry. Troubled by what Zarathustra had said next, the poetry-loving disciple asks about it. Zarathustra's words seem to have been calculated to elicit just this question, so that the consequent instruction on the authority of poetry might be given. The disciple's question, "Why did you say 'The poets lie too much?' ", asks about the warrant for Zarathustra's claim, but it seems to arise less from a desire to challenge that claim than from a desire that his teacher's authority be made indubitable. Zarathustra's harsh claim about poets has induced an unwelcome misgiving in his disciple. But rather than remove his disciple's unease with assertions of his reasons, he forces him to face other, still less welcome questions about the warrant for his teaching.

As befits the poet who said that poets lie too much, Zarathustra's first response is evasive and cunning. He has been asked for reasons but, alleging forgetfulness, is coy about giving them. Of course he has not forgotten them; there will come a time when he will be able "to speak of everything and pour out all his reasons" (III. 9), but that will be in solitude, not with disciples.[57] Zarathustra does more than pretend to forget his reasons, he impugns all his opinions:

> It is already too much for me to retain all my opinions and many a bird has flown away.
> And sometimes I find in my pigeon coop a stray that is strange to me and that trembles when I lay my hand on it.

If this is what Zarathustra's opinions are like, who can tell the strays? Is his opinion about poets a stray? It must be up to the disciple to tell. In constructing the image of a pigeon coop to illustrate the problem of knowing what to believe, Zarathustra repeats for his disciple what Socrates had constructed for Theaetetus as they were under way on their mutual search for the distinction between knowledge and opinion.[58] Attempting to account for false opinion, Socrates had "shamelessly" likened the mind to a pigeon coop and had spoken of teaching and learning as the handing over and receiving of information. But the image had apparently foundered on the absence of a way of distinguishing the birds handed over from nonbirds handed over, true bits of knowledge from false, without constructing an infinity of such ridiculous pigeon coops. But Socrates' image is actually an image of the mind stocked with opinions that have been acquired. The birds are not bits of knowledge, as Theaetetus himself goes on to suggest, but bits of opinion, and judgment must be exercised to distinguish the true from the false; one must take them into one's own hands and judge for oneself. While Theaetetus is apparently left baffled by the conversation, he has himself found the way out; that he learned to follow that way may be seen in the praise accorded him at the opening of the dialogue, where he is said to resemble Socrates inwardly.[59] But what Zarathustra finds in his disciple is apparently no inner resemblance, for the disciple seems unable to take the birds of Zarathustra's opinions into his own hands and judge them for himself.

Following his Socratic challenge to his disciple, Zarathustra is able after all to recall his previously stated opinion for his disciple, though he does not yet give his reasons for it. Instead, he says he is a poet and propounds the appropriate puzzle for the disciple of a poet who claims that poets lie too much: "Do you believe that he spoke the truth then?" The disciple ignores the problem, saying only: "I believe in Zarathustra," even though the ground of his beliefs has just sabotaged his own authority and made the distinction between the truth and the lie the disciple's responsibility. Zarathustra smiles at his disciple's dilemma and shakes his head.

To counter his disciple's belief, he delivers a speech of particular cunning. Stanley Rosen calls it a "noble lie,"[60] but it is perhaps better regarded as Zarathustra's account of the grounds of noble lying. The speech quite understandably makes his disciple angry. Like Kierkegaard's Johannes Climacus, Nietzsche's Zarathustra will make things hard for his followers, as hard as possible, but not any harder than they are.[61] In this long speech and in the next, he gives the reasons that he had alleged to have forgotten. Although the speech is in the first person—"*We* do lie too much"[62]—and therefore seems to intensify the problem of the liar, it opens assuming a "someone" who in "all seriousness" occupies a standpoint outside poetry, the author of the statement that poets lie too much, for whom that statement is simply and unparadoxically true. That someone would seem to be the nonpoetic or philosophic knower, because the main accusation asserts that the ground of poets' lying is ignorance. To mask that ignorance, poets produce intoxicants that all too often prove poisonous. Because of their ignorance poets are pleased by the poor in spirit, by those still poorer in spirit than themselves. They become flatterers, or, as Nietzsche said in his previous book, "The poets were always the valets of some morality" (*GS* 1)—here, in the context set by the allusions to Goethe, valets of the morality of the "Eternal Feminine," for the poet's flattery is aimed at attracting young women and at learning what old women tell one another in the evening. Because of their ignorance and because of their suspicion that the secret way to knowledge is barred to those who have learned anything, poets believe in the "wisdom" of the people, of those who have learned nothing.

But all poets believe something else as well, something that makes the way to knowledge the way through the tender sentiments. Specifically, the poet learns a little of those things that exist between heaven and earth when he lies in the grass or under lonely bowers with his ears pricked up. Attentive to nature in this way, experiencing the onset of tender sentiments, "poets always fancy that Nature herself is in love with them and creeps to their ears to tell them secrets and amorous flatteries." This is the only time in *Zarathustra* that the word *nature* is used, and it is used to describe the product of poets' amorous fancies. From this one use, nature would appear to be nothing but a poet's fancy, inaccessible in itself. But Zarathustra himself is engaged in an inquiry into "Life." Will its fruit too be a poet's fancy? Or should we believe that he speaks the whole truth when speaking as a poet for a disciple's edification? In learning to judge for himself the inflated claims of his beloved poets, the disciple will have to judge for himself whether his master's poetry withstands the criticism it dares to make of its own kind.

What the poets allege to have heard of nature through their tender attentiveness, they then parade before all mortals as stories of the immortals who exist between heaven and earth or even above the heavens. Zarathustra states categorically that all gods are parables created by ignorant poets, who, through the flattery of the still more ignorant, seek to inflate themselves. The seeming narrowness of this apodictic judgment on the gods attests to a great expansion of the function of poetry and the task of the poet. In particular, by narrowing to the single source of poetry the greatly divergent gods of masters and gods of slaves, Zarathustra demonstrates the adaptability of poets in choosing their own masters or the morality that they serve. The ingenuity of poetic invention serves the master who best serves the poet, the poet himself thereby ascending to the highest mastery.

Speaking as a poet, Zarathustra tells of being drawn heavenward into the kingdom of the clouds on which poets set their colorful but bastard husks, which they name "gods and supermen," empty husks just light enough for their places in the clouds. He says "gods and supermen"[63] twice, setting his own most honored creation, the superman, among the clouds alongside the despised creations of other poets. This speech makes the disciple angry, the only time in the book a disciple expresses anger at Zarathustra. But the anger would seem to have been provoked purposefully by a poet attentive to his audience, for it serves the necessary purpose of forcing the believing disciple to test for himself the differences between Zarathustra's opinions and the apparently similar opinions of other poets. In particular, Zarathustra has mocked the poets' claim to have a special ear to nature through which she whispers her secrets to them. But Zarathustra the poet has himself just composed a song and a speech that claimed a special ear to nature through which she revealed her secret to him. Furthermore, he has mocked the poets' invention of gods and supermen in the presence of a disciple drawn to him by his poetry of the superman. Is his own teaching on nature and man merely a poet's fancy grounded in ignorance and paraded before the still more ignorant in order to elicit their admiration and their submission to his creations? The admiring and submissive disciple does well to grow angry at his master for this assault on his discipleship. The only time in part II that Zarathustra speaks in private to a single disciple, he does so in order to free him from the subservience of discipleship and to initiate him into his own judgment. The lesson continues in the final speech in this chapter.

Zarathustra falls silent, and in the speech after his long silence he is apparently lost in inwardness. But the speech describes the poets' parading for an audience; it is itself a parade for his audience of one disciple that pretends that no audience is present, while giving what the audience has asked for, the reasons for the judgment that poets lie too much. In this lying stance that makes his reasons clear, he speaks of poets in the third person, as if he is the someone who in all seriousness knows what the poets are ignorant of.[64] He accuses lying poets of superficiality. Because they have not thought enough about the deepest matters, their feelings, consequences of their thought, have not descended to the ground of things. The superficiality of poets seems to lie in their not being philosophers, their best reflection having been on sensual passion and boredom, not on the fundamental matters. Further, poets are not pure enough, because they have dared to muddy their shallow waters to give the appearance of depth. Their impurity testifies to a failure of responsibility; those who come hungry to them, as Zarathustra has, receive only a stone[65] or the severed head of an ancient god. Performing for his ignored disciple, the poet Zarathustra ends his indictment of poets with a parable of performance. In their need for a public, poets always preen themselves before spectators, albeit spectators of the most common sort. The charge is the same one that Ion had been tricked into making against practitioners of poetry like himself when, implicitly denying the divine possession he had earlier avowed, he reveals that his art exists for its audience, as he peers out from behind his mask to delight in his success in being what they want him to be and pay him to be.[66] Though said to begin with eyes peering inward, Zarathustra too must be peering outward from behind his mask of poetic possession to read his audience's reaction, not in order to take pleasure in his success, but to ensure that his disciple grow in salutary anger and test for himself his own poet's waters.

Zarathustra is not the only one to tire of the poetic spirit, for that spirit will eventually tire of itself. But the poet's revulsion at his own peacock display does not take the form that Zarathustra's takes. The poetic spirit turns on itself, flagellating itself in shame with a penitent's punishment. It turns to willful deprivation, stripping itself of its poetic finery and laying bare its origins "in the foul rag-and-bone shop of the heart."[67] Out of those who indulged the spirit's inventiveness will grow those who force poverty on it. Doing penance for having been the teachers of mankind who created gods and supermen out of their own need for immortal glory, the poets, like those other penitents of the spirit, modern knowledge-seekers (II. 13), will atone by teaching worship of the stone. Schooled by intellectual probity, they experience embarrassment and distaste at rhetoric and artistic pretension, and come to practice instead a poetics of renunciation that forces their hard conscience on their audience of buffalo.[68]

Unlike the previous speech in this chapter, in which Zarathustra is not differentiated from other poets, this final speech raises him above all poets in both knowing and feeling and apparently separates him from their need for an audience. But his speech is made for an audience, because his task is inseparable from an audience, if separable from an audience of buffalo. As that task now stands, disciples have to be transformed from obedient believers into knowers who judge for themselves Zarathustra's claim to superiority in mind and heart.

Purporting to tire of poets, Zarathustra does not tire of poetry. Poetry will continue to be the medium of his achievements, but it will distinguish itself from previous poetry in a way suggested by Nietzsche himself when he dares to boast in *Ecce Homo* that "a Goethe and a Shakespeare would be unable to breathe even for a moment in this tremendous passion and height," and that "Dante is, compared with Zarathustra, merely a believer" (*EH*, "Books: *Zarathustra*," 6). Embarrassment at Nietzsche's immodesty[69] ruins the irony that invites the reader to judge for himself the possible grounds for such an outrageous claim: the immodest aim of Zarathustra's poetry is to give a new direction to the stream of mankind. Just as Nietzsche's conception of the philosopher as commander and legislator forced him to conclude that Kant and Hegel were mere philosophical laborers, so his conception of the power of poetry to create worlds diminishes the magnitude of Dante, Shakespeare, and Goethe. *Beyond Good and Evil* is silent on Plato when comparing philosophical laborers to commanders, and *Ecce Homo* is silent on Homer when comparing Zarathustra's poetry to that of Dante, Shakespeare, and Goethe. The silences may well provide a measure of the ambition that can move a poet or philosopher, an ambition for "influence, incomparable influence" (*WB* 8).

One of Zarathustra's criticisms of poetry concerns the poet's self-consciousness as performer, or the limitation that comes from the poet's obedience to Horace's stricture "to profit or to please."[70] But the more fundamental criticism—that the poet, through ignorance of the ground of things, turns to the creation of gods and supermen for the unworthy end of inflating himself in the eyes of the more ignorant—is made by a poet who claims also to be a philosopher who has glimpsed the ground of things as will to power. According to the new poet and philosopher, philosophy can no longer sustain its classic, Platonic claim to a higher station than poetry on the basis of the superior ontological status of its objects; neither poetry nor philosophy can in the fundamental sense be mimetic. Mirror turns lamp in Zarathustra (to use the language of Yeats), and the soul in its one highest activity creates and brings the world under a rule.[71] But from Zarathustra's perspective this is an ancient story, repeated again and again. What was once a bold metaphor in the history of thought on poetry—"the poet maketh a new Nature and so maketh himself as it were a new God"[72]—becomes in Zarathustra's account a description not only of what has always moved the highest poetry or philosophy, but also of the labor that falls to the new poet and philosopher, the superman. The superman thus embodies to the highest degree what Coleridge called the "esemplastic power," the power of both the "primary imagination" and the "secondary imagination" as Coleridge understood that distinction in its application to the ordering of perception and the conferring of meaning.[73] Recognizing man's "shaping spirit of Imagination," that "sweet and potent voice" from the soul of man "enveloping the Earth" in "a light, a glory, a fair luminous cloud,"[74] forces Zarathustra beyond mere criticism of the ignorance and vanity of poets, beyond mere appreciation of the world-making power of previous poets, to his own poetry of eternal return.[75]

Nevertheless, Zarathustra is no Romantic. In this chapter, as elsewhere (for example, *GS* 370; *BT*, "Self-Criticism," 7), Nietzsche repudiates the Romantic tradition with its doctrine of a Fall into intellect, its claims to special access to a special reality communicated in a special mode, its view of Art as the Tree of Life and of Science as the Tree of Death, a view that has severed poetry from science, thought it murder to dissect, and prepared a deliverance from science through the Image. The pervasive strength in the twentieth century of that tradition has made it seem that the poet Nietzsche must side with poetry so construed; even if he had a scientific period, it was, one says, supplanted by poetry and prophecy. But for Nietzsche, poetry and science, or music and insight, occupy warring camps only insofar as each is in the grips of a theory. Part IV presents a skirmish in this war, poetry having surrendered to Romantic theory, and science to positivist or mechanical theory. The contemporary spokesmen of poetry and science who there defend their ideologies are overcome by Zarathustra's comprehensive view of a poetry endorsing the "cleanliness and severity" of science and "hardened in the discipline of science" (*BGE* 210, 230), one that grounds and furthers scientific inquiry into beings.

Zarathustra's criticisms of poetry, coupled with his own poetry in solitude, force one to ask about the aims of Zarathustra's poet, Nietzsche. Although Zarathustra has an audience for his criticism of poetry, he dismisses even his animals before he sings his songs of solitude in part III. Still, his poet records those songs for an audience of "all and none," thereby making public Zarathustra's deepest privacy and parading before an audience poetry apparently free from the imperatives of an audience. The very existence of the solitary songs in *Zarathustra* shows that solitary speaking is not the goal of the poet of Zarathustra. The book is the record of a quite singular solitude, for it is Nietzsche's account of the ambitions of his own solitude. Because he has the whole future of mankind on his conscience, those ambitions must be made public even if they are, in a way, not fit to be uttered, or fit only for fable. *Beyond Good and Evil* has it just right, when its prose gives way at the end to poetry that shows Nietzsche's song of solitude to be shared by Zarathustra. Judging by Zarathustra's account of himself, this poet is moved by something other than a love of fame. Although he says at first that he is moved by a love of mankind, by the gift-giving virtue, he comes to understand that virtue only after discovering what moves the wisest men (II. 12; III. 10). Aspiring to the highest form of gift-giving, the most spiritual will to power, he prepares himself in solitude to become the new poet who brings to mankind the world-transforming poetry of eternal return.

In "On Great Events" (II. 18), Zarathustra sails away from the blessed isles on a voyage of discovery that will teach him, in addition to the lesson on revolution that he sailed away to learn, a lesson about his disciples who inhabit the blessed isles of his hope. They fail him a second time, and he is forced a second time to shake his head. The disciples again fail where they might be expected to fail, for Zarathustra's flamboyance and his teaching on conflict and revolution predispose them to see as "great events" mysterious and wondrous spectacles like the one recounted here. But a subdued Zarathustra ignores the spectacle, while quietly and indirectly teaching his disciples the stillness of the truly revolutionary events. Because they scarcely listen to the quiet teaching addressed to another, concentrating instead on the spectacle of a flying Zarathustra descending

PART II   133

to the underworld, they show themselves to be devoted to what Zarathustra
calls a "shadow" of his teaching.

That shadow, which Zarathustra has not yet brought under control,
transforms him into a mythic figure, a miracle-worker believed by the sailors
to have performed the supernatural deeds customarily associated with
great and redemptive heroes. Zarathustra's own talk of flying and of going
under is translated by the credulous sailors into literal deeds of flight and
descent to the underworld. Like the disciple disposed to belief in the previous chapter, the sailors, who hold the mysterious Zarathustra in "love
and awe," believe his words literally and through their faith in the fantastic
transform him into a shadow of himself. But the narrative of the chapter
demythologizes the great events reported by their alleged witnesses; it says
that Zarathustra "took ship" to the island to which the myth says he flew,
the island regarded by the people as a gate to the underworld. He took
ship in order to learn from a teacher of revolution domiciled on the island;
his actual journey and conversation, fabulous enough in themselves, appear
decidedly sober beside the impossible tale told by the sailors, which the
disciples are eager to believe. Reports of Zarathustra's powers continue to
grow among the people in a shadowy way; in subsequent chapters they
will appeal to him for healing miracles as confirmation of the tales they
have been told (II. 20), and in part III other sailors will expect deeds similar
to those these sailors report (III. 2). But in this chapter, the first to call
attention to the public shadow he casts, Zarathustra resolves to bring that
shadow under stricter control, lest it ruin his reputation. As "the wanderer"
who casts the shadow, he can determine where it falls; what appear later
as aspects of his shadow may well be the shadow brought under control,
the image he desires to have among a credulous public in order to serve
his reputation.

The impossible tales of the sailors were made possible by Zarathustra's
unexplained disappearance for five days. He had visited a fire-spewing
island on which he spoke with a fire-spewing monster, a hound of hell, a
revolutionary "overthrow devil," from whom he had wanted to learn, but
whom he ends up instructing on the nature of great events. In the setting
of a great event made mythical, Zarathustra relates his conversation about
great events with the creature of the underworld, the modern revolutionary
who would effect the "greatest" event, the revolutionary overthrow of the
modern state.[76] Zarathustra begins the conversation with a political speech
of inflated rhetoric, announcing that he shares with his interlocutor, the
fomenter of revolution, the view that the skin of the earth is diseased, and
that one of the diseases is mankind. But for him political revolution is itself
a disease of the earth's surface, even though it presents itself as an act of
healing. It was to get to the bottom of this riddle of the revolutionary's
self-presentation that he had journeyed to his lair. He draws him out of
hiding by raking at his teachings, charging that revolutionary rhetoric
speaks of deep changes and of freedom, while being merely superficial

and bound to an ideology. According to his own view of historical change, the world turns "not around the inventors of new noise, but around the inventors of new values," for "the greatest thoughts are the greatest events" (*BGE* 285). Revolutionary rhetoric serves only to support a crumbling order of church and state, the modern state and its revolutionary opponent feeding one another's fictions, each needing the other to certify its own necessity and desirability.[77]

The first words that Zarathustra's attack draw from the revolutionary express an ignorant scorn: "Church, what's that?", or in a more contemporary translation: "How many divisions does the Pope command?" Zarathustra counters the scorn by charging that the revolutionary is himself a religious zealot and should recognize in the church an image of himself. Nor does Zarathustra distinguish between the church and the modern state in this respect. All three—church, state, and revolutionary—believe that they hold conflicting views about the belly of things; but all three belong to the same camp as sects of the same religion, and each is possessed by the passion of sectarians against the heretics who stand nearest to them.[78] As a sectarian of the democratic religion, the only religion viable in the political ecclesiology of the modern world, the socialist or communist revolutionary sees himself as the fundamental opponent of the liberal state, with the church no longer relevant. When Zarathustra repeats the modern state's rhetoric claiming that it is the most important thing on earth, the revolutionary can no longer contain himself and almost chokes on his envy, thereby fulfilling the mission for which Zarathustra had set sail by confirming his suspicion that modern revolutionary fervor springs from a poisonous envy. In a setting that distinguishes the earth's surface from its underworld in political terms, one in which conventional surface and revolutionary underworld each sees the other as diseased and itself as pure, Zarathustra shares only the judgment of each that the other is diseased, while maintaining that both belong to the surface. But despite the discredit visited upon revolutionaries by their modern models, there exists a fire-hound worthy of respect, for whom the heart of the earth is gold, even if its surface is diseased: the true revolutionary or superman who brings a new teaching around which the world will turn anew.[79]

The teaching on great events addressed to the plotter of revolution is lost on the disciples; they scarcely listened, so anxious were they to tell Zarathustra of the miraculous journey to the underworld reported by the sailors. While he has harrowed the underworld as befits a hero, he renounces their pious interpretation of his journey. He says that they must have seen his shadow and draws a distinction between "the wanderer and his shadow," purposing to keep his shadow under stricter control. But to control the shadow he casts, he will have to control his wanderings or give an account of them that will be fitting for credulous disciples. Still, the disciples are hardly to be blamed for their belief in a Zarathustra capable of miraculous deeds that seem like great events. In particular, they can be forgiven their belief that he is an "overthrow devil," for this is precisely how he thought of himself on his return to them at the beginning of part II and how he has presented himself since then. The chapter closes with Zarathustra's quiet reflection on the story told him by his disciples. He wonders what to make of it, particularly of what the ghost cried: "It is time! It is high time!" In asking *"For what* is it—high time?" Zarathustra seems to be asking about the event that matters most, the coming of the superman. He learns from his voyage to the island and from the report of miracle it engenders, that it is high time for what he had thought was still a long way off. His storming for the sake of disciples for the sake of the superman who is still a long way off begins to appear fruitless, because the disciples show themselves capable only of crude belief in mysterious deeds and untested belief in his words, even when they are unwelcome words (II. 17). If disciples called into being by a revolutionary teacher cannot be the way to the superman, then it is high time that another way be found, the way that will be shown through the narrative of the rest of part II and of part III. "The stillest hour," referred to in the conversation with the teacher of the decisive revolutionary hour, returns personified at the end of part II in order to teach him that his own stillest hour, his own greatest event, lies ahead of him. Zarathustra will learn that the ghost's words ("It is high time!") were the first of three signs intended to teach him to renew his solitude through a break with his disciples and to effect in himself what he had long thought could be effected only through them (III. 3).

"The Soothsayer" (II. 19) is linked to the previous two chapters by the third failure of the disciples, this time of the disciple whom Zarathustra loved most, and by the third shaking of Zarathustra's head. The beloved disciple fails where he could be expected to fail; he fails because he too, in love and awe of Zarathustra, is only a believer who cannot permit himself to think that his master could suffer the terror he describes in his nightmare. Nevertheless, the nightmare is Zarathustra's own, and it provides him with insight into mankind's imprisonment without at the same time providing insight into the means of redemption. Only the next chapter, "On Redemption," will interpret the nightmare and intimate the means of redemption.

At the beginning of this chapter, without introduction or warning, a Soothsayer utters a prophecy. For only the third time in the book a teaching contrary to Zarathustra's is allowed to speak for itself, but now Zarathustra has no self-assured joke as an answer, as he did the first time, when the old teacher of virtue spoke (I. 2). Instead, the Soothsayer's prophecy transforms him and causes him to grieve for his teaching, as he did when he heard Life's teaching in "The Dancing Song" (II. 10). The prophecy announces both a teaching—"all is empty, all is the same, all has been"[80]—and a closely related faith—that all action is pointless. The imagery of this teaching and faith depicts a drought that sears a parched earth, drying up even the final hope of drowning for the despairing one condemned to live on. The prophecy of the Soothsayer is that this despairing teaching and this faith without hope will descend on mankind as a great sadness. In his response Zarathustra acknowledges immediately the truth of the prophecy but does not assent to the despairing teaching itself. He is "transformed" by the prophecy because he knows it to be true; mankind is now facing the "long twilight" of nihilism. This is the first appearance of a teaching now to become prominent. Although the teaching on nihilism is discovered in the Soothsayer's words, it is deepened by the nightmare caused by those words, as well as by later observations on the present age by Zarathustra himself, now become a seer (III. 5–8). Instructed by the Soothsayer, Zarathustra comes to understand what nihilism will mean for the history of mankind and for his own teaching. This understanding causes a shift away from the hopeful expectations indulged until now by the progressive Zarathustra, the maker of disciples better than himself. Here, in the midst of the failures of his disciples, the prophecy of the long twilight turns him despondent like those described in the prophecy; he too begins to despair of his harvest.

His only words about the Soothsayer's speech concern his fears for his own teaching. How can his light be preserved in the darkness he now knows to be coming? More specifically, how can his teaching survive, if entrusted to disciples to carry it further? Zarathustra knows that the Schopenhauerian pessimism of the Soothsayer is false, for "the heart of the earth is of gold," but insistence on such a teaching can carry no weight if the Soothsayer's prophecy is true. What transforms him and causes his grief, his three-day fast, and his nightmare is this single matter: how to preserve his teaching from extinction in the coming age of nihilism. The fate of his teaching is the most serious matter, because it alone gives meaning to the earth. But while his nightmare seems at first simply to confirm the necessity of despair, it turns out to be a kind of gift, a revelation into the cause of despair, including the despair of the Soothsayer, for it provides the wakened Zarathustra with the insight that he has heretofore lacked regarding what mankind—himself included—needs to be redeemed from, revenge on the past. Neither Zarathustra nor his beloved disciple know the meaning of the nightmare when he first tells it, but the meaning is said to be imprisoned within the nightmare itself. By the time the chapter closes, Zarathustra has grasped everything that has happened, and when, in the following chapter, he releases the meaning of the nightmare, he begins to release the imprisoned dreamer himself. He thereby shows how the deficiency of his teaching may be surmounted, how the provisional teaching of a herald can be transformed into the definitive teaching. If the problem is the past, the solution cannot be the future: the nightmare opens Zarathustra's eyes to the enigma of eternal return.

The nightmare is set in melancholy but is neither the cause of the melancholy nor its solution. The melancholy is caused by Zarathustra's fear for his teaching, and its solution will be intimated only in the next chapter. His account of his nightmare is divided into two parts: the first describes the situation of the dreamer, the second the event that led to his awakening. The dreamer is the life-renouncing watchman of the night in the lonely mountain castle of death. Accompanied by darkness, loneliness, and silence, he watches over the glass coffins of death, out of which gaze at him that in which life has been overcome. But he possesses the rustiest of all keys for the creakiest of all gates. The event that led to his awakening began with three echoing strokes on the gate. But he is unable to open the gate, for this time his keys do not work. When the great wind tears the gate open, it throws up a black coffin whose contents lead to his awakening, but not to his illumination, for it is his own cry of terror that awakens him.

Zarathustra would seem to be the dreamer, for he uses "I" throughout, but the beloved disciple "quickly" advances the interpretation that the dreamer who cries in terror symbolizes Zarathustra's enemies. For the beloved disciple, Zarathustra has to be the wind that opens locked doors for those imprisoned, just as he is the black coffin with its grimaces and laughters. But this beautiful speech of gratitude and encouragement is refused by Zarathustra, for he knows that he is the dreamer. Still, though the beloved disciple is wrong, he has good grounds for his interpretation, for the Zarathustra of that interpretation is true to what Zarathustra has presented himself as being. The beloved disciple's spirited rejection of the literal interpretation shows that this best of disciples has in love and awe faithfully followed what Zarathustra the herald has said of himself. "Your life interprets to us this dream," says the beloved disciple, and he proceeds to show how Zarathustra's life as he himself has presented it legitimates the interpretation that he is the liberating wind and the mocking laughter. Furthermore, this interpretation aims to bring comfort to Zarathustra on the essential point, for the disciple promises that his teaching will not perish in the long twilight ahead because he and his fellow disciples will remain loyal to it. The beloved disciple's interpretation is praiseworthy in being true to the Zarathustra whose disciple he is, the teacher of his own awakening. But he is not praised for it because, in a way that he could not have suspected, the one who has awakened him has come to see that he has himself not yet awakened from the essential nightmare.

Zarathustra offers no interpretation of the nightmare beyond his refusal of the beloved disciple's interpretation. But the chapter immediately following, "On Redemption," supplies the clues for it deals with redemption from the nightmare that has imprisoned mankind hitherto, from which no one has ever been redeemed, and from which it seems no one ever could be redeemed. These clues, which are themselves opaque at first, unlock Zarathustra's nightmare, for they show mankind to be imprisoned by what is itself entombed: the past, in glass coffins out of which peer, relentless and unwillable, the lifeless givens of "it was." The details of man's imprisonment belong to the next chapter; to release the imprisoned meaning of the nightmare, it is enough to know that it is the past that imprisons.[81]

In the first part of the dream, Zarathustra is waiting and watching, as befits a herald. Having given up on all the living, he waits among the coffins in which life has been overcome. It is not enough to see this simply as a setting of death or of his death, for the next chapter interprets "death's victory" and "life overcome" in reference to the whole of the past as dead and gone. What gazes lifelessly out at him from glass coffins is the whole of the past, passed out of life into dusty eternities, visible but inaccessible, as if under glass. Having given up on all that is present, with the past beyond his reach, he waits among the tombs for his redemption out of the future.

Why is the event that awakens the dreamer more terrifying than the situation in which he finds himself? The answer must be that the first part of the dream does not preclude hope, for the watchman does possess keys, albeit the rustiest of keys to the creakiest of gates, presumably the keys and gate most seldom used. If the dreamer is imprisoned in the unwillable past, the keys would seem to unlock the gate to the future, to his hope of the coming superman. The dreamer says that the gate has been opened, and although there was terror in opening the door to this future, there was even more terror in the deathly silence that followed its closing, the silence in which the dreamer waits, not even knowing if time is passing, if the future is drawing near. In this situation with its keys and gate, hope is not precluded, and when the three echoing strokes evoke from the despondent, but not despairing, watchman the cry, "Who is carrying his ashes to the mountains?", the question recalls the two previous uses of that phrase, both in relation to Zarathustra, in contexts that suggest it to be the symbol of his will to regeneration (Prologue 1; I. 3). But here the phrase is used of another and suggests the hope of the watching and waiting herald that redemption from the past is possible through one who is yet to come, one for whom it is high time.[82] But while the dreamer possesses keys that he thought opened this gate, and while he now exerts the greatest effort, he cannot open the gate to the hope that knocks. When the gate is opened by a force other than his own, what appears is itself a coffin, out of which laughter spills. The laughter does not stem from joy as the beloved disciple would like to believe, but from mockery directed at one who had foolishly hoped for a redeeming future. In the mocking laughter that breaks forth from "a thousand grimaces of children, angels, owls, fools and butterflies big as children," the dreamer experiences the terror of extinguished hope.[83] Whereas Zarathustra had sought to be delivered from the past by the future, it is the past itself that appears through the gate to the future, a black coffin of the dead and gone that mocks him in its pastness, in its inaccessibility to will. In coming out of the future, the black coffin shows the bondage of every future to its past: imprisonment on the high mountain points to the fatedness of present and future; temporality as fate has been the nightmare of the most ascendant human spirits. The Soothsayer's prophecy is confirmed directly in the nightmare, for the future from whence his deliverance was to come throws up before Zarathustra only more of the same, another coffin, but one filled with mocking laughter for the one who dreams of a redemptive future. The dreamer who had hoped that someone would come to deliver him and mankind, some superman made to appear through doors opened by his own teaching, now has his hopes dashed by the appearance out of the future of a mocking laughter that binds it to the unredeemed past.

The dream is a despairing dream offering no escape to the dreamer. It shows Zarathustra that if his teaching is only the call to a superhuman effort to prepare for the future superman, which is what it has been until now, it will perish in the coming nihilism. And yet the dream is also a revelation, for it reveals to Zarathustra not only the grounds of his own despair, but the grounds for the despairing judgment made by all the wisest, that life is no good. In the next chapter Zarathustra interprets his dream in a way that his beloved disciple cannot. The lonely mountain castle of death appears as the prison of time, and man as "a spectator on the past" whose "loneliest melancholy" is that he cannot "break time and time's desire," which turns all futures into irretrievable pasts, into lifeless forms peering out of glass coffins. The nightmare of nihilism reveals mankind's fundamental imprisonment; but the nightmare is a gift, for it allows the one who suffers it a glimpse of the possibility of redemption.

Although "The Soothsayer" gives grounds for despair, it ends with Zarathustra looking to a new possibility. The nature of that possibility is left obscure, just as it was at the end of the previous chapter, where it was expressed only in the question, "For what is it high time?" But the way to the new possibility is at least suggested, for it is precisely his beloved disciple's misinterpretation of his nightmare that leads Zarathustra to understand it. After that disciple spoke, the other disciples crowded around, wanting to persuade him out of his sadness. But like one returned from a long voyage, he looked at them and did not recognize them; perhaps now he sees them as they are, and not as he had wanted them to be. When the disciples raise him up and set him on his feet, he suddenly grasps everything that has happened and can appear again to them as he has until now appeared to them; but they can never again appear to him in the way that they have until now appeared, for he knows that he cannot entrust his teachings to believing disciples. At the end of "The Soothsayer," he addresses them as "my disciples" for the only time in part II—after they have failed him three times. He shakes his head a third and final time, having seen the essential limitation of all his disciples. But his last words in this chapter are for the Soothsayer, and they hint at what he has seen to be necessary, for it is high time that an ideal opposite to a nihilistic pessimism be discerned more precisely, and that the earth be redeemed from a teaching that has transformed it into a desert under an evil moon.

He returns to the Soothsayer's image of a parched earth and promises him a sea in which he can drown. That "sea" is the coming teaching of eternal return, the teaching that redeems mankind from its nightmare, for when the Soothsayer's teaching next appears, embodied in the Dwarf, it is banished by the thought of eternal return (III. 2). In part III, after his redemption, Zarathustra will once again speak of the Soothsayer's prophecy, but then as overcome (III. 13). If the Soothsayer can still reappear in part IV to repeat his prophecy, it will not be an exact repetition, for Zarathustra will be secure against it. In its new form, it prophesies that the victory which Zarathustra has won is beyond even the most superior men, and that the teaching will perish after all because no one but Zarathustra is capable of maintaining it (IV. 2).

WISDOM DISMAYED (CHAPTER 20)

"On Redemption" (II. 20) is the most astonishing of all the chapters of *Thus Spoke Zarathustra*. Under the great stress of his nightmare and what it has disclosed to him, Zarathustra breaches an imperfectly learned reticence to reveal what it is that mankind needs to be redeemed from. But that revelation shows that even he is not yet redeemed, and that the requirements of redemption seem to be beyond man's capabilities. "On Redemption" releases the meaning of Zarathustra's nightmare and shows it to be mankind's nightmare, one from which no man has yet awakened, but from which Zarathustra will set himself the task of awakening. The revelation of this chapter occurs because Zarathustra experiences "dismay": he is appalled or paralyzed with fear at the feeling of being undone. Beginning with an address to a crowd and passing to an address to the disciples, the chapter reaches its climax with Zarathustra speaking only to himself. The scorned hunchback is acute enough to notice what the disciples in their love and awe have probably still not noticed, that Zarathustra speaks one way to the people, another way to his disciples, and yet another way to himself. What he says to himself concerns the fate of mankind as he has now come to understand it. While what he says to the people and to his disciples is aphoristic and laconic, what he says to himself is terse to the point of being oracular. Nevertheless, its terseness encapsulates an amplitude that covers the whole history of mankind and mankind's thought. What Zarathustra addresses to himself equals in range what he had addressed to the wisest in his discovery that philosophy is will to power. But in this chapter on wisdom, he completes what he had addressed exclusively to the wisest by revealing the characteristic shared by all wisdoms hitherto: as the highest form of life, as the most spiritual will to power, wisdom has been in the service of revenge. Containing the final mention of will to power in the book, this chapter elicits, as in a premonition and for the first time, the thought for which the book exists, eternal return, the thought with which the most spiritual will to power overcomes revenge and achieves redemption.

The chapter announces its importance by opening with Zarathustra crossing the great bridge. In his crossing he is surrounded by a crowd of cripples, whose representative, the hunchback, offers him a special temptation that reveals his growing reputation among the people as a mysterious worker of miracles, one who could perhaps be the means of their redemption by removing their burdens. The people have learned from him, but they can be persuaded to believe in him fully only through healing miracles.[84] Given by invitation the opportunity to win the people and fulfill the aim that first brought him down the mountain, Zarathustra refuses them as before they had refused him. He refuses thereby the way of the miracle-worker, the temptation that he had told his disciples would eventually come to those who aimed above the people (I. 11). The temptation comes from the devil, and to surrender to his request for miracles would destroy the redeemer.

Speaking to the hunchback and the crowd of cripples, Zarathustra practices his teaching on pity. He sees his apparent hardness of heart as just and as having been learned from them. His justice is a refusal to harm the cripples by removing the diseases that give them their sense of worth. He thereby avoids the revenge that the healed would vent on the one who deprived them of their worth. But if he has learned from the cripples that they need their crippledness, his speech will later show that he has learned something else: that in some undisclosed way the crippled are needed by the one who wills to be whole. For now, he turns from those who are defective in their bodies to those thought not defective, those who are esteemed geniuses by the people, but they too appear to him as cripples, "inverse cripples," whose single exaggerated faculty has caused the atrophy of all other faculties. In this speech to the crowd and the later speech to his disciples, Zarathustra emphasizes the acuteness of his own faculty of sight; what his eyes have seen, no others have ever seen; still, the hypertrophy of his eye has not cost him the atrophy of his other senses.

Having turned away the people and the great among them, he turns to his disciples, but in deep dismay.[85] Dismay is the uncharacteristic mood of this most important of speeches, dismay, the feeling of being deprived of moral courage in the prospect of peril. In the face not of cripples, but of a universal crippledness, Zarathustra loses the customary courage of his contempt and gives voice to the peril glimpsed in his dark nightmare. Beginning as an address to his disciples, his great speech of dismay grows increasingly private under the downward spiral of its own insight until it finally recounts his private vision of a universal fall and a redemption that seemingly could never be enacted. That private vision, briefly glimpsed, ends abruptly. When he catches himself in the midst of this most rash of his public speeches, he falls prey suddenly to terror, for he has spoken his innermost dismay to his disciples, the friends before whom he has followed his own counsel on friendship and dressed himself better than he is in order to inspire their surpassing of his image (I. 14).

He begins with a description of how he has seen mankind until now, as "fragments and limbs of men," as "dreadful accidents." Cursed with this ability to see, he is unable to bear the present and the past; he would not know how to live at all were he not also a "seer" of what is to come. On the bridge with cripples he is more than a seer, he is

> a willer, a creator, a future himself and a bridge to the future—and, alas, also still like a cripple on this bridge.

All but the last of these characteristics refer to the essential matter of the future. This visionary, willful, creative bridge to the future had once before referred to himself as a cripple (II. 6), but as one long since healed. Now his actual crippledness has been made clear to him by his nightmare. But if he is a cripple to himself, what can he be to his disciples? He asks for them the question that they have often asked for themselves, "Who is Zarathustra to us?",[86] and answers, as they do, with questions. The first questions describe four pairs of alternatives:

> Is he a promiser? Or a fulfiller? A conqueror? Or an inheritor? A harvest? Or a ploughshare? A physician? Or a convalescent?

Where does he stand in the historic process of redemption that he has himself described—near the beginning as its herald or at the culmination as its heir? Before these questions can begin to be answered, he asks a different set of questions, again in a series of alternatives, this time involving qualities that question his previous claims about himself:

> Is he a poet? Or one who is truthful? A liberator? Or one who binds? A good man? Or an evil man?

Of the possibilities raised, he affirms only that he is a poet, one whose poetry seeks to unify what is now only fragment, riddle, and dreadful accident—a reaffirmation of his opening speech to the people (Prologue 3) and his closing speech to his disciples (I. 22, §2), in which, against the background of a heretofore accidental evolution, his poetry challenged mankind to the creative acts that master chance and create the superman. Up to this point, his questions can be answered in a way that is consistent with what he has so far presented as his task, but now his questioning takes him further. His first use of the word *redeemer* in the chapter on redemption pictures him as able to bear being human only because to be human is to be the redeemer of accidents or chance, but he now defines precisely what the accident or chance is from which mankind must redeem itself:

> To redeem the past and to transform all "it was" into "thus I will it"— that alone should I call redemption.

This new definition of redemption through willing the past carries him back to the first speech that he made upon returning to his disciples (II. 2), in which he named will "the liberator." Now, however, he adds the new

and decisive point taught him by his nightmare: "The will is still a prisoner."
The teacher of redemption through the will now sees the will as "powerless"
against "it was," the lonely mountain spectator of the coffins of "it was."
The will is "powerless against that which has been done," against accident
that has become necessity. Its very nature is thwarted by the sheer givenness and pastness of the past, of which it is not just the spectator, but
the "angry spectator" who sees the past as in glass coffins unreachable by
the will. In his earlier accounts of the will's hatred of necessity, Zarathustra
had taught that all gods and ideas of permanence must be destroyed because they imprisoned the creative will within the unwillable (II. 2), but
now he has discovered a new, less tractable prison enclosing will's power.

> The will cannot will backwards; that it cannot break time and time's de-
> sire—that is the will's loneliest melancholy.

Time, personified as desiring, imprisons the will. "Time's desire" is its
inexorable movement from future possibility through present actuality to
past necessity, where it enters glass coffins, visible but immutable. The
creative will is situated in time's passage yet inexorably opposed to it, because the creative will is directed forward into possibility, against the
movement of time into past necessity. To break the prison of time's desire
and practice the mastery to which it is impelled, the creative will would
have to learn either to break time's desire or to will backward. But Zarathustra's nightmare suggests something else about time's desire: the glass
coffins do not simply contain what is dead and gone, for they break open
into the present with mocking laughter. Every present is shaped by its
past; the unwillable, unalterable past imprisons present and future to its
dispensations. What comes at us out of the future is already fated, for no
present begins anew but is always already situated as just this moment
in just this train of moments. The future had once made the past and
present bearable for Zarathustra, but now it is not enough. Not just those
from whom he has turned away in dismay are cripples; the creative will
itself is crippled. Zarathustra's dismay arises from the discovery that there
is after all something that encompasses man within an unwillable given.
It is not "the world" or "God" that limits him, but "time's desire," "time
and its 'it was.' " Like all limits encountered by the creative will, it is a
curse, for it thwarts what the will to power is in its most spiritual form.

According to this speech of dismay, it is not mortality as such, the
becoming that ends in death, that poisons the creative will's response to
time's passage, but the becoming that is imprisoned in the unchangeable.
From this point onward, the speech recounts the reaction of the creative
will to its discovery of its imprisonment, the encounter of the victory-loving
spirit with the final Asia that the god says is not its to conquer. It thus
becomes clear that what Zarathustra has experienced in his nightmare,
the creative wills of the best and most powerful of men have also experienced. In explaining the image of prison and prisoner from the nightmare,

this speech makes clear that the will that rages in its prison is the most unbridled will, the most spiritual will to power of the wisest. The nightmare is the shared experience of those of the highest will: moved by the most unrestrained will to power, they experience the most intolerable limit to their will in time's passage. Zarathustra does not speak of the imprisonment felt by all men, but only that felt by the teachers of men; he speaks not about the prisoners in the cave, but about those who have been released from the cave and have climbed upward only to discover on the lonely mountain top an imprisonment more onerous still. Possessed by the cruel compulsions of the victory-loving spirit, they have stood within their fatedness and known themselves accursed. Knowing themselves not to be good enough, while knowing themselves to be the best of men, they have of necessity drawn the conclusion that life is no good and have taken their revenge. Mankind has borne the sorrows of the accursedness of the best.

The creative will grows mad in its prison of unbreakable time, but it grows creatively mad, inventing mad forms of redemption from its prison. That the past is not recoverable and alterable, that it cannot roll away the stone of "it was," is the creative will's "repressed fury." But the creative will forces itself to believe that it has rolled away the stone through its schemes of redemption. Here, Zarathustra's teaching on revenge takes its most comprehensive form as he reports cryptically that the interpretations of the human condition that have prevailed until now all stem from revenge, the creative will gone mad in its prison of time. The teachings that have housed mankind have turned the earth on which he dwells into a prison or a cave. The creative will that is the liberator turned to punishing, for when the will is not free to will completely, it wills its own destruction as the appearance of redemption. Or, as Nietzsche said later, in the formula that expresses this claim perfectly, "The will would rather will nothingness than not will" (*GM* III. 1, 28).[87]

When Zarathustra announced to the teachers of equality that their will to equality was a desire for revenge (II. 7) and to the wisest that their wisdom was a will to power (II. 12), he had not brought revenge and will to power together in a way that united them as mutually grounding all interpretations of life hitherto. But the gaze into the most life-denying way of thinking afforded by his nightmare makes clear that the stream of mankind has been directed by the will to power as revenge, and he can now give a precise and comprehensive definition of revenge introduced with the emphatic repetition of a discovery:

> This, yes this alone is *revenge* itself: the will's ill will against time and its "it was."

Will turned sick with revenge, ill will, directs itself not simply against passage, but against passage insofar as it fixes what has passed into the forever past, sealed in the glass coffins of Zarathustra's nightmare. The will's ill will is directed originally, but only originally, against the "it was" that it

cannot control. Revenge against the past defines the will's manner of relating to what is given, to its situatedness in time; but revenge expands its
range beyond the "it was" and takes revenge on the temporal as such,
because the unreachable, unwillable past fates present and future.[88] In
these curt stanzas of "On Redemption," in which he defines revenge and
describes how it gains "spirit," Nietzsche gives his account of the universal
fall. All men are defective, mankind is a disease, because the creative will,
which is the essence of man in the experience of the highest men, fell sick
to revenge. The creative will has found that the world is not lovable because
the creative will is not free; raging against its condition, it has invented
redemptions for itself that are curses on its condition and on mankind.
The acquisition of spirit by the passion for revenge has been the great
event in the history of man's self-interpretation, for it has interpreted to
him the accursedness of his being. Spirit is "the life which cuts into life"
(II. 8), and while the famous wise had to be told what spirit is, the wisest
do not, for they too have experienced it. In the wisdom of the wisest, in
those who have experienced the tragedy of their own creative will or spirit
of victory as intolerably thwarted by the unalterable, revenge has turned
spiritual. Sublimated into image and concept revenge has punished intolerable life and placed a curse on all human things.

> The spirit of revenge, my friends, that was till now the subject of man's
> best reflection; and where suffering was, there should punishment always be.

The best reflection of poets until now has concerned mere sensual passion
and boredom (II. 17), but the best reflection simply, that of the most spirited
men, concerns the nature of things and has been undertaken in the spirit
of revenge.[89] This well-cultivated and implacable spirit of revenge masked
itself behind the name "punishment" and took it upon itself to mete out
punishment wherever it suffered. But because the creative will always suffered, and suffered in its very being, the spirit of revenge had to punish
life itself, and did so with teachings that proclaimed life to be a punishment.
In the dismay and revenge that could not roll away the stone of "it was,"
"cloud upon cloud rolled over the spirit." Zarathustra's speech thus turns
to specific "preachings of madness," but the scope of the indictment remains universal, for while these preachings are all forms of justice, they
provide the ground for an understanding of the order of things. In Heidegger's language, they show how revenge is understood metaphysically
in Nietzsche's thought as the disposition that determines man's stance
toward things as a whole. Revenge, as the ground of justice hitherto,
grounds all teachings on the whole.

Each of the four forms of justice described by Zarathustra is deprived
of its characteristic way of redemption in his account, for each is seen
only as revenge against life as it is. In calling itself "punishment" and undertaking acts of justice, revenge feigns a good conscience by means of a
lie, a lie that not only interprets the suffering of the creative will but creates
the punishment under which mankind has been obliged to live. A long,

unidentified history of revenge precedes the madness contained in the poetic articulateness of the first preaching of madness characterized by Zarathustra:

> Everything perishes, therefore everything deserves to perish.
> And this is itself justice, that law of time that it must devour its children.

This mad justice is most reminiscent of the justice of ancient Kronos, but it could be taken to be characteristic of tribal societies generally, the justice of the ancestral way which demands that the children be consumed by the forefathers or exist in order to tend the forefathers.[90] Seen in this way, the first preaching of madness is the introduction to a comprehensive series on the forms of justice that recounts the experience of Western man, moving from Greek philosophy and Christianity to the modern, or the decayed modern of Schopenhauer.[91] The second preaching of madness is a philosophical formulation that echoes the philosopher Anaximander in teaching that things are ordered morally according to right and punishment; existence itself is a punishment redeemed by annihilation. The third preaching of madness intensifies this order of punishment in the manner of Christianity by making punishment eternal in a logical manner.[92] The fourth preaching of madness, the Soothsayer's doctrine, promises redemption through the will becoming not will, a redemption that is annihilation when existence is simply will.[93] At the end of his list, Zarathustra says to his friends that he led them away from such madness when he taught that "the will is a creator." But the final stanzas confirm that, while he knows what redemption would be and announces it in a terse formula, not even in his own teaching has the creative will achieved redemption from revenge.

When Zarathustra's speech of dismay turns finally to the possibility of genuine redemption, he treats it even more cryptically than he had treated revenge, for his speech now turns completely inward, and being addressed to himself, has no need to explain or persuade. Nevertheless, the character of redemption becomes clear, both from the description of revenge and the brief formula for redemption:

> All "it was" is a fragment, a riddle, a dreadful accident—until the creative will says to it "But thus I willed it!"
> —Until the creative will says to it "But thus I will it! Thus shall I will it!"

The creative will must respond differently to its imprisonment than it has hitherto; mankind is to be redeemed from the teachings of the wisest of all ages by an altogether novel sense of its temporal condition, arising from a creative will that wills "it was" in past, present, and future tenses. Until the creative will speaks this way, the accidental past remains an unwillable necessity that fates it to revenge. The creative will has never yet spoken a complete affirmation of time and the accidents of time, the temporal beings, including the limbs and fragments of men; yet this affirmation of the totality of beings as they are—historical beings, beings fated by unalterable time to be what they are—this alone would unharness the will from the madness of revenge.

Zarathustra's speech ends in a series of questions pointing to what is necessary. Embedded in the questions is a single declarative utterance stating the fundamental matter, for it identifies the creative will, the agent of redemption, with the will to power.

> And who taught [the will] reconciliation with time, and something higher than all reconciliation is?
>
> Higher than all reconciliation must that will will that is the will to power —: but how shall that happen? Who has taught it also to will backwards?

Zarathustra's questions just before he names will to power speak of two dispositions that differ from revenge: reconciliation with time and something higher than all reconciliation. Reconciliation, the ending of hostility and opposition between the will and time's desire, would mark the termination of man's historic revenge against time in an acceptance of the necessity of "it was." But how can such a reconciliation be accomplished when the past is experienced as a prison by the creative will to power? Zarathustra's answer lies in what he says about will to power when he names it for the final time in the book. Although reconciliation and "something higher" are both necessary if revenge is to be overcome, it is that "something higher" that the will to power must learn to will if there is to be redemption. The highest will does not will mere reconciliation, however desirable that may be in the face of the long history of revenge. The nameless "something higher," that "something higher" so ostentatiously not named, goes far beyond any reconciliation with the unalterable past. The longed-for harmony of will and time's desire, the longed-for redemption from the curse placed on temporal things by the madness of revenge, comes to light as possible for the highest, creative will in one way only. It must learn to say to the past that peers out of the glass coffins of the dead and gone, the past of fragment and accident that is the human past and that has brought mankind to this moment: "But thus I willed it!"

The conclusion implied, but not named, in Zarathustra's formulation of the problem of redemption is that the will to power that wills the past, and hence wills what is higher than all reconciliation, wills eternal return. The final naming of "will to power" is the first intimation of eternal return, not because the latter supersedes the former, but because eternal return arises out of will to power as its consequence. The will to power as redeemer overcomes and replaces the will to power as revenge when it wills the eternal return of beings as they are. Redemption comes not through the abandonment of will to power, but through an enactment of the most spiritual will to power. As the agent of redemption, the will to power learns the most affirmative willing of itself and all that is and has been, an "unbounded Yes to everything that was and is."[94] The creative will is not merely reconciled to the unalterable past, it does not simply love fate or love the fated; it "says Yes to the point of justifying, of redeeming even all of the past" (*EH*, "Books: *Zarathustra*," 8).[95] It is the complementary will of the "complementary man in whom the rest of existence is justified" (*BGE* 207). It expresses not revenge but gratitude, and in its gratitude gives its highest gift to the whole of which it is a fated fragment: "But thus I willed it!" This is the glimpse of the opposite ideal afforded the one who has gazed into world-denying pessimism to its nightmarish bottom and thereby discovered its grounds. This glimpse finally makes clear the relationship between the Soothsayer's prophecy, Zarathustra's nightmare, and the possibility of redemption. The prophecy of the coming nihilism causes Zarathustra's nightmare, but that nightmare is a much more comprehensive insight into the negating will, the final episode of which is the Soothsayer's teaching, but which includes the reckless vengeance wreaked by mankind's teachers until now. Zarathustra's vision of redemption is not simply an antidote to the prophesied nihilism, but to the whole history of mankind's curse on nature and natural beings. The ideal glimpsed is not yet open to articulation, however, for it is an ideal that Zarathustra is not yet able to will. Past and present still lie under the curse of mad teachings, and the new ideal seems like an "Impossibility." The work of part III will consist in articulating the new ideal and learning how to will it.[96]

Zarathustra's teaching gradually comes to light as a comprehensive teaching on being and time, one that judges all previous teachings on being and time to have been marked by revenge or by a poisoned refusal of temporal beings as they are. When Zarathustra arrives at these cumulative insights into being and time and the teachings of the wisest of all ages, his own task at last becomes clear as the task that he has heretofore assigned to the superman, that of undoing the curse of the hitherto wisest and redeeming mankind from its fall into revenge at the way things are. It is now clear how the stream of mankind is to be redirected, how the new house of becoming is to be built. Being as will to power and time as perpetual passage must be willed by the creative will; the immutable mutability of beings, their unalterable way, is affirmed by the most spiritual will to power when it wills their eternal return.

"That man be redeemed from revenge" (II. 7) is the essential matter, and it is still a future matter at the end of "On Redemption." But the chapter shows that redemption cannot come through liberation from the will or liberation from time as passage, for neither the will nor time as passage can be suspended by man. Redemption is liberation from revenge which gained spirit and preached the madness that man is blameable and punishable for his very nature and the madness that man can overcome his blameable nature either by liberation from time or by liberation from the will. The only redemption from revenge is for the creative will to see the extent to which the character of the world is unalterable and to will the eternal return of beings as they unalterably but accidentally are. Eternal return is the essential teaching after "On Redemption" has revealed the nature of Zarathustra's nightmare, or the nightmare of the wisest that has cursed all mankind until now. Redemption from revenge is achievable only by a will that would not have the earth be other than it is, other than what its accidental history has made it, a will that speaks its redeeming word to the temporal beings: Be the fleeting beings that you are.

The teaching of eternal return thus first comes to light as the teaching which solves the problem of revenge against the unwillable past, where that problem and no other is the cause of the teachings of madness which have cursed mankind hitherto. Although not all men feel this hatred of life, all have been forced to discover themselves within teachings that presuppose it. Cursed by its teachers, malleable mankind has been obliged to stream forward holding high the ark of their mad teachings. Eternal return comes to light in the discovery of its necessity as the teaching symptomatic of the love of life, for it neither repents of the past nor rejects it nor takes revenge on it; rather, it rejoices in the whole of the past and wills it just as it is. In the traditional language of philosophy, the connection between will to power and eternal return is the connection between fact and value. Discovery of the fundamental fact prepares the way for the positing of the highest value; discovery of the fundamental fact makes possible a form of human life, evaluating life, that aligns itself with life as a whole. Eternal return as the most comprehensive affirmation of life grounded in the insight into life as will to power provides the measure for "purely naturalistic values" (KGW VIII 9 [8] = WP 462) that meet an "objective value standard" (KGW VIII 10 [137] = WP 707).[97]

"On Redemption" shows that the teaching of eternal return is subsequent to, and dependent on, the discovery of will to power, Nietzsche's fundamental discovery. As the only chapter to show this essential link, it is the pivotal chapter, the turning point of the whole book. It sets in motion the process that culminates in redemption in "The Convalescent" (III. 13). Nietzsche does not repeat the formula for redemption in that chapter, but there the most spiritual will to power wills something higher than any reconciliation. Because the redeeming teaching is made possible and desirable by the discoveries about will to power and revenge, these discoveries mark the essential stages on the way in to *the* enigmatic teaching in Nietzsche. After this first report on its necessity, Zarathustra is occupied with eternal return above all else, for it is now his task to enter that teaching.

Neglect of the narrative structure of Zarathustra has, it seems to me, resulted in forfeiting the connection it so laconically shows between will to power and eternal return. Heidegger, who takes pains to be true to Zarathustra's literary form and to take his bearings "from some landmark in Nietzsche's own terrain,"[98] nevertheless misses the essential connection of eternal return and will to power supplied by "On Redemption." In his second lecture series on Nietzsche, in the summer of 1937, Heidegger argues that for Nietzsche, "will to power is the ultimate fact" and asks how the thought of thoughts, eternal return, is related to the ultimate fact. But Heidegger supposes that "Nietzsche failed to pose" this "decisive question."[99] Failing to see both Nietzsche's posing of the question and his communication of the answer in "On Redemption," Heidegger is required to invent his own answer, one that makes eternal return the fundamental teaching out of which the teaching on will to power arises. Eternal return becomes the metaphysical "stamp" of Being on Becoming, that aspect of metaphysics that names the way of being of all beings just as will to power names their constitution.[100] Twenty-five years later, at the end of his final and most penetrating series of lectures on Nietzsche, Heidegger gathered his comprehensive perspective into a single question: Does Nietzsche's thinking lead us across the bridge to the highest hope, redemption from revenge?[101] His answer is that Nietzsche's thought of eternal return is itself a way of revenge. Although Heidegger's lectures perform the great service of affording access to the encompassing scope of Nietzsche's thought, and although they pose the fundamental question that Zarathustra himself invites his audience to pose, there is no reason to be satisfied with Heidegger's answer, an answer that comes too soon, without consideration of the chapters in part III that exhibit the teaching of eternal return as the letting be of beings.

That Heidegger's answer comes too soon can be seen in his interpretation of the last *Nachlass* fragment analyzed in this last course on Nietzsche:

> We have created the heaviest thought,—*now let us create the being* for whom it will be light and easy! . . . Celebrate the future, not the past. Create the poetry for the myth of the future! Live in hope! Blessed moment! And then close the curtain again and turn our thoughts to firm and present purposes" (*KGW* VII 21 [6]).

According to Heidegger, the curtain always remained closed on Nietzsche's thought of thoughts, even for Nietzsche. But the fragment he cites is part of a much longer note from the fall of 1883, a preparatory, programmatic summary of the main events of part III. Its imagery already contains major elements of the poetry of part III that open the curtain on eternal return and allow it to be glimpsed in its redemptive power. The closing of the curtain referred to in the note follows the revelatory act of part III and is required by the tasks at hand, the warfare undertaken in Nietzsche's next books. Could Heidegger's judgment that the curtain always remained closed indicate that part III of *Thus Spoke Zarathustra* remained closed to Heidegger, in spite of his remarkable powers of interpretation? Part III is the sole writing of Nietzsche's whose purpose it is to open the curtain on his thought of thoughts. Whether it succeeds must be decided by the details given there, but a preliminary indication of the inadequacy of Heidegger's interpretation can be seen in what he thinks he is able to discern behind the always closed curtain: eternal return is the myth of the machine age that serves to justify total machination through poetry, to naturalize it and humanize it, as if it were Nietzsche's blessing on the iron age in which he found himself; as if Nietzsche had, unknown to himself, surrendered completely to his age.[102]

"On Redemption" ends with a dialogue that points to the decisiveness of what Zarathustra has just revealed. After reaching the peak, where will to power is named and the connection between will to power and eternal return revealed, he breaks off suddenly and looks with shock at his disciples. This shocked glance breaks the inwardness of his speech of dismay. Present again on the bridge with his disciples, the hunchback, and the crowd of cripples, he surrenders to terror of the most extreme sort as his eyes turn outward and he is forced to see that his uncontrolled speech has had an audience. His terror is for his disciples alone, however, and his eyes pierce their thoughts to the thoughts that must be behind their thoughts as they view their master fallen into dismay and speaking of a universal despair. Now they will know that the nightmare truly was his. Zarathustra recovers himself and utters a confession: "It is difficult to live with men because silence is so difficult. Especially for one so garrulous." It is not the disciples who respond to the excuse addressed to them, but the ignored hunchback. He had covered his face for the speech that so vehemently refused his opening appeal. But he had listened intently, as is demonstrated by his telling commentary that Zarathustra speaks one way to the cripples and another way to his disciples. Zarathustra has a cruel answer for this observation: "What's surprising about that? One may well speak to a hunchback in a hunchback way." The hunchback's answer acknowledges that there are grounds for speaking in a special way to a special audience: "With pupils one may well tell tales out of school." But then he adds his own tale for pupils out of school: "But why does Zarathustra talk differently to his pupils—than to himself?" For that shrewd question Zarathustra has no answer, because he knows that he has said too much in revealing the problem of redemption or the nightmare from which no one is redeemed. In the next chapter, which reflects on the hunchback's unanswered question, Zarathustra inquires into the prudence of hiding himself. In "On Redemption" he has not hidden himself.

PRACTICAL WISDOM (CHAPTERS 21–22)

After the imprudence of Zarathustra's speech of dismay, one might expect "On Human Prudence" (II. 21) to be a speech in praise of prudence. However, after dividing prudence into its various kinds, it recommends abandoning one kind of prudence, thereby anticipating Zarathustra's indulgence of imprudence. Prudence is the virtue of Zarathustra's snake (Prologue 10), and until now Zarathustra has simply admired and called attention to it. But now prudence appears in a new light, for only one kind need be practiced, the kind he failed to practice in the previous chapter. Practicing a more prudent speech, especially in the hearing of his disciples, Zarathustra will have to abandon all prudence in thought; his now moderate speech will mask his now immoderate thought. Following this insight, Zarathustra engages in moderate speech to his disciples (II. 22), and a few hours later starts out toward his immoderate, "impossible" thought (III. 1).

The prudence of the title is not simply the prudence befitting humans, but the prudence Zarathustra has heretofore exercised toward them: it has been prudent for him to believe mankind to be more capable than it is. But he sees now that his prudence has made him, as prudence ought, solid and weighty, slow of step, unfit for the risk of ascent and flight; in being prudent, he too has been made politic and calculating in working for good ends,[103] for him the end of the superman. In abandoning that prudence, he now undertakes the imprudent. Fittingly, it is in this chapter on prudence that he says more about the superman than anywhere else in part II. For the way to the superman has been barred by his prudence about mankind, but now his imprudence opens a new way.

Zarathustra invites his friends to unriddle his heart's "double will" and then unriddles it for them.[104] Although his will is swept upward to the superman, it is also held downward by his prudent love of mankind. To be released from that prudent hold would free his will for the flight upward. Of the four forms of prudence, the first three have to be abandoned and the fourth practiced that much better. To abandon the first three is to free himself from what is best in mankind, the hope, entertainment, and pleasure mankind affords. Cutting that anchor frees him for his flight, but his flight requires the fourth form of prudence. If mankind is no longer to be hidden from his eyes, he must be all the more hidden from theirs. It is prudent to hide what he is because now he is most imprudent; what he now undertakes is rash, icarian, impossible, and were even his disciples to learn of it, they would shake their heads; for there are some things that no man can do—no man can fly, no man can redirect the stream of mankind, no man can say to the past, "But thus I willed it!"

In the final chapter of part II ("On the Stillest Hour," II. 22) Zarathustra performs his prudent act of masking himself before his disciples by presenting himself as weak and divided in will, as still only a herald, though he has seen and accepted for himself with a single will the task that the superman must undertake. In this final chapter of part II, as in the final chapter of part I, he takes leave of his disciples with a reflection on gift-giving. He begins and ends his speech by asserting that he gives all that he has to give, but both the speech and the question with which it ends suggest that the most important things have not been said, that even one so garrulous as Zarathustra has learned how to be silent. Although this speech comes at the end of part II and seems to bring to a close the matters with which it deals, part III, which opens on the same night, just after he has left his disciples, begins with Zarathustra speaking to himself about the very same matters. The first speech of part III thus shows the last speech of part II to be an instance of Zarathustra speaking differently to his pupils than to himself. At the beginning of part III he speaks to himself about his reasons for leaving his disciples and entering solitude. What he said to his disciples about his departure emphasized his division of heart (II. 21), but what he says to himself emphasizes his singleness of purpose in the face of the task that he has now assumed as his own. To his disciples he prudently portrays himself as less than he is and less than he is determined to become. Saying that he tells them everything in order that their hearts not harden against him, he tells them only what it is necessary to tell them if their hearts are not to harden against him. The opening image of part III reveals what has happened at the end of part II: Zarathustra departs covering his tracks. But although the speech at the end of part II contains his last words to his disciples in the book, they are not his last words to them absolutely, for he still needs disciples (see III. 3) and will return to them at the end of part IV.[105]

For his disciples, Zarathustra creates a dialogue between himself and his "Stillest Hour." The dialogue appears to be an enactment of the double will disclosed in the previous speech, but here there is no suggestion that it is in the process of being replaced by a single will. The commanding will that would move him higher appears as a woman, his "terrible mistress," whereas Zarathustra himself, arguing his unfitness and failure, appears as the weakness of will that refuses her challenge. He chooses to present himself to his disciples on this final occasion as a whimpering, ineffectual man commanded by an imperious woman; he presents himself as unfit for the highest task without saying what that task is.[106]

The speech opened with a question—What has happened to Zarathustra?—to which it purported to give the answer; but it ends in a way which suggests that the answer has not appeared. That something has happened is evident even to the disciples, who see him troubled and driven away from them. This time they have no departing gift for him, but he has for them the gift of his prudent clothing. He blames his "terrible mistress" for the necessity of his departure and names her "my Stillest Hour," the hour of his greatest event (II. 18), which has come to light as the creation of a new good and evil to redirect the stream of mankind. Adopting a stance that avows complete candor, he tells those unable to interpret his nightmare something that happened in a dream, a dialogue about what he knows and what he wills. There is no dispute over what he knows, only over what he wills, though neither what he knows nor what he wills is ever identified in this speech that alleges to say all. Still, the preceding and succeeding speeches all point to the new knowledge and the new will as eternal return. Zarathustra knows what has to be willed for mankind to be redeemed from revenge but presents himself as not able to perform that act of will. Although he alleges in this dialogue related for his disciples' sake that he lacks the will to rule, it is precisely this that comes to light in part III as Zarathustra's virtue, as the real meaning of the gift-giving virtue that defines him (III. 10, 12, §21). As the final words of the dream dialogue show, his teaching has ripened into the discovery of the one thing necessary for the will to power that would achieve redemption; but, he tells his disciples, he lacks the necessary resolve. Addressing his friends directly for the last time, he alleges that they have heard everything, but then adds a riddle that should make them doubt his candor and lead them to wonder what is being held back by the one who, in leaving them years before, described himself as pure gift-giver ready to give everything for the sake of the superman. The gift-giver ends with a question that the disciples ought to consider for themselves about their gift-giving master: "Am I stingy?"[107] The last image they have of him is this riddle of stinginess in a speech alleging weakness, and the image is augmented by his loud weeping. After this indulgence, he disappears into the night, and his disciples never see him again in the book.

But the reader of the book sees him an hour or two later ascending resolutely to the task that he now knows to be his. He takes a path not yet trodden by any man; he goes alone and leaves no tracks; over the path is hung the sign "Impossibility" (III. 1). Zarathustra's return to solitude signals his abandonment of his role as herald. The evolutionary hope for a greater Posterity constructed on the shoulders of the best men of the present must be put aside by the one who has discovered both the incapacity of his disciples and precisely what is needed for redemption. He has learned that he cannot entrust his teaching to disciples, and that his teaching on the will to power and revenge requires of himself the culminating deed of willing eternal return.

Part III

The philosopher as we understand him . . . [is] the man of the most comprehensive responsibility who has the overall development of mankind on his conscience.

—NIETZSCHE, *BGE* 61

THE ACTION OF PART III

Part III is the climax and culmination of *Thus Spoke Zarathustra*, the part for the sake of which the two previous parts exist. Zarathustra here enacts the event toward which the book has been moving and brings to fulfillment what had been Nietzsche's intentions for him since being "overtaken" by Zarathustra on the long winter walks around the Bay of Rapallo in 1881–82. Zarathustra becomes the teacher of the "highest formula of affirmation that is at all attainable," eternal return (*EH*, "Books: *Zarathustra*," 1).[1] A few days after he finished part II, Nietzsche stated in a letter to Köselitz (13 July 1883) that part III might take him years to complete. In fact it took six months, the actual composition occurring again in ten days of inspiration. Those few days in January 1884 were, as Nietzsche immediately reported to Overbeck (letter of 25 January 1884), the "happiest two weeks" of his life, the completion of the "mariner's tale" he had been living "since 1870."[2]

Part III is more overtly dramatic than the other parts, though the action is still unobtrusive and is, as always, in the service of the speeches. The action begins with Zarathustra's separation from his disciples (III. 1) and his departure on a sea voyage (III. 2–4); he sails away from "the blessed isles" that had symbolized his hope at the beginning of part II.[3] He no longer looks to disciples to advance his teaching in the way that he now knows to be necessary. His "most abysmal thought" is the goal of his sea voyage, but the confrontation only begins there. The thought remains in the background during his renewed wanderings among men (III. 5–8). As a consequence of these wanderings, his assessment of the present age grows more ominous, making his own task all the more imperative. When he finally returns to his solitude (III. 9), he is capable of weighing the world according to his new measure (III. 10–12). After this preparation he wills eternal return and is redeemed (III. 13). The animals sing their grateful praise and then steal away, leaving him in complete solitude to sing his own songs of praise (III. 14–16). After completing these songs, Nietzsche thought that his book was complete (letters to Köselitz, 1 February 1884, and Rhode, 22 February 1884; see *EH*, "Books: *Zarathustra*," 8).

The climactic event that brings Zarathustra's course to its close and completes his entry into Nietzsche's philosophy is his "redemption" through willing eternal return. Redemption occurs in "The Convalescent" (III. 13) but its meaning is deliberately obscured by having it occur offstage, out of everyone's view. The book ends with reports of that event, beginning with the clearest, that given by Zarathustra's animals. But not only does their report lack Zarathustra's special authority, Zarathustra twice criticizes it; moreover, he is not able to comment on their final and most extensive account because he does not even listen to it. His own report is contained in a private speech to his own soul (III. 14) and in two songs sung by his soul (III. 15, 16). Zarathustra's understanding of the most important event of the book must be sought in these chapters but they are dark and resist entry. The culminating event of the whole book is concealed in Zarathustra's most private inwardness.

At the beginning of part III Zarathustra alludes to this hidden quality of what is to come by saying that he covers his tracks, and that he takes a path over which hangs the sign "Impossibility" (III. 1). Later he says that he draws circles around himself, making this former public speaker ever more unapproachable (III. 12, §19). But that hidden event at the end of Zarathustra's trackless way, that "Impossibility" obscured by the circles drawn around it until it lies at the center of some new labyrinth, can be interpreted, for Zarathustra's life interprets it for us. So ostentatiously hidden by having its hiddenness pointed to, this event is enclosed in a narrative that allows Nietzsche to parade it as a mystery before his audience, just as Zarathustra once paraded a mystery before a disciple, desiring thereby that the mystery be questioned and unraveled (I. 18). The hidden event cannot be merely the private achievement of a solitary man who has outgrown all possible audiences. From beginning to end, Zarathustra has measured his own success in terms of the future of mankind. Part III does not abandon that measure by surrendering to some private salvation but instead shows itself to be the fulfillment of the world-historical ambitions unveiled in parts I and II as the responsibility of some superman.

Part III is characterized by Zarathustra's progress, but also by his retrospection. Because his earlier actions must be assessed for the sake of actions still anticipated, retrospection occurs in every chapter of the first half of part III (1–9), as preparation for the decisive and conclusive actions that follow in the second half. Zarathustra's most comprehensive review of his career occurs, appropriately enough, at the beginning of his new account of his public teaching (III. 12), the pattern of retrospect and prospect characteristic of part III being repeated there in miniature. What he learns from his own career makes possible his final ascent. Through that ascent, Zarathustra enters Nietzsche's philosophy, to employ the metaphor of the entrance hall Nietzsche used in letters; he becomes a "philosopher," to employ that word in the elevated sense used by Nietzsche in *Beyond Good and Evil;* or he takes upon himself the labors of the superman, to employ the image of *Zarathustra* itself. In the depiction of these labors, Nietzsche runs the greatest risk of being seen to be an intolerable boaster, a risk acknowledged in Zarathustra's refusal to speak about his task to anyone but himself. He has masked himself to his disciples (II. 22) and will mask himself to others (III. 5–6), for his task is not fit to be spoken. Nevertheless, what he has attributed to past teachings he must attribute to his own; the novel teaching that aspires to replace the old teachings must aspire to the same scope and standing; if mankind's past and present have been ruled by the wisest and their revenge, the novel teaching must aspire to rule the coming age with a wisdom free of revenge. Nietzsche observes the appropriate moderation about his immoderate task through the literary devices of *Thus Spoke Zarathustra,* while Zarathustra observes the appropriate moderation by practicing prudent speech even with his animals.

Zarathustra has taught that the coming superman will be the founder of the new people, his acts resembling those of the founders of the thousand peoples hitherto (I. 15). The superman will fulfill the threat made to the wisest (II. 12) to destroy the ark of their values that the people have carried forward; he will replace it with a new ark of values that the people of the future will carry forward. In performing this act of destruction and construction the superman will end the nightmare of revenge and teach mankind how to love the earth. Zarathustra's act of willing eternal return presents itself as that foundational act. It is no wonder that when Nietzsche completed part III, he believed he was finished. He was finished. The essential task envisaged for Zarathustra had been brought to its culmination.

Nevertheless, the completed founding enacted in Zarathustra's poetry at the end of part III entails additional deeds or a founding of a more directly political sort, which is alluded to in the final, apocalyptic image of "Seven Seals." In the final, apocalyptic book of the New Testament, which is about to become an old testament, a book of seven seals is unsealed to bring to pass the final battle between Christ and Satan for the earth. Nietzsche borrows the image of a book of seven seals to close his own book and to intimate the political consequences of the new teaching brought by the founder of the thousand-and-first people. Although *Zarathustra* properly ends with part III, making part IV an afterthought, part IV is nevertheless a useful addendum, for it helps us to understand the action of part III and of the book as a whole by showing that the completion present in part III is not simply the end. Part IV shows, as part III in its own way had already shown, that another descent must follow the final ascent, a movement downward as legislator or commander to effect on earth the political consequences of the teaching won in solitude.

RESOLVE (CHAPTER 1)

Part III begins on the same night part II ended. It is midnight, and Zarathustra has just left his disciples to set off as a wanderer back to his solitude. The three speeches in this chapter entitled "The Wanderer" look to the past and the future, while describing Zarathustra's present resolve. They anticipate a theme prominent in part III, ascent and descent, and are given serially, one during ascent, one at the height, and one after descent.

The speech made during ascent shows Zarathustra to be resolute in facing his most difficult task. It corrects his last speech to his disciples made only minutes or hours before. Speaking to his disciples, he gave prudent reasons for entering solitude; he covered his tracks by depicting a challenge that he alleged he was unwilling to meet. Speaking to himself, the wanderer does not need to cast a deceptive shadow, but is able to affirm his willingness. In part III, he will frequently practice his new prudence of appearing to be less than he is. Now that he is no longer following a way along which to send disciples, but a way that is his alone, he has no need to appear to be more than he is (I. 14). His now moderate mask covers the most immoderate task, one whose dimensions come increasingly to light in part III, beginning with this resolute speech of ascent.

Speaking to his heart, Zarathustra claims to be master of all accident, with nothing befalling him that he cannot take as his own. Earlier, for the benefit of his disciples, he had said that the new challenge came to him uninvited and unwanted, as if from outside himself, and he had avowed an unwillingness to accept it, asserting that it was not his. That earlier dialogue had begun with what Zarathustra knows, but only here does he say what it is, that he stands before his "final peak," the one deferred longest because hardest and loneliest. Having just enacted a dialogue between his "Stillest Hour" and himself for the sake of his disciples, he now speaks to himself regarding what "the Hour" calls for and willingly accepts all that it presents as his task. The Hour announces that he is on the way to his "greatness," his "destiny," the task of commanding that he had openly refused before his disciples. Speaking first of his kind and last of what is his alone, the Hour affirms that there is now no path behind him; he takes a way that is not a way for followers to take.

Zarathustra's ascent calls for the oddest sort of climbing; no ladders suffice, and he must learn to climb on his own head, far above his own heart, for his ascendant mind must tether his passionate heart. Invoking the Old Testament yearning of the homeless for a land flowing with milk and honey[4] in order to condemn that yearning as corrupting, the Hour challenges him to look away from his heart's yearning and to cultivate hardness. But when this mountain-climber looks away from himself, he must not be as eager or importunate as his kind have been in seeking their enlightenment, for their eagerness has condemned them to see only the "foreground" of "all things." Zarathustra's desire to gaze into the ground and the background of all things requires a patience that other knowers have lacked. In order that his desire be satisfied, he must learn to ascend not only above himself but above "all things," until the stars themselves are encompassed by his ascent, and he is able to look down on them. What the Hour demands will be anticipated on the sea voyage (III. 4) and accomplished and described in the final song (III. 16).

Zarathustra's mood, though not his resolve, changes when he reaches the top of the mountain and stands in silence gazing out over the sea below. The brief speech at the summit asserts his readiness, but in a mood of sadness. It begins emphatically with Zarathustra saying, "I know my lot," the very word emphasizing the fatedness that, according to the Hour, Zarathustra must master.[5] His readiness for his "last solitude"[6] is readiness for descent into the deepest pain. Descent and ascent, going under and flying, belong together as the two poles of Zarathustra's mastery of his lot.

The third and final speech is made after his descent to the sea. The opening of part III parallels the openings of parts I and II in enacting an initial ascent followed by a much longer descent, but Zarathustra's speech here after his descent and his reflection on that speech presage the ways in which part III will be decisively different from the two previous parts. Beginning by describing the sea, he ends by addressing comfort to it. In his earlier speech about poets (II. 17) he had taken the sea as a model for the vain spirit of poets that postures for an unresponsive audience. Here the image is reversed, and the sea becomes Zarathustra's audience as he laments his inability to release it from its bad dreams. But he catches himself in this folly of comforting the sea and laughs at himself, the bitter laugh of one who often fails to discriminate in his love; his foolish speech had been grounded in rash love. Rash love has always been his danger, the danger of hermits who are all too ready to squander their love on unfitting recipients. But this talk of rash love makes him think immediately of the disciples whom he has just left behind, and his laughter turns to anger, for he has loved his disciples most rashly. The thought of his all-too-trusting love makes him laugh when he catches it comforting the sea, but it makes him angry when he thinks of his disciples. His anger, however, is directed at neither his disciples nor his love, but at the thought implied in what he has just said, the thought that he loves his disciples only because of his rashness in love and not because they are worthy of his love. His anger condemns his thought as wronging his friends, but his anger cannot refute the truth of his thought; his love of his disciples and his hopes for them *were* rash, being grounded only in his need to love and hope. He again cries at the separation from his disciples, as he had earlier that night, but this time he cries bitterly and alone, out of both anger and longing, anger at himself for his thought and its truth, and longing for his disciples.[7]

At the beginning of part III, as at the beginnings of parts I and II, it is Zarathustra's love for mankind that moves him to action. Earlier that love had moved him downward to mankind and to disciples in order to give the gift of a teaching that would initiate the long ascent to the superman. Now, moved still by love of mankind, he descends to his own lot and destiny, to the depths necessary to achieve the ascent to the superman that the Hour requires. The opening of part III begins the enactment of the heroic in exactly the way defined by Nietzsche in *The Gay Science:* "What makes the heroic? At the same time to set out to meet one's highest suffering and one's highest hope" (268).

THE ENIGMATIC VISION (CHAPTERS 2–4)

The next three chapters belong together as the account of Zarathustra's sea voyage, the voyage that is to take him to his most abysmal thought. But he seems not yet ripe for his thought, for it appears only in a vision. The first speech (III. 2) on board ship is made to an audience of awed sailors two days after setting sail; the second and third (III. 3, 4) are made to himself. All three are anticipations of the voyage of the spirit that Zarathustra will later undertake in his solitude.

"On the Vision and the Riddle" (III. 2) has a special prominence because it contains the book's first explicit presentation of the teaching of eternal return; still, its accessibility is compromised by the manner of presentation, as the title suggests. Zarathustra addresses a specific and special audience and presents his thought as a vision that he has had, a terrifying "premonition." The audience is invited to exercise the faculty toward which its talents and pleasures in any case direct it—guessing. Later, Nietzsche provides clues that educate the guesses by showing Zarathustra's premonition becoming Zarathustra's deed. Nevertheless, what is accomplished in the deed will still have to be guessed at, even after its enactment. The vision and the subsequent deed show that the confrontations recounted are not symbolic of some general human overcoming of discouragements, but are rather the specific overcoming of the specific threat that dismays the one who has understood mankind's fall into revenge and the necessity of willing eternal return. This first account of eternal return, in the book that exists for this thought and is now two-thirds over, shows the final achievement to be Zarathustra's singular deed.[8]

Zarathustra's very presence on board the alien ship had caused stirrings among the sailors, for someone else had boarded at the blessed isles and had provided the foreign sailors with rumors and stories about him. As these rumors about the miracle-worker spread, so too did "a great curiosity and expectation," a mood of anticipation that must have grown in the two days during which Zarathustra, sunk in his own sadness, remained inexplicably silent. The speech he finally makes, set in the mystery and expectation created by his very presence and by his long silence, identifies its appropriate audience at its beginning and near its end, offering instruction on how to approach what he is about to tell them. In *Ecce Homo*, a book that begins and ends by expressing concern about how he is to be read, Nietzsche repeated this description of Zarathustra's audience as a description of the readers he himself sought. Before quoting Zarathustra's words there, Nietzsche spoke of his "perfect reader" as "a monster of courage and curiosity," who is in addition "still somewhat pliable, cunning, cautious, a born adventurer and discoverer (*EH*, "Books," 3). Although Zarathustra attributes to the sailors the qualities of spirit Nietzsche thought necessary in his best readers, it is not plausible that Zarathustra, having just faced the shortcomings of his long-trained disciples, was seeking his true followers among these sailors. They are instead symbolic of the spirit of adventure, the uprooted passion for novelty in love with the undiscovered and the uncharted, hard but still somewhat pliable. Nevertheless, though the actual sailors can not themselves be the men Zarathustra needs as followers, it may well have served his purposes to address his vision of eternal return to them. His previous encounter with sailors (II. 18) showed them to be prone to tell fabulous tales and to carry the report of them from port to port. The last tale told of Zarathustra by sailors led to his resolve to bring his shadow under control. This vision of eternal return that he now tells the sailors may well cast a shadow of the sort he desires to have. To an audience with a propensity for the fabulous, one that has been prepared by both rumor and his ostentatious, unwonted silence, Zarathustra presents a vision that describes two heroic labors and taunts his listeners to draw the obvious conclusion that they are the deeds of Zarathustra himself. Death to the spirit of gravity and death to the heavy black snake—these are the heroic deeds of the one who is eventually to become known to men as the teacher of eternal return. Zarathustra has as yet given no inkling that it is his lot to be the teacher of eternal return, for he has just learned that this teaching is necessary for redemption. After long consideration, he breaks his mysterious silence to cast this shadow that will not ruin his reputation, the shadow that will prepare the way for the teaching he will eventually bring.

Zarathustra's audience of sailors must duplicate the feats of the heroic Argonauts, but they are to be even more heroic than one of the greatest of those ancient heroes, Theseus, because they are to deny themselves the assistance accorded Theseus, they are not to "grope with cowardly hand after a thread." Specifically, he denies his audience the form of assistance most commonly relied on by philosophy, the form that will be explicitly parodied in the vision; for where they are able to *guess*, they will hate to *deduce*. The chapter that begins to unveil the thought of eternal return starts out by shunning all assistance, whether dependence on a thread granted by Ariadne or on a "thread of argument" followed by deduction.[9] As the conflict in the vision shows, Zarathustra and his kin rejoice that the fundamental matters are not simply explicit and accessible, not simply subject to proof or deduction. Zarathustra's enigmatic vision presents an account of "all beings," but it is not the impossible goal of that vision to make all beings thinkable. Nor does he choose enigma simply as a rhetorical vehicle for lovers of riddles, one that can be smoothed out into unambiguous answers. Enigma belongs to Zarathustra's presentation because enigma stands at the heart of things. But that the whole is enigmatic is not the deplorable prelude to melancholy or despair; rather, it is a blessing on things. Zarathustra and his kind, bold sailors gifted with wonder, marvel at what rises out of mystery and perishes into mystery, while seeking ever to penetrate it. This new philosophic spirit, the new way of wonder, is here presented as a fight to the death with the old philosophic spirit; Zarathustra's spirit of grateful wonder does battle with its opposite, the spirit of gravity, the spirit of Socratic or "Alexandrian" man, rational optimists who demand that all beings be thinkable and follow the cowardly way of deduction or proof.

"The Vision of the Loneliest," the title given by Zarathustra to the "riddle" he saw,[10] has two main scenes: the first portrays an act performed by Zarathustra against the spirit of gravity, the second an act performed by an unidentified young shepherd, Zarathustra himself being only an observer, albeit an interested and engaged observer. The first and longer scene is interrupted by a paean to courage, Zarathustra's act of gathering his own courage in order to face his deadly enemy. Nietzsche divided the chapter into two numbered parts, the break occurring at the point at which Zarathustra has gathered the courage for his encounter; the summoning of courage is thereby made the decisive matter grounding the action of both scenes; courage is the virtue that makes possible the triumphant deeds of "the loneliest."[11]

Zarathustra's vision, a thing seen though not by ordinary sight, occurred "not long ago" as a "premonition" depicting events that belong to his future. He saw himself ascending a steep mountain path at sunset, climbing upward in defiance of what pulls him downward, "abyssward," the spirit of gravity, his "devil and archenemy." The spirit of gravity appears as a half dwarf, half mole, perched on his shoulder, but this apparition is only one of the forms taken by that spirit of whom "they say" that "he is the master of the world" (II. 10). Because Zarathustra's later encounter with the spirit of gravity (III. 11) shows it to be the rational spirit of Socratism or Platonism, the spirit that has mastered the world in various Platonisms for the people, it seems plausible that the modern or Schopenhauerian pessimism that here threatens to master Zarathustra is in fact the final outcome of Platonism, its last possible form. Dwarfed or shrunken, Platonism no longer harbors the rational optimism that there is some alternative to mortal life, something higher or better; there is only wretched life, life that is no good. To defeat the spirit of gravity, Zarathustra will have to master this late, decadent form in himself. What is at stake in this conflict is not merely Zarathustra's despair but mastery of the world.[12]

Only in this vision does the spirit of gravity speak, and his words are like lead in Zarathustra's ear, drawing him downward. Zarathustra is addressed as a "stone" that has thrown itself high, "the stone of wisdom," the philosopher's stone, the stone shot high into the heavens, even to the stars and the heavenly divinities crushed by the stone. While praising the force and trajectory of this stone, the spirit of gravity asserts its authority over it, for all stones fall back to gravity's center, subject to its downward pull, and the stone Zarathustra is no exception. Falling back to earth, Zarathustra will be the cause of his own "stoning"; his effort to fly above the spirit of gravity will end in self-inflicted despair. With this threat of death, the spirit of gravity's speech prepares the way for the fight to the death enacted in the vision.

Zarathustra gathers himself for that fight to the death in his speech to himself on courage. It takes place in the oppression of the long silence following the spirit of gravity's threatening words. The something within that he calls courage *(Mut)* has killed every failure of courage or every dismay *(Unmut)* until now, and, having gazed in deepest dismay into the grounds of the Dwarf's teaching (II. 20), he now summons his courage for a battle to the death. Courage is identified as an instrument of death, the best *Todschläger* with which to club every enemy to death. But courage must attack, and in the attack there is always *klingendes Spiel,* triumphant martial music, that may well cover a less than triumphant sense of danger or dismay. Like Theseus preparing for the heroic death-dealing deed, Zarathustra sings the praises of his death-dealing club.[13] Zarathustra's attacking courage belongs to the long history of human courage, though it has nothing whatever to do with the steadfastness or loyalty defined as "political" courage by Plato's Socrates, for it is not a defense of things already held.[14] Zarathustra's courage is not blind, it is not built on faith or obstinacy; nor is it simply reckless, risking danger for its own sake. It is coupled with insight and takes on the challenge posed by the dismaying history of revenge; it is the courage of a lion grown subtle, Theseus schooled by philosophy.[15]

According to Zarathustra's account of human history, courage is what defines mankind. Mankind was not granted dominion but achieved it through courage. But human courage now faces a new enemy; having overcome every pain until now with martial bravado, it faces the deepest pain, identified as having three aspects: dizziness, pity, and death itself, aspects which exemplify the Schopenhauerian character of the pain now experienced by the human spirit. Courage must first club to death the dizziness felt at the edge of an abyss, the dizziness of the knower to whom the groundless character of the world has become apparent. Zarathustra's patient will to see through the foreground of all things into their ground and background (III. 1) has caused the abyss to open before him, Schopenhauer's abyss, as seen by Nietzsche, the abyss of revenge into which the imprisoned will falls. Dizziness could cause him, a "stone," to fall into the madness of that abyss. Courage must next club to death pity—Schopenhauer's virtue, which Nietzsche defines as "the practice of nihilism" (A 7), the compensatory practice of the knower dizzied by the abyss. Pity is the deepest abyss, that out of which no ascent is possible, for when one peers into the ground or background of human life, one peers into suffering; pity, the passion that draws one down to the suffering, keeps one from ascending beyond human pain to victory over pain. Finally, courage must club to death even death itself; it does so with words in which there is a great deal of martial bravado, words that presage the affirmation of life in eternal return: "Was *that* life? Well then! Once more!", words that Schopenhauer maintained could not be uttered by one who knows that life is suffering.[16] It is clear from this hymn to courage that Zarathustra and the spirit of gravity are not polar opposites existing by virtue of one another in an endless oscillation of ascent and descent; rather, they are contraries or deadly enemies. Mastery for one is death for the other; as both speakers in the vision attest, "I! or You!" To club the Dwarf to death is to club to death the whole rational, Socratic tradition, culminating in Schopenhauer's overt condemnation of life.

After Zarathustra has summoned his courage, the second part of the chapter begins. He addresses the spirit of gravity simply as "Dwarf." Claiming to be the stronger of the two, he challenges the Dwarf on two matters: first, that he does not know Zarathustra's "most abysmal" thought, and, second, that he "could not bear it." The polemical speech that follows this challenge is a deed of courage with the most grave intent of clubbing to death its hearer.

The Dwarf takes the baited challenge for he is overcome with curiosity. Leaping from Zarathustra's shoulder, he squats on a stone opposite him; the combatants face one another over Zarathustra's most abysmal thought. Zarathustra draws attention to a gateway at which they have halted, a gateway that faces two directions simultaneously. Two paths come together in the gateway, and no one has ever walked either to its end. The long lane "back" continues for an eternity, the long lane "out" for another eternity. The two pathways "contradict" one another; they come together in the gateway, on which is written "Moment." From the perspective of the present moment, the paths to past and future appear contradictory, each leading further away from the other; concentration on the present with its alternative directions thus makes time appear to be linear. Having created this impression of linear time, Zarathustra engages the Dwarf with a question: Do the paths eternally contradict one another, as they appear to do? The Dwarf answers the riddle "contemptuously," for he is certain that he can easily know and easily bear the "abysmal thought" with which Zarathustra has apparently challenged him. His conclusion about time is grounded in his view of truth, for he is the rational spirit that now knows all truth to be crooked, to be hidden by appearance that makes truth elusive. Consequently, he knows that the linearity of time apparent from concentration on the present moment is illusory, that time is a circle.[17]

With the position of his deadly enemy clearly stated, Zarathustra can now deliver the lethal thought that will club the Dwarf to death and enable him to ascend unimpeded. The spirit of "heaviness" has made things too "light" for himself, and what Zarathustra says now will make the thought that time is a circle too heavy for the Dwarf to bear.[18] Appropriately, given the spirit of gravity's identity as the rational spirit, Zarathustra's speech takes the form of a deductive argument that draws a conclusion from the premise granted by the Dwarf. The premise is stated in the indicative and is followed by a series of questions in which there is one further use of the indicative. Then the scene changes completely, and the Dwarf disappears. The argument presented by Zarathustra intensifies the Dwarf's own thought that time is a circle. From the gateway of the present moment an eternal lane runs backward; if time is a circle, an eternity lies behind us. On the basis of this premise Zarathustra then asks: Must not all things that can happen have happened in the eternity of the past? In his argument with the Dwarf he does not add the premise that Nietzsche knew to be necessary when he wrote out versions of this argument in his notes, the premise later supplied by Zarathustra when he speaks of the finitude of force (III. 10).[19] The Dwarf does not respond to the question implying that this present moment has already been, and Zarathustra moves to the more telling point about the future, more telling to the Dwarf who faces the future with resigned loathing, with "ill will" against time and its pointless cycles. Zarathustra then asks whether all things are not so knotted together that the movement of this moment into the past draws with it all coming things and so, too, itself? Zarathustra himself answers in the indicative: "For whatever of all things *can* run; also in this long lane *out*—it *must* run once again!" The Dwarf has no answer easy or otherwise to this argument of Zarathustra's courage. The once curious and contemptuous Dwarf is completely stilled by Zarathustra's argument. Zarathustra's final series of questions make this moment more eerie and the thought of the return of this moment still more devastating to the Dwarf. Now, in the moonlight on this lonely mountain, he must contemplate that this moment will eternally recur for him and not be annihilated. Zarathustra has intensified the cyclical view of the Dwarf; for it is not similar things that come and go in an endless enervating cycle that thwarts all ambition, as the Dwarf had maintained in threatening the ambitious Zarathustra. Rather, Zarathustra says in threatening the Schopenhauerian Dwarf, exactly the same things return, precisely as they were and are. This vision, which contains Zarathustra's first unveiling of the thought of eternal return, makes it a weapon that deals death to what hates life, a weapon that slays what has mastered the world until now.

Played out before those who love to guess, this vision of combat by argument crushes the one who loves to deduce. Recognizing why the spirit of gravity cannot laugh at this argument, the guessers can still ask why he lets himself be crushed by it, rather than ignoring it or refuting it, or saying to it: "This argument must be considered one of Nietzsche's thought experiments which fails"?[20] What has been proved by this argument? Regarding the difficult problem of what can be theoretically proved with respect to eternal return, this chapter seems to go out of its way to mock syllogistic or formal argument as a way of dealing with fundamental questions and to diminish the logical force of this particular argument by putting it in such an unusual context and assigning it such an unusual use. The only deductive argument ever made by Zarathustra in the whole book occurs as part of a vision and is addressed only to those who desire to guess, rather than deduce. Deduction is alluded to as an act of cowardice or submission unbefitting the adventurers whom he addresses. The argument itself is used to club to death Zarathustra's rationalist archenemy. The argument begins by accepting the premise of the opponent and leaps too soon to the crushing conclusion; it is an enthymeme, omitting a premise that Nietzsche knew to be necessary to the conclusion. Finally, it is embellished in its crushing conclusion with chilling images. Still, it succeeds in banishing the deductive or rational spirit, which must see the argument as binding—but in what sense? Must the spirit of gravity yield because it was he who provided the premise of cyclical, infinite time? If so, Zarathustra has made it too easy for himself by having his rational opponent surrender without an examination of the premises, without a question about the suppressed premise, or the steps to the crushing conclusion. It seems to me that the most fitting guess is that the rational spirit crushed by the argument is that spirit in its modern skeptical and pessimistic form, the form it takes in Schopenhauer, the last possible Platonist, the one most ruined by dismay. The rational spirit in this dwarfed form has moved from dogmatism to skepticism with respect to the limits of rational argument: theoretical proof cannot demonstrate the fundamental features of the whole beyond the conclusion that it is a wretched whole of blind will. What the spirit of gravity glimpses in Zarathustra's argument is that when pure reason is understood to have limitations to which he too assents—as an instrument whose origins must be guessed at (I. 4; D 123), one that is unsupported by the webs of any cosmic spider (III. 4)—then reason itself can be reasonably employed to support the ideal that is the opposite of world denial. The interpreting, evaluating being, standing within the enigmatic whole and daring to grasp more and more of its particulars through the adventurous will to inquiry, can be so well disposed to that whole and to himself to say to the whole marvelous spectacle: "Once more!" This is not the response of the spirit of gravity, but with the aid of Zarathustra's club, it can see that this response, like its own, is grounded in a disposition of which it is symptomatic, a fundamental value in keeping with the fundamental fact. The spirit that has ruled the world now glimpses, through argument, that its hegemony is threatened by the new ideal that can make its case with probity and plausibility. The vision thus shows Zarathustra carrying out the threat to the hitherto wisest made in "On Self-Overcoming," and doing so in the way appropriate to them. What the guessers can reasonably conclude is that Zarathustra has had a vision of combat in which he clubs to death the spirit of gravity with its own invention; like Theseus with Periphetes the cripple, he wrests the death-dealing club from his enemy and kills him with his own club; like Theseus, he fits the punishment to the crime, and brings Reason itself to reason.

This grave play with argument on the all-important matter of eternal return shows that Zarathustra makes no exception for his own teachings in his critique of the place of argument in philosophy. Although Zarathustra's way is the opposite of a sacrifice of the intellect (*BGE* 23), he does not yield to the superior authority of formal argument, as if arguments based on evident premises and following universal rules of inference could be the way to discover and demonstrate the fundamental features of the world. Zarathustra has not arrived at the teachings of will to power and eternal return by a process of deductive argument based on some still more fundamental premises. Furthermore, although he has presented his teaching of will to power as his discovery of the enigmatic but fundamental phenomenon, his teaching of eternal return has not been the result of submitting to phenomena at all, for the phenomena themselves cannot give evidence that they eternally return even if they eternally return.

In the first part of his vision, Zarathustra has performed for the spirit of gravity what a "demon" performed at the end of *The Gay Science*, in the first presentation of the thought of eternal return in Nietzsche's writings (341). With the same spider afoot in the same eerie moonlight, the thought whispered by the demon takes possession of the one to whom it is whispered.[21] Only two responses are possible for the one controlled by the thought of eternal return: either he casts himself down, cursing the bringer of the message, or he blesses the bringer of the message: "You are a god and never have I heard anything more godlike!" In either case, the one possessed by the thought is transformed as he is. In taking possession of the Dwarf, the thought of eternal return crushes him by forcing him to see the full implications of his view that time is a circle. What had been possible to bear becomes unbearable when, instead of the meaningless cycles of dying generations, each similar to the one before, the exact same beings return eternally, and he too, with his malign antipathy toward those beings. The Dwarf is crushed by the antipathy that accompanies his reflection on temporal beings, slain by his own malignancy.[22] In this symbolic way, the old tradition slays itself: the tradition that has mastered the world with its rational gravity in search of eternal security and that now lies in the ruins of its necessary pessimism, is finally "stoned" to death by the thought that life as it is emerges eternally out of the enigmatic whole. Life has her way with this virtuous description of her. Eternal return is a "selective principle" (*KGW* VII 24 [7] = *WP* 1058), not because it selects out this or that event to eternally return, but because the thought that every event eternally returns selects out for stoning by the philosopher's stone those capable of being possessed by a thought, those for whom life is thought and who have brought civilization under a rule, the traditional teachers of mankind who have judged that life is no good. Those whom the thought does not take possession of, those for whom life is something other than thought, will, presumably, live their lives in the medium of opinion, with a greater or lesser degree of assent to the thought around which the history of mankind turns. But, inasmuch as they carry forward the ark of values created by the wisest, Zarathustra's victory over the spirit of gravity will mean that, with time, their opinions will be those shaped by the truth of eternal return. In this way, the selective thought of eternal return is "the great cultivating idea" (*KGW* VII 25 [227] = *WP* 1056; *KGW* VII 26 [376] = *WP* 1053), for it cultivates a human stance toward life and beings and encourages the nurture of a love of life; in that love, the new people mankind will experience its ennoblement and enhancement.

In the image of the Dwarf the transforming thought of eternal return confronts the spirit of Socratic rationalism with its historic impotence (II. 15): it cannot render all beings thinkable, though it can, in its final theoretical form, completely resign from the contemptible world, and in its final practical form, in its full and ultimate consequences in the universal and homogeneous state of modernity, undertake to render all beings into standing reserve for our employment and assume a practical mastery of manipulable nature. That the whole tradition of Socratic rationalism is at issue here, that this is the rational spider that spins in the moonlight, is suggested by the section of *The Gay Science* just prior to the transforming words of the demon: that section (340) displays the meaning of "the dying Socrates" by solving the riddle of his last words. Himself moved by a demon, Socrates is the philosopher whom Nietzsche accords the highest possible praise, for he admires both the courage and the wisdom of everything Socrates did, said, and left unsaid; Socrates possessed the two greatest virtues and exhibited them both in his every deed. But he broke silence on his deathbed to betray that for him life is a sickness. "Socrates, Socrates *suffered life!*" "Oh friends, we have to overcome even the Greeks," the greatest of whom condemned earthly life and whose condemnation is betrayed not only in his dying words but in the Dwarf, the dying form of what he set in motion.

How can we be spared the theoretical and practical consequences of Socratic rationalism? If the first part of Zarathustra's vision shows how the greatest weight crushes, the second shows the other transformation for there "the one transformed" is depicted in the act of transformation. The vision thus portrays the two paradigmatic possibilities named in Nietzsche's first presentation of his thought. When the thought gains possession of the young shepherd, he finds it possible to respond in the way set forth in "On Redemption." He takes responsibility for the whole of the past; his

"But thus I willed it!" is higher than any reconciliation and says to all that came before, "Once More!" That this is the transformation awaiting Zarathustra is suggested by the final section of *The Gay Science* (342), for there Zarathustra begins, the young shepherd begins the transformation that will yield the other paradigmatic response to eternal return, the response that hears in it the words of a god, words that make possible the convalescence from the long sickness that has judged life a sickness, words that are addressed to beings as a whole and to one's own being and that spare and shelter them as they are. It is this response that the rest of *Zarathustra* depicts, the coming to be of the new shepherd, the teacher of eternal return. The final three sections of *The Gay Science* thus disclose Nietzsche's task in its historic dimensions, by moving from the dying Socrates to the decisive paradigms to the birth of Zarathustra. Furthermore, the section immediately preceding these three final sections (339) suggests that the fundamental issue in affirming eternal return is the problem of nature. In that compact section entitled "Life is a woman," Nietzsche describes the privileged moment in which, by a lucky accident, the clouds momentarily part to afford the viewer who happens to be properly situated a glimpse of the peaks of nature in sunlight. Those peaks are the most beautiful works of nature, and for the viewer to be properly situated to view them he must already have removed the veils from the heights of his own soul. Then he is able to see the work of nature that is his soul confirmed and reflected in the peaks of nature now visible to him—Socrates in sunlight. That such moments occur so seldom is itself an enticement to life, its most powerful enchantment. In Zarathustra's vision, as in the final sections of *The Gay Science*, the spectators who love to guess and who love it that the whole is enigmatic are entertained with a visionary version of the greatest spectacle: the mighty antagonism of Nietzsche and Socrates that presages the fundamental turn in the history of human things.

Zarathustra's speech to the Dwarf ends on the whispered question, "Must we not all eternally come again?" That thought is fatal to the Dwarf, but Zarathustra confesses that he himself was afraid of his thoughts and the thoughts behind his thoughts. That he fears this thought has been known since its first intimation in "On Redemption" (II. 20) and from the chapters in which it is anticipated as his final challenge (II. 22; III. 1). What he fears clearly cannot be the same as what crushes the Dwarf; but what does he fear? What is the heavy black snake that crawls into his throat when he thinks of eternal return?

At both its beginning and end, the second scene of the vision emphasizes the singularity of "The Vision of the Loneliest"; what will happen when the vision is enacted has no like. For if Zarathustra had once, in childhood, heard the like of the dog's howl, he had never seen the like of its cause, and, at the end of the scene, he hears something the like of which he has never heard, laughter so sovereign and so singular that he is haunted by the need to laugh that laughter himself. But first he must enact the chilling scene that made that laughter possible. In the second scene of his vision, in contrast to the first, Zarathustra is only marginally a participant, and what he sees leaves him with a longing that will move him to do what is necessary to reenact the young shepherd's deed.

The scene has two parts, one of unparalleled horror, the other of un-paralleled laughter. The horror is the vision of the young shepherd, the leader who tends his flock assisted by his dog, now "writhing, choking, convulsed," because a heavy black snake hangs out of his mouth, having taken possession of him by biting itself fast in his throat. Zarathustra tries in vain to pull the snake out and then cries out to the young shepherd to bite off its head. At just this point Zarathustra breaks into the narrative to invite his audience of adventurers to do what they love to do and are clever at doing, to guess the meaning of his vision. Before relating the climax, he asks them to unriddle what he saw and, three times, just who the shepherd is. He helps his guessing audience by beginning to identify the heavy black snake as "everything heaviest and blackest" and by putting the event in somebody's future. Having thus invited his listeners to guess that it is a vision of himself, he describes the final event in which the shepherd bites off the head of the snake and is transformed.[23] The transformation makes him "no longer human," for he is capable of laughing as "never yet on earth a human being has laughed." The effect of this vision on Zarathustra is the same effect of envious emulation that gods would have had on him had they existed (II. 2). Having heard a laughter that is no human laughter and having not laughed it himself, he wonders, "How do I endure to go on living!" But his longing to laugh it himself transforms his wonder; "How could I endure to die now?" At the end of the speech that denied what he could not emulate (II. 2), he had referred to what moved him as the merest shadow glimpsed within the ugliest stone, mankind, the shadow of the superman. But now that the shadow has begun to take shape, his passion to emulate what he has glimpsed drives him onward; moved by his envy of the highest, he prepares to achieve in himself what his vision has presented as possible for a man.

The easy guess that the transformed, laughing shepherd is the super-man requires the less easy corollary that, when the vision is enacted by Zarathustra, Zarathustra becomes the superman. The second part of the vision contrasts the heavy black snake of suffering with the laughter that follows once the suffering has been overcome. When the head of the snake has been bitten off and spit out, as it is in "The Convalescent," Zarathustra, the one who wills eternal return, is redeemed. Here he tells this vision as a "premonition" to an audience of adventurers; there, alone with his an-imals, he performs the deeds of the vision.[24] The heavy black snake sym-bolizing Zarathustra's fear is clearly not Zarathustra's snake symbolizing his prudence and present later to sing of his redemption. In Heidegger's interpretation the heavy black snake is the symbol of nihilism, and the brief interlude between the two parts of the vision is itself a return to nihilism, to the prehistory of the thought of eternal return.[25] But the heavy black snake cannot be nihilism as Heidegger understands it, for it is an implication of eternal return and not its long prelude. All guesses regarding its identity must be grounded in Zarathustra's explanation of it in "The Convalescent" (III. 13). There he gives it two separate and specific identities: first, it represents Zarathustra's horror at willing the eternal return of the small man; second, his horror at the teaching of the Soothsayer; the two horrors belong together. If redemption comes only when the past is willed, then it requires willing the small man. What Zarathustra sees and fears is that the small man or, in the crueler imagery of "On Redemption," the fragments and pieces of men, must be willed not simply as the evolutionary stage prior to the highest man, who will refute and supplant him. The small man must be willed as necessary to the highest man in his highest affirmation, for the prophecy of the Soothsayer is true, even if his teaching and his faith are false; there is no historic redemption in some novel future in which mankind will be perfected and the imperfect past redeemed by being the prelude to this perfect future. What Zarathustra fears marks the beginning of a great transformation in his teaching: whereas he had taught that mankind's redemption would come through the achievement of the future superman, he now sees that the outcome of the long history of Socratic rationalism requires as the way of redemption the willing of eternal return. But to will that purposeless play of mortal things, to shelter and shield all things from the marauding fury of vengeful human will, is to will the whole order of beings, including the lowest and most contemptible. Possessed by the thought of eternal return, Zarathustra almost chokes on his own form of revenge.

Both scenes of the vision are premonitions, for neither the victory over the spirit of gravity nor the victory over the heavy black snake has yet been achieved. Still, the images of "The Vision and the Riddle" amplify the formula for redemption given in "On Redemption" by picturing what redemption or willing eternal return will effect. Although the thought of eternal return entails many questions, the answers to which are by no means clear, Zarathustra himself is not deflected into questioning. What impedes his way is not insufficient insight, but insufficient courage, the courage to say to the past that includes the small man, "But thus I willed it!" As it comes to light in Zarathustra's vision, willing eternal return seems to present him with a variant of the problem of theodicy: Why does life need what seems to refute life, what is small and deplorable in mankind (II. 6)? In justifying the ways of life to man, Zarathustra too faces the problem of evil as the fundamental puzzle, whose solution calls for an act of willful courage.

The next two chapters belong together. In the first ("On the Happiness Contrary to Will," III. 3), Zarathustra, having overcome the "riddles and bitterness" he has experienced since leaving his disciples four days previously, now finds himself in a mood of unexpected happiness, which grows until it breaks into the praise of the next chapter ("Before Sunrise," III. 4).

The narrative introduction to the first speech situates it in a mood of recovery after he has set himself once again on the way of his "destiny." There is no audience for this speech or the next, for each intimates what his destiny is; before audiences he prudently masks his destiny in duplicity (II. 22) and riddles (III. 2). The speech on the recovery of his destiny is delivered to his "jubilant conscience" and is a speech about disciples. Given in the afternoon, it begins by recalling two previous afternoons, that on which he first found his disciples and that on which he returned to them.[26] This retrospective beginning exemplifies the whole speech as a calm and affirmative reevaluation of his course since the prologue; a Zarathustra now clear about his destiny provides the perspective from which his career hitherto can be judged. This speech confirms the shift in destiny required of the herald by the incapacity of his disciples and by his own insight into what is needed. After the failures of his disciples chronicled in part II, Zarathustra never again speaks of "disciples"; instead he now begins to refer to them as his "children."[27]

At the beginning, Zarathustra recalls his descent in search of a haven for his happiness, his descent to mankind and to disciples to give them the gift of his teaching. At the end, his happiness refuses to obey his command to abandon him and to take refuge in his disciples, who themselves must be sad and bitter after his abrupt departure. This refusal by his happiness ironically shows his mastery over it; it shows as well the shift in his destiny, for his happiness is no longer to be sought through disciples. Hitherto, he has sought one thing only, to have "a living plantation of his thoughts," disciples in whom his planted thoughts could grow and through whom would be achieved his "highest hope" of the superman. Recalling his insight at the end of the prologue that he needed "companions," he reminds himself that companions were not to be found but had to be created by his teaching. The creator of disciples once saw that act as the fulfillment of his task, but now he knows himself to be in the "middle" of his work, not at its end. Now that the disciples are not the means to perfection, Zarathustra must perfect himself for their sake. Like Descartes, another teacher who needed followers, Zarathustra has come to know the nature of followers: they are like ivy that climbs no higher than the trees supporting it and that often tends downward again after having reached the top.[28] Like Descartes, he has come to realize that he must do all the essential work himself. Still, after his own perfecting work has been done, followers of a certain sort will be necessary.

Having described where he now stands, he describes where his children stand: they are small and fragile plants, still sheltering one another from the wind. Zarathustra, the storming wind of the opening of part II, now sees more realistically what his disciples are capable of and what they need. They are still "blessed isles" to him, and one day he will transplant them so that each may learn to stand alone; only then will they be fitting symbols of "indomitable life." They will be of his kind and race only when they are able to write Zarathustra's will on Zarathustra's tablets. Nothing is said here in private, as it was in public at the end of part I, about disciples denying him and finding their own way. The disciples will be his companions, fellow creators and fellow celebrants, insofar as they follow his will and his tablets; they will follow their wills wherever he wills (Prologue 9).

In thinking of his own testing to come, his own perfection, Zarathustra is led to reflect on the signs that called him away from his disciples: the wanderer's shadow (II. 18), the longest boredom (II. 19), and the stillest hour (II. 22). All told him that it was high time. What kept him chained down was his imprudent love of his children, his double will (II. 21). But all the signs saying "it is time" were not enough for the reader of signs to break his double will. For that to occur, his abyss had to stir, and his thought bite him. Only then could he take the necessary steps that set him on the way to his destiny. In this review of his recent past, the event referred to as decisive is the discovery of what is necessary for redemption (II. 20), eternal return. He now willingly acknowledges that abysmal thought to be uniquely his own, whereas, for the sake of his disciples, he had found it necessary to allege that he was not worthy of it (II. 22). When this retrospective speech turns finally to anticipation, the series of events to follow is made precise: after he has found the strength to summon his thought, the next step will be to overcome himself in "something still greater," after which a victory will "seal" his perfection. The "seal" of Zarathustra's perfection occurs in the final chapter of part III, "The Seven Seals," while the other two events, summoning his thought and the "something still greater" occur in the chapters preceding that finale (III. 13–15).

Meanwhile, secure in his coming destiny, he grows mistrustful of the happiness that settles around him. He instructs it to possess his children instead, who now find themselves alone. As evening comes and "the sun sinks," Zarathustra awaits the coming of his unhappiness; but although he waits through the whole night, it never comes. The next speech is the speech of his happiness, the happiness of the new philosopher.

"Before Sunrise" (III. 4) is, as Eugen Fink says, "of the highest significance."[29] As the secret speech of Zarathustra's aspiration, it is one of the rare speeches that makes explicit his most fundamental insight and mission. It could be seen as another "Night Song" (II. 9), but whereas the darkness of the night sky had evoked in him poisonous envy, the open sky between night and day kindles in him "godlike desires." On board ship on the open sea, he stands in the pure abyss of light that marks the transition between the starry blackness of night and the sun-dominated brightness of day, a moment in which no heavenly bodies are visible. In this momentary emptiness and openness of light Zarathustra delivers the most rash of his speeches, recounting private aspirations of the most unrestrained sort. Now that he has overcome his envy of night's receptivity, he aspires to emulate the one thing still enviable, creative deeds that enclose the earth within a sacred canopy. The religious language of this hymn to the sky expresses his experience of the sky as open and innocent, an experience utterly different from the experience of the heavens under which mankind has long labored. For Zarathustra the open sky elicits a quickening of desire, an elevation and ennoblement of man as an earthly being. This new experience of the sky grants a twofold responsibility: first, to destroy the antique notions according to which mankind lives out his allotted days on the earth under the sway of the heavens; second, to confer a blessing on earthly things that will be like a heavenly dome in providing security and well-being, a sheltering vault of open sky over the earthly things. Having journeyed to the underworld and found the earth to have a heart of gold (II. 18), Zarathustra here ascends to the sky and finds in its openness a blessing for the earth. For the first time mankind can find itself at home on the earth under this open sky. But while emulating the most enviable, Zarathustra shuns being envied or being seen as enviable; therefore, he resolves to emulate not only the great deeds that enclose the earth under a new sky, but also the silence practiced by the open sky. Like the sky that he here addresses as kin, he will observe silence about the deepest matters, a politic silence that will spare him envy and spare his friends and followers what in any case belongs only to himself and sky.

Zarathustra's speech to the sky is made in the happiness that came contrary to his will. It begins by confessing secret godlike desires enflamed in him by contemplation of the sky; it will end on the same theme of desire, after having revealed the insight that grounds such desires or makes them a responsibility. Only in the final chapters will these desires be transformed into deeds by the willing of eternal return. Addressing the sky with a parable, Zarathustra says that just as beauty shrouds the gods, so the heavens now hide their stars in the beauty of light. Earlier, he had defined the beautiful in relation to the visible and the invisible: "When power becomes grace and descends into the visible: Beauty is what I name such descent" (II. 13). According to this definition, the beauty of the sky in this moment of openness is a gracious act revealing to him its nature. His wisdom ascends from visible beauty to invisible power and apprehends the utter silence of the heavens. "Revelation" is granted to him not by the heavenly bodies or "gods," but precisely by the open light that dims them; "revelation" is afforded by the surrounding depth and silence, whose encompassing beauty is speechless or dumb. This privileged revelation makes him a friend of the open sky, for now they have in common "grief and terror and ground."[30] Sharing these things means that Zarathustra's knowledge of himself provides him with knowledge of the sky; they are kin, "sister souls," who have "learned everything" and therefore possess together the secret behind the things aloft or the highest things. "Psychology is once again the way in to the fundamental problems" (BGE 23); the secret of the highest beings harbored by the sky is the secret harbored too by the most spirited being, the man Zarathustra.

Having fulfilled the single goal of his "whole will" to fly into the open heavens, he joins the sky in looking down from a great encompassing distance at the "necessity and purpose and guilt" that rain on the earth below. Seen from below, "necessity, purpose and guilt" can seem to be imposed by the very heavens under which earthly beings must live, but, seen from above, they are clouds that obscure the open depths of the sky. But the open sky was clouded for him by his own passion as well, by his very hatred of the clouds that others drew across the sky. Such clouds of interpretation and passion have robbed him of "the immense, unbounded yes and amen saying" of the open sky. But the theft was twofold, for the skies have been robbed of "the immense, unbounded yes and amen" of the man Zarathustra, a robbery that will come to an end in Zarathustra's final song, "The Yes and Amen Song" (III. 16).

Unlike Achilles, Zarathustra would rather sit in Hades, an underworld without a sky, than see bright sky stained by such clouds. But he does not curse himself to that underworld, because clouded opinions are not the only ones possible. Instead, he pictures himself as the keeper of the lightning bolt who will one day strike down the clouds that mask the purity of sky. He will perform the deed that silent sky will not perform for itself, thereby justifying its silent but affirmative ways, clearing the sky of necessity or purpose, and clearing man of the guilt he has felt for his very being under the clouded sky.

In the midst of the curse that he places on the old teachings about the heavens, Zarathustra reports a principle of his teaching: "He who cannot bless should *learn* to curse!" That teaching, whose provenance is clear— it fell from the open sky and not from some evil moon (II. 19) or any other heavenly being—has been placed by Zarathustra in his own heavens as a star, a point of guidance present on even the blackest nights. While the open sky is indeterminate and can fully ground neither this teaching nor that, and while it harbors even teachings that pervert its openness, the one who speaks in vindication of the open sky can take a certain guidance from its openness, for the open sky implies that bringing a curse is higher than half-hearted uncertainty, and bringing a blessing is highest of all. By setting this teaching as a guiding star in his own heavens, Zarathustra intimates the status of all teachings under the open sky: even the firm stars, to say nothing of the passing clouds, are set in the firmament by man's will, but some accord with the openness of the sky, whereas others do not. Those teachings, those "human constructs of domination" (*KGW* VIII 11 [99] = *WP* 12B) that have set themselves in the heavens as earth's necessity, purpose, or guilt, will be justly cursed by the new teaching on earth and sky.

Given the condition that the sky surrounding him be pure and deep, that he be surrounded by the unbounded, Zarathustra can confer a blessing on all things. In the long fight to free his hands for this blessing, he has mastered the art invented by Theseus whereby the smaller and weaker are able to defeat the larger and stronger, the art of wrestling that Plato himself mastered. What is the heavenly blessing that the artful wrestler Zarathustra seeks to give to earthly things? In the images of his song, the redemptive blessing sets over every single thing its own "round dome, its azure bell and eternal security." His "yes and amen," that says to every single thing eternally return, sets over each thing an open sky of security, not a security anchored in the curse of some alleged divine purpose or some mechanical necessity, but in the highest human affirmation of things. Zarathustra's blessing on things is a sheltering vault of blue sky, a letting be, an allowing, a sparing. Because the heavens do not speak, because they are absolutely silent, man is free to speak the blessing on things that they be just as they are. His blessing does not do violence to things but allows them to become themselves, luminous and intense in their evanescence. When Zarathustra prophesies the return of a god, it will not be a god who drops from the skies but one who appears from across the sea, a god born of the earth, whose return is made possible by the blessing on earthly things conferred by mortal man. The blessing of eternal return permits mortal man to be at home on the earth under the open sky, and it permits the return of gods who consecrate the world of mortals. Eternal return is the teaching that lets beings be.

"Blessed is he who blesses thus," says Zarathustra after describing his blessing: it is not the poor in spirit who are blessed, nor is the kingdom of heaven their reward.[31] The eternal security granted things by the teaching of eternal return is a baptism in the well of eternity that gives all things a new name (see III. 9, 13); it is a baptism "beyond good and evil," beyond the way of naming that has blessed and cursed until now. Long schooled in the grave baptisms of good and evil, mankind will need time to learn that in naming the heavens that stand over all things "accident, innocence, chance and playfulness," and in naming the source of purpose or necessity the "rational spider," the new baptism is in fact a blessing and not a blasphemy. Freed of all rational, teleological, or mechanical necessity by "Lord Chance,"[32] all things are released into the play and dance that will later be sung by Zarathustra's animals (III. 13). In this new poetry of the transitory, life itself is worthy of the highest affirmation and need "never stoop to a mechanical / Or servile shape, at others' beck and call."[33]

Although no sovereign rationality governs earthly things, there is, nevertheless, a seed of reason strewn among things, which, like leaven, makes a kind of wisdom possible, a new wisdom about the heavens. The new wisdom detects no traces of the supernatural in the heavens. Contrary to ancient wisdom, the heavens do not declare the glory of God,[34] nor does their regular motion provide the necessary undergirding for man's moral life.[35] Contrary to modern wisdom, the immensity of the heavens made evident by modern astronomy does not reduce man to something subhuman; the starry heavens above mankind do not "annihilate" his "importance as an animal creature," requiring recourse to some "moral law within" in order that man be secure in his ancient dignity.[36] The sky above Zarathustra is neither the ancient heavens of Aristotle nor the modern heavens of Kant; it neither commands nor annihilates, but in its depth and silence affords man the highest responsibility. Zarathustra's experience of the open sky does not cause him to shrink in obedience or bewilderment; rather it causes a quickening of desire, an elevation and ennoblement that raises him to what Nietzsche named in his next book "the complementary man," man whose unbounded yes and amen to beings complements them in their being and lets them be the beings that they are. In this way Zarathustra enacts what Nietzsche had described under the title "My task" in one of the first notes outlining his new Zarathustra project: "the *dehumanization* of nature and then the *naturalization* of man after he has achieved the new concept of 'nature' " (*KGW* V 11 [211]).

With the reaffirmation of Zarathustra's godlike desires, the moment of pure light passes, and the morning sky grows red with approaching dawn. Has he spoken the unspeakable? No, sky's blush signals the danger of betraying their secret to approaching day. Day is coming, and the world is "deeper than day has ever thought," words that become the refrain of deep midnight after Zarathustra's redemption (III. 15, §3). Not everything is permitted to be spoken in the presence of day. The silence of the sky judged by the perspective of bright day is a kind of ignorance or stupidity. Day wisdom mocks all infinite worlds: its brightness conquers night's darkness and proves its superior penetration.[37] But it is precisely the overconfidence of day wisdom that is penetrated by Zarathustra; still, that overconfidence is not openly disputed, for night wisdom steals away before forceful day. His own daylight wisdom, the bright blessing of eternal return, will not itself bring into the daylight the midnight wisdom of will to power on which it depends.

Zarathustra's speech to the heavens vindicates the heavens but only as emptied of heavenly bodies. Contemplating the heavens as man has done from time immemorial, Zarathustra, in a mood of happiness contrary to his will, draws his lesson from that brief and passing moment when, bathed in diffused light, the sky is empty and silent. No heavenly bodies are present to give evidence to the senses of a regularity and order superior to the earthly or of gods responsible for that order. What appears to Zarathustra's joyful contemplation is an open and indeterminate universe of chance and spontaneity. Insight into that enigmatic universe shows the impossibility of a complete rational, teleological, or mechanical explanation of things. But not only is no state of perfect explicitness attainable, its very impossibility is a blessing. The heavens ordain nothing and maintain silence about what is ordained, and it is precisely for that reason that they are lovable.[38] It is a blessing on earthly things that they are not governed by a purpose from beyond them, that they are not responsible to some order of being higher than themselves. Under the open sky, it falls to human beings, to mankind raised to the highest power, to do in word what the heavens manifestly do in silence: let be. "Where is the ring that in the end still encircles man?—is it the world?—is it God?" It is the open sky, whose permissive allowing comes to word in the human affirmation of the ring of eternal return, the azure dome of security placed over each thing. "God is dead, everything is permitted" thus comes to have a quite unexpected meaning, one free of the horror evoked from the good and the just by the destruction of the ground of their virtue, one far beyond the exaltation evoked from the the free spirit by the death of the rational spider, a meaning that takes literally "everything is permitted" by allowing each thing the freedom to be the thing that it is. In this permitting man "raises himself to justice" (*KGW* VII 26 [119] = *WP* 259); he does justice to things by allowing them to be what they are and exhibits what Nietzsche had earlier required of the new thinker, "justice and love for all that exists" (*D* 43).

The metaphors of enclosing and encompassing that Zarathustra employs to describe his blessing on things do not imply some limitation on man, as if Nietzsche called on himself and others to live within an arbitrarily drawn in horizon he knew to be a delusion. If the knower who inhabits the open whole of heaven and earth supplies as the highest affirmation a sheltering vault over all things by willing their eternal return, that vault does not limit or forbid inquiry. The penetration of the heavens by modern astronomy is not a curse on mankind, forbidding him to think well of himself, for it is with the aid of such penetration that man comes to a proper sense of his dignity among natural beings and to a proper sense of the dignity of natural beings as a whole.

Nor does the open blessing of eternal return falsely elevate mankind as the supposed master of natural beings with the right of dominion over them—a powerful modern relic of the "preposterous over-evaluation of mankind" (*KGW* VIII 11 [148] = *WP* 30)[39] that turned him into the earthly regent of the rational spider. As eternal return thus gradually comes to light in part III, it becomes apparent that Heidegger's "new beginning," his meditations on mortals and gods and earth and sky, bring him near to a Nietzsche that he need not lose. The Nietzsche to lose is Heidegger's, a Nietzsche to whom violence has been done, a Nietzsche who is ostensibly the teacher of "the absolute humanization of all being," the teacher for whom man is "measure and center, ground and goal of all being," the teacher who carries out the final stage of Descartes' project to make man the master and possessor of nature, a teacher who has let himself be entirely dominated by the essence of technology in order to prepare the way for the superman who will be able "to steer and deploy individual technological processes and possibilities" and will be fit for "an absolute machine economy" with which he can institute "absolute dominion over the earth."[40] On the contrary, on the contrary, Nietzsche is the teacher of the dehumanization of nature and the naturalization of man, the teacher who frees natural beings from the imposition of an order alien to them.

Zarathustra had begun his going under by addressing the sun, the most prominent of heavenly bodies, and by proclaiming his likeness to the sun both in his bright wisdom and in the openness with which he would give it to others. Now he praises the wisdom of the open sky as superior to the wisdom of the sun, for the silent wisdom held and withheld by the open sky encompasses the wisdom of the sun. To learn fully the new wisdom of the open sky means not only to learn the new speech that does justice to things, but to learn a lesson of silence, the silence of sky shrouded by what apparently "speaks" in the heavenly bodies. Zarathustra's pact of silence with the sky does not betray itself by silence but covers itself with speech.[41] The growing brightness of coming day, under which the pact is made, is emblematic of the coming chapters, which occur in daylight. While speaking to many audiences with what seems the greatest openness and recklessness, Zarathustra keeps silent on the things spoken to the open sky. The new public speech is politic speech that shields him from envy while opening him to anger and inviting a declaration of war against him. But his public speech is not the most significant shroud over his silence. The most important speeches of all, those of eternal return, are themselves daylight wisdom, a beautiful shroud for the midnight wisdom that can never come to speech. In the songs of the animals and in Zarathustra's final songs (III. 13–16), power becomes grace and descends into the visible. Shrouding itself in beauty, Zarathustra's wisdom loves to hide.

Zarathustra's flight into the open sky demonstrates the precedence of ascent over going under, while not canceling the importance of going under. His effort to throw himself high, for which he was congratulated by the spirit of gravity itself (III. 2), is here an ascent beyond all heavenly bodies into the open heavens that is their encompassing abyss, their groundless ground. This ascent into the groundlessness of the whole precedes in time and rank the new descent, making it possible by enflaming him with godlike desires to bring mankind a new encompassing light. His ascent into the abyss beyond all stars, including "the great star" that is the sun, counters Plato's image of ascent out of a cave of darkness into the light and order of a permanent sun. Even more directly, it counters the ascent that Socrates relates to Phaedrus, in which the soul ascends above the heavens to the place of which no earthly poet has sung, where true being dwells, visible to the gods; according to Socrates, it is the visible fragments of that order that lead Necessity to impose its order of rank on the souls of men.[42] Zarathustra's ascent into the depth and silence of the open heavens denies that the visible fragments give primacy to necessity; it shows that the earth is not bounded by anything that can give weight and bearing to human things. That gaze into "the ground and background of all things" that the Hour had identified as Zarathustra's will and had said would come when he had climbed above himself until every star was below him (III. 1) is a liberating gaze, which frees his hands to confer a blessing on earthly things, a new weight and measure, a "revaluation of all values."

In this speech Zarathustra duplicates and surpasses the feats of Lucretius's godlike Epicurus.[43] Driven by a passionate manliness of mind and will to be first, Zarathustra too is a conqueror who flies beyond the flaming ramparts of the world, the sun and the stars, breaking through the secure and ordered limits that men have posited as the encompassing frame of things. But when he returns from his inquiry into the things aloft, he does so not simply as a teacher who brings a sobering report of the perishability of supposedly eternal things, one who has no greater aim than to establish a community of the wise on the margins of the world of the foolish. He returns trembling with godlike desires to encompass the world within a new ring, to enclose the earth under a new sky. Like Aristophanes' Socrates, Zarathustra has seen that beyond the clouds there lies only vortex or chaos out of which all things emerge.[44] Although chaos could, in the way Strepsiades fears, succeed to Zeus's place,[45] Zeus's place could, in the way Aristophanes seems to teach, be taken by the Clouds themselves. In Aristophanes' play, the Clouds aim to become the city's gods and even, by virtue of their true standing, gods acknowledged by all cities or cosmopolitan, global gods who spare the men made civil by Zeus's reign the chaos consequent on his fall. Or, from a standpoint outside Aristophanes' play, uncrowned Zeus could be replaced by firmer, more stable inventions, such as eternal forms or eternal causes or by the Lords Necessity, Purpose, and Guilt, or some other rational spider. Zarathustra's perspective on all such clouds and gods is that they veil a kind of vortex or chaos neither malevolent nor dismaying even if utterly indifferent. The "highest" is in this way seen to be subhuman, and the human is seen to be highest. This insight, which is by no means new, is accompanied by a sentiment that is new: it is a state of blessedness that the human be highest. Mankind need not be sheltered from the silence of the heavens, but only from the clouds invented to mask that silence.

In freeing Lord Chance from bondage to Lords Necessity, Purpose, and Guilt, Zarathustra liberates chance from the rational principle of ground, the principle that nothing is without reason. He thereby frees chance from the bondage of a rational, teleological or mechanical interpretation, or from the spirit of gravity, which has acted as if it ruled everything high (III. 2). Zarathustra has discovered that gravity's rational rule is not authenticated or certified by the heavens. Although the spirit of gravity has become master of the world, its mastery is not grounded in some necessity beyond the world. Zarathustra's insight into the heavens equips him to defeat his archenemy in the battle for mastery of the world, to overcome the "teleotheology" of Socrates that has granted historic sway to universal forces that transcend human beings,[46] to overcome the "ontotheological" tradition that has dominated Western thought since Plato.[47] The god who returns under the blessing of Zarathustra's teaching will not be all-seeing Apollo, but a new patron of philosophy, a god who himself philosophizes, for the whole of which he too is a part is an elusive, enigmatic, marvelous whole, worthy of the inquiry of a god.

THE HISTORY OF THE NEXT TWO CENTURIES (CHAPTERS 5–8)

The four chapters after the sea voyage (III. 5–8) recount Zarathustra's renewed travels among men. In showing how he now presents himself to
others, they show a Zarathustra who chooses to appear as something less
than he is. Three of the four chapters (5, 7, 8) display in public the effect
of his vows of prudent silence, while the fourth (6) reflects on silence,
stating in private that public display is required of the one who desires to
guard his silence. In these chapters Zarathustra wanders on the mainland
after his sojourn on the blessed isles and his sea voyage. He likens himself
to a river flowing back to its source (III. 5), the inverse of the river flowing
to the sea, to which he likened himself when he last left his solitude (II.
1). On his way he delivers speeches to all who will listen (III. 5). He also
speaks privately to one who takes himself to be honoring him by imitating
his teaching (III. 7); and finally, at the end of his public speeches, he speaks
to that special audience of former youths in the Colorful Cow to whom
he had addressed the speeches in part I (III. 8). The new public speeches
are completely silent on will to power and eternal return, a silence not
surprising, given the special audiences and circumstances of the earlier
speeches on these matters (II. 12, 20; III. 2). However, they are now also
silent on the superman, a silence that is surprising, given the earlier need
to persuade others to take up the task of the superman. This new silence
demonstrates how completely Zarathustra has abandoned hope in others
as a means to the superman, visible now to him not merely in a shadow
(II. 2) but in a vision (III. 2).

   These last speeches to the public make manifest Zarathustra's transformation as a public speaker. Having once been "all mouth" (II. 1), he has
now learned ironic speech.[48] In these public speeches he seems to conform
to Kierkegaard's judgment in *The Present Age* that the individual cannot
help his age but can only express that it is doomed. But these speeches
do not provide definitive guidance on the question of Zarathustra's relation
to his age, for although they are the final speeches given in public in the
book they nevertheless mark a provisional interlude in his relation to his
age. When he enters solitude after these speeches, he does not simply
abandon public speaking, for there he prepares and practices new public
speeches to be delivered at some future date. In these speeches the individual Zarathustra attempts to say much more than that the present age
is doomed. These later, definitive public speeches require that the present
speeches be seen as provisional, the speeches of one who is no longer
herald of the superman but one who is not yet the bringer of the definitive
teaching. They are the speeches of one who learns more than he teaches.

   Since his descent in the prologue to cure the earth of the deadly consequences of the death of God, Zarathustra has come to learn the truth
of the Soothsayer's prophecy of "the long twilight" of nihilism. Chronicler
of the next two centuries (*KGW* VIII 11 [411] = *WP*, Preface 2), of the future

that now lies in his past, Zarathustra has learned what Nietzsche had already taught in *The Gay Science:* when gods die, men play with their gruesome shadows for centuries on the walls of their caves (108–09). These shadows of God that darken men's minds are the theme of the new speeches, for although Zarathustra is no longer the herald of a new hope, he cannot bring himself to be a distant observer, ironic and detached, like the Epicurean god described at the end of the chapter on religion in *Beyond Good and Evil.* Epicurean detachment, the sweetness derived from contemplating the distance between others' suffering and one's own intense pleasures, is impossible for one who has the future of mankind on his conscience; such a one must take up a "divine hammer" and cry out his condemnation in "anger, pity and horror" (*BGE* 62); the hammer speaks in these chapters on contemporary nihilism.[49]

Zarathustra's return to mankind signals a return to smaller matters than those addressed on the sea voyage; he himself has grown in such a way as to make contemporary things seem smaller to him now. "On the Virtue that Dwarfs" (III. 5) shows that he is already well known to the people to whom he returns, and that his teachings are a scandal to them. His return to men after his ascent to the heavenly things resembles the philosopher's return to the cave in Plato's *Republic*, and the people's hatred and suspicion of him repeat what Socrates expected of the cave-dwellers.[50] Zarathustra protects himself from the people by a species of careful talk that only appears to be unbridled. Although such talk freely enflames the anger of the people, it achieves its calculated success by never awakening their envy, for he never hints at how intensely pleasant his own pursuits are. His seemingly intemperate speech hides the intemperate aims that it is not fit to utter. Although he has gained a reputation for being a miracle-worker, he is a speaker without standing in the people's eyes; he has neither wealth nor followers who are not fools (III. 7); he is a stranger and a hermit, who would hardly be thought enviable if he did not call attention to his enviability.[51] Zarathustra's public speeches now refrain from inciting either the poisoned envy of the small or the emulating envy of the potentially great; they have a completely different purpose from the public speeches of part I, which depended on the dangerous but useful passion of envy to work their effect on potential followers, seen then as Zarathustra's potential superiors.

The first section of the chapter "On the Virtue that Dwarfs" gives the reason for Zarathustra's renewed wanderings among men: he wants to find out for himself whether mankind has progressed. He sees evidence that men have grown smaller, have moved even closer to last men, and among the small, he has to stoop to accommodate himself to their scale in the manner shown in his coming speeches.[52] Each of the two main sections of this chapter begins with Zarathustra stating, "I walk among this people." The first time he adds, "and I hold my eyes open" (2), the second time, "and I let many words fall" (3); one section of the chapter

PART III   183

thus describes what he observes among men, the other section what he says to them.

Zarathustra sees (2) that the people cannot forgive him for not envying their virtues; perhaps they even envy him his freedom from envy of them. He is a stranger among them and therefore arouses suspicion, but their words about him show that his reputation as a miracle-worker has grown among them, perhaps through reports brought back by the sailors to whom he had related his vision. They fear that he will bring the plague; although he suffers the little children to come unto him, the people pull their children away, fearing that he will cast spells on them.[53] In the middle of his speech he repeats its opening line, emphasizing what his now open eyes can see, that the people are made small by their teaching on happiness and virtue. His description of this teaching and its consequences expands his account of the last man. Most offensive to the Zarathustra who teaches self-overcoming is the universal presence of a teaching of servitude, even on the part of the masters. He sees in all the virtues of modern men the desire not to be harmed, to live lives of comfortable self-preservation inoculated against the primary fear. Mankind's virtues have thus been transformed into the vice of cowardice, the modest yielding of happiness to others in order to gain one's own modest happiness, a domestication that has been christened "moderation."

Zarathustra says (3) that it is futile to talk to the people. In describing what he nevertheless says, he makes it evident that he is not, or at least not always, a practitioner of "that impish and cheerful vice, courtesy" described by Nietzsche near the end of *Beyond Good and Evil* (284) as among the appropriate masks for a philosopher. But the words that Zarathustra lets fall among the people mask him from them, nevertheless, for the reputation he acquires makes it seem that he is the most unrestrained and irresponsible nihilist. To those shocked and hurt by his godlessness, he loves to shout, "I am Zarathustra the godless." To those who teach resignation in the face of whatever grace or chance may bring, he identifies himself as one who transforms what chance brings into what he wants it to be. Wondering why he speaks what no one can hear, he ends by speaking to himself. In private he unfurls his threat to the yielding resignation of modern man, a final confrontation in which they will shrivel and dry up, becoming like parched grass awaiting the flames of a prairie fire. He will consume them in flames on the day of the Great Noon, thereby contrasting the effectiveness of fire with the futility of speech, even if the object of fire and speech are the same. As he says near the end of his speech, he has become his "own precursor," the hour he heralds being his own hour.

Unlike the speech on the last man, which it resembles in other respects, this speech reflects no hope that the audience can be shamed into worthier virtues by being taught to see their present virtues as he sees them. He addresses men with no expectation that they will be changed by his words, but also with no belief that the future depends on their being changed.

The future depicted in the promised Great Noon includes great wars in which Zarathustra will destroy what is now unreachable through his words. While his hour is not yet come, part IV will end with Zarathustra descending again to men in order to bring about the Great Noon (IV. 20). The Great Noon will now appear more frequently as the name of the decisive hour. Announced first as a promise to disciples (I. 22, §3), it appears here as a threat to those who are not (III. 7, end; III. 10, end; III. 12, §§3, 30; III. 13, §2; IV. 13, §2; IV. 20).[54]

"On the Virtue that Dwarfs" says that Zarathustra made many speeches during his wanderings, but none of them betray his own most private and enviable thoughts and pleasures. "On the Mount of Olives"[55] (III. 6) shows a Zarathustra who has retreated into that unmentioned privacy during his travels among men, and who sings a song on how to seem.[56] It tells of others who have enjoyed a silence that they wanted to hide, but it alleges that their attempts to veil their silence all failed, for they served only as invitations to clever and suspicious unriddlers, the "nutcrackers" who, like Zarathustra (III. 10, §1; IV. 7; see also II. 16), delight in forcing into the open what would prefer to remain hidden.[57]

The Zarathustra who privately praises silence is now frequently in the marketplace keeping his eyes open and letting many words fall, a Zarathustra viewed with suspicion and fear by the citizens. His song of silence begins and ends as a praise of winter, home of the Hyperboreans, reached neither by land nor sea, a place calling for a hardness that offends modern tastes (A 1). But Zarathustra also loves summer, and however much he hides himself in a wintry coldness, his greatest praise of winter is for the art that he shares with it, the art of silence that covers his beloved summer. His praise of the silence of the winter sky recalls the pact made with the open heavens in "Before Sunrise." Now that he has come to share the secret of the open sky, he waits impatiently for the gray white light of a winter dawn, which often hides the sun completely. He asks who learned the art of silence from whom but realizes that the question of origin does not yield a simple answer, because such good things spring spontaneously and joyously into existence from a thousand sources. Zarathustra (Nietzsche says openly) has learned this art of concealment so well that he has completely hidden his "ground and final will" from the clever nut-crackers.[58] His art of silence "has learned not to betray itself through silence"; his speech deflects attention from his silence by making it seem that he is incapable of irony, a speaker for whom it is impossible to leave anything unsaid. His many wintry speeches in the marketplace on matters other than his own pleasures hide the existence of his pleasures and the fact that they concern his "ground and final will." His wintry hiding is necessary to kill with cold the many flies and mosquitoes (I. 12) that surround him as he walks among men with his eyes open, for their envy could never tolerate his summery happiness were they to learn of it. Only his practice of ironic speech makes possible for him what Xenophon's Simonides says is "the noblest and most blessed possession among men," being happy while not being envied.[59] Through what he lets men see of him, he lets men pity him; he also lets them hope that he is racked with misery and that he will one day perish in misery from his evil thoughts; he lets their anger and their fear express itself in the sweet hope of his demise. He does not encourage them to envy him through any intimation that it is intensely pleasurable to have come to understand human things in a fundamental way and to aspire to take a hand in them and change their course.

"On Passing By" (III. 7) brings the wandering Zarathustra unexpectedly to the gate of the great city. He has taught that the city is decadent (I. 13; II. 8), but now he hears his own teaching about the city from one who has learned to imitate it. This is the fourth time he has listened to another teacher (see I. 2; II. 10; II. 19), but this time he hears what purports to be his own teaching from the mouth of one who sees himself as faithfully mirroring it. The people, by now well familiar with Zarathustra's teaching, have named this man "Zarathustra's ape," but the narrative and Zarathustra himself call him a fool. After meditating on the speech of the fool, Zarathustra does not enter the city, for he learns from the fool that the time has finally come to "pass by." Zarathustra is the only audience for the fool's speech, which quotes verbatim from his own political teaching as given both in his first speeches (I. 11) and during his present wanderings (III. 5), and which imitates his own speech in some respects of phrasing and cadence. Zarathustra's condemnation of modern urban democracy, particularly its pursuit of commerce, its sensuality, and its practice of the virtue of service, which reduces the spirit to the lowest common level, receives in this aping form a novel and vulgar expression.

The would-be follower who makes this speech to Zarathustra alone presumably intends to elicit the master's praise for carrying his teaching further. But while the fool's speech apes Zarathustra's, it coarsens the imagery and repeats five times the advice to spit on the city.[60] What Zarathustra hears in the fool's abuse and vituperation is his own teaching of contempt for the last man unrelieved by the great longing for something higher; he hears what can be made of his teaching by imitators moved only by vengeance or envy. Far from eliciting praise, the fool's foaming speech elicits a disgust that Zarathustra expresses in similarly coarse imagery. To stop this teaching that purports to be his, he finds it necessary to do what he was forced to do once before with a teaching purporting to be his: to silence it by putting his hand over its mouth (I. 18). One wonders what Zarathustra's action would have been had Nietzsche had even an inkling of the damage that would be done to his teaching by such alleged followers who loved it that Nietzsche's critique fed their prejudice and their vengeance and who succeeded in making his teaching appear irremediably evil.

After suggesting that the fool's words bring harm to himself by ruining his reputation, Zarathustra shows how little these misjudgments matter to him. His final speech follows a long silence in which he contemplates the great city before whose gates he stands. He addresses both the city and the fool, for they resemble one another in their insusceptibility to being made better or worse by his words. Whereas the fool's judgment on the city culminated in his command to spit on it, Zarathustra's judgment culminates in his calling down a pillar of fire to consume it.[61] The difference between Zarathustra and the fool who apes him is an essential difference in what moves each of them, but whether by revenge or love, each is, nevertheless, moved to condemn the city. To the citizens, Zarathustra's motive of love could hardly be thought to excuse his judgment. His much stronger curse on the city, which the citizens have already heard (III. 5), brings "the sword of judgment" (III. 10) against its corruption, the apocalyptic biblical imagery indicating, from the received texts themselves, the extent of the revolution to be brought about by his new teaching.

In parting from the fool, Zarathustra gives him the gift of a teaching on parting: "Where one can no longer love, there should one—*pass by!*" With that, he passes by both the fool and the great city to whose gate he had unexpectedly come. The conclusion could well be drawn (although it commits the fallacy of affirming the consequent) that Zarathustra can no longer love either the fool or the city. Zarathustra and the fool have the same advice for each other based on a contradiction that each can see in the other but not in himself: to abide in the place that is loathed corrupts the one who loathes. Having learned to pass by, Zarathustra ends his wanderings among the people, who by now identify his teaching with the poisoned form mouthed by his ape. He returns to his cave after one additional act of passing by.

"On the Apostates" (III. 8) is the final speech of Zarathustra's second descent to mankind. Having refused to enter the great city, he enters the city "that he loved," the Colorful Cow, where he had delivered the speeches of part I and found his disciples; but he enters to deliver a speech on passing by. Its special audience consists of youths for whom he had once had hopes, some of whom had once even danced to his wisdom. They are the apostates of the title, for they have broken with what once held their loyalty and have embraced new beliefs. Zarathustra's speech, which describes their new beliefs and the need for belief, could have been subtitled "On Belief." His perspective on belief is given in the first section as the setting for his speech. Himself a knower, and as a knower necessarily courageous, he describes his former audience as believers, and belief as cowardice. The once fundamental distinction between knowing and believing is grounded on the still more fundamental distinction between courage and cowardice.

Zarathustra's speech on belief presents itself as a description of the "hour," the times in which youths turn desperately to new and old beliefs, while those who are no longer young grow skeptical of their old and once comforting beliefs. This final public speech contains what he has learned about that "most uncanny of all guests," nihilism, described by Nietzsche in precise detail in the years following *Zarathustra*.[62] To the believers for whom he had once had hopes, Zarathustra speaks of their present age as a twilight doomed to a coming night, suggesting only by the merest hint that he harbors hope for a coming day. His "bright silence" does not suggest, as Nietzsche did later, that he is the one who has lived through the long night of nihilism, that he is the philosopher who must now "look backwards" to explain to others what is still coming, "the first perfect nihilist of Europe who, however, has even now lived through the whole of nihilism to the end—who has left it behind him, under him, outside of him" (*KGW* VIII 11 [411] = *WP*, Preface 3).

The chapter has two parts; in the first, Zarathustra speaks to himself on what the youths have become; in the second, to the youths themselves. Before he addresses them, he once again addresses himself with an injunction to take courage (see III. 2)—now the courage to relinquish his hopes for them. Having lost the courage that once drew them to his teaching, they now willingly say of themselves, "We have become pious again." Could Zarathustra be to blame? He absolves himself, seeing them as blameable because they share the vice of cowardice to which almost all fall prey. He has shared the fate of all who bring a novel teaching: at first to capture as followers only "corpses and jesters," second only "believers." He gathers the courage to pass by his former friends who have become believers again, but first he speaks to their faces in order to shame them, not to reform them.

Revival of belief is the predominant feature of the hour, an evening hour in which pious hunters sent out by ancient, as well as novel, sects stalk wounded quarry for new adherents.[63] Zarathustra presents himself as one who can "hear and smell" what arises in the darkness of this hour: "closet cults" and sects, of which he lists seven, with variants of Christianity predominating alongside other more novel beliefs such as those of Schopenhauer and Wagner.[64] New believers appear in the approaching night, but a new unbelief also appears as the seventh item he lists, an unbelief of nightwatchmen, a new form of apostasy. "Last night at the garden wall," Zarathustra overheard five sayings about ancient things in a dialogue between old men that reflected a new honesty or intellectual probity about their old God. This is the honesty that Zarathustra earlier saw as the youngest virtue (I. 3) and that Nietzsche described as the historic consequence of the Christian truthfulness that draws one inference after another against itself, destroying Christian dogma, Christian morality, and, finally, in its most striking inference, questioning the will to truth itself (*GM* III. 27). The old nightwatchmen do not draw all the inferences that truthfulness forces on Christendom, only the first one, the one that kills the Christian God as loving and attentive father. In this hour in which youths turn pious, their fathers grow secretly skeptical. The old men know that it is the nature of the old to demand that its authority be simply believed; they themselves want to be honored as authoritative by the belief of their sons, but they can themselves no longer believe in the old story of the fatherhood of God. They have themselves been far better fathers than God the father, and they renounce their sonship to an absent father who has never proved his fatherhood by fatherly deeds but has demanded instead only blind belief in his paternal authority. In the nihilism of the coming night Zarathustra hears the fathers turn in melancholy away from their ancient beliefs while the sons turn in cowardice to the same beliefs and to novel ones. This twilight of belief and unbelief accompanies the death of God, the event that sent Zarathustra into the mountains in the first place, the one whose immediate antidote he had once believed he could offer the people.

While the Christian God is fated to die in a long twilight of piety and impiety, the death of the ancient gods was different. The lie had been told that they "twilighted" into death in the growing light of the new God, but Zarathustra maintains that they died in a different and godly way. They died laughing when "the most godless saying" proceeded from the mouth of one of them, an old grimbeard of a god, jealous enough to forget himself and say, "There is one God! Thou shalt have no other gods before me!"[65] Laughing and rocking in their chairs, they died repeating, "Is that not divinity itself that gods exist but no God?" Thus there was only one God, but no divinity. Now the death of that God causes the long twilight of nihilism that was disclosed to Zarathustra by the Soothsayer and studied in his own wanderings among men. His last parabolic words in public suggest that the immortal ones who died laughing at the birth of the single God could perhaps be reborn in the laughter at his death, a possibility to be confirmed by the events of Zarathustra's redemption.

The last speech that Zarathustra delivers to men resembles his first speeches in describing the present as the time of the death of God. But because he has since learned of the long twilight in which piety is still possible and practiced even by those who once danced to his teaching, his last words are not simple declarations of what to do now that God is dead. "The greatest recent event"—that the old God is dead (GS 343)—is now viewed more ominously than it was years earlier when he expressed amazement that the old saint in the forest had not heard of it. It is the event that he now knows will occupy "the next two centuries" of European history (KGW VIII 11 [411] = WP, Preface 2), if only as a "pathological transition stage" (KGW VIII 9 [35] = WP 13). What lies on the other side of the night of nihilism is barely hinted at in his final speech to the newly pious. He ends his public speaking seeming to announce that his age is doomed. Kierkegaard, himself a public speaker, had said that every man should be chary of speaking about essential matters with anyone but God and himself.[66] "Zarathustra the godless" has grown chary of speaking about essential matters with anyone but himself. Although these guarded speeches promising doom are his last words to the public, his approaching solitude is marked by the rehearsal of public speeches. In solitude the audiences for his new tablets are only imagined, but the speeches he rehearses demonstrate that he will return to mankind to deliver a new teaching for the overcoming of nihilism.

ZARATHUSTRA'S SOLITUDE (CHAPTER 9)

Zarathustra's return to the solitude of his cave is a homecoming, a return from the alien to the near and familiar ("The Homecoming," III. 9). He will remain in solitude for the rest of part III—that is, until the end of the book as Nietzsche thought while writing it. The return to the cave ends the travels that had begun with high expectations at the beginning of part II. Addressing the solitude he had then abandoned, he attributes to it the qualities of a mother, supplying her with words for his welcome home. She speaks like a mother who always knows best and scolds him for not having learned earlier that he belongs with her. Zarathustra and his solitude both take speech as their theme and contrast the openness possible in solitary speech with the guardedness and superficiality necessary in public speech.

The first words he supplies his mothering solitude recall his earlier departure from her (II. 1) and quote his parting words in an act of self-mockery, for those words had celebrated the breaking of silence. Now that the unfaithful Zarathustra has returned to solitude, having learned the necessity of silence, faithful solitude promises him that here he need not practice silence, for here he can talk freely about everything and pour out all his reasons; he no longer needs to hide his reasons or even hide that he has reasons for the sake of disciples needing instruction (II. 17). To a Zarathustra newly returned from his lessons in guarded speech, solitude makes a promise of what will be possible now that his speech can proceed unguardedly. In the speech of his solitude—in the final seven chapters— "all things" will come to word, and it will ring as praise in the ears of all things that one would speak justly with them.

When Zarathustra responds to the invitation of his solitude to speak freely, he addresses her with a celebration of the kind of dialogue possible between them. In contrast to speech between Zarathustra and others, speech between Zarathustra and solitude can proceed without being halted by questions and without complaints arising. Speaking for himself, he confirms emphatically what solitude has claimed is possible for his speech:

> Here words and word shrines of all being open up before me; here all being wants to become word; here all becoming wants to learn from me how to speak.

Zarathustra has never before used philosophy's comprehensive word *being* except to ridicule its use by those whose inventive speech purported to have discovered the meaning of being (I. 3). When speaking with the range and ambition of those who spoke of "being," he had spoken of "all beings" (II. 12). Now, encouraged by his solitude, he claims for the first time that all "being" wills to become word in his speech. But in the same sentence in which he first uses philosophy's traditional word to name the goal of his own speech, he collapses philosophy's traditional distinction by adding also that "all becoming wills to learn speaking" from him. Not simply being and becoming, but being as becoming comes to word in his speech. The claims of this speech anticipate later speeches in which all things will be seen to come joyfully to speech and to have a blessing conferred on their playful way by Zarathustra's speech.

Having affirmed what will be possible, he again follows the lead of his solitude by contrasting solitary speech with what he has learned of the limitations of speech among men, with whom forgetting and passing by are the best wisdom. This chapter on the relation of speech and being twice contrasts the primary or authentic speech of Zarathustra, the speech of philosophy in which being itself comes to word, with common speech in which primary matters are veiled in idle talk. Such public talk betrays into superficiality the deepest mysteries of human existence, leaving them in a state of complete neglect while seeming to address them. Zarathustra can now congratulate himself on having put behind him his "greatest danger," earlier referred to as his heart's double will (II. 21). Now that he has abandoned the form of prudence that anchored him to mankind, he can terminate the form of public speaking that his single virtue, the gift-giving virtue, had once forced on him. His gift had intended to reform mankind through persuasion, but even his persuasive speech had turned common in the marketplace in which it had been given. Zarathustra's gift-giving virtue takes a different form in the solitude he now enters.

THE NEW MEASURE OF THINGS (CHAPTERS 10–12)

The speeches of Zarathustra's solitude divide into two groups, each fulfilling in its own way the promise that all being will come to word in his speech. In the first group (chapters 10–12) Zarathustra enacts a new measure of things. He thereby acts on the belief Nietzsche had expressed in *The Gay Science:* "What do you still believe in? In this, that the weight of all things must be newly determined" (269). Believing in the necessity of that task and freed from the constraints of speech addressed to others, Zarathustra in his solitude weighs specific values and legislates new values. Although his legislation is said explicitly to be incomplete (III. 12, § 1), its character is clear as a total revaluation of all values. These chapters exhibit a mood of expectancy as he awaits his final return to mankind. They are the guide to his public task as it has survived his previous failures to move the public. The second group describes the decisive event that fulfills the promise of his solitude more literally, the event of redemption in which all being comes to speech in the songs of eternal return (chapters 13–16).

"On the Three Evils" (III. 10) begins with a dream (§ 1) that sets the mood and the task for the coming day (§ 2). In his final dream before waking, Zarathustra weighs and blesses the whole world; standing apart from the world, beholding it as separate from himself, he finds it, under the right conditions and for the proper person, "measurable," "weighable," "encompassable,"[67] "unriddleable." This sweet dream contrasts with the three dreams of part II: the welcome dream at the beginning in which he is granted permission to return to his disciples (II. 1), the nightmare which revealed that mankind needs to be redeemed from revenge at the past (II. 19), and the commanding dream reported at the end that forced his break with his disciples and sent him back into solitude (II. 22). The sweet dream of Zarathustra's solitude confirms the powers of his solitude, which have grown since the first dawn of the prologue. Whereas at that dawn the sun blessed his happiness without envying it, here jealous dawn awakens him from his sweet dreams. But how could his dream have had the necessary time, strength, and insight to weigh the world? It must have been secretly informed by his day wisdom, for it alone could ground this most ambitious dream to measure the worth of things as a whole. Nietzsche said later that evaluations of the world as a whole make sense only as "symptoms," and that *"the value of life cannot be estimated."* But the context in the *Twilight of the Idols* for that emphatic declaration measures Socrates as in agreement with all the wisest hitherto in judging of life that *"it is no good"* (*TI*, "Socrates," 1, 2). The judgment made by the wisest of all ages is symptomatic of their hatred of life and of their will to revenge. Zarathustra's own evaluation of the whole world, his dream, could itself be seen as only symptomatic, albeit symptomatic of the opposite "physiology." His judgment that sees life as good and wills its eternal return could be taken to be as groundless as the uniform judgment of the wise hitherto if some ultimate ground be sought beyond things themselves. But his judgment, grounded in the disposition of the judge or in "the great stupidity" that he is (*BGE* 231), nevertheless accords with the openness of things; his most spiritual will to power is attuned to the will to power of things. The openness of the sky, the groundless ground of things, accords best with a teaching that does not cloud its openness. His dream, caused by his day wisdom, dreams of setting a great star in the open heavens, eternal return, the sun of his new affirmative daylight wisdom. It is grounded in his own being, which predisposes him to dream this dream rather than that dream, and it accords with the newly discovered way of beings as a whole.

Both driver and the thing driven, combining the contemplative virtue with driving force, Zarathustra's dream has in fact weighed the world. In asking himself if his day wisdom caused his dream, he contrasts it with his night wisdom or midnight wisdom. Although here his day wisdom may seem to eclipse his night wisdom, its brightness making sport of it, Zarathustra affirms the superior depth of his night wisdom (III. 4, 15–16). It befits day wisdom, even Zarathustra's, that its brightness seem to drive off a wisdom that is dark and that loves to hide. His day wisdom is said to "mock all 'infinite worlds.'" It must therefore mock the "infinite world" of his night wisdom, which faces the "unbounded," the abyss of light (III.

4), and which is deeper than day has thought (III. 15). His day wisdom can be seen as the now rising sun whose brightness hides the silence of the sky and his midnight wisdom. In its mockery of what encompasses it as the surrounding, unbounded heavens, Zarathustra's day wisdom speaks a formula for its own act of daylight mastery: "Where force is, there *number* becomes Queen:[68] it has more force." Number has more force than force, number masters force. All infinite worlds are reduced to finite measure by day wisdom; force itself is finite and is mastered by its calculability, by being made determinate; mere force is formed and controlled by its reduction to the calculable. This is a pregnant if singular saying for the mastering Zarathustra; this once, in his daylight, world-weighing, world-mastering wisdom, he speaks a formula akin to the will to mastery through calculation so omnipresent in modern philosophy since Descartes, whose mathematical physics or whose reduction of force to number promises to make men the "masters and possessors of nature" and to turn the world into a garden.[69] It is this promise alone that forced Descartes to publish his work. Similarly, the promise of Zarathustra's day wisdom forces him to descend again to mankind after he has completed by himself the tasks of his night wisdom, bringing in that descent a new teaching that aims to eclipse Descartes' teaching of possession and dominion. But despite its bold mockery of infinite worlds and its successful mastery of force through the calculable, despite its techniques of reasoning and calculation that enable it to transform a determinate world through speech, day wisdom, even Zarathustra's, is itself enclosed within unbounded and indeterminate heavens that mock its mockery with encompassing depth and silence.

After announcing the bold and mocking saying of his day wisdom, Zarathustra returns to his dream and its remaking of the "finite world" hitherto so cursed by human wisdom, a remaking not to be accomplished by number or the method of mathematical physics. The images of the dream evoke a world prior to the curse of human evaluation, the world of Eden, but his dream adds to those images of apple and tree the image of a "shrine," something handmade, joined by human enterprise. In the dream the world presents itself as at his disposal, to be enjoyed, not completely enigmatic, though not completely evident either, for complete evidentness would cause wisdom's sleep and the triumph of the mechanical. In Zarathustra's dream the world presents itself as a human thing for human enjoyment, humanly good, even though humans predicate evil of it.

When Zarathustra awakens, his day wisdom is able to weigh three things immediately—sensual pleasure, the passion to rule, and selfishness. What Zarathustra desires to master are the reigning evaluations of man and the world and not the world itself. The grave evaluations that have cursed human things have weighed them from a center of gravity external to them; the open heavens liberate by refuting the possibility of such a center. Still, Zarathustra's thought does not release things into mere weightlessness. According to the imagery of this speech, eternal return will master the world by defeating the spirit of gravity, and superseding it by a new center of gravity true to earthly things. This speech also suggests the appropriate relationship between will to power and eternal return: the midnight wisdom of will to power makes possible and desirable the daylight wisdom of eternal return, a teaching symptomatic of the disposition to affirm and in accord with the enigmatic character of the whole.

Gratefully remembering his dream, the wide-awake Zarathustra undertakes to weigh the three things judged most evil in the world and to free each from its ancient curse. Each of the three most accursed things is a human passion. Like the wisest hitherto (II. 12), he weighs them knowing himself to have accepted a great risk in being judge, avenger, and victim of his own law. He casts three questions on the scales, and each receives its answer in one of the accursed things: sensual pleasure is the bridge over which the now passes into the hereafter; the passion to rule is the compulsion that compels the high to stoop to the low; selfishness calls the high to climb still higher. The three passions all belong to human aspiration as the driving force moving humans toward the future, toward mastery, and toward greatness. Each of the three is linked to the next, and each is embodied in Zarathustra himself: the first shows what he shares with all men, the second what he shares with the few who seek power, and the third what he shares with the very fewest, the wise who legislate values. This chapter shows what moves Zarathustra by identifying the passions to which he finds himself subject or to which this commander is obedient. But, while moved by passions cursed by traditional teachings, he is spared their curse by the nobility of the passions themselves; having these passions is the condition and mark of nobility.

Zarathustra must curb his brief praise of the first "evil," sensual pleasure or pure lust, for fear that his praise will be misunderstood. Though he is the teacher who also extols chastity (I. 13), respects the virtue of continence, and himself practices self-restraint, Zarathustra praises sensual pleasure, the passion that moves human beings forward into the future through procreation. Further, the sensual pleasure enjoyed by a man and a woman is itself symbolic of "a higher happiness and the highest hope." The "fence" around his thought obscures what is signified by the symbol of sensual pleasure; but the words "highest hope" suggest the marriage between those "stranger still than man and woman," the marriage that is consummated at the end of part III when the chaste Zarathustra "marries" the woman Life. Sensual pleasure is not itself the highest happiness, but rather is symbolic of it as a passion that masters the present for the sake of a fruitful future in its progeny. For the chaste Zarathustra himself, sensual pleasure is sublimated into pleasures whose progeny are historic.

The central passion to be redeemed from its curse is the passion directed not at the single other but at all others, the political passion to rule

(*Herrschsucht*) that compels the high to stoop to the low. At the end of his account of this passion Zarathustra reveals its presence in himself by confessing that this is the passion he once called "the gift-giving virtue." His account of *Herrschsucht* thus unriddles his own most characteristic virtue, but without disowning it. The passion to rule is first depicted in images that demonstrate its terrible power over the one ruled by it, the ruler himself, and only later in its terrible power over the many ruled by the master ruled by the passion. The many learn to curse that passion in the ruler, while the ruler takes himself to be accursed by it and disowns it. But this doubly cursed passion creeps high even to the pure and solitary, to the most spiritual, compelling even them—even him, for Zarathustra must now be thinking of himself—to stoop down from his solitary height to rule. Here in his solitude, while freeing the three most accursed things from their curse, he knows that his solitude can never be sufficient for him. His own passion to rule, the translation of his victory in solitude into a gift for mankind, is the desire of the high to stoop to the low not out of compassion but as ennobling spiritual rulers. Zarathustra hesitates to call that desire for descent "passion,"[70] because the name could seem to demean an act of noble manliness. No one has found an adequate name for this force behind the act of mastery, a name with which to baptize it and confer virtue on it as the longing felt by the highest or most spirited, a name by which to ennoble it—though many have found names by which to debase it. Once Zarathustra had a name for this longing that he thought adequate, "the gift-giving virtue." But that name is no longer adequate, nor is the name "passion to rule," for he now calls it "the Unnameable." Unnameable is the active longing to rule to which the high are subject. The desire here left nameless is the political aspect of what Nietzsche later called "philosophy" when speaking of philosophers as "commanders and legislators" (*BGE* 211). The wisest are moved by the desire to give things the weight, measure, and stamp of their own thinking and to provide the people with the ark of values that they can carry forward as their treasure. Schooled by Nietzsche's use of the phrase in *Zarathustra*, at the point where the will of the wisest is unriddled (II. 12), and in later works in which the imperial ambition of the few philosophers is identified, one might expect that here, where Zarathustra refers to this longing as "unnameable" and as ill-served by naming it mere "passion," the name "the will to power," "the most spiritual will to power" would be introduced (*BGE* 9).[71] But Zarathustra pointedly avoids giving the name that he had used earlier and that Nietzsche would later use frequently for the phenomenon of ruling that he here describes. The use of that name is thus confined to parts I and II of *Zarathustra* where its extent is discovered and the responsibilities conferred by its discovery are glimpsed. In part III will to power is not named by the one who has learned politic speech; instead it is described and practiced by the one who was once the teacher of "the gift-giving virtue" and is now the practitioner of "the passion to rule" or the "unnameable" passion of the highest. The gift-giving virtue with which the book opened is present at its end, though now in a form more easily understood because no longer masked by a "virtuous name" which fails to name what is truly virtuous in the act of the high stooping to rule.

The third accursed passion follows from the previous two by being the passion that moves the highest individual not forward into the general future of mankind nor downward bringing the gift of his rule, but still higher into what he alone can achieve. Zarathustra named this passion "selfishness" when he taught the gift-giving virtue (I. 22, § 1), and here he proposes no new name but retains the old, accursed one.[72] The presence of this passion moves the highest or Zarathustra himself to aim for the highest goal. The highest soul is subject to a passion; its commanding is obeying; the highest natures yield to nature. Selfishness is linked to the passion to rule. Speaking not of the unnameable will to power but of what belongs to a "powerful soul," Zarathustra describes the love of victory that moves such a soul and what its highest victory is. To such a soul belongs a transfigured body in which all things are mirrored; the self-enjoyment indulged in by such bodies and souls names itself "virtue," and from the perspective of this virtue good and bad are not only distinguished but take on a form of the sacred; "good and bad" provide a canopy of protection resembling a sacred grove around such a rejoicing self. This account of selfishness focuses on the "bad" or on vice as seen from the perspective of the virtue that is the love of the highest self for itself. From this perspective the primary, even the sole, vice is cowardice, of which Zarathustra identifies many forms, ending with the yielding pacifism of Christianity. All types of cowardice are seen as belonging to a slave mentality brought to effective focus in the priestly teaching according to which giving selfishness a bad name is a virtue. Ending with prophetic words gleaned from the Bible,[73] Zarathustra promises or threatens that at the Great Noon at which much will be revealed, the "sword of judgment" will be raised against the teaching that condemns the self. The chapter that opened by weighing the world in a dream thus ends by promising the sword of judgment against other evaluations of the world. The selfishness of the most powerful soul seeks a victory that is no private victory; moved by its own most powerful passion, it seeks to overturn the evaluations that have cursed the noble passions and ruled the world until now.

Perhaps because of its emphasis on the freedom to be won by the highest self, an emphasis necessary to the fable depicting that self in its self-overcoming, *Zarathustra* seldom mentions a factor prominent in Nietzsche's accounts of what the self is to be delivered from in the new teaching of selfishness: the myth of personal responsibility, "the metaphysics of the hangman," according to which human beings are fully at their own disposal, a myth that has made it possible to affix guilt, justify punishment, and influence behavior, particularly through the incorporation of guilt and punishment by conscience. Exploding this myth is essential for the love of self in all selves; this is the "great liberation—only thereby is the innocence of becoming established again" (*TI*, "Errors," 7,8).[74] In its selfishness the most spiritual self achieves a teaching that is a gift of liberation to other selves, a gift of reconciliation and gratitude for being the selves they are. Zarathustra's selfishness is indistinguishable from complete public spiritedness or the love of mankind. His selfishness is a kind of selflessness or cruelty toward the self that demands of it what is hardest. Driven by a love of victory that it simply discovers and honors as its unteachable spiritual fate (*BGE* 230–31), the powerful soul that is Zarathustra's finds that it cannot be satisfied except by the greatest possible service to others. The desire of Zarathustra's soul, its selfishness, liberates him from the desire for lesser things such as comfort, riches, and immortal glory; it demands of him the most difficult undertaking, that of redeeming the world from the curse under which it has lain from time immemorial and of founding a new order on the earth.[75]

Zarathustra's weighing of the world continues in "On the Spirit of Gravity" (III. 11), where he confronts his mortal enemy in a way that finally exposes it completely.[76] The imagery associated with the spirit of gravity has a prominence afforded no other image in *Zarathustra*; it persists from beginning to end and is underscored in six separate chapters (I. 7; II. 10; III. 2, 11, 12, §2; IV. 17). The spirit of gravity is singled out as Zarathustra's "devil," his most dangerous and most present enemy. Although it makes its only direct speaking appearance in Zarathustra's vision, where it is "half dwarf half mole" (III. 2), this seemingly low or diminished form does not exhaust its powers of appearing, for the spirit of gravity is, "they say, 'the master of the world' " (II. 10). As such it is the force holding everyone in thrall, and the present chapter provides a most remarkable description of how that force is exercised.

When he first identified the spirit of gravity as his devil, Zarathustra spoke prematurely of his own "walking," "running," "flying" over that spirit as if the antidote to gravity were levity (I. 7). But the appealing gaiety of that speech is supplanted when the spirit of gravity next appears in "The Dancing Song," where it is first identified as "the master of the world" (II. 10). No victory over what masters the world is gained in that song. When the spirit of gravity finally takes shape and speaks, it is crushed by Zarathustra's thought (III. 2), but that victory, an image in a vision, is only symbolic of a victory yet to come. Although the vision shows what the coming deed will effect, it is only in the present chapter that the spirit of gravity is fully identified; only here does it become obvious why the spirit of gravity merits the name "master of the world," and why victory over it would inaugurate a new age. The account given here shows that it is worthy of its name and reputation as the force that has given all things a weight that seemed intrinsic to the things themselves. The spirit of gravity is Zara-

thustra's special devil because, as master of the world, it signifies what
must be mastered if Zarathustra is to give a new weight to things; it is
Zarathustra's special devil because of Zarathustra's special task. The spirit
of gravity appears most frequently as the enemy to be defeated by Zarathustra's ascent or ultimately his flight, by the movement contrary to going
under, the descent made prominent by its appearance at the beginning,
by its frequent repetition, and by the animals' benediction that Zarathustra's
going under is ended (III. 13). Whereas the animals use the image of going
under to crown his course, Zarathustra uses the image of ascent, celebrating
his victory over the spirit of gravity in the image of flight. The precedence
of ascent over descent is confirmed by his final words in part III, his "alpha
and omega that all that is heavy become light," where he himself becomes
light and soars on wings of his own making into skies of his own making
(III. 16, §§6, 7). Zarathustra's most important victory is over the spirit of
gravity.

The imagery associated with the spirit of gravity has an arresting and
essential component added to it when Zarathustra says of his "abysmal
thought," eternal return, the means of victory over the spirit of gravity, that
it has its own terrifying weight or gravity (III. 3). In his first announcement
of the thought, Nietzsche had named it *Das Grösste Schwergewicht*, "the
greatest weight," "the heaviest burden," or even "the most solid center of
gravity" (GS 341). The weightiness or gravity of Zarathustra's thought points
to the decisive matter in his victory over the spirit of gravity, for that thought
is not to be understood as simply opposition to gravity, but as a new center
of gravity from which all things derive a new weight. Zarathustra "replaces"
all boundary stones rather than simply removing them; he redraws the
boundaries within the unbounded that he has glimpsed. Heidegger says
that, while asking "if there is still gravity or weight in things or whether
every possible center of gravity has vanished from things, Nietzsche's
thought ... wants to give things weight again."[77] Nietzsche's thought is a
new weighing from a center of gravity supplied by the affirmative will that
wills eternal return. The imagery of weighing the world, characteristic of
all four chapters prior to Zarathustra's actual willing of eternal return (III.
9–12), shows that his final victory, his becoming a "bird," is no mere freedom
from gravity, no mere "explosion into the air," to use Hegel's relevant criticism of those who would escape the gravity of their own setting in the
historical.[78] Zarathustra's "heaviest" thought gives a new gravity to human
actions; it does not simply oppose all gravity with an unbearable lightness
of being.

Entitled "On the Spirit of Gravity," this chapter has as its theme the
distinction long known to philosophy between nature and convention.
Focusing on the nature of man, it reveals the process whereby mankind
has come to its conventional interpretation of its nature. In keeping with
his practice of abandoning the old language of philosophy, Zarathustra
avoids the terms *nature* and *convention*, speaking in the main part of the

chapter of the love of "one's own." Acknowledging the universal predominance of a certain kind of love of one's own, he advocates a new love of one's own by distinguishing what is genuinely one's own from what is conventionally one's own or one's own only by acquisition. He reveals the secret power of the spirit of gravity to be that process whereby man has learned to love as his own a self that is secondary or invented, the self of the clansman or citizen created by weighty tradition. This chapter provides a commentary on "The Thousand Goals and One" (I. 15) by revealing the secret process by which one comes to honor as one's own a people's good and evil. Here, where his point is not to honor peoples or their founders, Zarathustra brings the spirit of gravity to light as the master of this world, whose mighty force has everywhere grounded convention on the gods or nature, thereby creating a conventional self that purports to be one's own while actually being inimical to one's primary, but obliterated, "own." The spirit of gravity is the force that ties one's deepest loyalties to external matters that come out of the past, bearing the weight of grave tradition and certified as one's own by every authority that counts.

But the enemy can be identified more specifically still.[79] As the Platonic language of "one's own" suggests, Zarathustra's special enemy is Plato and Platonism. Whether in its pure philosophical forms, which will to make all beings thinkable, or in one of the many Platonisms for the people, which translate that purity into a popular religion, his enemy is what has mastered the world as the view that mankind is ultimately responsible to something outside itself, that human beings are by nature or by God fitted for obedience or reverence before what is universal and transcendent. Our tradition trains us in obedience, makes us civil or grave, by teaching us that it belongs to our highest nature to serve what is immeasurably higher than ourselves, thus eradicating "one's own" for the sake of a new and learned sense of "one's own," a second nature said to be superior to the first. Our Platonism, our gravity, trains us to regard belief in the transcendent as the condition of the very possibility of human dignity and a humane community. If that teaching has now shriveled into a dwarf of its former self in the Soothsayer, in Schopenhauer, the last possible Platonic philosopher; if Platonism is now only the view that the world as it exists ought not to be and that the world as it ought to be does not exist (KGW VIII 9 [60] = WP 585); if we are now fitted only for despair, the spirit of gravity still rules and needs to be conquered by a different spirit, one that does not set out from the judgment that life is no good without some supplement.

The battle with the spirit of gravity, the central fable of *Zarathustra*, is reproduced with names in the great preface to *Beyond Good and Evil*. The enemy is Plato and Platonism for the people, our branches of the dogmatism that has until now mastered the world. Plato's dogmatism— the invention of the pure spirit and the good in itself that makes all beings thinkable—once bestrode the world as a monstrous and frightening mask, and the long modern fight against it has created a magnificent tension of the spirit, the like of which has never before been experienced on the earth, a tension now felt as the need and distress of nihilism. For the philosopher who experiences that tension, it may be clear that all dogmatism lies on the ground, but even in its shrunken, pessimistic forms, Platonism rules mankind's view of itself. Another of those shrunken forms, the democratic enlightenment that is the heir to Christianity, tempers the distress and threatens to unstring entirely the tense bow that could project mankind to future goals. Coupling the nihilistic despair of the Schopenhauerian philosopher with the threat of universal rule by the last man and his pleasures, the preface to *Beyond Good and Evil*, like the book itself, suggests that there is a higher goal, the goal set forth in *Zarathustra* as fatal to the spirit of gravity.

The chapter on the spirit of gravity opens playfully, showing how the parts of Zarathustra's body oppose the grave, how his body, his self (I. 4), what is most his own, is far from what is one's own by custom. How his mouth speaks, his hand writes, his feet run, and his stomach digests all point to a bodily order different from gravity's order. His is a transformed body, one that is birdlike as the final, extended image suggests; his manner is to sing and to fly and thereby to overcome the spirit of gravity. The promised song and flight of the birdlike Zarathustra belong to the final acts of the book (III. 15–16), though the second part of this chapter anticipates those songs and describes the victory they enact.

The spirit of gravity as educator has, by a secret process, succeeded in becoming the master of the world. Therefore, the one who teaches men to fly will have moved[80] all boundary stones and baptized the earth with a new name, "the light," in place of the old name, "the grave." Opposition to flightless gravity is achieved through love of one's self, the selfishness of the previous chapter. Zarathustra claims that "love of the neighbor" is the subject of the best lies told by the spirit of gravity, though "the spirit has told many lies about the soul." To discover the soul worthy of love, it is now necessary to engage in the labor of overcoming those many ignoble lies. The Platonic lies about the soul are neither noble nor necessary, though Plato's Socrates alleged that they were both, while showing how love of the neighbor or of one's fellow citizens is grounded.[81] Plato has Socrates cast his lot with the spirit of gravity even after he has understood the process whereby a lie replaces the truth, whereby convention "nobly and necessarily" replaces natural origins and lyingly grounds one's loyalty to one's "own" things as one's people's things. The *Republic* itself introduces new lies about the soul in the "ministering poetry" of book 10, for Plato tells the lie that the soul is immortal, hoping to ground the decency of young men who no longer believe that they must be just because Zeus is just. In Nietzsche's view Plato "wanted to have *taught* as absolute truth what he himself did not regard as even conditionally true: namely the separate existence and separate immortality of souls" (*KGW* VIII 14 [116] = *WP* 428). While opposing this "calamitous" "soul atomism" that has been taught longest and best by the Platonism for the people that is Christianity, Nietzsche has no desire to renounce the "ancient and venerable" hypothesis of the soul. His new version of the soul hypothesis, what his spirit teaches about the soul, includes such conceptions as "mortal soul," "soul as subjective multiplicity," and "soul as the social structure of the drives and affects" (BGE 12).

In contrast to Jesus, who transformed the old commandments respecting the other into new commandments respecting the other,[82] Zarathustra's act of conferring worth on the self does not appear as a commandment at all but as a special art. This subtlest of arts which practices love of one's self, presupposes in its practitioner the best of qualities, because what it seeks, "one's own," has been best hidden by the spirit of gravity, which has created the political or social animal man by making his primary love a love of others. In contrast to these submersions of the self in the other, Zarathustra elevates as most lovable the self of a certain sort of self. The classical distinction between love of one's own and love of the good collapses for the artist who discovers in what is his own what is most lovable or what is good in itself.

How has the spirit of gravity succeeded in making it seem that what is worthy of one's love because lovable in itself is external to one's self and demands the suppression of the self? Speaking of how the spirit of gravity has "created" what it willed, Zarathustra uses the impersonal "one"—"one gives," "one allows," "one hears," "one forgives," "one forbids"—calling attention thereby not only to the universality of the commandments of custom, but also to their impersonality, the uncertainty of their source of authority. The conventions embraced as one's own come out of the past bearing the weight of unquestioned authority, though their origins are in fact misty or hidden. Almost from the cradle "one gives us"—Zarathustra says as the representative of what all men have undergone at the hands of authoritative tradition—grave words and values, "good and evil." "One suffers the little children to come unto him" so that these words may be given as the inheritance that alleges to teach us our nature, while actually creating what eventually seems to us to be our nature. And we who have all been schooled or burdened by the spirit of gravity, "haul loyally what one has given us." Should we perspire under our acquired load, one confirms its necessity by reassuring words; one says to us, "Yes, life is hard to bear!" But Zarathustra says, "Only man is hard for himself to bear!" and the reason is that man hauls on his shoulders much that is alien which passes as "one's own." Man is like a camel who has willingly knelt to be laden with foreign cargo. Especially desirous of this burdening is "the strong, weight-bearing man in whom dwells awe and reverence."[83] But now the camel spirit undertakes a new burden, as described in Zarathustra's earlier speech (I. 1), the burden of separation from everything thought to be essential or sacred until now. In the language of *Beyond*

Good and Evil, the reverent spirit climbs the last rung on the ladder of religious cruelty and sacrifices God himself (55). Zarathustra agrees in part with the judgment of the burdened that there is much about one's own that is hard to bear. Because of the presence within of much that is ugly, mankind has done well to acquire the art of masking, for that art creates a noble shell around that shameful core. Nevertheless, the art of shell building has been abused, and wretched shells have come to hide what is good in man. This long process of hiding one's own with a shell alleging to be one's own has made it difficult to discover what man is in himself, or what the soul is, and whether it is worthy in itself. The heart of man, deepened and made enigmatic by the historic sway of the spirit of gravity, now requires an art of nuance in order to discern what is good in it. For Zarathustra there can be no simple return to nature or to the nature of man once the lessons of the spirit of gravity have been scraped away, for man is what the spirit of gravity has made of him. Man is the being determined by his history, and Zarathustra too must say, "Let us not be ungrateful" to the spirit of gravity (*BGE*, Preface), because "this tyranny, this capricious, this rigorous and grandiose stupidity has *educated* the spirit" (*BGE* 188), and the long spiritual warfare against it has now created a magnificent tension that brings the most distant goals within reach, including among them a new natural man achieved through ascent (*TI*, "Skirmishes," 48).

The final part of the chapter shows how to break the hold of what the spirit of gravity has created. "The mole and dwarf" who says that good and evil are anchored in the nature of things and hence binding on everyone is silenced quite simply by the one who says, "This is *my* good and evil." This liberating first step away from the spirit of gravity breaks the authority of the ancestral words given almost from the cradle, words that have been "the greatest power on earth." The affirmation based on personal taste[84] that this is my good and evil (see I. 5) renders the spirit of gravity mute, breaking his power, which from the beginning has been the power of speech by which peoples, speaking their good and evil to their offspring, dripping lead into their ears, have robbed them of their own by giving weight to the ancestral. Guided by his taste and freed of the bonds of gravity that once tied him in love to what was allegedly his own place and allegedly his own things, his home and the lake of his home, Zarathustra now freely chooses where he will make his home, and what he will identify as his own things. He has won the right to be guided by his taste through a long process of self-instruction, "standing and walking and running and jumping and climbing and dancing." But these stages on life's way which liberate from the spirit of gravity culminate in another learned act, flying, the activity that is learned last, for one does not fly into flying. Zarathustra's learning to fly is the last of his deeds; he thereby breaks free of the weightiness of the ancestral curse and frees his hands to bless all things (III. 4, 16).

The spirit of gravity has no single name; it is both willing and unwilling to be called Zeus;[85] it is not any single founder of any single people but the way of founders hitherto. The spirit of gravity stands for the way of the ancestors, the way that provides fresh blood for old ghosts. While the ancestral gods of mere family or mere city have long since been swallowed up by greater successors, those successors still secure the ancestral way. Whether in the shape of Clouds or eternal Forms grounded in the Good, or some Platonism for the people, Christian or modern, the way of the ancestors continues in the universal rule of the other. The spirit of gravity maintains forcefully that its way is simply necessary, that "The Way" be grounded in the gods or God or Nature or History. The spirit of gravity can even demonstrate that some such ground belongs to the fundamental requirements of the city by demonstrating that it has been a feature of every city or people hitherto. It can even quietly hold that God does not exist while arguing that it is necessary to invent him or to lyingly teach that he exists in order to preserve the city from nihilism and tyranny. Zarathustra is the teacher of new fundamental requirements for the city. He is thus the most modern of teachers, committed to the historical sense and engaged in spiritual warfare against what has prevailed until now and against what seems demonstrably necessary. Because of the sway of the spirit of gravity, there is for Zarathustra no question of return, not even to the ancient temple to whose columns he found it necessary to be bound. What he seeks to establish is an experiment with something that has not yet existed among men, love of one's own, where one's own is identical with the good. But this most modern of teachers takes the ancient way of peoples; he aspires to hang over mankind a new faith and love, a new table of values to ground the praiseworthy, the good, and the holy, not out of loyalty to the ancestral but out of loyalty to the earth.

Zarathustra's speech on the spirit of gravity as educator ends in a manner consistent with its beginning, emphasizing the singularity of the way he has taken. It ends in a declaration easily misunderstood as simply an invitation to a permissive and yielding relativism that would reduce Zarathustra's way to his personal opinions, which could be set alongside all other opinions as of equal merit: "This—is now *my* way—where is yours? ... *The* way—does not exist!"[86] It belongs to Zarathustra's way that no apodictic ancestral voice legislate the way or punish waywardness. He has just said that man cannot fly into flying; in learning the preliminary steps to the highest act of flying, he has himself taken many routes, devious and questionable, and along the way he took, he always hated to ask after the way. But whereas he has asked only reluctantly, many have asked him eagerly about the way. In a chapter with frequent references to a way of gravity whose hold is still felt, Christianity, Zarathustra here draws a further contrast between himself and Jesus. After speaking of the way to be taken and hearing a disciple ask eagerly about the way, Jesus said, "I am the way."[87] But when the teacher of the ladder of achievements for overcoming the spirit of gravity is asked about the way by those eager to fall into the gravity of some way, he says, "This—is now *my* way—where is yours?" This is the teacher who has had to modify his hopes for his disciples because, like all disciples, they depended on him for making the way; he has now learned to parry the question of the way by inviting the questioner to his own way, for *"The* way—does not exist!" The Zarathustra who has learned the necessity of ironic speech turns aside those who would make him a new center of gravity in the old way of gravity. In Zarathustra's way no absolutely grave commandments emanate from some Commander whose very existence as Absolute Sovereign or tyrant dictates that there be The Way. Zarathustra's way liberates from all forms of the spirit of gravity, including that final and most dangerous form, the universal and homo-geneous way of the last man that abolishes all difference or directs it into the madhouse. Although Zarathustra is the teacher of the global people, mankind, he refuses the tyranny of a universal morality grounded in some supposed God, Nature, or History; the whole is an enigma, a permissive openness offering no ground for a universally valid way.

Nevertheless, the one who refuses a universal way now prepares him-self in solitude for the sovereign task of weighing the world anew. Zara-thustra has discovered that the way of the wisest is the passion to rule; he has not refused that passion, even if he has refused what it has hitherto legislated. In the very next chapter he appears as a new legislator creating new tablets for mankind and smashing old ones. Through his final act he becomes for the rest of mankind, for those who will ever learn only to stand or to walk or to run or to jump or to climb or to dance, the new legislator who finds in himself that which is most lovable and who stoops to rule because he is moved by an "unnameable" passion or a will to power. The way he takes is named "Impossibility"; it is the new route that opens to him alone, but one that enables him to create a new way of making things matter, a thousand-and-first goal for the new people mankind. Still, it belongs to Zarathustra's legislation that the new tablets be only "half-written" (III. 12, §1); they do not dictate chapter and verse but provide only boundary stones within the unbounded by which a variety of tastes true to the earth can express themselves and create their own ways.[88]

The voice of the new legislator speaks in "On the Old and New Tablets" (III. 12).[89] This is the longest chapter in the book, and it contains Zara-thustra's final weighing of the world prior to the culminating events of redemption. Like the two previous chapters, it reviews his public teaching and reforms it. While awaiting his redemption, the now solitary Zarathustra prepares himself for a final return to mankind in order to bring the new legislation that will fashion the people mankind out of the thousand peoples that have existed hitherto. This is the most important account of Zara-thustra's public teaching, because it shows how that teaching is to be for-mulated subsequent to all the lessons learned in the course of addressing the public. Schooled at last by his errors and his audience, he now prepares half-written tablets that will bring the earth under a new rule. Appropriately, this final account of the public teaching is silent on its ground; the daylight wisdom brightens away the midnight wisdom. It is silent on the superman as well, except in retrospect (III. 12, §§3, 24). Zarathustra no longer teaches that mankind or disciples must be dedicated to the task of evolving a superman. Instead, one finds the outline of a "new nobility," leaders and teachers of men reconstituted by the teaching true to the earth, eternal return. The right of the new nobility to rule will have to be wrested from "the good and the just" who now shepherd mankind; consequently, the new public teaching ends on a call to hardness for the spiritual warfare to be fought on behalf of the future of mankind.

In his retrospective account (§§2, 3) of his attempts to move mankind into the future that he alone has envisaged, Zarathustra recalls the main points of his earlier teaching. He now knows that he sounded like a fool then, like a "preacher of repentance" whose "wild wisdom" ranted at an audience that could never comprehend. For, while they occupied a present that seemed complete and firm, he had flown into distant futures where everything was in flux; whereas they believed that only the permanent could be divine, he had seen a future where the play of becoming was divine. Even in this vision of the future the spirit of gravity is present. The grave view according to which only the unchanging can be sacred seems inextinguishable from human things, for it is present, if no longer master, in the future of sacred becoming envisioned by Zarathustra.[90]

While retrospectively recalling his flight into the future (§3), Zarathustra names the superman for the first time in part III. The word will be used once more by Zarathustra in a similar retrospective setting (III. 12, §24) and, for the final time in part III, by the animals (III. 13). No longer a feature of the public teaching now being assembled, the superman is visible only in the acts undertaken by Zarathustra himself. The section that begins by naming the superman (§3) deals primarily with redemption, now seen as an event in his own future. He repeats exactly the definition of redemption given earlier (II. 20); but now, in solitude, he can say freely what caused terror when intimated in dismay to his disciples, that he himself is not yet redeemed. But he awaits his redemption, that act in which he will say to the "it was" that has drawn the curse of the wisest hitherto, "But thus I willed it!" It is only here, not during or after his redemption, that Zarathustra repeats this essential formula for redemption. Describing the course of events he now plans, he says that only after he has redeemed himself will he return to his disciples; only then will be the right time to die.

The long speech that follows this review of his career is given to an imagined audience of brothers to whom will fall the tasks of the new nobility. Although Zarathustra's new legislation (§§4–6) begins with commandments of overcoming that repeat things already said to disciples, these lessons too seem intended for those already long schooled in his teachings. They are no longer enjoined to perform the tasks preparatory to a superman, but the tasks of spiritual warfare that secure the new teaching against the old. What remains unwritten in the new legislation is the precise way of overcoming that each must write for himself; the boundaries that can be commanded outline a noble disposition toward life sworn in an oath. The new legislation will require of its first adherents that they be sacrifices, victims of the still reigning customs of good and evil. They will be victimized by the only language available to them, the language of good and evil shaped over the centuries by what they oppose. In again insisting that his friends become more "evil," Zarathustra himself accedes to a language that is not his own, one by which he will be victimized, for it will be said that he is calling on his friends to invent as yet unimagined instruments of cruelty with which to inflict new tortures on mankind. His own teaching is beyond good and evil, beyond the terms of measurement first introduced by Zarathustra/Zoroaster as metaphysical realities. "Evil" is a label invented to inflict harm; it is itself an instrument of punishment (§10). Because the "good" is what is customary or ancestral, "evil" is what opposes the ancestral (*HH* I. 96). In acceding to its use, Zarathustra calls on his friends to be still more adamant in drawing down on themselves the vengeful judgment that they are teachers of evil. Having disclosed the roots of the ancestral as the work of the spirit of gravity, he calls on his friends to become completely evil, to break utterly with the ancestral ways. To earn the vengeance of the good, Zarathustra's friends are to practice a virtue first introduced by Zarathustra/Zoroaster, truthfulness, a virtue closed to the good and the just because they have surrendered their minds to the spirit of gravity and its supposedly noble lies (§7).

Having introduced the theme of truth with the accusation of a systematic lying by the good, Zarathustra turns to the fundamental question of philosophy: being, or the meaning of being. In an age in which transcendence rules, the river of becoming is spanned by man-made planking (§8), and the one who proclaims that "all is flux" is easily refuted, even by the simpletons who point to the apparent permanence of the planking of transcendence over the river of flux. But when the hard winter comes, the river itself seems to freeze into permanence, and the cleverest, no longer persuaded by planks of transcendence, are persuaded by the icy permanence to hold the nihilistic variant of the teaching of transcendence, that everything is the same, nothing changes. Zarathustra is a spring wind, breaking up that permanence, and making evident to the wise and simple alike the sovereignty of becoming. This historic task of breakup also requires attacking the superstitions of ancient determinism and modern freedom (§9) and the mendacity of biblical commandments (§10).

In two sections, both of which are reflections on past and future, Zarathustra's new public speeches turn directly to his political teaching (§§11, 12). They give content to what Georg Brandes called Nietzsche's "aristocratic radicalism," [91] a political stance not included within the modern spectrum of politics here depicted in its two extremes of tyranny and mass democracy. The setting for Zarathustra's reflection is his compassion for the whole of the past because it is fully at the mercy of the present. It is not permitted to be what it is but is distorted by every present into a prologue of itself, as if the past existed in order to have this outcome. In the modern age the whole of the past is threatened in two ways, first by the possibility of a tyrant powerful enough to read it as existing only for the sake of his appearance. His power would commission a base rewriting of history in order that the past underwrite his present; the past would be constrained to appear as a series of stages leading to him as its necessary and desirable outcome. This modern tyrant is not the mighty spirit capable of preserving and willing the whole disparate past with his "But thus I willed it!"; he is instead "a shrewd monster" whose pleasure and displeasure transform that past into History now allegedly made meaningful by its outcome in himself. The second way in which the whole of the human past is threatened in the modern age is by the lordship of the mass, who exist in a foreshortened present, completely forgetful of anything older than their grandfathers. Reflection on the annihilation of the past by the two modern political extremes of tyranny and democracy leads Zarathustra to a third political possibility, one not connected to the present dialectically; it will not arise through some historical necessity, for not even this finger of God plays a part in human history (*BGE* 203). Zarathustra's new politics depends totally on his powers of persuasion. In attempting to persuade his friends of the poverty of the present age and the possibility of a new age, he is required to speak a language disturbing to their ears—and now further debased by those who aped his speech in some respects of phrasing and cadence—the language of "a new nobility."[92] In introducing the idea of a new nobility, Zarathustra makes a theological suggestion by referring to his parable: "Is that not divinity itself that gods exist but no God?" (III. 8). Just as base monotheism drove out the noble variety of many gods, so the political monotheisms of modern tyranny and modern mass democracy forbid the variety that is the precondition of nobility. A new political polytheism, a plurality and variety of noble forms, must supplant the base uniformity of political monotheism. Though compelled to use the discredited language of aristocracy, Zarathustra shows that the new nobility is to be distinguished from all previous nobilities for, unlike them, it does not base itself on pride of descent, on its ancestors or claims about ancestors. It spares the past the indignity of noble lies perpetrated by every previous aristocracy to ground its spurious claims. It looks away from the land of the ancestors toward a "children's land." While the new nobility differs radically from the old by basing itself on the future, not the past, it redeems the whole of the past, allowing it to be what it was, for it holds that "nothing that is may be subtracted; nothing is dispensable" (*EH*, "Books: *Birth*," 2). "The eye of the nihilist . . . is unfaithful to his memories; it lets them fall, lose their leaves," and the modern political nihilisms let the whole of the human past fall into forgetfulness (*KGW* VIII 10 [43] = *WP* 21). The new nobility, while engaging in an act of founding that loves posterity, preserves in memory the whole of the human past by not letting it perish into dialectics or ignorance.[93]

The "new nobility" is a political concept, but politics has been enlarged by Zarathustra to include principally the acts of the educator. In Zarathustra's public teaching the new nobility seems to replace the superman, its plurality and variety seeming to supplant the singularity of the one superman in whom the history of mankind would be justified. But the superman teaching cannot be replaced by the teaching on the new nobility, for the latter is not comprehensive enough; tasks once thought to be the responsibility of the superman still need to be accomplished, and they are not assigned to the new nobility. Mankind is in need of a redemptive teaching that will end the rule of revenge and weld mankind into a single people, not a homogeneous people but a people of noble variety. Zarathustra prepares himself for that new teaching, the teaching of eternal return within which a new nobility can take its various ways. His teaching educates the educators with half-written tablets. Although Zarathustra says that he is only "a prologue to better players" (III. 12, §20), he nevertheless brings the essential teaching within whose permissive boundaries those better players can play. The new nobility are the friends and followers needed by Zarathustra for the tasks of investigation and instruction that carry forward what he has already grounded. Nietzsche's books after *Zarathustra* are all fishhooks cast for such followers (*EH* "Books: *Beyond*," 1).

As vulnerable as the ancient nobilities are the ancient wisdoms, for their teachings against life are ennobled now only by their age (§§13–15). Modern wisdoms, heroic in their way (§18), embody, nevertheless, a nihilistic hatred of earthly things (§§16, 17). Knowing that both his motives and his teachings will be perverted by parasitical critics (§19), Zarathustra repeats and expands many admonitions already given (§§19–29) while exhibiting a new awareness of his audience's sensibility by apologizing for his cruelty on the grounds of its necessity (§20). Old lessons on warfare, friend and enemy, the mass, and passing by (§21) lead Zarathustra once again to the theme of ruling. The rule of kings, like the rule of princes (§12), is past, having been succeeded by the rule of commerce, with everyone calculating his own self-interest in even the meanest circumstances. Zarathustra yearns for a time when a people will say to itself, "I want to be—*master* over peoples!" The lesson he draws runs counter to an old teaching on ruling: "For, my brothers, the best should rule, the best also want to rule! And where the teaching runs otherwise, there—the best is *lacking*!" The teaching seems to have run otherwise among the wisest hitherto,[94] and Zarathustra concludes that where the conjunction of power and wisdom is left to grace or chance, it does not occur, and the best is not achieved. The education that makes this conjunction possible is treated in a parable (§22) in which the best are portrayed as inexorable "beasts of prey," incapable of being domesticated even by a society sufficiently desirous of taming them to give them whatever they want. Zarathustra wants to rear these lions in our midst; he wants such beasts of prey to be nurtured until they become capable of the greatest tasks. Only the birds are still above such men, but when men learn to fly, their ambition will be boundless, as depicted by Zarathustra's act of flying at the end of part III.[95]

The peroration of Zarathustra's public speech brings to a fitting climax this final outline of what will be required of the friends of his teaching. Building with rising intensity to the harshest tablet he will set before his friends (§27), he imagines their shocked response (§28) and, granting its legitimacy, shows them how to overcome their initial horror (§§29–30).

The one who has grown wise about ancient origins (§25) and understood peoples and their foundings finally aspires to found a new way, one in which power and wisdom come together. All foundings have been accompanied by great eruptions and dislocations, and this one will be no exception. It will be an exception, however, in being built on the true insight that all peoples till now have been experiments, and even that the whole history of peoples has been an experiment. Mankind is not the result of some "contract" implying consent and equality among the contracting members, but rather of a series of commandings that have created communities of the obedient. But now in human history there appears a time of special eruption, for the new founding must be directed against those whose dominion threatens the experiment that is mankind with perpetual failure, "the good and the just" who refuse to see that mankind is an experiment (§26).

Just here, as he prepares to announce the harshest consequence of his public teaching, Zarathustra finds it prudent to note that he is only the second to have understood the good and the just, Jesus being the first. Still, the second understands them better, having not only seen into their hearts, but having also discovered their very land and soil. Their hearts show the necessity of their being Pharisees, for they value their own things and, out of gratitude for their superior sanctity and merit, crucify those who invent their own virtues. The one who has gone further and discovered their land and soil has discovered that they necessarily hate most those who break their tables of values and inscribe new ones, and that their hate grows out of the soil of envy. Envious of what they cannot duplicate, they confer on themselves the names of goodness and justice and stand loyal to the ancestral past. The Pharisees of the modern age, the modern good and just who have spread their virtue across the globe and who know themselves to be the successful outcome of the whole upward arc of history, represent a special danger to the human experiment because their continued dominance, their successful opposition to the new creative founding, would terminate the experiment too early and make the last man the lamentable end of the whole magnificent experiment. If the worth of mankind depends on continuing the long experiment, then it follows that "the harm done by the good is the most harmful harm"[96] because "they crucify the whole human future," not just one revolutionary teacher. This insight first came to Zarathustra at the end of the prologue (9); he knew then that the enmity between himself and the good would have to be a fight to the death. Now, having prepared his imaginary audience of brothers by discrediting the goodness of the good and showing how the good imperil the future, he announces his harshest public demand (§27): *"Break, break the good and the just!"* Faced now with the statement that they must break not only the teachings, but those who teach them; faced too with arguments showing this act to be the necessary conclusion of Zarathustra's public teaching, the audience of friends, already long habituated to hard demands from their teacher, nevertheless shrinks back in terror (§28).[97] Zarathustra does not soften his hard saying, but he does explain metaphorically the necessity of their fright and how it can be overcome. The good and the just have led mankind to believe that it rests secure on firm land under fixed heavens. That assurance comforted mankind until it was discovered that mankind was in fact adrift on high seas. The discoverer of mankind's drift is also the one who charts the course for its future. Those trembling in terror over the disclosure of what that course will cost, are instructed to think rather of the cost of continued allegiance to the discredited old. Adrift on a stormy sea, they are to count as nothing the imaginary "fatherland" taught by the good and the just but are to steer toward the "children's land" that Zarathustra has taught them to imagine.

Those told to break the good and the just are those who are to become the new leaders and teachers of men. They must be prepared to break the old teachers in whose teachings they have been raised. To "break" the old teachers is not blood lust, no trace of which can be found in Nietzsche's work. This too is a half-written tablet, and just how it is to be implemented in a sense true to Nietzsche's teachings can best be seen in Nietzsche's own acts of war, his own "dynamite": books—but books so deft, so subtle and enticing in their explosiveness, that they clearly succeed in the aim here announced; they break the good and the just. Of course these are the words of "a teacher of evil." But knowing that he would be so characterized, Nietzsche took pains to show just what "evil" means, and just what is hidden in the historic civility appealed to by the teachers of good and evil who raise that charge against him.

The call to courage at the end of the public speech of the new lawgiver concludes with a parable on the desirability of hardness (§29). Like a diamond teaching its kin, soft coal, Zarathustra promises his trembling brothers rewards of the most intense pleasure, rewards that can come only from hardness, from that condition which yields to no other and gives its imprint to millennia. The reason now given for cultivating the hardness that can break the good and the just is the attainment of bliss experienced by the most powerful, the perfectly hard, the absolutely unyielding. The final tablet hung over his trembling brothers by the new lawgiver gives the order: "Become hard!"[98]

But this too is a half-written tablet, and Zarathustra's friends will have to learn what it means for themselves. They are given a lesson in what it means, however, when Zarathustra, having confronted his friends with the hardest task required of them, ends by addressing himself with the hardest task required of him (§30). He speaks only to his will, the part of him that impels him onward to hammer out of unyielding stone the image of beauty he glimpses as a shadow within it (II. 2), the part that is invulnerable (II. 11), the liberator and joy-bringer (II. 2, 20), the part that must learn to say to the past, "But thus I willed it" (II. 20), the part that in its totality is the will to fly (III. 4), and that has learned to speak in a mastering way even to mastering chance (III. 5, §3). His prayer of hardness to his will asks that he be preserved for "one great victory," here anticipated as the Great Noon, when he himself will be the cloud heavy with lightning; annihilating other sources of light, he himself will be the sun of his Great Noon. As the end to Zarathustra's final account of the public teaching and what his friends will be responsible for, this closing prayer points appropriately to what he is responsible for: he will bring the teaching of eternal return, the comprehensive blessing on things, within which the various tasks of the new nobility will find their place.

REDEMPTION

The last four chapters of part III of *Thus Spoke Zarathustra* contain the event for the sake of which the whole book exists. They belong together in that they collectively provide the necessary perspectives on the event of redemption or Zarathustra's deed of willing eternal return. They are the final chapters of the book according to Nietzsche's plans while writing them.

Schooled by Zarathustra's life and discoveries, the reader comes to the climactic event forewarned as to its nature. Learning what is possible and desirable from long exposure to Zarathustra alone, the reader of *Thus Spoke Zarathustra* has been taught by a privileged glimpse into the darkest matters that life is will to power and that the most spiritual will to power has determined the course of human history and taken revenge on life. He has been taught by the most private of speeches that above Zarathustra there are only open, indeterminate heavens, which kindle in him godlike desires. Attentive to Zarathustra, the reader will have been tutored in unrestraint or freed of his convictions regarding what restrains man or is possible for man. Carried in this way into the formidable temple of wisdom by a power other than his own, the reader glimpses as decisive an act that would otherwise be thought patently impossible, redemption for mankind and the earth.

Redemption occurs in the way that it must for the one who has defined it and stated that no one as yet has been redeemed (II. 20). Although it is not redefined in these chapters, it is said to have just occurred (III. 13, §2).

For redemption to occur, Zarathustra must say to the past, "But thus I willed it!" This act of willing the whole of the past occurs in "The Convalescent" and is celebrated there and in the three chapters that follow. In "The Convalescent" a conversation between Zarathustra and his animals presents two notably different accounts of redemption. The animals then steal away, leaving him alone for a completely private dialogue with his redeemed soul (III. 14), which is followed by a song and a dialogue in which Zarathustra speaks and dances with Life (III. 15), and by the marriage song of Zarathustra and Life, in which she is given his name, Eternity (III. 16). The accounts of redemption in all four chapters occur on the seventh day after his encounter with his "most abysmal thought." The final song is sung just after the bell tolls midnight on the seventh day, thereby heralding the coming of the new day. This interconnected series of perspectives on the event of redemption comprises the most detailed account of the teaching of eternal return in all Nietzsche's writings and thus provides the essential access to what Nietzsche took to be his most important teaching, indeed, the most important teaching simply.

The Convalescent (Chapter 13)

This chapter presents Zarathustra's redemption. It also solves the riddle of "On the Vision and the Riddle" (III. 2) and gives the most direct statement of the meaning of eternal return. Still, the act of redemption remains obscure because it occurs offstage, and the direct statement of eternal return contains its own riddles, first because it is spoken not by Zarathustra but by his animals, and second because their speeches are depreciated by Zarathustra's smiling comments on them.[99]

Zarathustra is the convalescent, the one who recovers from the universal sickness that has infected all mankind, the madness of the teachings of revenge based on man's felt imprisonment in time. The root of *genesen* ("convalesce") means "to come through alive," or "be delivered," senses that apply directly to Zarathustra's convalescence in light of his interpretation of mankind hitherto as fallen or self-cursed. It also means "to return joyfully home," thereby making Zarathustra's convalescence his ultimate homecoming (III. 9), his return to his own. He is thus related to ancient Nestor, whose name is based on the same root and means "the one who always returns," in tribute to his valor and his ability always to come through alive, even when Herakles killed his eleven brothers and when Poseidon ruined the homecoming of other Greek heroes at Troy.

Like "On the Vision and the Riddle," its prelude, "The Convalescent" has two parts, the break again falling near the beginning, just after courage has been summoned for a decisive encounter. The courage gathered here, however, is not summoned in a vision, but for Zarathustra's actual encounter with his most abysmal thought. This encounter, on the first of the seven days covered by the chapter, is followed by seven days during which he lies as if dead; on the seventh day he recovers and speaks with his animals. The encounter is staged as a combat between two resolute enemies, although here, unlike the visionary encounter with the Dwarf, the speech of only one of the combatants is reported. The encounter occurred in an early morning not long after Zarathustra's return to his cave. In the presence of his animals, he speaks the decisive words that awaken his abysmal thought for the first time, an awakening after which there is no going back to sleep.[100] Zarathustra identifies himself first as the cock crow of the abysmal thought that belongs to his depth, then, after hearing it stir, as the godless advocate of life, suffering, and the circle, an advocacy that in its most extreme form wills eternal return. His advocacy distinguishes his teaching from the Soothsayer's godless teaching, which also knows life to be suffering and time to be a circle; but it also distinguishes his teaching from that of the wise of all ages who have judged temporal life to be no good.[101] Zarathustra's thought responds to his command; it comes forth through his will to an encounter or struggle. It speaks, but Zarathustra does not report what it says. Instead he forces the clasp of hands that forces his perpetual embrace of this thought.

The first part of "The Convalescent" ends with this embrace and the nausea it induces. In the second part Zarathustra falls down in a trance, and when he finally comes to himself, he remains prone, neither eating nor drinking, for seven days. The speeches of this chapter interpret these events, with the animals speaking of joy and transformation and Zarathustra speaking only of his nausea. It is said six times that his recovery took place on the seventh day, making clear that a new creation has taken place; the scene of recovery recalls many other details of the biblical story of Eden, though with essential differences. On the seventh day Zarathustra sits up, in a garden of fruit gathered by his eagle; he takes an apple into his hand and finds it sweet and good. New knowledge has come to him. His snake is with him in this garden in which a new naming of all things occurs, a naming that is a blessing on the things named.[102]

The animals break the silence of the seven days, having judged by Zarathustra's movements that the time had come to speak. The dialogue between Zarathustra and his animals consists of seven speeches. The animals continue to bring comfort to the convalescent in their four speeches, as they had earlier brought him food and remained beside him day and night. But while the ministering animals initiate the dialogue, it is brought to a close by Zarathustra's inattentive silence, which causes them to creep away. Each of Zarathustra's three speeches begins with a smiling depreciation of the animals' preceding speech, though twice he says that they know well what has happened. In each of his speeches, but especially in the central and longest one, he speaks of his redemption in a markedly different way from the way the animals speak. The dialogue, as well as the whole ascending course that Zarathustra has taken, points to the interpretation of that difference; it is not simply attributable to the difference between man and all other beings or between man and the animals, nor

to the difference between authentic man and all other men. Rather, it is
the difference between this particular man and all other beings. Although
the animals' speeches are different from his, they are not false or mistaken
as Heidegger claims; Heidegger expects too much from the animals in ex-
pecting them to speak as Zarathustra speaks.[103] In being different from
Zarathustra's, the animals' speeches are appropriately different for they
represent the point of view of things redeemed, not that of the redeemer.
In the language of fable in *Zarathustra*, the animals come to speech in
order to pronounce the blessing of beings on the one whose teaching
blesses them. The animals' speeches are songs of gratitude, sung by beings
whose place in the order of things is different from Zarathustra's. Whereas
in the prologue Zarathustra stood below them, both in pride and prudence,
he now stands above them in both respects, as they acknowledge by
creeping off to allow him his private songs of redemption. Given the heights
to which he flies in these songs, it is to be expected that even his animals
would stand below him in pride and insight.[104]

The animals speak most clearly the meaning of eternal return, but
although their speeches can be seen as appropriate and true, they are not
simply guides to the meaning of eternal return as some commentators
have assumed.[105] Both the animals and Zarathustra sing songs of redemption, but the differences in their songs point to Zarathustra as the
supreme singer whose song effects redemption. In scope his words match
those of the wisest and most powerful of men, though in content they
differ completely. In the political language made appropriate by his understanding of peoples, Zarathustra's words are those of a founder, whereas
the animals' words are the loyal words of those who discover themselves
within the realm founded. When the animals' perspective on eternal return
is measured against that of Zarathustra, the animals can be seen to have
gone astray, if playfully and permissibly so, when they claim too much,
when they claim to know Zarathustra's own most private experience. The
animals remain in innocent ignorance of that experience, which is recorded
for all and for none in the final three chapters.

The animals' first speech invites Zarathustra to stand up and step out
into the world that awaits him like a garden. In speaking for the first time
in the book the animals speak on behalf of "all things" and say that all
things have been awaiting his awakening to bless him and minister to him;
their speeches are the vehicle of this ministering gratitude. Like Siegfried,
who temporarily won the power to understand the song of birds, Zarathustra understands the song of the animals; the animals have not won
the power of human speech; rather Zarathustra has won the power of
understanding the song of natural beings. The redeemed Zarathustra is
attuned to the celebration of life expressed in the animals' song.

Zarathustra's first speech after his redemption speaks of language. Its
first words depreciate the animals' words as "chatter," albeit refreshing
chatter that turns the world into a garden for him. While the animals say
the world simply is a garden, Zarathustra insists on the bridging effect of

words which seemingly, but only seemingly, bring together what is essentially apart. His first words show that what exists as a garden for his animals covers a reality that is open and indeterminate for him, for he knows what the world is as his animals never can. His speaking is more than chattering, for his words and tones are gifts bestowed on things for the sake of man, who refreshes himself in the things named; with the beautiful foolishness of speech, "man dances over all things." These words in praise of speech assert man's responsibility to name all things, including the animals;[106] speech thus enacts, in a way, man's dominion over all things, but now as man's dance over all things, as the justice done to things by the most spiritual of things. In this way, all being comes to word through Zarathustra, and all becoming learns from him how to speak (III. 9). But the bridging effect of language causes forgetfulness, sweet forgetfulness, of the fundamentally elusive character of beings and of the fundamental experience that "there is no without."

At Zarathustra's invitation the animals chatter on. But they contradict what he has just said, for in response to his claim to "dance away over all things," they say that "all things themselves are dancing." Their perspective is stated at the beginning of their second speech: "To those who think as we do, all things themselves are dancing." But Zarathustra is not one of those who think as the animals do. The animals belong to the dancing things; they do not fly over them as he does. In saying something different from what he says, the animals cannot know better than he does. He describes their song immediately afterward as a "lyre-song," a ditty, a trivializing thing. But while their song cannot be his song, it is not for that reason simply false or simply trivial, as Heidegger maintains, taking the animals to be like the Dwarf, symbolic of an inattentive humanity blameable for not grasping the essential matter in eternal return. Heidegger is required to separate the animals from Zarathustra by his view that eternal return cannot be a cycle of the same things, but must be something very like the *Entschlossenheit* of *Sein und Zeit*. But in judging the animals mistaken, Heidegger states too radically the difference between them and Zarathustra.[107] It would hardly be fitting at the climax of the book to record a beautiful song by the honored animals and mean it to say nothing at all about the teaching for which the book exists. Moreover, what the animals say is close to what Zarathustra said in his vision and what he will say in the next chapters; to speak of redemption as willing the past is quite in keeping with the animals' interpretation of a joyful recurrence. The difference between what Zarathustra and his animals say is a difference of perspective, where the perspective gained by Zarathustra is singular, the action of the most spirited of beings, while the perspective sung by the animals is general, the response of beings to the most spiritual blessing on mortal things. As the one who dances away over all things, Zarathustra is the one whose most spiritual will to power releases things into their dance; those who think as the animals do are the things released into their dance by the act of naming and blessing.

Zarathustra's speaking has its own kind of unrestraint, but the animals' speaking is unrestrained precisely where his has been restrained, for it purports to describe the very character of "being" as such. In speaking of being, the animals are able to adopt the optimistic language of philosophy that Zarathustra has always avoided.[108] Unlike Zarathustra, who has seen the open, unnameable character of the whole, the animals speak freely and easily about the whole; they speak as metaphysicians who make metaphysics a joyful science of recurring beings. The animals, in their way, platonize. As believers in the commensurability of speech and being, in the power of *logos* to bring reality to word, they beautify the nearest, the timely, the around-us.[109] In speaking freely of being, they transform the whole of being into becoming, as Zarathustra himself had done (III. 9). Their platonizing replaces the grave Platonism that lies in the ruins of despair. Their metaphysical poetry celebrates time and becoming; it is praise and justification of the transitory (II. 2). The animals sing confidently of the wheel of being, the year of being, the house of being, the ring of being, and the beginning of being in every instant.[110] Their knowledge of being is joyful even though, from the standpoint of the traditional teaching about being, their song is a wretched song celebrating the meaninglessness of things, for the animals do not bow to the lords Necessity, Purpose, and Guilt. They celebrate a nonteleological coming and going of things, an endless joyful ring in which all things dance. In their song a sane view of mortal beings takes shape, one that eternalizes them out of sheer joy at their being. The song of the redeemed world tells of a new allowing, in which things are permitted their impermanence by the one who places an azure dome of eternal security over the impermanent things. Although the ways of Zarathustra and other beings are different, they are not contradictory. The teaching on the superman in *Zarathustra*, and, more generally, Nietzsche's teaching on the philosopher, holds that it is the way of mortal man raised to the highest power in the wisest men to give the things of the earth their meaning, while it is the way of all other things to reveal themselves in the openness conferred by legislating man. What Zarathustra has learned from the wisdom of the wisest is that all things fall under the power of man's naming; through the exercise of that power, earthly things have hitherto fallen under the curse of man's revenge against time. Only a naming free of revenge does justice to earthly things and frees them from that curse; on the morning of the new creation Zarathustra hears the song of earthly things freed by that naming.

Zarathustra's next speech is the central and longest speech of the chapter; its twenty-two verses give his own account of what has happened and solve the riddles of the young shepherd and the heavy black snake. The narrative comment at the end provides the perspective on the whole by saying that Zarathustra "remembered his sickness." The purpose of the speech is to give Zarathustra's account not of his redemption, but of the sickness from which he has redeemed himself, and to identify what he himself feared in his thought.

He begins with a smiling depreciation of the animals as "buffoons and barrel organs" but says that they well knew what had to be accomplished in seven days. It is not necessary to hold as Heidegger does that Zarathustra's comment on the animals' knowledge is ironic, pointing to their ignorance.[111] What Zarathustra credits the animals with knowing is the solution to the riddle, for he speaks as the shepherd into whose throat the heavy black snake had crawled, as if that were what they knew. With a smile he accuses them of having made a lyre song out of his act of biting off the head of the snake. Their lyre song makes no reference to the symbols of Zarathustra's vision; rather, it transforms them into a new symbolism of recurrence, as is evident from the song itself and from Zarathustra's description of it, for *Leier–Lied* suggests something that is repeated over and over. But the lyre is also the instrument that brings harmony to cosmic disorder, Apollo's instrument, which, in the hands of an Orpheus, both appeases the infernal powers and tames what is wild on the earth, causing the very trees and stones to array themselves in regular patterns around the music of the lyre. The animals' lyre song fashions a new world of appearances out of Zarathustra's deed, a new world of bright Apollonian surfaces that beautifies in the loveliness of its music the enigmatic and Dionysian vision that makes this new world of appearances possible. In Zarathustra's own songs of redemption the Dionysian flute replaces the Apollonian lyre.[112]

To those who know that Zarathustra is the young shepherd who has bitten off the head of the snake, Zarathustra now describes the horror of it. He speaks of his redemption as behind him, though he is still sick from its effects. His speech shows him to be convalescing and not yet to have laughed that triumphant laughter which, when first he heard it in his vision, moved him with the imperative need to duplicate it. He accuses the animals of cruelty in having watched his suffering. The charge would seem to be unfair, for they have ministered to him and not left his side for seven days except to gather food for him; it would be fitting only if the animals resemble men, only if their ministering too, secretly delights in the need of the great to be ministered to by the less great. But Zarathustra turns from the falsely anthropomorphized animals to man, the cruelest animal, whose cruelty is exercised on himself. According to his accusation, man's cruelty to man grows out of the natural order of rank that obtains among men, for that inequality leads to the conclusion that the highest and greatest things possible are closed to most men, and to the further conclusion that the simply highest and greatest things are closed to even the highest and best of men. Nature has been unjust to mankind and must be punished for its injustice. But man's cruelty extends punishment to the whole natural order of which he is a part. Suffering from nature's inhumanity, humanity has found its happiness in teachings that compensate for that injustice, the preachings of madness recounted in "On Redemption." The poets, who have sung the meaning of life for all mankind, have avenged themselves on nature as spokesmen for this perceived injustice. If life has her way with them and their teachings, if they go the way of all flesh, their teachings in some form still direct the stream of mankind. Zarathustra catches himself in his accusation of life's accusers: is he himself merely accusing? He could defend himself by maintaining that his accusation is not of life but of life's accusers, that it arises from a different perspective on the natural order of rank, a perspective from which the low is seen to have mastered the high, thereby bringing it low. Besides, his accusation is new: who till now has accused mankind of not being great enough in its evil?[113] But such defenses are useless, for it becomes clear that his accusation too is against life insofar as it seems to need what is low. Furthermore, his accusation too must arise from the source of all accusations against life. When the thought of eternal return takes possession of him, he experiences horror at having to will what has accused and accursed life. That horror and its degree must arise from his own passion to avenge himself on those whose vengeance has poisoned life for mankind. Whereas he had once envisaged a future free of what is low, that future is now known to be impossible: life needs the whole order of rank that it has generated. The heavy black snake that fastens itself in Zarathustra's throat is the recognition that, far from exercising sweet revenge on the small and vengeful, he must will their eternal return. That the great weight of this thought threatens to crush him shows that he too is afflicted by a form of the universal human sickness of revenge. His accusation is not only against life's accusers, but against life for needing such accusers. With no friends to lash him to the noble pillars of an ancient temple, he must master by himself the revenge he still harbors. He, the man who experiences himself as ascendant in the order of rank among human beings, must overcome the revenge of his own soul and say to that whole order of rank, "But thus I willed it!"

In the gathering momentum of Zarathustra's solution to the riddle of the heavy black snake, a momentum that concentrates on the horror of willing the small man, a brief aside ascribes to the snake a second identity, the teaching of the Soothsayer: "Everything is the same; nothing is of worth; knowledge chokes." Only here are the Soothsayer's words given a focus on knowledge (see II. 19; III. 12, §16; IV. 2). Having been taken possession of by the thought of eternal return, Zarathustra is almost choked by the view that "knowledge chokes." Does Schopenhauer's knowledge, his insight into life as endless meaningless cycles, require Schopenhauer's judgment that life is no good? What almost chokes Zarathustra is the possibility that what is highest and best in man, his spirited inquiry into himself and the world, must itself end by choking mankind. This second implication of taking eternal return with the greatest seriousness is different from the first. Whereas biting the head off the heavy black snake requires that he affirm the eternal return of the small, it requires that he deny the Sooth-sayer's judgment on knowledge; to one aspect of what almost chokes him he must say yes, to the other no. In the songs that follow, Zarathustra recounts the grounds for his judgment that a knowledge of life, far from choking the knower, elevates and exalts both knower and known. Knowledge does not require the Soothsayer's conclusion. As *Beyond Good and Evil* puts it, the one who pursues a life-denying pessimism to its bottom glimpses the opposite ideal of a world-affirming human being who wants what was and is repeated to all eternity (56).

Zarathustra's remembrance of his own part in the universal human sickness continues to its end with a repetition of the nausea implied in the thought of willing the small man, but it culminates in the acknowledgment that his accusation against mankind is an accusation against all existence. This confession of his sickness at its deepest level is broken off by the animals, who halt his remembrance at just that point at which the narrative of the event was halted in the first section of this chapter, at the threefold repetition of horror.[114] The animals' refusal to permit him to continue allows him only to identify the heavy black snake, not to recount his means of victory over it. Zarathustra's speech on eternal return here is thus decisively limited by the desire of the animals to hear and to sing only the new music of the newly redeemed earth. He does not insist on speaking further to an audience not desirous of hearing the grounds on which their own celebration of life is founded. Only after the animals have completed their lyre song will he repeat to himself the words and songs of his own redemption.

Still, what he has been allowed to say by the animals eager to celebrate makes clear the nature of the bite that severs the head of the heavy black snake. It cannot be renewed optimism about what is possible for mankind through elimination of the small man, the optimism that had previously sustained him. The discoveries of "The Soothsayer" and "On Redemption" destroy that optimism by showing that redemption depends on the will taking responsibility even for what it judges to be small and detestable in man and willing the whole natural order of rank. Gilles Deleuze has argued that Zarathustra's thought of eternal return is "selective," that Zarathustra engages in merely apparent collusion with his animals on the matter of a cycle of the same things, and that "the small, petty, reactive man will not recur."[115] But if the thought were selective in this way, if it did not will the whole through willing the eternal return of the same things, the small man would hardly be a problem for Zarathustra. He almost chokes on the thought of the small man precisely because willing eternal return is not selective in this way but requires taking responsibility for the small. Zarathustra thus fulfills a prayer uttered by Nietzsche seven years earlier: "May sane reason preserve us from the belief that mankind will at any future time attain to a final ideal order of things, and that happiness will then shine down upon it with unwavering ray like the sun of the tropics: with such a belief Zarathustra has nothing to do, he is no utopian" (WB 11).[116] Life needs a hierarchy of human beings; there is no redemptive future like the one pictured in the earlier speech in which the high is utterly free of the low (II. 6). Eternal return precludes the millennial dreams of insane reason, even Zarathustra's, and when he is able to overcome the remembrance of his sickness, he too, like his animals, is able to pronounce the death of the Future a blessing. Still, although the will says to the whole of the heretofore unwillable past, "But thus I willed it!" and thereby wills even the small man who exists in past and present, it does not face the willable future with the expectation of the Soothsayer, that it will simply be more of the same. From where Zarathustra now stands in the passage of time, an alterable future lies ahead, willable by the one with the whole future of mankind on his conscience. With regard to that alterable future, Zarathustra's thought is "selective," blessing or crushing those who can be possessed by a thought. If it belongs to "the bone-structure of human nature" (WB 11) that the small man exist, it does not belong to that bone-structure that the teachings of revenge should hold sway. The teaching of eternal return alters "the very much alterable judgments of mankind" (WB 3) and in that way promises a sane future.

Thus the affirmative will of eternal return does not forbid itself every no. Beyond good and evil, it is not beyond good and bad; it is not the affirmation of an ass, braying its yes to everything (III. 11, §2). The eternal security of beings achieved in affirming their eternal return implies a no to that way of being with beings that curses them or alters them out of the mad judgment of their accursedness or worthlessness. To do justice to beings requires a refined human sensibility which is grounded in an affirmative will but which schools itself in a complementary no—not the no of what is forbidden, for nothing is forbidden, but the no of what it forbids because of its desire to permit. The no that complements the yes of eternal return is the no to the historic way of being with beings that culminates in the theoretical resignation of modern, Schopenhauerian philosophy, and in the practical aggression of the modern will to transformation which takes all beings standing reserve to be put into the service of mankind. The no complementary to Nietzsche's most important teaching is a refusal of the modern theoretical and practical consequences of Platonism, a no that is not blind to what is great in those consequences, for it clearly recognizes the place of inquiry and adventure in the human enterprise and grounds it anew. But, in affirming all beings and in affirming as highest in human beings the impassioned inquiry into beings, the teaching of eternal return points toward a science liberated from the Baconian and Cartesian impulse to "the effecting of all things possible," a science that knows in principle that it can provide limits to the will to alter because it can teach itself in each specific case the no appropriate to its affirmation of all that was and is. Eternal return is present in *Zarathustra* only in song; it is not transformed into the gravity of prose. Nevertheless, translation into the prose of science of what it warrants and what it forbids is presumed by the role that Nietzsche assigns to his most important thought.

Breaking off the speech in which Zarathustra remembers what had almost choked him, the animals invite him to sing, telling him that singing is appropriate to convalescence. When he responds, in his final speech of this chapter, he again acknowledges that the animals know what has transpired in the seven days. Once again this acknowledgment of what they know need not be seen as ironic, for they are right in saying that he needs to sing. His songs in the next chapters are, nevertheless, not sung at their invitation, for he had already invented that comfort for himself on the seven days. Although the animals know that he must sing, they do not know his songs, and for these songs to be sung, they must creep away.

The final speech of the animals is introduced by Zarathustra as another "lyre song," and it ends with him not even listening to it, for he does not notice when they fall silent. Both his introduction and his inattention separate the song from Zarathustra himself, the song that most emphatically presents the idea of a literal eternal return of the same things. Zarathustra had said twice in response to the animals' earlier speeches that they well know what has happened, but it is in this final song that they make the most extensive claims to knowledge, and to these knowledge claims Zarathustra has no response. The animals claim to know who Zarathustra is, what he teaches, and what he would say to himself were he to die now. They know him as the teacher of eternal return. Although they claim to know what he teaches, their knowledge of eternal return contains neither the horror that Zarathustra had experienced nor the courage that he had needed in order to will it. As stated by the animals, the teaching lacks the elements most emphasized in Zarathustra's own accounts. But more than that, according to the lyre song of the animals, the teaching is a discovery. It states the truth about the world in which they play, a truth that the world yields willingly to the playful participant within it. But it is Zarathustra, not the animals who is schooled in the way of philosophy; he knows that this teaching too is enacted by the most spiritual will to power, that it too is a gift given to the world by the wisest and most powerful who stoops to bring the world under a rule. Teacher and taught have different perspectives on the teaching of eternal return, but this difference is necessary according to Zarathustra's teaching on the wise and the less wise; what the wisest effects in his teaching, mankind carries forward like an ark of greatest worth. The literal celebration of eternal return, the teaching attributed to Zarathustra by his celebrating animals, names the new world of appearances called forth by the will of the wisest who has seen most deeply into things.

As attested by their spokesmen's words, "all things" are freed into their existence as transient by the teaching of eternal return. For those existing joyfully within it, the eternity of eternal return is neither beyond the transience of things nor after it; it is neither the eternity of being taught by Plato's Socrates to lie beyond the world of becoming nor the eternity of well-being taught by modern philosophers to lie ahead, in a golden age to be established by industrious men. Rather, it is the eternity of transience and passage itself, the eternal running and running out of the hourglass that marks the great year of being as the great year of becoming. The animals sing of the new freedom permitted by the teacher of eternal return, who teaches all beings that they may be the birds of passage that they are; they are not, in Milton's words, with weeping and with sighing sent to their mortality by some immortal one.[117] Under the aegis of the mortal Zarathustra, they are allowed their coming and going. Their song is one of gratitude, in which all beings, released into their becoming by the new teacher, give thanks for that release. No longer does man, the most spiritual being, aim to have dominion over all beings, "over the fish of the sea, and over the birds of the air, and over the cattle, and over all the earth, and over every creeping thing that creeps upon the earth";[118] man takes his place among the animals as the most spiritual animal. Although Zarathustra's highest act is always presented as a commanding act of will, that mastering will blesses beings as they are. The highest commanding appears as an allowing; the highest nature provides the natural or earthly things with a heavenly dome of security by willing their eternal return.

The third thing that the animals claim to know is of a different order, in that it presumes access to Zarathustra's most private knowledge. They think they know what he would say to comfort himself at the point of death. Zarathustra has just spoken of the comfort he invented for himself in the seven days of his suffering, but that comfort is presented in the following three chapters to which the animals are not privy. While claiming to know his most private thoughts, they are not permitted audience to those private thoughts. What actually comforts him and what the animals think would comfort him are in fact quite different. The reader of *Thus Spoke Zarathustra* is privileged to draw a contrast not accessible to the animals who measure all experience by their own: whereas the animals' hymn provides them with a private and personal comfort, Zarathustra comforts himself with the completion of his labors to enclose the earth under the dome of the sky. Still, for all their differences, neither Zarathustra nor the animals comfort themselves with anything like the perpetual being or immortality that has served as one form of mankind's revenge against mortal life. Moreover, both Zarathustra and the animals comfort themselves; they are not, like the comfortless Soothsayer, ruined by the ruin of revenge's comforts. Claiming to speak the comfort that Zarathustra will speak to himself at the end of his life, the animals' words seem to represent what they would say to themselves were they at the point of death. They sing the comforting thought of recurring natural cycles, the sting of death removed by the knowledge of return to the selfsame life. In belonging to the causes of eternal return, they will their own return.[119] Their love of life as it is makes the thought of eternal return consoling; but their solace is not a sop, for they desire only to be again exactly what they are now. Their understanding of death does not make death a refutation of life. Death is not the center of gravity from which all life is weighed and found wanting; what the animals desire is mortal life just as it is, ending in death. The tragedy of death is lightened by the comedy of return; but the tragedy is not removed, for mortals still need to be comforted. Zarathustra never speaks this way; he never speaks as if the teaching of a return to the selfsame life is a source of solace for him. Just as the animals see the earth to be a garden, whereas he knows the reality masked by the garden, so the animals find solace in his teaching, whereas he appears neither to find it nor to need it. The animals give expression to a salutary form of Zarathustra's teaching.

The animals' account of what is comforting in the teaching of eternal return offers no comfort to those who desire life to be other than it is, for what returns is "this same, selfsame life in the greatest things and also in the smallest."[120] The animals are so well disposed toward themselves that their affirmation of themselves is an affirmation of the whole of which they are a minute and transient part. The words that follow this affirmation of life as it is end the animals' song by describing the career to which Zarathustra himself returns. Viewing Zarathustra's life from the perspective of his death, they treat it as a completed whole, its beginning not distinguished from its end, but simultaneously present: the Great Noon yet to come is as present as the opening announcement of the superman. In this summary of his life, as in their other speeches, the animals assign to Zarathustra an exalted role as the teacher of the view they are certain is true. But they attribute too little to him, nevertheless, for they remain ignorant of the role that he has in fact played with respect to that teaching. Beyond making clear that to him their version of his teaching sounds like a lyre song, Zarathustra makes no effort to give them the more complete view of his life and work that he will recount when alone. It is fitting that they think of his life and teaching as they do, because, as the narrative of *Zarathustra* has made clear, only the wisest can have a complete understanding of what is aimed at by their teachings. The animals' version does not need to be corrected, nor do they need to give him his due, for to give him his due would contradict their understanding of the way of beings. Zarathustra's labors would be, from their perspective, an impossibility; they would believe the sign placed over his way at the opening of part III. How could the animals believe that Zarathustra is the author of the view that they are certain is simply true? For them, its being true requires that it have no author, but only spokesmen or teachers. The way of the wisest remains a mystery for those not simply wise, for those who carry forward the ark of values created by the wise. Nevertheless, Zarathustra has discovered that life is will to power, and that the most spiritual will to power is an act of commanding that founds a way of thinking and being. The wisest have always been rulers, though the ruled have never understood themselves to be under the sway of spiritual rulers. Zarathustra's silence in the face of his animals' characterization of his life continues his own masking of himself as legislator. It shows that he is still governed by the necessity that he appear to be less than he is, that he speak differently to himself than to his pupils. His prudence now flies higher than his pride.

The speeches by the animals solve a serious narrative problem in *Zarathustra*, the problem of stating, in a way that avoids presumption, just what is effected by Zarathustra's redemption. Their speeches describe the experience of the new people, mankind, those brought into being by the gift of the new teaching, those for whom it is light and easy (*KGW* VII 21 [6]). The dialogue between Zarathustra and his animals portrays the difference between the complete understanding held by the founder of the teaching and the incomplete understanding of those who live within what he has founded. As a new expression of the old distinction between knowledge and opinion, it is an aspect of Nietzsche's own platonizing, his beautifying the near.

In the animals' speech about being and time, in their metaphysical speech, being is transformed into becoming and celebrated as becoming. The "true but deadly teaching of sovereign becoming" (*UD* 9) is affirmed in a way that overcomes its deadliness. To the animals, Nietzsche's teaching is a return to nature, to the natural cycles of birth and death. But their metaphysical speech is not Zarathustra's speech. His speech, based on his gaze outward to the open, indeterminate sky and his gaze inward to the will to power, reflects Nietzsche's view that man must be "made natural" or "naturalized" with the "pure, newly discovered, newly redeemed nature" (*GS* 109); that he must be "retranslated into nature" (*BGE* 230). The return to nature in the speech of the animals is for Zarathustra an "ascent—up into the high, free, even terrible nature and naturalness where great tasks are something one plays with" (*TI*, "Skirmishes," 48). The return to nature celebrated by the animals has therefore a natural ground, an act of conferring performed by the most spirited man, himself a natural being whose commanding is obeying. In obedience to nature, in obedience to his own nature, the highest being prescribes eternal return to all natural beings.[121] The animals' version of eternal return can be seen as the culmination of Zarathustra's injunction to be loyal to the earth, a loving reconciliation with beings as a whole; Zarathustra's act, however, is "higher than any reconciliation" (II. 20). The animals' speeches are not the guide to Zarathustra's own understanding of his teaching; only in his own final, private speeches is that guide to be found.

On the Great Longing (Chapter 14)

When the animals have finished their song, they wait in silence for Zarathustra to respond. Because he does not notice their silence, he cannot have noticed their song, at least the end of it, the part that alleged to tell him his most private thoughts; instead, he is engaged in those most private thoughts. The animals honor his silence as a dismissal and steal away for the first time in seven days. They thus remain ignorant of Zarathustra's conversation with his soul, the conversation related for all and for none in the next three chapters, the final chapters as Nietzsche thought while writing them. The words spoken here are the most important words, for they are the culmination of Zarathustra's whole course and give his private account of his redemption.

The first chapter relating his private thoughts presents a carefully structured conversation with his soul.[122] Twenty-two times Zarathustra says, "O my soul." The first eleven times speak of the past, recording his gifts to his soul or how he has redeemed his soul. The conversation then moves briefly into the present with a description of his soul. Finally, following the only words of his soul in the book, it turns to the future, basing a prophecy of what is to come on what his soul has become. With its structure of past, present, and future (suggested also by the first stanza) this chapter provides guidance to Zarathustra's career as a whole: his redemption is now in his past, but it requires future deeds, which are the subject of prophecy. That prophecy confirms that he must descend once more (see III. 12, §1) to bring mankind the Great Noon he has anticipated. "On the Great Longing" depicts the longing to which Zarathustra's soul is subject even subsequent to its redemption.

The first half of the dialogue is one-sided, for Zarathustra is the only speaker; in eleven salutations to his soul he celebrates himself as gift-giver to his soul. His soul listens silently as he recounts the gifts that have made it what it is. With eleven different verbs he states what he has done to enable his soul to achieve its present redeemed condition. The chapter builds in intensity toward the words of his soul, words that when they are finally spoken, seem wrong—jarring, even dispiriting words in that they do not, as the animals' words do, express gratitude to the gift-giver. Yet the words are the very words he anticipated and they make possible his final gift to his soul.

The dialogue gives the impression of being a contest between a male and a female, a manly or spirited Zarathustra who provides for his receptive, female soul or who has given his pliant soul the form it has come to have, a form that makes it a sister soul to the soul of the open sky (III. 4). In his speech to his soul he pictures himself as a storm of spirit, blowing over his soul as sea. He is "the life which cuts into life" (II. 8), a spirited male seeking the highest victory; his spirit has given his receptive, waiting soul all that it requires to be fruitful in the way appropriate to it. Zarathustra is superior to his soul in a way that he is not superior to his spirit: he commands his soul, whereas he is obedient to his spirit, yielding to it and allowing it free reign. This difference reflects the fundamental difference: he creates his soul, whereas he simply finds himself with his spirit. His spiritedness is the gift of his nature that enables him to create the soul he here describes, the redeemed soul whose song will redeem the world from the old songs of revenge. Redemption depends on his creating his soul, while it depends on his simply having the spirit that he has.

Zarathustra's account of his gifts to his soul is not chronological; it begins with the final matter, the gift of a teaching about time that shows his soul how to speak of present, past, and future and how to dance the redemptive "ring dance over all Here, There and Yonder." Utterly alone, his eyes closed to everything around him, he speaks of complete openness, a total lack of shame at what his soul now is, even before the highest observer (see I. 14). His soul has attained its redeemed, innocent condition because his spirit has strangled the strangler called "sin." His spirit has murdered what has murdered man's soul until now, and with that murder has come a right of speech to say no and yes, to curse and to bless in a way that places the azure bell of allowing over all things. His spirit has freed his soul from bondage to the already made or to the past that has turned other souls to revenge. Because of this freedom, his soul knows a passion for the unmade things, the future things, things that come to be through the songs of his soul.

After murdering the murderer, he taught his soul a second lesson, a lesson on speech as the mastery that persuades "the very ground" of things. Such speech is a daylight wisdom or force that persuades all things to be drawn up to its heights. He shares this mastering speech with "you who are wisest," with those whose will to truth is a will to power. But whereas their will has desired to make all beings thinkable or to transform all beings into something they are not, Zarathustra's will permits all beings the elusive mystery of their transience. In likening his soul to the sun in its passionate desire to draw up the sea (II. 15), he replaces Plato's unnatural image of the sun, for it is no longer the grave image of the permanent Good, beyond being in dignity and power, and holding all being in permanent intelligibility and permanent being. When, shortly after, he names the good of his soul, he shows that the new good permits all beings their impermanence. Glaucon laughed when Socrates' gravity posited a ground beyond the permanent ground of eternal being. But, though given tentatively, Socrates says, and under compulsion, and as mere opinion, the sun as symbol of the permanent Good came to characterize the grave Western ideal of eternal worth of eternal things eternally thinkable. But that sun sets, that whole constellation sets, when Zarathustra's songs cause his sun to rise.[123]

The mastery practiced by the persuasive speaking of Zarathustra's soul knows no mastery beyond itself; he has conferred upon his soul names that spell out its destiny—"Encompassing of Encompassings," "Umbilical Cord of Time," and "Azure Bell"—and these names grant to his soul the ambitions opened to him by his insight into the open sky and the ambitions of the wisest. Picturing his soul as receptive earth and himself as the one who waters it, impregnates it, even, Zarathustra speaks of having given his soul "all wisdom" to drink. Wisdom is an intoxicating drink, of which he has given his soul two kinds: new wine, or all modern wisdom, and old wine, stronger and more intoxicating, the immemorially old wine of ancient wisdom. His manly deeds have not been in vain, for his soul, once mere soil to his sky, has now been transformed from receptive earth to growing vine; he has created out of his soul's receptivity a plant imbued with his own features. The image of his beautified soul standing as a vine before him brings him into the present, a present known only to himself and his redeemed soul. While the present condition of his soul is the result or creation of all his past gifts, it demands, nevertheless, a further gift, and he presents it with a prophecy describing the future as its own offspring.

The image of Zarathustra's soul as a living vine governs the second half of the dialogue. Though his soul stands before him as a vine whose fruit promises intoxication, it is in a state of waiting. But Zarathustra alleges that he has now given everything to his soul, and that, while she stands ripe, he waits empty-handed. It is as a member of this waiting pair that Zarathustra's soul comes to word for the first time in the book.[124] Her seemingly ungrateful words are just the right words to address to one who holds, as Zarathustra does, that it is more blessed to give than to receive, especially just now, when he has recited his list of gifts. Her words are given "smilingly" but not gaily; they are wry words, but even more, combative words, for although they acknowledge the fullness achieved through his gifts, they question the worth of mere fullness. In questioning the worth of contentment with one's own perfection, they question the finality of any state of perfection and suggest that there is a desire that comes with the fulfillment of one's desires, as Zarathustra had himself indicated when speaking of the highest desires (III. 10). Her words are therefore "full of melancholy":[125]

> Which of us should be thankful?—should the giver not be thankful that the taker took? Is giving not a pressing need? Is taking not—compassion?

The words of Zarathustra's soul confirm the truth of his experience of gift-giving by implying that his emptiness is more joyful than her fullness, that the giver rejoices in the gift more than the receiver. She too knows the gift-giving virtue and knows it as he does, as the "nameless" passion inadequately named "the passion to rule," the passion grounded in the highest selfishness of giving oneself in the act of stooping to rule. Like the sun at the very beginning of Zarathustra's course, she can question the worth of her happiness if she lacks those on whom she can shine. Zarathustra is delighted by the words of his soul, challenge though they be; he seems to have expected them or awaited them, for he has the perfect response.

But first he expresses his delight in his soul and her longing, a longing not fulfilled by its redemption. This state of his soul and the words that issue from it delight him and move him to tears—precisely because she is not herself in tears over her melancholy. It is "the good" of his soul, even "the super-good" or the good beyond the good in dignity and power, that she wills not to complain or to weep. As its author or creator, Zarathustra knows his soul completely, and he cites as the grounds for her smile the words that she speaks to herself: "Is all weeping not a complaint? And all complaining not an accusation?" The simple words of his soul exhibit the highest victory, for even in its deepest longing, his soul is free of the will to revenge. The ground of the new wisdom or the new speech is a soul created free of lamentation over its existence. Privy to the most private and noble words of his own soul, Zarathustra is moved to tears that neither complain nor accuse. But he still has something to teach his soul, for his hands are in fact not yet empty; the gift-giver can teach his soul to give.

Having understood the need of his redeemed soul, he now gives it his final gift. The gift is twofold, advice and prophecy, the advice of singing and the prophecy of what will happen when his soul sings. This is the comfort he invented for himself on the seven days; this is his convalescence or his growing hale and healthy again. He does not follow the advice of his animals and make a new lyre for new lyre songs. His songs are of a different order, one that masters the master of the lyre; they are not the songs of Orpheus, but of the victor over Orpheus. The songs of Zarathustra's soul will be sung in the next two chapters (III. 15–16); here he only invites them and prophesies the results of their being sung. Like the songs of the animals, they fulfill his description of poetry's responsibility to speak the best parables, not of the intransitory, but of time and becoming, in praise and justification of transitoriness (II. 2).

The poetry he now speaks to his soul belongs to the order of prophecy. The song of his soul will still the roaring sea, and over the sea grown still a boat will glide, a golden marvel of a boat, around which all things, all good bad marvelous things, will leap and spring. Animals large and small and everything with light feet will run to the golden miracle of a boat and to its master, the vintager with his diamond-studded vine knife. That master is "the great freer" of Zarathustra's redeemed soul, who frees her from her fullness by receiving her gift, allowing her to become the gift-giver. "The nameless one—for whom future songs will first find a name" is Dionysos, who arrives again as he arrived in ancient Athens in a miraculous boat over seas stilled by song; he arrives bringing the gift of earthly celebration, attended by dancing beings who draw him through the streets in the boat on wheels. "Almost two thousand years and not a single new god," laments Nietzsche in *The Antichrist* (19), but in the secret heart of his book for all and for none, Zarathustra prepares the return of Dionysos.

The master who comes in the golden boat is not the master of Zarathustra's soul. The great freer of Zarathustra's soul is not her redeemer. Zarathustra is the master and redeemer of his own soul; the one who comes is permitted to appear by the song of his soul. When the prophecy is given, Zarathustra's soul "glows and dreams," and, drinking "thirstily at all deep and resounding fountains of comfort," draws Dionysian metaphors and images from them for the future songs that already bring its melancholy to repose. The final gift that he gives to his soul is this gift of Dionysian dithyramb. The dialogue ends with Zarathustra repeating his soul's question; who should be grateful to whom? But he does not insist on gratitude from his soul; he wants to hear her songs so that they might both be grateful, both be emptied givers, both be fulfilled in the longing downward for power that now brings Dionysos back in his golden boat. Dionysos, the god who always comes for the first time, the god who comes bringing joy and horror, the ancient god of the mysteries of rising and dying, a god dismembered and reassembled, is the god who appears from across the sea to reap the harvest of Zarathustra's songs. Two of those songs appear in the next chapters, Dionysian songs that partake of the mystery of Dionysos's coming and depict that mystery as a dance (III. 15) and a marriage (III. 16), the marriage made possible by the dance. It does not fully illuminate the dance and the marriage to say that they reenact the fundamental story, the perpetual story, of Dionysos and Ariadne; nevertheless, the songs partake of that mystery or present the mystery as a mystery.[126]

Thus Spoke Zarathustra has moved toward the event of redemption as the crowning event. But redemption proves to be a prelude to events yet to come that can be prophesied in the mysterious and veiled words appropriate to epiphany. The songs of Zarathustra's soul permit the reappearance of a god godly enough to have laughed himself to death at the ungodly word that there is only one God (III. 8). The god who comes is a god not of being, but of coming and becoming, of rising and dying; he is a god whose nature it is to die, but whose dying presages birth. The god who comes to harvest the fruit of Zarathustra's song comes to celebrants, dancers and singers transfigured by joy at his coming.

In the official tradition of Athens, Dionysos is the last god to join the honored twelve on Olympus, a latecomer but one who comes even to the Olympians with force, wresting membership in the twelve from modest Hestia, goddess of the hearth, of the sacred things of the ancestral home, the nearest yet oldest things. As a latecomer to a world already ordered among the sacred powers, he forces Apollo himself to relinquish to him his sanctuary at Delphi for the winter months. But in his forceful coming even to the gods, there is the suggestion that the youthful Dionysos is the most ancient of gods, whose origins are always dark.[127] When Dionysos comes to men, he comes as Exekias painted him coming, from across the wine-dark sea in a black ship accompanied by springing dolphins, friends of man from the depths of the sea, and bringing with him the gift of divine madness, fruit of the earth friendly to man. He comes to celebrants who dance and sing at his coming and strew flowers in his path, but he comes to men too, with force and violence, for "Dionysos is a judge" (KGW VII 41 [7] = WP 1051). The earthly god who comes to settled orders, to once wild places settled by the heavenly music of Orpheus's lyre, comes with the hardness required to transform a heavenly order, to tear it apart, leaving only a sweet and haunting memory of things past. Dionysos punishes those who try to ignore his coming, like the daughters of Minyas in Orchomenus, who wanted only to be left alone to live as they had always lived among their settled things. But Dionysos punishes most terribly those whose loyalty to their old gods makes them resist his coming, as did Lycurgus in

Thrace and Pentheus in Thebes. The Dionysos who appears in *Zarathustra* is not the god of drunken playfulness, the jolly "Bacchus and his crew" depicted by Renaissance painters and Romantic poets, who arrived at the Greek gods through the Romans and reduced Dionysos to a domesticated merrymaker. The Dionysos who appears in *Zarathustra* appears to a joyful mankind, but he is the hardest and cruelest god, the god said by the Olympians to have been driven mad by jealous Hera and to imbue his followers with madness. The hardness that Zarathustra requires of his followers is a cruel hardness exhibited by the seemingly youthful and soft Dionysos, the hardness of the panther sacred to Dionysos.[128]

The manner of Dionysos's coming in *Zarathustra* repeats the manner of his coming in the ancient world, but it is his coming at all that is most mysterious. In a note concerning the possibility of new gods written four and a half years later, Nietzsche says: "Zarathustra himself, of course, is only an old atheist" (*KGW* VIII 17 [4, §5, May–June 1888]).[129] Zarathustra's godlessness is emphasized throughout the book. How can the godless Zarathustra comfort his soul with the prophecy of a god's return? Is Zarathustra's godlessness merely part of the shadow he needs to cast? Since arguing that gods must be destroyed because they limit man's creativity and thus imperil what gives mankind worth (II. 2), Zarathustra has discovered the truth of will to power and of the teachings of revenge that have held mankind prisoner. He has looked into the depths of the open heavens, discovering there not gods but an abyss of letting be that comes to human speech in eternal return. It is a consequence of this speech that Dionysos reappear on the earth as the mastering god hard enough to destroy the teachings of revenge. That mastering god prophesied by Zarathustra does not come as Zarathustra's master, as one who encloses the range of his godlike desires. Nor does he appear at the end of the book as a last-minute acknowledgment of a sacred order enclosing the earth. Rather, the order of earthly beings is itself seen as sacred, as worthy of the highest affirmation because it is not enclosed within anything higher. Dionysos is not a god who encloses human creativity within a perfect or heavenly order; he is an earthly god who himself philosophizes or inquires into the enigmatic marvel of things. There are no sky gods, for it is the earth that generates the sacred things. In applying this sickle to the myth of Uranos's generative powers, Nietzsche allows even the open skies to be what they are. To believers in the old God, as to free spirits only recently freed from that God, whose freedom is not yet such that it permits them to hear of God and gods (*BGE* 295), Zarathustra presents himself as godless. But to comfort his soul, he prophesies the return of a god who will appear as master and reap the harvest sown by his teachings. Dionysos does not return as some *deus ex machina* come to solve some unmanageable dilemma for mortals; he will appear only after the highest victory of the mortal Zarathustra, in a world made habitable for him by a mortal. He will be reborn not from the womb of Semele or the thigh of Zeus, but from Zarathustra's music.

What appears in a prophecy in *Zarathustra* is presented in a somewhat more sober mode in *Beyond Good and Evil*, a somewhat more sober book. Nietzsche the philosopher is there masked as a free spirit who makes clear the order of rank separating philosophy and all other human pursuits, including religion. Like "the philosopher of the future" and unlike the modern intellectuals whom he criticizes, Nietzsche seems very well to "know what religions are good for" (57) and to be prepared to exercise philosophy's rightful rule over religion. At the end of *Beyond Good and Evil* too, Dionysos returns, and there too his "last disciple and initiate" hints at where he stands with respect to his god. With a book that opens by calling Christianity Platonism for the people or by bringing philosophy and religion together in such a way as to show that religion is the fitting handmaiden of philosophy, a book that reaches its climax by showing the true philosopher to be the legislator who knows what religion is good for, and that ends with the arrival of the god himself, it can hardly be supposed that the philosopher who composed it grew forgetful of his own understanding of religion's place with respect to philosophy. In *Thus Spoke Zarathustra*, as in *Beyond Good and Evil*, religion is given to the care of philosophy. Zarathustra enacts the rule of philosophy over religion, but hardly as a triumph of antitheological ire or as a triumph of free spirits or humanists or refined atheists. The rule of philosophy over religion permits the reappearance of the god. It is a vindication of the gods. While maintaining the rule of philosophy, the Zarathustra who prophesies the mysterious reappearance of Dionysos leaves to Dionysos the things of Dionysos.

Zarathustra could thus be said to repeat the apparent piety practiced by Socrates, who founded a city in speech but apparently left to the oracle the practices of religion.[130] With respect to the sacred matters, Socrates, while omitting to mention that he has already legislated what the stories of the gods will be permitted to tell, appears to allow only the ancestral interpreter to speak; that interpreter speaks as if he possessed an authority higher than that of any mere human legislator or founder like the philosopher Socrates. So too Zarathustra, having prepared the way for the god, apparently yields to the greater authority or to what must appear as the greatest authority to have authority at all. But in the *Republic* Socrates makes his appeal to "Apollo at Delphi," not to Dionysos. In his first book Nietzsche understood this pious Socratic appeal to Apollo in a unique way, as the human murder of the god Dionysos. There, when not speaking in salutary parables that attribute the death of the gods to their laughter, Nietzsche argues that it was Socrates who banished Dionysos, and not Jehovah through his proclamation of himself as the one God. Zarathustra's parable to apostates seems to mask the truth about gods and mortals, that gods no more cause their own death than their own birth. According to the philosopher Nietzsche, the philosopher Socrates is "the one turning point and vortex of all so-called world history" (*BT* 15). That turning point can be construed religiously as the banishment of Dionysos and the elevation of Apollo, the heavenly god who held in being *Nous* and *Logos*, who made all beings thinkable and speakable, and who, in the religion of the victorious Platonism for the people, Christianity, became a transformed, though still jealous, Jehovah. Although Socrates' kindred spirit Euripides confessed abjectly at his end in *Bacchae* that Dionysos could not be driven out after all, and although Socrates himself at his end practiced music, if paltry music out of his own misgivings, in "so-called world history" the Socratic spirit succeeded in driving out Dionysos by means of its intoxicating promise of a Logos capable of grasping and showing Nous. But now the whole process of "so-called world history" has become world history and has become clear to Nietzsche, who stands "deeply moved, at the gates of the present and future." Though himself a "contemplative man," to whom it has been granted that he witness these tremendous struggles and transitions, the struggles themselves have, "alas," charmed their contemplative beholder to take part and to fight. As that fight unfolds, it is not Kant or Schopenhauer or Wagner who finally provide the music that revives the spirit of tragedy and drives out the Socratic, rational spirit of gravity that once drove out Dionysos under a scourge of syllogisms; it is the song of Zarathustra's soul. And if the adversary is "the one turning point and vortex of all so-called world history," who, through his intoxication of his followers, could transform a local event in Athens into world history and give his imprint to millennia, then the one who wins the victory over him wins a world-historical victory that will for millennia be hailed as the beginning of the new epoch. Socratic rationalism, the many-colored cloak of those who are wisest, has now itself been understood in its grounds. Long before, the ugly Socrates had appeared beautiful and had in the beauty of his rational optimism corrupted the most beautiful growth of antiquity, Plato. The force of Socratic rationalism had rent that most beautiful artistic veil that had been drawn over the terrible and tragic truth expressed by Silenos, associate of Dionysos: "What is best is utterly beyond [man's] reach: not to be born, not to *be*, to be *nothing*," and "the second best for you is— to die soon" (*BT* 3). Socratic rationalism had refused both Silenian truth and the art of tragedy that had remade that ugly truth into a magnificent affirmation of mortal life; it had attempted to make all beings thinkable, or permanent and beautiful. But the dream vanished, as Nietzsche says of one of its late, pale forms, Kantianism (*BGE* 11), and with its disappearance came the reappearance of Silenian wisdom in the teaching of the Soothsayer or in modern nihilism. This reappearance brought about by the honesty of the sublime modern inquirers promises the possibility of a new artistic affirmation of the seemingly deadly truths of existence. "The tragedy begins," says the first entry in Nietzsche's writings mentioning Zarathustra (*GS* 342). *Thus Spoke Zarathustra* comes to its climax in songs that anticipate the return of the god of tragedy, the earthly god of earthly life.

   In the tragedy of *Zarathustra* Nietzsche undertakes for himself "the supreme task" that he had earlier ascribed to Richard Wagner in Bayreuth:

"retention of the sense for the tragic," "the one hope and one guarantee for the future of humanity," for "all the ennoblement of mankind is enclosed in this supreme task" of consecrating the individual to something higher than himself (*WB* 4). After *Zarathustra* there is no longer any need for Nietzsche to feel "ashamed and afraid in the presence of the Greeks," as he had while "still concealed under the scholar's hood," while still feeling that "in their presence everything one has achieved oneself, though apparently quite original and admired with sincerity, suddenly seemed to lose life and color and shrivel into a poor copy, even a caricature" (*BT*, "Self-Criticism," 7). Moved by this shame and by his spirited love of victory to emulate what is highest, moved too by a love of mankind that refuses to permit its ultimate fall into the gravity of nihilism, Nietzsche undertakes to supply the music for the reappearance of tragedy and the god of tragedy. Tragedy is the artistic affirmation of the deadly truth about human things and all things. It refuses pessimism and nihilism and does not flee the world known to be mortal. It does not ground the earthly things in some cosmological or rational necessity of supposedly greater dignity or take revenge on the earth for being what it is. Nor does it engage in the masked revenge of a hopeless optimism that the earth might be made other than it is. While freeing man from "the terrible anxiety which death and time evoke in the individual," tragedy opens the possibility for the individual that "in the briefest atom of his life's course, he may encounter something holy that endlessly outweighs all his struggle and all his distress—that is what it means to have a sense for the tragic." Death and time face not only the individual, however, but the whole of humanity, for who can doubt that it too will die out? This unflinching modern clarity about human destiny sets the goal for humanity, the supreme task for all of approaching time: so to grow together, for one and for all, that humanity as a whole goes forth to meet its impending extinction with a sense of the tragic. The tragedy of *Zarathustra* aspires to this supreme task (*WB* 4).[131]

When Dionysos appears through Zarathustra's song, it is not to a world already inhabited by a panoply of divinities. He is not obliged to win the favor of regnant gods by some such act as leading Hephaestus back to Olympos and reconciling him with angry Hera. He need concede nothing to Zeus or Apollo or Ares or Pan, all gods who no longer exist. Rather, he appears in a world scarred by the death of the one God and by his gruesome shadows, the shadows of a refined atheism, or the complete desacralization of the earth left over from the vengeful judgment that only the heavenly can be sacred, and that the earth has fallen to the infernal powers and must be escaped or changed utterly. The coming of Dionysos to this godless world does not signal the return of the Olympians in whose court Dionysos was always an alien, even if he was conceded a temporary place. His return is not their rebirth; the religion prophesied by Zarathustra is not some aesthetically motivated reconstruction of classical divinities, as if a new age could be constructed by piecing together the beautiful shards of a lost age. When Dionysos returns in Nietzsche's writings, he brings only Ariadne.

In giving names to his soul in "On the Great Longing," Zarathustra withheld the name that Nietzsche himself gave to this whole chapter in his working manuscript: "Ariadne." The chapter in which Zarathustra comforts his soul with the prophecy of Dionysos's return is also a chapter that evokes the mystery of Ariadne, Dionysos's mysterious quarry and bride. Neither Dionysos nor Ariadne is named in this chapter; nor are they named in the subsequent two chapters, one of which reenacts their mysterious labyrinthine dance, while the other heralds their marriage. The unnamed presence of Dionysos and Ariadne at the end of the book fulfills the promised overcoming of the merely human or heroic, the overcoming of Theseus in need of a thread which Zarathustra had promised the heroic modern knowers: "Only when the hero has deserted the soul does there approach it in dreams—the super-hero" (II. 13), the god himself.[132] In its final three chapters *Zarathustra* moves beyond the heroic to the superheroic by alluding to the ancient mystery of life itself, as celebrated in the union of Dionysos and Ariadne.

Nietzsche alluded to this mystery as fundamental on other occasions as well. It is the great hunt seen from the perspective of the hunted in the "Lament of Ariadne" (IV. 5). The hunter is there described in a way that elevates him beyond what Zarathustra could be permitted to say of himself. In *Ecce Homo* Nietzsche provides a commentary on the final events of *Zarathustra*. "Who besides me knows who *Ariadne* is!" (*EH*, "Books: Zarathustra*," 8), Nietzsche says and supplies a mysterious answer where there had as yet been no thought even of a question. Both the question and answer illuminate the final songs of *Zarathustra*, for they occur in the most extensive account that Nietzsche ever gave of that book. After describing Zarathustra as experiencing "himself as *the supreme type of all beings*" (6) and stating that in him "the concept of the 'superman' has . . . become the greatest reality," after elevating him to the highest rank possible in a way of thought given to a new order of rank, Nietzsche says, "But that concept is the concept of Dionysos himself." Having identified Zarathustra and Dionysos in this way, Nietzsche says that Dionysos speaks dithyrambs when speaking to himself; as an example of dithyrambic speech, he reproduces "The Night Song" in full, calling it "the immortal lament at being condemned by the overabundance of light and power . . . not to love." That "immortal lament," "the suffering of a god, a Dionysos," is followed in *Zarathustra* by "The Dancing Song." But the Dancing Song does not fully provide the answer to this dithyramb of immortal lament, though Life herself appears there and in the appropriate way offers herself as the answer. *Ecce Homo* does not give the full answer either, but it points to the answer already given in *Zarathustra* by saying that the answer to the Night Song or to Dionysos's lament is Ariadne. The problem of the Night Song is restated exactly in "On the Great Longing," the chapter that Nietzsche had originally entitled "Ariadne," but the problem is there restated by Zarathustra's soul, and the answer to the problem, given by Zarathustra to comfort his soul, is the coming of Dionysos. Dionysos comes to Ariadne as the answer to her need to give; Ariadne comes to Dionysos as the answer to his need to give. Dionysos and Ariadne appear as the fundamental pair, the complementary pair, each being the answer to the other's lament. This is the dual coming that occurs in the two songs that end *Zarathustra*. In "The Other Dancing Song," Ariadne or Dionysos's quarry appears as Life herself, while Dionysos or Life's hunter appears as Zarathustra. In the final song the great marriage of Dionysos and Ariadne appears as the marriage of Zarathustra and Eternity. According to the hint of *Ecce Homo*, therefore, the final three chapters reenact successfully the anticipations of the three songs of part II. The lament of the Night Song is answered by On the Great Longing; Zarathustra's separation from Life by virtue of his wild Wisdom in the Dancing Song is ended by Zarathustra's dance with Life in the Other Dancing Song; the "resurrection" and victory anticipated in the Song at Grave-side are enacted in the Seven Seals.[133]

The mystery of the final songs of *Zarathustra* evokes the ancient mystery of Dionysos and Ariadne, though who but Nietzsche knows who Ariadne is, to say nothing of Dionysos? In order that the peak of *Zarathustra* not disappear completely in the clouds of Nietzsche's most mysterious preoccupation, and in order that that peak not be drawn down to the conventional lowlands it exists to surmount, one must remain schooled by Nietzsche alone and not by the sobriety or gravity he expressly has his Zarathustra overcome. The peak of *Zarathustra* mixes levity and intoxication with a new kind of gravity and sobriety: the history of mankind is at stake in Zarathustra's songs, for they aim to bring to earth again the sacred mystery of Dionysos and Ariadne and to terminate the ruined effort of the spirit of gravity to banish that mystery.

The Other Dancing Song (Chapter 15)

The title of this chapter is the only one that all but repeats an earlier title, a repetition inviting a comparison. The Dancing Song began with a prose passage that set the context for the song, stated its purpose, and identified its audience. "The Other Dancing Song" has no such prose introduction; it needs none, however, because the preceding chapters have provided the necessary setting. They have shown that this is the song of Zarathustra's soul subsequent to his redemption, sung in the complete privacy of his cave with his eyes closed. Given the promise of the previous chapter, this song sings the return of Dionysos and does so in a precise, if enigmatic, way. Disciples are not present, nor do young girls dance with Cupid. Life is present again, however, though this time she and Zarathustra are completely alone, and this time they dance together. Before, it was he who turned to his wild Wisdom after first turning away from Life as one who speaks ill of herself; now, it is Life who turns to Zarathustra's wisdom, summoning her apparent rival in words of careful jealousy to which Zarathustra responds in a way that calms her jealous fears. Wisdom is not personified, though she still plays the important role of Life's rival for Zarathustra's love. But now the dissonance of the earlier song is resolved, the three having become two, Zarathustra's wisdom having been transformed into a love of Life. Zarathustra is no longer a mere suitor for Life like "the other old carps"; their dance culminates in a speech showing that he, like no other, has achieved an intimacy with Life that fits him for marriage to her. This dancing song is not followed by the coming of melancholy evening, or by a graveside song that can only make promises of rebirth. It is followed by a song that completes the dance by transforming it into a procession preparatory to the consummating marriage.

But for all its difference from "The Dancing Song," this is nevertheless "The *Other* Dancing Song," and it can be asked whether this, too, is "a mocking song on the spirit of gravity"? What place does this song have in the long battle against the spirit of gravity? Judging by the series of events described by Zarathustra in his confrontation with the spirit of gravity (III. 11), this song is not a mere mocking song but is, together with the song that follows, the essential account of the complete victory over the spirit of gravity, the victory that frees his hands for the blessing on things, the azure dome of eternal security that lets things become what they are. Here Nietzsche "solves the yes-saying part of his task" (*EH*, "Books: *Beyond*," 1).

This dancing song at the climax of Zarathustra's course describes a great hunt, one that is in deadly earnest. It is not mere fishing; there are no nets or golden fishing rods. A dialogue with two speakers, Zarathustra and Life, this dancing song begins exactly as the first one began, with Zarathustra looking into Life's eyes. But this time he does not sink into the unfathomable; instead, he sees in Life's eyes a vision of a boat that glitters on dark waters. Life no longer has a golden fishing rod, because Zarathustra no longer needs to be fished out of the dizzying unfathomable. The golden boat in Life's eyes submerges and surges on her nocturnal waters; it is like a "swing," and the vision of it causes Zarathustra's heart to stand still with passion. The vision in Life's eyes is a Dionysian vision, the boat a sign of Dionysos's arrival, its rocking and swinging a portrayal of the happiness that knows no goal but life itself, one that the Greeks pictured in a young girl's swinging, her swing kept in pointless but joyful motion by a satyr's push.[134] Life casts a questioning glance at his feet, and her glance is itself like a swing. She clicks her castanets, the instruments of Dionysos's dancing maenads.[135] The dance that follows this invitation is described in a series of twenty-one rhymes.

Zarathustra is filled with passion by his vision and, responding to Life's invitation to dance, leaps at her, but she flees, her hair streaming and flying the way the maenads' hair streamed in the wild head-tossings characteristic of their dance.[136] In this impassioned proximity to Life, he learns from her crooked glance crooked ways, the ways of guile and treachery (as he had earlier reported to the wisest, II. 12). Life both draws and repels him, and as her hunter he both loves and hates her. As the hunter who catches living game, Zarathustra is Zagreus,[137] the great mythical hunter, and he too risks dismemberment. Life draws him in the hunt, fleeing his grasp repeatedly; he "dances" after her, following the slightest trail. He fears that they will lose their way in caves and thickets, for Life is an owl and a bat who wants to confuse him. She has learned howling and barking from the hounds that always accompanied Dionysos on his hunt, and although Zarathustra feels danger at her mysterious presence, he gathers his courage for the challenge: does she want to be his hound or his doe, his help or his quarry?[138] Suddenly she is near him, and he adopts the strategy of appearing to be the hunted; feigning a fall, he calls attention to his vulnerability and lies before her pleading for grace. Prone, he tempts her to the tenderer paths of love, creating a picture of pastoral and Dionysian languor in a still and leafy glade by a lake as the sun sets and a shepherd plays his flute. Appealing to her exhaustion from the hunt, he invites her to let him carry her to the lakeside. But she does not yield to his temptations, for though she was close enough to touch his face, her hand leaves only scratches as she moves away, and he curses her as a "supple snake" and a "slippery witch."

With this refusal Zarathustra tires of the hunt, and the mood changes for the last time in the song. Now—at the end of the first section of this chapter—he gathers his courage as he had at the end of the first sections of earlier chapters for other important encounters (III. 2; III. 13). The manner he adopts toward Life is the manner under which the second part of the chapter is played out, a commanding manner that forces Life to change her response to him. She is not now simply quarry, but cornered quarry. So far, he has chased and tempted her, but he says he has had enough of playing the "sheeplike shepherd." Now she will dance to the tempo of his whip, for, in coming to the woman Life, he has not forgotten the whip. In response to Zarathustra's whip, Life finally yields; under the force and violence of his commanding presence, a now yielding and responsive Life begins to speak. But her words are marked by guile, for she fears her hunter and doubts his motive. Nevertheless, these words spoken under the threat of his whip draw from him the secret words that transform them into lovers and prepare them for their marriage.

Life answers the newly resolute Zarathustra by denying that the whip could have been the means of transforming her; still, she stands transformed. But her final transformation, in which she shuns guile and welcomes him as lover, does not take place until she hears his whispered words of love. For now, the dance continues as a hunt, as he searches for the real meaning of her veiled and cunning words. No longer unwilling and distant, no longer enflaming him by her distance, she grows yielding and submissive under the whip. Confessing her tender thoughts, she speaks in a way designed to please him of their kinship "beyond good and evil," of their being alone on their own "island," their Naxos, and their own "green meadow." She who had evaded and thwarted him now says that they must be good to one another, given their likeness and aloneness. But her speech continues to be coy and guarded, for she treats it as simply given that they do not love one another from the "ground up" or from the heart. In alleging easily that she does not love him from the heart, she masks her suspicion and fear that he does not love her from the heart. But she says that she is "well-disposed towards him and often too well," and her sly words repeat exactly the words he had earlier used in her presence to describe his feelings for her rival, wild Wisdom. Now Life says openly that she is jealous of that wild Wisdom just as Wisdom was jealous of her. But Life's jealousy is different in that it acknowledges the necessity of her rival; although she calls her rival "a crazy old fool of a Wisdom," it is precisely his love of his Wisdom that makes him lovable to Life; if his Wisdom left him, Life says, so too would she. Life evidently loves best the wisest of men, and loves them for their wisdom. Nevertheless, she has learned with good reason to be suspicious of these best of men, for it is they who have said that she is no good and have imposed on her their own virtues. When it is time for him to speak, Zarathustra will not have to withhold the truth from the woman Life, as he had from the woman Wisdom; when he tells Life the truth, she will see that this wise man in fact loves her from the heart, and she will be able to respond with the disclosure of her own love from the heart.

Before Life continues her speech, she gazes thoughtfully around her and behind her, assuring herself of their utter privacy for what she is going to say next. What she says provides the reason for her suspicion of Zarathustra's love, her fear that he loves his Wisdom more than Life herself, as all the other old carps have done: he is not loyal enough to her; what he says and what he thinks are contradictory; for, while saying that he loves life, he thinks that he will leave life soon. She knows that between the twelve long tolls of the midnight bell, he thinks of his mortality, of the term placed on his love of life by death. Does he, like all the wisest hitherto, judge that life is no good because it ends in death?

Life's speech is an appeal to the most spirited man not to abandon her in favor of a vengeful wisdom that condemns life for not being other than she is—as she has always been abandoned by the best and wisest men. Although life eventually has her way with such men and abandons them, she must abandon them sadly and jealously, because she has had to surrender them to an old fool of a woman. But just now, when she accuses Zarathustra of unfaithfulness, she forces him to think of her unfaithfulness; Life is not true to what she loves, for she allows it to die. Life had said defiantly in her earlier private conversation with him that she abandons everything she loves, becomes the opponent of what she creates, and watches its demise (II. 12). Now, in the altogether different intimacy of this lovers' dance, she forces him to answer the essential question: Is Life's unfaithfulness, his own mortality, grounds for judging her no good? Zarathustra's answer relieves Life of her fears and rescues her from her jealousy by assuring her of his love. His answer proves that he loves her from the heart, that the consummation of his midnight wisdom does not come at the cost of his love of life, that his love of wisdom is a love of life itself.

But the answer that removes Life's jealous fears is not an answer that Zarathustra shares with anyone but Life. He answers her "hesitantly," in her ear, between her "tangled yellow foolish tresses." She is astonished that he knows what no one knows. Earlier she had yielded to him her secret that she could be fathomed as will to power, but this new secret she has not told him.

What has Zarathustra said? When the narrative disappears at its peak into something spoken but not reported, does it disappear into a mere puzzle or riddle that cannot be solved? Or are Zarathustra's unreported words to Life the completely obvious words of a "holy open secret" that belongs to Zarathustra and Life, words that the narrative dictates as simply necessary, words that name the eternal return of life? The exact exchange in the dialogue provides essential clues in favor of this answer. Life has just confronted Zarathustra with his mortality, the fact that at deepest midnight he knows that he must leave life. Though set in Life's confession of her jealousy and emphasizing his choice between Life and Wisdom, these words still affirm indirectly that Life will have her way with him whatever he choose. In emphasizing his mortality, her words convey the grounds on which he could conclude that she does not love him from the heart and is therefore not worthy of his love from the heart; her words give him the opportunity to say, as all the wise have said, that immortal wisdom is worthy of being chosen over mortal life. His answer to her final words—"You want to leave me soon!"—affirms his mortality: "Yes," he will leave her soon. However, this necessity is not a refutation of life, for his "yes" is followed by a "but"—"but you also know ...," and this "yes ... but" suggests that the whispered words are some variant or other of the expected phrase, "I will eternally return." Having heard the highest affirmation of life that can ever be achieved (*EH*, "Books: *Zarathustra*," 1), and having heard that affirmation arise out of the deepest awareness of mortality, Life now knows that he loves only her from the heart. Still, her response leaves the great enigma intact: "You *know* that, O Zarathustra? No one knows that.——" Does Life know that? Does anyone *know* that? Still, Life's question and assertion, however problematic they render any final knowledge claim about eternal return, do not refute Zarathustra's whispered confession of love but acknowledge it and accept it; she reciprocates his love from the heart, and the complementary pair of Zarathustra and Life prepare to marry. It may even be that Zarathustra, the teacher of eternal return, teaches even Life eternal return, for in the next song he gives her, for the first time, the name Eternity.

The words unspoken by the narrative but spoken by Zarathustra to Life must have demonstrated his love for her, but they can do so only because they are at the same time the words of his wisdom, for Life would abandon a wise man who abandoned his wisdom. What Zarathustra whispers to Life is what no wise man has ever whispered to her, that she is of all things the sweetest. He loves her as she is and does not aim to alter her. His wisdom wills her eternal return as she is; it "replenishes and gilds and immortalizes and deifies Life" (*KGW* VIII 14 [11] = *WP* 1033). Zarathustra's secret words must name eternal return, because any other words would make the narrative progress of the book unintelligible. Zarathustra's course has long pointed to the willing of eternal return as its climax, and here, in the poetry relating that climax in parables that praise and justify time and becoming, his whispered words will Life's eternal return. These are the secret words that name the highest; they are, according to the hierarchy said to be present in all tables of value (I. 15), not merely praiseworthy words, or good words, but sacred words symptomatic of the disposition that in the most unrestrained way says yes to life.[139]

But Zarathustra brings the whip when he goes to the woman Life. What is the meaning of the whip? Is it symbolic of that mastery of nature that aims to alter her ways, to give her new and better ways? In speaking of the whip Zarathustra says that Life will dance to the tempo or rhythm set by his whip. In speaking earlier of rhythm under the title "On the origin of poetry," Nietzsche had spoken of it as the fundamental power of poetry: with rhythm added to their petitions, men thought that they could better impress even the gods. As for men themselves, rhythm could compel them to yield not only their feet but their souls. Rhythm is the invention of Apollo, and with it Apollo learned to bind even the goddesses of fate (GS 84). The crack of Zarathustra's whip provides the new rhythm for the dance with Life, the new measure that binds even Life by giving her a tempo or a time to keep, the time of eternal return. He does not whip Life into submission by imposing some virtue on her that is not her own, nor does he seek to alter Life's unalterable ways; he considers her ways and wills their eternal return.[140]

On this day on which he convalesces from the act of his redemption, Zarathustra hears the bell toll midnight. He thinks not only of death when he hears the bell, but also of marriage and offspring. What the midnight bell tolls constitutes the third section of the chapter, in which a line of verse follows every toll except the twelfth, after which there seems to be silence. But in fact, after the bell tolls twelve, the marriage song is sung, in the next chapter. The song of the midnight bell is sung in Life's presence; its name is "Once More," and its meaning, "to all eternity," according to Zarathustra's commentary on the song given to the superior men (IV. 19, §12). Life and Zarathustra, alone on their island, hear the heavy tolling of the bell, and he tells Life what his thoughts are at deepest midnight. What she hears are words meant especially for her, though they are public words that proclaim to all mankind that life alone is worthy of the highest love.

The song begins by calling mankind to attend to the speech of deep midnight; the public bell sounds a public address. Deep midnight's speech begins by acknowledging a long sleep and a deep dream from which it is now awakened. Its deep dream confirms that the world is deeper than day has ever thought. The unsuspected depth of night is a deep woe, but one that is transformed into a still deeper joy. The two depths of awakened midnight speak different and contradictory commands; its woe commands Life to depart, while its joy (according to the line following the eleventh toll, the last line of the chapter) commands Life to eternally return. Whereas woe longs for a different life, joy loves this life just as it is. The commanding voice of joy sings the marriage song after the twelfth toll. Unlike the will of the hitherto wisest, which has given voice to woe and commanded life to depart, Zarathustra gives voice to joy and commands that Life become eternity.[141]

In marrying the woman Eternity, the only woman from whom he has ever desired children, Zarathustra does not marry some woman whom he meets for the first time at the end of his course. For, in marrying Eternity, he marries Life, but in the act of marrying bestows upon her a new name. "Eternity" is the name that Zarathustra wills Life to take. As is appropriate for a bride, Life receives a new name from her husband. Just as Dionysos, in marrying mortal Ariadne, raised her to the heavens and placed her immortal among the stars as Corona Borealis,[142] Life is valorized "Eternity" by Zarathustra's love.

The Seven Seals (Or: The Yes and Amen Song) (Chapter 16).

The toll of the midnight bell introducing the final song marks the passing of one day and the arrival of another; Nietzsche ends his book on the image of passing and arriving. What passes is the world created by the wisdom that tells Life to depart; what arrives is the new world created by the wisdom that names life Eternity. This new world has its own weights and measures; around its new center of gravity all objects are arrayed and find their new value.

The last chapter is the only one with a pair of titles. The pair enables Nietzsche to close his book on his own affirmation of "Yes and Amen" and at the same time to close on the image of finality used by the world that is passing, Christianity's image of a book sealed with seven seals. The last chapter of part III seals the fifteen previous chapters with seven seals; thus, in a witty fashion, Nietzsche continues his pattern of making each part, like the book of *Revelation*, contain twenty-two chapters.[143] By naming the last chapter of the last part "The Seven Seals," Nietzsche ends his own sixty-six chapters by invoking the sixty-sixth and final book of the Bible, thereby signaling the passing of what was once a new testament. The original book sealed with seven seals found no one worthy to break the seals and open the book until the Lamb Jesus returned and broke them one by one, thereby bringing the age to a close and bringing the earth to an unearthly end. In breaking the seven seals, Jesus loosed pestilence on the earth, the breaking of each seal bringing new waves of destruction, the seventh seal alone containing seven angels with seven trumpets, each bringing new destructions, some so terrible that even John was forbidden to report them. With the seventh trumpet of the seventh seal came the final battle of Christ and Satan on earth, followed by the passing of the old and hated earth and the appearance of a new earth and a new heaven. What was hated most about the old earth is abolished, for in the new Jerusalem there is no night, and death shall be no more.[144]

Grim vengeance does not intrude into what is shown of the seven seals that seal *Thus Spoke Zarathustra*, but the book and the breaking of its seals are surely meant to loose storms on the earth, though not the earthly doomsday devoutly wished by Christian eschatology. At the end of *Zarathustra* a new battle for the earth is proclaimed; in bringing his fire to the earth, Zarathustra, too, brings not peace but a sword.[145] By borrowing the final symbol from the old revelation, he proclaims the arrival of terrible battles between irreconcilable forces. If Zarathustra's final song is a song of joy and a marriage song, it is still the song of "The Seven Seals," and those seals contain what Zarathustra has maintained since the end of the prologue, that he is also a bringer of destruction. "For a temple to be built a temple must be destroyed" (*GM* II. 24), and Nietzsche reaffirms this aspect of *Zarathustra* in *Ecce Homo*, where, "speaking theologically," he says that after *Zarathustra* God himself becomes the devil, and the one who made all things too beautiful turns to destruction, for "the devil is merely the leisure of God on that seventh day" (*EH*, "Books: *Beyond*," 2).

The eschatological symbolism of the Bible is also reflected in the marriage that ends *Zarathustra*, for the final event in the book of *Revelation* is the marriage of the victorious, imperial Christ to the purified Church, the New Jerusalem.[146] Still, despite its biblical title and marriage theme (and lesser parallels such as "The Alpha and Omega"[147]), the imagery of Zarathustra's final song is not primarily biblical. Nor are the images of the marriage song primarily Dionysian, though the marriage of Life and Zarathustra parallels that of Ariadne and Dionysos, and specific Dionysian images such as lightning and a violent coming are utilized in the song's description of Zarathustra. The images of the song are drawn primarily from *Zarathustra* itself, for its seven stanzas provide a summary of the portrait of Zarathustra developed in the book. Celebrating himself serially as soothsayer, destroyer, creator, bringer of harmony, seafarer, dancer, and finally, supremely, flier, Zarathustra demonstrates his fitness for marriage to Life.

Each of the seven seals repeats the same threefold pattern, beginning with a conditional statement, drawing a conclusion, and stating the same necessity as consequence. The consequence of Zarathustra's seven transformations is that he is able to confer upon Life the name "Eternity." Life is the only woman from whom he wants children. The one who finds a worthy friend only in the heavens whose secret he shares and keeps finds a worthy bride only in Life herself. What he meets and what he sees answers to the "danger and play" that a "true man" wants from a woman; finding that in Life, he is prepared to give her what she must desire of him, for "everything about woman is a riddle and everything about woman has one solution: pregnancy" (I. 18). In willing the eternal return of Life, or in danger and play bestowing upon Life the name Eternity, Zarathustra too desires offspring. Whereas the animals comfort themselves with thoughts of their own eternal return, Zarathustra, in thinking of children, thinks of the line and race that will follow his midnight marriage to Life; he thinks of what will dawn, or what will be fathered, what will spread itself throughout the earth as a consequence of the teaching of eternal return.

In thinking now of children, he is not thinking only of his disciples. He has performed the deed that he had said was necessary when he first called his disciples his "children" (III. 3): he has perfected himself by willing eternal return. In so doing, he has made it unnecessary for disciples to take the way named "Impossibility" or to attempt to throw the golden ball of his teaching further than he could throw it. Perfecting himself has authorized his return to his children as the teacher of eternal return and the bringer of the Great Noon (IV. 20). But the "children" of the complementary marriage of Zarathustra and Life are not merely the disciples already drawn to him. Given the world-historical scope of the marriage song, its children must be those many generations to come who will inhabit the world altered by the teaching of eternal return. They are the myriad of men and women who, liberated from the spirit of gravity and the teaching of revenge, will live joyfully within the earthly garden of mortal things. The fable of Zarathustra concludes with the global consequences of the teaching of eternal return and the religion of Dionysos; under the open sky the new global people mankind takes its place among the mortal beings as the conscious celebrant of those beings.[148]

Seven times Zarathustra affirms his passionate desire for marriage with with life willed eternal. The descriptions preceding these seven affirmations give the most exact description of the redeemed Zarathustra. His final account of himself sings of the fulfillment of the godlike desires enflamed by his discovered kinship with the heavens; it sings the enactment of the "nameless" lust to rule by the most spirited being whose highest victory creates a new earth. All seven conditional statements describe what Zarathustra has made of himself.

Zarathustra is first a soothsayer, full of the soothsaying spirit that calls forth a new future. Reviving an earlier image of the superman, as well as an image of Dionysos, the lightning-bringer, he pictures himself as a heavy cloud pregnant with redeeming lightning wandering between past and present. Such pregnancy is blessed, but the one pregnant in this way, the one who will kindle the light of the future, must for a long time loom over the present like a threat. "For the most powerful thought, many millennia are required—long, long must it be small and weak" (*KGW* V 11 [158]).

Looking from his future to his past in the second stanza, Zarathustra recounts his actions. Like Dionysos himself, he has come with force and violence. In anger he has broken graves open, moved boundary stones, and tumbled old law tablets into deep chasms. In mockery he has blown away the decayed standards of Christianity, rejoicing in his destruction. He can even love the monuments to old gods when they stand in ruins open to the new heavens.

In the third stanza he asserts his ascension to the place of divinity whence the earth is ruled. He shares the "creative breath" that compels accident itself to dance to his dictates. In this stanza that bore the title "Dionysos" in Nietzsche's manuscript, the conclusion repeats and makes emphatic the claim first put conditionally with respect to the gods and cosmic order: that the earth is the table on which they play their divine games of dice; that it heaves and breaks at the creative new words of the gods, now, finally, the word of loyalty to the earth.[149]

In the middle stanza of his marriage song Zarathustra pictures himself drinking a full draught from that receptacle in which "all things" are blended together. He is the one who brings about a new blending or ordering of all things, transforming fire into spirit, the passions into something higher and more spiritual. He is the grain of redeeming salt whose savor blends together the good and evil that had been held furthest apart in the old mix of things. The tumult and bedlam of Zarathustra's mixing bowl brings near what once was far off, what once was said to belong to the superman, and in its "evil" mix makes recognizable, as nearest or one's own, the mortal soul that has been concealed by the spirit of gravity.

The fifth stanza invokes the sea as an image of the "unbounded" that permits untrammeled inquiry into the great enigma of things. Zarathustra is qualified for his marriage with Life by his passion for the undiscovered, his rejoicing that the settled shoreline falls away before the adventurous inquirer and that the open sea challenges him to the joyful science of discovering new shorelines of the knowable. Certified by Zarathustra's marriage to Life, mankind's spirited inquiry into uncharted space and time does not aim at the effecting of all things possible. The goal of Zarathustra's science is not the technological mastery of nature, but the discovery of nature's secrets under the eternal security granted nature by willing its eternal return as it is.

The images of dancing and flying that have been associated from the beginning with the victory sought by Zarathustra provide the culmination of the marriage song. His virtue has been a dancer's virtue; in the rapture of the dance, laughter erupts, a laughter in which all evil is present. But this is an adequate evil, one great enough in its opposition to the settled good to upset it entirely and thereby to sanctify itself and absolve itself. This transforming laughter must be the very laughter that Zarathustra heard in his vision and resolved to emulate. His conclusion announces what has always been fundamental for him, victory over the spirit of gravity, the transformation of the heavy and grave into the light and easy, of the body into a dancer, and of the spirit into a bird. The "bird" into which spirit is transformed conquers the spirit of gravity through the birdlike acts of singing and flying in the final stanza.

This last stanza brings the marriage song to a close with the encompassing flight into the open sky. In the depths of his free and unencumbered flight his "bird-wisdom" spoke to his freedom, asserting both the permissive openness of the whole and the legislative power of speech. Zarathustra's

bird-wisdom is a wisdom of which his bride need not be jealous, for it
freely affirms in speech that Life herself is desirable while recognizing that
life is ungrounded in anything higher; it beholds the open, enigmatic character of the whole, while at the same time lauding and loving it. The bird-
wisdom commands Zarathustra to "Behold" and causes to be seen that
there is no "above" and no "below," no up and down natural to things as
their orienting ground. The birdlike one, free of the gravity of fixed form,
can throw himself "around," "out," "back." After beholding this vision of
the groundless whole, he is commanded by his bird-wisdom: "Sing." He
is to speak no more, for mere speech belongs to the heavy and grave. To
those who are light, "all words lie," and Zarathustra is the lightest. In not
commanding silence, even after it has made him see the lying way of words,
his bird-wisdom commands a way with lying words that is different from
the way of gravity. Rather than speak the grave word of some rational spider,
he is to compose with words a new way of "bridging" that which is eternally
separate. "It is sweet that words and tones exist," lying though they be,
for they are gifts given to things so that mankind may be refreshed in those
things. Thus spoke Zarathustra in his first speech after his redemption;
but his animals interrupted, purporting to correct his account of the way
of words and tones by giving a pious and loving interpretation of the dance
of things themselves, as if things themselves danced, as if things themselves
had an up and down. Having curbed his speech for their sake, he returns
to his own account of words and tones in his marriage song, showing the
power of words for the one who flies highest, far above his eagle. All words
are lying words, but among them are words that confer the blessing of
which the animals sang, the blessing of an up and down that allows mankind to refresh itself in things and provides for earthly things, the things
beneath his snake, the heavenly dome of eternal security that lets them
be what they are. The coming species mankind will inhabit a world blessed
by the words of his songs. For, though they are, like all words, lying words,
they refresh mankind and transform the world into a garden.

    In light of the bird-wisdom that ends *Zarathustra*, the "brave birds"
whose song brought Nietzsche's earlier book *Daybreak* to a close are revealed as in fact modest birds that show by contrast the immoderate ambition of Zarathustra's bird-wisdom. The birds of *Daybreak* end that book
too on the image of flying, but when they find their solitary final perch,
they are encouraged by the thought that "other birds will fly farther." No
such encouraging word need be imagined by the bird-wisdom that brings
Thus Spoke Zarathustra to a close, for Zarathustra has himself learned to
fly beyond all boundaries, to defeat the spirit of gravity that would bind
him to some center other than the centering on life that he ordains. His
final flying is the transcendent act, the encompassing of the earth by the
most spiritual human will to power, a complementary will to power that,
out of love for life, desires the eternal return of life. With this consummating
act, Zarathustra shows the way in to Nietzsche's philosophy, to the historic
achievement that replaces the spirit of gravity with a new human spirit.

Conclusions: Nietzsche as Educator

> Through Nietzsche we are all *able* to educate ourselves *against*
> our age—because through him we possess the advantage
> of really *knowing* this age.
>
> —NIETZSCHE, *SE* 4[1]

The fabulous tale told in *Zarathustra* of a world grown old and worthy of destruction and of a new world a long way off but worthy of being built does not tell but allows to be guessed just what responsibilities Nietzsche thought fell to him as a consequence of his having become a philosopher, the first philosopher to see through to the grounds of Socratic rationalism and to glimpse the opposite ideal of wanting all that was and is repeated to all eternity (letters to von Meysenbug, May 1884, and von Stein, 22 May 1884). From *Zarathustra* one learns that Nietzsche means to found a world on the teachings of will to power and eternal return.

WILL TO POWER

In *Thus Spoke Zarathustra* will to power comes to light as the most fundamental matter in Nietzsche's thought; it names what is true of all beings and hence of the highest beings. In the language avoided by Zarathustra but used by Nietzsche in his next book, it names what is true of nature and of philosophy. In *Zarathustra* will to power appears first as the ground of the greatest power on earth (I. 15), then as the still more fundamental secret of life itself (II. 12). The discovery of will to power is not only the primary discovery with respect to nature and philosophy; it also transforms the discoverer, assigning him his task, for the discovery reveals that the wisest have had dominion, that philosophers have been the secret spiritual rulers whose ark of values the people have carried forward, an ark of Socratic or rational optimism that willed the thinkability of all beings. Mankind has been given to the care of the wisest and most powerful beings whose wisdom and power came to be experienced as the passion to rule. Thus will to power as truth led to will to power as art, where the greatest art is the founding art that hangs a new tablet of the good over a people.

When Zarathustra discovered that life is will to power, he concluded immediately that the will to power as art, the most spiritual will to power, had moved the wisest hitherto (II. 12), but he did not conclude immediately what the new founding art must be, or that it must be his art. Although it was clear to him that the new founding art must be undertaken not for the sake of this or that people but for mankind as a whole because of the global spread of modern states, just what that founding had to be became clear to him only after his discovery that the wisest hitherto had been moved by revenge at the unbreakable tyranny of the past. The rule of the wisest hitherto is now threatened, not because their will was corrupt in being a will to power, but because their will to power was corrupted by revenge. The discoverer of will to power must will the eternal return of life as it is and ground a new world of experience for human beings by breaking the hold of the teachings of revenge. Because it opposes the old teaching in the most fundamental way possible, the creative act of willing eternal return is necessarily an act of war that strikes down the spiritual rulers of the age. But it is also an act of creation that establishes a new form of the greatest power on earth, a new good or standard of the highest value. After the wars that the new creation inaugurates will come a new era marked by the judgment even by the wisest that life is good or desirable for itself.

Nietzsche's presentation in *Zarathustra* of the fundamental discovery of will to power takes pains to show that there are limits on the possibility of teaching it. Although it is the most comprehensive of truths with respect to its applicability to all beings, with respect to its relevant audience, it is a limited truth. Zarathustra addresses its discovery only to "you who are wisest," and invites them to reason together with him on the truth that unriddles their wisdom and terminates their ancient sway. But when he sets off in part III on the path along which his will to power impels him, a path not yet trodden by any man, he takes care to leave no tracks. Later, having effected his own redemption, he does not try to persuade the animals that their experience of being and time is less fundamental than his own. Nor does he, in the preparation of his half-written tablets, include an account of will to power or of the groundless ground of those tablets. His reserve is not practiced for reasons of delicacy, for he opens his hand on many a dangerous truth. Because he knows that hidden truths draw attention to themselves, and that skeptical inquiry belongs to human beings as part of the highest enterprise which is philosophy, to write as Nietzsche does is to loose inquiry and to taunt the interested few to pursue where their fancy leads. Nietzsche need not feel chagrin before the nutcrackers who discern in his words an esoteric or ironic content; he does not keep secrets, he tends them in a fitting way.

It can hardly be expected that Nietzsche would forget his own lessons on what can be taught and, in his next books, engage in acts of instruction with respect to the will to power that *Zarathustra* had shown to be impossible or undesirable. The later books all share the limitations with respect to teaching will to power that *Zarathustra* had shown to be intrinsic to the fundamental phenomenon. But in addition, they all share a more overt limitation, in that it is not their purpose to chronicle the discovery of will to power and its consequences. In *Ecce Homo*, Nietzsche directs his readers back to *Zarathustra* for the account of how he solved the "yes-saying" part of his task. Reviewing his books, he says, "From this moment forward"—from the completion of *Zarathustra* forward—"all my writings are fish hooks," "a slow search for those related to me," those who would choose to become his friends in the tasks that fell to him because of the discoveries chronicled in *Zarathustra*. Nietzsche, like Zarathustra, goes in search of those "who will to follow themselves—wherever I will" (Prologue 9), those who "inscribe my will upon my tablets" (III. 3).[2] The books written after *Zarathustra* have the appearance of being the last word on Nietzsche's philosophy simply because they were the last to be written before his breakdown, but they are preliminary books, "no-saying," "no-doing" books intended to win friends for the immediate tasks.

With respect to will to power, the fishhook that is *Beyond Good and Evil* occupies a special position because, in taking as its theme philosophy past and future and the present task facing philosophy, it reveals the most about philosophy and its ground.[3] But "the art of silence is in the foreground" of this book (*EH*, "Books: *Beyond*," 2), and it must be read with attention to its silences. Nietzsche announces clearly enough the presence of the art of silence, for he says that he makes use of a distinction "formerly known to philosophers" between "exoteric and esoteric," wherein the esoteric looks down from above on what is below. The presentation of the view from above requires irony, one of whose modes is the art of successfully appearing more stupid than you are (*BGE* 288). The need for this appearance of relative stupidity follows from Nietzsche's judgment that "when a philosopher these days lets it be known that he is not a skeptic everyone is annoyed" (208), especially the free spirits to whom the book is addressed. "The need for concealment" (40) that has dictated that no philosopher "ever [express] his real and ultimate opinions in books" (289) dictates a specific mode of concealment for the philosopher Nietzsche. In a book that assigns the greatest responsibility to the philosopher as the one who knows what religions are good for, who knows how to order the politics of fatherlands, who commands and legislates how the world ought to be, and who has the whole future of mankind on his conscience, the philosopher Nietzsche must conceal himself behind the mask of a free spirit. Having shown the utter immoderation of philosophy, he must allege moderately that he shares only the spirit of those to whom the book is addressed or for whom the hook is cast, possible kin, though as yet merest novices in relation to the one who has already flown highest and farthest and views things from above. This art of writing enables Nietzsche simultaneously to attract potential kin and keep at a distance those "who listen in without permission" (30). Near the end (295) the author theatrically lowers his mask (his mask of Apollo) to suggest his actual identity with respect to his god Dionysos, whom he here puts on his stage. This subtle suggestion, like others throughout the book, makes it possible to penetrate the foreground silence and to understand that in this book too, as in *Zarathustra*, Nietzsche enacts a battle between philosophers, the protagonists being Plato and Nietzsche, with the whole future of mankind at issue.

Plato may be the most beautiful growth of antiquity, but he is responsible for having invented the "most dangerous of all errors so far" (Preface). So successful was he in employing his strength—"the greatest strength any philosopher has so far had at his disposal"—that since Plato, "all theologians and philosophers" have been "on the same track" (191). But not any longer. Against Plato, Nietzsche maintains a novelty that is said to be "far from innocuous," namely, that "the gods too philosophize." If the gods too philosophize, if they are not simply wise as Plato's Diotima taught, then for all beings, even the most gifted, the whole remains an enigma of becoming. Flattering the gods with omniscience is homage that need no longer be paid. Thus will to power, the Nietzschean name for the enigmatic whole, must itself name the whole enigmatically. It is not what "pure spirit" purely grasps with respect to the whole; it is not the solution to the mystery of the whole, but the statement of its mystery. The teaching of will to power replaces the most dangerous invention, the pure spirit and the good in itself, the dogmatic invention which, though it "lies on the ground," still determines our view of things by leaving us in "need and distress" (Preface).

Will to power first appears in *Beyond Good and Evil* in "On the Prejudices of Philosophers," in a section telling the truth about Stoicism (9). But that truth is the truth about philosophy as such, for Stoicism is presented as the paradigm of "an old eternal story" about philosophy: "Philosophy is this tyrannical drive itself, the most spiritual will to power, to 'the creation of the world,' to the *causa prima*." In this book will to power first appears as the insight that solves the riddle of the hearts of "you who are wisest." As a preface to his most precise statement about the reasoning of the Stoics and of philosophy as such, Nietzsche says that Stoicism is moved by "some abysmal overreaching pride" to entertain a "mad hope" of tyrannizing nature. Stoic reasoning, and philosophic reasoning generally, begins with the nature of the reasoner and moves to nature as a whole; because the reasoner is able to tyrannize himself or to master nature in himself, and because he is himself a piece of nature, it seems to follow that nature lets herself be tyrannized and—his proud madness tells him— by him. Philosophy's proud madness is the tyranny of nature grounded in the philosopher's successful tyranny of himself.

This account of philosophy, though it appears as the critique of Stoicism, in the chapter on the prejudices of philosophers, is not simply a condemnation of philosophy. Like *Zarathustra, Beyond Good and Evil* points to the necessity that the philosopher, the most spiritual and most powerful of beings, rule, that the philosopher, after discerning "to what extent the character of the world is unalterable," "set about improving that part of it recognized as alterable," especially "the very much alterable judgments of mankind" (WB 3). In the chapter ironically entitled "We Scholars," Nietzsche shows how little he surrenders philosophy's right to rule. "The most spiritual will to power" is not a mere prejudice of some proud philosophers, for it is required of all "genuine philosophers," including the "philosophers of the future," that they be *"commanders and legislators,"* that "they say, 'thus it shall be!' " Genuine philosophers are the ones who "first determine the Whither and the For What of man." "Their will to truth is—*will to power*" (211). Although will to power first appears in *Beyond Good and Evil* in the critique of philosophy as proud madness, the book teaches what Zarathustra was shown learning, that will to power names what simply belongs to philosophy as the ruling art. Is there then a philosophical rule that is not proud madness? Or, in the language of *Zarathustra*, is there a philosophical rule not moved by the spirit of revenge? On this question *Beyond Good and Evil* observes almost complete silence, for the answer is eternal return, a topic unsuited to a no-saying book. Still, once, in a reserved and appropriate way, eternal return is glimpsed as the ruling ideal opposite to the old proud madness (56).

In discovering that philosophy was will to power, Zarathustra discovered the enigma that the highest commanding is itself an act of obedience, and that the one who would rule is himself ruled and yields to that rule (II. 12). This hint about philosophy, that it is itself a piece of nature, or that nature expresses itself in its highest form in philosophy, is expanded in *Beyond Good and Evil* in three sections that offer a detailed account of Nietzsche's experience of "spirit" (229–31), and that can be read as a commentary on Zarathustra's aphoristic definition of spirit as "the life which cuts into life" (II. 8). The account occurs in the chapter entitled "Our Virtues," under the general theme of the cruelty that human beings exercise on themselves. The argument of the first section (229) is that civilization is sublimated or spiritualized cruelty exercised on the self. Most of the examples involve forms of religious cruelty or self-denial, but the final example is that of "the seeker of knowledge" who is said to perform a "rape" on "the basic will of the spirit," which Nietzsche claims is a will to ease. But this claim about the basic will of the spirit requires a long explanation, for Nietzsche has to teach the meaning of spirit to those who have come to experience it as a will to ease (230). The basic will of the spirit is what "the people call 'spirit' "; it is a mastering will that seeks to subdue everything around it and that orders the world according to its needs: it assimilates the new to the old, the manifold to the simple, and overlooks or rejects the contradictory. Thus the world comes to be shaped by the people's mastering will that aims at ease. In opposing this spirit, the seeker of knowledge opposes what had appeared as the same as all living things in seeking comfortable self-preservation; his spirit seems to oppose life itself. His is a spirit unknown to the people and to the wise famous among them (II. 8). The one who experiences that spirit wills to see things profoundly, manifoldly, fundamentally; he wills to cut into the appearance, the unity, the mask that the basic will of the spirit has created through its mastery. The one moved by this "inclination" of spirit, or possessed by the greatest spiritedness, experiences it as an acute cruelty of conscience and taste, and just here, in his description of the seeker of knowledge who is at the disposal of a cruel spirit, Nietzsche speaks of "we free, *very* free spirits." There are virtuous words that would serve to define such a spirit, but they have already been used by the opposite spirit and have become the property of their misusers; it is better to let those words go than to try, in the chapter on "Our Virtues," to reclaim them. Instead of assuming virtuous titles, those moved by the cruel spirit of knowledge must proceed with their work of recognizing "the frightful basic text of *homo natura*," or what is unalterable about man. What falls to this spirit is a more than heroic task calling for virtues that combine in superior measure those of Oedipus and Odysseus, for such a one must be able both to gaze into the most frightful truths without putting out his eyes and to hear the siren song of the metaphysical bird-catchers without succumbing to it. The task for one who sees and hears in this way is "to retranslate man back into nature." Having defined his task, the one to whom it has fallen asks himself before the rest of us what the rest of us ask him: Why obey that cruel commanding spirit? "Why have we chosen it, this insane task?" The best or the most civil answer that can be given by the one who has asked himself this question a hundred times is given in the next section (231): his obedience is itself not chosen but given. It is part of his unteachable ground, "the great stupidity" that cannot be interrogated but to which he yields. It is the obedience of the most commanding spirit described by Zarathustra in his discovery that life is will to power.

While the most spiritual will to power comes to light as what is given in the philosopher's nature, will to power in general comes to light in *Beyond Good and Evil* (as in *Zarathustra*) as the way of nature as such. There has been a connection between the nature of the philosopher and nature as such since the beginning of philosophy: the first section of *Beyond Good and Evil* to mention will to power (9) had suggested that previous philosophers had based their conclusions about nature on their experience of their own nature. But in this very section the philosopher who has discovered philosophy's tyranny of nature implicitly claims simply to know nature. The Stoics are mistaken about nature, not simply because they attribute to it a form that it does not have, but because they attribute to it a form that is different from the form that it does have, that it has independent of attribution. Nietzsche thus begins his description of nature, one of the most important themes of the book, with seemingly dogmatic assertions. Those assertions, already problematic on the basis of what Nietzsche says about the tyrannical prejudices of philosophers, become emphatically problematic when Nietzsche introduces himself as "an old philologist" long schooled in the distinction between a text and the interpretation of a text (22). The text in question is nature. The old philologist chastizes the new physicists for taking as text what is only interpretation, the supposed laws of nature. They read into nature a human convention and in "nature's conformity to law" implicitly posit some commanding lawgiver and the requirement of obedience and the possibility of transgression (GS 109). Modern physics serves a modern democratic politics and gives a "humanitarian emendation" to nature, correcting it in the interests of egalitarianism, as if nature too were democratic and demanded equality before the law. Lamenting this egalitarian atheism that refuses everything high, including gods, the old philologist says that "somebody might come along," moved by different interests and by an art of interpretation opposed to theirs, and find in nature a will to power any description of which would be hampered by the accumulated anthropomorphism of the available language. In his countercase the old philologist seems to claim access to the text itself, and the physicists, now schooled in the philological art of interpretation, make eager use of the objection with which he has supplied them, dismissing his novel reading of nature as will to power as itself only interpretation. "So much the better," says the old philologist. It is desirable that even physicists learn a little philological caution and not rush to precipitate conclusions in the service of their political masters, that even physicists learn what "is perhaps just dawning on five or six minds" about physics, that it too is only an interpretation of the world (14).

But is a salutary relativism the best that the old philologist can offer in defense of his own interpretation of the basic text? Has he removed all grounds for legitimating interpretations or giving them warrant? Or could the old philologist have found a new route to the interpretation of nature? The next section, the last on the prejudices of philosophers, begins to answer these questions. It too speaks of will to power but does so by taking it to be a teaching that leads to a thousand dangerous insights that it is better to keep away from if one can. Having invited his readers to desist if they can, Nietzsche proceeds to flatter them if they can't. What will face readers cured of the prejudices of the philosophers and ready to confront the dangers of a new interpretation of nature will be a new investigation of the soul, the venerable hypothesis of the soul being one that the new psychologist wants to retain, having freed it of the calamitous "soul atomism" of Christianity (12). This new study of the soul reveals the nature of the whole, for subhuman nature comes to light through the study of the highest or most spiritual nature. The old philologist has in fact a better answer for the physicists, although the physicists may choose to avoid the dangers faced by the philologist turned psychologist turned philosopher. But the way to the fundamental problems suggested here is not novel, for Nietzsche says that psychology must "again" be recognized as the queen of the sciences, must "again" be "the path to the fundamental problems." Study of the soul is the Socratic way already taken by philosophy according to the account of philosophy just given, and it is the way specifically taken by Zarathustra. Still, the results of taking that old way may turn out to be novel. Despite its opening critique of the way taken by philosophy, *Beyond Good and Evil* shows that what comes to light in the philosopher brings to light the whole with which philosophy has to deal.

The arguments necessary to make a case for what is claimed about will to power in the first part do not appear until well into the second part (36) and are then given only tentatively, as befits a method described as temptation. The reasoning uses philosophy's language of appearance and reality and moves from what is given to what must be supposed about what is not given when one follows a conscientious method. The initial supposition is that what is given as real is only "our world of desires and passions." Granted access to the reality of his drives, the experimenter then asks if it is not permitted to suppose that what is given in the drives is sufficient for understanding "the so-called mechanistic (or 'material') world" as like in kind. That world would then have the same rank of reality as the affect known immediately only in ourselves; it would be "a more primitive form of the world of affects," a "preform of life" in which "everything lies contained in a powerful unity" prior to undergoing the developments of the inorganic, organic, and spiritual processes in terms of which that world articulates itself. Conscientious method (or "the economy of principles," 13) not only permits, it requires that such an experiment be made. Conscientious in this way, the experimenter posits "will" as the force accessible in instinctive life and as the ground of mediate knowledge of the world. The final supposition, identified as Nietzsche's own principle, is that if our entire instinctive life could be explained as the development and ramification of one basic form of the will, will to power, "then one would have gained the right to determine *all* efficient force univocally as—will to power." The most comprehensive conclusion is thus drawn about the world on the basis of the successful explanation of instinctive life as will to power: "The world viewed from inside, the world defined and determined according to its 'intelligible character'—it would be 'will to power' and nothing besides." The intelligible character of the world, what can be grasped as intelligible by the only available route, depends, just as its having "a 'necessary' and 'calculable' course" does (22), on its being will to power.

Here, as in *Zarathustra* (as well as in the center of the part of *The Gay Science* (309, 310) that anticipates *Zarathustra*), Nietzsche indicates that his solution to the problem of the knowledge of reality utilizes the intellect for the examination of the soul. Unlike "all the young theologians of the Tübingen seminary" who, following Kant's lead, rushed "into the bushes looking for faculties" for intuiting the reality made inaccessible by Kant's strictures on the intellect (11), Nietzsche does not invent some new faculty for intuiting reality; his inquiry into the soul does not sacrifice the intellect (23). Nor does he avail himself of the grace of History, which, in a privileged moment, reveals to its philosophical or revolutionary student the meaning of reality as process. Nietzsche's way repeats what Schopenhauer regarded as "the most characteristic and important step of my philosophy," which he described as forcefully as Nietzsche does subtly: "A way from within stands open to us to that real inner nature of things to which we cannot penetrate from without. It is, so to speak, a subterranean passage, a secret alliance, which, as if by treachery, places us all at once in the fortress that could not be taken by attack from without."[4]

As soon as he has forced his free-spirited readers to view the world from the inside, Nietzsche permits them to give vent to the horror expressed often enough by Nietzsche's readers (37): "What? Doesn't this mean, to speak popularly: God is refuted, but the devil is not—?" The free spirits who "no longer like to believe in God and gods" (295) would like even less to have to believe in the devil. Nietzsche responds emphatically to their earnest concern; addressing them as friends he says: "On the contrary! On the contrary!" The contrary of what his friends fear would be that the devil is refuted but God is not. In this way Nietzsche indicates for the first time in this book that his teaching on will to power, or the world seen from the inside, could well be a vindication of God or gods. The form that vindication will take is alluded to in other passages (most especially 295) and is suggested by his words of comfort to his friends: "And, as to the devil—who forces you to speak popularly?" Nothing forces the free spirits still to speak a remnant of a popular theology that divides heaven and earth between God and the devil and makes the earth the devil's. Nevertheless, through his own adoption and inversion of this old way of speaking, Nietzsche can provisionally accommodate his own teaching to the vulgar speech still spoken by worried friends who fear his teaching because they are, while free spirits, only partially free of the clumsy dogmatism that two thousand years of Platonism for the people has made second nature. If the vulgar speech must still be endured, then it is necessary for now, for purposes of expiation, to think of the transcendent God as the devil. Only gradually can a new speech about the world be introduced, one that sees the world from the inside as will to power and confers a blessing upon it, instead of abandoning it to the devil. Such speech, the philosophy of the future, will vindicate the gods, permitting the return of earthly gods judged devils or of the Devil by the teaching that still lingers as a gruesome shadow needing to be vanquished even in the free spirits who are, of all Nietzsche's contemporaries, the most like him.[5]

The teaching of will to power as disclosed in *Zarathustra* and *Beyond Good and Evil* suggests that nature is continuous or of one kind and that at the same time nature is hierarchical or exhibits an order of rank. "The absolute homogeneity of all events" (*KGW* VIII 10 [154] = *WP* 272) that permits them to be designated comprehensively as will to power also permits an order of rank among beings that distinguishes levels of organization without losing the rich ambiguity of beings or compromising their individual variety. In that ordered whole, responsibility falls to the highest beings, for nature is in some measure subject to their acts of interpretation. The Stoics are in part right in the conclusion they draw from their own tyrannized natures, for nature does let herself be tyrannized. She has yielded to the impetuous force of the most powerful men as if she were mere matter, malleable at their command. But the discoverer of will to power and of the most spiritual will to power, the discoverer of the way of all beings and of the highest beings, finds a new responsibility given to him for ending the tyranny of malleable and immalleable nature, for willing an order that is "true to the earth" after discovering what is unalterable. This new responsibility requires a courage quite unlike that of popular existentialism faced with grim mortality. Nietzsche's courage takes its bearings not from considerations of personal authenticity, but from concern for the future of mankind.[6] But Nietzsche's courage is also not the courage that invents ever new ways to deconstruct what is already standing or coming to stand. In his wonderful description of Nietzsche as nomad philosopher, whose marauding acts bring terror to all men of settled conviction but liberation and pandemonium to all free spirits, Gilles Deleuze expresses gratitude for one of the fundamental deeds of Nietzsche's philosophy but stops short of acknowledging what Nietzsche sees as the consequent responsibility of a new creation.[7] The courage Nietzsche requires of himself is courage for a new act of ordering, a new daylight wisdom whose relation to night wisdom is not refusal or horror, a daylight wisdom that is true to the earth seen from the inside as will to power and nothing besides.

As Homer has it, the river Okeanus flows without end around the island of order legislated by the gracious gods.[8] Plato's Socrates, protesting that this view grants primacy to perpetual flux and eventually generates teachers who bring down even the order of the gods,[9] takes issue with the whole array of teachers generated by Homer and with Homer himself, and undertakes to make the perimeters of the world more secure through a teaching of a permanent order superior in dignity to the impermanent, even impermanent gods. Nietzsche takes issue with the whole array of teachers generated by Plato and with Plato himself and undertakes to create a new island of order amid the surrounding flux, the order of eternal return. Nietzsche enters what he calls "the complete, the genuine antagonism" between Plato and Homer, the advocate of the beyond and the deifier of the near (*GM* III. 25). He enters on the side of Homer, though there can be no question of returning to Homer or even of desiring such a return.[10]

ETERNAL RETURN

Thus Spoke Zarathustra makes clear that the fundamental sense of will to power is ontological, in that it names the enigmatic essence of all beings. But it also makes clear the historic consequences of that ontology, for will to power is not a teaching that carries to some logical culmination modern teachings on power that have as their end "the effecting of all things possible." Will to power requires the affirmation of eternal return, the affirmation that lets beings be what they are. In the last stanza of the last chapter Zarathustra's bird-wisdom triumphs over the spirit of gravity with a new language that names beings anew. The affirmation of eternal return is a gift given to beings that construes them as lovable or desirable in themselves, and not, like Plato, as some "spume that plays/ Upon a ghostly paradigm of things."[11] Zarathustra wills the eternal return of beings not grounded in anything more grave than themselves. It refuses revenge on beings, or it refuses to will that they be other than they are. "Why is there something rather than nothing?" remains an enigma that challenges inquiry; but that there is something, that there are these beings, remains a marvel that draws from the most spirited being the blessing that lets them be what they are.

Beyond Good and Evil, in its own reserved way, also points to the necessary connection between will to power and eternal return. After having hinted to his friends that it is a vindication of God to see the world from the inside as will to power and nothing else, Nietzsche allows his new ideal to be glimpsed in a different way—appropriately enough in the chapter on religion. Religious cruelty has demanded its supreme sacrifice and has sacrificed God for the stone, stupidity, gravity, fate, the nothing (55); "all of us already know something of this" cruelty of honest nihilism. But the one who has thought it through to its depths "may just thereby, without really meaning to do so, have opened his eyes" (56) on the ideal opposite to the old ideal of renunciation and sacrifice, the new ideal of the saint of eternal return who does not merely resign himself to "whatever was and is" but shouts insatiably, "Once more," to the whole marvelous spectacle of which he himself is a part. Nietzsche again entertains a possible objection: "What? And this would not be *circulus vitiosus deus?*"—Is the circle of eternal return a refutation or a vindication of God? This playful ambiguity had been put more starkly in Nietzsche's first report of his thought of eternal return, for there the one who hears this thought is either crushed by its demonic gravity or moved to say to the one who brings the thought: "You are a god and never have I heard anything so divine" (GS 341).[12]

Zarathustra presents the affirmation of eternal return in two ways, as what Zarathustra wills and as what the animals experience. In the less ecstatic formulations of *Beyond Good and Evil,* these two ways could be said to be reflected in the necessity that religion pass into the care of philosophy. Zarathustra's noble words of eternal return transform the world

into a garden inhabited by beings like ourselves who sing a version of
Zarathustra's song that makes it sacred and simply true. This sacred song
acknowledges "the sense of tears in mortal things" but affirms their coming
and going in the noble wish for their eternal return just as they are. Zarathustra anticipates that the songs of his soul will bring the return of the
earthly religion of Dionysos, which celebrates the divinity of earthly things.
Through the philosopher Zarathustra, the religion of Dionysos triumphs
over the vengeful religion of Father Sky who wills that Mother Earth be
other than she is, the patriarchal religion whose modern adherents embrace
an arid atheism and humanism (*BGE* 22), having been wised up about the
futile faith of their forefathers that this defective earth is only a foretaste
of the true world in the sky. It triumphs over the religion of last men, who
take themselves to be the fully corrected versions of mankind inhabiting
the fully corrected earth. Zarathustra's act of philosophical legislation is
a mystery lived less mysteriously by the religious animals and by his "children" to come. The mystery of eternal return as the lived world of Zarathustra's animals can be elaborated into a theory of beings and time, for
the lyre song of the animals, like that of Orpheus (*GS* 286), reorders the
very trees and stones in celebration of a new world of appearances, a believer's world or a lover's world.

    Thus Spoke Zarathustra and *Beyond Good and Evil*, by demonstrating
that will to power is the name both for what is and for the most spiritual
act of the highest being, show thereby that it cannot be the nature of beings
to participate in any transcendent or rational order of God, Nature, or
History. But what threatens Plato and the Platonists, where both Christianity
and modernity are interpreted as Platonisms for the people, is not simply
the revelation that their teaching is grounded in will to power or the revelation that their will to power is based on revenge. Their dominion is
threatened by the new act of will to power that replaces their teaching
with a new evaluation of beings and actions. Deaf at last to the siren song
of the metaphysical bird-catchers that runs, "You are more, you are higher,
you are of a different order" (*BGE* 230), the new singer creates new songs
that elevate the present order. Willing the eternal return of beings and
actions gives them a new center of gravity; it provides a new measure of
the grave, after the old forms of gravity have been exploded. Eternal return
is Nietzsche's teaching on the good, on that for the sake of which one does
whatever one does.[13] It confers gravity on things themselves, not by im-
porting a pale reflection of something that is good in itself, external to
things, but by willing the thing itself simply as it is. This teaching is no
"substitute" for the good or for God, as if regret governed its choice, as if
in sadness one moved from a greater to a lesser perfection. Rather, it celebrates the replacement of the ancestral past, and of transcendence, and
of the Future as the giver of gravity, for the gift of gravity is man's rejoicing
at the way things are. Still, willing eternal return, as the act of the most
spiritual will to power that naturalizes man or retranslates him back into

nature, builds on the whole history of man. It conquers the rule of non-sense and chance that has moved mankind through domestic gods, civic gods, cosmopolitan gods, God, and cosmopolitan atheism, and it does so through a human act of will that says to this whole past, "But thus I willed it!"

Although eternal return presents itself as in a certain fashion "lying words," it is not a lie in the sense of being a salutary veil generously placed over things that are otherwise by a teacher who knows best and who shelters noninquirers from a truth that harms. Although the teaching of eternal return may well shelter those who share Zarathustra's love of life but lack his perspective, and although they may be led to formulate eternal return in a metaphysical way never employed by the philosopher Zarathustra, eternal return is the necessary teaching that will be arrived at by the most diligent of those who share his spirit of inquiry and his love of life and loyalty to the earth. These inquirers, schooled by Zarathustra, or perhaps moved along his path by its self-evidence, will repeat Zarathustra's experiences and will come to see the warrant for his teaching when all beings are seen to be will to power and all teachings seen to be "symptomatic" of "moral intentions" (BGE 6), for this teaching raises to the highest degree the intention to affirm beings as they are. Such inquirers will not themselves be the bringers of the teaching, for Zarathustra has won a precedence that cannot be impaired, even by the "better players" he expected would follow. The teaching of eternal return is the focal point of the new "faith and love" that the creator Zarathustra hangs over the people of the future (I. 11). In the words of "On the Thousand Goals and One" (I. 15), it is "the law of overcoming" that legislates for the thousand-and-first people, mankind. It is what causes the new people "to rule and conquer and glitter to the dread and envy of its neighbor," what it accounts "the high, the first, the measure giver, the meaning of all things," "the ladder on which it ascends to its hope." Eternal return provides a new table of overcomings that defines in a new way the ascent from the praiseworthy to the good to the holy. At its height it names what is affirmed by the new "saint of knowledge" (I. 10), the one driven by his love of life to praise the beloved to the highest degree. Although it would, as always, be given to few to be saints, it would be given to the new people as a whole to recognize what is saintly. Nietzsche naturally shrank from using such still disreputable words as *holy* or *sacred* or *saintly* as words of praise when addressing those who "no longer like to believe in God and gods" (BGE 295). But such words can be reclaimed by the way of thought that celebrates the earth as the highest and invites Dionysos back as celebrant. Such words acknowledge the sacred as a fundamental requirement of the new people, not out of some high-minded concession to the weak-minded who may stand in need of such things, but as a recognition of the experience of the highest.[14]

Zarathustra makes clear that the teaching on eternal return opposes any teaching on the linearity of time that points toward some future eschatological fulfillment of time. Nietzsche's Zarathustra thus overthrows what Zarathustra/Zoroaster had bequeathed to mankind, prophetic religions that force mortal life to be lived under the terrible gravity of a future Day of Judgment on which eternal doom or eternal bliss will be decreed. But Zarathustra's teaching of eternal return also opposes the Zoroastrianism in the modern teaching of progress, even in the form that it took in his own original public teaching: the works of time are not in need of redemption by any future, not even the one constructed by the human enterprise of creating the superman.[15] As a public teaching therefore, eternal return replaces the superman teaching. It seems to me that one of the greatest single causes of the misinterpretation of Nietzsche's teaching is the failure to see that the clearly provisional teaching on the superman is rendered obsolete by the clearly definitive teaching on eternal return. That there is no call for a superman in the books after *Zarathustra* is no accident, but rather an implicit acknowledgment that the philosopher of the future has already come in the one who teaches that the weight of things resides in things and not in some future to which they may or may not contribute. Zarathustra's teaching on an order of rank and the passion to be first now finds its place within the boundaries of a teaching that maintains that the highest good is earthly life, and that the highest affirmation of earthly life wills its eternal return. Such a teaching does not abandon an order of rank that honors the high, but it does surrender the need to put that order of rank in the service of some superman. The superman, if the word can still be used, is the one who has brought the teaching of eternal return.

In presenting the teaching for which it exists in the form of an enigmatic vision, *Thus Spoke Zarathustra* does not prepare the way for less mysterious presentations of this teaching in less mysterious books. The published works after *Zarathustra* are in fact less mysterious, but they do not present an exposition of eternal return, although they refer to it occasionally as the essential matter.[16] In the progress of teachings which is Nietzsche's work, *Zarathustra* begins where the later works end; it begins with the death of God, and hence with the need for a new teaching, and ends with the achievement of the needed teaching, the philosophy of the future. As for Nietzsche's notes, they testify to the importance of eternal return by consistently making it the culminating teaching of the work he was planning as the presentation of the completed structure of his philosophy. According to notes written when Zarathustra was to be the one to make that presentation, he is to relate eternal return "as a *mystery*" (*KGW* VII 20[10]). In keeping with the enigmatic character of this teaching, the notes do not attempt to clear up the enigma with some non-enigmatic explication. But the notes do make prominent by repetition a matter almost foreign to *Zarathustra* and the other books, theoretical proof of eternal return as a truth about the cosmos. Notes from as early as 1881 and as late as 1888 contain arguments for the cosmological truth of eternal return. The details vary, but typically they consider the implications of conceiving the world as infinite with respect to time and finite with respect to possible states. The arguments usually follow a *reductio ad absurdum* form, arriving at the conclusion of eternal return in two steps. Either the whole has a goal, or it has no goal. If we assume that it has a goal, we are forced to ask why the goal has not yet been reached, given infinite time and finite possible states. Not having arrived at the goal proves the impossibility of so arriving, hence the whole has no goal. This whole exists either as continued variety or as the eternal return of the same. If we assume continued variety, we contradict the necessity that the infinity of time allows all possible states, of which there are a finite number; hence, the whole is the eternal return of the same.[17]

What status did Nietzsche intend these arguments to have? It seems impossible to answer this question on the basis of the notes themselves, for they have no setting to guide their interpretation or to secure their authority in a speaker. Their interpretation must therefore be accompanied by the caution appropriate to ignorance regarding their intention. *Zarathustra*, on the other hand, exists in order to present the teaching of eternal return, and what it suggests provides boundaries for the application of the projected arguments. Although the arguments in completed form predate *Zarathustra*, a truncated version was allowed to appear in the book in a setting (III. 2) that diminished the significance of argument through a whole battery of devices. The view argued for in the notes is then stated by the metaphysical poets, Zarathustra's animals, but their metaphysics is held at a distance by Zarathustra, for whom speech bridges the eternal cleft separating beings. When the opportunity arises for Zarathustra to affirm eternal return, he whispers it to Life offstage—and she says in response, "No one *knows* that." Zarathustra's teaching as a whole celebrates as liberation the impossibility of a rational order fully accessible to human reason. Assuming the superior authority of *Zarathustra* over sketches of arguments left in note form, it seems necessary to conclude that the enigmatic vision of eternal return is not a theoretically demonstrable truth about the cosmos, but in Nietzsche's view, something higher, the ideal opposite to world denial, the highest attainable form of affirmation, the lover's construal placed upon becoming.

Why then are there such arguments at all in the notes, and then right up to the end? Nietzsche takes pains to show Zarathustra engaging in a strategic presentation of his teaching on such subsidiary matters as the human soul and the modern state in order to win a hearing from those trained to think otherwise and reluctant, as always, to yield the firm ground of the obvious. Nietzsche himself engages in careful instruction of the new physicists and of scientists in general in order to open to them the possibility of a new interpretation of the fundamental matters. It seems plausible that the long-rehearsed arguments for eternal return could themselves be put to such heuristic ends. Because we are not pure minds who come to ourselves in a purely rational order, eternal return is not fully demon-

strable theoretically, but the arguments Nietzsche develops show that teleological and mechanistic views are far less plausible, that a case can be
made in the discourse of science, as in the discourse of poetry, for the
comprehensive view that accords with the deepest affirmation of things;
that the authoritative sciences of physics and cosmology are not to be set
aside in affirming eternal return, but can themselves be used to demonstrate
its plausibility. It was no mistake on Nietzsche's part, as has so often been
alleged, on grounds that here he understood himself poorly, to want to
find a quiet university library in which to study contemporary physics for
five years after completing the fundamental work in *Zarathustra*. Having
learned as a philologist, a scientist of the human sciences, the necessary
limitations on the interpreter and thus on the interpretive speech of even
the natural sciences, he wanted very much to find ways in which that
speech could be brought into accord with the fundamental speech of philosophy. Rule of the sciences by philosophy does not consist in the willful
suppression of unfavorable scientific arguments and the willful invention
of favorable ones. Nietzsche construes eternal return as "the most scientific
of all hypotheses" (*KGW* VIII 5[71] = *WP* 55), the one that, far better than
teleological or mechanical hypotheses, accords with what cosmology can
tell us about the ultimate questions of being and time. Nietzsche's understanding of the nature of fundamental teachings and of the natural
sciences leaves room for concord that does not depend on compromising
intellectual probity.

Perhaps a form of Kantian language is applicable: the mystery of eternal
return is a "regulative idea," a "postulate." But if it is a regulative idea,
beyond the possibility of either theoretical or experimental confirmation,
it is not, like God, freedom, and immortality, removed from confirmation
in order to be sheltered from refutation. Arising after the destruction of
Kant's three pure rational ideas ("one grew older, the dream vanished"
BGE 11), eternal return is an affirmation of the world disclosed by the
tenacious probity of modern philosophy and modern science, the world
whose fundamental mystery is will to power. If eternal return is a postulate,
it is not a postulate of practical reason grounded in the supposed fact of
the moral law, but a postulate of the judgment of the most spirited being
in his disposition toward things. It is not an "as if" story, a useful fiction,
but the most spiritual expression of the will to power, a human disposition
that shelters the transient things by willing their eternal return.

When *Zarathustra* is taken as the guide to the interpretation of eternal
return, that teaching comes to light in a way that refutes Deleuze's praise
of Nietzsche as "the only thinker who makes no attempt at recodification,"[18]
for it appears precisely as the "recodification" of the world. Decodification
or skepticism that is active and deconstructive, total war against the temple
that now stands, is necessary and desirable according to Zarathustra; but
it needs to be augmented by acts that Zarathustra understands to be still
greater, founding acts that secure the earth under an open sky through a

new standard of the highest good. Nietzsche knew that his acts of de-struction could well mislead the readers most akin to him, and he took special precautions against the conclusion that they might draw, that his aim was purely destructive. Privately, he said in a letter to Lou Salomé (23 November 1882): "Don't *you* be deceived about me—*you* surely don't believe that the 'free spirit' is my ideal?"[19] But she was not deceived; she did not believe that the "free spirit" was his ideal. During the intense days of con-versation in the hidden valley of Tautenburg, where the leafy walk and the steep inclines closed out everything extraneous to their considerations of the essence of religion, and where Nietzsche disclosed to her, for the first time to anyone, the thought of eternal return that had come to him a full year earlier, she made the accusation in her notebook that Nietzsche's thought was a new "religion." In her accusation she congratulated herself on being above all religion. Because the free spirit was her ideal, she could believe herself to be above Nietzsche, for he had fallen out of skepticism into religion, and she was annoyed.[20] Nietzsche took the annoyance of free spirits very seriously and addressed his next book to them in order to parry the annoyance that they would feel when they discovered, as Lou Salomé had, that the philosopher Nietzsche was no longer a skeptic. In *Beyond Good and Evil*, the new "school for the *gentilhomme*," where the gentleman is conceived "more spiritually and more radically" than ever before, modern free spirits are educated out of their annoyance at the new philosopher for having overcome their newly won ideal. Beguiling speech and an art of silence entice them away from the nearest, their most modern and radical free-spiritedness, toward the farthest, *Zarathustra*, where "the new world conception" is depicted in its discovery (*EH*, "Books: *Beyond*," 2; *KGW* VIII 14 [188] = *WP* 1066).[21]

Zarathustra presents eternal return as a historic novelty that differs from all previous teachings in not being an act of revenge. As Zarathustra understands his teaching, it must be distinguished from other views which may seem to resemble it,[22] for teachings on the recurring cycles of nature are obviously not novel and include among their variants the view that turns those cycles into the eternal return of the same things.[23] Nietzsche knew very well that the Stoics taught a doctrine with the same name, but he could reasonably maintain that the Stoic teaching was not the precursor of his own, and that he did not learn it from them, because his teaching, unlike theirs, does not involve a resigned submission to the necessity of natural cycles; nor does it have an ulterior motive.[24]

But Nietzsche's refusal of predecessors for his most important teaching is countered in a more telling way by Heidegger. Heidegger's Nietzsche is the fulfillment of Western philosophy as a whole, and in particular of mod-ern philosophy, understood as the way of thinking in which certainty re-sides in the subject construed as will in a reality of will, a subject whose highest aim is mastery, and who sees the world as resource or standing reserve at his disposal.[25] Eternal return is recognized by Heidegger as

Nietzsche's thought of thoughts, the thought that must be understood if Nietzsche's thought as a whole is to be grasped. If Nietzsche's thought as a whole brings modern philosophy to its culmination, then his thought of thoughts must express modernity's understanding of being and time. Eternal return, "the high point of meditation," "the peak," may well remain shrouded in thick clouds, "in a darkness from which even Nietzsche had to shrink back in terror," but it yields clarity nevertheless to Heidegger, the one who is able to interpret the thought in its unthought historical necessity. Heidegger judges that the eternalizing of passage in eternal return expresses "an aversion to mere transience," a "supremely spiritualized spirit of revenge," the final expression of the human will's will to its own eternity. No "mystical fantasy," it expresses what is already omnipresent in the modern technological desire for perpetual mastery, for "what is the essence of the modern dynamo other than *one* expression of the eternal return of the same?"[26] This lame reading is the only one possible if eternal return is to be aligned with modern technological dominance. But making the song of eternal return a hymn to machinery runs counter to everything that Nietzsche himself said about it. Eternal return sings not of bodies machined eternal, but of mortal bodies, the things of a day. It does not express a secret desire to achieve permanence but celebrates the impermanent. It is not a song of dominance but of sheltering and letting be. It is not a song for the "tough, industrious race of machinists and bridge-builders of the future," for it is not a work song but a song of play and playfulness (*BGE* 14).[27]

Heidegger's alleged penetration of the clouds surrounding eternal return does not take its bearings from Nietzsche, nor does it think it needs to, for it holds that Nietzsche remained trapped within an unperceived horizon of metaphysics. Given its historicity, its insertion into a process that fated it in a way inaccessible to it, Nietzsche's thought has to be refused by Heidegger in its two basic claims, the claims to have understood being and to have understood time. Being and time escaped Nietzsche. Will to power and eternal return, uprooted from their Nietzschean ground as the fundamental phenomenon and its highest affirmation, have to be rerooted in their allegedly actual ground, the history of Being. The real meaning of will to power and eternal return has to be supplied by a thinker other than Nietzsche, whose horizon encloses his. But if will to power and eternal return become visible in *Zarathustra* as something other than a fulfillment of their alleged historical antecedents, as something more than historical statements of what is true for us and only for us, then Nietzsche's history of thought recommends itself as more penetrating than Heidegger's. It is not encumbered by the absolute opaqueness of Being that results from the absolute historicity of meaning. It is therefore open to what the history of human inquiry has actually discovered about man and the world. In part because of what it learns from that history of discovery, it is also open to the discernment of the fundamental phenomenon and to its affirmation.

That discernment and affirmation of being and time show how Heidegger's radical historicism can be refused. *Zarathustra* shows not only how Nietzsche can be rescued from the Heideggerian shadow that threatens to ruin his reputation, but also how Heidegger can be found as a follower of Nietzsche, whose *Holzwege*, for all their illumination and power, dwindle away before reaching the clearing opened by Nietzsche's thought. The warrant for such a Nietzschean reading of Heidegger becomes more fully apparent with a consideration of Nietzsche's own understanding of the new beginning or the founding task.

NIETZSCHE'S FOUNDING

Ecce Homo asserts what *Thus Spoke Zarathustra* had shown narratively, that "the concept of the 'superman' has here become the greatest reality"; Zarathustra "experiences himself as the *highest type of all beings*" (*EH*, "Books: *Zarathustra*," 6–8).[28] According to *Zarathustra* the superman is the founder of a new people. He imitates other founders in hanging a new table of values over a people, but he differs from other founders in having understood the act of founding through his insight into the thousand peoples. He aims to found the global people, mankind, by creating a table of values free of revenge and loyal to the earth. Nietzsche shows Zarathustra the founder taking a route not yet trodden by any man, a route that discovers and introduces entirely new modes and orders to the earth.

Is what Zarathustra claims to be a novel founding of global proportions in fact only the latest extension of modernity, founded earlier by other thinkers moved by godlike desires?[29] Driven by an ambition akin to Zarathustra's, "if ambition it can be called,"[30] Francis Bacon and René Descartes set forth a philosophy of power that founded the modern world view.[31] Guided by the love of mankind, by "charity" and "generosity," they undertook to transform the world into a garden through the conquest of nature, with the aim of eventual planetary mastery by man, Baconian or Cartesian man. Having learned that "nothing is more difficult to deal with nor more dubious of success nor more dangerous to manage than making oneself the head in the introduction of new orders,"[32] these students of Machiavelli wrote fables, holding that, "even to this day, if any man would let new light in upon the human understanding, and conquer prejudice, without raising contests, animosities, opposition or disturbance he must go in the same path [the path of fable] and have recourse to the like method of allegory, metaphor, and allusion."[33] Bacon's fables included the rewriting of ancient myth, Descartes' the rewriting of his own life.

Bacon's *Wisdom of the Ancients* includes an account of "Orpheus, or Philosophy" in which the fable, "though trite and common," is made to explain natural and moral philosophy or the whole of philosophy and thus the task of the philosopher Bacon. Although Orpheus was a "wonderful and perfectly divine person," he nevertheless fell prey to two shortcomings, one of which caused his failure in natural philosophy, the other his failure in moral philosophy. An Orpheus cured of his shortcomings would save philosophy from its failures and enable it to fulfill Orpheus's ambitions. Orpheus's music made his ambitions seem realizable, for it tamed the infernal powers, the powers of nature that had taken his beloved Eurydice from him in death. Taming the infernal powers is the task of natural philosophy, whose "noblest work" is "the reinstatement and restoration of corruptible things" and, "in lesser degree, the preservation of bodies in their own state, or a prevention of their dissolution and corruption." Orpheus's failure in natural philosophy, his failure to subdue nature and win back the mortal Eurydice from the dead, came about "through the impatience of his care and affection." All subsequent philosophy until Bacon shared this flaw of impatience and therefore failed to subdue nature. But philosophy also shared the consequence of this flaw, Orpheus's sad turn to moral philosophy, the turn most prominent in Socrates. Having turned away from the noblest work, the mastery of nature, thwarted Orpheus applied his taming music to civil society and succeeded in domesticating the wild beasts, causing them to forget their natures and to listen attentively, moved no longer by "revenge, cruelty, lust, hunger or the desire for prey." The very trees and stones hearkened to the precepts of moral philosophy and submitted to the discipline that philosophy ordered for them. But even the political realm founded through Orpheus's music had a sad end, for into the orderliness effected by Orpheus's gentling lyre there erupted the wild and dominant music of the flute brought by Dionysos's women. Drowning the ordering music of Orpheus, the music of the passions caused latent nature to burst forth and civil order to disappear into the chaos whence it had sprung. Lacking the power to control either the natural decay of mortal things or the fury of Dionysian passions, philosophy hitherto has brought only temporary order before being torn apart by forces it cannot master.

Bacon's fable of the power of philosophy points to a new Orpheus grown most powerful, an Orpheus grown patient with respect to overpowering mortality and subtle with respect to the disordering din of the passions. Bacon's fable points to Bacon's own philosophy, a natural philosophy equipped with the experimental method and the patient will to conquer nature, and a moral philosophy equipped with the rewards of both temporal and eternal well-being. The fable of Orpheus points to the fable of *New Atlantis*, to the fabulous society that will exist forever, founded by Bacon's music, the society that is under way to the complete mastery of nature, that surrounds itself with a line and race of inventions that makes life sweet and that, where necessary, is permitted by Bacon to anticipate satisfactions of a different order in a heaven yet to come.

But the heirs of the modern world view have conferred the honor of being their founder or father not on Bacon but on Descartes. Born posthumously as the father of modern philosophy, Descartes practiced the gift-giving virtue under the name "generosity," "the key to all the other virtues."[34] Cartesian generosity, like Zarathustrian gift-giving, begins in a relation of the self to the self but entails the political consequence of doing good to others and even, moved by the joy of glory, of doing "great things" for others.[35] The great things Descartes undertakes are shown in the preface to the first book that he published, *Discourse on the Method for Rightly Conducting One's Reason and for Seeking Truth in the Sciences*. In that preface Descartes, with appropriate discretion, makes an example of him-self, ending with the high-minded warning that he will refuse the greatest offices on earth should they now be offered to him on the basis of what he recounts as his achievements in that first book.[36] Early in part 1, the *Discourse* invites its reader to think of what follows as a "fable," an account of fabulous labors that have secured a new foundation for the "clear and steady knowledge of everything that is useful for life"; it is a fable which says that fables are able to "awaken the mind" "when read with discretion." Read with discretion, Descartes' heroic fable of his life shows how he faced the problem of introducing new teachings or of giving the world the gift of a novel wisdom that it could not know it wanted. The *Discourse* also says that it is a "history" and that even the most accurate histories must omit many matters. Those who govern their own conduct by examples drawn from such fables and histories fall into "the extravagances of the knights of our novels and to concocting plans that are beyond their powers." Descartes' fable and history presents a hero not susceptible of imitation, in that only one master can create the perfect foundation from which a new people can arise. At the opening of part 2 he lets it be known that he is faced with the problem of being the legislator of a new people. Knowing that a new legislator will be opposed by those who have the laws on their side, Descartes chooses to shelter his novelties by presenting them as if they are no threat to the fundamentals of the old teaching that they are to replace. In part 3, after showing how he arranged provisionally to shelter himself, to be resolute, and to be happy while pursuing the definitive mat-ters that afforded the most intense pleasure, Descartes quietly likens himself to Socrates on trial and in that striking way indicates that he too learned politic speech from the fate of Socrates. Desiring, therefore, to appear wor-thy of the reputation for wisdom bestowed on him because of his skeptical questioning, he labored for eight years on the creation of a public teaching that is subsequent to and different from the teaching on nature on which he had labored for the previous nine years and which the public teaching shelters while encouraging—for doesn't he prove in part 4 that he too, a wise man with strange views on nature, believes after all in God and the immortal soul? When the teaching on nature is finally introduced in part 5, the teaching that contains "several truths more useful and more im-portant than all I had previously learned or hoped to learn," or than every-thing contained in the part proving the existence of God and the human soul, it is presented as if it were true only of a "new world," "somewhere

in imaginary space." Availing himself in this way of the immunity accorded
a mere imaginer, the founder of the new world sets forth the principles
of the science that will create that world, imagining even a human being
without a "rational soul" and accounting for all human behavior on the
basis of the body—except for what is added at the end as allegedly dependent on the rational soul. But it is made apparent that the rational
soul, like the rational God, is added for political reasons, to succor those
humans (and their shepherds) with no better view of themselves than to
judge that without an immortal soul they are no better than flies or ants.
The sixth and final part of the *Discourse*, Descartes' presentation of his
extraordinary debate with himself on whether to publish his discoveries,
speaks explicitly of the benefits of his method. His original inclination to
make his work public changes to disinclination in the face of the punishment meted out to Galileo and his own determination "never to write anything that could turn to someone's disadvantage." Recognizing that his
thoughts on "the speculative sciences," like his thoughts on "moral conduct" do not, by themselves, warrant publication, he is persuaded to publish only by his physics: publishing his physics is an act of generosity that
procures the general good of all men, because his physics teaches a
"knowledge that is very useful in life" and that will "make ourselves, as it
were, masters and possessors of nature." In his effort to do great things
for others, Descartes gives mankind a method that will lead "to the invention
of an infinity of devices that would enable us to enjoy without pain the
fruits of the earth and all the goods one finds in it," and to a new queen
of the sciences, medicine for both body and mind, through which "we
might rid ourselves of . . . even perhaps also the enfeeblement brought on
by old age." To publish his physics, however, requires that he publish his
otherwise expendable thoughts on the speculative sciences and on the
principles governing moral conduct, for the prudential reasons of shelter
and utility that he has already made clear. Knowing that he cannot entrust
to followers any essential step of his work since an inventor knows his
invention best, Descartes must perform all the fundamental work himself,
leaving his teachings in a form that others will be able to utilize without
ruining. Patience will be necessary, or "several centuries" will have to pass,
"before all the truths that can be deduced from these principles have been
so deduced," but if "the most intelligent of men" undertake the investi-
gations based on this method, "I trust that posterity may behold its happy
issue."[37]

Descartes' teaching on the gift-giving virtue or generosity seems quite
restricted at first, because it confines itself to what alone truly pertains to
a person, the free disposition of his will.[38] But because Descartes is the
teacher of the method that leads to the mastery of nature, all restrictions
on what pertains to the will—including the provisional maxim that restricts
Descartes' will to the conquest only of himself and not of fortune—must

be understood in terms of the expansion of will made possible by its mastery of nature through the instrumentality of the new science. Although Descartes' teaching on generosity apparently confines self-satisfaction to the will that alone is at man's disposal, his act of generosity in proffering a method for the conquest of nature greatly expands the range of will and readies for man's disposal what had previously been thought to be beyond his will, to be grace or chance, or to be as far outside man's reach as "possessing the kingdoms of China or Mexico" or of having "a body made of matter as incorruptible as diamonds," all matters provisionally outside man's powers of conquest until brought within imaginable reach by Descartes' gift. Whereas the sweetest of the passions is the good done by ourselves, and the sweetest of joys is self-satisfaction because its cause depends only on ourselves,[39] the sweetness of glory, dependent to a degree on others, can nevertheless be savored in confident expectation of its accrual by the one who gives to all others the means whereby their lives can be enjoyed.[40]

This modern founding or the godlike desires already enacted by the fabulous deeds of Bacon and Descartes has been taken to be the founding that Nietzsche merely extends. *Zarathustra* does in fact exhibit parallels with their great founding work, for it too is a fable in their sense, a representation of deeds thought impossible, fabulous deeds undertaken on behalf of mankind by one who is not to be imitated but in some sense obeyed. As a fable it encapsulates no mere moral platitude but world-altering events whose goal is to edify, or to ennoble and elevate. Success in the spiritual warfare carried forward by Bacon and Descartes and other great modern thinkers—for what has modern philosophy been but anti-Christian? (*BGE* 54)—meant that Nietzsche did not need fable to shelter himself from a reigning dogmatism in quite the way that they did; nor did he need fable to shelter mankind from deadly truths uncovered by modern philosophy and science. The immediate benefit of fable for Nietzsche is that it enabled him to present the impossible task that fell to him without offending good taste. Taste having become the standard of measure, the author of the new task gives it to Zarathustra, someone younger and stronger. If, a full century after the creation of the fable, we point to Nietzsche as the actual author of the deed, there is no offense. Not only is it important to know that such a man once lived; it is even more important to know what that man thought his task to be. The lasting benefit of fable therefore is that it presents the spiritual task of the next centuries in spiritualized form. *Zarathustra* is not a fable of spiritualized love and war that "really" means to celebrate brutalized love and war, lust and bloodlust. Those old accusations accuse Nietzsche in the way that Soul accuses Self in Yeats's great Nietzschean poem "A Dialogue of Self and Soul." There Soul shames Self by ridiculing its dreams of love and war, but Self withstands Soul's shaming, for it knows itself to be a lover and a warrior in an elevated sense. In the way shown by *Zarathustra*, Self's victorious spiritual war against Soul assassinates the old soul concept, freeing Self for its highest affirmation of itself:

> I am content to live it all again
> And yet again,

and in that affirmation,

> We must laugh and we must sing,
> We are blest by everything,
> Everything we look upon is blest.

It is the lasting benefit of fable to be able to present this historic task of spiritual love and war as an enticement that cultivates and educates, calling into being a world of order that would not exist apart from it.

But Nietzsche's fable of *Zarathustra* makes clear that a new beginning is required, a beginning that does more than merely extend the world founded by Bacon and Descartes. The insurgent reading of the history of philosophy presented in *Zarathustra*—one that makes possible the recovery of their founding deeds—shows that the novelty of the modern founding is decidedly incomplete. This incompleteness comes to light concentrically in its Christianity, its Platonism, and its spirit of gravity. For Nietzsche, Christianity, "the greatest calamity for mankind till now," remains an essential element of modernity, not simply as the civil religion in whose house the scientific and commercial revolution has of necessity been introduced, but even where it has been supplanted by the religion of progress, for that religion too carries forward Christianity's successful "slave revolt in morality" (*TI*, "Skirmishes," 47; *GM* I. 10). If that slave revolt succeeds in mastering the planet, it is still not necessary to think of it as masterful or noble, for its complete victory over the planet would be no more paradoxical than its complete victory over Rome. In Zarathustra's imagery, modern teachers such as the preachers of equality (II. 7) and the famous wise men (II. 8) spring directly from the older priestly teachers, whose vengeance brought low the mighty.

But to locate the modern founding within Christian vengeance against the conditions of earthly life is not comprehensive enough. The godlike desires of modern founders are one form of the desires set in motion by the single turning point in all so-called world history, by Socrates, whose rational optimism initiated philosophy's attempts to subdue and improve the earth through "the unshakeable faith that thinking, following the thread of causality, can reach the deepest abysses of being, and that thinking is in a position not only to know being but even to *correct* it" (*BT* 15). Plato is the greatest example of a philosopher-founder engaged in the Socratic task of knowing and correcting being. Corrupted by the "wicked Socrates" (*BGE*, Preface), Plato called into being the realm of permanent ideas as the rational ground for an orderly cosmos, an orderly polity, and an orderly soul. Such a teaching counsels awe before the permanently given and legitimates the rational optimism of Socrates. It also prepares the ground for other ways of construing the cosmos as rationally ordered, for it is the first installment in the long "fable" that has sustained Western thought and culture (*TI*, "Fable"). Nietzsche intimates something further about the one with "the greatest strength that a philosopher till now has had at his disposal" (*BGE* 191) when he says that he is a "complete skeptic" about Plato (*TI*, "Ancients," 2) and that Plato's integrity is not beyond question (*KGW* VIII 14 [116] = *WP* 428). Perhaps because of his own discoveries about the necessity of careful speech, as recounted in *Zarathustra* and *Beyond Good and Evil*, Nietzsche was able to rediscover Plato's esotericism, his art of ironic speech. In Nietzsche's account Plato emerges as the philosopher who knows himself to be "the antithesis of the moral man" in that he is the "critic of all customs" who aims to become "the lawgiver of new customs" (*D* 496). As a lawgiver who intends "to take in hand the direction of mankind," Plato arrogates to himself immediately the right to lie (*KGW* VIII 15 [42] = *WP* 141), for he knows that being must be "corrected" by lies, that even the good city needs to be founded on noble lies of divine origin and an order sanctioned by founding gods. But the lawgiver Plato undertook to ground lies that go far beyond what he presented as the necessary and salutary lies of a civil religion; in the *Republic*, having made a place for ministering poetry, he adds the poetic lies of immortal souls judged by just gods.[41] Just as the spirit of gravity found it necessary to tell lies about the soul (III. 11), so Plato "wanted to have *taught* as absolute truth what he himself did not regard as even conditionally true: namely, the separate existence and separate immortality of 'souls.' " Having carried on the moral work of Zarathustra/Zoroaster in this way, Plato invents its final ground in an enigmatic vision beyond demonstration: an idea of the good that holds all being and all beings in its yoke.[42]

While fascinated by the spectacle of Plato's lying, Nietzsche the philologist was not deflected into the perhaps interminable philological inquiry into what Plato really believed; nor was Nietzsche the immoralist deflected into outrage at Plato's world-historical presumption. Rather, disputing Plato's judgment about the fundamental requirements of the city and man, Nietzsche follows his lead or imitates the greatest example by conducting a campaign on the same level of seriousness, with the whole future of mankind on his conscience. In the long twilight of what was set in motion by Plato, Nietzsche rekindles the battle of gods and giants already kindled at the level of philosophy by Plato himself. The ancient writers had taught that in their battle with the earthborn giants, the heavenly gods had chosen to conduct their campaign under the cover of darkness. In this darkness the gods still needed mortal aid; only the mortal Herakles could kill the earthborn giants whom the gods could only maim or temporarily overpower. What was taught covertly by the ancient writers is taught covertly by Plato, the new Herakles. Demoralizing stories of the battles of gods and giants will not be permitted in the purified theology of the city built through the philosopher's speech. Thus future generations will have no recollection of an earthly rule prior to the violent crimes that established the heavenly gods, the present rulers about whom the lie will be told that they never lie, never change their shape, and are responsible only for good.[43] In the presence of inquirers who still have that recollection, the mortal Plato comes to the aid of needful gods unable to slay the latest giants whom the earth has raised against them, giants who hold that being itself is "nothing but" power or the capability either to affect something or be affected,[44] to command or obey. With the aid of the mortal Plato the heavenly gods triumph over these latest earthly giants, for, like all giants till now, they are powerful but brutish; they are half barbarians whose brutishness is exposed in that ugliness which is inarticulateness or lack of refinement in speech: these powerful brutes need to be told what they really think by one who speaks like a god, even a philosophizing god.[45] Once they have been told what they think, once they have been identified, they can be killed or dismissed by rational proof.

The giants brought to refutable speech by Plato hold beliefs quite like those of Aristophanes' Socrates, that vortex rules the gods. Such giants are easily slain, for they lack caution and are politic neither to the old gods nor to aspiring new ones like the Clouds. Plato's Socrates has learned politic speech, by means of which he lyingly appears to side with the ancestral gods and the gods of the city while introducing new gods neither ancestral nor civic. The new gods are cosmopolitan; like clouds they appear over all cities, but unlike clouds they do not change their shape; they do not imitate the things in whose presence they find themselves; rather, things imitate them, for they are the eternal forms of mutable things. Thus a Platonic imprint is given to millennia by the one who says "I Plato am the truth" (*TI*, "Fable"). But the earth continued to generate giants, as the ancient writers assumed it would, and in Nietzsche the battle of gods and giants is rekindled from the side of the earthborn giants by a giant who has learned the art of beautiful and persuasive speech, a giant who speaks like a god and who brings the ancient battle out from under the protective cover of darkness. His speech requires a renaming of gods and giants, for now it is the gods who have slumped into inarticulateness and have to be told what they really think. Their "embarrassed blush" reveals the truth of the charge that their beautiful words are grounded in the most brutish of passions, vengeance against an earthly life that they judge to be no good. Victory by the sweet-speaking giant who teaches what the heavenly gods really say permits the return of earthly gods not moved by revenge, Dionysos and Ariadne, whose survival once depended on conceding the lie that they had heavenly or Olympian origins. Acknowledging without terror "the great cosmic stupidity" or the subhuman character of the heavens alleged to house the highest, Nietzsche rejoices at the death of the always questionable teleotheology initiated by the Platonic Socrates in the form of a noble lie. Contrary to appearances, his rejoicing is a vindication of the gods, for his teaching is the contrary of the conclusion drawn by worried free spirits that "God is refuted but the devil is not" (BGE 37).[46]

Nietzsche's history of philosophy makes clear that locating the modern founding within Platonism is still not comprehensive enough. As the inventor of a Greek and philosophic translation of the moral vision founded by Zarathustra/Zoroaster, the Platonic Socrates may be the one turning point and vortex of all so-called world history, but what he founds is itself a modification of the way founded by the spirit of gravity, the ancestral way brought into the open by Zarathustra (III. 11). Plato's city built in speech can be understood as an effort to secure the authority of the ancestral in nonancestral ways, to secure the holy city by the unholy means of philosophy. In the introduction of his novel teaching Nietzsche opposes the most comprehensive wisdom of the ages, as well as its Platonic, Christian, and modern modifications. As Zarathustra makes clear, the immediate task requires that the most firm opposition be directed at what stands now; however useful the genealogy of modern morals may be for exciting suspicion against them, there is no need to vanquish forms of the dream that have already vanished. Having gazed into the grounds of Western thought and being, Nietzsche opposes most directly what he interprets as a decayed form of the spirit of gravity, decayed Platonism, decayed Christianity, virulent modernity. What he opposes appears in two forms in Zarathustra: a theoretical form, the last possible Platonism for the wise, the dwarfed form of the spirit of gravity, Schopenhauer's philosophy, which tempts the modern thinker to resignation and despair; and a practical form, the last possible Platonism for the people, represented by the "last men" and their managers, "the good and the just." The historic identity of the last men is perhaps blurred by the literary fiction governing the presentation of particulars in Zarathustra; for they necessarily appear without their modern machinery, "the infinity of devices" that makes possible their state of ease. Nevertheless, they are the final regents in "the Baconian succession," heirs to Bacon's and Descartes' science of nature, with its aim of complete technical management of nature, civil society, and the human body, just as they are heirs of Christianity, Socratic rationalism, and the spirit of gravity. Zarathustra shows that both theoretical and practical modernity are the outcome of a long historical process governed by the spirit of gravity, and that this process must be opposed fundamentally by exposing its ground and opening a new route to the opposite ideal.

In introducing his novel teaching, Nietzsche does not share the problem faced by Plato's Socrates, the problem of introducing a novel teaching under the pretence that it is ancient.[47] As his hesitation intimates, Socrates knows that he will not be able to get anyone to believe such novel truths in his own generation, but Glaucon's answer to the problem of belief intimates that even such novelties could become believable in the way utilized by the spirit of gravity, the way of tradition described by Socrates as the obliteration of natural origins through beliefs about origins acquired in a time prior to the formation of memory; they will themselves become the deepest available memories.[48] When speaking for once to the authoritative multitude of his fellow citizens, Socrates alleges that his practice is merely obedience to the ancestral authority that they acknowledge, aware that if he spoke otherwise or acknowledged the true ground for his practice, they would be even less inclined to believe him.[49] Inclined not at all to believe Socrates when he gives the ground or warrant for his thought, Nietzsche himself, in his public speaking, appeals for warrant to the authoritative modern oracle of the future, the new age to be ushered in by the Great Noon. But then isn't such a teaching after all a relapse into "Zoroastrianism," into the view that the whole of history is justified by its end? Such a relapse cannot be avoided altogether by the historical sense which affirms that the particular route taken by mankind has made the definitive difference in opening the present possibility of total affirmation. Nor can Zoroastrianism be avoided in the sense that the achievement of the new teaching requires that it be fought for. But Nietzsche's teaching differs from Zoroastrianism in being preserved by sane reason from the madness of utopianism (WB 11). His appeal to the authority of the future is an appeal to a time beyond the ancestral teachings of revenge, a time not ruled by permanence and ease, but by life, suffering, and the circle, by the love of earthly life that wills the eternal return of mortal beings.

In the face of the great danger of becoming the chief promoter of this novel enterprise that affects everyone's interests, and in the face of the difficulties of directing it, bringing it to a successful conclusion, and maintaining it after that conclusion, Nietzsche seems to have learned from his great protagonist Socrates to make himself fascinating in the way that Socrates is fascinating. Pondering "The Problem of Socrates" from the side of Socrates' charm, or wondering how it was possible for the ugly Socrates to charm even the most beautiful growth of antiquity and to make himself the one turning point of world history, Nietzsche concludes that there were three reasons (TI, "Socrates," 8, 9): that Socrates provided a novel *agon*, that he was a great erotic, and that his experience was symptomatic of what others were just beginning to experience. This third reason points to the basic matter: that what Socrates presciently saw and mastered as a chaos of instincts in himself was beginning to appear in others as a consequence of the Athenian decline. To the best of the new generation, Socrates seemed a very savior who already knew the solution to what they were just beginning to experience as a threat. Although Nietzsche judges that to have to fight against the instincts as Socrates did is already to be lost, the example of Socrates' charm is still useful for him. Though Nietzsche has flown into the furthest future and must now return to his own past to face that future with others, he knows that his own case cannot be an exception. To show himself already master of the chaos of instincts that others are now coming to experience only as the first stages of half barbarian threat is to make himself fascinating. Nietzsche's writings, his fables and fishhooks, draw to him those with whom he can share his vision of what is coming.

Made fascinating by his unparalleled capacity to bring to enchanting speech what others are beginning to feel inchoately as their own fate, does Nietzsche ultimately fail those whose hopes he raised by his enchantment? Does Nietzsche the educator betray his student by being after all just another teacher of revenge? The long route taken through *Thus Spoke Zarathustra* makes clear that Nietzsche does not fail his friends, that he is, as he almost said he was, the genius of the heart worthy of being followed. The inherent improbability of such a claim for any teacher is intensified in Nietzsche's case because his work finally fell out of his control. Having learned from Schopenhauer, Nietzsche the educator came to covet and eventually possess the "iron nature" of the philosopher that alone could preserve him from what he saw to be the three intrinsic dangers that threaten the philosopher's ruin: not having a single companion of his own kind, despair at the deadly truth, and melancholy and longing posed by the profound desire to fulfill both the saint and the genius in him (*SE* 3). Despite the immense scrupulousness and rectitude practiced by Nietzsche in consequence of the responsibility that fell to him as a philosopher, and despite his iron nature, he was betrayed by many "scars and open wounds" not of his own making. "The death of the poet was kept from his poems," Auden said of Yeats. No one could say the same of Nietzsche. The spiritual death that cost him control of his unfinished work delivered it over to fortuity, to calamities like his sister and her Archive, purveyors of a Nietzsche legend perversely tailored to fit a political movement utterly contrary to Nietzsche's own spirit and teachings; here were the purported followers and disciples who, like the fool of part III of *Zarathustra*, put some of Nietzsche's phrases and cadences into the service of their vengeance, thereby making Nietzsche appear to be a teacher of evil in a sense quite different from the sense appropriate to every revolutionary teacher.[50] But worse still was the cruel accident of his madness itself, not simply because his personal fate came to color the fate of his work, but far more because it left his work incomplete. What remained for Nietzsche, as I see it, was not the ascent of some peak even higher than the one ascended by Zarathustra, for that ascent had made possible the insight into the fundamental phenomenon and the teaching of eternal return based on it. What remained, rather, was a descent in order to become the teacher of eternal return who could show how that teaching provided "a new center of tremendous forces" that would "revolutionize the entire system of human pursuits" (*SE* 8)[51] and show too the way to political responsibility for those enchanted into his orbit by his demolition of the old tradition and his promise of virtues loyal to the earth. Nietzsche had fitted himself for that task and said, after the completion of *Zarathustra*, that he must now live a few years longer to complete his task.[52] His breakdown came just as he was experiencing the "great harvest time" (letter to Overbeck, 18 October

1888) for which he had so long prepared, and it has deprived us of the "most independent book," the "Revaluation of All Values" on the basis of eternal return (*TI*, "Skirmishes," 51). In the absence of Nietzsche's own agenda for the long spiritual warfare that his writings provoke and advance, it is necessary now for us to formulate that agenda as best we can from the works he did write, recognizing all the while that ivy can climb no higher than the tree supporting it and may even tend downward again after it has reached the top.

Any consideration of the particulars of Nietzsche's agenda must judge Nietzsche by the new standard by which he condemned both ancient and modern teachings on nature and human nature, revenge. Specifically, is Nietzsche's teaching an extension of the vengeful conquest of nature that it discerns in modernity? Though the word *nature* is used only once in *Zarathustra*, and then in mockery of poets who claim to have communed with her (II. 17), the recovery of nature is fundamental to Nietzsche's task. The immensity of that task, its improbability, perhaps even impossibility, is emphasized by Zarathustra in his precarious efforts to remake his audience. For Nietzsche there is absolutely no question of something called "invincible nature" eventually regaining "its dominion," as Rousseau alleged it always would, even against modern states.[53] Not even this finger of God plays a part in the future of mankind, not even nature herself can be counted upon to erupt in protest against those who would subdue her. In speaking of the recovery of nature, Nietzsche does not revive the lie of optimistic dependence on benevolent forces greater than man, nor the lie of a prehistoric or premodern naturalness, a state of nature once lived innocently by mankind. "I still hate Rousseau in the French Revolution," Nietzsche says, for the return to nature of "this first modern man" was merely a modern translation of one aspect of Christian antinature. Because "there has never yet been a natural humanity," what Nietzsche means by a return to nature is not a going back but "an ascent—up into a high, free even terrible nature and naturalness" (*TI*, "Skirmishes," 48; *KGW* VIII 10 [53] = *WP* 120).

In his attempt to recover nature from its Platonic, Christian, and modern interpretation, Nietzsche can speak in the name of nature against the goal of the mastery of nature that originated with "the famous wise" (II. 8). Extending the view that mankind had a quarrel with nature, they taught mankind to believe that the quarrel could be won by technological means, for nature was not perverse or fallen, only careless or niggardly.[54] Their will to the mastery of nature aimed at that "humanitarian emendation" of nature (*BGE* 22) that introduced the democratic instinct into nature itself. Control of nature promised to eliminate the order of rank separating the exceptional one who appears by chance and the many unexceptional ones who appear by chance. Grounded in a vengeful will to alter, the technological will to the effecting of all things possible creates a global homogeneity that surmounts the suffering and inequality of the thousand peoples. The consequence of the single vision of this new and aggressive Platonism for the people is modern man, whose apparent variety masks the machined uniformity of its sacred way, technological democracy. While seeing it as primarily a surrender to the general will to ease (*BGE* 229–30), Nietzsche discerns a second essential feature in "our whole modern existence": insofar as it is not weakness, insofar as it is "power and consciousness of power," it gives the appearance of sheer hubris, even when measured against that standard of hubris the ancient Greeks. There are three kinds of modern hubris: "*Hubris* is our whole stance toward nature, our rape of nature with the help of machines and the heedless inventiveness of technicians and engineers." Hubris is also our stance toward God and our stance toward ourselves, a rape of ourselves (*GM* III. 9). The hubristic rape of nature, God, and man has become the task of the heedless, who have rough work to do, and who do it with a rough materialist imperative (*BGE* 14).[55] Himself the accidental or natural exception whose massive undertaking on behalf of mankind is based on the natural accident of what is given to him, "the great stupidity" that he is (*BGE* 231), Nietzsche aims to recover nature from the hands of those who judged nature to be faulty and mankind to be her victims.

Zarathustra addresses the question of modern science and revenge most directly in part IV, though even there Nietzsche abstracts from the specifics of technological mastery in order not to mar his book's setting. Nevertheless, Zarathustra corrects the typical misunderstanding of science held by its representative practitioner. The superior modern men assembled in part IV learn from him that science need not be grounded in the passion of fear but can find its legitimation in the passion of adventure. Dynamic contemplation need not turn to active transformation of the thing investigated, for science can be detached from the historic will to alter, a will grounded in fear and revenge, and be attached instead to the will to discover the tightly held secrets of the beloved, a will grounded in gratitude and justice. The will to mastery intrinsic to the modern Baconian or Cartesian project is not identical with the will to mastery exhibited in Zarathustra's ascendancy to the mastery which is philosophy. This ascent questions the modern linkage of science and technology, of knowing and making, and forces us to ask: How can a mastering will to know assign limits to the conquest of nature and let the thing known simply be the thing that it is? How can science be impelled by wonder and yet be free of the will to alter?

Nietzsche's answer is: by having science pass into the care of the philosophy of the future, eternal return. Science carried out under the imperative of eternal return would be a sheltering science, Nietzschean science. To affirm eternal return is to construe both time and being in ways inimical to modernity's understanding of them and to overcome its revenge against time and being. With respect to time, the teaching of eternal return opposes the single-minded trajectory of modern technological science, its linear or progressive development spurred by the belief in the perfectibility of corruptible bodies and the insatiable will to alter them. In its opposition to modern, progressive time, eternal return cannot be interpreted as the view of time appropriate to the age that finally achieves the technological correction of existence, as Heidegger argues. For, with respect to being or beings, the teaching of eternal return opposes the corrective aims of modern technological science. Those aims could be said to be the achievement of the permanent in two earthly forms, each visible in the veiled promises of Bacon and Descartes to master the natural laws of decay: a technological global society that is immune to the fate of all societies hitherto, and individual bodies "even perhaps also" made immortal through the technology of medicine. While recognizing the possibility and desirability of progress in the sciences through the spirited drive that carries the inquirer higher, further, deeper (or even through less noble drives [*BGE* 206, 207]), Nietzsche's teaching of eternal return opposes the terminal hope for permanent bodies in a permanent social order with the exultant play of mortals among the mortal things. With respect to time and beings eternal return opposes the modern hope for the eventual technological subjection of nature, exposing that hope as a species of vengeance, one form of Socratic rationalism that holds that existence can be fully understood and corrected. Nietzsche's teaching replaces both the need for that hope and the nihilistic hopelessness occasioned by its demise; it affirms the existence of temporal beings that appear out of a fundamental mystery and disappear back into it, and it affirms as part of man's being the passion to study their ways. The teaching of eternal return seems to me to be the essential element in Nietzsche's program to bring science under the care of philosophy—a seemingly preposterous program given the reduced state of philosophy, given philosophy's capture by sciences already in the grip of an unarticulated philosophy. Nietzsche seeks to remedy this "unseemly and harmful shift in the respective ranks of science and philosophy" (*BGE* 204) while grounding science as mankind's passion to inquire.

The rudiments of Nietzsche's affirmation of science can be gleaned from the way in which he accords praise and blame in *The Antichrist* (59; see also 60–62): highest praise for ancient science because of the foundations that it has successfully laid; highest blame for Christianity because it has robbed the world of the harvest of that whole preliminary labor. And it was *preliminary* labor, the necessary foundations for the scientific work that would occupy thousands of years. While all the presuppositions for a learned culture, all the scientific methods, were attained by the ancients, Nietzsche makes emphatic that their central achievement, the single presupposition that would have made possible a tradition of culture and the unity of the sciences, was their achievement of the art of reading well. This primary art of nuance, what Nietzsche went so far as to call "the best gain of life" (*BGE* 31), philology where everything is text, is the presupposition even of the natural sciences, the imperial sciences of modernity that now require careful schooling in the art of nuance from the old philologist (*BGE* 22). Science that passes into the care of the old philologist, science governed by Nietzschean philosophy, is different from the science of those "with nothing but rough work to do" (*BGE* 14). It is a joyful science, a science of artful inquiry in the service of the nobility of nature. For such a science even labor

> is blossoming or dancing where
> The body is not bruised to pleasure soul,
> Nor beauty born out of its own despair,
> Nor blear-eyed wisdom out of midnight oil.[56]

The long spiritual warfare against the dogmatism that has robbed mankind of the harvest prepared by ancient science has created a productive tension of the spirit that promises to set mankind back on the path of inquiry and adventure, now deepened and enlivened, made finer and more subtle by that warfare, made Nietzschean (*BGE*, Preface).

Nietzschean science first appears as a possibility in a setting dominated by a technological science that knows no assignable limits to its conquest of nature, its correction of nature's alleged failures such as mortality, an order of rank, male and female. Although it perceives grave dangers in these corrective undertakings and detects a motive of vengeance at the heart of them, Nietzschean science does not arise in the hoary name of the unalterable. It does not speak for the gravity of a natural law confirmed in the starry heavens above or for the gravity of a moral law inscribed within; it does not speak for any unalterable laws with which man dare not tamper. Nietzschean science speaks a more nuanced tone, for it speaks in the name of alterable, vulnerable nature, nature susceptible of being whipped into correction. It speaks its opposition to technological science, not because that science fails but because it seems likely to succeed. It judges that what is due beings is more than their humanitarian manipulation or their transformation into standing reserve for human use. Commissioned by his insight into the fate of modern man, given authority to act by his recognition of the impending danger and by that alone, Nietzsche teaches a new way for human beings to exist among beings, the way that wills their eternal return out of love that there be such beings. Limits to the conquest of nature must be assigned, for there are none to discover, and the assignment of limits derives its imperative from the lover's will that wills eternal return. To will the eternal return of beings generates a new conduct toward beings, one that preserves, allows, and spares. In this amazing way, one discovers in the "immoralist" Nietzsche the transcendence of justice over technology.[57]

As Heidegger's lectures on Nietzsche between 1936 and 1940 descend into rancor against him, they achieve their lowest level in their account of justice in Nietzsche. During the tense summer of 1940, with Britain apparently about to fall to Germany's air attacks, France already having fallen, Heidegger is able to assure his students that the enemy's act of destroying its former ally's fleet is an example of justice according to Nietzsche.[58] By this propaganda trick Heidegger reverses the usual propaganda about Nietzsche's political paternity and makes it seem that Nietzsche is the ideological father of English-speaking justice, the enemy's justice, which unashamedly justifies even the most brutal acts of war. In an essay written at about the same time,[59] justice appears as the fifth of five fundamental terms in Nietzsche's philosophy, as what would, in the case of any writer but Heidegger, be called the practical or moral consequence of the already recounted theoretical standpoint. Heidegger's account of justice comes to focus on two notes: "Justice as building, separating, annihilating mode of thinking, out of value judgments; highest representative of life itself," and "justice, as function of a wide-ranging power, which looks out over the little perspectives of good and evil, thus has a wider horizon of interest— the intention to preserve something that is more than this or that person" (KGW VII 25 [484], 26 [149]). Heidegger holds that these notes demonstrate that for Nietzsche justice was nothing but the justification of modern freedom, and thus of man's absolute dominance of the earth in the service of the enhancement of power. But in the light of Zarathustra these rich, but unguarded and unpublished, notes yield quite a different sense. The value judgment that is the highest representative of life itself is the judgment that says to life, eternally return. This mode of thinking results in a justice with three activities: building, separating, and annihilating. The central activity of separating out is effected by the great weight of the thought of eternal return, which blesses or crushes, builds or annihilates. That thought annihilates the view that desires to take revenge on life and it builds on the earth the home in which mortals dwell under the open sky, awaiting the return of Dionysos and Ariadne, gods of earth. Justice, the function of the wide-ranging power of the teacher of eternal return, looks out over the little perspectives of good and evil. Beyond good and evil, beyond the narrow perspectives according to which moral categories are properties of things themselves, beyond Zoroastrianism and Platonism, the wide-ranging power of the new thinker encompasses the widest horizon of interest, taking into account more than the preservation of the few things judged good among that totality of things judged evil, which once included the human and still more the animal and still more the material (GM III. 28). Grounded not in the perspective of this or that person, some little perspective which humanizes nature to nature's disadvantage, grounded rather in the insight into nature free of all anthropomorphism and moved by the intention to preserve the whole of natural beings, the new justice derives its warrant from that "high spirituality" which is "the spiritualization of justice" and not its brutalization, from that gracious severity "which knows that it is commissioned to maintain in the world the order of rank, even among the things, and not only among men" (BGE 219).[60]

An agenda for Nietzschean science requires consideration of the precise ways in which that justice is to be enacted. "Is there a measure on the earth?—There is none." Nietzsche shares Hölderlin's judgment but, in the poetry of eternal return, indicates the way to the assignment of measure. Zarathustra's way promises to place an azure dome of eternal security over the transient things, and the translation of this poetry into the sober prose of the sciences would mean the assignment of limits to conquest and alteration. Because man cannot help but imitate in action his vision of the nature of things,[61] the moral imperatives for particular cases would be worked out within the horizon provided by the new ideal of eternal return, for that ideal gives a "new grounding of normative thinking," an objective basis for value judgments.[62] Regulated by this ideal, the sciences would themselves contribute to the goal of making the earth a home for man.

One of Nietzsche's prose translations of the azure dome of eternal security appears in *Beyond Good and Evil*, in which he never once speaks of a superman, but speaks instead of a "complementary man" as the highest human achievement (*BGE* 207; see also 28). In the complementary man the most spiritual nature complements nature, or completes and perfects what without him is mere fragment. His yes to nature in its mortality, its order of rank, its being male and female, complements nature with an unbounded Yes to everything that was and is.[63] The complementary man thus personifies the high spirituality that, so far from being the atavism of some premoral or presocial condition, is instead the refinement and strengthening of mankind's spiritual qualities, "the synthesis of all those states which one ascribes to men who are 'only moral' " (*BGE* 219). Such high spirituality expresses itself in the justice of letting beings be. But this affirmation not only shelters everything that is from the heedless inventiveness of technicians and engineers, it shelters everything that was from the fall into forgottenness, for the past that it wills it desires to recover. "The eye of the nihilist . . . is unfaithful to his memories; it lets them fall, lose their leaves . . . and what [the nihilist] does not do for himself, he also does not do for the whole past of mankind: he lets it fall" (*KGW* VIII 10 [43] = *WP* 21). In the teaching of eternal return willed by the complementary man, the whole of the natural and human past is seen as worthy of preservation in human memory, and mankind's spiritual qualities are affirmed by being grounded in their natural history. It is not enough that the complementary man simply will the past that made him possible—this past, this once. Rather, he must give his unbounded yes to everything that was and is, the yes of eternal return, for the saving force grows where the greatest danger grows, and the greatest danger grows out of the European past, the danger posed by the historic conquest of nature which knows no assignable limits and by the historic forgetting of the natural past which assigns it to nihilistic oblivion (III. 12, §11). The yes of eternal return grants nature its eternity and the past its remembrance, and it does so by a postulation, an act of love on the part of the most spiritual nature, who stands at the end of a long chain of natural and historical accident, the "least likely of all beings."[64] To affirm himself means to affirm every particular of the whole of which he is a part, and to place the azure dome of eternal security over those particulars.

Complementary man, superman, Dionysos, Zarathustra are not fully synonymous, but they share a quality that defines them: each is needy, incomplete, a lover. In the search for a complement Zarathustra's career is paradigmatic; while remaining incomplete in himself, he finds a lover from whom he desires children. Life, Ariadne, Earth, Nature are not fully synonymous, but they too share a quality that defines them: each is needy, incomplete, a lover. The relationship of man and nature is a problematic complementarity, ruled not by a whip but by a complementary love. Nietzschean science, as depicted in both Zarathustra and the complementary man, is characterized by a spirit meant to infuse all the branches of science. The spirit of the lover drives out the spirit of the engineer and of the nihilist; science passes into the care of the philosopher who says to life, eternally return. Nietzschean science runs the risk of the vulgarity of man's management of nature and of a cheap elevation of man above the ranks of all living things as their presumptive liberator. However, Nietzsche's agenda need not be measured by the standard of some Nietzscheanism for the people, but by the nobility of natural man's affirmation of the marvel of natural beings.

Although contemporary inquiry is far from identifying itself as Nietzschean, it seems to me that it would gain much by becoming self-consciously Nietzschean. It would gain a new perspective on the character of inquiry in general, for Nietzsche makes it possible to ground and legitimate inquiry into being and beings as the way of the most spiritual being. Man inquires into the whole of beings as a part of those beings, not as their rightful conquistador but as participant with them in the marvel that is the whole of becoming. Speaking to scientists in general as he had spoken to the physicists on whom it had not yet dawned that physics too is only interpretation (BGE 22, 14), Nietzsche warns that they should "above all ... not wish to divest existence of its *rich ambiguity*" (GS 373). His admonition warns scientists and scholars especially of any mechanistic interpretation "that permits counting, calculating, weighing, seeing, and touching, and nothing more." While the old philologist can assign the name "will to power" to the fundamental phenomenon, he assigns it knowing that no name is adequate, for each is "a weakening and attenuating metaphor," and that this most fitting name leaves the heart of things elusive, opaque, tempting, taunting. But more than this, the sciences can gain from Nietzsche the understanding that they are aspects of a comprehensive teaching. Within the horizon of Nietzsche's philosophy, inquiries conducted in the natural and human sciences would know how to answer the grave charge that they are nihilistic or conducted in the oblivion of eternity and in ignorance of the highest good. Through the philosopher Nietzsche, philosophers of the future and inquirers in general can discover how to affirm life as good in itself when viewed from the inside as will to power, and to affirm the eternal return of temporal life as the highest ideal. In this way the sciences are freed from the uneasy conscience of nihilism, a feeling Nietzsche had earlier described when he said that for many, scientific work is pleasant to engage in but unpleasant to find out about (HH I. 251). Science grounded in Nietzsche's philosophy has no fear of what it may discover, for it does not set out needing to prove or refute anything; it serves no vested interests requiring a world of a certain sort; it is no mere specialization while giving spirit to specialists in every field of inquiry; it is impassioned, but not voluptuary, for it is fueled by the passion at the heart of man, wonder.

Nietzsche understands all science to be interpretation—which is not to diminish it, for it deprives science only of its dogmatic self-interpretation, an interpretation that one of its own refined disciplines, philology, has come to see as inappropriate. The scientific interpretation of things opens itself to revision, a characteristic it exhibits in revising its own claims for itself. Those claims needed time to free themselves from the long prevailing dogmatism in the midst of which modern science arose and against which it had to make holy war to establish itself. But if science is interpretation, it is far from arbitrary, nor will its revisions be arbitrary but interpretations of a more comprehensive and adequate sort, provisional products of its organized skepticism. For in Nietzschean science, convictions have no rights of citizenship, and all hypotheses remain "under police supervision, the police of mistrust" (GS 344). New hypotheses will mean the replacement "of the improbable with the more probable, possibly one error with another" (GM, Preface, 4). The comprehensive teaching of eternal return is also interpretation, but it is clearly not arbitrary, for it arises out of the insight that being is will to power and that the most spiritual will to power has brought mankind to the modern predicament of nihilism and dominance, and it arises out of the disposition to rejoice in things. Rooted in insight and disposition, it states a taste, and in matters of taste there is the greatest disputation. But the new taste has taste enough not to degrade itself before some standard purportedly higher or firmer than itself. It is not dogmatic or blunt, but savors and discriminates, having been educated by the long struggles of the spirit that it has come to understand. Refined, subtle, informed, the new taste that wills eternal return provides the open sky of affirmation under which the human and natural sciences can proceed.

Eternal return is not some antiscientific myth, some salutary lie intended to shield mankind from deadly truths not fit to utter. As the ideal that grounds and rules a new age of inquiry, it loves intellectual probity and loves to loose inquiry into its own rule. It does not fear inquiry or the disclosure of the truth behind its rule, for it is founded on the fundamental phenomenon and on its affirmation. Within the strictures of the supreme

art of philology, the art of reading well, it knows and celebrates the un-
doubtable core of truth in modern philosophy and science.[65] For the
teaching of eternal return is not "radical historicism," which reduces all
conceptions, including those of physics, biology, and psychology, to the
realm of myth or to the fated sequence of true dispensations of historical
being; nor, in the language of a parallel philosophy of science, does it suppose all scientific statements to be paradigm-relative. Nietzsche's "ontogeny
of thought" (HH I. 16, 18) is not bound to suppose that Aristotle's cosmology
is as true as Galileo's or as that of contemporary cosmologists. It weans
mankind from the no longer salutary lies of Socratic rationalism, not only
because they are obsolete, but because they are base, and because they
are false.

Nietzsche provides not only a new grounding for science, but also an
indispensable example of how scientific investigation is to proceed, indispensable because it investigates the provenance of the sciences themselves and hence of its own practice. On the Genealogy of Morals shows
the sciences, including Nietzsche's, to be the latest and noblest forms of
the ascetic ideal whose earlier forms are far from noble. Although this
genealogy must be a "polemic," it is also an exercise in gratitude or familial
piety by a descendant fascinated by his roots. It is a local or family history
portraying the lines of descent from forebears who are forceful and interesting, if not themselves noble in the way of their descendant. But their
descendant's nobility expresses itself in part as a refined taste in moral
matters that is very far from self-congratulation, for he knows that he is
not the author of himself.[66] In tracing his lineage, he gives thanks for his
existence. Although he is moved by the monumental in history and exemplifies the critical spirit, he is above all an antiquarian whose own things
or whose "city" has become the whole of human things. Finding himself
within this city as its latest offspring, he "reads its walls, its towered gate,
its rules and regulations, its holy days, like an illuminated diary of his
youth and in all this he finds himself again, his force, his industry, his joy,
his judgment, his folly and his vices" (UD 3). Knowing its roots, the particulars of its coming to be, such a spirit must take part and fight on behalf
of its own things, the natural and human things.

Nietzschean science is served by Nietzschean politics, the highest by
the high. Opposed to the conception of time and being in the Western
past, both ancient and modern, Nietzsche's politics does not seek the return
of something still earlier or the establishment of something non-Western.
Mankind bears the indelible marks of its accidental history, and that history
is neither repented nor regretted by Nietzsche. Schooled in the "historical
sense," the great virtue of modern Europe, "our" virtue (BGE 224), Nietzsche
recognizes that, while fully accidental and hence open to having been other
than it was, the past of the contemporary age has in fact been Platonism
and the Christian and modern Platonisms for the people. Although even
its latest virtue, the historical sense, has ignoble roots in Europe's self-

contempt and longing for something past or alien, it can no longer be thought ignoble to have ignoble roots: gods and heroes stand at the head of no ancestral line, ennoblement through noble origins is now an unusable lie, now that no genealogy ascends through unbroken dignities to the beginning of the world. The particular accidental past of Europe and of Nietzsche is Platonism—"As a plant I was born in a churchyard, as a man in a pastor's house," said Nietzsche at nineteen ("Mein Leben," 18 September 1863)—and it is this particular European past into which we are all born that has educated the spirit and through that long education created "a magnificent tension of the spirit the like of which has never yet existed on earth" and made possible "the goal" (*BGE*, Preface), the highest human achievement, the complementarity of human nature and nature expressed by Zarathustra.

This European past, which presents the greatest danger and makes possible the highest goal, has become a global fate. Faced with a planetary fact, with a Europeanization of the world that has already, in Descartes' words, taken possession of the kingdoms of China and Mexico or, in Marx's words, drawn "all nations, even the most barbarian, into civilization," Nietzsche responds with a planetary politics, a "great politics" that also begins in Europe, but in a unified Europe prepared for the undertakings Nietzsche prescribes for it (*BGE* 208). The politics of the new people mankind, while fully acknowledging the global fact established out of the thousand peoples of the past, stands opposed to the teaching on man and world that has created that fact. In its opposition, Nietzsche's politics made free use of an inflated rhetoric of warfare, now rendered offensive and unusable by the experience of twentieth-century wars. Nietzsche's anticipation that the twentieth century would be marked by global wars is not prescience; the wars he anticipated and even desired and kindled were not the wars that were actually fought. In declaring war and plotting war, Nietzsche's books invite his readers to enlist in the wars that he did fight, spiritual wars against powers with a secure hold on the allegiance of almost all mankind. In the risky business of war rhetoric, Nietzsche has come out decidedly a loser, since a few dangerous phrases from *Zarathustra* set in a reading of Nietzsche's life and work that sounded as if it should have been authoritative in that it came from his own sister, his "Lischen," made it seem that Nietzsche had a passion for bloodletting, and that he shared the general belief in the power of a good shooting war to redeem a decadent society. Though he chose to be an exile, a "good European" who surrendered his German citizenship and claimed no other, Nietzsche's name came to be associated with the wars of what had been his own people, his subtle words of liberation and permission twisted into complicity in the most appalling crimes. Had one of his final, mad wishes actually been carried out—"I am just now having all anti-Semites shot" (letter to the Overbecks, received 7 January 1889)—it is not only Nietzsche's reputation that would have been spared. Nietzsche's free use of the rhetoric of warfare makes it all too easy to overlook the fact that the essential warfare is spiritual warfare against global adversaries who have the laws on their side, and that even that warfare is a means to an end and not an end in itself. Nietzschean politics does not endorse the iron age of which it is a part; it ignites the great spiritual warfare for the sake of the Dionysian age.

Nietzschean politics arose in a setting dominated by an imperial technological science that implied global hegemony and the completion of history in a universal and homogeneous state. Nietzsche protested the leviathan of the universal state and its citizenry of last men, but, in elevating as superior the old way of peoples, can Nietzsche's politics of a new people do anything other than carry forward the homogeneity intrinsic to modern technological science? Certainly, the specific grounds of the thousand cultural and religious particularities hitherto cannot be sustained by Nietzsche's thought. In understanding the grounds common to Cyrus, Theseus, Moses, and Romulus, it can lend its support to none of them. Its probity undermines the exclusive ancestral grounds of any people's way. Can the fruit of those grounds be preserved in some different way by the people mankind? Founded on intellectual probity, the people mankind could never fool itself into believing any one of the ancestral ways, or into believing that by lending support indiscriminately to every one of the thousand ways it could adequately support any of the ways whose character has been their passionate exclusivity, their evocation of the dread and envy of their neighbors. Now it is modernity itself that evokes the dread and envy of its neighbors, and all contemporary peoples are its neighbors. Nietzsche's teaching presents itself as having no one way but as following, nevertheless, the path of peoples marked out by the exclusive way of each of the thousand peoples. A return to the way of peoples, though not to the way of any one historic people, would be a turn to a new faith and love, a new table of values, one that recognizes the ascending rank of the praiseworthy, the good, and the holy. A new law of overcomings would bring the new people under a rule, eternal return, a rule that is not monotheistic, that does not command uniformity or homogeneity but that grants to the diverse bush of life, and to its diverse branch, human life, the multiplicity that is part of its glory. Under the rule of eternal return, Nietzschean science is not moved by a will to alter, but by a preserving and remembering will; it therefore exults in variety and novelty and nuance; it is grateful to the given things while refusing the customary explanations of their givenness. It belongs to the agenda of Nietzschean science to secure the assertion that there exist nonancestral grounds for a love of ancestral things, one's own things, one's home and the lake of one's home.

In part IV of *Zarathustra*, the agenda of responsibilities left to followers is addressed to those called "the lords of the earth" (IV. 19, §7; see *KGW* VII 25 [137]). In that now chilling phrase, Nietzsche does not look forward to those who have presumed to lord it over the earth in our century, but backward to those friends of Plato who carried out the interpretive tasks of Platonism over the centuries and succeeded in bringing the world under a rule that held for millennia. Those tasks took time and had time, as do the interpretive and political tasks left to the friends of Nietzsche—though Nietzsche's writings do not simply await the coming of such friends but act to create them. A somewhat better phrase for his followers is the one Nietzsche used earlier in *Zarathustra*, "a new nobility"; but whereas Zarathustra may permit himself such flattery to attract followers, Nietzsche's account of "our virtues" shows how unseemly any pride of place would be, given his increased delicacy in moral matters (*BGE* 230). A better phrase still would be the more sober one used in *Beyond Good and Evil*, "the philosophers of the future," though that phrase is also too elevated, given the definition of the philosopher in that book. An even more appropriate one would be "philosophical laborers," understood in Nietzsche's honorable way to refer to those engaged in the enormous and wonderful task of inquiry within the horizon provided by Nietzsche's philosophy. Friends of Nietzsche in any case, Nietzscheans, whose projects in Nietzschean science and Nietzschean politics clearly do not need to be begun tomorrow. One does not need to be an enemy of Nietzsche to see his "incomparable influence" everywhere, in philosophy, in the contemporary sciences of nature and man, and in political and social movements loyal to the earth.

Enactment of the Nietzschean agenda in science and politics promises a new sense of the sacred, a return of Dionysos and Ariadne. The free minds addressed by Nietzsche do not like to hear of God and gods, for we rightfully celebrate our newfound liberation from the tyrannical God after centuries of spiritual warfare. Nietzsche's vindication of the gods has nothing to do with the jealous sovereign of the Bible or with its many humanitarian reinterpretations; on the basis of Zarathustra's speech to syncretistic disciples (II. 2), no biblical theology could in good conscience claim Nietzsche as its prophet. Unlike heavenly gods, the earthly Dionysos is well-disposed toward mankind, for he experiences mankind's woes while himself being a philosopher. With Ariadne, Dionysos symbolizes the fundamental complementarity. But the incompleteness of Nietzsche's work leaves the religious aspect of his agenda particularly fragmentary—and it is this aspect that most requires special authority to be spoken. Those dialogues on Naxos—what a book they would have made had Nietzsche survived to complete it (*TI*, "Skirmishes," 19).

Nietzsche's teaching opposes "you who are wisest"; it opposes the wisdom of the ages, the ancestral wisdom that has brought the weight of the fathers to bear on all subsequent generations, demanding and receiving fresh blood for old ghosts. In declaring a break with what has hitherto constituted wisdom about the fundamental requirements of the city and man, the comprehensive wisdom of the spirit of gravity, it specifically opposes the fragment of that wisdom which still reigns, Platonism and its descendants. Eternal return is the heart of Nietzsche's teaching, because it accords the highest honor to the evanescent beings of which the whole consists. Guided neither by ancestral gods nor by philosophical and cosmopolitan idols nor by some lodestar of future paradise, guided rather by its own insight into the whole of beings, and granted responsibility by this insight to maintain those beings, Nietzsche's teaching shows the way to the highest affirmation of natural beings, the new justice that shouts insatiably "Once More!" to the whole marvelous spectacle of which the grateful celebrant is a momentary witness.

Appendix: Part IV—An Interlude Between the Main Acts

THE ACTION OF PART IV

It was fitting that part IV of *Thus Spoke Zarathustra* be privately printed and circulated secretly in only a handful of copies among Nietzsche's friends, for the existence of a fourth part violates the ending of part III. Everything points to the end of part III as The End. It is, as the animals say, the end of Zarathustra's going under. Zarathustra's private songs invite the harvester, the god Dionysos, whose coming brings the end of the old order (III. 14). Zarathustra successfully concludes his courtship with Life in his dance with her, and the midnight bell tolls the completion of his wisdom (III. 15). In the final song (III. 16) Nietzsche seals his book with seven seals that mark the doom of the old order and the dawn of the new, the sixty-six chapters of *Zarathustra*[1] thus ending with a repetition of the apocalyptic symbol from the sixty-sixth and final book of the Bible. Zarathustra's final song, an "Amen Song," is a marriage song, another echo of *Revelation*, bringing to a happy end his dance with Life. Furthermore, when Nietzsche finished part III, he said that his book was finished.[2] And when he published the complete book in 1886, two years after completing part IV, he published only three parts. In *Ecce Homo*, too, he said that he was finished with Zarathustra when he finished part III ("Books: *Zarathustra*," 4). As Nietzsche conceived it while writing it and as he presented it to the public, the book ends with part III.

But now it ends with part IV, a part that Nietzsche sent to a few select friends with instructions not even to whisper of its existence;[3] and though he whispered of its existence himself in *Ecce Homo* ("Why I am so Wise," 4),[4] his last known reference to it is in a plea made to Köselitz on 9 December 1888:

> Now a *serious* matter. Dear friend, I want to have *all* the copies of Zarathustra *four* back, in order to secure this unpublished work against all the accidents of life and death.... If after a few decades of world historical crises—

wars!—I publish it, then that will be the *proper* time. Please, try as hard as you can to remember *who* has copies. I can think of: Lanzky, Widemann, Fuchs, Brandes, probably Overbeck. Do you have Widemann's address? How many copies were there? How many have we still got? There may be a couple in Naumburg.

Lovely weather in every respect. . . .

Nietzsche therefore did think that there could come a time decades hence when its publication would be thinkable, but his friends thought it best not to wait and saw to its publication only four years later, in the fall of 1892, when Nietzsche was in no position to object.[5]

When it appeared in public, it bore the title "Fourth and Final Part." This is a title Nietzsche gave it, and it is in fact final in that it is the last part he wrote. But judged by its content, its being entitled "final" is not nearly as appropriate as another title that Nietzsche gave it. "The Temptation of Zarathustra: an Interlude," a title that he called "more exact," "more descriptive," "its proper title in view of what already transpired and what follows" (letters to Fuchs, 29 July 1888, "An Entr'acte"; to Brandes, 8 January 1888, "Ein Zwischenspiel"). That part IV is more exactly and descriptively entitled an interlude becomes obvious after a consideration of the whole series of events in part IV; but it is also confirmed in miniature by its very beginning and very end, where Zarathustra speaks of his happiness and his work. Although he has achieved his happiness prior to part IV, his work, that which most concerns him, still lies ahead of him at the end of part IV. What had "already transpired" prior to this interlude, parts I–III, can be understood as the achievement of Zarathustra's happiness, his love of life culminating in his willing eternal return. The action of the interlude, "The Temptation of Zarathustra," is self-contained and concludes with Zarathustra's temptation behind him. It concludes, however, on the anticipation of Zarathustra's work, the events associated with the Great Noon.[6] Though that work now lies much closer, part IV is not final in the sense that it includes that work. As an interlude it does not add anything essential to Zarathustra's course, for it falls between the achievement of his happiness and the resumption of his work. It shows how his work could be jeopardized were he to yield to the temptation represented by the superior men of his age. Part IV implies further events to follow, and notes written while Nietzsche was composing it confirm that he was then planning subsequent parts in which Zarathustra would fulfill the promise of his work by descending to bring the Great Noon to mankind.

The oddness of "The Fourth and Final Part," then, is twofold: it appears after the book has already ended once, and it is not itself an ending. The oddness arises from Nietzsche's changing intentions for his Zarathustra. After finishing part III, he referred to his whole book as the "entrance hall" to his philosophy (letters to Overbeck, 8 March and 7 April 1884, and to von Meysenbug, end of March and 1 May 1884). Having shown Zarathustra to have completed the act of entering the teaching of eternal return, Nietzsche for a time thought he would spend "the next six years working out a scheme which I have sketched for my philosophy" (letter to Köselitz, 6 September 1884).[7] But he then came to think that he should entrust the teaching of his philosophy to Zarathustra, who would then be shown becoming what the animals said he was, "the teacher of eternal return." Had this new plan been carried through, Nietzsche's Zarathustra book would have become both the entrance hall and the completed structure of his philosophy. His new intention called for many other parts, but he wrote only one, part IV. Nietzsche abandoned these extensive new plans after finishing part IV, though he did not abandon his plans to set forth the teaching that Zarathustra had been shown entering. Abandoning Zarathustra involved making good on his earlier "Resolution: I want to speak and no longer Zarathustra" (*KGW* VII 25 [277] Spring 1884). Thus began the plans for his own speaking in a book usually projected as bearing the title "The Will to Power," or "Revaluation of All Values."[8]

Thus Spoke Zarathustra as it exists today is therefore a whole (parts I–III) plus a fragment (part IV) of a larger whole that does not exist. Still, despite its confusing position as the "Fourth and Final Part," despite its intrinsic privacy and secrecy which leaves all but a few friends uninvited, despite its not being essential to Zarathustra's happiness or his work, it is pleasant to have part IV. Nietzsche shows in the carnival of part IV, in a manner not at all in keeping with his customary "impish and cheerful vice, courtesy" (*BGE* 284), that the best men of his age fall short of what is necessary for his teaching. Even with them, however, "much is still possible" (IV. 13, §15); even they finally come under Zarathustra's sway and yield to a height that they can recognize if not scale. It is a shame that nobody got this proud joke—just as it is a shame that so many have misunderstood the superior men of part IV as parodied fragments of Nietzsche himself, as if his hard joke on the best of his contemporaries were a joke on himself.

It is more than a joke, of course, for Nietzsche's seriousness, the part of him which knew that he was a destiny and which required that he govern himself with the greatest scrupulousness and rectitude, necessitated his saying in a variety of ways, some more comic than others, that mankind must become "stronger, more evil, more profound." Zarathustra himself says such words in a Dionysian setting (III. 15, §2). Dionysos says them in Nietzsche's next book, in which Nietzsche himself had to feign a flinch in the face of his god's cruel words so as to maintain his standing among the earnest humanitarians, the free spirits for whom the book was written (*BGE* 296). In keeping with Nietzsche's seriousness, part IV shows how and why the superior men of a democratic age lack what is essential for the task that Zarathustra sets for his "children." Part IV is an interlude that demonstrates how necessary hope is to Zarathustra's undertaking. Although much is possible for the best men of his age, part IV points to different men still to come, those whom Zarathustra's teachings have made stronger, more evil, and more profound—for Nietzsche's books are written to inculcate the virtues they propound, to create the audience that does not yet exist and will not exist unless he creates it. "Everything contemporary is importunate" (SE 3), but part IV shows Zarathustra successfully resisting the temptation of his best contemporaries while not surrendering hope for his children.

As a private performance to which only a few friends are invited (and to which the superior men themselves were not invited), part IV contrasts with the public performance it parodies, Wagner's *Parsifal* that "abortion gone mad of a hatred of knowledge, spirit and sensuality" which won the public in July and August of 1882 (NCW, "Wagner as The Apostle of Chastity").[9] The theme of *Parsifal* is redemption through pity, which is achieved by the pure fool Parsifal; that of part IV, the resistance to pity by the already redeemed Zarathustra, who never was a fool (though he had certainly been foolish, as he confesses to the superior men themselves [IV. 13, §1]). In "The Temptation of Zarathustra," pity, far from being redemptive, is the temptation that, if not resisted, would cast him down from his height.

Nietzsche's motto for part IV announces that its most important theme is pity. Pity or compassion for man had been the target in many of Zarathustra's earlier speeches (I. 9, II. 3; see also III. 2, 9), and he had acknowledged it as his own temptation after seeing the failure of his disciples and discovering his own double will (II. 21). In part III, however, he defeats this double will and ascends to his own redemption, and in part IV, now redeemed, he faces and passes the "ultimate test" of pity. This test God had failed, and as a consequence of his failure God died. Zarathustra has this information from the devil, though who is devil and who is God is open to question, judging by Nietzsche's aside to his friends in *Beyond Good and Evil* (37). Zarathustra is not tempted to pity as others pity, he is not tempted to pity the pitiable. He has freed himself of pity for the low through long cultivation of hardness of heart. His final temptation is to pity what is highest in man. Such a temptation to pity is in fact the temptation to despair of man. If the zenith of human greatness is represented by the superior men of part IV, Zarathustra must surrender to the despair to which the Soothsayer had invited him at the beginning of part IV (IV. 2), despair at there being no "blessed isles" where his teaching can find harbor. If Zarathustra's "fishing" with the bait of his happiness (IV. 1) lures only the men of part IV, sufferers who suffer from themselves and not from mankind (IV. 13, §6), then the Soothsayer wins, and Zarathustra's redemption is a useless passion.[10]

It is customary to complain about part IV and to regard it as an embarrassment to those who want to admire Nietzsche's art. It is judged to be an artistic failure in that it carries the book's excesses beyond what is thought acceptable.[11] But this aesthetic judgment deflects attention from the most important difference between part IV and the other parts. In the first three parts Zarathustra is under way to his happiness, to the act of understanding and will recorded in part III. These parts require of him that he engage in motion, that he learn and enact for himself what he had at first regarded as the task of another whose herald he was. Zarathustra's temptation in these parts is to remain at rest, to despair of his ability to do what is necessary when the crowd and then the disciples prove unable to accomplish what his teaching demands of them. At the end of part III, having completed the essential movement to his midnight wisdom, Zarathustra comes to a kind of rest in his happiness. Because the way to his wisdom is now complete, part IV presents him with a different temptation, the temptation to motion, to the movement of being drawn by pity down to the superior men. Zarathustra triumphs in part IV because he hardens his heart and remains at rest.

If there is to be a complaint about the artistic merit of part IV, it must be about the portrayal of the superior men. This is no confederacy of dunces come to put Zarathustra's genius to the test; his temptation has meaning only if these men are seen as the best men of their age.[12] But in the encounters with Zarathustra, they can seem low and laughable, fit objects for Zarathustra's pity and even for ours. The explanation for this apparent failure must be that the perspective on the superior men is that of Zarathustra alone, the highest perspective. Though men of stature—two kings, the last pope, a philosopher, a scientist, a murderer of God, the greatest poet of the age—all appear in order to honor him, they are puny and faulty to Zarathustra, because he brings a new measure of what is high in man. Because we, as privileged viewers of a private party, share for a pleasant moment the view from his place in the order of rank, these tall and lofty men seem low to us too.

The best commentary on this aspect of part IV is Nietzsche's last composition, *Nietzsche Contra Wagner*, that quietest and most serene of all his books, though it deals with the greatest tempest of his life. Four years after *Zarathustra*, Nietzsche here explains his problem of perspective in part IV, the problem of presenting the superior men as high. *Nietzsche Contra Wagner* speaks of "superior men," their "corruption" and "destruction," and of the problem they present for a "born psychologist and unriddler of souls," in that "others venerate, admire, love and transfigure where he has *seen*."[13] The men who appear in part IV are worthy of veneration, and Zarathustra himself wants to venerate and admire them; but he is unable to do so because his perspective from above forces him to see the "whole inner haplessness of the superior man." Zarathustra's temptation parallels Nietzsche's own after his break with Wagner because Wagner was the greatest man he ever met and, Nietzsche thought, perhaps even the greatest man of his age. *Nietzsche Contra Wagner* shows why Zarathustra's ultimate test must be against pity. Part IV of *Zarathustra* is an exhibition of "the hardness and cheerfulness" required of one who always views mankind from above, who, while "seeing" the "exquisite cases" who appear before him, refuses to be drawn down by pity for them. Although the action of part IV must always be seen as a temptation that comes to Zarathustra from below, that "below" must be seen as the humanly high.

ZARATHUSTRA'S HAPPINESS (CHAPTER 1)

Part IV opens quietly with a portrait of a now white-haired Zarathustra in solitude, still awaiting the work he knows must come. The title of the opening chapter, "The Honey Offering," emphasizes a ruse that Zarathustra must sustain with his animals. He has to allege that he is going to make an offering, but his assertion is a mask, which shelters even his animals from what he has become. Though honey is another invention and gift of Dionysos, Zarathustra makes no offering. Now prouder and cleverer than his animals—whom in privacy he refers to as his "pets"—he must curb his speech for their sake and tell them fine lies that preserve the truth for his solitude. Part IV thus opens by calling attention to the necessity that Zarathustra mask himself in his speech as an act of courtesy. He hides his happiness from his animals, just as he had hidden it from men (III. 5). He hides the fact that his happiness has no need to make offerings by allowing his animals to attribute to him a kind of natural piety familiar to them (III. 13). Zarathustra's ruse also hides his *work* from his proud and clever pets. His first words in part IV distinguish in this private way between his happiness and his work and show that, while he has achieved his happiness, his work still lies ahead.

Once Zarathustra has dismissed his animals and climbed to the peak, he can speak in the complete candor permitted by solitude. This speech at the beginning is one of only three private speeches in part IV, the others falling at the middle and the end (IV. 10, 20). In private he corrects the image of honey of the opening chapter; it is not an offering, but the lure of his happiness held out to others. He is a hunter or a fisherman, one with a golden fishing rod (II. 10). Part IV will be an account of superior contemporaries lured by his sweet bait; they are not those whom he aimed to catch, but he overcomes the temptation to despair at the yield, knowing that his happiness will eventually lure the friends he seeks, and that his work will transform them into the followers he needs.

Zarathustra's private speech states that he must eventually descend once more to mankind (see III. 12, §1), though only when his sign appears (IV. 20). In contrast to the opening of part II, Zarathustra is neither patient nor impatient; he knows that his time will come, the time of his *Hazar*, the thousand-year Zarathustra *Reich*.[14]

A MORNING OF ENCOUNTERS (CHAPTERS 2–9)

The first visitor to arrive at Zarathustra's cave on the following day appears first as a shadow cast alongside the shadow Zarathustra casts. Startled at first by his unexpected visitor, Zarathustra eventually welcomes the Soothsayer as a guest at his table, as he had in part II (II. 19). But the Soothsayer does not reciprocate his host's graciousness; he brings the bacillus of his despair to Zarathustra's cave with the intention of infecting Zarathustra. He warns of the arrival of others who will ruin Zarathustra's solitude, as they will ruin the cheerfulness that he affects for his guest. The temptation that the Soothsayer anticipates and over which he will preside is the temptation to despair of ever succeeding in his work, a temptation that could cast him down from the mountain height of his happiness.[15]

The cry of need that they hear affords Zarathustra an opportunity to prove the Soothsayer wrong by finding and welcoming the one who has cried out and by showing him that there is happiness in his cave. He hears the cry of need as the cry of a single man, the superior man, and that misapprehension governs his reaction to each of the men he meets in the next hours, none of whom seem to be a superior man. Only later does he realize that the cry is the collective cry of all the men whom he has met, and that each is a superior man. That realization will move him to pity them and to despair of his teaching (IV. 11).

In his search for the superior man, Zarathustra first meets two kings leading an ass. His startled remark on seeing the royal procession lacks delicacy but serves to elicit the kings' royal reflections on mere good manners. Appropriately, it is the kings who introduce the political theme of the rule of mass man in modern democracy, one of the main themes of part IV. All who appear in part IV are above the mass, but each in his own way bears indelible traces of the elevation of the mass, traces that they will attempt to erase during the ass festival that they devise at the end of the day. The kings have brought the ass for the kingly one whose coming they await, just as the ass was brought to Jesus for his entry into Jerusalem as king.[16] The one they await will be higher than any king; he will be the highest man, the king of kings. In his delight at their words, Zarathustra presents the kings with a blasphemous rhyme that he says is not fit for everyone's ears. But the long-eared one who is present listens in anyway and provides his first commentary (see IV. 12, 17): the ass, symbolic of the mob, brays its accompaniment to the rhyme that fixes the birth of Jesus as the moment at which things started to go awry, ending the rule of kings and making possible eventual rule by the mob.[17] The kings are pleased with Zarathustra's rhyme, and the King on the Right, the more loquacious of the two, reports that Zarathustra's enemies have continued to show his image in a mirror as the image of the devil (see II. 1), but that they themselves have not been repelled by this image because they remember his noble words. The words they admire are the martial words of "On War and Warriors" (I. 10), words that stirred memories of their ancestors' manly heroism. The king speaks eagerly, and his words are more ferocious and bloodthirsty than Zarathustra's ever were. Zarathustra offers no criticism of this interpretation, but only because, minding his manners, he is able to control himself and suppress his ridicule of refined and peaceful kings who speak so eagerly in praise of bloody war.

In "The Leech" Zarathustra steps on a man inadvertently and then proceeds to insult him with a parable meant to calm him. After the man has given an account of himself, reconciliation with Zarathustra becomes possible, but only because Zarathustra curbs his tongue and remains silent about the gulf that separates them. Though he identifies himself as "the Conscientious of Spirit," the man is referred to throughout the chapter as "the one stepped on." He is the embodiment of the scientific and scholarly spirit, strict and single-minded in pursuit of knowledge, even though the object of his pursuit has no grace to charm the senses, and the knowledge he wins no apparent moral or edifying application. He has made one tiny part of the knowable things his kingdom; he is at home here but only here, for he is candid in admitting that what he knows is bounded on all sides by comprehensive ignorance. Still, he takes himself to be secure in what he knows and is proud both of his mastery of his subject and of what that mastery has cost him. This high-minded specialist literally cuts into himself for the sake of knowledge, and he quotes Zarathustra's definition of spirit— "the life that cuts into life"—as his inspiration and justification. Although Zarathustra here refrains from further stepping on the scientific and scholarly spirit, he will later find it necessary to speak out against the conscientious interpretation of science given by its representative who supports himself, after all, with a moral interpretation of his work, for he thinks of it as part of mankind's great project to overcome the primary passion of fear (IV. 15).

The next encounter, with the fifth or central figure invited to his cave, exceeds all the others in subtlety and importance. He here meets not simply an admirer but a rival, whose rivalry can only temporarily be appeased, for it breaks out again later as a contest for those drawn to Zarathustra (IV. 14–16). The rivalry with the Old Sorcerer, who describes himself as the "greatest man of his age," exemplifies the old rivalry between poetry and philosophy by bringing it to a focus in two personages. What begins here is an emblem of Nietzsche's perspective on his encounter with Wagner, Nietzsche contra Wagner being artistically transformed into Zarathustra contra the Old Sorcerer, though Nietzsche ensures that what happens between Zarathustra and the Old Sorcerer turns out better for both.[18]

In this chapter for the first time Zarathustra thinks that the man he meets could be the superior man whose cry of need has sent him on his search. He comes to recognize that he is wrong only at the end of the Old Sorcerer's song. That song is the first of three songs in part IV that reappeared in 1888 in Zarathustra's Songs or Dionysos Dithyrambs. None of the songs of part IV are sung by Zarathustra; two are sung by the Old Sorcerer, while the third, sung by the Shadow, is played on the Old Sorcerer's harp. After hearing the Old Sorcerer's first song, Zarathustra repudiates the singer but not the song, for the words portray his own Dionysian experience.[19] The frenzied antics of the Old Sorcerer, the appearance of poetic possession and inspiration, reproduce the Dionysian ecstasy in which the god possesses his human mouthpiece,[20] but all the while the Old Sorcerer keeps a watchful eye on his audience of one, secretly exulting in his success at drawing out Zarathustra's pity. The song sings of an unwelcome possession, a capture by a superior force that cannot be resisted. The images of the song all refer to the inexorable and terrifying coming of Dionysos, the hunter, the torturer, the hangman god, who comes without word, without interpreting his coming, but who comes to possess totally the one to whom he appears. The song achieves its greatest intensity at the end, where Dionysos's appearance is finally embraced, though its terror is undiminished. In *Dionysos Dithyrambs* the song is entitled "Lament of Ariadne" and is the climactic seventh song that affirms the coming of Dionysos to Ariadne and affirms the love of life in its suffering.

Both Zarathustra's accusations and the Old Sorcerer's defense make use of Zarathustra's earlier critique of the poet (II. 17), the greatest poet thus conceding the truth of the critique. In their dialogue, as in his song, the Old Sorcerer cannot avoid donning masks of beauty or deference in order to charm Zarathustra. But Zarathustra, vulnerable to deception because he cannot afford to be cautious (II. 21), is ultimately immune to the Old Sorcerer's magic because he knows that his every appearance is merely calculated and that he is only his appearances. Subdued by this recognition of his pitiable state, the Old Sorcerer yields to Zarathustra's unmasking, but his yielding is itself calculated, in that it aims to evoke Zarathustra's pity for a condition no longer subject to remedy. If he is nothing but his masks, his contempt at being what he is is genuine, or so alleges this man of many guiles who must suspect that Zarathustra too is a penitent of the spirit, like himself, however much he may fear that Zarathustra harbors something unalterable the like of which he has never known. Zarathustra apparently accepts the confession of self-contempt and compliments the Old Sorcerer for possessing the youngest virtue, honesty. But he does not look into the eye of the Old Sorcerer, the eye that can strike green lightning, when he speaks the words that honor him for aspiring to something great. In the long silence that followed, he then closed his eyes completely to appearances. Finally he speaks with politeness and guile, feigning acceptance of the Old Sorcerer's final pose, the pose that flatters Zarathustra by calling him a "saint of knowledge" (I. 10). He invites the Old Sorcerer to continue his search for greatness in his cave and to ask advice of his animals, those proud and clever animals whose advice he himself no longer seeks. Zarathustra says that he has never yet found a great man and questions whether the modern age could cast up such a man; even if it could, it would not be someone whom the age itself would acknowledge as great— he says to the one who claims greatness and is acknowledged by the age as great. Mere boys can deflate that empty greatness, he says; did that old fool think that he could tempt Zarathustra? Zarathustra's guileful speech does him good, and he leaves the Old Sorcerer having transformed his anger into laughter.

In the next three chapters (IV. 6–8) Zarathustra meets men with profound complaints against Christianity. In the first he sees a priestly nature whom he would prefer once again to pass by (II. 4), not suspecting that

he is the last Pope and that God is dead for him too. Neither does the last
Pope recognize Zarathustra, even though he is searching for him. The last
Pope is a servant who is lost without his master; he experiences no liberation in the absence of his master, only defenselessness in a hostile world.
While seeking the last remnants of piety in order to comfort himself, he
has discovered that even the old saint of the prologue is dead; now he
seeks Zarathustra, whose piety is of a different sort. Having identified
themselves to each other, these two old theologians of the death of God
at first compete over who is the more godless, Zarathustra having identified
himself as godless as if to refute the Pope's attribution of piety to him. The
old Pope proves himself more godless in one respect at least, in that Zarathustra, having never suffered from the death of God, has never needed
to be consoled or compensated as has his faithful servant. Still, the Pope
is not one in whose teaching of godlessness Zarathustra can rejoice, at
least not immediately (III. 5, §3). In yielding to the superior godlessness of
the last Pope, Zarathustra seeks to learn from him how God died: is it true
that he died of pity? Selectively quoting the motto of Part IV, he graciously
suppresses the source of this opinion, the devil, but the Pope does not
answer until Zarathustra has encouraged him, the bereaved, to feel free
to speak ill of the departed. Cheered by Zarathustra's permission, the servant reports on his lord's passing. His report is true, but being the report
of a servant and of a servant blind in one eye, its perspective is faulty, and
it lacks depth perception. Fully a monotheist, with a monoculist way of
seeing and explaining, he does not know that "when gods die they die
many kinds of death," and he learns only later that with gods, with immortal
ones, death is always only a prejudice (IV. 18, §1). Nevertheless, the servant
had spied out the secret ways of his secretive lord and now brings to word
his long-harbored loathing. Having surrendered his will to this lord and
master, he came to discover that his master had grown decrepit and had
surrendered his own will to mastery long before he actually expired. For
the servant without a will of his own, God died of his decrepitude, requiring
no murderer. Zarathustra the godless also feels free to speak ill of the dead
and refines some charges that Nietzsche had already expressed in *Daybreak*
(91) giving the old Pope good reasons for thinking himself well rid of a
master who held his servants blameable for his own failures and who took
revenge on his own, for such a God offends good taste. The last Pope apparently hears better than he sees, for he detects some god or other behind
Zarathustra's harsh words against his dead master. Having all his life seen
God as secret cause, he now detects in Zarathustra's piety and honesty
the voice of some god who will take Zarathustra "beyond good and evil."
The last Pope then conducts a service, a laying on of hands, in which he
blesses Zarathustra as one who will bless. Zarathustra acknowledges his
incapacity to remedy the Pope's sadness, for it will abide until the resurrection of his God—but the remedy comes later in the day when the
Pope's God is resurrected, taking upon himself the form of an ass.

The death of God finds another adequate explanation in the next chapter, in which the Ugliest Man declares himself to be God's murderer. The Ugliest Man is ugly not because he murdered God; rather, he murdered God because he was ugly and could not tolerate a God who insisted on seeing the ugliest, pitying it, and reminding its victim of its presence. " 'Is it true that God is present *everywhere?*' a little girl asked her mother; 'I think that's indecent'—a hint for philosophers!" (GS, preface of 1886). With a similar sense of decency and pride, but more to hide, the Ugliest Man sees God's offense as even more serious and takes his revenge on the shameless witness by murdering him. When Zarathustra first sees and hears the Ugliest Man, he too is struck down by pity, but he does not admire his pity as a virtue, even though he is vulnerable to it. Instead he desires to be hard of heart and to cultivate his sense of shame at shameful ugliness, for, as the Ugliest Man says, great misfortune, great ugliness, and great failure need to be respected as what they are, not simply pitied. Though Zarathustra has seen his ugliness, he is spared the revenge against the witness by his shame at what he witnesses; shame honors the Ugliest Man, whereas pity shames him. The Ugliest Man's long speech confirms Zarathustra's teaching on the danger of pity from the perspective of the one pitied. He prefers the Valley of the Snake's Death to the crowd of virtuous pitiers. In his extraordinary ugliness he knows himself to stand above the crowd that has been taught the virtue of pity by Jesus, a teacher he derides. While he well knows the uses of pity, he virtuously refuses them. His murderous deed is a humanitarian blow struck on behalf of mankind, which cannot endure the existence of such a witness. Zarathustra recommends that he speak to the proudest and wisest of the animals and learn from them; the Ugliest Man thereupon attends not only to Zarathustra's animals, but also to the dumbest and most dogmatic of animals, the ass, for it is he who devises the ass festival, finding thereby a way to comfort himself. Of all the men Zarathustra meets that morning, only the Ugliest Man persuades him to think that perhaps he is the superior man.

In the next chapter Zarathustra encounters a reformed version of the "Sermonizer on the Mount" who no longer addresses the poor but the cows, for theirs is the kingdom of heaven.[21] The Voluntary Beggar, the one who wants to beg, desires to learn happiness on earth from the contented cows and imagines that they are about to address their secret to him. But he is also a seeker of Zarathustra, for he believes that he can learn happiness on earth from him too. It is his own peaceable teaching that, "unless we return and become as cows we shall never enter the kingdom of heaven," and "verily what would it profit a man if he gained the whole world and did not learn this one thing: how to chew the cud."[22] But he has nobility, for above all he wants to overcome his revulsion at the world, and he interprets both the sacred cows and Zarathustra as having succeeded in this regard, whereas he himself is filled with revulsion and rancor against the very ones in whom he had once placed his hopes, for the poor have now become the mob. In this way he assents to Nietzsche's account of the religion founded in his name and repudiates the apostle Paul, whose interpretation of him replaced the glad tidings with the worst of tidings, a movement of peace with one of revenge (A 42; see D 68).

The last encounter is with a special man, for however much the others might admire Zarathustra and respect his teaching, this man is Zarathustra's Shadow, having become his follower and attempted as best he could to live by his teaching. For its sake he has abandoned everything and undertaken great journeys, which he describes in his speech. But his wanderings have ended in self-contempt and lament, for they have not taken him home though he has always yearned for home. Adherence to Zarathustra's teaching has made him a nihilist, but not a cheerful nihilist, for he fears that he will never find a home, and he has no desire to always wander. Zarathustra had tried to escape this encounter with the one who has been made a nihilist by his teaching, but he finally concluded that he could not outrun his Shadow—just when his Shadow was growing weak from the exertion of following him, a weakness that could have turned to despair. Hounded by the nihilistic shadow his work casts, Zarathustra recognizes that he will be unable to escape the conclusion that his teaching is nothing more than a "rebound from 'God is truth' to the fanatical faith 'All is false' " (KGW VIII 2 [127] = WP 1). He can for now offer no helpful advice, for the Shadow knows as well as Zarathustra does the dangers he faces. Calling him a "free spirit" and a "wanderer,"[23] Zarathustra can only warn him that he may bring his wanderings to a close too early and find himself at home in some narrow dogmatism. Both know his problem to be the lack of a goal for his wanderings, but can Zarathustra teach him a goal? He makes no such promise when he invites him to his cave, promising only a rest and a home for this evening.

NOONTIDE SOLITUDE (CHAPTER 10)

At the center of part IV, for a brief moment at midday, Zarathustra's solitude is portrayed. What comes to light is a duality, an inclination in two directions, toward his happiness and his work. Here, as at the beginning and the end of part IV, his solitude is revealed as a repetition of the happiness achieved at the end of part III, with the difference that in part IV no effort of overcoming is involved, no striving beyond the peak earlier and definitively achieved. There is nothing here that was not in the songs at the end of part III, for there is no progressing beyond that happiness, nor can it be diminished. Here, as in part III, Zarathustra's work is simply what falls to him as a result of the achievement of his happiness. He was sent on his way that morning by his work, his search for the superior man. In the course of that search he had in fact encountered superior men, but without recognizing them as such; now at noon he experiences a moment of relief from the morning's strange adventures. The images of "At Midday" are uniformly Dionysian and draw frequently on images employed in the previous parts to depict Dionysian perfection.[24] Under a gnarled tree embraced by a laden grapevine, Zarathustra speaks out of an intoxication not induced by wine. He addresses his soul as a ship that has crossed the sea and now lies at rest in a quiet bay, bound easily to the earth, loyal to the earth, its journey forever over. His soul desires to sing, but he opposes her and instructs her in what he has learned about happiness. His soul remains still until he tries to rouse himself from his momentary blissful sleep in order to resume his task. She speaks of a contrary desire to remain at rest and, languid and peaceful, enjoy the world's perfection. In this dialogue, witnessed only by the silent heavens, Zarathustra reveals himself, even in his perfection and the perfection of the world, as not a simple unity of soul and spirit, not even a seamless harmony of parts. In his transparency to himself he remains in part female soul, tempted to remain at rest, at home in his happiness, and in part masculine spirit, restless to undertake his work. Furthermore, the perfection of the world includes the anticipation of death, the acknowledgment of mortality, in which the abyss of noonday drinks the drop of dew back into itself. Even in the ecstatic vision of noonday, Zarathustra affirms the division and mortality of man and that he is subject to the return of melancholy. His perfection includes imperfection.[25]

AN EVENING OF ENTERTAINMENT (CHAPTERS 11–19)

Only when Zarathustra gives up on his fruitless search for the superior man and returns to his cave in the late afternoon does he learn to his astonishment that the ones "passed by" that morning were themselves superior men. When he finally speaks he manages only the most ambiguous welcome for those who have sought him out. The loquacious King on the Right answers in courtly politeness, praising him and promising better men to come, but Zarathustra's dismay is not abated, even though what the king says and the fact that a king says it bespeak a success unmatched by anything that he has yet achieved among men. He shrinks from the veneration both reported and offered by the king and makes it clear that it is not for them that he waits on his mountain. The rebuff contained in his first statement is partially obscured by the gracious witticism of the King on the Left, but he continues in an intemperate way to describe their shortcomings. Finally, in the presence of those who have come, he dreams of those who might have come, his "children," those whom he imagines have become "laughing lions" since his departure at the end of part II.

The grim Soothsayer, his early morning words of despair seemingly vindicated by the events of the day, now lightheartedly interrupts Zarathustra's speech to set in motion the preparations for "The Last Supper." His announcement alarms Zarathustra's animals, for they have brought home too little to feed even the Soothsayer. The King on the Left announces that the kings can supply wine for all. But Zarathustra is "a born water drinker" and the Voluntary Beggar refuses wine; therefore, because bread is lacking, both Zarathustra and the Voluntary Beggar partake of this last supper without bread and wine. Noting the lack of bread, Zarathustra quotes the words of Jesus that "man does not live by bread alone," but he replaces Jesus' next words, "but by every word that proceeds out of the mouth of God,"[26] with his own words, "but also by the flesh of good lambs of which I have two." Thus easing the anxiety of his domestic animals, he prepares to have the traditional Passover lamb killed for this last supper as well, except that here there are two lambs, and they are prepared with many spices and fruit, all of which the Voluntary Beggar refuses in favor of his customary seeds and water. Still, he shows himself capable of participating in the convivial mood, jokingly calling Zarathustra a glutton. Zarathustra in turn permits him his peculiarities; after all, he has no dietary law for everyone, his way not being The Way. But, in response to the stern asceticism of the Voluntary Beggar and to his embarrassment, he says that those who are of Zarathustra's kind must take the best for themselves, the best food, the purest sky, the strongest thoughts, the loveliest women. The King on the Right seems not to be made for joking, and his ponderous praise of Zarathustra for not being an ass receives its appropriate comment when the ass brays his "Ye-a."

At the last supper with his twelve (counting his own two animals and the ass) Zarathustra delivers a long after-dinner speech entitled "The Superior Man" (IV. 13). With its twenty short sections, it invites comparison with the thirty short sections of "On the Old and New Tablets" (III. 12). Whereas the latter was addressed to true but imaginary followers, the present speech is addressed to actual men who, though superior, are not the longed-for followers, and for whom his expectations are not high; whereas the earlier speech was addressed to young men, this one is addressed to old men whose ways are set and who themselves judge their ways to be failures; whereas that was freely given to those he sought out, this is given as the courteous act of a host to those who have sought him out; whereas that was an invitation to reckless acts for the sake of mankind, this counsels caution to those whose thought is only of themselves; whereas that ended on flying and on hardness, this ends on "how much is still possible," on laughing and dancing.

To this audience of old men, the first audience that Zarathustra has had since his own hair grew white, he recounts his foolish mistake at forty in bringing his message to the marketplace. In relating the events of the prologue and repeating all its main themes, he seems to be repeating his mistake of the prologue in addressing the wrong men. But this time he knows his audience, that they are not the kind of followers whom he ultimately seeks because they suffer from themselves and not from mankind (6). He counsels a reasonable limit on their aspirations, not only for their own sake, but more because their failure brings a bad name to aspiration itself (8). In being superior men they should have the pride to know that the very highest escapes them (*BGE* 213).[27] Honesty with themselves is their necessary, but rare, virtue, and that honesty does not preclude, but rather presumes, a healthy mistrust and a skill at lying, especially when it comes to keeping secret one's reasons or grounds. Zarathustra reveals the ground for keeping one's grounds secret: neither the mob nor the learned who grind everything small can respect worthy grounds. Those hearing this advice might well expect that he too practices what he counsels and keeps his grounds secret, and the difference between this speech and his speeches in solitude confirm that suspicion. Zarathustra's warnings (10–12) culminate in a repetition of the warning not to be virtuous beyond their powers (13). For their sake he tempers the instructions to "Firstlings" that he had prepared for his followers (III. 12, §6) and warns that the superior men should take care not to be "Lastlings." While acknowledging their failures, he counsels encouragement until there are no more grounds for encouragement, until mankind itself has turned out to be a failure (14). His encouragement of them (beginning at 15) brings his speech to a fitting, uplifting close, but one that assumes their irremediable fixation on the little perspective of their own wounded selves. That they are not the measure of man should be a consolation for them, as should the fact that there are many small good perfect things that have turned out well and that give delight. These gloomy men are finally to separate themselves from the teachings of a man of sorrows who cursed what he could not love.[28] No man of sorrows with a crown of thorns, Zarathustra ends by crowning himself with a wreath of roses and leading them into dance and laughter.[29] But in his apparent gaiety, he has kept his grounds secret, for, having invited the superior men to laugh and dance in his cave, he must flee into the fresh night air to escape them and the stifling air that they bring.

Meanwhile, taking advantage of Zarathustra's absence—his only complete absence from any event or speech in the book—the Old Sorcerer revives his rivalry with Zarathustra, the rivalry that failed when Zarathustra was his audience. Now alone with the superior men, this consummate actor alleges that he is about to suffer possession by an evil demon opposed to Zarathustra from the ground up. Alleging at the same time that he loves the now absent Zarathustra but that it is futile to attempt to resist possession by this evil demon, he looks cunningly around him twice; he is as much in control of himself now as when he sang the Dionysian song by which he attempted to snare Zarathustra. This song by this poet of many voices sabotages Zarathustra by a very clever means; addressing those well disposed to Zarathustra because he seems to promise them a saving truth, the poet avows that Zarathustra is only a poet. Diminishing him to the level of "Only fool! Only poet!" by implying that there is only poetry, only sorcery, he elevates himself, for who is the better sorcerer? Zarathustra is simply a sorcerer who has charmed himself into believing that he has escaped the fate of all sorcerers and can offer the superior men the saving truth they seek. If there is only poetry, if there is no text but only interpretation, it's time the superior men freed themselves, even from the true reading promised by Zarathustra. No wonder they all fly like birds into the net of his cunning—all except Conscientiousness Himself, the scholar who knows that the grounds of this deconstruction of Zarathustra must be false, because he knows that he knows the brain of the leech.

Before beginning his song, the Old Sorcerer notes that evening is now coming to all things, even the best things, even to Zarathustra who had once been like the dawning of a new day for them. In the first and last parts of the song he addresses his heart, whereas in the central part he is himself addressed by the all-seeing evening sun. The first and last parts begin with the same words, but the accusatory speech of the setting sun has changed everything, and the singer ends in resignation and sadness, having surrendered to the sun's accusations which reduce the truth-seeker of the opening stanza to a mere poet obliged to lie even to himself. The truth-seeker is neither mild nor innocent; he is turned to cruelty by an inner rage. Abandoning everything solid, everything sacred, he becomes a beast of prey, a cat, an eagle, pouncing on its unsuspecting quarry and tearing to pieces the god in man, laughing as he tears. When evening returns in the final part, it brings a murderous moon, a vengeful sickle that slices off the luxurious growths of the day, leaving them to sink lifeless into dark night. Himself a severed plant, the singer sinks into banishment from truth, "only fool, only poet."

Sung by an evil demon opposed to Zarathustra, the song laments the impossibility of any true teaching, even Zarathustra's. But the conscientious man of science and scholarship springs to the defense of truth. This ascetic, amusical Socratic, a modern, small-scale manifestation of the rational optimism that insists that all being be thinkable, insists in an impassioned speech not only that truth is possible, but that Zarathustra's truth is identical with the truth of scientific knowledge—and Zarathustra enters the cave in time to eavesdrop on this speech in his defense. Wrenching the harp away from the Old Sorcerer, he makes himself the defender of civility against the new barbarians who have abandoned the sure ground of scientific truth. A severe ascetic and moralist, the leech expert sees the others as narcissists, sensualists, aged lotus-eaters and flower children, who incautiously indulge the seething cauldron of desires that he suspects to be at the heart of man, suspecting it to be at his own heart. He holds the instinctual renunciation that he suffers to be virtuous since it is in the service of something higher, modern democratic civilization. The first outburst of the scientific conscience draws a quiet rebuke from the Old Sorcerer, who is enjoying his success at having charmed the other superior men into his net, and who now wants quiet in order that his message sink home to those more receptive to it than this ascetic scholar who lacks the spirit of music. But Conscientiousness Himself had discovered how different he was from the other superior men in their earlier conversations in the cave, and he now interprets that difference to them. Thinking themselves free, they fall prey to the lower passions that civilization has sublimated into something finer and more spiritual. Having become lax and flabby as guardians of the hard-won fruits of civilization, they risk a return to the swamp of superstition and magic, from which science has delivered man. The Old Sorcerer's doctrine of poetry threatens to demolish the enlightened civilization constructed by the long and arduous progress of science in its quest for certainty. History is progress and in its great march passes from religion to metaphysics to science. Although the human in man may spring from base origins, from fear, the fundamental passion directed at beasts without and beasts within, man transforms that fear into the one virtue that counts, science. From base origins comes the nobility that is science, the instrument of domestication or civility that tames wild nature by mastering it without and within. As the moral spokesman of civilizing science, sublimated, spiritualized fear, the conscientious man must protest what he sees in his colleagues, for he fears a rebarbarization of man, an upsurge of the passions that destroyed Orpheus and his work. Much rather this civilization with all its discontents than an eruption of the beast in man.

Unaware that he is on trial before the superior men and thus unable to speak against the subversion of his thought by the sorcerer, Zarathustra can and must repudiate the moralist defense of both his thought and science itself offered by the conscientious spirit of modern science and scholarship. His ambitions for philosophy's leadership of science depend on his refuting this view of the end of science. The ground of both Zarathustra's thought and science is not fear but courage; they share a courage grown subtle and spirited, a spirit of adventure and joy in the unknown, a spirit expressed by Nietzsche in a note: "For many, abstract thinking is toil; for me, on good days, it is feast and frenzy" (KGW VII 34 [130]). Zarathustra's praise of science began with him throwing flowers, and it builds up to the climactic but unreported word *science* in a rhetorical repetition of the scientist's speech. His praise of science is drowned out for the collected company by their desire to praise him, for, not inappropriately, and in confirmation of his own relation to science, they shout "Zarathustra" where he shouted "Science." In this way they exhibit the aptness of his earlier parable of man and dog, which had properly offended the scientist (IV. 4): how little it would take for the one stepped on to become reconciled to the one whom he at first, in fear and surprise, perceived to be a powerful enemy because he had been incautious or unattentive; how little it would take for science to pass into the care of the new philosophy.[30]

The shouts and laughter of the superior men lift the heavy cloud of melancholy from their midst. But the Old Sorcerer, desiring to hold his advantage, speaks cleverly, attributing the newly lightened mood to the departure of his evil demon. Again he alleges that he has no control over it: "Did *I* create him and the world?" The answer is yes, he did create the evil demon just as he created the melancholy world that the demon brought. Now that they are of good cheer, he invites them to be of good cheer, as if he created that world too and did so while Zarathustra was angry—"Just look at him, he bears me a grudge." His final words cunningly aim to create the world of their response to Zarathustra by raising suspicions about him: whereas Zarathustra will overcome his grudge and come to love his enemy, the Old Sorcerer will take revenge for that—on his friends, the assembled company of superior men. Although his friends applaud this cunning speech, Zarathustra acts as if he has something to make up for and apologize for; he shakes hands with his friends, silently refuting the Old Sorcerer.

Only the Shadow speaks in the following chapter, and only because he fears that melancholy will return, should Zarathustra again leave them at the mercy of the Old Sorcerer; for, although the Shadow knows what the Old Sorcerer is, he is no match for him, and without Zarathustra he too would be possessed by this evil demon. Still, he succeeds in bringing his own good cheer, for his song of parody and mockery induces all the superior men to laugh at the Old Sorcerer. Played on the Old Sorcerer's harp, which the Shadow has rescued from the amusical scholar, the song of the Shadow transports these Europeans far from their European cave by ridiculing the Old Sorcerer for one of his worst roles, that of "apostle of chastity."[31] The Shadow is a wanderer who, like Zarathustra, has "seen many lands" (I. 15), and he has a nose able to test and judge many kinds of air, though it is less trained than Zarathustra's, for the cave air belongs to the purest that he has tasted. Though prey to a threatening melancholy and given to gloom, the Shadow sings a song that secures a new mood of good cheer and prepares the way for the ass festival. The song mocks a "good European" seated in a desert oasis attended by maidens of Paradise. The European's words praise chastity by denouncing sensuality—yet another European curse on one of the three most accursed things (III. 10, §2). In this paradise there is even a maiden with the name that Goethe gave to his own Persian lover in *West-östlichen Divan*, but it is a measure of this European's paradise that his culminating advice to the lovely and pliable Suleika is: "Be a man." Unlike Goethe, unlike Hafiz, he wants his women moral, manly, fully dressed, lest the desert he fears invade his paradise, a sensual, sexual paradise that he reads puritanically.[32]

The song begins and ends with a line that parodies European preaching of chastity;[33] "The desert grows, woe to him who harbors deserts within!" is said by the European to be a worthy beginning, "solemn in an African way." But it is solemn only in a European way, for the European loves his moral superiority. But his morality causes ignorance of his actual situation: while enjoying an oasis surrounded by a desert, his perverse moral reading of his situation interprets the oasis as chastity and the desert as sensuality, whereas all the images of his speech suggest that the oasis is sensuality and the desert chastity. He likens his being swallowed by the oasis to Jonah's being swallowed by the whale and even wonders if the whale could have been as pleasant for Jonah as his haven is for him—but he doubts it, for he is a European and it is European to be skeptical. Continuing the sexual imagery that he employs in unwitting parody of himself, he likens himself to a ripe date not yet tasted, but assailed by little flying insects, still smaller and more sinful wishes involuntarily called forth by the presence of Dudu and Suleika. Still, the air of this paradise is as good as ever fell from the moon. Is this an accident, or could it be that it comes from wantonness as the old poets supposed? As a doubting European and a moralist, he must doubt that dangerous supposition. He looks at the palm tree and considers its ways; it seems to him to sway rhythmically at the hips, like a dancer tempting the one who watches to do the same. But instead of dancing, he falls into the grip of a saddening thought, for is the palm tree not like a dancer who has lost a leg? In vain has he searched in the secrets of her skirts for that other leg. It is gone, gone forever. Did it flee in fear of an angry lion? Was it gnawed off by that beast or broken in pieces? The thought seems too much to bear but the courageous European, trained in the view that life is hard to bear, gathers his strength in order to rally the courage of the gentle hearts of Dudu and Suleika: "Do not weep," he says to Dudu; "Be a man," he says to Suleika. But those injunctions may not be enough. Perhaps what is needed is "something bracing," and he gathers himself for a grave exhortation in the last stanza. "Blow, blow again bellows of virtue." "Roar once more, roar morally." Thus, this European who can, like Luther, "do no other, so help me God," pours forth the denunciation that will elevate and edify and turn maidens into men: "The desert grows: woe to him who hides deserts within!"[34]

This song is followed as it must be followed by tumult and laughter, even from the melancholy superior men who are themselves stern Europeans schooled in doubt and moralism. Zarathustra is pleased by their gaiety, but his approval is tempered by aversion to the tumult they cause, and he finds it necessary to flee the cave again. Having been completely absent for the Old Sorcerer's song, absent although an eavesdropper for the Conscientious Spirit's speech, and only reluctantly present for the Shadow's song—presence and absence illustrating his relationship to the speeches—Zarathustra is now outside again, but his thoughts are on the superior men and what he hears transpiring inside. His interpretation of what he hears and smells reveals once more that he is not hard to fool, although this time his hope attributes to what he hears not too much but too little. At first he correctly understands the superior men to be taking his way to convalescence. But then he is fooled by the most striking event of the day, the ass festival. When the cave grows still and he smells incense burning, he peers in on the superior men and sees a festival that he interprets as an act of piety. They have devised a festival for themselves, as he thought they would, but, to his astonishment, it is a religious festival in which they kneel before the ass.[35] The Ugliest Man, who is responsible for devising the whole festival, also provides the litany for their collective worship, eight stanzas of new theology, showing why the ass is worthy of

all praise and honor and wisdom and thanks and glory and strength.[36]
The ass quite literally bears their burdens and takes upon himself the form
of a servant;[37] he is patient and never says no. He is trainable and tractable,
for whoever loves his God chastizes him.[38] He finds the world he has created
good and says nothing but yes to it,[39] thus he is seldom found wrong. He
is a rebuke to no man, for he is unpretentious, and if he has spirit at all,
he successfully hides it. But everyone believes in his long ears, or wants
to, for despite hearing everything, he denies nothing. He has created the
world after his own image,[40] as dumb as possible. He is no moralist whose
way is straight,[41] and he cares little about what men take to be straight or
crooked, for his kingdom is "beyond good and evil." He turns no one away,
neither beggars nor kings, and he does better than merely suffering the
little children to come unto him,[42] because to the sinners who entice him
he consents.[43] He is known by the fruits he eats, since as far as he is concerned, men can well gather figs of thistles,[44] it being the wisdom of a god
to be pleased with a thistle.

At this point in the litany, which could have gone further, Zarathustra,
braying louder than the ass, leaps into their midst and pulls them up from
the ground. His words are exactly the wrong words and reveal the misunderstanding that has caused him to lose control of himself. He attempts
to shame them, to make them feel mortified at the thought that someone
might have been watching and caught them in this act. Zarathustra the
shocked moralist attempts to shame the very men who suffer from shame
and self-contempt. But they are unrepentant and do not submit to his
attempt to humiliate them. Instead, the five he singles out for special in-
terrogation provide such roguish answers, such wry and buffoonish answers that Zarathustra is finally able to understand the true nature of their
festival and to answer in kind.

His first question is for the old Pope: how could he of all people, God's
vicar on earth, reconcile himself to the worship of an ass? The Pope, alleging
superior enlightenment on matters concerning God, offers a maxim whose
wisdom he assumes will become evident to Zarathustra the godless: "Better
to worship God in this form than in no form at all." His second reason,
his insight into the danger of teaching that "God is a spirit," shows that
he renounces his old form of worship not in the name of just any worship
but in the name of this superior form; rather an ass than the God who is
a spirit, because the ass is palpable and cannot threaten a believer like
himself with the terror of unbelief.

Zarathustra's question to the Shadow asks how he can consider himself
a free spirit when he engages in such worship. The Shadow's answer is
fittingly evasive: it's not his fault that the old God lives, it's the fault of the
Ugliest Man; besides, says the Shadow who has seen many lands, with
gods, death is always only a prejudice.

To the Sorcerer, Zarathustra says: "What you did was a stupidity: how
could you, you clever one, do something so stupid," to which he receives

what is perhaps the finest answer of all, an answer worthy of the greatest artist: "O Zarathustra, you are right, it was a stupidity and it was hard enough to do it." He who can create worlds has not created this world of ass worship; he has yielded to the creativity of the Ugliest Man. But in doing so, he has shown how he yields to the age that has created the worship of an ass or of the mob. In a setting of ass worship, the modern worship that has replaced Christianity, the Old Sorcerer does what is necessary. He is no more disposed to believe in such stupidities than are the rest of the superior men, but he knows at least as well as anyone else how to flatter the ass, however stupid it may be and however difficult it may be for him to do it. In this way Nietzsche relieves his Old Sorcerer of the necessity of having to "sink down, helpless and broken, before the Christian cross." He is allowed instead to exemplify Nietzsche's preferred, but impossible, reading of *Parsifal*, the wishful thinking that it is intended as a joke, an epilogue and satyr play in which Wagner says farewell in a manner worthy of himself (*NCW*, "How I Broke with Wagner," 1; "Wagner as Apostle of Chastity," 2,3).

In turning to Conscientiousness Himself, Zarathustra asks if his stern conscience is not aroused against such worship. On the contrary, he replies; worship of the ass does his conscience good. His answer is analytic and gives precise grounds, for in his carefully considered way he does not proceed without his reasons. His reasoning in defense of the new piety shows that he can mimic other famous wise men who have not believed in the people's gods but whose eccentricities have been tolerated by the people because their reasoning serves the people's superstitions (II. 8). While quietly remaining an atheist, he finds that God in this new form is most worthy of being believed in, and for two reasons. First, according to the pious of all ages, God is eternal; thus, having time, he should take his time; thus, he should be as slow and dumb as possible. Second, what has too much spirit might well become infatuated with stupidity and folly. His own spiritedness forces him to cut into his own life and deny himself such comforts, but, to take a text from Zarathustra (IV. 4), if the wisest proceed in the crookedest ways, as the evidence shows, then Zarathustra himself could become an ass and fall into some dogmatism.

Zarathustra turns finally to the Ugliest Man, the one who has devised the festival and benefits most from it, as his transformed, sublime appearance makes clear. Both the questioner and the questioned show themselves to be tricksters. Zarathustra's questions assume that the newly awakened God is the God murdered by the Ugliest Man. "O Zarathustra, you are a rogue!" says the Ugliest Man, implying that Zarathustra knows far better than he does whether *that* God still lives or lives again or is completely dead. One thing the Ugliest Man does know, although this too is known better by Zarathustra, for it was he who taught it to the Ugliest Man: one kills best by laughter (I. 7). What Zarathustra should know even better than God's murderer is that though that God is dead, he still lives, for when gods die, men play with their shadows in caves for centuries (*GS* 108), and that to drive off those gruesome shadows, to leave forever the Valley of the Snake's Death, laughter is necessary. The superior men are still sick from Christianity and its dead God, and they need such parody, such incantations and spells, as an exorcism to purge themselves of its melancholy, long, withdrawing roar. The Ugliest Man continues his murder of God, but now he may well be cured of his need for revenge, for his gleeful litany that kills by laughter transforms him and makes him sublime.

The litany, together with the five answers given to Zarathustra's in-credulous questions, teach even Zarathustra a lesson in death-of-God the-ology. Out of a kind of religious cruelty these melancholy men had sacrificed God for "the stone, stupidity, gravity, fate, the nothing"; but having fallen prey to pessimism and melancholy, they have now achieved, if only for a moment, in their mocking worship of the ass, something of the opposite, world-affirming ideal that expresses itself in self-affirmation (*BGE* 55, 56). Their new god, everyone's new god in the age that they live in, bears even them no grudge; in seeing what kind of god they need, they see what kind of men they are and the ways in which they are laughable. As superior men and unbelievers, they well know that their age bows down to the ass, to the dumbest and slowest, to the grayest and poorest in spirit, to that which least discriminates, which says yes to anything. Having despaired of their democratic age, which subjects itself to the standard of the mob, they are able, in the good air of Zarathustra's cave, to transform their despair into a festival of derision. The present religion—"and if you listen closely the only religion preached today" is the religion of pity (*BGE* 222)—has its hold over them broken by the evil incantations they devise. No wonder Zarathustra is now pleased with them, for their apparent abasement, at first so horrifying to him, hides a pride that can only be enhanced by their having put one over on their superior host. Easily fooled, because too grave in matters of religion, he does not have to take his stick to those who fooled him this time, but rather, is schooled by their wry buffoonery to take plea-sure in their blasphemy as a belated participant; although he enters their festival late, he enters as its crowning participant, a role that they are pleased to permit him. Speaking in praise and acceptance of them, calling them "my friends" for the first time, he tells them not to forget their festival, nor that they invented it in his cave. He assumes the fitting, ascendant role in keeping with their festival: "Do this in remembrance of me."[45]

Now that they have become friends, Zarathustra admits them, as far as is possible, to the acme of fellowship with him, the celebration of life in eternal return. Together they leave the cave and go out into the night for the final song of part IV, "The Nightwanderer's Song."[46] But before the song, "the most astounding event" on this whole astounding day takes place, for the Ugliest Man speaks to exhibit the gratitude that enables even him to affirm life. For the sake of this one day he is, for the first time in his life, content to have lived his life. Even he, through the festival in Zarathustra's cave, has become so well disposed toward himself and his life on earth that he is able to repeat for himself the words of Zarathustra's courage: "Was that life? Well then, once more!" (III. 2, §1). The one who invented the litany for the ass festival now invites his friends to join him in his affirmation of life, and the narration here takes on the style of a teller of ancient tales relating a now famous event from once upon a time about which many apocryphal tales have been told.

When he hears the great affirmation of the Ugliest Man, Zarathustra almost swoons and his thoughts take him back to the songs that brought part III to its climax and close. Now, as the bell once more tolls midnight, the nightwanderer relates the song of the midnight bell and becomes for the superior men what the animals had said he would become, the teacher of eternal return. In this song mankind is called to attention (3), for the hour come round at last heralds a new task, but "who has heart enough for it?—who shall be be lord of the earth? Who will say: thus shall you run, you big and little rivers?" (4). The hour that presents this daytime task to mankind is the hour of midnight, but what midnight speaks is fit only for fine ears, for at midnight the very graves wail their demand that the dead be redeemed, that the past be willed (5). The old bell of midnight that rings out of the depth of the world is to Zarathustra already a sweet lyre (6). Though it rings with the pain of our fathers and forefathers, though the whole past cries out for redemption in its ring, that pain and suffering mysteriously ripen into joy. Can the superior men sense the sweetness in this mystery? Midnight resists the betrayal of its mystery, the soiling touch of importunate day (7), for midnight is pure, and only the purest deserve to be what midnight's wisdom can make them, lords of the earth. As midnight wisdom turns away importunate day, Zarathustra turns away the superior men who have come in search of his wisdom (8), but he turns them away to a god, to Dionysos, who, though unnamed, is present in the pain and joy of this song of intoxication, for a god must undertake the daytime task that the world demands. Zarathustra gives in his song what Nietzsche gave just as enigmatically and cryptically in *Beyond Good and Evil* (55, 56), a glimpse of the opposite ideal afforded the one who thinks world denial and pessimism to its depths. The sober speech of the intoxicated poet Midnight, "Woe is deep," reflects its inquiry into life, but so too does its affirmation of the profounder depth of joy. But what grounds that affirmation? The severed grapevine is allowed to speak the Dionysian affirmation of mortal life (9), that death belongs to mortal life, not as its refutation but as a consequence of growth and ripeness. Whereas woe speaks deeply and wants a form of life, it does not want its own life, but a life transferred outside itself into heirs or afterlives that are different. But joy speaks more profoundly, for it wants its own life most deeply, it therefore wants everything eternally the same. Who is Nietzsche's Zarathustra? (10): the wise man who teaches the superior men the grounds for eternal return. He reveals that ground only after adding to his list of contradictions the assertion that the wise man—and not only the poet—is also a fool, that wisdom itself is founded on an enigmatic vision. In his argument he makes use of the moment of joy that the superior men have just experienced. If they are to follow the Ugliest Man a second time, if they are to say to life, "Once More," for the sake of that moment of joy, then they must also be prepared to say, "To all eternity," for all things are intertwined. Joy in this one moment grounds an unbounded yes to everything that was and is; for the sake of this one fragment, joy wills the whole of which it is a part. This is the way to love the world (11), to will every moment and every being, for joy is hunger and thirst after the world while knowing its pain and suffering.[47]

Have the superior men learned Zarathustra's song (12) through his commentary on it? Have they learned how to move beyond the expiation of their ass festival, beyond even the affirmation "Once More" to which the Ugliest Man invited them, to Zarathustra's festival, the affirmation of eternal return? They sing the song together at midnight, but when the laughing lion roars the next morning, they resume their cry of need. These superior contemporaries who are still suffering from the modern world are not the men Zarathustra needs, the future lords of the earth, those hardened to the lion's roar, the purest, the least known, the strongest (7), the new nobility who are the spiritual preceptors of the new age, Zarathustra's "children," to whom he descends at the end of part IV. Nietzsche privately permitted himself this spectacle of instructing the best, albeit needy, men of his age in his most important teaching, and he permitted himself the disclosure of their weaknesses, which in some measure he shares, for, having "created the heaviest thought," the task at hand is to "create the being for whom it will be light and easy" (KGW VII 21 [6]).

ZARATHUSTRA'S WORK (CHAPTER 20)

The final chapter of part IV repeats the events of the opening section of the prologue, the very end thus repeating the very beginning; but in between Zarathustra has come to understand the work that must be done, and that he must be the one to do it. The narrative that has become kingly chronicle now has Zarathustra rise and gird his loins, like Elijah when he saw the sign of the cloud no bigger than a man's hand rising out of the sea,[48] but what Zarathustra sees is not a small cloud but the rising sun. He addresses the sun with the opening words of the prologue, thereby showing that his happiness still depends on having those on whom he can shine. But the latter are not the superior men still fast asleep in dreams that reflect on his mysterious midnight teaching. When he thinks of his work, he knows that they are not his proper companions (Prologue 9) because they lack the ear of obedience that his proper companions must possess. When the superior men awaken, their gaiety is intact, and they form a procession to greet Zarathustra. But the cry that they emit when frightened by the laughing lion's roar is still a cry of need, and it calls Zarathustra back to his work and enables him to interpret the events of the previous day. Their cry had tempted him to the final sin of pity for the superior men. Having experienced that pity, he is able to set it behind him out of hope for his children, hope to be realized through the work that now awaits him. Part IV ends with Zarathustra rising like the morning sun from behind dark mountains, rising to the Great Noon that he will celebrate with his children, those on whom he will shine with the teaching loyal to the earth, those for whom the teaching of eternal return will be light and easy.

If the sign of Zarathustra's descent can make us think of Thucydides—"the lion laughed here"[49]—it can make us think too of Nietzsche and Nietzsche's descent or his appearance among men; for, inasmuch as it is to him, and not to any of the superior men among his contemporaries, that we now look to discover a humane teaching loyal to the earth, Nietzsche has earned a laugh on even the most superior of his contemporaries, but, as is fitting for a thinker of his refined sensibility, that laugh, though the laugh of the king of beasts, is a peaceable and not a vindictive laugh, accompanied as it is by a whole flock of doves.

Notes

NOTES TO INTRODUCTION

1. Janz, *Nietzsche*, 1. 398ff.

2. See Duschesne-Guillemin, *The Western Response to Zoroaster*, and Jackson, *Zoroaster*. Legend made Pythagoras a student of Zoroaster. The earliest reference to Zoroaster in extant Greeks writings is in Plato *Alcibiades* 1. 122a. For Nietzsche's earlier references to Zarathustra, see "Zarathustra vor Also Sprach Zarathustra," in Montinari, *Nietzsche Lesen*. Diogenes Laertius, on whom the twenty-three-year-old Nietzsche had written a prize-winning essay, refers to Zoroaster (I. 2) and interprets his name as "star worshipper" (I. 8), but modern authorities interpret it as "old camel" (Jackson, *Zoroaster*, 12–14, 147–49). Nietzsche understood it to mean "golden star," but only after he had written part I (letter to Köselitz, 23 April 1883). Schopenhauer, *Parerga und Paralipomena*, II (Paralipomena, ch. 15, "Über Religion," §179) had argued for the Zoroastrian origin of Judaism.

3. The only historical personage named in the book besides Zarathustra is Jesus.

4. This is not to say that his other books lack structure. In *Ecce Homo* Nietzsche reports Ritschl's judgment that even his student essays were planned "like a Parisian *romancier*—absurdly exciting" ("Books," 2).

5. The usually unacknowledged practice of ignoring the dramatic action and interpreting the speeches as if they had no essential order or setting has been defended on the grounds that the book has "no ordered development ... or ... direction of argument or presentation. [It] may be entered at any point" (Danto, *Nietzsche As Philosopher*, 19–20); and on the different grounds that "there is little meaning in his structure; each disquisition relies on itself alone; his repetitions are seldom elucidations" (Knight, *Christ and Nietzsche*, 195).

6. On the controversy surrounding the use of the notebooks, see the defense of their use by Montinari, one of the editors of *KGW*, in "The New Critical Edition." However, the dramatic conclusion of Montinari's "Nietzsches Nachlass," in *Nietzsche Lesen*, seems to me not to be credible: "The disaster in Turin came when

Nietzsche was literally finished with everything" (118). In effect Montinari's conclusion adduces a new reason for Nietzsche's breakdown: he had nothing to do.
But Montinari's conclusion in no way follows from the evidence he assembles. To
say that the years spent reflecting on and preparing a Hauptwerk, whose main
themes were to include nihilism, a critique of philosophy, an account of eternal
return, and the religion of Dionysos, actually came to complete fruition in *Twilight*
and *Antichrist* does not do justice either to Nietzsche's reflections or to those two
books. Although I have used the notebooks to illustrate various points, all the main
aspects of my interpretation derive from the published texts.

7. Nietzsche applied this metaphor to himself after being pleased to see it
applied to him in a review of *Beyond*; see Janz, *Nietzsche*, II, 495–98.

8. The straightforward narrative, culminating with Zarathustra entering
Nietzsche's teaching and awaiting the day of his return as teacher at the end of
part III, is apparently confounded by the existence of part IV, a part that Nietzsche
kept strictly private. But Nietzsche's private description of it as an "interlude between
the main acts" is precise and illuminating. The first of those main acts, the entering
of Nietzsche's teaching, is portrayed in the first three parts of the book; the other,
the teaching of Nietzsche's teaching, or the bringing of the Great Noon, is not made
explicit at all, for it awaits Zarathustra even at the end of part IV. Justification for
this interpretation of part IV is given in the Appendix.

9. Heidegger, *Was Heißt Denken?*, 75; English trans., 75. I have also found the
writings of George Grant especially valuable in attempting to understand Nietzsche,
for Grant, a thinker schooled by Heidegger and Strauss, is able to make Nietzsche's
issues speak English and to show that "the thought of Nietzsche is a fate for modern
man" (Grant, *Time as History*, 45). I have benefited from other interpreters throughout in ways I hope I have made evident; quarrels with them have been confined
to notes for the most part.

10. Strauss, "Note on the Plan of *Beyond Good and Evil*." I have also benefited
from transcripts of Strauss's three courses on Nietzsche, especially the 1959 seminar
on *Zarathustra*.

11. Where biographical information seems relevant, I have not hesitated to
use it. But in attempting to understand the relation between Nietzsche's life and
writings, I have tried to be guided by Nietzsche's judgment about his worst readers:
"The worst readers of aphorisms are their author's friends if they are intent upon
guessing back from the general to the particular instance to which the aphorism
owes its origin, for with this pot-peeking they reduce the whole effort of the author
to nothing, and thus they only deserve it when, instead of a philosophic outlook
or instruction, they gain nothing but, at best—or at worst—the satisfaction of a
vulgar curiosity" (AO 129).

NOTES TO PART I

1. Kant, *Critique of Practical Reason*, "Conclusion."

2. This image is first used in *Gay Science* where the experience of descent
is called "the happiness of a god" (337).

3. Imagery of descent and ascent is also prominent in *Daybreak*, where solitude requires a move downward until the solitary becomes a "seeming Trophonius,"
an "underground man" who becomes human again by ascending to the company
of men as speaker (*D*, Preface, 1), and who ends his report on the underworld on

the theme of flying (574, 575). In addition to the specific symbols of climbing, dancing, and flying in *Zarathustra*, the abundance of *über-* words indicates the importance of the theme of ascending or transcending. See Löwith, *Nietzsches Philosophie*, 181; Kaufmann, *Nietzsche*, 309.

4. Fink, *Nietzsches Philosophie*, 70.

5. See, e.g., the poem at the end of *BGE*, the sections that end parts II and III of *GM*, and *TI*, "True World."

6. As is frequently the case, the arbitrary paragraphing of Kaufmann's translation makes the structure of the speech more difficult to detect.

7. Scheier interprets the scene in the marketplace as theater with the crowd as modern spectators, descendants of the theoretical or Socratic culture whose greatest fear is boredom and greatest need entertainment (*Nietzsches Labyrinth*, 153–56).

8. See Nietzsche's complaint about the misunderstanding of the word *Übermensch* as "an 'idealistic' type of a higher kind of man" (*EH*, "Books," 1). Alderman, fearing "an elitist doctrine" that would hold "that some men because of their power, spirituality or intelligence are over other men as their masters," interprets the superman teaching in as democratic a way as possible (*Nietzsche's Gift*, 27).

9. The only later mentions of *Übermensch* are in *GM* I. 6; *TI*, "Skirmishes," 37; *A* 4; and the three references in *EH*, all of which refer back to *Z* ("Books," 1, "Zarathustra," 6; "Destiny," 5). The first mention is in *GS* 143.

10. With respect to Nietzsche's view of evolution, some of the early sections of *Antichrist*—themselves an opening address of sorts, as the beginning of Nietzsche's *Hauptwerk*—could be read as balancing Zarathustra's one-sided rhetoric intended to ennoble and move the people. Nietzsche makes it clear that his view is less anthropomorphic than Zarathustra's speech implies. "The problem I pose is not what shall succeed mankind in the sequence of living things" (*A* 3). While putting man "back among the animals," Nietzsche does not indulge the "vanity" that "mankind had been the great hidden purpose of the evolution of the animals. It is by no means the crown of creation, every living kind stands beside it on the same level of perfection" (*A* 14).

11. Heidegger, *Was Heißt Denken?*, 24; English trans., 57; *Nietzsche* II, 129; English trans., IV. 86.

12. Montaigne, *Raymond Sebond*, ch. 2. Nietzsche has the highest praise for Montaigne, "this freest and strongest of souls": "The fact that such a man wrote has increased the joy of living on this earth. . . . I would side with him if the task were to make oneself at home on the earth" (*SE* 2). But the implication is that this is not the task, and that Nietzsche therefore cannot side with Montaigne.

13. Earle, "The Paradox and Death of God," 81.

14. Gen. 1:26; see 28–30; Gen. 9:2; Ps. 8.

15. Heidegger, *Was Heißt Denken?*, 22; English trans., 53.

16. Bacon, *Wisdom of the Ancients*, "Prometheus."

17. Locke, *Essay*, 2.20.§6.

18. See Plato *Laws* 646e–647d on the uses of shame.

19. Strauss, "Three Waves of Modernity," 97. For a description of last men as "the growing majority in the northern hemisphere as the modern age unfolds," see Grant, *Time as History*, ch. 4. See *HH* I. 235 on the homogenizing effect of the modern state and on the responsibility of the philosopher to oppose that uniformity

in order to keep alive the possibility of philosophy. See *WS* 218, 220, 288, for the homogenizing and centralizing effect of modern technology.

20. See also *HH* I. 109: "The danger arises that man might bleed to death from the truth he has recognized."

21. For the connection between the last man and the good and the just, see *EH*, "Destiny," 4, and *A* 17. See also *GM* I. 11–12, for last man and modern man. On the last man see also *D* 49, a reflection on the uses of past and future as means of dignifying man.

22. On Jesus' opposition to the Pharisees as "the good and the just," see *A* 27.

23. Matt. 4:19.

24. *HH* I. 275 says of the trained cynic: "He can scold to his heart's content and thereby rises high above the sensation range of the animal. . . . The cynic remains only negative." Later Zarathustra says that those who are of his kind will have only corpses and jesters as their first companions (III. 8). When he says later that only a jester believes that mankind can be leaped over (III. 12, §4), he would seem to be referring only to himself, for the jester of the prologue gives no evidence of believing that mankind can be leaped over, only that its fools, its aspirants to greatness, can.

25. In Matt. 8:22 the one who would bury his dead is also called away to a task. See II. 14 and III. 9 on grave-diggers.

26. Machiavelli, *The Prince*, ch. 6.

27. Zarathustra thus learns the lesson stated in *Daybreak: "The evil principle.—* Plato has given us a splendid description of how the philosophical thinker must within every existing society count as the paragon of all wickedness: for as the critic of all customs he is the antithesis of the moral man, and if he does not succeed in becoming the lawgiver of new customs he remains in the memory of men as 'the evil principle' " (496).

28. Zarathustra resolves never again to speak to the people; his one speech to the people in part II (II. 20) and the more extensive such speeches in part III (III. 5) are given out of necessity and do not compromise this resolve. Two later reports of the coming of his new insight (III. 12, §§1–3; IV. 13, §§1–3; see also III. 9) show how essential it is to his career.

29. The attribute of Zarathustra's snake is *Klugheit*, which combines the English senses of cleverness and prudence. Nietzsche does not use the customary German word for the virtue of the serpent, *listig*, which has the connotation of low cunning (see Gen. 3:1, 14; compare Matt. 10:16). While *klug* is used to describe the last men, *klug* and *Klugheit* are especially important with reference to Zarathustra's own prudence (II. 21). *Klugheit* is also used for the Aristotelian virtue of prudence.

30. Nietzsche studied these symbols in a book on ancient symbolism; see Janz, *Nietzsche*, II. 230–32.

31. Gen. 3:14–15. See Fink, *Nietzsches Philosophie*, 70. On the symbolism of the eagle and the snake, see also Heidegger, "Who Is Nietzsche's Zarathustra?," in which the animals are seen as emblems of eternal return. For a history of the symbols in relation to Zarathustra, see Thatcher, "Eagle and Serpent in Zarathustra."

32. Matt. 10:16.

33. Scheier places extraordinary significance on the division of the prologue into ten sections, their content allegedly providing the pattern that is repeated in divisions of ten throughout the book (*Nietzsches Labyrinth*, 147–53, 167–70). Although

this works reasonably well for parts I and II, each interpreted as having opening and closing chapters framing two sets of ten chapters, it does not work well for the sixteen chapters of part III (see 214). Moreover, Scheier provides no rationale for the pattern, nor does he explain why he thinks it important to look for the centers of the various parts, chapters, and speeches. Nevertheless, his account of *Zarathustra* is instructive regarding important transformations in Zarathustra's teaching.

34. Plato *Republic* 509b. See Dannhauser, *Nietzsche's View of Socrates*, 249–50.

35. See Heidegger, *Question Concerning Technology*, 106–07.

36. Plato *Republic* 517a.

37. See Strauss, *On Tyranny*, 26.

38. Plato *Republic* 537e–539a, 494d–e.

39. Ibid. 327a–c.

40. Ibid. 520b, 347a–e.

41. Ibid. 493e–502a.

42. On the basis of a distinction regarding two kinds of rhetoric made by Nietzsche in an early essay, Shapiro argues that the rhetoric of *Zarathustra* is the play of imagination that does not aim at persuasion; it is Greek rather than Roman, from Demosthenes rather than Cicero. Shapiro develops this thesis into a useful analysis of the differences among the four parts of *Zarathustra*. Nevertheless, with regard to part I, the main claim obliterates Zarathustra's declared purpose for his speeches; they aim at persuasion above all else. ("Rhetoric," 347–85).

43. See Matt. 5:21–48.

44. The Colorful Cow is a different city from the one in which the speeches of the prologue were given, as might be expected in view of the hatred aroused by those speeches. Zarathustra is later said to be two days' journey away from his cave when in the Colorful Cow (III. 8), whereas the town of the prologue is only a half-day's walk away.

45. Plato *Republic* 557c–d, 558a–b.

46. For example, Fink maintains that the camel represents "man under the burden of transcendence" (*Nietzsches Philosophie*, 70). But Heller, correctly in my view, describes the camel's way as "the fundamental truth of Nietzsche's existence," and so of Zarathustra's (*Disinherited Mind*, 307–09). In the drafts of this chapter Zarathustra is described as the one who bears much (*KGW* VII 4 [237]; 5 [1, #162]). A later note entitled "The Way to Wisdom" (*KGW* VII 26 [47, Summer–Fall 1884]) describes the three necessary stages on the way to wisdom, but without the symbols of the camel, lion, and child. The first step requires a better "revering and obeying and learning" than has yet been in evidence.

47. Yeats, "The Phases of the Moon." In this poem Yeats names Nietzsche's spiritual qualities and assigns him what Heller calls "the highest office ever assigned to him in the varied history of his reputation" (*Disinherited Mind*, 337). Robartes, describing the phases of the waxing moon as they gather in strength, says:

> Eleven pass, and then
> Athene takes Achilles by the hair,
> Hector is in the dust, Nietzsche is born,
> Because the hero's crescent is the twelfth.

48. Subsequent speeches in part I develop the distinction between lovers of honor and lovers of victory (esp. I. 8, 10, 14), whereas the later parts show Zarathustra

to be a lover of victory of the most unrestrained sort. Zarathustra's most extensive definition of spirit contrasts the lover of victory with a certain kind of lover of honor or fame (II. 8). On this distinction, see Craig, "The Timocratic Man in Plato's *Republic*."

49. I. 8 is the first chapter to mention the heroic after I. 1. See also II. 13, where what is hardest for the heroic spirit is defined in a new way.

50. In *Beyond* this inclination of spirit is described as a "ladder of religious cruelty," whose last rung is the sacrifice of "whatever is comforting, holy, healing"; the consequence of such heroic sacrifice is the worship of "the stone, stupidity, gravity, fate, the nothing" (*BGE* 55). The next section (56) describes the next transformation. See also the cruel "inclination of spirit" of the "seeker of knowledge" in 229–31.

51. On the limitations of the child image, see Fink, *Nietzsches Philosophie*, 71: the play of the child is not yet the full Dionysian world play. Typical of treatments that ignore the context is Magnus, "Aristotle and Nietzsche: 'Megalopsychia' and 'Übermensch,' " 276–81, in which the three transformations are generalized into the ideal of the superman. Alderman interprets the passage as describing essential features of "the creative person," not of those who would become Zarathustra's disciples (*Nietzsche's Gift*, 30–34). The transformations have been interpreted as a history of the human spirit by Dannhauser, "Nietzsche," 793, 800.

52. "Chairs" inadequately translates *Lehrstühlen*, which implies teaching positions with institutional authority to which youth defers in being schooled.

53. Other chapters in part I in which a setting is given are 8, 18, 19, and 22.

54. Compare Plato *Apology of Socrates* 40c–e; *Republic* 571c–572a.

55. In his insightful comments on this chapter, Dannhauser contrasts Zarathustra with Socrates (*Nietzsche's View of Socrates*, 253–54).

56. For Zarathustra's commentary on this chapter, see III. 12, §2.

57. "Afterworldly" inadequately translates Nietzsche's coinage *Hinterweltler*, which sounds like *"Hinterwäldler,"* a word for a complete rustic or backwoodsman. Nietzsche first used this word in *AO* 17.

58. As indicated by this speech about being, Zarathustra abandons the traditional terminology of philosophy and even the words *philosophy* and *philosopher*. He avoids naming any single philosopher. Only very rarely does he use the terms *being*, *becoming*, and *nature*, moreover, he avoids altogether technical terms of university philosophy such as *metaphysics, epistemology, aesthetics, ethics*, and *logic*, and Nietzschean terms such as *nihilism, revaluation*, and *Dionysian*. Still, the language employed by Zarathustra has the same comprehensive range and ambition.

59. See *BGE* 45, 269, on "the great hunt," or the work of the psychologist. The psychologist in Nietzsche's sense is a physician of culture; "he never seeks himself. . . . We have neither the time nor the inclination to rotate around ourselves" (*KGW* VIII 14 [27, 28] = *WP* 426). In his investigation of moral phenomena, the psychologist Zarathustra might well give the impression of "gazing around haphazardly in the blue after the English fashion" (*GM*, Preface, 7). The strictures of fable forbid him (unlike his philologist creator) from taking advantage of the color that "is a hundred times more vital for a genealogist of morals than blue: namely *gray*, that is, what is documented." Nevertheless, it is clear that Zarathustra has read the relevant documents.

60. Although the soul here seems to be eliminated by the mature speech of knowers, Zarathustra later makes clear Nietzsche's view that abandonment of the

calamitous error of the Christian teaching on the soul does not require that the psychologist abandon the "soul-hypothesis" as such (*BGE* 12).

61. Zarathustra's counsel on the virtues remedies what the young educator Nietzsche feared was being dòne to youth through modern education, which "can cut off at the roots the strongest instincts of youth: its fire, defiance, unselfishness and love, damp down the heat of its sense of justice, suppress or regress its desire to mature slowly with the counter-desire to be ready, useful, fruitful as quickly as possible, cast morbid doubt on its honesty and boldness of feeling; indeed, it can even deprive youth of its fairest privilege, its power to implant in itself the belief in a great idea and then let it grow to an even greater one" (*UD* 9).

62. Aristotle *Rhetoric* 2. 22.

63. This battle of the virtues could be the chaos still present in man that makes possible the birth of a dancing star (Prologue 5). Zarathustra's apparently inflammatory invitation to "evil" presupposes a Nietzschean analysis of good and evil, according to which "evil" is opposition to the "good" or customary. "To be evil is to go against tradition" (*HH* I. 96).

64. Rosen holds that when Zarathustra says that "all gods and afterworlds" are creations of the despairing body (I. 3) he is being "more categorical and more careless" than usual; he cites as evidence Nietzsche's "regularly favorable mention of Dionysos" (*Limits of Analysis*, 202). But Dionysos receives no mention in *Zarathustra* and does not make his mysterious appearance until the end of part III. In part I all worship of gods is condemned as unworthy subjection, grounds for a different understanding having not yet surfaced.

65. On hardness of heart, see Ps. 95:8; Matt. 19:8; Mark 10:5; 16:14; Heb. 3:8, 15; 4:7. The biblical word for "hardness of heart," *sklerokardian*, is not found in Greek authors.

66. Aristotle *Rhetoric* 2. 8. See also Rousseau, *Second Discourse*, pt. 1: "Commiseration will be all the more energetic as the observing animal identifies himself more intimately with the suffering animal." This occurs in the argument demonstrating that pity is a natural sentiment.

67. Strauss, *Thoughts on Machiavelli*, 49–50, 81–82.

68. A less aphoristic account of the exegesis of the aphorisms of *Zarathustra* occurs at the end of the preface to *Genealogy*. With regard to the exegesis of Zarathustra's aphorisms, especially their connectedness, see also Nietzsche's warning that the worst readers are "those who proceed like plundering soldiers: they make off with what they can use, stain and confuse what is left and bring disrepute upon the whole" (*AO* 137).

69. Plato *Phaedrus* 258d, 273d, 274b–278b. See the interpretation of the *Phaedrus* in Klein, *Plato's Meno*, 10–23. There are other remarkable similarities between the *Phaedrus* and these two chapters (I. 7, 8). In the *Phaedrus* Socrates speaks alone with one young man whom he loves. The conversation takes place under a very tall tree outside the city and concerns what moves one beyond the city. They speak as friends, or, more particularly, Socrates engages in an act of befriending, the nature of which is to draw the young man away from a passion that holds him down. They speak of love, the passion that leads the soul upward, one of four divine madnesses, the gift of Aphrodite and Eros, a madness in which there is reason. The soul of the lover ascends to the highest things on wings that can be be lost or broken; it flies with divine madness, the gift of Dionysos, the dancing god, the god of purifications who releases the dancer from what weighs him down

by dancing through him. Reaching the height, led by Zeus, leader of souls, themselves Zeus-like, "of a philosophic and commanding nature" (252e), such souls, through the eye, "the keenest sense" (250d), look out over everything as at a divine banquet (247b). The madness of song or poetry, gift of the Muses, inspires the speaker, while the madness of prophecy, gift of Apollo, enables him to discern the destiny of souls.

70. Empedocles (Diels fragment 24): "Stepping from summit to summit, not to follow a single path of words to the end."

71. Aristotle *On the Parts of Animals* I. 5, 645a15.

72. §§5, 12, and 17 are addressed to "my friend" or "my brother"; §20 to my brother contemplating marriage; §§7, 9, and 13 have no addressee; and §18, Zarathustra's teaching on woman, seems to require a special privacy that is effected by two interlocutors.

73. The symbol of lightning has a different use here from its first use in the prologue (3). There, the lightning prophesied by Zarathustra is the superman himself, whereas Zarathustra is a warning drop of rain. Here Zarathustra is identified with the lightning that the young man's envy threatens to call down upon himself. This parable of the tree and the lightning is repeated in all its main details in *Gay Science* (371) (1886) under the title "We Incomprehensible Ones." In his analysis of envy based on this chapter, Shapiro ("Nietzsche on Envy," 5) speaks of "the downward spiral of silent envy" and quotes Nietzsche's statement on such envy from *Assorted Opinions and Maxims* (53); "Ordinary envy is wont to cackle when the envied hen has laid an egg, thereby relieving itself and becoming milder. But there is a yet deeper envy that in such a case becomes dead silent, desiring that every mouth should be sealed and always more and more enraged because this desire is not gratified. Silent envy grows in silence."

74. See Homer *Iliad* 11. 784; 6. 208.

75. Aristotle *Rhetoric* II. 10, 11.

76. See Hillesheim, "Nietzsche Agonistes," 343–53. In *Daybreak* Nietzsche says: "The older Greeks felt differently about *envy* from the way we do; Hesiod counted it among the effects of the *good,* beneficent Eris, and there was nothing offensive in attributing to the gods something of envy; which is comprehensible under a condition of things the soul of which was contest; contest, however, was evaluated and determined as good" (38). See "Artistic Ambition" (*HH* I. 170): "The Greek artists, the tragedians for instance, composed in order to conquer; their whole art cannot be imagined without rivalry. Ambition, Hesiod's good *Eris,* gave wings to their genius." Such ambition does not measure itself by the approval of the viewer, but by the approval of the artist himself; the artist "wished to *be* more excellent," not merely esteemed as such. Hesiod's description of a good and bad Eris, or strife, occupied Nietzsche repeatedly; see *WS* 29, "Envy and its Nobler Brother." Nietzsche's praise of Heraclitus in *Philosophy in the Tragic Age of the Greeks* (1873) singles out Heraclitus's elevation of the contest to the fundamental cosmic principle of justice: "It is Hesiod's good Eris transformed into the cosmic principle" (5–6). It is noteworthy that the other Eris leads to Orphism, a form of resignation and the judgment that life is no good. Hesiod's account of a good and bad Eris occurs in *Works and Days* 11. 10–34; see also the single Eris of *Theogeny* 223–33. In a book that makes Nietzsche the obviously sufficient grounds for turning against modern teachings on ethics which he allegedly represents (*After Virtue,* 121–22), MacIntyre accuses him of having misunderstood heroic virtue by reading it anachronistically as

"*self*-assertion," or modern individualism. But what Nietzsche praises is not so much the heroic virtue of Achilles and other Greek heroes, but a culture of admirers of Achilles culminating in Alexander. Nietzsche aims not to duplicate ancient heroes, but to duplicate ancient admiration; Nietzsche's own admiration is not for Achilles (however modernized) but for that way of stationing oneself toward the admired which intends to surpass it.

77. This speech to the young man refers to the noble more often than any other speech. For the political aspects of nobility, see especially III. 12, §§11, 12. The public dangers threatening noble youths are explained in I. 10, 11, in a way reminiscent of Socrates' account of the dangers faced by such youths through flattery of the public in Plato *Republic* 494b–c. The account of the utility of monumental history in *Uses and Disadvantages of History* (2) describes the uses of the great in a way that is relevant to the young man thwarted by Zarathustra: the high points of humanity are linked across the millennia; the man who aspires to greatness is preserved from despair by the knowledge that the great which "once existed was in any event once *possible* and may thus be possible again." No reward beckons such men "unless it be fame," and the happiness they seek is "often that of a people or of all mankind." Nietzsche's praise of great men sounds a note heard again in Zarathustra's search for worthy companions: "Suppose someone were to believe that it required no more than a hundred productive men, raised and active in a new spirit to put to an end the cultural refinement which has now become fashionable in Germany, how it would strengthen him to realize that the culture of the Renaissance was raised on the shoulders of such a group of one hundred men." In encouraging the young man on the mountainside to admire what stands higher than he does, Zarathustra aims to create in him the spirit of gratitude that Nietzsche had earlier expressed for the singular and noble Heraclitus: "It is important to learn from such men that they once existed" (*PTG* 8).

78. Sensual pleasure, the theme also of "On Child and Marriage" (I. 20), is revalued much later as the first of three so-called evils (III. 10).

79. This chapter contains echoes of Nietzsche's own search for disciples, most notoriously Lou Salomé, though he had, like a pirate, long been *auf Menschenraub*, as he said in a letter to another possible disciple, Reinhart von Seydlitz (24 September 1876). The infamous episode with Lou, "a pity forever," has at last and to Nietzsche's honor been definitively described by Binion in *Frau Lou*. With astonishing perspicacity and analytic precision, Binion has set straight the record doctored by both Lou and Nietzsche's sister: "In this contest between fabler and forger, the one sure loser was Nietzsche himself" (169). Nietzsche continues to lose to the fabler in Janz's recent biography, in which the account offered by the "clear-sighted and honest" Lou is credited, even though it has been demolished once and for all as Lou's "first large-scale autobiographic hoax" by Binion (158; see 148–71 for his analysis of her book *Friedrich Nietzsche in seinem Werken* [1894]). Perhaps Janz (who does not cite Binion) gives Lou as much credit as he does because he wants to assign her a task dear to himself: he presents Lou as the last hope for saving Nietzsche from his crazy doctrine of eternal return (*Nietzsche* II. 149–52). On one matter concerning *Zarathustra*, Binion is misleading, however; apparently forgetting what he had said on page 54, Binion claims that "the first conception of *Zarathustra* dates ... from his encounter with Lou" (102, n. p), thus crediting Lou with fathering the book on Nietzsche (101–02, 118). In fact, the first plans for the book were made a year earlier than the first conversations with Lou, which took place in May 1882. See *KGW* V 11 [195] Spring–Fall 1881.

80. Here I follow Pangle's perceptive analysis in "The 'Warrior Spirit,' " 143, 146–48. He interprets chapters 9–12 as a series of speeches describing an ascent through "the four mainstays of contemporary culture," the religious establishment, the military, the state, and the marketplace of ideas. See Dannhauser, *Nietzsche's View of Socrates*, 38–39.

81. Envy of this kind is reflected in the obsolete English usage "a virtuous envy," emulation without malevolence. The *Oxford English Dictionary* records that envy could be used in its aphetic form *vie*, meaning to vie with one another or contend for mastery.

82. Much later (III. 5) Zarathustra will need to deflect the people's envy (though not their anger), by keeping silent on his happiness, thereby implicitly denying that he is enviable.

83. "Looming as a cloud over all of Nietzsche's insights" is his "praise of war." Beginning his essay on "The 'Warrior Spirit' " with this judgment, Pangle succeeds in dissipating that cloud by following the warrior spirit through its transformations in *Zarathustra* up to the spiritual warfare between the commander Zarathustra and his peers, the wisest men of the past, in part II. See Nietzsche's account of his wars (*EH*, "Wise," 7); also, Kaufmann, *Nietzsche*, 386–90, and Eden, *Political Leadership*, 113. On the misuse of Nietzsche's war rhetoric prior to the First World War, see Stromberg, *Redemption by War*. Janz goes so far as to wonder if a Nietzsche grown old and authoritative could have helped to spare mankind the First World War (*Nietzsche* III. 57). Nietzsche's actual influence on Germany with respect to the First World War, as opposed to what was alleged by propaganda on both sides, is set forth in Thomas, *Nietzsche in German Politics*, esp. 125–31. Thomas discusses the legend "that German soldiers went to war in 1914 with Nietzsche in their hearts and *Thus Spoke Zarathustra* in their kit bags" (103–04). See Kuenzli, "The Nazi Appropriation of Nietzsche," and Sokel, "Political Uses and Abuses of Nietzsche." See also Stackelberg, "Nietzsche and the Nazis."

84. On Nietzsche's political philosophy, see also *BGE* 208, 240–56; *GM* II, 12; *TI*, "Skirmishes," 38–44; *SE* 4; and Dannhauser, "Nietzsche."

85. Nietzsche's teachings on peoples and their faith and love is expanded in *Antichrist* (16, 25, 57); the gods that ground the common life of historic peoples are there praised as necessary and life-enhancing. Compare *GM* II. 23. *BGE* 251 contrasts European nations with peoples; see also 242.

86. Matt. 4:9.

87. Strauss, *What is Political Philosophy?*, 55.

88. See Lessing, *Nietzsche*, "Das neue Reich (1870)." Zarathustra's speech on "The New Idol" can be understood as the act of a "flatterer" according to Plato's story about a matter needing a great deal of guarding. The flatterer persuades the changeling children raised in the great and noble "family" which is the state that they have been lied to about their origins, and that they do not owe their existence to the family to which they have until now been loyal. Although he cannot tell them what their true origins are, the flatterer may well be able to tell them something novel about the end to which they ought to direct themselves now that their old loyalty is broken (*Republic* 537d–539b).

89. Plato *Republic* 430c.

90. See III. 12, §21; *BGE* 61, 211 affirm the rule of the philosopher. Similar conclusions about Zarathustra's political aim can be drawn by contrasting the appeals of Zarathustra and Lucretius to talented young men. When Lucretius attacked the political realm in his appeal to the politically ambitious Memmius, he

was careful to do so in a setting that seemed at first to honor Rome and Rome's founders and founding goddess. Only gradually does the honor tarnish to dishonor as the exertions of politics, the improbability of their successful consummation, and the vulnerability of even the successful, are contrasted with the firm pleasures of Epicurean friendship and a knowledge of the way things are. Openly spurning modern politics, Zarathustra calls his followers to solitude, but to a solitude that differs from the detached fellowship of Epicurean philosophers, not only in its singularity but, more important, in being merely provisional. Zarathustra and his companions are not permitted the tranquil observation of human things afforded Epicurean philosophers and their gods for they are required to intervene with a divine hammer in their hands (*BGE* 62).

91. I owe some of the main points of the analysis of this chapter to Pangle, "The 'Warrior Spirit,' " 143, 146–48.

92. Plato's account of rival claims on the talented young man contrasts the insistent flattery of the public with the gentle charms of the philosopher; despite the reserve of the philosopher's approach, the city organizes private plots and public trials against its rival (*Republic* 494a–e).

93. Yeats, "Meditations in Time of Civil War," VII. Nietzsche emphasizes the absence of a desire for fame in his account of Heraclitus (*PTG* 8).

94. Nietzsche returns to the theme of *Parsifal* in part IV.

95. 1 Cor. 7:9; but see also the whole of ch. 7.

96. In the life of the ascetic priest, chastity means something quite different; see *GM* III. 11.

97. Bacon, *Essays*, "On Friendship."

98. In this title the thousand is separated from the one by avoidance of the more customary *Von tausendundeinem Ziele*, "On a thousand and one goals"; note also the unusual capitalization of *one* following the customary noncapitalization of *thousand.*

99. Nietzsche's account of peoples in *Antichrist* describes a natural hierarchy with three levels, closely resembling the three classes based on natural suitability in Plato's *Republic* after the philosopher has been added. It also resembles the description of the ancestral city in Fustel de Coulanges, *The Ancient City*. *Genealogy* (II. 17, 18) speaks of "the most involuntary unconscious artists" who are the founders of states, "those artists of violence and organizers who build states." See also "The Greek State" (1871): "the creation of the military genius—with whom we have become acquainted as the original founder of states" (*KGW* III, 2. 269).

100. Jaspers, *Nietzsche and Christianity*, ix; *Nietzsche*, 287.

101. Homer *Iliad* 11. 784; 6. 208. With respect to the Greek passion to be first, see Lucretius's praise of his Greek master Epicurus (I. 62–79) and his intimations about himself (I. 923 ff.; IV. 1 ff.). On Greek admiration of Odysseus and his capacity to be first, see *D* 306.

102. Herodotus 1. 136, 138.

103. Exod. 20:12; see Eph. 6:2–3.

104. See Neumann, "Nietzsche, The Superman, The Will to Power, and The Eternal Return," 289. Neumann relates Zarathustra's fourth example to suggestions for a united Europe and Germany's place in that unification in *Beyond* (208–13). See also *BGE* 256.

105. Virgil *Aeneid* 12. 838; see 7. 202–04; 6. 851–53; and Fustel de Coulanges, *The Ancient City*, 142–46.

106. See *The Prince*, ch. 6, on the founders Moses, Cyrus, Romulus, and Theseus.

107. See the "great politics" that require the unification of Europe (*BGE* 256, 241–43).

108. Rom. 12:20. See Nietzsche's comment in *AO* 57.

109. See II. 22, where Zarathustra cries uncontrollably on leaving his disciples.

110. Zarathustra had spoken about woman in I. 7, where wisdom is a woman, as well as in I. 13, 14.

111. Of all Zarathustra's teachings on conventions, this one is the nearest to traditional teaching, echoing God's words to Eve (Gen. 3:15) as well as Greek and Roman practice. But despite its traditional sanction, it is the one that he treats with greatest caution, and one that has proved an unwelcome embarrassment to many of Nietzsche's readers—see, e.g., Kaufmann, *Portable Nietzsche*, 120; *Nietzsche*, 22, 42ff., 84. Compare the acute analysis by Platt in "Woman, Nietzsche, and Nature," the conclusions of which are compromised, however, by his mistaken judgment that "Zarathustra never marries" (38). Bertram lists a series of judgments that have been made about Nietzsche's views on women (" 'God's *Second* Blunder,' " 275, n.1) and argues that Nietzsche's thought on woman is far from being hostile, and belongs moreover, to his essential thought on nature. See also Thomas, *Nietzsche in German Politics*, Appendix, an insightful interpretation of I. 18, which follows the theme of women and the whip through subsequent chapters. See Mencken, *The Philosophy of Friedrich Nietzsche*, 174–91.

112. Derrida's sport with Nietzsche's sport with woman never acknowledges the old woman's gift; see *Spurs*, 50–51, 64–65, 94–95, and 98–101. Derrida acts as if Nietzsche's sport with woman freed him of "his foolish hopes of capture" (54–55), whereas, in fact, it made possible the complementary capture that is marriage. Derrida can thereby suppose that Nietzsche writes as a woman (56–57); in remembering the forgotten umbrella, Derrida forgets the remembered whip. In taking Nietzsche to be elevated to the "Eternal-Feminine" instead of to its masculine complement (see II. 17), Derrida takes Nietzsche to be giving permission to an infinite play of interpretation or deconstruction; but Zarathustra's sport with the woman Life precludes that he himself ends with deconstruction.

113. Machiavelli, *The Prince*, ch. 25 and 6.

114. Bacon, *The Great Instauration*, "The Plan of the Work." "By the help and ministry of man a new face of bodies, another universe or theater of things, comes into view" (Bacon, *Description of a Natural and Experimental History*, in *New Organon*. Bacon's earlier reference to "a chaste, holy, and legal wedlock" makes the offspring "a blessed race of Heroes or Supermen" (*Masculine Birth of Time*, 72).

115. Luke 1:37.

116. In *Beyond* the sections on women (232–39) follow the description of the most spirited natures (230–31) and are introduced both as "*my* truths" and the truth about woman *an sich*.

117. For conclusions drawn by others, see II. 17; II. 20; IV. 3–9; and esp. III. 7.

118. The parable that Jesus explains to his disciples is the parable of the tares (Matt. 13:24–30, 36–43), which also concerns justice and harm to enemies.

119. After saying that the Prince has to pamper men or extinguish them, Machiavelli says that if one has to hurt men, it should be in such a mode that there is no fear of vengeance (*The Prince*, ch. 3).

120. Plato *Republic* 331d–336a, 537d, 539a.

121. Descartes, *Discourse*, pt. 3.

122. Matt. 16:24–26.

123. On the gift-giving virtue, see Fischer, "The Existentialism of Nietzsche's Zarathustra," and Beatty, "Zarathustra." Both accounts fail to consider Zarathustra's rethinking of this virtue after part I. Shapiro elaborates the image of the staff into a general account of metaphor in Nietzsche ("Zarathustra's Hermeneutics Lesson").

124. A note for this speech explains its "cats and wolves" as those who take without giving and would rather steal than take (*KGW* VII 4 [100]).

125. Eden provides a lucid account of Nietzsche's new individualism (*Political Leadership*, 101–03).

126. On modern selfishness, see *SE* 4. Selfishness is revalued at III. 10.

127. Compare the five signs of the spirit in Jesus' disciples, Mark 16:17–18.

128. Scheier, *Nietzsches Labyrinth*, 173.

129. Matt. 24:3 ff.; 26:41.

130. See Exod. ch. 4, 7.

131. See Isa. 43:20.

132. Matt. 10:39; see also Matt. 10:33, Jesus' promise to his disciples that if you deny me I'll deny you.

133. See Aristotle *Poetics* 1452a 7–10.

134. On the meaning of the Great Noon announced enigmatically as a promise to disciples, see III. 5. The prophecies uttered at the very end of "Zarathustra's Speeches" serve as a useful agenda for interpreting subsequent epochs in Zarathustra's life. In *Ecce Homo* ("Books: *Birth*," 4) Nietzsche again refers to the Great Noon and to the chosen people while describing *Wagner in Bayreuth*. His description makes clear that *Wagner in Bayreuth* is of special importance for the reader of *Zarathustra*.

135. Nietzsche had to wait many anxious months for the actual appearance of part I after rushing it to the publisher on 14 February 1883, because the printer and the publisher were both occupied, and with causes inimical to Nietzsche, the printer with 500,000 hymnbooks for Easter, and the publisher with anti-Semitic causes (letter to Köselitz, 1 July 1883). The first copies were sent from the publisher in August. Part II, on the other hand, completed by 13 July 1883, was back from the publisher by 5 September.

136. Dannhauser, *Nietzsche's View of Socrates*, 264.

137. Reichhold, *Attische Vasenbilder*, 26.

138. Aristotle *Rhetoric* 2. 22.

139. Rosen, *Nihilism*, 74.

140. Aristotle *Nichomachean Ethics* 1119b–1125a; see Kaufmann, *Nietzsche*, 382–84.

141. Phil. 2:7. See the account of charity in Weil, *Waiting for God*, 137–57.

142. I Cor. 1:27–28.

143. Luke 1:52.

144. See Becker, *Heavenly City*, 119–68.

145. Locke, "Of Property," *Second Treatise of Government*, ch. 5.

146. Kant, *On History*, 113–16. While encouraging a consciously held ideal of history that postulates progress as "a justification of Nature—or, better, of Providence," Kant marveled at the oddness of the means that makes "earlier generations appear to carry through their toilsome labor only for the sake of the later," while "only the latest of the generations should have the good fortune to inhabit the

building on which a long line of their ancestors had (unintentionally) labored without being permitted to partake of the fortune they had prepared" (*On History*, 114).

147. Hegel, *Philosophy of History*, 20–37.

148. Cited by Mazlish, *Riddle of History*, 81.

149. Voegelin, "Nietzsche, the Crisis and the War," written toward the end of the second World War, is a superb summary of Nietzsche's political relevance. The limitation of his conclusion regarding Nietzsche's "perhaps hopeless and futile" attempt is best indicated by his failure to discuss eternal return.

NOTES TO PART II

1. Hesiod *Works and Days* 166 ff.; Pindar *Odes* 2. 68 ff.; see Plato *Republic* 519c–d.

2. The differences that have been noted between parts I and II usually involve a difference in emphasis, not in teaching. Dannhauser says that part II is "more creative, more destructive," and that "the primary target of destruction is no longer Christianity but philosophy" (*Nietzsche's View of Socrates*, 255). In analyzing the rhetoric of part II, Shapiro finds it "reductive" because "metonymical"; all experience has been reduced to will and thereby turned into a series of oppositions and dichotomies ("The Rhetoric of Nietzsche's *Zarathustra*," 357–59). Rosen, distinguishing the two parts as the "morning" teaching and the "afternoon" and "night" teaching, concentrates on the inadequacy of the disciples and takes Zarathustra's main task to be rhetorical, the discovery of how to vary his speech in such a way as to render his thought intelligible to the disciples (and the reader). He concludes that "there is no essential difference between the teachings of the first and the second parts" (*Limits of Analysis*, 205). Pangle's incisive account of part II notes that its opening chapters (2–7) are a polemic addressed "to followers who have spent years in withdrawn meditation upon, and discussion of, his earlier appearance among them" ("The 'Warrior Spirit,' " 151). Only in the central chapters on wisdom (8–13) does Zarathustra address his peers; there he presents what Pangle takes to be the foundation of his teaching, the ground on which it can be adequately judged (160–70).

3. See Eden, *Political Leadership*, 61. No book known to me is as persuasive as Eden's in presenting the political ambitions of Nietzsche's philosophy; here is no "effete Nietzsche diddling with the literati" (69) but a Nietzsche fully occupied with the legislative task of philosophy. Remedying what he identifies as a "shortcoming of most treatments of Nietzsche's politics ... the absence of any consideration of Nietzsche's attempt to continue the forward motion of modern science" (270, n. 11), Eden shows that "Nietzsche's philosophic politics is, in the first instance, leadership of science" (74). But in my view even Eden does not go far enough with Nietzsche. His ground-breaking analysis of *Beyond* does not lead him into *Zarathustra*, and perhaps for that reason he judges Nietzsche to be a "nihilist," the more polite modern denunciation replacing the now forbidden "teacher of evil."

4. Yeats, "The Statues."

5. Part I of *Zarathustra* had been completed on the Bay of Rapallo in January 1882. Six months later Nietzsche was in Rome, "the least congenial city for the poet of Zarathustra" (*EH*, "Books: *Zarathustra*," 4). He reports, however, that he was able to challenge even those inappropriate surroundings; he inquired at the former residence of the pope as to whether there was a quiet room where a philosopher could work. The work he had to do was part II, which he began in Rome

and completed, again in ten days of inspiration (early July 1883), in Sils Maria, where the "fundamental conception" of the book, eternal return, had first come to him two summers earlier.

6. Nietzsche's original title was "The Second Daybreak."

7. Zarathustra's animals are with him at the beginning and the end of the prologue, at the beginning of part II, and during the decisive event of part III (III. 13); in part IV they are present at the beginning and the end, as well as for the events in the cave (IV. 11–20).

8. Zarathustra never refers to his disciples as "disciples" in these opening speeches; he calls them "disciples" only after they have failed him (II. 19).

9. Nietzsche's original title for this chapter was "On the Gods."

10. Plato *Alcibiades* 1. 105a–c. In a note identifying his proper audience, written in the spring of the following year (1884), Nietzsche quotes the young Theages: "Each of us would like to be master, if possible, over all men, and best of all, God" (Plato *Theages* 126a). Nietzsche adds: "This attitude must exist again" (*KGW* VII 25 [137] = *WP* 958).

11. This account of the gods, aiming at the greatest breadth in order to destroy all external limit, does not distinguish the relatively more worthy gods created in imitation of a master's self-admiration from the gods or the "holy God" of slaves. This distinction is important, however, in accounts of the gods in other settings: *HH* I, "The Religious Life," esp. 114; *BGE* 45–62, esp. 49, 260; *GM* II. 23.

12. *GS* 84 ends by quoting a poet to lend force to Nietzsche's criticism of a practice said still to be followed by "the most serious philosophers," namely, that of quoting poets to lend force to their ideas. Nietzsche says he quotes Homer— "The poets tell many lies"—but he's lying.

13. Strauss, "Notes on Lucretius," 84–85.

14. In works that name names Nietzsche attacks more overtly than Zarathustra can the supposition that Christian virtues can be retained after the destruction of the Christian God. See *TI*, "Skirmishes," 5 (re "G. Eliot," the English translator of Feuerbach's *The Essence of Christianity*). Nietzsche's "greatest ridicule" is reserved for "intellectual democrats" who "want to maintain a content to 'justice' and 'truth' and 'goodness' out of the corpse they helped to make a corpse" (Grant, *English-Speaking Justice*, 77).

15. Compare Matt. 22:37–39.

16. This chapter "might be thought to be a response by Nietzsche to some intelligent but hostile reader who has decided he can satisfactorily explain the Zarathustra of Part One as merely a new, anti-Christian version of the priestly type" (Pangle, "The 'Warrior Spirit,' " 152–53). My account of this chapter owes some important points to Pangle's enlightening discussion.

17. The heart and mind of the priest of priests, the apostle Paul, are interpreted this way in *Daybreak* (68). Zarathustra's speech attacks only Christian priests, the form of the priestly that tempts his disciples; it omits the history of the priestly that Nietzsche provides on other occasions. See especially *A* 17, 27, 49, 53; *GS* 351; *GM* I. 6, 7; III. 11–23; *TI*, "Errors," 7; "Improvers," 2, 5; see also Pangle, "The Roots of Contemporary Nihilism," 56 ff., and Neumann, "Superman or Last Man?," 11–13.

18. "In a remarkable stroke of prescience, Zarathustra foresees that his teaching about the death of God, about 'creativity' and the subjectivity of all values, will be appropriated and exploited by the anti-Christian, anti-ascetic Left" (Pangle, "The 'Warrior Spirit,' " 154).

19. On the order of rank and a natural aristocracy, see *BGE* 275 and *A* 57.

20. In "Homer's Contest" (1872) Nietzsche described the godlike aspirations of the Greeks in words very like those used here, and in one of his last essays (*TI*, "Ancients"), he uses similar words. See also *TI*, "Socrates," 8–10, and *D* 544.

21. *Gerecht*, "just," is pronounced like *gerächt*, "revenged." Nietzsche utilizes this pun on other occasions as well; see II. 5; II. 20; also I. 19.

22. Homer *Odyssey* 12. 39 ff., 158 ff.

23. Heidegger, "Who is Nietzsche's Zarathustra?," 76; *Was Heißt Denken?*, 35, 45–48.

24. Three years later, in the 1886 preface to *Daybreak*, Nietzsche speaks in a way that clarifies his historical judgments in this chapter. Rousseau is "the moral tarantula" who bit both Kant and Robespierre, poisoning them with the moral fanaticism of a secularized Christianity, creating in one a revolutionary philosopher, in the other a revolutionary actor, both speaking on behalf of "the good and the just." See *KGW* VII 25 [130]. Nietzsche's "hatred" of "Rousseau in the French Revolution" is expressed in terms similar to those of "On the Tarantulas" in *Twilight* ("Skirmishes," 48). In *Antichrist* the themes of "On the Tarantulas" receive a less metaphoric analysis, but there too, Nietzsche invites enemies to a contest for the future of mankind. Revenge is seen as the fundamental motive of Christianity and its modern heirs, although Jesus himself is conspicuously exempted (27, 32, 35, 36, 40; see also *Z* I. 21). Christianity is said to be the historic movement that "cheated the world" of the fruit of the "ancient temple" of Greece and Rome (56–62). On revenge see also *GM* I. 8, 14–16, where Nietzsche quotes examples of "sweet revenge" from Christian authors. On modern teachings of equality as heir to Christianity see *BGE* 201 and Schacht's sensible defense of the propriety of Nietzsche's view of inequality and the justice of his attacks on the teaching of equality (*Nietzsche*, 326–40).

25. Pangle. "The 'Warrior Spirit,' " 155.

26. See *GS* 193, where it is said that the secret joke of Kant's soul is to prove in a way that would dumbfound "the whole world" that "the whole world" was right. There is much in this chapter that rings of the wisest of the moderns, Hegel, especially the master and bondsman dialectic and the desire for recognition.

27. Eden, *Political Leadership*, 81. In an argument based on *BGE* 211, Eden makes a case for Montaigne as the modern founder par excellence, the inventor of the "new, untrodden way to make men greater," the way of "humanity," of the bourgeois gentleman (59–63).

28. Hesiod *Works and Days* 3–4.

29. See also II. 2, where Zarathustra is likened to Boreas, the north wind.

30. As Pangle suggests, this threefold classification of wisdom—the famous wise, the free spirits, and the free spirits metamorphosed into the wisest—is the basis of Nietzsche's new history of philosophy. "In effect, Zarathustra here insists that if we—and the wisest themselves—'test' this threefold conception of the life of philosophy in our historical researches into the greatest past thinkers and cultures, we will discover it to be *the* compelling interpretative approach" ("The 'Warrior Spirit,' " 162).

31. Nietzsche later called the Night Song the loneliest song that was ever written and reproduced it in full in *Ecce Homo* ("Books: *Zarathustra*," 4, 7). The three songs have been ignored by most commentators. See the dismissive comments by Kaufmann and Hollingdale in their translations of *Zarathustra*. Dannhauser's astute comments focus on the Dancing Song (*Nietzsche's View of Socrates*, 257–

59). Fink criticizes the tendency to read the songs as expressions of particular personal experiences of Nietzsche and notes that they occur at a decisive point in the book; still, his comments do not show what is decisive about the songs (*Nietzsches Philosophie*, 78–79). Pangle's interpretation of the songs ("The 'Warrior Spirit,' " 160–66) leads to the heart of the matter but seems to me to have serious shortcomings; see below, n. 41.

32. Earlier occasions are lessons that Zarathustra addressed to his heart: Prologue 2, 5, 7, 9, 10; I. 2; II. 2.

33. The other occasions mark his decisive lessons about others: his rejection by the people in the prologue and his departure from his disciples at the end of part II.

34. For Scheier, the Night Song marks the turning point of *Zarathustra*, numerically inasmuch as it is the halfway point, the thirty-first of its sixty chapters, and in content inasmuch as it follows the break with traditional wisdom (II. 8) and exposes the dilemma of modern wisdom to which the whole second half is to provide the answer, the dilemma of the groundless ground (*Nietzsches Labyrinth* 179–89).

35. *Unergründlich* contains the word for ground or first principles, or elements.

36. Literally, "between four eyes"; this German expression for a *tête-à-tête* strengthens the image of eyes present at the beginning and end of Zarathustra's conversations with Life.

37. See prologue 10, where Zarathustra wonders if he is still alive, after the crowd has rejected his wisdom.

38. On the harm potentially done a heroic spirit by a woman's love, see *HH* I. 431, 434; Nietzsche's reflections on Xanthippe are also relevant in this context (*HH* I. 433, 437). See Strauss's comparison of Socrates' treatment of Xanthippe and Ischomachus's treatment of his wife, especially what is implied in the outcome Strauss finds it desirable to supply for Ischomachus's instruction of his wife (*Xenophon's Socratic Discourse* 156–58, 166.)

39. In the Song at Grave-side more than anywhere else in *Zarathustra*, the greatest events in Nietzsche's own past come almost to the surface, his friendship and hopes for Wagner and his break with him. Hollinrake demonstrates definitively just how much *Zarathustra* as a whole is "an anti-Wagnerian manifesto" (*Nietzsche*, 120), albeit recognizing that it is much more besides. Here, where the emphasis is on the person, Nietzsche also suggests the injury caused by the behavior of Lou Salomé and Paul Rée. In a Christmas day letter to Overbeck in 1882 (part II was completed the following summer), Nietzsche wrote that their actions toward him were "the *very best* opportunity of proving that for me 'all experience is useful, all days holy and all humans divine'!!!! All humans divine." See Binion, *Frau Lou*, 100, 104, and 75. Binion relates the "lucky bird omens" of this song to Nietzsche's belief that he had seen an eagle omen in Lou Salomé (104; letter to Köselitz, 4 August 1882). Though that "eagle" was only an "owl monster," Nietzsche can now sing like Prinz Vogelfrei—not only Prince Free *as* a Bird, but Prince Free *of* a Bird. The lament of the Song at Grave-side is echoed in the 1886 preface to *BT*: what marred Nietzsche's first book above all was that he allowed the Dionysian experience to be eclipsed by Schopenhauerian and Wagnerian elements foreign to it.

40. See Plato *Republic* 492a, 493a, 496a–e.

41. For Pangle, the interpretation of these songs is decisive in judging Nietzsche's thought as a whole, and his account of Nietzsche's warrior spirit comes to its focus here, for at this point, Pangle holds, Nietzsche attempts to ground and vindicate his spiritual warfare with the whole tradition; here "is the real bedrock, the fundamental empirical presupposition of the Will to Power doctrine" ("The 'Warrior Spirit,' " 163). Here, therefore, we allegedly see Nietzsche's failure to provide the evidence that would compel or incline us to take the side of his taste in the spiritual warfare against the wisest hitherto. In my view, Pangle has pursued the appropriate question to the appropriate place but has found, nevertheless, an inappropriate answer, for two reasons: he misreads the songs and misjudges their importance. He misreads the songs by making them too general, what the wisest moderns, few as they are, experience in their highest moments, rare as they are. More specifically he makes the Night Song the inescapable dilemma of the philosopher as founder, for his creation is either too great or too meagre; he fathers either patricidal sons or ineffectual ones. Having set the dilemma, Pangle provides, in his interpretation of the Dancing Song, a Heideggerian escape: the founder or procreator image of philosophy can quietly die because it is replaced by philosophy that articulates the historical truth of the age. By taking the way of radical historicism, the creative thinker is spared patricidal sons; and though he may seem to spawn shoals of unworthy ones, they all adopted him as father. He speaks what is true of his age, as others of his kind have spoken what was true of theirs. This interpretation of lament and escape makes the Song at Grave-side a problem because it is quite unnecessary, and Pangle treats it gingerly: perhaps it is the creative soul's repetition of lament and escape. Pangle thus makes Zarathustra's fluid and singular situation static and general. But, as Zarathustra's singular experience of a novel insight, the songs are more naturally explicable, it seems to me, in the way that Zarathustra himself suggests: the lament is temporary, the answer permanent; but the permanently true answer is not yet fully in hand, for it promises a more complete recovery to come.

Pangle misjudges the importance of these songs by exaggerating it, for, important as they are, they are not sufficient for a final judgment on Nietzsche's thought. At its very climax part III contains three songs that repeat the issues of these songs in a way that completes them; only after those songs have been interpreted are we in a position to judge Nietzsche's thought as a whole, but Pangle does not treat those songs. His essay thus broadens its focus too soon and constructs a case against Nietzsche before pursuing the warrior spirit through part III. While succeeding in showing how Nietzsche can be saved from the cloud created by his praise of war, Pangle leaves him under a different, if much more elevated, cloud: Nietzsche is not the teacher he would like to be because he fails to repeat Socrates' reserve. He posits a goal rather than probing every goal; he becomes a sectarian, too religious, too moral, still a poet. By becoming the Plato of his own Socrates, he betrays what is highest in mankind, the hard Socratism of sheer, impassioned wonder. In my view, this praise of Socrates at Nietzsche's expense (by one who knows what "Socrates would doubtless say" to Nietzsche: he would tell him to alter the hopeful conclusion of the preface of *Beyond*) requires ignoring Nietzsche's critique of Socrates and the Socratics, ignoring his history of Socratism to the present, and ignoring his goal as set out in part III.

42. Nietzsche uses the present participle of *sein* in its substantive form

(Seiende); although singular in German, the word functions as a collective noun that needs the plural in English in order to distinguish it from being *(Sein)*.

43. That "life" is coextensive with "all beings" is made apparent by Heidegger, *Nietzsche* I, 277–78, 341–43; Fink, *Nietzsches Philosophie*, 80; and Schacht, *Nietzsche*, 234–53.

44. The original title of this chapter was "On Good and Evil."

45. Whereas Zarathustra avoids the word *nature* even where it seems necessary, Kaufmann's and Hollingdale's translations use that word at this point.

46. German can say this with substantive participles that avoid the word *thing*: *Alles Lebendige ist ein Gehorchendes*: "Every living is an obeying."

47. This imagery of stealth and capture for the discovery of the fundamental matter is present in Schopenhauer's account of the discovery of will in *The World as Will and Representation*, vol. 2, suppl. to ch. 18. The fabulous language of *Zarathustra* is far from being the only one available to Nietzsche for his intimations of the fundamental phenomenon. In *Gay Science* and *Beyond*, but especially in notes refined for his Hauptwerk, he employs a language closer to the traditional language of philosophy. The central sections of *Gay Science*, part IV, the part that prepares the way for *Zarathustra*, raise the possibility of discerning the fundamental truth of all beings. In the section entitled "Will and Wave" (310), the secret of the wave is also the secret of the will discovered by the speaker to be his own secret; but the speaker vows a loyal silence about their shared secret, for they are also of one kind in the way they disclose their secret (see also *GS* 240). The parallel passages in *Beyond* show how psychology is once again the way in to the fundamental problems (23), how the truth of the soul leads to the truth of life and the truth of being (36), how the spirit of the discoverer of these truths differs from spirit as customarily experienced (230–31), and, with playful malice, how the route so traversed to the secret heart of things leads to the vindication of the gods (37). Schacht (*Nietzsche*, 52–117, 140–86, 187–253) provides a detailed analysis of Nietzsche's explorations of the metaphysical and epistemological problems of will to power, with special concentration on the notes collected in *Will to Power*. He painstakingly demonstrates how Nietzsche refined and transformed terms borrowed from existing realms of discourse. *Chaos, perspective, creation, instinct*, as well as the fundamental *will to power*, when interpreted in the new, Nietzschean sense, exhibit a coherence and plausibility not otherwise evident. By carefully deciphering Nietzsche's subtle employment and adaptation of the available language, Schacht is able to show that no contradiction exists between Nietzsche's critique of metaphysical knowledge and his claim to possess it.

48. Yeats, "Supernatural Songs" XII, Meru.

49. See *KGW* IV 5 [23] Spring–Summer 1875: "The stupidity of the will is Schopenhauer's greatest thought when thought is measured by the criterion of power. . . . No one would name the stupid God."

50. See Eden, *Political Leadership*, 88–91.

51. A note from the summer in which Nietzsche completed part II gives the words of the final stanza of this chapter to Ariadne in a dream (*KGW* VII 13 [1, p. 453]).

52. Like his Zarathustra, Nietzsche has to return from the futures that he alone has occupied if he is to address even his most progressive contemporaries in an idiom that they will not find offensive. The whole of *Beyond*, addressed to "free minds," is a return from the future marked out by *Zarathustra* (*EH*, "Books: *Beyond*," 2).

53. Nietzsche's working title for this chapter was "On the Contemplatives." The power of the contemplatives and Nietzsche's own place among them is indicated in *GS* 301, and *D* 41.

54. Calder plausibly reads this parable as Nietzsche's last public reference to the controversy with Wilamowitz over the scholarly merits of *Birth* ("The Wilamowitz–Nietzsche Struggle," 251.

55. While he here criticizes the practice of the "nutcracker," he later refers to "divine nutcrackers" (III. 10) and is himself presented with a problem as a nut to crack (IV. 7). In *Genealogy* (III. 9) Nietzsche refers to "we nutcrackers of the soul." See *BGE* 206, 207, on modern scholarship.

56. Hegel, *Philosophy of History*, "Introduction."

57. See IV. 13, §9, for a reason for keeping reasons secret.

58. Plato *Theaetetus* 196c–200d.

59. *Ibid.* 143e–144d.

60. Rosen, *Limits of Analysis*, 200.

61. Kierkegaard, *Concluding Unscientific Postscript*, 164–66, 340.

62. The drafts of this speech are in the third person (*KGW* VII 10 [17, 21]) or addressed to poets in the second person (13 [18]).

63. This is the only time that *Übermensch* appears in the plural in *Zarathustra*. Its first use in Nietzsche's books occurs in the plural in a context that also involves the creation of gods and supermen (*GS* 143).

64. The valuable account of "On the Poets" in Shapiro, "The Rhetoric of Nietzsche's *Zarathustra*," concentrates on the deconstruction of metaphor as an act of perpetual play and shows how Zarathustra implicates himself in that deconstruction. Still, by failing to note the transition from "we" to "they" for the final lengthy speech, Shapiro does not seem to give due weight to the poet Zarathustra's claim to be different from other poets.

65. Matt. 7:9.

66. Plato *Ion* 535e.

67. Yeats, "The Circus Animals' Desertion."

68. See Heller, "Nietzsche—Philosopher of Art." Despite this insight into the modern poetic aesthetic that favors a spare and ironic self-reflection, Nietzsche wrote his most important work in a style decidedly contrary to such taste. Given his account of the penance practiced by both modern poets and modern heroes of knowledge (II. 13), Nietzsche would have been glad to refuse the lessons in thrift urged on him by his critics. Still, he has had to pay a high price for his refusal of the reigning rhetoric. *Ecce Homo* ("Books: *Birth*," 4) states that the poetic style of *Zarathustra* "is described with incisive certainty and anticipated" in *Wagner in Bayreuth*, 9. There, in an analysis of Wagner's language and the problems of communication that he faced, Nietzsche distinguishes communication in mythic form from communication directed at the theoretical man. Avoiding communication directed only at the theoretical man and desiring to influence the feelings, Nietzsche, a poet and sculptor of language whose work is intended only to be read, and who consequently has at his disposal only concepts and words, puts himself under the sway of rhetoric. But he faces a very serious problem. Not only has the language of myth and fable "been deeply debased and disfigured, transformed into 'fairy tale,' the plaything of the women and children of the degenerate folk and quite divested of its miraculous and serious manly nature" (8), but passion, or what he wants to bring to speech, is rarely loquacious in life. Thus the attempt to elevate language by having it express exalted and noble passions runs the risk of appearing

artificial. Whereas Wagner was afforded devices of gesture and music in the solution of this problem, Nietzsche has to depend solely on language for the production of the desired effect.

69. For example, Kaufmann, *Ecce Homo*, "Editor's Introduction," 2.

70. Nietzsche's classification of music in *Daybreak* fits this criticism of poetry: it is not "innocent" enough when it does not think "wholly and solely of itself," when it acts in consciousness of "hearers and listeners and effects and failures" (255).

71. Yeats, "Nineteen Hundred and Nineteen."

72. See Barfield, *Saving the Appearances*, ch. 19, esp. 198. See also Barfield, *History in English Words*, ch. 11, "Imagination," for an account of the shift from mimesis to creativity.

73. Coleridge, *Biographia Literaria*, ch. 13.

74. Idem, "On Dejection—An Ode."

75. In the context in which Nietzsche mentions the order of rank among poets, he speaks of a *"world-governing* spirit, a destiny" who "first creates truth" (*EH*, "Books: *Zarathustra*," 6).

76. Nietzsche planned a more elaborate visit to the underworld: *KGW* VII 13 [2,3 pp. 466, 469]; *KGW* VII 10 [28, 29].

77. See *TI*, "Morality," 3. Only in this chapter does Zarathustra name the "state" after part I.

78. The political character of a church is defined in opposition to any state in *Gay Science:* "A church is above all a structure for ruling that secures the highest rank for the *more spiritual* human beings and that *believes* in the power of spirituality to the extent of forbidding itself the use of all cruder instruments of force,— on this score alone the church is under all circumstances a *nobler* institution than the state.—" (358).

79. See *SE* 4 for a clarification of this chapter. There Nietzsche describes the threatening barbarism of modern times, when, sunk under the oppression of the modern state, in which everything is ruled by the crudest and worst of forces, "the egoism of the money makers," and "the military despots," men seek desperately for an image of man to elevate them. Of the three available candidates, those of Rousseau, Goethe, and Schopenhauer, Rousseau's has "the greatest fire and is certain of the greatest popular effect." In fact, "behind all socialistic tremors and earthquakes is Rousseauian man, moving like old Typhoeus under Mount Etna." When this volcanic giant erupts, it is an eruption of modern man's self-contempt directed at what has made him contemptible to himself:

> Oppressed and half crushed by arrogant castes and pitiless wealth, spoiled by priests and bad education, humiliated before himself by ridiculous customs, man in his distress calls on "holy nature," and suddenly feels that she is as far from him as any Epicurean god. His prayers do not reach her, so deeply has he sunk into the chaos of the Unnatural. Scornfully he throws away all the gaudy finery, which shortly before seemed to be his most human possessions, his arts and sciences, the advantages of his refined life. He bangs his fists on the walls, in whose shadow he degenerated, and cries for light, sun, forest and cliff. And when he cries, "Only nature is good, only the natural man is human!" then he is despising himself and longing beyond himself; a mood in which the soul is ready for terrible decisions, but which also calls up what is most noble and rare in its depths.

Still, in the book dedicated to Voltaire, Nietzsche says of "Rousseau's passionate idiocies and half-truths that have called awake the optimistic spirit of revolution: 'Ecrasez l'infame!' " (HH I. 463).

80. When these words are quoted later, slight variations are introduced (III. 12, §16; III. 13; IV. 2).

81. Or could the nightmare be Nietzsche's acknowledgment of a fundamental deficiency in his teaching?—that Zarathustra's teaching is essentially indistinguishable from the Soothsayer's nihilism, as Rosen suggests, honoring Nietzsche's honesty? Rosen gives an enlightening interpretation of this chapter (Limits of Analysis, 206–10) that assigns it extraordinary importance ("the puzzle of Zarathustra's ultimate teaching is treated most extensively in 'The Soothsayer' "). Nevertheless, Rosen does not give due weight to Zarathustra's transformations, treating this still early chapter as if it contained the "ultimate teaching" and provided the basis for a final judgment about Nietzsche's teaching. But it is just here, beginning with the nightmare and leading to "On Redemption," that the most fundamental transformation is set in motion.

82. The "Alpa" cried out three times by the dreamer may be a coinage based on Alp, the old High German word for nightmare, present in Alpdrücken, Alptraum. Or it may be the personified bringer of the nightmare (incubus in Latin and English), the demon who sits on the dreamer's chest causing evil dreams. Such demons came in female (incubus) and male (succubus) varieties, depending on the dreamer, and Alpa may be the female form who would visit Zarathustra with a nightmare. Nietzsche recounted a dream to his friend Reinhart von Seydlitz in the summer of 1877. "Nietzsche related laughingly that in a dream he had to climb an endless mountain path; at the top, under the mountain peak, he wanted to pass the mouth of a cave when out of the dark depth a voice called out to him: 'Alpa, Alpa—who is carrying his ashes to the mountain?' " (cited in the notes to "The Soothsayer" in the Studienausgabe of KGW XIV 306).

83. This image seems clear in its mockery, but what do the five sorts of faces symbolize? Are they five symbols of unredeemed wisdom as the next chapter might suggest?

84. See Matt. 15:30–31.

85. Unmut, whose root is Mut, courage, Zarathustra's characteristic attitude to what repels him.

86. See Matt. 16:13–17.

87. When commenting on this necessity of the will in Ecce Homo, Nietzsche remarks that it necessarily expressed itself in the ascetic ideal, for there was no alternative—"until Zarathustra" (Books: "Genealogy").

88. In interpreting "On Redemption," Heidegger argues persuasively that Nietzsche's focus on time's "it was" does not narrow time to one dimension, but highlights the essential character of time as passage. See "Who is Nietzsche's Zarathustra?", 72–73, and the apparently earlier and more detailed Was Heißt Denken?, esp. 39–40, 42–47, 76–78. Heidegger provides the essential commentary on Nietzsche's phrase "time's desire" by showing how time is defined by its passing into the past; its coming is a going that transforms it from possibility to dead and gone necessity. Nevertheless, Pangle seems to me to be right in arguing against Heidegger that the ill will of revenge is directed not simply against temporality but against temporality as fate ("The 'Warrior Spirit,' " 171–72).

89. See KGW VIII 15 [30] Spring 1888 = WP 765: "The instinct of revenge has

so mastered mankind in the course of millennia that the whole of metaphysics, psychology, conception of history, but above all morality, is impregnated with it. As far as man has thought he has introduced the bacillus of revenge into things."

90. See Eliade, *Cosmos and History*, 85–86, and Fustel de Coulanges, *The Ancient City*, bk. I and II.

91. Strong says of the four preachings of madness, "It is not hard to pick out who is meant," and he identifies the four as (1) Hegel and Anaximander, (2) Kant and Anaximenes, (3) Schopenhauer, (4) Wagner (*Nietzsche*, 225–28).

92. The phrasing suggests Christianity by referring to "it was" as the stone that cannot be rolled away; see Matt. 28:2; Mark 16:4; Luke 24:2. On the novelty of Christianity's eternal punishment, see *D* 72, 77.

93. See Schopenhauer's account of the passage of time as a dying in which the present continuously rushes into the dead past, in *World as Will and Representation*, I. 57.

94. Strauss, "Note on the Plan of Nietzsche's *Beyond Good and Evil*," 189.

95. The distinction between reconciliation and something higher may be the distinction between *amor fati* and willing eternal return. Amor fati would be the act of a lover who "wants to learn more and more to see as beautiful what is necessary" and thereby to become "one of those who make things beautiful." But higher still than *amor fati* is the act of the creative will that says to the whole of the past, "But thus I willed it!" (*GS* 276). This New Year's resolution of 1 January 1882, opens book 4 of *Gay Science*, in which is found the first introduction to the experience of the previous August, when eternal return first came to Nietzsche.

96. These events, from nightmare to redemption, are presented with astonishing economy in *Beyond*, a book one of whose functions is to so concentrate on the near that a way is opened to the far, to the most distant future traversed by Zarathustra (*EH*, "Books: *Beyond*," 2). After the account of religious cruelty that sacrifices God for the stone (55), Nietzsche turns to the one with the "asiatic and supra-asiatic eye," Zarathustra, who has gazed most deeply into the most world-denying way of thinking and has, without really meaning to do so, "opened his eyes on the opposite ideal, the ideal of the most high-spirited, alive, world-affirming human being . . . who wills to have *what was and is* repeated to all eternity, shouting insatiably *da capo* not only to himself but to the whole play and spectacle" (56). A remarkable passage in a book Nietzsche wrote more than ten years prior to *Zarathustra* illuminates both the curse on mankind described in "On Redemption" and the anticipation of redemption it describes (*UD* 1).

97. Schacht's chapters on "Value and Values" and "Morals and Morality" (*Nietzsche*, 341–475) demonstrate that "the standard of value with which Nietzsche operates in his 'revaluation of values' is for him neither conventional nor stipulative (nor, for that matter, merely symptomatic of his own constitution)" (394). "Nietzsche's 'naturalization of morality' thus involves the incorporation of moral theory into philosophical anthropology, in the context of which it loses its autonomy but acquires legitimacy" (464). Schacht's sensible and sober interpretation of Nietzsche's statements about value shows that Nietzsche's "new theory of value" (394–416) knows how to ground itself objectively, that valuations consequent on insight involve not merely the bestowal of value but its attainment (416).

98. Krell's felicitous translation (Heidegger, *Nietzsche*, I. 387; English trans., II. 124).

99. *Nietzsche*, I. 417; English trans., II. 156.

100. *Nietzsche*, I. 463–64; English trans., II. 199. On Heidegger's reading of the important note that refers to the stamp of Being on Becoming (*KGW* VIII 7 [54]), see Krell's comments in the English trans., *Nietzsche*, I. 19, II. 201, 256–57.

101. *Was Heißt Denken?*, 76, 46.

102. On the connection between will to power and eternal return in "On Redemption," see Löwith, *Nietzsches Philosophie*, 82; and Fink, *Nietzsches Philosophie*, 81–82. Despite his detailed study of "On Redemption," Strong can state that "there is no direct textual evidence" for "the notion that the will to power has something directly to do with eternal return" (*Nietzsche*, 276). Strong loses the essential link when he interprets the failure of the will to will the past as a necessary and perpetual failure of will (224) that can be overcome only by the abandonment of will to power (257). Missing what "On Redemption" shows about the link between will to power and eternal return, Arendt entitles her chapter on Nietzsche, "Nietzsche's Repudiation of the Will" and sees eternal return as an acceptance of the cycles of nature by a superman emptied of ambition or will to power (*Life of the Mind: Willing*, 158–72, esp. 168 ff.). Perhaps because it ignores "On Redemption," even Rosen's acute reading of *Zarathustra* arranges Nietzsche's teaching under the umbrella of reconciliation or amor fati without seeing reconciliation as a consequence of the "something higher" effected by the creative will to power (*Limits of Analysis*, 211–15). Another way of indicating this limitation in Rosen's insightful study can be given in his own terms: a study of Zarathustra's dreams, it omits the dream in part III (10) in which Zarathustra weighs the world and finds it measurable and masterable. Nehamas argues for an essential connection between will to power and eternal return on strictly metaphysical grounds: on the basis of the whole understood as will to power, to affirm one item in that whole, one's self, it is necessary to affirm the whole, for if a single property of the whole were different, the self would be a different self (*Nietzsche*, 141–69).

103. Aristotle *Nicomachean Ethics* 6. 5.

104. His double will is further unriddled at III. 3, and at III. 9 he proclaims victory over one side of his double will.

105. The whole point of part IV is lost, as well as the point of Zarathustra's separation from his disciples, if one carelessly assumes that the "superior men" addressed there are the disciples of parts I and II; see, e.g., Alderman, *Nietzsche's Gift*, 114 ff.; Rosen, *Limits of Analysis*, 205.

106. The dialogue is introduced as if the Stillest Hour spoke through the twelve strikes of the clock at the midnight hour—but then one hears only eleven speeches. Scheier implausibly transforms the very silence following the conversation into the twelfth strike (*Nietzsches Labyrinth*, 204–08). Does the laugh at the end stand for the twelfth? Or does the missing speech indicate that Zarathustra does not report to his disciples everything said in his conversation with his soul? In III. 15 the midnight bell again makes only eleven speeches but there the next chapter follows the final strike. Perhaps that is the case here too.

107. Hollinrake (*Nietzsche*, 78) describes a verbal parallel between this passage and Wagner's *Götterdämmerung*, act 3, sc. 1. Nietzsche's initial stinginess with the teaching of eternal return is shown by his refusal to speak to anyone about it for a full year after the momentous day in August 1881 when it first came to him and by the very few occasions on which he ever spoke to anyone about it (Janz, *Nietzsche* II. 80, 280). Part III of *Zarathustra* remedies that stinginess.

NOTES TO PART III

1. See Janz, *Nietzsche*, II. 79–81.

2. The house in Nizza in which part III (and part IV) was written was destroyed in an earthquake four years later. After observing the destruction, Nietzsche commented to a friend: "This has the advantage for posterity of leaving them one less pilgrimage site to visit" (Janz, *Nietzsche*, II. 514).

3. The geography of *Zarathustra* roughly reflects Nietzsche's annual travels between the Alps and the Mediterranean. Taken literally, it requires a cave in mountains on the mainland; a town nearby in which the speeches of the prologue are given; another city, the Colorful Cow, in which the speeches of part I are given, two days' walk from the cave (III. 8); islands to which Zarathustra sails at the opening of part II and away from which he sails at the opening of part III; neighboring islands, the isle of his youthful dreams (II. 11) and the volcanic isle where the sailors land (II. 18); the sea of the sea voyage (III. 2–4); and the mainland with many cities, including "the Great City" (III. 7), where he wanders after his return from the sea voyage. The blessed isles would have to be extensive and populous, since on them were found the crowd of cripples (II. 20), young girls dancing in a forest meadow (II. 10), and Zarathustra's enemies, as well as his friends (II. 1). The geography is even less precise than the imprecise historical setting, and, like natural things generally in the book, serves primarily as metaphor for ascent and descent, arrival and departure, danger and decadence. Still, the geographic setting, like the historic setting, is emblematic of an urban culture in decline, though without the specific technological accoutrements of the modern age, a necessary lack given the literary fiction of a nonspecific historic setting.

4. Exod. 3:8.

5. Nietzsche began the chapter of *Ecce Homo* entitled "Why I am a Destiny" by saying, "I know my lot," and describing the coming crisis of Western man in dramatic terms, with himself as "dynamite."

6. See "Die Sonne sinkt," the sixth poem of *DD*, and *GS* 309, a speech from the seventh solitude, which precedes the fundamental insight of 310.

7. Compare Matt. 26:75, where Peter "wept bitterly" after his betrayal of Jesus.

8. For analysis of this chapter, see especially Heidegger, *Nietzsche*, I. 289–97, 438–44; English trans. II. 37–44, 176–83; Rosen, *Limits of Analysis*, 211–14; Fink, *Nietzsches Philosophie*, 82–90.

9. See Small, "Three Interpretations of Eternal Recurrence," 100–01. Manuscript variants of this part of the speech connect it to Ariadne and "The Other Dancing Song" (III. 15).

10. Vision and riddle are thereby shown to be only one thing, not two. "The Vision of the Loneliest" is the title that Nietzsche originally gave to this chapter.

11. A similar unequal division into two parts at the point of summoned courage occurs in the two chapters most closely related to this one as the unriddling of the vision, III. 11 and III. 13. Chapter 15 of part III could also be interpreted as dividing into its first two parts at the point of summoned courage. See also the two divisions in III. 8, 10. Dannhauser notes that, "in Part III of *Zarathustra*, courage is the most highly praised and most frequently mentioned of the virtues. It is presented as an intellectual as well as a moral virtue" (*Nietzsche's View of Socrates*, 266 ff.).

12. The vision is trivialized if the Dwarf is guessed to be "the 'last man' in ourselves," as if this were not the vision of the loneliest but of all of us (Magnus, *Nietzsche's Existential Imperative*, 167). Alderman interprets the Dwarf as symbolic of Zarathustra's "own timidity and of his longing for something immutable and certain" (*Nietzsche's Gift*, 96), though the Dwarf's words say the opposite. Heidegger ignores the Dwarf's identification as the spirit of gravity and makes him simply inattentive humanity that takes everything superficially and knows nothing of despair or decision (*Nietzsche*, I. 308–09; English trans. II. 53–55.

13. It is Herakles who is customarily pictured with the club, but Theseus also used a brass-bound club in his first labor, the killing of Periphetes, and carried the club with him ever after.

14. Plato *Republic* 430c, a passage that makes clear that Socrates is acquainted with attacking courage as well; see Nietzsche's remark: "A very popular error: having the courage of one's convictions; rather it is a matter of having the courage for an *attack* on one's convictions!" (cited by Kaufmann, *Nietzsche*, 19). Courage is defined as the refusal to stick fast in *Beyond* (41).

15. When Nietzsche lists the four virtues of the philosopher (*BGE* 284), courage and insight are followed by compassion and solitude.

16. The climactic song of Zarathustra's dance with Life (III. 15, §3) is later given the title "Once More" (IV. 19, §12). In *World as Will and Representation* Schopenhauer had advanced as possible the affirmation of eternal return as long as one did not know the truth about the wretchedness of life (54), but when that is known, when life has been fathomed as it is, such a response becomes impossible, and one wills much rather absolute annihilation (59).

17. Commentators violate the image of the gateway by supposing that it is there to be entered, for that decisive or existential choice that transforms one's being in time. (See Heidegger, *Nietzsche*, I. 311–445; English trans., II. 56–181; *Sein und Zeit*, 65, 68a, 74; Rosen, *Limits of Analysis*, 213 ff.) But Zarathustra uses the gateway to trap the Dwarf into refuting the apparent linearity of time. The dwarf is crushed not by stepping into the gateway, but by the thought of its return.

18. Zarathustra's statement that the Dwarf's answer is too easy has been interpreted as meaning that it is completely false; see Stambaugh, *Nietzsche's Thought of Eternal Return*, 38: "For Zarathustra, time is precisely not a circle"; and Strong, *Nietzsche*, 264.

19. See the notes of 1881, in which the arguments for eternal return were first projected, arguments based on time as infinite and possible states as finite (*KGW* V 11 [148, 202, 203, 292, 311, and, for the counterarguments, 313]). See also *KGW* VIII 14 [187] = *WP* 1066, March–June 1888.

20. Schacht, *Nietzsche*, 265.

21. In the first note to mention eternal return, the idea of "taking possession" is expressed as incorporation or ingestion, the thought being taken into one's body and taking over one's being after the "fundamental errors," the "passions," and a "renouncing knowledge" have already been incorporated (*KGW* V 11 [141]).

22. That the crushing element in the thought is self-inflicted, the consequence of an already present antipathy toward life, is reflected in a note of 1882: "This thought is mild against those who do not believe in it; it has no hellfire, no threats" (*KGW* V 11 [160]).

23. *Ein Verwandelter*, the word used in "On the Three Transformations" (I. 1) and *GS* 341.

338 NOTES TO PAGES 170–78

24. Rosen's acute analysis of "On the Vision and the Riddle" becomes vague at this point, alleging unclearness on Nietzsche's part regarding the symbol of the shepherd: the clear implication that Zarathustra becomes the superman is held to be "inconsistent with Zarathustra's regular denial that he is himself, or can become, a superman" (*Limits of Analysis*, 214). Rosen's identifications of the symbols of the second half of the vision have the merit of being guesses, but they are not guesses guided by the clues in the vision or by Zarathustra's later enactment of it. Speculating on the shepherd, he says, "The guardian of the sheep may be the Platonic king or Christ," or the shepherd is "the human spirit that created the Christian perspective."

25. The identification of the snake with nihilism necessitates an interlude of 140 pages in Heidegger's account of this chapter (*Nietzsche*, I. 298–438; English trans., II. 45–75), the demise of the Dwarf and the advent of the shepherd are there grounded in the historic necessity of the thought of eternal return as the countermovement to the history of Western nihilism.

26. No reference has previously been made to the fact that he found his disciples in an afternoon; the return to the disciples occurs on an afternoon in the fall (II. 2).

27. The last reference to "disciples" in the book occurs in "On Redemption" (II. 20), and Zarathustra last addresses them as "my disciples" just when they have exhibited their incapacity (II. 19). He had earlier referred to them as "children" in the insulting close to II. 5, but not as *his* children. At the end of part I, anticipating his coming appearances to them, he referred to them as "children of one hope" (I. 22, §3).

28. Descartes, *Discourse on Method*, pt. 6.

29. Fink, *Nietzsches Philosophie*, 90; the significance that Fink sees emphasizes Zarathustra's insight, but not the actions consequent on it. Like Fink, Morgan sees this speech as "a song of innocence" (*What Nietzsche Means*, 307).

30. *Gram und Grauen und Grund. Grauen* is the term for the dusk of morning, the gathering light in which Zarathustra addresses the heavens.

31. Matt. 5:3–11.

32. *Von Ohngefähr*, said to be "the oldest honor on earth," means literally the title of nobility conferred on chance, "Lord Chance," and is a pun that sounds like "Von Ungefähr"—"from about . . ." or "from approximately . . ."—a phrase expressing uncertainty or indeterminacy regarding a thing's origins. The words of Zarathustra's blessing reflect the "unsound reasoning" of the "ungodly men" in the Wisdom of Solomon (in the *Apocrypha*) 1:16–2:2; see 2:21–24.

33. Yeats, "Meditations In Time of Civil War."

34. Ps. 19:1.

35. Aristotle *Physics* 196a25ff.; 199a3–5.

36. Kant, *Critique of Practical Reason*, Conclusion.

37. *Daybreak* (130) contains many preliminary reflections relevant to this chapter and speaks of Christianity's need to judge that the heavens are "not as stupid as they look."

38. In the different mood of *Human* Nietzsche says the same thing: "Whoever revealed to us the essence of the world would disappoint us all most unpleasantly" (*HH* I. 29).

39. See *GS* 346 on the "extravagant aberration of human vanity" that invented values that were "supposed to *excel* the value of the actual world."

40. Heidegger, *Nietzsche*, II. 127, 241, 61–62, 129, 165–6; English trans., IV. 83, 183, 28–9, 86, 117.

41. See *Daybreak* (423) for the silence of the sea and the silence of the sky and what the great muteness of nature described there evokes from the speaker Nietzsche.

42. Plato *Phaedrus* 247c–248e.

43. Lucretius *De Rerum Natura* 1. 62–79.

44. Aristophanes *The Clouds* 423ff.

45. Ibid., 380ff.

46. Strauss, *Xenophon's Socratic Discourse*, 148–49.

47. Heidegger, *Identity and Difference*, 54–61, 68–73.

48. "To speak differently to different people may be said to be irony in the proper sense of the word" (Strauss, *Thoughts on Machiavelli*, 40, where reference is made to Plato *Rivals (Lovers)* 133d8–e1; see Strauss, *The City and Man*, 51).

49. See Lucretius *De Rerum Natura* 2.1ff.

50. Plato *Republic* 516c–517b; see 482c–d.

51. Not being a prince, Zarathustra is as free as Machiavelli to ignore Machiavelli's advice to the prince that he avoid arousing hatred against himself. In avoiding the arousal of envy, Zarathustra practices Machiavelli's art of seeming: "Everyone sees what you seem to be but few touch what you are" (*The Prince*, ch. 18). Few will touch what is truly enviable in Zarathustra, and his art of seeming will not insist that he is enviable. One reason for avoiding the arousal of envy is given at the end of *Antichrist* (57).

52. On "the dwarfing of mankind," the road that modern man has taken, and "which can now be completely surveyed," see *KGW* VIII 10 [17] = *WP* 866: "Once we possess that common economic management of the earth that will soon be inevitable, mankind will be able to find its best meaning as a machine in the service of this economy—as a tremendous clockwork, composed of ever smaller, ever more subtly 'adapted' gears." See also *KGW* VIII 9 [17] = *WP* 890; *KGW* VIII 9 [153] = *WP* 898; *KGW* VIII 10 [11] = *WP* 888. On modern uniformity see *HH* I. 481.

53. Matt. 19:13–15.

54. In his account of *Daybreak* (*EH*, "Books: *Daybreak*") the book with which "my campaign against morality begins," Nietzsche describes the Great Noon as belonging to his task because he has seen "that mankind has so far been in the *worst* of hands." Therefore it falls to him to prepare "a moment of the highest self-examination for mankind, a *Great Noon* where it looks back and far forward, when it steps out from under the dominion of accidents and priests and for the first time poses, *as a whole*, the question of Why? and for What?" He also says that what he once described under "the idea of Bayreuth" belongs to the Great Noon (*EH* "Books: *Birth*," 4; see *WB* 8–11).

55. The Mount of Olives is Jesus' customary retreat (Luke 22:39), and it is at its foot, at Gethsemane, that he suffers in solitude while his disciples fall asleep (Matt. 26:30–46, Mark 14:26–42).

56. Nietzsche's working title for this chapter was "The Winter Song."

57. Zarathustra may be referring to the art of speech practiced by Plato and discovered by Nietzsche to be essential to Plato's undertaking. Zarathustra's invention of a bright, transparent silence discourages nutcrackers by leading them to believe that only the bright and transparent exists in his speech. Nietzsche's ostentatious flaunting of Zarathustra's invention has the opposite effect and is pre-

sumably essential to his undertaking. Like Zarathustra (I. 17), he seems to want to be asked what he's hiding.

58. The art of concealment is the only art that Zarathustra specifically claims to possess as an art; see the related art of having a shell, III. 11, §2. Zarathustra the gift-giver later refers to the art of giving as the "master art" (IV. 8) and speaks as one who has learned it well.

59. Xenophon *Hiero*, last sentence; see the commentary by Strauss, *On Tyranny*, 85.

60. See Zarathustra's advice on spitting (II. 6, end).

61. See Gen. 19:24, 25; Jon. 3:4, 4:11. In Luke 19:41–48 Jesus approaches the city of Jerusalem and weeps over it; he prophesies its destruction but enters it to correct it.

62. The word *nihilism* appears in Nietzsche's books only after the completion of *Zarathustra*. The most extensive analysis of nihilism in his books is found in *Genealogy*, where it is linked to *Zarathustra* by a hint indicating that the later writings are preludes to *Zarathustra*, clarifications of the hour in which Zarathustra appears. The analysis of nihilism in *Genealogy* is limited by the book's being "A Polemic" that contains only "preliminary studies" (*EH*, "Books: *Genealogy*"). Although lacking a resolution to the problem of nihilism, the book makes two promises at those decisive points where it says, "Enough! Enough!" and breaks off its analyses. The first comes at the end of the second essay and concerns the one "who must yet come to us," one who is "younger" and "stronger" than Nietzsche, Zarathustra. The promise Nietzsche here gives is one that he has already kept: Zarathustra shows the way out of nihilism. The second promise does not point backward to *Zarathustra* but forward to a new work; it occurs at the end of the third essay, after Nietzsche has extended his polemic to the ascetic ideals that eventually led to nihilism of the Soothsayer's sort. There, he promises to "probe these things more thoroughly and severely in another connection (under the title 'On the History of European Nihilism'; it will be contained in a work in progress: *The Will to Power: Attempt at a Revaluation of All Values*)." This promise he was unable to keep, but by July 1887, when *Genealogy* was finished, the analysis and overcoming of nihilism had already been achieved by Zarathustra and sketched out in elaborate notes. Some of these notes, which were expanded in the coming months, are collected under the title "European Nihilism" in *Will to Power*.

63. See *Daybreak* (64) on Christianity as a hunt that uses the device of inviting its quarry to despair. On nihilism and the revival of Christian belief, see *Gay Science* (347): "Christianity it seems to me is still needed by most people in old Europe even today" (1886).

64. While linking Christianity and the phenomenon of modern nihilism, *Zarathustra* does not describe the way in which nihilism sprang historically from Christianity, nor does it argue that "nihilism is rooted" "in one particular interpretation, the Christian moral one" (*KGW* VIII 2 [127] = *WP* 1).

65. See Exod. 20:3.

66. Kierkegaard, *Point of View*, 111.

67. *Erfliegbar*, capable of being circled by flight.

68. *Meisterin*, literally female master, mistress.

69. Descartes, *Discourse on Method*, pt. 6. Zarathustra here expresses for the only time a thought that Nietzsche long cultivated in notes; for the earlier notes see Nietzsche, *Philosophy and Truth*, trans. Breazeale, 20–21 n.; 35, §93; 58, §9; 87; for later notes see *KGW* VIII 6 [14] = *WP* 565 and 710. The formula of Zarathustra's

day wisdom is discussed in Small, "Three Interpretations of Eternal Recurrence," 96–97.

70. *Sucht* also means addiction, or control by some need.

71. Nietzsche had written "will to power" at the point where he first named the three accursed things, but deleted it from the final version; he also deleted the frequent references to "will."

72. *Selbstsucht*, literally, is the passion for the self. Because Zarathustra's speech deals only with the selfishness of the highest selves, it does not repeat the warning given earlier about a low selfishness (I. 22, §1), the "egoism" preached up by "English Utilitarians" "who undertake to advocate the cause of egoism as the cause of the general welfare" (*BGE* 228), and whose advocacy of egoism becomes the advocacy of other-directed service. "Selfishness is worth as much as the physiological worth of the one who has it" (*TI*, "Skirmishes," 33).

73. Matt. 10:26; 1 Cor. 3:13; 2 Cor. 5:10.

74. See *HH* I. 39, 107. See *GS* 356 on "the American faith of today which is fast becoming the European faith" that any role is a possibility for almost any man.

75. Strauss, *Thoughts on Machiavelli*, 286. "Selfishness" of the sort here described is exhibited in the single account of eternal return in *Beyond* (56): the one who shouts "Once More" to the whole play and spectacle at bottom affirms himself; here too, in the understanding of the good legislated by eternal return, the good is defined by the one who finds himself good. See *GM* I. 10.

76. "The spirit of gravity" is only marginally adequate as a translation of *der Geist der Schwere*, for "gravity" suggests only indirectly the two most direct connotations of *schwer*, heavy and difficult. "The spirit of heaviness" or "the spirit of difficulty" would be still less adequate, in that each lacks what gravity implies, a seemingly inexorable force that gives all things weight by drawing them to a center.

77. Heidegger, *Nietzsche*, I. 79; English trans., I. 66. When speaking of great historical changes such as those effected by Christianity and its demise, Nietzsche speaks of a changing "center of gravity." See *A* 42, 43; *KGW* VIII 11 [48] = *WP* 30; *KGW* VIII 14 [182] = *WP* 864.

78. Hegel, *Philosophy of History*, Introduction.

79. Rosen identifies the spirit of gravity as "piety toward tradition" (*Limits of Analysis*, 212), Dannhauser as "the spirit of objectivity and the spurious universality created by reason" (*Nietzsche's View of Socrates*, 267; see 265–76). Pangle ("Roots of Contemporary Nihilism," 48–50) in effect combines both suggestions, describing the spirit of gravity as manifested in a people's need "to establish its tasks as 'heavy' not only in the sense of difficult but also in the sense of anchored and lasting" (48) and as therefore connected with "man's drive to create and worship gods." Pangle's judgment seems to me to be just right: "The Socratic demand for rational universality is a radicalization of the pre-existing 'spirit of gravity' " (51).

80. *Verrückt*, "moved," "displaced," also names the condition of derangement or madness.

81. Plato *Republic* 414b–415d.

82. See Matt. 22:34–40; John 15:12.

83. This clause repeats I. 1 exactly, except that *Geist* becomes *Mensch*. *Ehrfurcht*, literally "awe" or "reverence grounded in the passion of fear," is far from being simply negative, as both I. 1 and the coming chapters show. On hearing that Lou Salomé was to marry, Nietzsche said in a letter to von Meysenbug (12 May 1887), who had also become disenchanted with her former protégé, "One must avoid this sort of person who lacks *Ehrfurcht*."

84. "Taste" is used ten times in this chapter to measure the most grave criteria. Compare II. 13, the other chapter in which Zarathustra's taste is most prominent.

85. Heraclitus, §32 (Diels).

86. These final phrases are the focus for Alderman's interpretation of Zarathustra as the teacher of a liberal relativism (*Nietzsche's Gift*, 52, 63, 78, 82).

87. John 14:1–6.

88. "The last thing [Nietzsche] is is a social reformer or revolutionary" (Nehamas, *Nietzsche*, 225). Nehamas's sympathetic study comes to this pallid conclusion about its revolutionary subject partly, in my view, because it wants to veer at all costs away from an "absolutist" interpretation of Nietzsche. For example, Nietzsche's perspectivism allegedly entails opposition to Platonism and Christianity primarily because they are "absolutist," not because they are base or false. Such judgments would ill suit Nehamas's Nietzsche, for whom all evaluations of life are inappropriate (135). Nehamas's interpretation, for all its value in illustrating the open character of Nietzsche's thought, seems to me to slight its still more important character as the new standard. Nehamas is thus spared the hard problem of how Nietzsche the legislator legislates a way of thought open to variety and alteration.

89. This "decisive" chapter was composed on the most difficult ascent to "the marvelous Moorish eyrie—Eza" high above Nizza (*EH*, "Books: *Zarathustra*," 4).

90. "It seems inevitable that the 'Spirit of Gravity' will in the future still dog the heels of 'Das Religiöse Wesen' " (Pangle, "The 'Warrior Spirit,' " 159–60).

91. In a letter to Brandes of 2 December 1887 Nietzsche approved of the term, calling it "the shrewdest remark I have read about myself till now."

92. Zarathustra uses the word *nobility* six times in these two sections and only twice elsewhere in the book (III. 4; IV. 3). On Nietzsche's "aristocratic politics" see Eden, *Political Leadership*, 49–52, 64–67.

93. The culminating act that wills the whole of the past can be seen as an expansion of the gratitude Nietzsche frequently expressed for the particular heritage that was his own; see especially *Ecce Homo*, "Why I am so Wise."

94. Plato *Republic* 519d, 520d–521b; see Lucretius *De Rerum Natura* 5. 1105ff. That philosophers want to rule is the conclusion of *Beyond* 207.

95. On raising lions in our midst, see Aristophanes *The Frogs* 1431–32. Does Nietzsche have *The Birds* in mind in this and other speeches about human ambition and birds? Peisthetairos would at least fit this account of superhuman ambition in the founding of a new order both human and divine. Nietzsche's high esteem of Aristophanes is shown by his readiness, for the sake of Aristophanes, to "*forgive* everything Hellenic for having existed." To understand what such forgiveness means, one must first have "understood in its full profundity *all* that needs to be forgiven and transfigured here"—namely, the consequences of Socratic-Platonic philosophy. Nietzsche says that nothing has caused him to meditate more on Plato's secrecy and sphinx nature than the fact that under the pillow of his deathbed was found a volume of Aristophanes (*BGE* 28). Nietzsche even swears by "Holy Aristophanes" when speaking of how modern women threaten modern men (*BGE* 232). On Aristophanes' greatness see also *HH* I. 125; *KGW* VIII 9 [157] = *WP* 380.

96. This is quoted and emphasized again near the end of *Ecce Homo*, where Nietzsche makes as clear as possible the nature of the hardness for which he calls (*EH*, "Destiny," 4).

97. Despite this emphatic requirement, Scheier supposes that Zarathustra's newly discovered necessity to affirm eternal return eliminates the necessity of destruction (*Nietzsches Labyrinth*, 208).

98. The steps followed by Zarathustra toward this hard requirement can be traced in Nietzsche's judgments about what is required of a teacher. In 1881 (*D* 330) he said: "*Not enough!*—It is not enough to prove something, one has also to seduce or elevate people to it." In a note written in the fall of 1883, he said: "It is not enough to bring a teaching: one has also to *violently* alter people in order that they accept it." The parable of the hammer was added to the end of *Twilight*. Many notes refer to eternal return as the hammer in the hand of the most powerful man, e.g., *KGW* VII 27 [80], VIII 2 [100, 129, 131].

99. What Rosen calls the "markedly rhapsodic character" of this chapter has discouraged interpreters from attempting to guess its riddles (*Limits of Analysis*, 214). Hollingdale even denies that it contains riddles, asserting in the notes to his translation that here eternal return is "stated in full and without disguise." Magnus is typical in quoting extensively from this chapter in which Nietzsche "unfolds his ontology in allegory" (*Nietzsche's Existential Imperative*, 170) while offering little in the way of explanation (171–76). The most extensive interpretation is Heidegger's (*Nietzsche*, I. 302–17, 444–47; English trans., II. 49–61, 181–83); see also Fink, *Nietzsches Philosophie*, 97–100, and Scheier, *Nietzsches Labyrinth*, 210–13.

100. This scene parodies act 3, scene 1, of Wagner's *Siegfried*, in which Erda the earth mother is resummoned by Wotan the wanderer only to be sent back to sleep again. For verbal parallels see Hollinrake, *Nietzsche*, 83, 117.

101. What it means to be the advocate of suffering is indicated by Nietzsche's earlier account of "the greatest causes of suffering," all of which concern man's spiritual nature: "That men do not share all knowledge in common, that ultimate insight can never be certain, that abilities are divided unequally." Mankind cannot be happy, moral, or wise in the face of this spiritual suffering; still, "this threefold incapacity" is tempered by the spell of art, which exists "so that the bow shall not break," and whose existence is "the guarantee of the unity and continuance of the human as such" (*WB* 4).

102. The garden scene reminds Heidegger of the philosopher of the garden, Epicurus (*Nietzsche*, I. 306ff.; English trans., II. 52ff.). Scheier interprets it as Midas's garden, the Dionysian garden where Silenos was tricked into drunkenness and forced to disclose his wisdom (*Nietzsches Labyrinth*, 221).

103. Heidegger, *Nietzsche*, I. 308 ff; English trans., II. 54ff.

104. The beginning of part IV shows even more decisively how things now stand between Zarathustra and his animals, for he there finds it necessary to deflect them from his private thoughts by cleverly told "fine lies" and, once out of their hearing, can refer to them, his eagle and his snake, as "pets" (IV. 1).

105. Danto (*Nietzsche as Philosopher*, 211, 212) does not mention that the animals speak what he quotes. Alderman (*Nietzsche's Gift*, 101) attributes some of the animals' words to Zarathustra. Löwith (*Nietzsches Philosophie*, 77) argues that the animals are superior in knowledge to Zarathustra because they live by nature what he can only achieve by art; but for Nietzsche, what is achieved by art is not lower than what is achieved by nature, nor are they fully distinct from one another. Scheier too gives a Christian interpretation of the animals but for him they are soulless beings whose song is a temptation to ignorant forgetfulness (*Nietzsches Labyrinth*, 222–23).

106. Gen. 2:19, 20.

107. Heidegger, *Nietzsche*, I. 308–10; English trans., II. 53–56. The animals are said by Heidegger to advocate the cheery optimism "that everything will come around again different and better," a view they explicitly renounce.

108. *Sein* occurs in the animals' speech five times, in all Zarathustra's speeches nine times, once with respect to the "being" of man (Prologue 7), six times in mockery of philosophy's pretensions (I. 3), and twice with respect to what his speech can effect (III. 9).

109. Strauss, "Note on the Plan of Nietzsche's *Beyond Good and Evil*," 175.

110. The animals' song contains a phrase—"the center is everywhere"—with a long history in philosophy, one that is open to both joyful and despairing interpretations. For the history and range of interpretations see Borges, "The Fearful Sphere of Pascal," 189–92.

111. Heidegger, *Nietzsche*, I. 309; English trans., II. 54.

112. See the transformed or drunken lyre of Zarathustra's "Nightwanderer's Song" (IV. 19, §§6, 8).

113. This is precisely the complaint of Dionysos at the end of *Beyond* (295).

114. *Genealogy* III. 14 describes Nietzsche's horror or disgust at the men of *ressentiment*; see also *UD* 9 and Scheier, *Nietzsches Labyrinth*, 216–18.

115. Deleuze, *Nietzsche and Philosophy*, 71.

116. Following Nietzsche's express instruction, I have "without hesitation put down the word 'Zarathustra,' where the text has the word 'Wagner' " (*EH*, "Books: *Birth*," 4).

117. Milton, "Ode on the Morning of Christ's Nativity."

118. Gen. 1:26; see also Gen. 9:2 and Ps. 8.

119. The animals' affirmation is reflected in a note from the summer–fall of 1884 on the "means of enduring" the thought of eternal return: "No longer the humble expression 'everything is merely *subjective*' but 'it is also *our* work!—Let us be proud of it!' " (*KGW* VII 26 [284] = *WP* 1059).

120. Omission of this statement enables Nehamas to interpret the animals' song as affirming only the infinite repetition of the cycles of nature (*Nietzsche*, 146–47).

121. See Strauss, "Note on the Plan of Nietzsche's *Beyond Good and Evil*," 189–90.

122. Fink calls this "perhaps the most beautiful chapter in the whole book" (*Nietzsches Philosophie*, 100). Heidegger holds that with this chapter "the whole work achieves its summit" (*Vorträge und Aufsätze*, I. 100).

123. Plato *Republic* 507a–509c. See "Ruhm und Ewigkeit" (*DD*).

124. Zarathustra earlier reported a single word said by his soul: "*Gesundheit!*" (III. 9).

125. "Melancholy" translates *Schwermut* correctly but cannot convey the remarkable combination of two words so significant for Zarathustra and so transformed by his thinking: *Schwere* and *Mut*.

126. There are other songs called "The Songs of Zarathustra," the *Dionysos Dithyrambs*, which Nietzsche prepared for publication in the summer of 1888, although they all stem from the Zarathustra years. These nine poems give an independent account of Zarathustra's career, repeating the essential events of *Zarathustra*. The first two and the climactic seventh appear in appropriate contexts in part IV of *Zarathustra*, and the last two were to be used as poetic epilogues to *Nietzsche Contra Wagner* and *Ecce Homo*, respectively. They depict Zarathustra in that mood of masterful serenity that spreads itself through all Nietzsche's later books, the mood of one who knows that he has time, that the essential deeds have been done. In his commentary to his new translation of the songs, Hollingdale, in my view, consistently misreads them in relation to *Zarathustra*, and draws what

seems to me to be the contrary of the appropriate conclusion: they represent "not so much repetitions of the grand central figure of *Thus Spoke Zarathustra* as alternatives to him" (Nietzsche, *Dithyrambs of Dionysus*, 87).

127. As Nietzsche himself held in his reconstruction of the history of Greek myth (*BT* 10). For Nietzsche, the coming of Dionysos prepared the highest phase of Greek experience through his conquest of the Homeric Olympians. According to some authorities, the god most opposed by Zarathustra/Zoroaster and finally overthrown by him was Dionysos; Nietzsche's Zarathustra makes amends for that deed too by his namesake. See Herzfeld, *Zoroaster and His World*, II. 543–61. For a history of views of Dionysos from antiquity to the present, with emphasis on Nietzsche, see Henrichs, "Loss of Self, Suffering, Violence."

128. In a note regarding what can be demonstrated about God, Nietzsche draws the conclusion that all fear: the God who would be demonstrable from the known world would not be humanitarian (*KGW* VIII 2 [153] = *WP* 1036). In his published references to Dionysos after *Zarathustra*, Nietzsche emphasizes his hardness. In *Beyond* that hardness seems to shame even his "last disciple and initiate," causing him to apologize coyly to his gentle, free spirited readers (295). In speaking of *Genealogy* in *Ecce Homo*, Nietzsche says: "Dionysos is, as is known, also the god of darkness," alluding to the acts of destruction undertaken in his book as themselves Dionysian. The 1886 addition to *Gay Science* (370) defines the Dionysian spirit and emphasizes destruction. The most extensive definition of the Dionysian is given in *Twilight* ("Ancients," 4, 5) and prepares the reader for the last, Dionysian section, Zarathustra's parable on hardness (III. 12, §29). In the book subtitled "How to Philosophize with a Hammer," this parable is entitled "The Hammer Speaks." *Ecce Homo* begins with Nietzsche referring to himself as "a disciple of the philosopher Dionysos" and ends by transforming that discipleship into a war cry; "*Dionysos versus the Crucified.*" Its description of the Dionysian occurs in the account of *Zarathustra*.

129. Nietzsche's comment on his Zarathustra appears in the fifth of five sections entitled "On the History of the God Concept." The first four are included in altered form in *Antichrist* (16–19), which then breaks off to consider a new topic, Christianity as contrasted with Buddhism. The published form thus suppresses the final section concerning Zarathustra. The section that Nietzsche chose not to publish adds a culminating consideration after the lament "Almost two thousand years and not a single new god": "And how many new gods are still possible!" There he reflects on his own religious instinct. Citing the inestimable, never too highly to be praised authority of Zarathustra, he repeats his words, "I would believe only in a god who could *dance*" (I. 7). Then, enigmatically and allegedly against the authority that he has just raised to the highest power, he says: "Zarathustra himself, of course, is only an old atheist." Finally, with respect to what Zarathustra said he would believe, he adds: "Understand him correctly! Zarathustra says indeed, he *would*—; but Zarathustra *won't*." Zarathustra, the highest authority, will never be a believer, even though he knows as well as Nietzsche does that many gods are still possible. (*Will to Power* [1038] is slightly different from *KGW* on the important matter of what Nietzsche reports regarding Zarathustra.) Pangle uses this note as one of three arguments to prove that "Zarathustra himself is not a superman." Recognizing the dubiousness of using a suppressed note to contradict what Nietzsche says explicitly in his published books, Pangle tries to give the note weight by making it Nietzsche's "only important explicit reflection on Zarathustra in the fragmentary *Will to Power*" ("The 'Warrior Spirit,' " 175–76)—as if it could possibly matter that Nietzsche's editors

selected only this one note, as if Nietzsche's notebooks were not full of important explicit reflections on Zarathustra, as if Nietzsche himself did not choose to omit this part of his longer reflection when he published it in *Antichrist*.

130. Plato *Republic* 427b–c.

131. *Ecce Homo* refers to the world-historical accent with which the tragic is here introduced ("Books: *Birth*" 4). Unfortunately, Hollingdale's translation of *Wagner in Bayreuth* omits the six lines that move from the mortality of the individual to the mortality of humanity itself, the ground of the new tragedy.

132. See *KGW* VII 13 [1, p. 453], where Ariadne says these words in a dream in the presence of Dionysos on a tiger; a panther and the skull of a goat are also present.

133. Definitive guidance to Nietzsche's mystery of Ariadne is not to be sought in the humanized, patriotic version of the Ariadne story preserved by the Athenian tradition. The relation of the Athenian hero Theseus to Ariadne and Dionysos as Nietzsche understood that relation can best be read in the "Satyr play" recorded at *KGW* VIII 9 [115, end] where Dionysos makes sport of a jealous Theseus who perishes in Ariadne's sport after she has denied him the thread that he needs. The scholarly account that comes closest to what Nietzsche hints at is that of Kerenyi (*Dionysos*), despite his frequent criticism of Nietzsche's *Birth of Tragedy*. Ariadne there appears as an early representative of the earth goddess (whose other names are Artemis, Kore, Demeter, Aphrodite), who was also goddess of the underworld and who belongs in marriage to Dionysos. See also Otto, *Dionysos*. On Ariadne in Nietzsche, see Reinhardt, "Nietzsche's Lament of Ariadne," although Reinhardt judges Zarathustra too narrowly, as if he were a mere Theseus. The index of the *Studien Ausgabe* of *KGW* lists fourteen references to Ariadne in Nietzsche's work excluding the letters, five in the published works (*DS* 12; *BGE* 295; *TI*, "Skirmishes," 19; *EH*, "Books: *Zarathustra*," 8; *DD*), the rest in the notes (*KGW* III 8 [37] 1869–74; VII 4 [55] November 1882–February 1883; VII 13 [1 on page 453] Summer 1883; VII 37 [4] June–July 1885; VII 41 [9] August–September 1885; VIII 1 [163] Fall 1885–Spring 1886; VIII 9 [115] Fall 1887; VIII 10 [95] Fall 1887; VIII 16 [40] Spring–Summer 1888). See also *KGW* VIII 1 [123]. The issue of Ariadne is skewed and obscured if more than pathological significance is ascribed to the three postcards that in his extremity, himself having become Dionysos, Nietzsche sent to the one who had become his Ariadne, Cosima Wagner, as if this breakdown into the psychotic could explain the force that the Dionysian had for him while he was at the height of his powers. See, e.g., Janz, *Nietzsche*, II. 433–34, 555–56; III. 28; and Hollingdale's comments in Nietzsche, *Dithyrambs of Dionysus*, 85.

134. Kerenyi, *Dionysos*, 170.

135. The erotic is present both as deed and symbol; see III. 10 where pure lust is also symbolic of something higher. In Euripides' *Bacchae* Pentheus suspects that the secret rites are merely erotic and supposes that he has unmasked them as base with that understanding. He also thinks that Dionysos's maenads are simply drunk, but he is wrong about that aspect of their worship too.

136. See Euripides *Bacchae*, 150, 181, 241, 493–94, 831, 930. Euripides explains that the maenads catch wild snakes and entwine them in their hair (99 ff.; see also 698, 768).

137. See Kerenyi, *Dionysos*, 80–89.

138. In "The Lament of Ariadne" (*DD* and IV. 5), Ariadne is the hunted who seems not to know what the hunter wants of her, whether the submission of a

hound or the death of a quarry; she even imagines that he seeks her only to kidnap her for ransom.

139. Resa von Schirnhofer reported that Nietzsche whispered to her (after looking around cautiously to ensure that no one would overhear) that the "mystery" whispered by Zarathustra to Life was "the eternal return of the same" (Janz, *Nietzsche*, II. 279–80). Are the spoken but unreported words of Zarathustra's abyss the same words (III. 13, §1)? If so, what he once heard whispered only to him, he can now whisper to Life, now that his most abysmal thought has taken possession of him.

140. Gadamer's account of Nietzsche and of *Zarathustra* comes to focus on this conversation, a "scene of infinite elegance and intricacy" and "the deepest point plumbed by [Zarathustra's] new wisdom" ("Das Drama Zarathustras," 10–11). But for Gadamer, the dialogue is intended to demonstrate the "irresolvable discord" between life and wisdom, not its resolution (13).

141. On the meaning that Zarathustra assigns to this song of the midnight bell see IV. 19. The evening bell that sounds in one of the most beautiful aphorisms of *Human* (I. 628) also reminds Nietzsche of mortal things and turns his thoughts to Plato's judgment that their mortality makes them unworthy of the greatest seriousness. But "Seriousness in Play" questions Plato's judgment.

142. Correcting the Homeric version according to which Artemis killed Ariadne at Dionysos's behest following her betrayal of him for Theseus (*Odyssey* II. 321–25), Hesiod records that Dionysos took the mortal Ariadne to wife and made her immortal (*Theogony* 947–49). In later Hellenistic and Roman worship, the marriage of Dionysos and Ariadne was corrupted into the centerpiece of a religion of heavenly immortality.

143. Nietzsche's many plans for the order of chapters within the different parts show that they were to number twenty-two. See e.g., *KGW* V 16 [83, 84], 20 [3, 8], 21 [3], 23 [10]. Part IV, however, has only twenty chapters.

144. Rev. 5:1ff. *Genealogy* I. 16 calls *Revelation* "the most wanton of all literary outbursts that revenge has on its conscience"; Nietzsche's intentions are hinted at in *Genealogy* (I. 17).

145. Matt. 10:34.

146. Rev. 19:6–9; 21:1–22:5.

147. Ibid., 21:6.

148. Schacht's comprehensive and sympathetic interpretation of Nietzsche seems to me to give too little place to eternal return and the religion of Dionysos. His willingness to read "beyond good and evil" as a "teleological suspension of the ethical" (*Nietzsche*, 457, 464) open to the exception and closed to the "herd," seems to me to be a consequence of minimizing the cultivating effect of eternal return and the religion of Dionysos in the transformation of the moral climate in which everyone lives.

149. A less ecstatic relationship of the philosopher-god to the earth is suggested in a note describing the more serene surroundings after the marriage, a conversation that took place on Dionysos's first visit to Naxos or presumably just after the marriage. While delivering a philosophical lecture on morals and physiology in which he praises the body as a complex of obeying and commanding, one of whose instruments is consciousness, the philosopher-god Dionysos is stopped by his audience Ariadne who can take this lecturing no longer. Her critique of his lecture reveals to Dionysos that she is two thousand years behind in her philosophical

education. It could well be that such backwardness is no shortcoming in Ariadne, that she has thereby avoided the whole philosophical corruption of Socratic rationalism. For she delivers her critique while fiddling with her famous thread, which could well take her to the heart of things without the Schweinedeutsch needed by her philosopher lord (*KGW* VII 37 [4]).

NOTES TO CONCLUSIONS

1. In this quotation I have followed Nietzsche's instructions and written "Nietzsche" where he wrote "Schopenhauer" (*EH*, "Books: Untimely Ones," 1, 3).

2. Nietzsche conducted his search not only through his books but also among his new acquaintances, all of whom were measured as possible students to whom he could teach his philosophy, possibly in some school like the ancient Greek schools of philosophy, possibly on a Mediterranean island, possibly Corsica, where Napoleon had his beginnings. Janz provides a fine chronicle of these attempts, though he judges it foolish of Nietzsche and even contrary to his philosophy which Nietzsche had the misfortune of understanding less well than his biographer did. See, e.g., Janz, *Nietzsche*, II. 267.

3. In the other books after *Zarathustra*, will to power appears infrequently, if sometimes prominently. The argument of *Genealogy* breaks near the middle of the middle essay (II. 12) for a brief statement of the theory of will to power: "In all events a *will to power* is operating"; "the essence of life [is] its *will to power*." This "major point of historical method" is emphasized though not explained; the brief interlude shows only the opposition of this method to the prevailing modes of explanation in morals against which the book is "A Polemic." The other direct references to will to power in the later books are: *GS* 349; *GM* II. 18; III. 7–8, 14, 18, and 23 (where Nietzsche describes the will to power of ascetic priests who remade the world in their own image); *CW*, Epilog; *EH*, Preface, 4; "Books: *Birth*," 4; "Books: *Wagner*," 1; "Destiny," 4; *TI*, "Skirmishes," 11, 20, 38; "Ancients," 3; *A* 2, 6, 16, 17.

4. Schopenhauer, *World as Will and Representation*, vol. II, suppl. to ch. 18. Nietzsche's notes also state clearly the way taken in his books; see, e.g., *KGW* VII 36 [31] = *WP* 619; *KGW* VIII 14 [82] = *WP* 689; and *KGW* VIII 2 [172] Fall 1885–1886 = *WP* 582. Complaints about Nietzsche's alleged failure to consider the ground for his claims about will to power neglect the suggestions of such passages. Kaufmann concludes that "Nietzsche was not at his best with problems of this kind" (*Nietzsche*, 204). Schacht's illuminating discussion (*Nietzsche*, 214–16, 231–34) of this "opening wedge," the point of departure whereby will to power "wins rights of citizenship in science" (*GS* 344), makes it a dual route through life and human life. While suggesting that biology and psychology are the paradigmatic sciences, replacing physics and its tendency to mechanics, Schacht emphasizes almost exclusively the route through life, and not, as Nietzsche does, the route through the most spiritual form of life.

5. After this argument will to power appears only infrequently in the book, but still in a way that assumes it to be "the essence of the world" (186) and assumes that "life simply *is* will to power" (259); for, though this be "an innovation as a theory, as a reality it is the *primordial fact* of all history" (see also 44, 51, 198, 211, 227, 257). What the teaching of will to power implies about man is suggested in §188, where Nietzsche claims to have discovered the one imperative of nature with respect to man's morality. Speaking at length about the tyranny against "nature"

necessary for any morality and noble achievement, Nietzsche always places the word *nature* in quotation marks, as if to express his reservation about claims made with respect to the "nature" tyrannized by morality. But there is one exception: at the end of the section Nietzsche quotes what he calls "the moral imperative of nature." The imperative of nature appears to be that "nature" be tyrannized, that man obey nature and command his "nature" into some form. Nature's imperative is not categorical, but if it is disobeyed, if mankind take the way of ease or "the basic will of the spirit," nature will have her way with disobedient mankind, and it will lose its respect for itself.

6. Nietzsche's courage is thus more authentic, more ambitious, and more historical, than Heidegger's Entschlossenheit in *Sein und Zeit*, for the latter means to depict a perpetual state of inauthenticity to which the perpetual features of authenticity are a perpetual challenge. Nietzsche's courage, on the other hand, is consciously situated in a particular culture, whose present he comes to understand, and for whose future he takes responsibility.

7. Deleuze, "Nomad Thought."

8. Homer *Iliad* 14.201, 302.

9. Plato *Theaetetus* 152e.

10. In addition to the accounts of will to power in *Zarathustra* and *Beyond*, there are extensive reflections in the notes. When consideration is given to the pains Nietzsche took to present this fundamental matter in his books, it seems obvious that the single most grave disadvantage of the notes is the lack of any setting. Whatever the final form might have been of the Hauptwerk Nietzsche was planning, and which he often referred to by the title "The Will to Power" in his notes (and in *GM* III. 27), it seems certain that it would have borne the character that Nietzsche said all his writings bore: it would be "very well guarded" (*KGW* VIII 2 [79]). The notes examine the implications of will to power in ways not followed by *Zarathustra* and *Beyond* and give further evidence that will to power is the fundamental matter in Nietzsche's thought, despite the relative and understandable silence on it in the books of the last years. The notes add reflections on two general matters implied especially in *Beyond*: nonatomistic reality and the relation between that reality and the phenomenal world. Any attempt to give an account of reality must avoid imaginable fictions like the monad or "the clod 'atom' " (*BGE* 12). Atomism and monadology, in drawing distinctions between objects and objects for subjects, develop doctrines of primary and secondary qualities, or of a rational and harmonic reality grounding "well-founded phenomena"; but such precise formulations of the nonphenomenal are forbidden the teaching of will to power, which names only the elusive ground of the "calculable" or "intelligible" or "necessary." Notes from 1888 speak of "dynamic quanta" as the necessary remainder after all constructs of form and thing have been rigorously thought away (see, e.g., *KGW* VIII 14 [79] (Spring, 1888) = *WP* 634, 635; see also *KGW* VIII 14 [81] Spring 1888 = *WP* 689). The specifics necessary to save the appearances in this account of reality as "dynamic quanta" are not fully elaborated in the notes beyond the numerous accounts of phenomenal qualities ("concepts, species, forms, purposes, laws") as constructed under compulsion by the subject (e.g., *KGW* VIII 5 [22] Summer 1886– Fall 1887 = *WP* 522). While acknowledging that "rational thought is an interpretation according to a schema that we cannot throw off," these notes do not analyze the subjectivity of the subject with respect to some necessary structure of compulsions in the manner of Kant. They attempt neither a metaphysical deduction of categories or a transcendental deduction, but they do give the rudiments of the "deduction"

appropriate to Nietzsche's task, the historical or genealogical deduction that rel-
ativizes and radicalizes the categories, not justifying their employment but as-
certaining its consequences. Employment of such falsifying categories as Unity,
Identity, Permanence, Substance, Causality, Being (*TI*, "Reason," 5) may be a custom
necessary for the existence of beings like ourselves, but Nietzsche is not satisfied
to leave it at that. He aspires to discover what can be said about the fundamental
events of nature, the deeds to which our perceiving and thinking always add a
doer, as if it were able to know the dancer from the dance (*GM* I. 13). To name the
fundamental events "will to power" is a beginning. Some of the thoughts in the
notes reached polished form in the sections of *Twilight* entitled "Reason in Philosophy" and "The Four Great Errors." See Schacht, *Nietzsche,* 212–53.

11. Yeats, "Among School Children."

12. In addition to celebrating eternal return, *Beyond* refers to the return of
something natural that one tries to drive out with a pitchfork (264), the rabble
whose eternal return almost caused Zarathustra to gag on this teaching. Both the
divine and crushing qualities of eternal return are thus intimated in *Beyond.*

13. See Plato *Republic* 505d–e.

14. In willing eternal return, Zarathustra fulfills Nietzsche's New Year's resolution of 1882 to become what he was not yet, one who sees "as beautiful what
is necessary in things: then I shall be one of those who make things beautiful.
Amor fati: let that be my love henceforth!" (*GS* 276). This first occurrence of amor
fati in Nietzsche's published writings stands at the beginning of the part of *Gay
Science* that prepares for *Zarathustra* and thus for the teaching of eternal return.
The other three occurrences are in writings of 1888. In *Nietzsche Contra Wagner,*
it appears in a retrospective context of gratitude for his sickness (Epilogue, 1). In
Ecce Homo it is Nietzsche's "formula for greatness in a man that wants nothing
to be different, not forward, not backward, not in all eternity"; it is also Nietzsche's
own "inmost nature" ("Clever," 10; "Books: *Wagner,*" 4). See also the uses of amor
fati in *KGW* VIII 16 [32] = *WP* 1041 and in a letter to Overbeck in the summer
of 1882.

15. *KGW* VIII 2 [127] = *WP* 1. See *GM* III. 27. See also *KGW* VIII 11 [72, November
1887–March 1888] = *WP* 708: "The present must not under any circumstances be
justified by a future, nor must the past be justified for the sake of the present."

16. See the end of *TI* and *EH*, "Books: *Zarathustra,*" 1, 6.

17. A late example that attempts to secure its premises regarding infinite time
and finite states is "The new world conception" (*KGW* VIII 14 [188] = *WP* 1066,
Spring 1888). Arguing against a mechanistic account of the world, Nietzsche claims
that if a state of equilibrium were possible, it would already have been reached in
the infinity of time past; its not being actual shows that it is not possible. Because
a mechanistic conception of the world implies movement toward a state of equilibrium, it is thereby refuted. Nietzsche then turns directly to a nonmechanistic
view, his own view that the world is will to power, and argues that it requires
eternal return:

> If the world may be thought of as a certain definite quantity of force and as
> a certain definite number of centers of force—and every other representation
> remains indefinite and therefore useless—it follows that, in the great dice game
> of existence, it must pass through a calculable number of combinations. In
> infinite time, every possible combination would at some time or another be
> realized; more: it would be realized an infinite number of times. And since

between every combination and its next recurrence all other possible combinations would have to take place, and each of these combinations conditions the entire sequence of combinations in the same series, a circular movement of absolutely identical series is thus demonstrated: the world as a circular movement that has already repeated itself infinitely often and plays its game *in infinitum.*

See the account of this argument in Combee, "Nietzsche as Cosmologist," and the critique of it in Danto, *Nietzsche as Philosopher,* 206. Heidegger's way of putting the argument generalizes it: if becoming is the character of all beings, what is the character of all becoming? Because all being as will to power must be continually becoming and have no end, being as a whole must have no end but always recur and bring back the same (*Nietzsche,* II. 37–38; see I. 369–70; English trans., II. 108–09, for another statement of the proof). On the matter of proof and eternal return, see Heidegger, *Nietzsche,* I. 365–95, esp. 367 and 377–78; English trans., II. 106–32, esp. 107 and 116–17.

18. Deleuze, "Nomad Thought," 143.

19. Quoted in Janz, *Nietzsche,* II. 168; see also Binion, *Frau Lou,* 96.

20. Janz, *Nietzsche,* II. 149; Andreas-Salomé, *Friedrich Nietzsche,* 222.

21. On the back cover of the 1882 edition of *Gay Science* Nietzsche declared that it marked the end of a series of books whose goal was the construction of a new image of the free spirit. *Zarathustra* therefore does not have that goal.

22. Löwith, *Nietzsches Philosophie,* 113–26; see also 179, 99. Löwith interprets Nietzsche's effort to overcome Christianity through the teaching of eternal return as itself a return to a pre-Christian, Greek conception of time, noting in passing how little Nietzsche adds to earlier Roman arguments against Christianity's notion of time besides "Christian pathos" (124). Löwith well recognizes, nevertheless, that Nietzsche's concept of eternal return contains elements that are quite un-Greek and spring from the biblical tradition (125–26). The latter considerations seem to me to successfully counter the accumulated arguments of his chapter and to point to the historic singularity of Nietzsche's teaching, not to its being an attempt to repeat Greek thought.

23. See Eliade, *Cosmos and History,* esp. 112–30.

24. "This doctrine of Zarathustra *could* in the final analysis already have been taught by Heraclitus" (*EH,* "Books: *Birth,*" 3). See *KGW* VIII 14 [187] = *WP* 1066: "I have come across this idea in earlier thinkers: every time it was determined by other ulterior considerations (—mostly theological, in favor of the *creator spiritus*)."

25. *Vorträge und Aufsätze,* I. 105 ff.; *Nietzsche,* I. 231–42; English Trans., I. 200–10; for "standing reserve" (*Bestand*) see esp. *The Question Concerning Technology.*

26. *Vorträge und Aufsätze,* I. 118; see also *Was Heißt Denken?* 40–44.

27. See the critique of Heidegger's interpretation in Fink, *Nietzsches Philosophie,* 172–73, 186–89. Fink's critique, however, depends on severing eternal return from will to power.

28. The notes also assume that Zarathustra has become the superman after part III; see, e.g., *KGW* VII 20 [10]: "Zarathustra relates, *out of the happiness of the superman,* the *mystery* that everything returns."

29. See Heidegger, *Nietzsche,* II. "Der Europäische Nihilismus," 31–256. See Grant, *Time as History,* for Heidegger's reading of Nietzsche as culmination and expression of modernity.

30. Bacon, *New Organon,* §129.

31. On Nietzsche and Descartes, see Heidegger, *Nietzsche*, II. 189–92.

32. Machiavelli, *The Prince*, ch. 6; *Discourses*, III. §35.

33. Bacon, *Wisdom of the Ancients*, Preface.

34. Descartes, *Passions of the Soul*, §161.

35. Ibid., §§153, 156.

36. Descartes, *Discourse*, pt. VI, last sentence.

37. Descartes, *Principles of Philosophy*, Preface.

38. Descartes, *Passions of the Soul*, §153.

39. Ibid. §§63, 153.

40. This interpretation of Descartes' intentions owes much to Caton, *The Origin of Subjectivity*, and Kennington, "Descartes."

41. Plato *Republic* 607c–621a.

42. On Plato's right to lie, see *TI*, "Improvers," 5, and *KGW* VIII 11 [54]. On his "absolute skepticism toward all inherited concepts" while teaching the opposite, see *KGW* VII 34 [195] = *WP* 409. Speaking of the philosopher as a great educator to whom "uncanny privileges" must be granted, Nietzsche says that such an educator "never says what he himself thinks but only what he thinks of a thing in relation to the requirements of those he educates. In this dissimulation he must not be detected; it belongs to his mastery that one believes in his honesty.... Such an educator is beyond good and evil but no one must know it" (*KGW* VII 37 [7] = *WP* 980). Everyone knows that Nietzsche is beyond good and evil. Still, the youngest virtue requires of him that he shun "the absolute lack of moral integrity" exhibited by those for whom it does not matter whether a thing is true but only the effect it produces" (*KGW* VIII 10 [184] = *WP* 172). Nietzsche is still virtuous in the way shown in *GS* 344 and *GM* III. 24; though the family history of morals demonstrates that the honesty of science, its "I will not deceive," is the latest form of the ascetic ideal, here too, ignoble origins are not a refutation and do not compromise the nobility of what they have produced. Intellectual probity is the inescapable piety of the new teacher.

43. Plato *Republic* 378c–383c.

44. Plato *Sophist* 247d, e.

45. Ibid., 216b.

46. Regarding Nietzsche's *Auseinandersetzung* with the great Greeks, see Eden, *Political Leadership*, 109; 121–33 for the contest with Thucydides.

47. Plato *Republic* 414b–415d.

48. Ibid., 537e–539d.

49. Plato *Apology of Socrates*, compare 20c–23b with 37e–38a.

50. See Peters, *Zarathustra's Sister*, and Kaufmann, *Nietzsche*, 3–16.

51. Nietzsche quoted the last clause from Emerson.

52. Janz, *Nietzsche*, II. 288 ff.

53. Rousseau, *On the Social Contract*, II. 11. On Rousseau and the appeal to nature see *SE* 4.

54. On Christianity's antinature teaching see *EH*, "Destiny," 7; also the early comment that Christianity's "battle against the natural man has created the unnatural man" (Spring–Summer 1875, *KGW* IV 5 [51]), and *WP* 266.

55. See Heidegger, *Vorträge und Aufsätze*, I. 5–62.

56. Yeats, "Among School Children."

57. "The transcendence of justice over technology" is the theme of Grant's *English-Speaking Justice*, though Grant does not think Nietzsche affords that transcendence; see 69–89.

58. Heidegger, *Nietzsche*, II. 198; English trans., IV. 144.
59. Heidegger, "Nietzsches Metaphysik," in *Nietzsche*, II. 257–333; see also "Die Wahrheit als Gerechtigkeit," in *Nietzsche*, I. 632–48.
60. Translation taken from Strauss, "Note on the Plan of Nietzsche's *Beyond Good and Evil*," 187.
61. Grant, *Technology and Empire*, 72.
62. Schacht, *Nietzsche*, 422.
63. See Strauss, "Note on the Plan of Nietzsche's *Beyond Good and Evil*," 180, 185, 189.
64. Eden, *Political Leadership*, 129.
65. Grant, *English-Speaking Justice*, 86–87.
66. Strauss, "Note on the Plan of Nietzsche's *Beyond Good and Evil*," 187–89, 190–91.

NOTES TO APPENDIX

1. See above, p. 240.
2. Letters written after the completion of part III consistently state that *Zarathustra* is complete in three parts; letters to his publisher Schmeitzner, 18 January 1884; Overbeck, 25 January 1884; his mother, draft of January/February 1884; Köselitz, 1 February 1884; Schmeitzner, 6 February 1884; Overbeck, 6 and 12 February 1884; Rohde, 22 February 1884; Laban, beginning of March 1884; von Meysenbug, end of March 1884; von Schirnhofer 30 March 1884.
3. All letters mentioning part IV insist on secrecy: to von Gersdorff, 12 February 1885; Köselitz, 14 February 1885; his printer Naumann, 12 March 1885 (in which he asked that all traces of the manuscript developed through the printing process be destroyed or sent to him and extracted a guarantee against misappropriation of copies by Naumann's employees); Köselitz, 14 March 1885; his mother, 16 April 1885; his sister, 7 May 1885; Widemann, 31 July 1885. After mailing a copy to von Gersdorff, he wrote immediately (7 May 1885) fearing that he had not wrapped it properly and that it could fall into the wrong hands. To the end, part IV remained for him what he had said it was to his mother (16 April 1885): a secret gift to be bestowed as a courtesy on a few friends.
4. Another whisper occurs in the 1886 preface to *Birth*, 7.
5. See Janz, *Nietzsche*, III. 131–37, 144–50.
6. See esp. I. 22, §3, III. 12, §1, and IV. 20. These references to future events do not demonstrate that Nietzsche always intended to extend the book until the events had been depicted; they do demonstrate, however, that Zarathustra's *work* was to continue beyond what Nietzsche had already described.
7. See also a letter to Overbeck, 7 April 1884, in which the time is said to be five years.
8. For a sample of notes for additional parts to *Zarathustra* prior to the writing of part IV, see: *KGW* VII, 25 [249, 305, 322, 453] Spring 1884; also *KGW* VII 27 [23] Summer–Fall 1884. For those written during the work on part IV, see *KGW* VII 31 [2, 9] Winter 1884–85; 32 [14, 15] Winter 1884–85. For those dating from after its completion, see *KGW* VII 34 [199] April–June 1885; 35 [73, 74] May–July 1885; 39 [3] August–September 1885; *KGW* VIII 2 [71, 72, 129] Fall 1885–Fall 1886. Perhaps the most concise and representative of all the many plans is that in *KGW* VII 25 [322]. Zarathustra's return effects a great crisis (e.g., *KGW* VII 25 [322] and 27 [23]); his

task is the preparation of men fit to master the earth (*KGW* VII 25 [305, 307], 26 [243]), the future "lords of the earth" (*KGW* VII 25 [134, 137, 247]; 26 [269]; 27 [23]; 35 [73, 74]; 39 [3]). He teaches a new "order of rank" among men (*KGW* VII 26 [243, 258]; 35 [73, 74]; 39 [3]; *KGW* VIII 2 [71, 72]) and confers the right to rule on "the law-givers of the future" (*KGW* VII 34 [199]; see also 26 [258, 407]; 34 [201]; 35 [74]). Behind his practical teaching lies the mystery of eternal return (*KGW* VII 25 [322, 323]; 27 [23]; *KGW* VIII 2 [71, 72]) and Dionysos (*KGW* VII 25 [2, 101]; 26 [243]; 29 [66]; 31 [17]; 34 [191, 101]; 35 [45, 73]; 42 [6]). Scattered among notes mentioning plans for the next parts of *Zarathustra* are many notes in which Nietzsche describes his own task as identical to Zarathustra's: "*My task: to force humanity to resolutions which will decide the whole future. Highest patience—Careful—to* SHOW *the* TYPE *of men who are permitted* to face up to this task" (*KGW* VII 25 [405]). "*Who shall be lord of the earth?* That is the REFRAIN *of my practical philosophy*" (*KGW* VII 25 [247]; see also 25 [137]). In the notes, plans for Zarathustra blend into plans for a major new work in which Nietzsche will speak in his own voice (see, e.g., *KGW* VIII 2 [71, 72, 74]). In the many plans for that work Nietzsche repeats all the most important topics that were to have been constituents of Zarathustra's teachings on his return (*KGW* VIII 2 [74, 100, 131]; 7 [1–8, 64]; 9 [1, 164]; 10 [58]; 14 [137]; 18 [17]; 19 [8]; 22 [14], the last two under the title "The Revaluation of All Values"; see also *TI*, Preface, and *A*, Preface, where the title is also "Revaluation of All Values").

9. Hollinrake, *Nietzsche*, 123–71, gives details of the parody of *Parsifal*.

10. For an analysis of the problem of pity for superior men as it appears in *Beyond* 268–77, see Eden, *Political Leadership*, 105, 118–20.

11. Typical in this respect, though not in others, is Fink, *Nietzsches Philosophie*, 114–15. A minority view of the merits of part IV is effectively presented by Hollinrake, *Nietzsche*, 138 ff., in part on the basis of his understanding of it as a parody of *Parsifal*. An appreciation of part IV from a different perspective is found in Ogilvy, *Many Dimensional Man*, 175 ff. See also Alderman, *Nietzsche's Gift*, 113–36, and Shapiro, "Festival, Parody, and Carnival in Zarathustra IV."

12. See Fink, *Nietzsches Philosophie*, 117.

13. This section of *Nietzsche Contra Wagner* is entitled "The Psychologist Speaks Out."

14. See Rev. 20:1–10. *Hazar* is the Persian word meaning millennium or thousand; *KGW* VII 25 [148] speaks of the Persians as the first to have thought of history as a totality, a sequence of developments each presided over by a prophet whose *hazar*, or *Reich*, lasts a thousand years.

15. Matt. 4:1–11. For Gadamer, part IV is intended to answer the question, Is eternal return a possible truth, one that the superior men can share? Their failure is the failure of the teaching itself as well as Nietzsche's acknowledgment of that failure ("Das Drama Zarathustras," 11–12, 14–15). Gadamer's account thus sides with the Soothsayer in judging that eternal return, although it may contain a kernel of nostalgia for a beautiful moment once upon a time, is a worthless teaching because not even the superior men are fit for it.

16. Matt. 21:1–7; Zech. 9:9.

17. This little verse presenting Zarathustra's version of the history of mankind is in its own way a popular version of that history, one fit for the powerful in that it attributes to religion what is possible only for philosophy and treats an event in the history of religion as if it were the one turning point of all world history (*BT* 15).

18. The Old Sorcerer is not explained by seeing him as Wagner; rather, the Old Sorcerer is one of Nietzsche's attempts to explain Wagner. Nietzsche says in the epilogue to another of his books on Wagner: "Let us recover our breath in the end by getting away for a moment from the narrow world to which every question about the worth of *persons* condemns the spirit" *(CW)*, and the Old Sorcerer can be seen as a successful escape from that narrow world of persons to a consideration of the phenomenon of the great modern artist. For an effective reading of the Old Sorcerer as Wagner, see Hollinrake, *Nietzsche.* My analysis differs from Hollinrake's, however, especially on the interpretation of the ass festival.

19. On mistakes about the song and the singer, see *Gay Science* 370 (included in *NCW* as "We Antipodes"), in which Nietzsche explains that he was fooled into attributing to Wagner the Dionysian spirit, because he had not yet perfected his art of "backward inference from the work to the maker." Wagner is called an "old sorcerer" in the afterword to *The Case of Wagner.* Hollingdale mistakes the singer of the song for its subject and thus finds Nietzsche's two uses of it, here and in *Dionysos Dithyrambs,* an "artistic blunder" that makes the poem "irresolvably ambiguous" (Nietzsche, *Dithyrambs* of *Dionysus,* trans. R. J. Hollingdale, 84).

20. See Euripides *Bacchae* 136 ff.

21. Matt. 5:3.

22. Matt. 18:3; 16:26.

23. He is like those Nietzsche addresses and advises in *Beyond.* The notes refer to him as the "good European"; see *BGE,* Preface, 241, 243, 254; *HH* I. 475.

24. The phrase on the perfection of the world—"Did not the world become perfect just now?"—used four times, perhaps reflects a statement of Emerson's in which the perfection referred to is *nature's* perfection; see letter to von Gersdorff, 7 April 1866. At I. 18 the phrase is used in a different sense. The noon of great Pan is described in *WS* 308. Löwith (*Nietzsches Philosophie,* 99–112) reads the noon image in part IV as the consummating moment in *Zarathustra*—and as a hopelessly confused mixture of Greek and Christian symbolism.

25. See Ogilvy, *Many Dimensional Man,* 250.

26. Matt. 4:4.

27. See Eden, *Political Leadership,* 93.

28. In Luke 6:25, Jesus wished woe on those who laugh now.

29. Nietzsche selected five verses from the last three sections of this speech as the final words of his "Attempt at a Self Criticism" *(BT);* they show how much was still possible for the victims of Romanticism who interpreted his first book as itself Romantic, as essentially Wagnerian.

30. On the misinterpretation of science by its spokesmen, see *BGE* 22 and *GM* III. 23–25.

31. See *NCW,* "Wagner as the Apostle of Chastity." In *Genealogy* (III. 1–5) Nietzsche analyzes the ascetic ideals of the artist as expressed in Wagner's praise of chastity.

32. When speaking of the apparent antithesis of chastity and sensuality, Nietzsche praises Goethe and Hafiz for judging this unstable equilibrium to be one more attraction that seduces to existence (*NCW,* "Wagner as Apostle of Chastity," 2).

33. Unfortunately Heidegger has made this resonant line famous as a paradigm of Nietzsche's denunciations, as if it referred to modernity and not sensuality (*Was Heißt Denken?,* 19 ff.).

34. The lines added in *Dionysos Dithyrambs* name the cause of woe, "sensual passion" or "pure lust":

> Stone grinds on stone, the desert wolfs
> down and spews out
> Stupendous death gazes glowing brown
> and *chews*—its life is its chewing . . .
> *Do not forget, man, extinguished by pure lust:*
> *you—are the stone, the desert, you are death.*

In the *Dithyrambs* the song properly follows the prose introduction from this chapter of part IV, the only prose in the whole of the *Dithyrambs*. Dropped in many editions, the prose setting is necessary to separate the song from Zarathustra, who was never one to curse accursed Eros as a desert. If the poem is read, as Hollingdale suggests, as "a lightly disguised recollection of a visit to a brothel," it is no wonder that it "seems an irrelevant and capricious insert" to part IV (Nietzsche, *Dithyrambs of Dionysus*, trans. R. J. Hollingdale, 79).

35. This ass festival shares only the ass with the various late medieval ass festivals conducted under the auspices of the Church, in which the ass represented the promise of the coming savior. Here the ass itself is worshipped as the savior. Salaquarda's survey of the metaphor of the ass in Nietzsche's writings ("Zarathustra und der Esel") shows that it stands primarily for convictions and the holding of convictions. But his interpretation of the ass festival itself is less persuasive, for it turns the superior men into complete asses, which is not in keeping with their becoming Zarathustra's friends and celebrating with him the Nightwanderer's Song.

36. Rev. 7:12.

37. Phil. 2:7; Isa. 53:4–5.

38. Heb. 12:6.

39. Gen. 1:31.

40. Gen. 1:26.

41. Matt. 7:13.

42. Matt. 19:14.

43. Prov. 1:10.

44. Matt. 7:16.

45. Luke 22:19; 1 Cor. 11:24.

46. The earlier title, followed in most editions, is "The Drunken Song." "*Das Nachtwandler-Lied*" could also mean "The Sleepwalker's Song," but the point of the song is wakefulness in the night.

47. This argument to persuade the superior men differs from what persuades the most superior man in *Beyond* (56): there, willing eternal return is based on self-affirmation. It differs, too, from the perspective presented by the animals, in being an argument based on one moment of joy; in this respect it could be seen as the positive analogue of the argument used against the spirit of gravity (III. 2).

48. 1 Kings 18:46.

49. An ancient commentator's remark on Thucydides's reaction to I. 126. 3. See Calder, "The Lion Laughed."

Works Cited

NIETZSCHE'S WORKS

Werke. Kritische Gesamtausgabe, ed. Giorgio Colli and Mazzino Montinari. Berlin: Walter de Gruyter, 1967–78.

NIETZSCHE'S WORKS IN TRANSLATION

Beyond Good and Evil, trans. Walter Kaufmann. New York: Vintage, 1966.
The Birth of Tragedy and the Case of Wagner, trans. Walter Kaufmann. New York: Vintage, 1967.
Daybreak, Thoughts on the Prejudices of Morality, trans. R. J. Hollingdale. Cambridge: Cambridge University Press, 1982.
Dithyrambs of Dionysus, trans. R. J. Hollingdale. London: Anvil Press Poetry, 1984.
The Gay Science, trans. Walter Kaufmann. New York: Vintage, 1974.
Human All Too Human: A Book for Free Spirits, trans. Marion Faber, with Stephan Lehmann. Lincoln: University of Nebraska Press, 1984.
Human All Too Human; Vol. 2: Assorted Opinions and Maxims, The Wanderer and His Shadow, trans. Paul V. Cohn. New York: Russell and Russell, 1964 (1909).
On the Genealogy of Morals and Ecce Homo, trans. Walter Kaufmann. New York: Vintage, 1969.
Philosophy and Truth: Selections from Nietzsche's Notebooks of the early 1870s, ed. and trans. Daniel Breazeale. Atlantic Highlands: Humanities Press, 1979.
Philosophy in the Tragic Age of the Greeks, trans. Marianne Cowan. Chicago: Regnery, 1962.

The Portable Nietzsche, trans. Walter Kaufmann. New York: Vintage, 1954. Includes *Thus Spoke Zarathustra, Twilight of the Idols, The Antichrist, Nietzsche Contra Wagner,* and an abridged version of "Homer's Contest."

Selected Letters, trans. Christopher Middleton. Chicago: University of Chicago Press, 1969.

Thus Spoke Zarathustra, trans. R. J. Hollingdale. Harmondsworth: Penguin, 1961.

Untimely Meditations, trans. R. J. Hollingdale. Cambridge: Cambridge University Press, 1983. Contains *David Strauss: The Confessor and Writer; On the Uses and Disadvantages of History for Life; Schopenhauer as Educator; Richard Wagner in Bayreuth.*

The Will to Power, trans. Walter Kaufmann and R. J. Hollingdale. New York: Vintage, 1968.

OTHER WORKS

Alderman, Harold. *Nietzsche's Gift.* Athens: Ohio University Press, 1977.

Allison, David B., ed. *The New Nietzsche: Contemporary Styles of Interpretation.* New York: Delta, 1977.

Andreas-Salomé, Lou. *Friedrich Nietzsche in seinen Werken.* Vienna: Konegen, 1911.

Arendt, Hannah. *The Life of the Mind: Willing.* New York: Harcourt, Brace, Jovanovich, 1978.

Aristophanes. *The Birds, Clouds, Lysistrata, Frogs,* trans. William Arrowsmith et al. New York: New American Library, 1984.

Aristotle. *The Complete Works,* ed. Jonathan Barnes. 2 vols. Princeton: Princeton University Press, 1984.

Bacon, Francis. *The Great Instauration and New Atlantis,* ed. Jerry Weinberger. Arlington Heights, Ill.: AHM Publishing, 1980.

———. *The Masculine Birth of Time,* in *The Philosophy of Francis Bacon,* trans. Benjamin Farmington. Chicago: University of Chicago Press, 1964.

———. *The New Organon and Related Writings,* ed. Fulton H. Anderson. Indianapolis: Bobbs-Merrill, 1960.

———. *Wisdom of the Ancients,* in *Works,* Vol. VI, 687–764, ed. J. Spedding, R. L. Ellis, and D. D. Heath. New York: Garrett Press, 1968.

Barfield, Owen. *History in English Words.* London: Faber and Faber, 1962.

———. *Saving the Appearances.* London: Faber and Faber, 1957.

Beatty, Joseph. "Zarathustra: The Paradoxical Ways of the Creator," *Man and World* 3 (1970): 64–75.

Becker, Carl. *The Heavenly City of the Eighteenth-Century Philosophers.* New Haven: Yale University Press, 1932.

Bennholdt-Thomsen, Anke. *Nietzsches Also Sprach Zarathustra als literarisches Phänomen.* Rev. ed. Frankfurt am Main: Athenäum, 1974.

Bertram, Ernst. *Nietzsche: Versuch Einer Mythologie.* Berlin: Bondi, 1918.

Bertram, Maryanne. " 'God's *Second* Blunder'—Serpent, Woman and the *Gestalt* in Nietzsche's Thought," *Southern Journal of Philosophy* 19 (1981): 259–77.

Binion, Rudolph. *Frau Lou, Nietzsche's Wayward Disciple.* Princeton: Princeton University Press, 1968.

Borges, Jorge Luis. *Labyrinths.* New York: New Directions, 1964.

Calder, William Musgrave III. "The Lion Laughed," *Nietzsche Studien* 14 (1985): 357–59.

———. "The Wilamowitz-Nietzsche Struggle: New Documents and a Reappraisal," *Nietzsche Studien* 12 (1983): 214–54.

Caton, Hiram. *The Origin of Subjectivity: An Essay on Descartes.* New Haven: Yale University Press, 1973.

Colli, Giorgio. *Nach Nietzsche.* Frankfurt am Main: Europäische Verlaganstalt, 1980.

Combee, Jerry H. "Nietzsche as Cosmologist: The Idea of the Eternal Recurrence as a Cosmological Doctrine and Some Aspects of its Relation to the Doctrine of Will to Power," *Interpretation* 4 (1974): 39–47.

Craig, Leon H. "The Timocratic Man in Plato's *Republic.*" Paper presented at the Fourteenth Annual Meeting of the Northeastern Political Science Association, 18–20 November 1982.

Dannhauser, Werner J. "Nietzsche," in *History of Political Philosophy,* ed. Strauss and Cropsey, pp. 782–803.

———. *Nietzsche's View of Socrates.* Ithaca: Cornell University Press, 1974.

Danto, Arthur. *Nietzsche As Philosopher.* New York: Macmillan, 1965.

Deleuze, Gilles. *Nietzsche and Philosophy,* trans. Hugh Tomlinson. New York: Columbia University Press, 1983.

———. "Nomad Thought," trans. David Allison, in Allison, ed., *The New Nietzsche,* pp. 142–49.

Derrida, Jacques. *Spurs: Nietzsche's Styles,* trans. Barbara Harlow. Chicago: University of Chicago Press, 1979.

Descartes, René. *Discourse on Method,* trans. Donald A. Cress. Indianapolis: Hackett, 1980.

———. *Passions of the Soul,* in *Philosophical Works of Descartes,* trans. Elizabeth S. Haldane and G. R. T. Ross. Cambridge: Cambridge University Press, 1967.

———. *Principles of Philosophy,* trans. V. R. Miller and R. P. Miller. The Hague: Reidel, 1984.

Duschesne-Guillemin, J. *The Western Response to Zoroaster.* Oxford: The Clarendon Press, 1958.

Earle, William. "The Paradox and Death of God," in William Earle, James M. Edie, and John Wild, *Christianity and Existentialism,* pp. 66–87. Evanston: Northwestern University Press, 1963.

Eden, Robert. *Political Leadership and Nihilism: A Study of Weber and Nietzsche.* Gainesville: University Presses of Florida, 1983.

Eliade, Mircea. *Cosmos and History*, trans. Willard Trask. New York: Harper Torchbooks, 1959.

Euripides. *Bacchae*, trans. Donald Sutherland. Lincoln: University of Nebraska Press, 1968.

Fink, Eugen. *Nietzsches Philosophie*. 3d rev. ed. Stuttgart: W. Kohlhammer, 1973.

Fischer, Kurt Rudolf. "The Existentialism of Nietzsche's Zarathustra," *Daedalus* 93 (1964): 998–1016.

Fustel de Coulanges, Numa Denis. *The Ancient City*. New York: Doubleday Anchor Books, orig. 1864.

Gadamer, Hans-Georg. "Das Drama Zarathustras," *Nietzsche Studien* 15 (1986): 1–15.

Goicoechea, David. *The Great Year of Zarathustra (1881–1981)*. Lanham: University Press of America, 1983.

Grant, George. *English-Speaking Justice*. Notre Dame: Notre Dame University Press, 1985 (1974).

———. "Nietzsche and the Ancients: Philosophy and Scholarship," *Dionysius* 3 (1979): 5–16.

———. *Technology and Empire: Perspectives on North America*. Toronto: House of Anansi Press, 1969.

———. *Time as History*. Toronto: CBC Systems, 1969.

Hegel, G. W. F. *The Philosophy of History*, trans. J. Sibree. New York: Dover, 1956.

Heidegger, Martin. *Die Frage Nach dem Ding*. Tübingen: Niemeyer, 1962.

———. *Holzwege*. Frankfurt am Main: Klostermann, 1950.

———. *Identität und Differenz*. Pfullingen: Neske, 1957. Translated as *Identity and Difference* by Joan Stambaugh. New York: Harper and Row, 1969.

———. *Nietzsche*. 2 vols. Pfullingen: Neske, 1961. Trans. David Farrell Krell. 4 vols. New York: Harper and Row, 1979–86.

———. *The Question Concerning Technology*, trans. William Lovitt. New York: Harper Colophon Books, 1977.

———. *Der Satz vom Grund*. Pfullingen: Neske, 1957.

———. *Sein und Zeit*. Tübingen: Niemeyer, 1967 (1927).

———. *Unterwegs zur Sprache*. Pfullingen: Neske, 1959.

———. *Vorträge und Aufsätze*. 3 vols. Pfullingen: Neske, 1954.

———. *Was Heißt Denken?* Tübingen: Niemeyer, 1961. Translated as *What is Called Thinking?* by Fred D. Wieck and J. Glenn Gray. New York: Harper and Row, 1968.

———. *Wegmarken*. Frankfurt am Main: Klostermann, 1967.

———. "Who is Nietzsche's Zarathustra?" trans. Bernd Magnus, in Allison, ed., *The New Nietzsche*, pp. 64–79.

Heller, Erich. *The Artist's Journey Into The Interior and Other Essays*. New York: Vintage, 1968.

———. *The Disinherited Mind*. Expanded ed. New York: Harcourt, Brace, Jovanovich, 1975.

————. "Nietzsche—Philosopher of Art," *Nietzsche Studien* 12 (1983): 443—53.

Henrichs, Albert. "Loss of Self, Suffering, Violence: The Modern View of Dionysus from Nietzsche to Girard," *Harvard Studies in Classical Philology* 88 (1984): 205–40.

Herzfeld, Ernst. *Zoroaster and His World*. Princeton: Princeton University Press, 1947.

Hillesheim, James W. "Nietzsche Agonistes," *Educational Theory* 23 (1973): 343–53.

Hollingdale, R. J. *Nietzsche, the Man and His Philosophy*. Baton Rouge: Louisiana State University Press, 1965.

Hollinrake, Roger. *Nietzsche, Wagner, and the Philosophy of Pessimism*. London: George Allen and Unwin, 1982.

Homer. *The Iliad*, trans. Robert Fitzgerald. New York: Doubleday, 1974.

————. *The Odyssey*, trans. Richmond Lattimore. New York: Harper and Row, 1968.

Jackson, A. V. Williams. *Zoroaster, The Prophet of Ancient Iran*. New York: Columbia University Press, 1898.

Janz, Curt Paul. *Friedrich Nietzsche Biographie*. 3 vols. Munich: Carl Hanser, 1978.

Jaspers, Karl. *Nietzsche, An Introduction to the Understanding of his Philosophical Activity*, trans. Charles F. Wallraff and Frederick J. Schmitz. Tucson: University of Arizona Press, 1965.

————. *Nietzsche and Christianity*, trans. E. B. Ashton. Chicago: Regnery, 1961.

Kant, Immanuel. *Critique of Practical Reason*, trans. Lewis W. Beck. Indianapolis: Bobbs-Merrill, 1956.

————. *Critique of Pure Reason*, trans. Norman Kemp Smith. New York: St. Martin's Press, 1965.

————. *On History*, ed. Lewis White Beck. Indianapolis: Bobbs-Merrill, 1963.

Kaufmann, Walter. *Nietzsche: Philosopher, Psychologist, Antichrist*. 3d ed., rev. and enlarged. New York: Vintage, 1968.

Kennington, Richard. "Descartes," in *History of Political Philosophy*, ed. Strauss and Cropsey, pp. 395–413.

Kerenyi, Karl. *Dionysos, Archetypal Image of Indestructible Life*, trans. Ralph Manheim. Princeton: Princeton University Press, 1976.

Kierkegaard, Søren. *The Concluding Unscientific Postscript*, trans. David F. Swenson and Walter Lowrie. Princeton: Princeton University Press, 1941.

————. *The Point of View of My Work as an Author: A Report to History*, trans. Walter Lowrie. New York: Harper and Row, 1962.

Klein, Jacob. *A Commentary on Plato's* Meno. Chapel Hill: University of North Carolina Press, 1965.

Knight, G. Wilson. *Christ and Nietzsche, An Essay in Poetic Wisdom*. London: Staples, 1948.

Kuenzli, Rudolf E. "The Nazi Appropriation of Nietzsche," *Nietzsche Studien* 12 (1983): 428–35.

Lessing, Theodor. *Nietzsche*. Munich: Matthes und Seitz, 1985 (1925).

Locke, John. *An Essay Concerning Human Understanding*, ed. Peter H. Nidditch. New York: Oxford University Press, 1979.

———. *Two Treatises of Government*, ed. Peter Laslett. Cambridge: Cambridge University Press, 1967.

Löwith, Karl. *Nietzsches Philosophie der Ewigen Wiederkehr des Gleichen*. 3d rev. ed. Hamburg: Felix Meiner, 1978.

Lucretius. *De Rerum Natura*, trans. Rolfe Humphries. Bloomington: Indiana University Press, 1968.

Machiavelli. *The Prince*, trans. Leo de Alvarez. Dallas: University of Dallas Press, 1978.

MacIntyre, Alisdair. *After Virtue: A Study of Moral Theory*. Notre Dame: Notre Dame University Press, 1981.

Magnus, Bernd. "Aristotle and Nietzsche: 'Megalopsychia' and 'Übermensch' " in *The Greeks and the Good Life*, ed. David J. Depew, pp. 260–95. Indianapolis: Hackett, 1980.

———. *Nietzsche's Existential Imperative*. Bloomington: Indiana University Press, 1978.

Mazlish, Bruce. *The Riddle of History*. New York: Harper and Row, 1966.

Mencken, H. L. *The Philosophy of Friedrich Nietzsche*. Port Washington, N.Y.: Kennikat Press, 1967 (1913).

Montaigne, Michel de. *In Defense of Raymond Sebond*, trans. Arthur H. Beattie. New York: Ungar, 1959.

Montinari, Mazzino. "The New Critical Edition of Nietzsche's Complete Works," *Malahat Review* 24 (1972): 121–33.

———. *Nietzsche Lesen*. Berlin: Walter de Gruyter, 1982.

Morgan, George. *What Nietzsche Means*. New York: Harper Torchbooks, 1965 (1941).

Nehamas, Alexander. *Nietzsche: Life as Literature*. Cambridge, Mass.: Harvard University Press, 1985.

Neumann, Harry. "Nietzsche, The Superman, The Will to Power, and the Eternal Return," *Ultimate Reality and Meaning* 5 (1982): 280–95.

———. "Superman or Last Man? Nietzsche's Interpretation of Athens and Jerusalem," *Nietzsche Studien* 5 (1976): 1–28.

Ogilvy, James. *Many Dimensional Man: Decentralizing Self, Society and the Sacred*. New York: Harper and Row, 1979.

Otto, W. F. *Dionysos, Mythos und Kultur*. Frankfurt am Main: Klostermann, 1960 (1933).

Pangle, Thomas L. "The Roots of Contemporary Nihilism and its Political Consequences According to Nietzsche," *Review of Politics* 45 (1983): 45–70.

———. "The 'Warrior Spirit' as an Inlet to the Political Philosophy of Nietzsche's Zarathustra," *Nietzsche Studien* 15 (1986): 140–79.

Peters, H. F. *Zarathustra's Sister. The Case of Elisabeth and Friedrich Nietzsche.* New York: Crown, 1977.

Plato. *Alcibiades* I, trans. W. R. M. Lamb. Cambridge, Mass: Harvard University Press, Loeb Classics, 1917.

———. *The Apology of Socrates,* trans. George Grube. Indianapolis: Hackett, 1982.

———. *Ion,* trans. W. R. M. Lamb. Cambridge, Mass: Harvard University Press, Loeb Classics, 1925.

———. *Laws,* trans. Thomas L. Pangle. New York: Basic Books, 1979.

———. *Phaedrus,* trans. H. N. Fowler. Cambridge, Mass: Harvard University Press, Loeb Classics, 1914.

———. *Republic,* trans. Allan Bloom. New York: Basic Books, 1968.

———. *Symposium,* trans. W. R. M. Lamb. Cambridge, Mass: Harvard University Press, Loeb Classics, 1925.

———. *Theaetetus,* trans. H. N. Fowler. Cambridge, Mass: Harvard University Press, Loeb Classics, 1966.

———. *Theages,* trans. W. R. M. Lamb. Cambridge, Mass: Harvard University Press, Loeb Classics, 1917.

Platt, Michael. "Woman, Nietzsche, and Nature," *Maieutics* 2 (1981): 27–42.

Plutarch's Lives, trans. John Dryden. New York: Modern Library, 1967.

Reichhold, Karl. *Attische Vasenbilder: Der Antikensammlungen in München nach Zeichnungen von Karl Reichhold.* Munich: Beck, 1981.

Reinhardt, Karl. "Nietzsche's Lament of Ariadne," *Interpretation* 6 (1977): 204–24.

Rosen, Stanley. *Limits of Analysis.* New York: Basic Books, 1980.

———. *Nihilism: A Philosophical Essay.* New Haven: Yale University Press, 1969.

Rousseau, Jean-Jacques. *The First and Second Discourses,* trans. Roger D. Masters and Judith R. Masters. New York: St. Martin's Press, 1964.

———. *On the Social Contract,* ed. Roger D. Masters, trans. Judith R. Masters. New York: St. Martin's Press, 1978.

Rzepka, R., and Anuschewski, J. u. W. *Index zu Friedrich Nietzsche 'Also Sprach Zarathustra.'* Essen: W. Anuschewski, 1983.

Salaquarda, Jörg. "Zarathustra und der Esel," *Theologia Viatorum* II (1966/1972): 181–213.

Schacht, Richard. *Nietzsche.* London: Routledge and Kegan Paul, 1983.

Scheier, Claus-Artur. *Nietzsches Labyrinth: Das ursprüngliche Denken und die Seele.* Freiburg: Alber, 1985.

Schopenhauer, Arthur. *Parerga und Paralipomena.* 2 vols. Zurich: Diogenes, 1977.

———. *The World as Will and Representation,* trans. E. F. Payne. 2 vols. New York: Dover, 1966.

Shapiro, Gary. "Festival, Parody, and Carnival in Zarathustra IV," in *The Great Year of Zarathustra,* ed. Goicoechea, pp. 45–62.

———. "Nietzsche on Envy," *International Studies in Philosophy* 15 (1983): 3–12.

———. "The Rhetoric of Nietzsche's Zarathustra," in *Philosophical Style,* ed. Beryl Lang, pp. 347–85. Chicago: Nelson Hall, 1980.

———. "Zarathustra's Hermeneutics Lesson," *Mosaic* 14 (1981): 37–49.

Small, Robin. "Three Interpretations of Eternal Recurrence," *Dialogue, Canadian Philosophical Review* 22 (1983): 91–112.

Sokel, Walter H. "Political Uses and Abuses of Nietzsche in Walter Kaufmann's Image of Nietzsche," *Nietzsche Studien* 12 (1983): 436–42.

Stackelberg, Roderick. "Nietzsche and the Nazis: the *Völkisch* Reaction to Nietzschean Thought," *Research Studies* 51 (1983): 36–46.

Stambaugh, Joan. *Nietzsche's Thought of Eternal Return.* Baltimore: Johns Hopkins University Press, 1972.

Strauss, Leo. *The City and Man.* Chicago: Rand-McNally, 1964.

———. "Notes on Lucretius," in Strauss, *Liberalism Ancient and Modern,* pp. 76–139. New York: Basic Books, 1968.

———. *Natural Right and History.* Chicago: University of Chicago Press, 1953.

———. *On Tyranny.* Ithaca: Cornell University Press, 1963.

———. *Persecution and the Art of Writing.* Glencoe, Ill.: Free Press, 1952.

———. "The Three Waves of Modernity," in *Political Philosophy: Six Essays By Leo Strauss,* ed. Hilail Gildin, pp. 81–98. Indianapolis: Bobbs-Merrill, 1974.

———. *Socrates and Aristophanes.* New York: Basic Books, 1966.

———. "Note on the Plan of Nietzsche's *Beyond Good and Evil,*" in Strauss, *Studies in Platonic Political Philosophy,* pp. 174–91. Chicago: University of Chicago Press, 1983.

———. *Thoughts on Machiavelli.* Chicago: University of Chicago Press, 1958.

———. *What is Political Philosophy? and Other Studies.* Glencoe, Ill.: Free Press, 1959.

———. *Xenophon's Socratic Discourse.* Ithaca: Cornell University Press, 1970.

———, and Cropsey, Joseph, ed. *History of Political Philosophy.* 2d ed. Chicago: Rand-McNally, 1972.

Stromberg, Roland. *Redemption by War: Intellectuals and 1914.* Lawrence: University of Kansas Press, 1982.

Strong, Tracy. *Friedrich Nietzsche and the Politics of Transformation.* Berkeley: University of California Press, 1975.

Thatcher, David S. "Eagle and Serpent in Zarathustra," *Nietzsche Studien* 6 (1977): 240–60.

Thomas, R. Hinton. *Nietzsche in German Politics and Society 1890–1918.* Manchester: Manchester University Press, 1983.

Thucydides. *History of the Peloponnesian War,* trans. Rex Warner. New York: Penguin, 1954.

Voegelin, Eric. "Nietzsche, the Crisis and the War," *The Journal of Politics* 6 (1944): 177–211.

Xenophon. *Memorabilia, Oeconomicus, Symposium,* and *Apology,* trans. E. C. Marchant and O. J. Todd. Cambridge, Mass: Harvard University Press, Loeb Classics, 1923.

———. *Scripta Minora,* trans. E. C. Marchant and G. W. Bowersock. Cambridge, Mass: Harvard University Press, Loeb Classics, 1925.

Weichelt, Hans. *Zarathustra-Kommentar.* 2d ed. Leipzig: Meiner, 1922.

Weil, Simone. *Waiting for God,* trans. Emma Craufurd. New York: Harper Colophon Books, 1973.

Yeats, William Butler. *The Collected Poems.* New York: Macmillan, 1956.

Index

Achilles, 49, 62, 67, 110, 124, 175, 320n76
Aeneas, 62
Ahriman, 29
Alcibiades, 89
Alderman, Harold, 314n8, 317n51, 335n105, 337n12, 342n86, 343n105, 354n11
Amor Fati, 147–48, 334n95, 335n102, 350n14
Anaximander, 146, 334n91
Anaximenes, 334n91
Andreas-Salomé, Lou. *See* Salomé, Lou
Animals, man's relation to, 22, 178, 221, 280, 314n10. *See also* Zarathustra's animals
Ape, 60, 63; Zarathustra's, 184–86, 273
Aphorism, 45–46. *See also* Zarathustra's art of speaking
Aphrodite, 104, 109, 346n133
Apollo: and Dionysos, 16, 82, 180, 228, 230, 232, 248; and snake, 29; and Zarathustra's staff, 74; and the lyre, 216; and rhythm, 239
Arendt, Hannah, 335n102
Ariadne, 8, 103, 122, 232–34, 270, 278, 280, 285, 330n51, 336n9, 346nn132, 133, 347nn142, 149; marriage of, 109, 228, 240, 241; thread of, 162; "Lament of," 233, 295, 346n138
Aristocracy, 205–07. *See also* Nobility; Order of rank
Aristophanes, 180, 270, 342n95
Aristotle, 36, 46, 315n29, 324n133, 335n103, 338n35; on virtue, 41; on envy and jealousy, 42, 49, 77; on pity, 44; on magnanimity, 78; on the heavens, 177, 282
Art: highest art, 61, 120, 246; and convention, 61; "worth more than truth," 123; subtlest art, 200; and tragedy, 231–32
Art of reading. *See* Philology

Art of writing: Nietzsche's, 4, 7–9, 44–46, 246, 247; Plato's, 8, 45, 269–71, 339n57; Bacon's, 8, 263–64; Descartes', 8, 264–67. *See also* Zarathustra's art of speaking
Ascent: into solitude, 14, 154, 158–60; images of, 16, 30, 45–47, 75, 162, 313n3; in Zarathustra's vision, 162–69; to the sky, 173–80, 243–44; over the spirit of gravity, 197; into naturalness, 223, 274. *See also* Descent; Flying
Ascetic ideal, 93, 300; and science, 282, 302–03
Asklepius, 74, 82
Ass, 102, 219, 293, 296, 297, 300, 356n35; "ass festival," 305–08
Atheism: Zarathustra the godless, 7, 183, 188, 212, 229, 296, 306, 345n129; of last man, 24–25, 256; "refined atheists," 25, 230, 232, 251; veiled, 202, 307; "Zarathustra is only an old atheist," 229. *See also* "God is dead"
Athena, 109
Auden, W. H., 273

Bacon, Francis, 23, 57, 68; art of writing, 8, 263; and modern science, 125, 219, 264, 271, 275–76; as founder, 263–64, 267–68
Barfield, Owen, 332n72
Beatty, Joseph, 324n123
Becker, Carl, 324n144
Beauty: and the Greeks, 90, 98; defined, 122, 174; and eternal return, 216, 239
Being: and becoming, 30, 190, 205, 215, 221, 223; "the belly of being," 37–38, 81, 114, 116; and the highest beings, 89, 106, 174, 180, 221, 254; all beings, 112, 117, 119, 159, 162, 189, 225, 256, 257, 280; "thinkability of all beings," 112, 162; as funda-